THE SOCIOLOGY OF HEALTH AND ILLNESS

THE SOCIOLOGY OF HEALTH AND ILLNESS

R. KENNETH JONES
B.A. (Hons), A.C.E., Ph.D., FCoLLP, FRSA
Director of Teacher In-Service Training in Bophuthatswana
(Formerly Professor of Sociology at the University of Transkei)

1991
Juta & Co, Ltd

First published in 1991

Copyright © Juta & Co, Ltd
PO Box 14373, Kenwyn 7790

ISBN 0 7021 2441 9

Printed and bound by Creda Press, Solan Road, Cape Town.

TO MY DEAREST AMANDA,
without whom none of this would have been possible.

You are my true and honourable wife,
as dear to me as are the ruddy drops
that visit my sad heart.

W Shakespeare *Julius Caesar*

PREFACE

There has been awareness in the past few years that medical care must, if it is to be entirely successful, be linked to the total environment of the individual and his or her relationship to the society in which he or she lives. This has highlighted the importance of sociology and its application to medicine. Those who practise medical skills, both doctors and nurses, are often in their day-to-day work forced to deal with a large number of problems only indirectly related to physical illness. They are faced with the knowledge that many problems of physical illness itself are intricately linked with people's social and economic circumstances. In the hospitals and in the community all staff are becoming more aware of the way that social and organisational factors can influence the total care of the sick and dying.

The Sociology of health and illness is the first book of its kind in South Africa which attempts to give not only a broad introduction to sociology but also to relate it to such areas as the organisation of the health professions, sexual deviance, the structure of the modern hospital and the sociological approaches to illness and death. It provides, also, extensive coverage of the relevant prescribed nursing syllabi.

Although written primarily for doctors and nurses both in training and practice, this book will also be of interest to all those whose work is concerned with the care of people, for example health visitors and social and probational workers. It will also be of interest to the public in general.

The author, Professor R. Kenneth Jones, B.A. (Hons), A.C.E., Ph.D., FCoLLP, FRSA, is currently director of teacher in-service training in Bophuthatswana. He was previously Professor of Sociology at the University of Transkei, and has held similar posts at the universities of Botswana, Athabasca, Canada, Ulster Polytechnic, and the Open University in Britain, at all of which he specialised in medical sociology. He is the author of eight other books and has written extensively in journals and collections. He was a regular broadcaster for BBC Radio and Television, and is the Director of the film *The Politics of Sickness; Health in Transkei.*

CONTENTS

CHAPTER
ONE

SOCIOLOGY AND ITS RELEVANCE FOR MEDICINE

- the nature of sociological concepts
- social theory and medicine
- research design
- data collection

THE NATURE OF SOCIOLOGICAL CONCEPTS

What sociology is The origins of sociology can be traced even further back in time than to the French philosopher who gave the subject its name—Auguste Comte, usually known as the 'father of sociology', who lived and worked in the first half of the nineteenth century. Some have seen vestiges of the discipline in the Greek and Roman philosophers and also in the Schoolmen of the Middle Ages. Nevertheless it did not really gain respectability until the present century, when both American and European universities established departments. In Britain, following the pioneer work of Booth and Rowntree into the conditions of poverty at the turn of this century, sociology has developed a strongly empirical slant, coupled with a strong theoretical inheritance from social anthropology.

It is never easy, useful or wise to attempt a one-sentence definition of any complex subject. There are many such definitions in existence, most of them different, and although there is this difference, nevertheless reputable sociologists are in general agreement about the content of these definitions. In other words, requests for definitions of medical and paramedical fields might result in different verbal formulations, but for both these and sociology there would be quite wide general agreement as to the field of competence and expertise of these areas. As a subject, sociology is concerned with the study of *human relationships*, and more specifically the formulation and perpetuation of these relationships, and of the individuals who enact them, within the broad context of human society. Sociology seeks to explain how it is that human systems and organizations exist over time in a recognizable and ordered fashion. It also concerns itself with the apparent *order* of human relationships–and of the concomitant *disorder* when such occurs. Above all it realises that even cognitive and affective behaviour, the way we know things and feel things about the world, is socially formed.

No subject can be happily compartmentalised, least of all those in the social sciences. Sociology is closely related to economics, political science, history, social geography, psychology and social anthropology; indeed in the last two subjects it is often very difficult to establish any clear demarcation.

What sociology is not Sociology is not a kind of practical philanthropy which exists for the sake of helping people. It provides information equally for those who are misanthropic as for those who care deeply about others. Neither is sociology to be confused with either socialism or social work, although it is true to say that the major growth point of the subject was coincidental with the development of the great urban problems which heralded the rise of the latter. Sociology is not necessarily linked with any political stance, such as socialism, nor with a practice in society, but it is an attempt at understanding. Such understanding is available, certainly to social workers, but it is also available to nurses, soldiers, politicians and advertising men. Sociologists usually regard themselves as value-free, which means not that they themselves have no values but that these values must be eliminated as much as possible from the work that they are doing. It follows that the sociologist is also neither a 'do-gooder' nor social reformer.

Another confusion arises when the sociologist is regarded as a head-counter or statistician; this has been referred to as earthworm sociology. It is true that some sociologists have devoted enormous energy to asking 'how much?' or 'how often?'. Works such as that of the sexologist Kinsey have not helped to eradicate this image. The gathering of data, including statistical data, can often be a vital part of the sociologist's task, but eventually it has to be fitted into a sociological framework and interpreted sociologically if it is to count as sociology.

A further confusion is to regard the sociologist as a scientific methodologist. A number of practitioners have been guilty of using what has been termed outlandish jargon, often obtuse and pseudo-scientific. Lewis Carroll wrote, 'It seems very pretty (Alice said), but it's rather hard to understand'. Because the subject was in its infancy, and in the beginning uncertain of its status, sociologists resorted to using a language that they thought was scientific, covering up the defects of the subject in verbosity. However, all subjects suffer from this to some extent. Sociology can also be extremely lucid. Terminology is important for the sociologist simply because his subject matter is familiar. As we shall see later, not only does the sociologist deal with everyday phenomena in a special way, but he also uses as part of his technical vocabulary terms borrowed from day-to-day speech and situations, such as *role, class, community, culture* and *society*.

Finally, the sociologist is not a detached, aloof and superior being, anxious to gather data about his fellow men and feed such data into a computer system. Above all he is concerned with understanding society through the special 'spectacles' that his subject offers. In recent years some have argued that sociology is weighted, not towards the sciences, but towards the humanities, that it is not concerned with gathering facts nor with establishing causal reasons, but rather that it is a quality of mind that equips its practitioners to utilise information and reasons so that they may better understand themselves and the world around them. This has been called the *sociological imagination.* Through this self-consciousness they experience a revision of values. Others have placed it more in the area of philosophy and history than the sciences. The *verstehen,* or understanding method believes that sociology can make people conscious of facts and situations in the world simply by seeing how or what makes these facts and situations 'tick'.

Sociology as a science   Before looking at the scientific nature of sociology we must look at the distinguishing characteristics that go towards calling a subject a science. The word *science* comes from the Latin *scientia,* meaning knowledge, and although science is a certain type of knowledge, a more profitable way of viewing it would be as a way of looking at the world, or a way of thinking. The main method of scientific activity is the *hypothetico-deductive* method, the requirements of which are (a) general expectation, (b) an observation, and (c) a valid deduction. Most scientific observations are made because of some interest or expectation, and often there is no fast line to be drawn between pre-scientific or commonsense expectations and hypothesis. Science is *progressive* in a sense that the arts and humanities are not, so that Greek plays and philosophers, for example, are of interest today in a way in which early Greek science is not of interest to the scientist but only to the scientific historian.

Scientific thinking is essentially *methodological*: it is an orderly arrangement or construction of facts that constitutes science. The scientist is concerned with fact that is observable through the senses and capable of being treated through or by a particular method. Many think that it is the method which determines whether a subject is scientific or not. Any proposition or hypothesis of the natural sciences is dependent on what happens to exist in the external world, and the truth of these depends on what there actually is in the world, and on the use of induction by empirical observation or simple enumeration.

Science, then, seems to be characterised by the following activities: (a) collection of facts following observation; (b) a hypothesis explaining the relationships of the facts to one another; (c) testing the hypothesis, attempting to disprove it; (d) new facts may mean altering the original hypothesis; (e) the emergence of a general rule or law which requires universal agreement. Sciences are sometimes divided into the *exact* (mathematics) and *descriptive* (botany, zoology).

The kinds of questions that science can answer varies from 'Why are tides constant?' to 'Why can we predict eclipses?'. Certain kinds of questions which are called *metaphysical*–for example 'Why is there evil in the world?'–science could not answer, and indeed would not claim to do so. This is partly because we cannot answer such questions by pointing to empirical, or observable, facts which would help us in reaching agreement.

In science we often claim to have discovered something, but the act of discovery itself escapes logical explanation and description. We cannot, in other words, pinpoint the actual process of drawing an inference, and neither are there any rules for discovering something. To have a recipe for discovery would be already to have discovered. Many great scientific discoveries have been inspired guesswork, luck, or pure accident, and intuition plays no small part.

We turn now to considering sociology as a science. Some sociologists would say that the above formal scientific method, that is the stating of the hypothesis, the testing, and the consequent systematic description and classification, ought to be followed by sociologists, although some sociologists–even the majority–would suggest that sociology not only cannot but should not ape the physical sciences. It is often assumed that the logic underlying the social sciences is identical to the one which underlies the natural sciences, and that wherever generalization is possible, so also is science.

However, sociology, because of the infinite variety of the factors involved, is by nature incapable of the exactness possessed by the natural sciences. The difference between human and physical action is not simply one of complexity, and the difference of degree may really be a difference in kind. Only a poet would describe a brick wall as being in pain. The field of human behaviour requires a different framework to that of the natural sciences, and neither can supply the other with its own peculiar conceptual apparatus.

Objectivity and prediction

Sociologists, unlike medical scientists or physicists, for example, are involved in the stream of life of the very phenomena that they are studying. They are personally orientated to families, political systems, religion, and so on. They themselves have been, or are, or know others who are, deeply involved in many of the areas they study. Sociologists are constantly confronted by 'instant experts' on delinquency, new towns, the decline of institutionalised religion and so on. Some areas, such as race relations and religious behaviour, are more prone to this than others. The sociologist must, therefore, leave aside his personal views and prejudices, inasmuch as they are likely to affect the outcome of his research, and refrain from making moral judgements other than in terms of the beliefs of a given society. In practice it is as difficult for a sociologist to stand apart from his subject matter as it is for a doctor or nurse to assume the role of complete objectivity in dealing with certain patients.

Finally, a word about prediction in sociology. We can with relative certainty predict events in the natural sciences. But by the very nature of the subject matter we are unable to predict events in the field of social behaviour. If one's prediction of someone's behaviour is not fulfilled, this does not mean necessarily that one predicted incorrectly (as it would in the natural science analogy, in terms of inadequate theory, etc.) but possibly that this someone whose behaviour was predicted acted otherwise than the way it was predicted. That is, human beings are complex and also to a large extent free in their choice of actions. In the sense in which we use the word in the natural sciences there is no prediction in social behaviour. Even using the term loosely, sociology has not had the same success with predictions as other subjects. This is partly because of the newness of the subject but also because of meaning. That is, individuals are not simply creatures of instinct but interpret their situations. This factor means that different individuals interpret a situation along totally different lines. For example, a Buddhist places a different meaning on a symbol of a cross than a Christian. There are many *variables* in human actions of which the sociologist may have incomplete knowledge, and to predict or forecast with accuracy entails a reasonably complete knowledge of such variables.

The birth of sociology and its context

Some insight into the nature of sociology might be gained from looking at the context in which it first appeared as a scientific discipline. Comte thought of the subject as studying social phenomena in the same spirit as physical phenomena were studied. Others later felt that there were general laws of social action which were there to be discovered. The world at that time was in the grip of the Industrial Revolution which brought with it the appropriate advance in science and technology. It was not to be wondered that the early sociologists saw the subject as lying along the path of science for this was considered to be the ideal path, although this does not mean that they believed social behaviour followed laws as inexorably as did scientific phenomena.

Some suggestions as to why sociology is not a science

We have already mentioned that what the sociologist is expected to be objective about is by its nature more infinitely variable than the subject matter of the physical sciences. What predictability we have is *general* rather than *individual*; that is, we can say that people from a certain category tend to vote Conservative, but the individual is less predictable. Although sociology makes use of experimental method, a pure scientist would regard this as pseudo-experimental. Experiments in the social sciences, unlike those in the natural sciences, are very rarely repeated, or even capable of exact repetition.

There are two main differences between the subject matter of the physical sciences and the social world. We are within the social world and interpret it intelligently only because we project onto it our own experience. The physical world of chemical substances, brain tissues, neutrons, and protons do not affect us in the same way. The second main difference is that the movements of the physical world depend on a mechanical causality while movements of social phenomena are to be understood in terms of purpose and value and meaning. It is also to some extent true that human events are unique and incapable of repetitions.

Sociology becomes, therefore, something which is evaluative, critical and sympathetic. The practitioner becomes a professional pryer. It is in its methodology and in its intentions that sociology *can* claim to be scientific. In the former because it is concerned with objective empirical facts, and in the latter because it aims at exact description and explanation.

It is not a necessary part of the concept of sociology that it must be of use nor that it should be *for* something. Sociology is not to be defined in terms of uses. It is not social reform; it is not doing something for the community; it is not helping industry; it is not working for any one organization; it is not a body of fact; it is not a purely descriptive discipline. The concept of sociology involves the deliberate conveying of something of value in a manner which is lucid and coherent, and which conveys to the listener a need to strive towards understanding it. It undoubtedly has a practical use; but this is incidental to its real value in enabling the learner to understand the world in which he is an actor.

The use and application of sociology As an academic discipline, sociology, in common with a great number of other subjects, is *of no use as such,* being an attempt to understand rather than do. It is nevertheless the case that thousands of sociologists are applying their knowledge to some practical purpose, either in advertising, fighting crime, census studies, the planning of new towns, examining the social origins of disease, and so on. They are extensively used in government agencies and in areas of political decision making. For example, government plans to introduce changes into certain programmes concerning health, income and retirement benefits usually employ sociologists at the blue-print stage. Changes in our national education system are generally brought about after years of research by sociologists into areas such as ability, streaming, occupational choices for school-leavers. Problems in industry, both in its location and efficient functioning, are generally brought to the attention of social scientists.

Sociologists play a part in providing information on which decisions are taken in areas such as health, the army, the police, regional growth points, the re-organization of local government, and so on. On a smaller scale, they contribute to marriage-guidance counselling, group therapy, the organization of mental hospitals, and to the provision of data on which decisions which affect human relationships are based. Industrial sociologists play a major part in detecting day-to-day weaknesses in the social relationships of large commercial concerns. Only gradually, in this country, has sociology crept into the curriculum of schools, but it is increasingly recognised that in many respects it forms a valuable part of an individual's education. Many occupational training schemes have some element of sociology in them: for example, the training of clergy, the police, the probation officer, health visitors, and management.

In America, sociology has been important in the training of medical and para-medical personnel for some time. In this country, the training of future medical practitioners, either in general practice or the hospital service, has not kept pace with the real requirements of such training, which would adequately reflect the demands of modern industrialised society. General practice is increasingly being called upon to fill the role that was formerly entertained by the Church or the local friendly squire, and indeed deals with 96 % of all illness in Britain, for example. But the GP is completely ill-prepared to deal with many of the problems with which he is confronted in the U.K., often giving bad advice, or at the best advice no better than that which could be offered by a layman. Often he is unaware of the real nature of voluntary services or of the way in which they could compliment the health service. More and more patients are expecting a warmth of human relationship in their GP. Very important were the results of a recent survey conducted by the Office of Health Economics in the U.K. in which doctors listed the following as areas that they felt they should give advice; contraception 93 %; other marital problems 83 %; upbringing of children 67 %; employment problems 51 %. This is a further indication that doctors not only regard themselves as authoritative in non-medical matters, but also presumably that it is a reflection of the sort of advice that they *are* in fact asked for. In the 1980s doctor–patient relationships *are* important, but the other major areas in which he gives advice are sexual relationships and marriage, loneliness and old age, and psycho-social disharmony. A sound body of knowledge of the behavioural sciences, built into his training programme, would help the prospective medical practitioner to cope adequately with problems in these areas.

When we turn to the field of nursing, the situation is somewhat different. Nurses are altogether thrown into a situation with patients which involves greater contact over time. They get to know their patients much better than most doctors, and they share the problems of patients in ways that doctors do not. Often patients are nursed constantly for several months on end, and often it is the nursing staff who are with a patient at the last moments of his life. In many ways, therefore, sociology, because it deals with human situations and relationships, can offer much in this area in the way of assistance. A basic grounding in a discipline which deals with the nuances of social class, the development of individuals, the eccentricities of political, religious, and moral beliefs, the peculiarities of sexual and social behaviour, the meanings attributed to illness and death, the differences between the town and country dweller, the behaviour of individuals in small-group (perhaps ward) situations, the division of occupations, the social structure of the modern hospital, combined with a broad picture of trends in the sociology of medicine, will inevitably lead to a better understanding of the patient and finally to a more adequate system of nursing.

It has been necessary in the first part of this chapter to discuss the question of the *kind* of subject and the sort of knowledge that sociology offers. This is because questions arise as to whether sociology is a humanity or science, whether its methodology is scientific, what individuals think they mean by the term, the nature of concepts and models; all this is an important part of sociology and must be broadly understood before tackling some of the main areas of the discipline. It is important that the tools of the trade are mastered before we begin to use them. And unlike practical or technical subjects, questions such as these are encouraged.

Concepts and theories The meaning of *concept* falls basically into four categories. Generally speaking the term indicates an idea or notion. It is an abstract notion which becomes a tool of social inquiry. A second meaning is that it is a kind of unit through which we think on a smaller scale than a judgement, proposition or theory but still a necessary part of thinking. Again, concepts correspond to meaningful words and tend to be general rather than singular, 'concept of Cape Town' or 'concept of Amanda' rather than 'concept of it' or 'concept of and'. Lastly, concepts in the social sciences tend to be rather vague and are described as applicable or inapplicable, valid or invalid, useful or useless. (Gellner E. In: Gould J, Kolb W. *A Dictionary of the Social Sciences*. London: Tavistock, 1964.)

Theories embrace concepts and organise them into a system of meanings by explaining how they relate together. Theories enable us to organise seemingly meaningless facts or occurrences into a meaningful and coherent whole. Theories can be micro or macro. An example of the former is perhaps a theory of how one becomes an alcoholic. An example of the latter is what we might term 'grand theory', such as how is social order possible or what were the social origins of World War One. Generally, sociologists tend to acquire in their training one of three main sociological perspectives

The functionalist perspective One of the early sociologists, Herbert Spencer (1820–1903) viewed society as a kind of organism. Emile Durkheim (1858–1917) also shared this view. Human societies are like living structures and contain a head, limbs, etc. Each part of the organism has a function in relation to all the other parts and consequently plays a vital *function* in which each part relates to all the others. Such organisms changed over time due to natural evolution. We must remember that one of the dominant theories of the time was Charles Darwin's theory of *evolution*. 'Social Darwinism' influenced both British and American sociologists, and they held to the view that such Darwinian ideas as 'natural selection' and 'survival of the fittest' pertained not only in the natural world but also in the social world. Thus the fact that certain groups are higher in the social hierarchy, that class and social stratification are a part of the social world was ascribed to 'natural' processes of selection.

In recent times functionalism regained some status in the works of Talcott Parsons and Robert Merton. Such a theory regards society as integrated and balanced. Components reinforce each other and abrupt change is regarded as disruptive. Functionalism as a theory is a conservative one. Change much be paced or else it will be fragmentary. Merton subsequently asked for the consequences of certain elements in society, calling them *manifest* functions and *latent* functions, i.e. intended and unintended consequences. For example, medicine has a manifest function of caring and curing people who are ill. However, it also has latent functions such as attempting to control individuals, to bring them under the control of professional medical staff. An example of this is the manner in which the medical sphere has spread its authority to embrace not only disease but peripheral areas such as sexual 'deviance' (e.g. homosexuality) or alcoholism. These newly created 'diseases' are now medicalised in order to bring some form of control to bear on individuals who would otherwise be outside the norm of society. Another perspective introduced by Merton is that of *dysfunction*, when some 'spin-offs' from the manifest functions of some element in society have negative consequences. An example drawn from medicine is what Ivan Illich describes as *iatrogenesis*, by which he means that the medical system can have side-effects which are detrimental to the individual, for example too many antibiotics can have very negative affects on the individual's ability to provide an immunity against certain germs.

The conflict perspective Karl Marx, who, although born in Germany, spent most of his life in London, is probably the most significant sociologist. The majority of people regard him as the man who gave his name to several political movements such as Marxism and Communism although he himself states 'I am not a Marxist'. Through Marx's eyes we learn to see the world as full of *conflict* and *dysfunction* which, indeed, are inherent in all societies. Marx's famous picture of the world is based on the notion of class conflict, between those who own the means of production and those who do not. The final solution will come about by revolution with the overthrow of oppressive elements and the formation of a classless society. It must be remembered that Marx (1818–1883) has been dead for more than a hundred years. Much of what he said is now not true or his predictions have not materialised. This is not to say that there is not much of value in his writings. Nevertheless Marx's conflict perspective helps us to see the numerous conflicts at work in society, for example the conflict of interests between doctor and patient, between nurse and doctor, or between hospital administrator and medical staff.

Individuals are constantly competing for scarce commodities and instead of consensus there is a struggle to establish compliance and conformity by those who control these scarce resources. Far from being destructive, conflict binds essentially different elements into a common unity against specific goals. Such a perspective shows us that there are powerful interest groups in society whose position is based essentially on privilege, wealth and power.

The interactionist perspective The German sociologist Max Weber (1864–1920) first drew attention to the concept of *Verstehen*, or interpretive understanding, in which he stressed the importance of understanding situations and events from the point of view of the actors or participants. Social psychologists such as George Herbert Mead (1863–1931) analysed everyday social interaction between people. They emphasised the individual rather than what they considered abstract entities such as The Hospital or The School and argued that the latter were made up of the former. Mead emphasised language as the basis of communication, moreover human behaviour differs from animal behaviour because it is mostly purposeful or deliberate.

The interactionist perspective embraces *dramaturgical* theory which was expounded by Erving Goffman (1959). He viewed social interaction very much as a play in which the actors adopted specific parts. Individuals frequently 'improvise' and 'stage-manage' their lives and 'manage their impressions'. In other words, we present ourselves to others by playing a part. Goffman carried out several fascinating studies which included patients in mental hospitals and individuals born with some type of 'stigma' such as a physical or social deformity.

Symbolic interaction and ethnomethodology are two branches of interactionism which developed under the influence of phenomenology. Phenomenology is a school of philosophy which refers to the process by which we interpret objects or 'phenomena' which surround us in the social world. We interpret such objects by bestowing *meaning* on them. For example, when we enter the house of a stranger we perceive a chair which to us is an ordinary chair. The owner however, sees the chair as the one in which his dear mother died or which was given to him on his retirement from work. Similarly time and distance mean different things to different people. To the phenomenologist the world does not exist as a given objective reality. What does exist is bundles of meanings. A good example is a dying patient in a hospital. The 'situation' actually does not exist as one static reality because it means something entirely different to the patient, to the relatives (sorrow, greed, etc.), the harrassed doctor, the probationer nurse, the ward orderly, the experienced Sister, and so on.

Ethnomethodology attempts to test the basic assumptions underlying everyday social reality. We entertain a number of everyday taken for granted conceptions of the world around us and ethnomethodology sets out to try to understand how these conceptions and definitions of reality are constructed and shared in social interaction and everyday encounters. One of the originators of this particular perspective, Garfinkel (1967), devised a number of situations in which everyday assumptions and rules were violated. For example, he invited his students, when in their own homes, to behave towards their parents as though they were boarders or lodgers. The results were remarkable; family members demanded explanations and wondered whether their children were afflicted in some way.

For most of our waking lives we are engaged in some form of social interaction which requires not only participation but also interpretation. A slap on the face, for example, can be interpreted as: (*a*) two people quarreling; (*b*) actors in a stage play; (*c*) a father slapping a child; (*d*) a child slapping a father, etc. We talk about interaction being *symbolic* because we bestow meanings on objects and situations. A national flag, for example, can be viewed as a piece of cloth or encapsulating the spirit of a country, and a piece of wood constructed in a certain way as the Christian cross. The sacred Hindu cow is essentially no different from other cows apart from the meaning given it. We do not respond to individuals directly but rather to the way they are situated and the repertoire of meanings we place on what they say and do. Perhaps more obvious examples of how certain groups utilise symbols to present their identities to others are demonstrated by a study of nurses and punks (Travers, 1982) both of which groups demonstrate a symbolic power by their appearance and social behaviour. Another example of a carefully staged interaction is when a physician (generally male) carries out a vaginal examination of a female patient. The context is highly ritualised in order to exclude any suggestion of a sexual encounter. (Henslin, Briggs, 1971; Emerson, 1970).

An important aspect of social interaction is *non-verbal behaviour* by which we generally mean gestures, facial expressions and signs. Our posture, what we do with our hands and our facial expressions communicate a considerable amount of information over and above our verbal utterances. 'Body language' and physical propinquity (physical space between people) are considered important areas of non-verbal interaction (Argyle, 1969). Anthropological data has brought to our attention a variety of ways in which gestures can communicate the same message but in a different way. Consequently, gestures, to be meaningful, must be placed in a cultural context.

The physical proximity that individuals have to each other is also a means of communicating. We carry with us a private space that, if violated or intruded upon, brings a strong reaction. If we touch somebody when talking to them we are suggesting an extreme familiarity. When talking to strangers we 'distance' ourselves as we do also when addressing someone of a different race, age, or social class.

It is important in evaluating what we have described above to conceive of them as many different perspectives. This is because there is no one interpretation of social reality but multiple interpretations which generally fall into one of the three we have outlined. Often it is more fruitful to use a combination of perspectives in our analysis. For example, if we made a study of a hospital ward we could use the functionalist mode of analysis to bring out the bureaucratic structure, the roles that each individual plays and the positive benefits within the context of society at large and the economic system. A conflict perspective might highlight the racial or class tension that exists within the ward and the hospital at large, the disharmony between the administrative and the medical staff, the struggle for parity of wages, and so on. The interactionist perspective would, as the name implies, look in detail at the everyday social interactions, including staff/staff, staff/patient and patient/patient. It would most probably look at the manner in which rules are short-circuited (the key to the drugs cabinet) or the manner in which patients manipulate the nursing and medical staff or the utilisation of 'timetables' and so on, (Roth, 1963). Naturally, sociologists tend to fall into certain schools, advocating the superiority of the one they belong to against the other two. However, a fairer view would be the one that regarded all three perspectives as contributing their own special dimension.

Social theory and medicine Medical sociology is a relatively recent area of interest but despite its youth it is now an indispensable part of any medical training. It is fashionable to make the distinction between sociology in medicine and sociology of medicine. (Strauss, 1957) *Sociology in medicine* refers to the application and use of sociological concepts and techniques to facilitate the work of the medical profession. *Sociology of medicine* refers to a sociological analysis of medical practice and its practitioners in much the same way as sociology looks at other institutions in society such as religion and education.

Sociology *in* medicine is concerned with the ecology and aetiology of disease. It is now well established that there is a *correlation* (a relationship between variables that occurs regularly) between certain social factors and specific diseases. We know, for example that there is a correlation between schizophrenia and Registrar General Social Class V (unskilled workers). However, the '*drift hypothesis*' argues that perhaps the mentally ill are unable to cope with their work and families, etc. and consequently descend to class V. Another area of interest to sociology *in* medicine is in recognising the importance of social class in information about the attitudes concerning disease, health and health resources. There are quite broad differences between the social classes in their perception of illness and disease. This area has also concerned itself with labelling and deviance, but we deal with this in more detail in the next chapter.

The sociology *of* medicine concerns itself with such topics as the recruitment and characteristics of medical and nursing personnel and the paramedical occupations such as physiotherapy, dentistry, radiography and so on. It would be relevant to this particular discipline that in America, of the 10 000 students entering training in 1970 only 4,2 % were black, and only 2 % of the 250 000 physicians currently practising in America are black, (Kendall and Reader, 1972). The sociology *of* medicine also concerns itself with the training of health workers by writing books such as the one you are now reading or by contributing relevant aspects of sociology to lecture and training programmes. It is also concerned with analysing the role of doctors and how they relate to nursing and paramedical staff. Two further areas are those concerned with the analysis of medical organisations (for example, the modern hospital) and with the development of community health.

It is increasingly recognised that health and illness, and the methods used to treat them, are both historically and culturally bound. Several studies have tried to trace the emergence of modern medicine (Jones, 1986). Jones shows the historical context of resistance to the use of anaesthetic and the struggles for supremacy amongst medical factions. There is no doubt that culture decides on the nature of treatment for a particular disease or illness. Recent studies have shown that traditional treatment exists alongside western treatment in many countries of the world, including South Africa, (Jones, 1988; Elling, 1981). Every known society has socially organised health problems and the response to them, (Jansen, 1973).

The historical development of medicine led to the emergence of medical sociology as a distinctive discipline in the 1950s, (Twaddle and Hessler, 1977). At the beginning of the germ theory era, various early public health movements were instigated, resulting in the isolation of lepers into colonies and the drainage and irrigation systems of ancient Greece and Rome. These movements, during the nineteenth century in large industrial cities of England, culminated in the early epidemi-

MIDWIFE ATTENDING CHILDBEARING WOMAN SEATED ON OBSTETRICAL STOOL
Jacobus Rueff 1554, Engraving. (The Wellcome Institute for the History of Medicine)

ological work of Snow and his Broad Street pump in London, and led the way to a public awareness of the social aspects of disease and the social solution for many of them. The discovery of germ theory resulted in a new orientation on the part of the physician, namely a disease-orientation rather than a focus on the patient as a person. The era of post-germ theory has meant a concentration on the social sciences and medicine.

It soon became obvious that the isolation of germs and viruses was not the answer to the eradication of disease, even if this were in fact possible, (Dubos, 1959). Not only were physical and biological states recognised but also psychological and social states. (Twaddle, op. cit. p.14). The emergence of psychiatry was a further demonstration that germs were not a complete answer: there were many illnesses for which germ theory could not account.

The emergence of social epidemiology (the study of the origin, distribution, and means of transmission of disease in populations—see Chapter Nine) fixed the origin of disease very squarely in a social context. Specific diseases now became linked with specific occupations (asbestos workers and cancer, for example). Lifestyles became linked with stress-related diseases such as hypertension and mental illness. Demographic and epidemiologic pioneers include Snow and his investigation of the cholera epidemic in London, Chadwick, who separated water supplies and sewage disposal, Abraham Hume, who pioneered a social survey into health, disease and poverty in Liverpool, William Farr and others. The work of Hume, Frederich Engels and Charles Booth did much to highlight the terrible condition of the poor in industrial nineteenth century England.

More recently, McKeown (1971) has shown fairly conclusively that dramatic changes in mortality prior to 1937 were not the result of developing medical technology but rather due to improved food supplies resulting from better agricultural and industrial development. If we examine graphs for respiratory tuberculosis, bronchitis, pneumonia, influenza, whooping cough, measles and scarlet fever from about 1838 to 1970, the intervention by vaccine and chemotherapy had no perceptible effect on an already declining curve. Economic, political and social change outweighed technical advances.

The demographic and health survey contribution to medical care is outlined in other chapters. Twaddle (1977) outlines a number of other 'sociological' aspects which have been of benefit. The *organic tradition*, represented by Herbert Spencer, and the school of social Darwinism mentioned above, had an influence on medical concepts and care. The medical concept of a 'system' is directly inherited from the biological/human ecological model. Another contribution is the 'debunking' of tradition cited by Berger (1963). Here prestigious groups and ideologies are singled out for criticism. Durkheim's *Suicide* is a primary empirical study in sociology and although it utilised poor data and has been recently heavily criticised, (Douglas, 1967) it was extremely influential and can be regarded as the first medical sociology textbook.

Other sociological contributions in terms of social theory include the Chicago school on social change and cultural lag (i.e. political, social and economic knowledge lags far behind advanced medical technology). The Lynds' study of Middletown (1929 and 1937) were important contributions to medical sociology because they were the first to explore illness and health behaviour from the perspective of the community. Parsons' *The Social System*, published in 1951, was the first attempt to analyse medical practice and the role of the sick person. Finally, there is an overlap between medicine and sociology in their methodologies which utilise quantitative, experimental and predictive techniques.

Research design As a systematic study sociology has to come to terms with (a) the philosophy and logic of social inquiry and how it relates to sociological theory, and (b) a set of techniques appropriate to the area which we intend to study. Natural scientists do not appear as obsessed by *methodology* (a system of rules, procedures, principles, etc. that serve as a guide to scientific investigation). The nature of social investigation, unfortunately, is very much more difficult than that of the natural sciences. The very unpredictability of human behaviour compared with the behaviour of protons and atoms, for example, involves a series of often competing methodologies. The very act of trying to measure or observe another human being renders a change in the characteristics of the observed. This is not to say that such an effect is not also present in the natural sciences. The Principle of Indeterminacy formulated by Heisenberg is found in physics. In the quantum world we cannot observe a particle without illuminating it. However, the very act of illuminating it pushes it out of the way and consequently we observe a collision and not a particle.

In order to understand social behaviour it is necessary to understand the notions of cause and effect and, indeed, to separate the one from the other in the intricate web of social interaction. One important aspect of the relationship between cause and effect is the *variable*. This is defined as any characteristic which can change or differ. Variables are classified as qualitative (nationality, political party, occupation, sex) or quantitative (age, intelligence, wealth). If we seek to discover the correlation between malnutrition and infant mortality in Transkei, for example, or the relationship between hypertension and a high cholestoral level, we have to then distinguish between an *independent variable* and a *dependent variable*. The former is one that influences another variable. The latter is one that is influenced by a variable. Thus in studying the incidence of traffic accidents one of the areas we would examine would be alcohol intake (independent variable) and vehicle accidents. Alcohol consumption is perhaps only one independent variable. Others might be age, driving experience or even temperament.

It is important to realise that it is the relationship between variables that is important rather than the variables.

The sociologist looks also at *correlations*. We defined this earlier as the relationship between variables. In a recent study of measles and tuberculosis in Transkei a strong correlation appeared between these variables and malnutrition. Thus we generalise that both these diseases are what Waitzkin (1983) calls the 'second sickness', i.e. that they both arise from the condition of poverty. However, the high correlation between two variables does not distinguish a cause or effect nor necessarily any relationship at all! Robertson (1987) gives an interesting example of a high correlation existing in America between the sale of ice cream and the incidence of rape. If we equated a high correlation with a causal connection we would have to say that eating ice cream causes rape or, conversely that rape causes people to eat ice cream. .Neither position is of course tenable because we need to introduce an additional variable, the heat of summer! The earlier correlation between ice cream and rape is a *spurious* correlation, one that is a pure coincidence and not a causal relationship.

In nineteenth century England, William Farr noted an inverse relationship between altitude and deaths from cholera. This appeared to give support to the popular theory of the time that bad air was responsible for the disease (miasma = bad air). According to this theory, in areas of low altitude there would be a higher incidence of cholera. Indeed, the observed mortality 'is remarkably close to that predicted on the basis of the miasma theory. According to current knowledge, however, cholera death rates were high in areas of fetid air because they were areas of low altitude where water supplies were also less pure. It was the impure water, not the fetid air, which led to the high death rate from cholera.' (Mausner and Bahn, 1974.) This points the way to the introduction of *controls*, i.e. excluding other factors influencing the relationship between the two variables.

There are numerous difficulties encountered in the research process of social phenomena, which are not present in research in the natural sciences. These are generally regarded as the following:

1. Someone who is being studied always reacts in some way. The very fact that one knows that one is being observed alters our behaviour.
2. Individuals possess attributes which inanimate objects do not, such as personality and emotions. One would doubt very much the complete truthfulness of answers about the subject's intimate sex life, for example. Individuals prone to alcohol-related problems invariably underestimate their consumption. A temperate interviewer would also be more likely to overestimate responses when questioning a possible alcoholic.
3. There are a multitude of factors involved in the study of social behaviour. There is no simple answer to the rise of capitalism in western Europe and the emergence of the Protestant ethic. It is even

Medieval monasteries kept herb gardens for medicinal purposes, but the seventeenth century saw an explo-
sive growth of physic gardens, well stocked with exotics. The spirit of rationalism is evident in this engraving
of the layout of the Physick Garden in Chelsea: The stock has been maintained and the garden is now open
to the public.
(*BBC Hulton Picture Library*)

difficult to establish whether industrialised societies are more secularised than they were a hundred years ago.

4. Whereas natural scientists can establish a whole range of experiments on plants, neutrons, DNA molecules and even animals, sociologists cannot do so easily with humans. If there is some suggestion that child abusers have themselves been abused as children we cannot artificially create a situation which would produce this effect. The hypothesis that homosexuals are made and not born, i.e. that certain patterns and relationships in their formative years lead them to associate sexually with the same sex, is impossible to test by deliberately creating 'faulty' childhood environments.

5. Sociological research is itself a social process and sociologists are part of what they are examining. Sociologists have political commitments, are married or single, atheist or Christian, for example. A botanist studying mountain fauna is separate from the object of study in a way that a sociologist can never be.

These are serious impediments to the development of sociology (and the social sciences in general) along anything like the line of the natural scientists. The *hypothetico-deductive model* is an attempt at an ideal procedure. This model consists of a theory, a deduction, and finally an hypothesis. In reality what actually happens in science is far from the ideal model. One of the reasons is that science is itself a social activity. Scientists are not the detached, aloof, observers they are depicted as in films and television. There are heavily vested interests at work. A few years ago the late Sir Cyril Burt, a leading British psychologist was found to have fabricated his data on identical or uni-ovular twins. Some ten years ago a prominent Harvard medical scientist was found to have faked his results in over 100 research publications. Those scientists who discover something first obtain and retain the scientific honours. Thus we have all heard of Darwin but not of Wallace, each of who is credited with the theory of evolution. It is the American Edison who is credited with inventing the electric light bulb and not the Britisher Snow. Kuhn (1962) gave a very significant analysis of scientific innovation concentrating particularly on the scientific revolution. Scientists in a particular field develop a set of concepts and beliefs which Kuhn called a *paradigm*. A paradigm sets the boundaries of what constitutes the problem, the solution and the methodology. Eventually one paradigm is replaced by another, for example when the Ptolemaic theory of the universe was replaced by the Copernican theory. This in turn was replaced by Einsteinian theory.

One way of overcoming some of the problems of methodology which confront sociologists is to use an *inductive method of reasoning*. That is, rather than *deducing* a hypothesis from a theory, the sociologist *induces* a conceptual structure:

	HYPOTHETICO-DEDUCTIVE	INDUCTIVE
Step 1:	Theory	Observation
Step 2:	Deduction	Data gathering
Step 3:	Hypothesis	Analysis

Winch (1958) discussed at length whether it was the goal of sociology to explain or to interpret reality. Clearly these are two entirely different perspectives and we find that sociology has been split in terms of both its theory and methodology between the two opposing approaches. We will deal with this in the last section of this chapter but first it is useful to sketch some of the basic research methods, the nature of the research model and some ethical problems associated with research.

Natural scientists carry out a great deal of experimental and laboratory work. Occasionally in sociology individuals are introduced into an artificial setting as an *experiment*. This type of methodology is much more common in psychology or the biological sciences. Usually one group is the *experimental group* (exposed to the independant variable) and the other the *control group* (exposed to everything the experimental group is exposed to except the independent variable). The classic sociological experiment was conducted in 1939 at the Hawthorne factory of Western Electric. The management were keen to increase productivity and a group of researchers were invited to give their opinion on this. The researchers introduced a number of variables such as coffee breaks, extra lighting and so forth. However, whatever they did increased the productivity even when the researchers withdrew. It was subsequently discovered that the very act of being observed increased productivity. The women enjoyed the attention and worked harder simply as their way of rewarding the researchers for all the attention. This contamination of an experiment by the subject's anticipations about what the researcher is trying to discover is known as the *Hawthorne effect*. Good experimental design will have comparison (a group with which to compare) and control (a process by which we exclude alternative explanations). In addition it will also have internal and external validity. An experiment is internally valid if we can assert that the experimental stimulus was truly responsible for the differences found. It is externally valid if we can generalise the results beyond the particular time, place and design.

Another important method used frequently in research is *sampling*, that is, selecting a sub-set of a wider population for the purpose of study. We generally sample when we conduct a survey, which is a systematic method of collecting standardised information about specific characteristics of a population. The Transkei conducted a sample census, not the entire population but a representative sample of it, in 1985. If a survey requires the opinion of nurses concerning their working conditions it would probably be too large a task to question every nurse in South Africa. The answer lies in conducting a *random sample*, one chosen in such a way that every member of the population (in this instance nurses) has the same chance of being selected. By *population* we mean the total group the researcher is interested in, i.e. nurses, doctors, homosexuals, alcoholics, etc. The size of a sample does not guarantee its representativeness. A popular way of surveying is by means of questionnaires and interviews. These can be structured (closed) or unstructured (open). This area is a very complex one and we can do no more than mention it here. Suffice it to say that students intending to carry out even a small series of interviews or administer a small number of questionnaires must read the literature extensively. Otherwise, if they do not draw up their instruments very carefully they will be wasting their own time and that of the respondents.

A third method of research is using an *observational* study. This consists of accurate description and analysis, usually in the form of a case study, a complete and detailed record of a group, event or social process. There are two approaches to such studies that can be utilised. The first is that we can approach the group, tell them we are sociologists, and then simply watch what they are doing, or we can join the group by pretending to be alcoholic (a study of Alcoholics Anonyous), or an ex-mental patient (Recovery, Inc.) or a believer (religious sects and cults). These approaches are termed *participant observation*. The second approach is non-participant observation or detached observation. This is a method in which the observer remains aloof, and the subjects are usually unaware that they are being studied. Jones (1985) studied seven such groups including two religious sects, a group of problem drinkers, two ex-mental patient groups and a fundamentalist Marxist political sect. A famous study in America was described in Leon Festinger's book *When Prophecy Fails* (1956). The study was about a religious cult which held the belief that Jesus was coming to visit the earth in a flying saucer to save the select few! Polsky (1964) used participant observation with pool-room hustlers, Goffman (1961) used it in a mental institution, Wallis (1977) posed as a Scientologist and Lofland (1966) as a 'Moonie'. There are many arguments for and against such methods, ranging from ethical problems to methodological ones. Obviously, in many respects the insights gained by these methods are impressionistic or personal and the study is largely unreplicable. On the other hand the sociologist describes real-life situations.

The final method is that of using existing sources. By this is meant census reports, departmental reports, coroner's reports, historical records, health statistics, and so on. The Development Bank of Southern Africa, for example, publishes a complete file (continually up-dated) on all the homelands, including information on education, health, the economy and industry. The classic study by Durkheim, *Suicide* (1897), utilised existing suicide statistics and showed that suicide, far from being a highly individual action, was deeply embedded in a social context. Extreme caution must, of course, be used in regard to the reliability of the statistics and records used, even the official ones.

The *research model* is a tested method of carrying out research. Most sociologists would skip or omit perhaps one or two of the following seven steps but it is intended as a guide to any one intending to carry out a piece of research.

1. A definition of the problem. We do this partly by drawing on our everyday experience or reading the literature, once we have formulated an idea. Perhaps we do not want to research an area already heavily researched or perhaps we are drawn to an area because it is currently topical. e.g. child-abuse.
2. Review of the literature. The next step is to read extensively on and around the area of choice.
3. The research problem must be capable of being tested. To do this we have to put it in the form of an hypothesis. The researcher must also produce an *operational definition*, one that states a concept in a way that can be measured.
4. Select a research design, a survey, observational study, experiment or existing sources. It is possible to use more than one of these.
5. Data collecting. We must collect data which is capable of being analysed and handled within the time scale available. Often there is either too much data collected or insufficient data collected. As far as the latter is concerned it is simply not possible to revisit the field because a vital piece of information was omitted.
6. An analysis of the results. The range of analytical techniques is very wide. Generally they fall into qualitative (descriptive, literary, etc.) and quantitative (statistical).
7. Reaching a conclusion. This involved relating the findings to the general body of theory and research and to the initial hypothesis.

The ethical issues connected with carrying out research have been amply discussed in Bulmer (1982). Both medicine and sociology at times perform research which calls into question the ethical status of the action. In medicine various biomedical experiments with polio immunization in the 1930s rendered many children dead or paralysed. The development of the successful vaccine involved a large group who were given a *placebo* (harmless substance) in the knowledge that the placebo group was unprotected, some of whom would contract polio and become paralysed, or died, simply because they were randomly allocated to the control group, (Paul, 1971). A group of black American prisoners were withheld treatment for syphillis for twenty-five years to observe the affects. Doctors at the Sloan-Kettering Cancer Foundation injected live cancer cells into the skins of unsuspecting patients (Katz, 1972). Generally, in sociology, research is considered unethical under the following conditions:

1. *It harms participants.*
There are, in effect, hardly any examples of this except a few

experiments with LSD, exposure to violent television programmes and exposure to pornographic material.

2. *Invasion of privacy.*
   Generally this occurs when unobtrusive measures are used (Webb, 1966) that is, that they are being studied without their knowledge. The classic illustration is the searching of household rubbish in order to establish consumer behaviour in Tucson, Arizona.

3. *Informed consent.*
   Researchers should inform people they are being studied and also obtain their consent. However, many studies would be impossible to carry out if this were always the case.

4. *Application of research.*
   The researcher must not enter into a research project which might be used against people or groups in a manner which would hurt them.

5. *Deception.*
   The classic example is that of Humphreys's of homosexual acts in public lavatories in America (1970). He was able to observe hundreds of acts by posing as a 'watchqueen' or police lookout. He noted their car numbers and visited their homes after an interval of a year, on the pretext of carrying out a consumer survey. Humphreys was criticised for being irresponsible in noting the car numbers as these could have fallen into the hands of a blackmailer, and also for deceiving people by lying about his follow-up.

Data collection The general theory or set of theories which embrace science and scientific research is known as *positivism*. Positivism basically maintains that in both the social and the natural sciences sense experiences and their mathematical and logical treatment are the only source of all worthwhile information. The term itself, coined by the 'father' of sociology, Auguste Comte, comes from the French *positif*, meaning 'based on facts or experience'. Naive positivism maintains that social phenomena must be explained in terms of Newtonian mechanics with analogies drawn from the natural sciences. A later development were the *logical positivists* of the Vienna Circle, sometimes referred to as *neo-positivism*. The aims of logical positivism were to 'provide a secure foundation for the sciences . . . (and) to demonstrate the meaninglessness of all metaphysics . . . by the method of the logical analysis of all concepts and propositions'. (Weinberg J R. *An Examination of Logical Positivism*, London: Kegan Paul, 1936). The social world, from this perspective, replicates the natural world. Just as there are causes and effects in the natural world so there are in the social world. The world is consequently regarded as objective and given and it exists independently of any subjective feelings we may entertain about it. Positivist sociology began, historically, with Comte who designated sociology the 'science of society' whose task it was to uncover the 'laws' governing social behaviour just as the physical sciences did this in the natural world. Durkheim was an extremely influential positivist as were many

American sociologists in the 1940s and 1950s. These sociologists believe that we are born into pre-existing social structures which determine our socialisation and from which we learn to think in a particular way and act in a particular manner. By going one step further they argue that the methods used to study the physical world should also be used to study the social world. Durkheim believed in *social facts* which he defined in his book *The Rules of Sociological Method* (Chicago: University of Chicago Press, 1938) as: 'a category of facts with very distinctive characteristics; it consists of ways of acting, thinking and feeling, external to the individual and endowed with a power of coercion by reason of which they control him.' He further goes on to say that 'The laws of societies are no different from those governing the rest of nature and the method by which they are discovered is identical with that of the other sciences.'

Methods of data collection in positivist sociology include the experiment which we discussed above. This method is part of the process of systematically producing original data (primary data), including quantitative methods. Using secondary (existing) material, which we also mentioned above, includes the use of the comparative method as an alternative to the experimental method. Closely linked to the comparative method is the historical one. Both Weber and Durkheim utilised these methodologies, searching for causal relationships between two factors. Weber compared Europe with China in his search for a connection between Calvinism and capitalism, while Durkheim was interested in the connection between community integration and suicide rates, i.e. the higher the integration of support the lower would be the suicide rate. Marx, too, was concerned with establishing a scientific theory of society. Of the 'founding fathers' of sociology Comte was perhaps the most naive in the application of science to social phenomena, followed by Durkheim's incessant search for social facts. Marx thought, as do some of his disciples, that he had discovered the laws of social change. Weber, alone, was sceptical of sociology's ability to establish laws on a par with those existing in the sciences.

Anti-positivist sociologists take an entirely different and contrary point of view. Interpretive or qualitative methods fall into three categories, the in-depth interview, and participant and non-participant observation. These methods describe as accurately as possible the quality of social experience that the social actors themselves feel. The premise supporting the methodology is that the social world has no similarity to the physical world. Interpretists argue that the behaviour of individuals is not determined by pre-existing social structures but is a socially constructed product. There is no reality as such but merely the interpretation we give to the evidence which we gain *empirically* (through our senses). As W I Thomas, who worked closely with G H Mead, stated: 'If people define situations as real, they are real in their consequences.' Berger and Luckman (1963) described the process by which individuals construct their social reality as consisting of three stages:

1. Human beings create material and nonmaterial products. This is everything around us, which sociologists call *culture*. By material products we mean squash racquets, cities and computers, and by nonmaterial products theories of chemistry, the AWB, apartheid and Mondays.
2. These cultural creations become part of what we term reality, even though we have created them.
3. We describe elsewhere the process whereby we assimilate the reality of our culture. This process is termed *socialisation*.

As individuals are actors who interpret the world around them it is the purpose of methodologies to help us to understand these interpretations or meanings. The method of *verstehen*, puts us in the place of the individuals observed.

There are a number of anti-positivist methodologies used for data collection. Symbolic interactionists rely to a considerable extent on the analysis of talk, as a principle medium of communication. Often an analysis of talk takes the form of an *in-depth interview*. This approach is to be contrasted with the formal interview which is considerably more structured. Partly, of course, there remains the interviewer effect, similar to the Hawthorne effect outlined above. Sociologists must struggle hard not to influence their subjects. Often, too, those interviewed give the answers they want the questioner to hear.

As we have already mentioned, non-participant observation as discussed in the Hawthorne experiment was intended to be detached and aloof although it was found that the productive performance of the workers was influenced by social factors. In that instance it was the researchers themselves who influenced the results. However, participant observation involves the researcher taking part in the very social life he wants to study. Goffman used this effectively in *Asylums* (1968), as did Becker (1963) in his analysis of life in a medical school, *Boys in White*. An earlier study by Whyte (1943) of a group of Italian slum children was a major methodological contribution. A recent example is Patrick's (1980) study of a Glasgow gang.

The methodology of ethnomethodologists tends to differ from that of symbolic interactionists. Not only does the research act now become the object of observation but no amount of observation and description can arrive at a 'true' or 'proven' result. Interestingly, ethnomethodologists make use of the experiment. We mentioned earlier Garfinkel's experiment with his students where he asked them to pretend to be lodgers in their own homes. In terms of participant observation ethnomethodologists are keen on descriptions, or ethnographies as they term them. Finally, ethnomethodologists rely on what they term 'conversational analysis'. In one study Sacks (1967) carried out research into suicides' talk. He was particularly concerned with examining the transcripts of recorded telephone conversations between potential suicides and staff.

Finally, a word must be said in this section of the relationship between theoretical perspectives and method. No one doing research can stick faithfully to the boundaries of the sociological perspectives they adopt. This is partly because such perspectives are usually too general to be validated. Secondly, although certain perspectives usually encourage certain methodologies this is not always or necessarily the case. Many studies contain a mixture of methodologies, both interpretive and structural. Willis (1978) contains a mix as does Cohen (1972). Atkinson (1977) gives an interesting picture of the writer's theoretical development from straight positivism, through interactionism, to, finally, an ethnomethodological approach.

Sociology and medicine It seems astonishing that hysterectomies could ever become fashionable. Yet in nine years, between 1961 and 1970, the number of women undergoing this operation had increased from 43 350 to 61 020. Several reasons can be given for this increase, including the rise in the

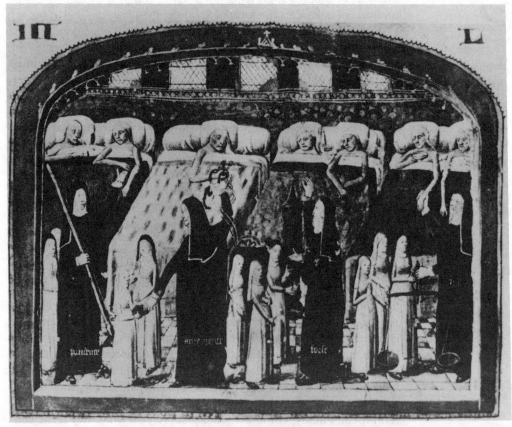

Sick ward of the Hôtel Dieu
(Fifteenth-century, Musée de L'Assistance Publique, Paris, France)

population and the feeling that operations of this kind are now surgically safer. There is even some evidence that a hysterectomy is becoming a middle-class status symbol. Further evidence from America suggests that one fifth of the operations performed there are unnecessary, including 50 % of tonsillectomies, 30 % of hysterectomies and 20 % of appendectomies, making a total of 2 000 000 unnecessary operations every year. Apart from factors such as incompetence in surgeons, and a greed for money from the fees, there is a strong pressure for such operations from the patients themselves. Another factor appears to lie in the training of doctors in America. That is, if there is an excess number of surgeons then it is possible that they will perform an excess number of operations. The American system also means that an empty hospital bed costs as much, or almost as much, as a full one, and the tendency is to fill these empty beds. The number of appendectomies performed in a given area, for example, does not relate to the number of people in that area that would be liable to have the operation performed but rather to how many surgeons and how many hospital beds there are in the area. People in areas with few surgeons and hospital beds appeared to exist quite happily with their appendices intact, and in areas with more surgeons and beds available produced a concomitant increase in appendectomies. In America hysterectomies are almost automatic for middle-class women over the age of 40, and a study at Columbia University put the figure of unnecessary operations of this sort at 33 %.

In Britain, the National Health Service pays for these operations, so the doctors and surgeons could not be said to have a money motive. Nevertheless there do appear to be unnecessary operations performed. Professor Neville Butler, Co-Director of the National Child Development Study, found that one third of all children who enter hospital in Britain do so to have their tonsils removed. Consequently, by the age of seven 16 % of British children are without tonsils. The surprising evidence was the variation of the rate throughout the country. In Wales 14 % of children had their tonsils removed, in the North of England 15 %, the South 17 %, and Scotland 21 %. Again, one local area can have fifteen times as many tonsillectomies as an adjoining area. Part of the reason for this regional and local variation lies in the services available, so that in an area where hospitals and surgeons are available then the operation is more in evidence. But there is also a general belief among the population as a whole that the removal of tonsils is conductive to health even if the child has not been ill. The higher up the social scale one goes the move likely the child is to be without tonsils. 15 % of unskilled manual workers' children have had their tonsils removed, while among the children of white-collar workers the figure is nearer 22 %.

These examples from America and Britain illustrate very clearly the scope and the contribution of sociology to medicine. In its origins sociology was concerned to establish itself as a scientific discipline and it turned readily to social areas and problems such as poverty and anomie, which were conditions highlighted by the industrial revolution. Medicine, for its part, developed in the nineteenth century heavily under the influence of biological germ theories of disease and relied on the laboratory and its techniques to give it respectability. Various factors can be seen as contributing to the convergence of the two subjects, as suggested by Coe.

1. Morbidity rates

The twentieth century has witnessed dramatic drops in the rate of epidemic disease, with the result that many of the population now live to feel the effects of chronic illness. Many of the population are reluctant to benefit from scientific advances such as screening tests. The changing pattern of disease has meant a shift in attention away from a single-cause theory of disease to the view that there are situations in common in the lives of individuals with some form of chronic illness which differ from those for individuals without evidence of such illness. Epidemiological studies have consequently become concerned with the life experiences and habits of individuals in society.

2. The rise of preventive medicine and the public health sector.

The spread of contagious disease in the population has been for the large part replaced by a wider concern for the ecology of any disease (how it is distributed in the general population). Many factors such as family background, type of housing, type of water, have now to be taken into account in the field of treatment. It is now clearly recognised that certain actions are bad for an individual's health, and a new area of health education has emerged. Of interest to the sociologist of medicine is the resistance to health measures from certain social strata of the population. This century has experienced the emergence of a total view of medicine with such concepts as community care, and techniques for measuring the level and type of health care that may be required by a particular area or community. Other growth areas include concern for the rehabilitation of individuals into families and communities after particular accidents and the increasing concern that certain occupations, e.g. work with asbestos, may carry with them grave risks.

3. The impact of modern psychiatry

Biological theories of the causation of disease broke down with the contribution of psychologists and psychiatrists that mechanisms other than biological ones could be involved. Such concepts as psychosomatic cause and stress began to play an important part in modern medicine. Mental illness, for example, came to be seen as having important social aetiologies, and the relationship of the patient with the physician was recognised as a very positive aspect of the treatment. In some cases the entire context of medical practice and the total environment of the patient became part of the milieu therapy.

4. Administrative medicine

More attention is now being given to the provision of medical facilities to regions in a way that would ensure a minimum of regional disparities. Hospitals themselves are becoming more humanised and patients given help in adjusting to their environment. The nursing profession has been among the first to employ social scientists in order to enhance the level of patient care, and indeed nursing schools have themselves been innovators of new perspectives.

By 1950 it was clearly seen in America, and to a lesser extent in Britain, that sociology, with its particular areas of study, had much to contribute to medicine. For example, the study of socialization, the family, the beliefs of individuals, social differentiation, the demographic and ecological techniques of social scientists, and the social psychological heritage of studying small groups and communities—all these had an important part to contribute to the field of medicine. Coupled with this the new view of health as not merely the absence of disease but the complete well-being of the individual, physical, mental and social, then it was but a short step to a conception of medicine as a social science.

Sociologists are increasingly employed as research workers, as lecturers in nursing and medical schools, and on psychiatric problems. With the growth of medicine, the contribution of sociology and its techniques will probably become even more relevant. Nevertheless, the four main perspectives of the sociology of medicine will still encompass those mentioned by Rodney Coe in 1970. First, disease in the population is neither random nor uniform but located in social groupings of various kinds. Because social structure imposes different life-styles on people this difference is often seen to provide clues to the origins of illness, an example being the incidence of bronchitis in unskilled labourers. Second, people respond to disease, and define it, in a predictable way from the perspective of their own culture and their own social class within that culture. Third, society erects a whole set of institutions to treat disease, whether it is the medicine man of the Trobriand islands or a modern teaching centre. Fourth, medical institutions for the treatment of the sick are supported in modern industrial societies by a vast array of other institutions, ranging from voluntary organizations to drug companies.

Disease and the sick person | The field of epidemiology is concerned with the way disease occurs and is distributed in a population, and it examines this distribution with the aid of different data before going on to construct logical chains of inference which explain the many factors that cause disease. The epidemiologist is concerned with the change in causes of death as well as simply the number of deaths. He has to rely to a great extent on official statistics on death, and although these may be accurate in modern industrialised societies there may still be some inaccuracy in the exact cause of death. In strongly religious countries suicide verdicts, as we have seen, need not necessarily give a reliable or true picture of the pattern. (See chapter nine, SOCIAL EPIDEMIOLOGY.)

The measurement of *morbidity* (the level of disease in the population) is a difficult task because there is no general agreement as to what constitutes a disease, the disease itself may remain undisclosed, treated disease may present a different picture to actual disease, and diseases tend to be under-reported. An important concept is *life expectancy* (the average number of years as measured from birth that an individual is expected to live measured by characteristics such as race, sex, and age). So for example we could compare rural with urban dwellers, and blacks with whites. The *incidence* of disease is the number of new cases of a disease which arise over a certain period of time, while the *prevalence* is the actual number or cases which exist at any given point in time.

The *rate* of disease is generally measured by epidemiologists in one of three ways. There is the *crude* rate (the number of people for a given unit of the population who possess the characteristics being measured for a particular unit of time), the *age-specific* rate (the number of deaths of people in a particular age-category divided by the number of people alive in that category at the middle of the year), and the *standardised* rate (for which age-specific rates are adjusted to compare age groupings in different populations). The standardised rate ensures that a fair comparison is made.

Epidemiological research methods involve the search for specific *disease agents*, factors in the *environment*, and *human* elements such as life-styles. Often a dramatic element is introduced in the work of the epidemiologist when he traces the source of a particular disease, or in the work which has been done on the correlation between cigarettes and lung cancer.

Some British examples One of the areas which lends itself to this particular aspect of the sociology of medicine is that of regional differences in the health of the population, and of concomitant regional responses in the preventive and general-practitioner services provided. By the use of epidemiological methods we can discover the distribution of mortality from all causes in England and Wales, for example. We find that large-population areas are high risk, and that Salford is second only to Berwickshire in its unfavourable mortality for males. Mortality from all causes for females tends to be concentrated in Southern Scotland, North and North-West England, Wales and sections of Northern Ireland. Research such as this can show that the average risk of dying in Burnley, for example, is 60 % greater than in Oxford, and that infant mortality rates are in excess in South Lancashire. Generally speaking the British Isles has two broad areas of disparity, one running from North of a line from the Humber to the Bristol Channel, and the other South of that line. Even when we look at mortality from accidents, regional variation is marked sometimes as much as 43 % in excess. The same general differentiation can be shown for mental illness rates and suicide, in

some areas the latter being 50 % above the national average. Bronchitis, tuberculosis, cancer of the trachea, lung and bronchus, morbidity from pernicious anaemia and breast cancer can also be
calculated by these methods. If we take the areas with a high excess
of breast cancer we must also consider that it tends to be most common
in women who are unmarried, married women who are childless, and
married women who have children but have not breast-fed them.

When we turn to examine the provision of health services we find
that these are relatively better in the South and East, despite the fact
that people in the North and West are at a higher risk of mortality.
Although the North and West are better off for hospital beds, the South
and East have large areas of relatively low provision. To complicate
matters there is an over-concentration of teaching hospitals in the
London area with a large number of consultants with merit awards.
Hospital costs per patient by regional hospital boards tends to have
wide variations within each region but no great difference between the
large regions to the North and South of the imaginary line from the
Humber to the Bristol Channel. Similar research can produce a
distribution for residence in mental hospitals and units by regional
hospital board, average list size of general practitioner, number of
school children per medical officer of country, and general dental
services by counties. The picture can be further elaborated by data
showing the distribution of overcrowding (over one and a half persons
to a room), household facilities (exclusive use of a cold and hot-water
tap, a fixed bath and a water closet), those on Income Tax Schedule E,
second-year sixth formers, income above the UK mean, the proportion
of children for whom free school meals are claimed, children granted
university awards, and so on.

Medical Until the consolidation of medical practice in Britain with the formation
practitioners of the General Medical Council in 1858, many of those practising
medicine were unqualified and came from a very heterogeneous background. It was not, perhaps, until the outbreak of the 1914–1918 war
that medical practitioners became competent enough to ensure a
patient more than a 50 % chance of benefiting from consultation.

The sociology of medicine includes in its sphere of inquiry surveys
and examination of trends in the composition and deployment of
doctors. Ann Cartwright's (1968) work has shown that of general
practitioners 5 % are women (based on her sample of 422); 13 %
qualified either during or after 1955; 25 % before 1934; 59 % have a
university degree and no further qualifications; 20 % have licentiate
qualifications only; only 4 % have an MD.

As many practitioners are employed as junior and senior hospital
staff as are engaged in general practice, and a strict hierarchy of office
exists from House Officer to Consultant. Some two thirds of Consultants have only a part-time National Health Service appointment, the
remainder of their week being in a private capacity. Half of the junior
hospital staff in England and Wales are from overseas. Since 1963 both

general practitioners and hospital practitioners have not increased to keep pace with the rise in population. There seem to be three reasons why this is so. Firstly, there was a serious error in forecasting future requirements and trends at the end of the 1950s. Second, the forecasters failed to allow for the rate of emigration from Britain to more remunerative nations. Thirdly, the career structure of medical practitioners has not taken into account the rapid technological progress. The Willink Committee, which was responsible for these gross errors, failed to take into account, or even to utilise, any sophisticated data and analysis whatsoever. For example, the increase in the general population is double what they forecast it would be by 1971, that is an increase of 7 % and not 4 % between 1955 and 1971. The forecasters also failed to take into account an increased demand for medical staff which would follow more advanced diagnostic and preventive techniques, and they also did not allow for an increased demand for practitioners following an increase in economic prosperity. Although the findings of this committee had disastrous consequences, they also had the effect of increasing the scarcity value of personnel and therefore giving them additional leverage in pay and status negotiations.

Much of the work of researching into medical practice has highlighted serious faults in such areas as the doctor–patient relationship, and displayed extreme apathy on the part of the general public to the work of medical personnel. It is uncertain exactly what sort of work that the role of the family doctor should adopt in the future. The education of medical personnel is often inappropriate for what is expected of them, and some studies have found both general and hospital practitioners ignorant of local authority services available for the patient's after-care, and unwilling to cooperate with health visitors and social workers.

Patterns of disease and the measurement of health One of the means of measuring the level of a nation's health is by the *infant mortality rate* of a country. Britain comes fourteenth in the world table compared with America's nineteenth position. Naturally, infant mortality is not an isolated factor but one which must be viewed in conjunction with housing facilities, industrialization, income and education. We must also consider the effectiveness and availability of local health services. South Africa is (all races) ranked eighty-fifth. If we took the white population only, the rank would be comparable to First World nations.

Post-neonatal mortality shows a marked regional variation, partly because respiratory weaknesses are linked with social and environmental factors. Neonatal mortality is generally the result of natal and prenatal malformations, which again can be linked to regional differentiation due to such factors as urbanization, occupation, income, sex, and so on.

The disease of the urban man

In Western nations large conurbations, as we have already mentioned, tend to display the highest rate of mortality, and the lowest levels are generally rural areas. No doubt respiratory disease is the important element which we must associate with city living, in large measure due to the pollution of the atmosphere, but also partly the result of the higher risk involved in being constantly in close proximity to others in crowded places. Pneumonia, cancer, and respiratory tuberculosis are all higher in urban areas than rural, but a great deal of further work needs to be done to determine whether city dwellers are more sophisticated in recognizing a need for treatment and hospitalization, or whether facilities are more available in urban than rural areas.

Income and disease

The U.K. Registrar General's classification of the population into five groups, as we have seen, is a useful research tool:
- Class, I, Higher professional and administrative occupations,
- Class, II, Employers in industry and retail trades and the lesser professions,
- Class, III, Skilled occupations,
- Class, IV, Semi-skilled occupations,
- Class, V, Unskilled occupations.

The common pattern in nearly all disease is that it tends to be concentrated in Classes III, IV and V, although naturally there are diseases which are peculiar to Classes I and II. For example, infant mortality among unskilled workers in the early 1950s was twice that among professional families. Despite the overall decrease in mortality between the early 1920s and the 1950s the *difference* between Classes I and V remained proportionate. Two reasons for this have been suggested. Firstly, the better educated are more able to make use of existing medical provision (as they are in most things) than the unskilled sector of the population, and secondly, because of the increase in social mobility, those who are in Class V are probably there because of a general ill-health or lack of ability, which is not the case with those who were in the same sector forty-odd years ago. Gastroenteritis and pneumonia are the chief contributors to infant mortality in the unskilled class, both of which, of course, are fully treatable.

In the adult male population Class I has a higher rate of mortality for coronary disease, leukaemia and Hodgkin's disease than Class V, but the reverse is true for carcinoma of the stomach, bronchitis and influenza.

Occupation and disease

Certain occupations appear to be more prone to certain diseases than others. The statistics are to be treated with caution because certain occupations attract individuals who are already disposed to develop certain illnesses. For example, we would expect manual workers to be fitter than those in sedentary occupations. Many who contract a disease due to performing a certain task subsequently change their work at the onset of incapacitating symptoms, and it is the latter occupation that is statistically recorded. Very often an occupational category slides over age differences and obscures them. In data of this type the information gathered from relatives is often false or inaccurate, as McKeown and Lowe indicate.

Occupational mortality can be calculated from all mortality taken together and from specific mortality taken singly. For example, doctors have a low mortality from all causes but a fairly high one from suicide and cirrhosis of the liver. High on the list of mortality from all causes are occupations such as glass blowing, mining and sandblasting, while low on the list are occupations such as teaching and herding sheep. Publicans and innkeepers have a high rate of mortality from all causes and the highest from cirrhosis of the liver.

Sex differences

It is indisputable that death rates for males are constantly higher than for females, mainly due to arteriosclerotic disease of the heart, bronchitis, cancer of the lung and accidents. In other words, the differences can be attributed to the different habits of males to females and to different occupations, rather than to biological origins. Strangely enough, morbidity rates are higher among women than men, which may be due to women being more ready to consult their doctors or having more time available to do so.

International variation

The statistics of the World Health Organization, despite difficulty in gathering facts for many countries with inaccurate records, nevertheless demonstrate clear differences in the incidence of disease between countries. Infant mortality rates, for example, vary from 20 per 1 000 live births in Holland, Sweden and Norway to over 120 in Egypt and Chile. In Africa and India it is probably over 200. Yet in modern industrialised nations arteriosclerotic diseases are high while in Africa, Asia and India it is infectious diseases which are predominant.

International variations are accounted for by a number of factors. One such factor, instanced by the spread of malarial infection, is the geographical and climatic condition of a country. Trypanosomiasis and yellow fever is dependent to an even larger extent on these conditions. Hot and humid climates provide a setting for the spread of disease by insects much more readily than colder areas. By far the most important factor, however, is the level of social development of a nation, when such elements as housing conditions, income level, and general level of education become significant. Consequently, even in the same country for example South Africa and the southern part of America, black mortality from all causes is generally very much higher than white mortality.

Measurement

Many mortality tables measure deaths from all causes for all ages, but obviously in many respects this is a crude measurement which disguises many of the subtleties. In 140 years, causes of death have grown from 100 to over 1 000, and just as the instruments for diagnosis and measurement become finer so the total picture becomes more detailed. Different measurement produces very different pictures. If we calculate the number of years lost in a working life, we get a very different perspective than if we calculate simply the leading causes of deaths from all causes for all ages.

An interesting study was done by MacQueen in Aberdeen, Scotland, on home accidents. Contrary to what one might expect, that such events are purely random, the study unveiled a number of interesting sociological facts. The highest accident rate was in children, especially pre-school children, with the elderly next. Non-gas poisoning was a particularly high risk with pre-school children, followed by burns and scalds. Surprisingly, but as already noticed when we discussed suicide and suicide attempts, there were variations in the month, day and hour of the accident. As we might expect, burns were more frequent during the months of December, January and February. Monday is the day of greater risk for women, old people of both sexes, and pre-school girls, although Saturday is the day of greater risk for school children, young men and middle-aged men. The time of accidents is generally between 10 a.m. and 12 noon for the elderly, toddlers and women. The picture that emerged was that the time of greatest danger was at the end of a busy period of household activity. When we come to look at the social and environmental factors involved in accidents we discovered that the widowed, divorced and separated of either sex were more prone to falling than if they were married, but this factor does not seem to affect other accidents. The old and alone were more prone, but accidents in children tended to increase with the size of household. The more rooms in a house the fewer accidents, and scalding occurred mostly in one-roomed households. Children whose fathers are unemployed were more prone to accidents than those whose fathers were in Social Class IV or V, but surprisingly children whose mothers worked were no more prone that those who did not. Work such as this can throw important light on situations and circumstances conducive to accidents and perhaps prepare the ground for a local authority home-safety campaign, and the work itself illustrates very well the use of measurement.

Morbidity measurement

We have already mentioned some of the ways of measuring morbidity and some of the problems associated with such measurement, such as definitions of health and the judgement of individuals. Again, a person may be ill and yet not conscious of the fact, and be ill from more than one disease at the same time. One of the ways round these problems is to have an exact definition of the index being used together with an indication of the *severity* of the disease. McKeown and Lowe found it useful to distinguish between illness most frequently complained of, illness which led to a person consulting a doctor, absence from work caused by illness, and illness requiring hospital admission. Research both in America and Britain has suggested that during one month, in an average adult population of 1 000 patients, 750 were likely to report one or more illnesses, some 250 would consult their GP and 9 would be admitted to hospital. This has been diagrammatically represented by Horder and Horder as shown:

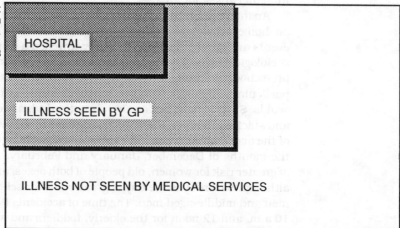

Source:
Office of Health
Economics.
Without Prescription.
London, 1968

HOSPITAL

ILLNESS SEEN BY GP

ILLNESS NOT SEEN BY MEDICAL SERVICES

Several tables have been constructed which show that individuals are more likely to consult GPs over some ailments than others. For example, they are more likely to go to a doctor if they are suffering from tuberculosis, anaemia, personality disorders, heart, respiratory and skin disorders, and diseases of the bone, than if they have coughs, chest pains, swollen limbs and joints, refractive errors, and so on. Some studies have been carried out on the extent of self-medication in the general population and this suggests that often as many as two out of three take some form of self-medication without prescription over a four-week period. Such self-medicants can include analgesics, skin medicines, lower respiratory medicines, tonics, vitamins and salts, sedatives, upper respiratory medicines, and ear and eye medicines, and laxatives and purgatives. The implication of this form of self-treatment are enormous. For example, should the pharmacists, so often described as the country's best-qualified shop assistants, play a more substantial role in the preparation and recommendation of non-prescription remedies, and perhaps also in giving advice to individuals on whether they should consult their doctors? This would certainly enhance the social status of this occupation and also call into question the legislative monopoly exercised by doctors over certain treatments. The 1968 Medicines Bill in Britain was intended to clarify the range of products suitable for self-medication.

The annual morbidity in an average general practice of 2 500 persons that a doctor might be expected to see each year would include upper respiratory infections (500), emotional disorders (250), digestive disorders (200), skin disorders (200). These are minor disorders. For more serious disorders he would expect to see pneumonia (50), 'anaemia' (Hb 70 % or less) (40), five new and ten old cases of coronary heart disease, new cancers (3), severe depressions (12), acute appendicitis (5), glaucoma (3), killed or injured in road accidents (17). On top of this there is a long list of chronic illness such as chronic arthritis, bronchitis, emotional illness, hypertension and asthma with which he must cope. In addition, there is a substantial caseload of sociomedical problems which the GP is expected to deal with, and for this he is given virtually no training and often is in the position of giving very inadequate advice. Problems such as the following no doubt were dealt with by the family physician some fifty years ago but society today has its own specialists qualified to deal with social pathology in a sophisticated manner. The sorts of problems one would designate as sociomedical are patients on Supplementary Incomes Benefit, the aged, lonely, broken homes, deaf and blind, alcoholics, delinquents, problem families, homosexuals, illegitimate births, and so on.

More females complain of ill-health than males, and of all people complaining only one in four had consulted a doctor during the preceding month of the complaint. The Central Office of Information survey in the U.K. which highlighted this also showed that only one person in eight has lost time from work. The types of illness complained about were most commonly rheumatism, digestive disorders and colds. The types of illness for which a GP was consulted were acute and chronic bronchitis, acute nasopharyngitis, influenza and acute tonsillitis. Surveys have shown that two thirds of the patients on a doctor's list can be expected to consult him during a given year.

Absence from work is generally due to bronchitis and other respiratory disease, and mental and psychoneurotic illnesses. The data, in this case certificates of incapacity, must be interpreted carefully because not all men, and certainly not women, are employed in a situation which requires a 'sick note'.

Illnesses leading to hospital admission are generally well-documented and reliable, although we must remember that the *sample* of illness is a highly selective one. Some illnesses require an automatic admission but others become treatable in a hospital depending on the socio-economic background of the patient together with the seriousness imputed to the illness by the GP. The general table of causes of admission in England and Wales display a clear bias towards diseases requiring surgery: injuries and accidents, malignant neoplasms, hypertrophy of tonsils and adenoids, diseases of the breast and female genital organs, diseases of bone and organs of movement, appendicitis. McKeown and Lowe make the very interesting point that this is the pattern experienced by medical students during their clinical years, and it is a pattern which bears very little resemblance to either what the general population claims to suffer from or which the GPs record as diagnosing.

Staff and patient bargaining processes It might be apparent so far that the sociology of medicine is concerned solely with epidemiological factors. This is certainly not the case at the present time although it probably was some twenty years ago. Freidson's work, *The Profession of Medicine*, and Goffman's *Stigma* are just two of many examples of the application of theoretical sociology to concrete instances to be found in the medical area. Roth's work examined the treatment of tuberculosis as a bargaining process. He argued that skilled service occupations attempt to control their clients by the utilization of specialised knowledge and vocabulary, and to some extent this is true of non-professional occupations. Most people in work endeavour to surround their practice with a mystique which prevents or tries to prevent others from encroaching on their prerogative. The medical profession is not exempt from this analysis because they, more than perhaps most occupations, have become *the* example of professionalization. Naturally no single occupation in practice stands alone in its autonomy. The doctor's goals never entirely coincide with those of his patient. For example, the doctor may wish his patient to stay in bed but the latter may wish otherwise. In this situation both may appear irrational to the other. Generally, this situation arises because the doctor has a specialised goal in mind (reducing bronchial infection) while the patient has a number of goals other than that of client. Roth found that the dilemma in tuberculosis hospitals was that between educating the patient about his disease to the extent of benefiting from the professional's advice but not to the degree of knowledge which would enable him to assume he knew as much as the doctor treating him. The key to effective decision making and service appears to lie in the control of information, because the client can evaluate the service he is receiving because he is (or thinks he is) in full possession of the facts. In a tuberculosis hospital patients can easily pool their information from respective contact with medical staff, and such information becomes a way of resisting the control of hospital staff. Most profession–client relationships follow a pattern of control and resistance to control, but generally speaking the social interaction takes the form of negotiation, whereby each participant relinquishes some aspect of his territory. Roth describes the treatment relationship as a form of conflict for the control of the patient's behaviour which is usually resolved by bargaining. A form of bargaining goes on in most social situations. Generally, one aspect of the bargaining relationship lies in the relative power of the participants. We are all familiar with the POW camp inmate who manages to 'outdo' his captors, or the Sergeant Bilko who, apparently helpless, manages to gain his desired goals. Unreasonable demands of the client are generally dealt with by the professional's use of subtle means.

If the demands of the clients, opposite to those of the professionals, are centered around fewer restrictions and earlier discharge then the latter can exert control. The client can threaten to leave, but the professional may consequently become alarmed that infection will be carried to others. In the ward Roth found that nurses could control patients by means of diet and medical treatment, but by the pooling of information it became apparent which nurses were 'soft' and which were 'hard'. Surgery is another area in which the bargaining process takes place. Patients may refuse to undergo an operation or may cajole a surgeon into performing an unnecessary operation, sometimes, as we have discussed, from motives of status.

Sometimes a 'deal' is negotiated whereby the staff allow the patient certain privileges in order that the latter will not discharge himself, and at times such privileges will be 'understood' by the patient and the staff member rather than explicitly stated. Roth continues in his analysis of the bargaining process by concluding that naked power and threats are not part of the process but it is rather a matter of A anticipating the reactions of B, who in turn is reacting to A, and so on. All along human behaviour in these social encounters is being anticipated and modified.

The myth of mental illness Szasz, an American psychiatrist, has cogently argued that the term 'mental illness' is a metaphor and that psychiatric intervention is a form of control. All involuntary interventions which involve 'diagnosis', 'hospitalization' or 'treatment' interfere with the individual. Psychiatric diagnoses are *stigmata* or derogatory labels that are used as a means for controlling behaviour which annoys or offends other people. Generally speaking, people who complain or suffer in relation to their own behaviour are labelled 'neurotic' while those who make others suffer or about whom others complain are labelled 'psychotic'. The argument he uses is partly sociological and partly philosophical but it remains an example of a systematic application of sociology to psychiatric medicine.

The doctor–patient relationship Work done on the doctor–patient relationship distinguishes it from other professional relationships such as social work (but not from law, for example) because the doctor 'accepts' a client or patient while the social worker is 'assigned' one. Freidson and others have shown that very often patients do not do what they are told by physicians. Just as there is ample evidence for a subterranean 'folk-culture' (the unknown gods of the English) existing alongside mainstream religion, so also there is strong evidence that the general population both diagnoses itself and consequently treats itself in relation to lay advice. The position is somewhat paradoxical as it is difficult to account for this at a time when the status and prestige of medical science has reached an all-time peak. The answer seems to lie, according to Freidson, in the perpetual conflict of the layman and professional worker's perspectives. He is essentially saying what Roth and others have also said. The practitioner is applying to a *case* a detached knowledge gleaned from his professional training. The client, on the other hand, is personally involved in judging and controlling what the physician is doing to him, with the consequence that while the goals of the respective parties are usually similar the means often differ.

Generally mistakes occur in the diagnosis either from incomplete knowledge or because the categories of diagnosis are inappropriate. He instances the confusion of typhus and typhoid until 1820, and the identification of syphilis with gonorrhea. A second source of error, however, resides in applying knowledge to everyday life. Medical science has only a limited number of categories into which to 'fit' the 'flow of reality'. Quite diverse elements of human experience therefore become both equivalent and ordinary. An example is the category of complaints in general practice designated as upper respiratory. Because they are so common they are considered ordinary, and because they are considered ordinary they become complaints which one is not permitted to display a great amount of fuss or suffering over. To the patient, however, the pains and the suffering are real enough. Furthermore, because a large number of complaints are diagnosed as upper respiratory in origin it becomes a simple clinical diagnostic matter to insert into the same category any single complaint which exhibits roughly the same features. Problems of diagnosis are real for the patient as well as the doctor. If the latter tells the patient not to worry, then when is it legitimate for the former to claim that his own special feelings are acute enough as to warrant special attention? Often the patient is crying wolf, but sometimes medical science is inaccurate.

The role of the professional in society is such as to entitle him to *a priori* trust and confidence, but it is a mistake to assume that *all* who occupy the role of professional automatically have bestowed upon them a special competence. Sometimes the professional prescribes a remedy which the client or patient was not led to expect. This is essentially a clash of culture, the cultural expectations of the client not being those of the physician or medical professional. The introduction of the social sciences into medical and nurse training stems partly from the assumption that something may be taught about 'the patient as a person'. But doctors and nurses and medical professionals in general can only comply with the patient's knowledge to a certain extent because often this knowledge is both bizarre and ignorant. To comply wholly would result in the professional relinquishing the specialised knowledge which marks him off as a professional. At some point, presumably when the doctor or nurse can no longer concede, the patient must change in order to comply with the expectations of the professional. But education of the patient in order to better understand medical knowledge has the unfortunate concomitant of also making the educated layman more critical of professional performance.

Finally, it is well documented that medical professionals do not perform as competently with patients from the equivalent or higher socio-economic bracket. If the professional is from a higher social class, then this is an additional source of leverage to add to his specialised knowledge.

CONCLUSIONS

Some of the salient features of the sociology of medicine have been touched upon in this chapter. Other areas that the subject concerns itself with are important enough to devote an entire chapter to, for example a sociological approach to the social structure of the modern hospital (Chapter 7), the nursing profession (Chapters 3 and 7, responses to disease and death (Chapter 8), and so on. The relevance of the other chapters of this book, for example those on the family, social class and social deviance are such an integral part of the sociology of medicine as to leave no doubt that they deserve a separate treatment in order to do them full justice. The sociology of medicine is much more than the epidemiological study of medicine, and even more than the study of social medicine (which limits itself usually to epidemiology and the medical 'needs' of society). It is the application of a subject respectable in its own right to another subject respectable in its own right, in the sure knowledge that each will benefit. Historians of medicine could argue, no doubt, that social consequences in the field of medicine have always been with the best of the practitioners. However, the last few years have heralded an increasing search for social factors in the causation of disease and indisputable evidence that many chronic diseases have their aetiology in socio-psychological factors. More important, perhaps, is the emergence of a sociological body of theory and methodology able to cope with the complexities of the subject.

SUMMARY

1. Sociology is concerned with the study of social relationships rather than a kind of practical philanthropy. It relies on a systematic observation of facts which are themselves verifiable.
2. Sociology offers a unique look at society and brings out the relationships between social structures and institutions and individuals.
3. Concepts are notions or ideas which are incorporated into systems of meaning or theories.
4. Functionalism is one of the three major perspectives of sociology. It views society as integrated and balanced. Change, when it occurs, must be slow and considered. It is a consensus, structuralist perspective because it stresses the agreement people share over moral values. It is therefore a conservative theory. Its methodology is positive.
5. Conflict perspectives include Marxism and social action theory, from Marx and Weber respectively, and are also structuralist in nature. These theories emphasise conflict and dissonance as the basis of society.
6. Interpretive sociology is either symbolic interactionism or ethnomethodology. It is opposed to the structural perspectives and the positivist methodologies. It is concerned with the meanings individuals construct in relation to the things around them rather than the way society shapes the individual. It embraces phenomenology as a basis of explanation.
7. It is important to realise that the major perspectives can be used together in the same study. They are not necessarily exclusive.
8. Social theory relates to medicine in a number of ways which are divided into sociology *of* medicine and sociology *in* medicine.
9. In research design we can trace cause and effect by establishing correlations between independent and dependent variables. Some control has also to be introduced.
10. There are a number of sources or error in the research process. By observing someone we may well affect their behaviour; individuals can underestimate or overestimate their responses; social behaviour is extremely complex.
11. We cannot create artificial environments; research is itself a social process.
12. The hypothetico-deductive model implies a theory, deduction and hypothesis. It is more suitable for the natural sciences than the social sciences.
13. Methods of research include the experiment, the survey, the observational study, non-participating and participating observation, and existing sources. The research model is an ideal one from which we often deviate (in practice).

14. Positivist methodologies and interpretive or interactionist methodologies overlap but they also have their own distinctive methodologies appropriate for their theories.

15. Sociology relates to medicine in a number of ways which we outline briefly. They will be followed in more detail in subsequent chapters.

IMPORTANT TERMS

age-specific rate	case study
concept	conflict perspective
control(s)	correlation
crude rate	dependent variable
dramaturgical theory	drift hypothesis
ecology	empirically
ethnomethodology	existing sources
experiment	functionalst perspective
Hawthorne Effect	hypothetico-deductive method
iatrogenesis	independent variable
interactionist perspective	life expectancy
logical positivists	manifest and latent functions
metaphysical	methodology
morbidity	non-verbal behaviour
observational study	operational definition
organic theory	phenomenology
participant observation	non participant observation
placebo	population
positive	primary and secondary data
qualitative	quantitative
random sample	research model
social darwinism	social facts
spurious correlation	standardised rate
survey	symbolic interaction
theory	unobtrusive measures
variable	verstehen

SELF ASSESSMENT QUESTIONS

1. Discuss the nature of the sociology and its relationship to the other social sciences.

2. In what research situations would you utilise either qualitative or quantitative methods? Can you think of, or have you read about a piece of research that combines the two?

3. Compare and contrast the strengths and weakness of the major sociological perspectives.

4. What are the main contributions sociology can make to medicine?
5. Discuss, with examples, the major problems confronting the sociologist in the research process.
6. Outline some of the ethical (moral) problems encountered by social scientists in the research process.

SOCIOLOGICAL ASPECTS OF HEALTH AND ILLNESS

- defining health and illness
- illness as deviance and deviance as illness
- the sick role
- culturally induced illness

Florence Nightingale
(Wood engraving, *Harper's Weekly*, 6 June 1857. National Library of Medicine, Bethesda, Maryland)

DEFINING HEALTH AND ILLNESS

Health and illness do not exist in isolation but within a specific socio-political, cultural and interactive context. Most of us think that we know what health and illness are but the matter is not as simple as it appears. The World Health Organisation, for example, defines health as 'a state of complete physical, mental and social wellbeing, and not merely the absence of disease or infirmity.' When doctors and patients come together they also bring with them lay and professional definitions and conceptions of illness. Sometimes these are congruent and sometimes they differ to a considerable degree. Sometimes, of course, doctors also disagree amongst themselves and from time to time disease entities are no longer categorised as such, and new diseases are identified and drawn into the medical frame of reference.

Labelling theory, identity theory Our behaviour towards others is generally characterised by what we know or think about that person. We attribute *labels* to others, by which we mean the process whereby individuals and groups define certain behaviour as acceptable or undesirable. The process of attributing labels is believed by sociologists to alter behaviour, even to the extent, as we shall see later, of producing deviance. Therefore terms such as 'illness', 'sickness' and 'health' constitute part of this process of labelling and we should begin by examining the way in which these labels come to be applied.

Sickness

When people are designated sick by others or decide that they themselves are unwell, a shift of identity takes place. 'Sickness' as a social identity is specifically the concern of sociology. In contrast, 'disease' is a purely medical matter discovered by diagnosis and investigation.

Illness

People often wake up in the mornings and define particular feelings they experience or think they experience, as 'illness'. Usually, but not always, individuals experience these feelings which lead them to define themselves as ill because the feelings are accompanied by physical events such as an influenza virus or damaged muscles or broken bones. However, feelings of illness *can* occur in the absence of disease symptoms and sometimes disease symptoms can occur in the absence of illness.

Disease

By this we mean the biological malfunctioning of certain organs and areas of the physical body which can generally be measured by occupiers of specialised roles.

Medical definition: illness and disease as sickness

An important psychosocial approach to the behaviour by healthy people when they try to avoid illness was formulated by Irwin Rosenstock (1966) and Becker (1974). This theory owes much to Festinger's theory of *cognitive dissonance* and Lewin's *positive and negative valences* (values). Briefly, these theories posit that people live in life spaces composed of regions with negative and positive values. An illness has a negative value which has the effect of pushing a person away from that region. People are attracted to regions with positive values. In the figure below it is indicated that by following a particular action we would reduce susceptibility, and if the disease occurred, its severity would be reduced. This health belief model has been successful in a number of preventive health behaviour studies such as the seeking of dental care. Limitations of the health belief model include the fact that it is has been applied only to voluntary behaviour. A positive aspect of the model is that it stresses the importance of an individual's subjective interpretation, which in many instances can be more important than objective medical diagnosis. For example, a patient who feels well often discontinues treatment, in spite of a medical need for further treatment. This phenomenon is called compliance—the patient complies with his subjective experience of feeling well again, rather than with the instructions of the doctor. We see this often among rural blacks in the treatment of T.B. or hypertension where there are often no recognisable symptoms.

The health belief model

Source: Marshall H. Becker (ed.), *The Health Belief Model and Personal Health Behaviour* (San Francisco: Society for Public Health Education, Inc., 1974), p. 334.

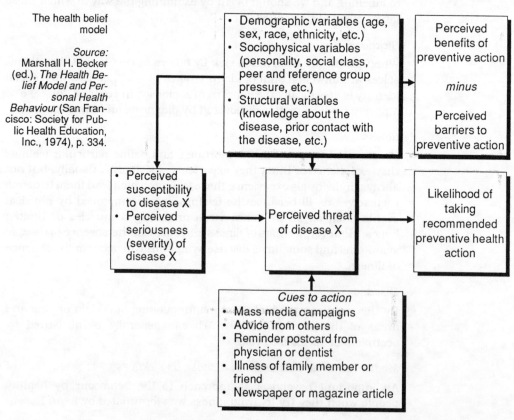

Illness behaviour Medical perspectives usually fall into four areas:
1. the germ theory of disease
2. epidemiological theory
3. the mechanistic concept;
4. the cellular concept (causes of chronic and degenerative diseases).

Generally, diagnosis is made within the parameters of one or more of these four. Some doctors would say that 'disease is any state that has been diagnosed as such by a competent professional.' (Twaddle, 1977, p.98) This glosses over any question of ambiguity of interpretation which arises constantly in practice.

Doctors generally rely on two categories of evidence, *signs* and *symptoms*. These are different from each other and certainly not objective. Signs are observable phenomenon such as raised arterial measurements, temperatures, laboratory results, etc. They are objective and quantifiable. Problems arise in the interpretation of physical signs in instances of alleged child abuse, as reported by the media. Doctors have on occasions misinterpreted certain physical damage as indicating sexual abuse. Symptoms are not always objectively manifested. The patient in this instance complains of pains or aches or general weakness. Thus symptoms are generally regarded as soft data which do not in themselves define health status.

Laypersons generally regard illness as the ability or non-ability to carry out activities. Being sick means feeling ill, having symptoms, and not being able to do what one could normally do. Thus the layman uses a notation of deviance (from the normal standard) as part of the definition of illness. Mechanic (1968), however, suggests that some illnesses such as appendicitis have obvious symptoms, whereas others, such as early stages of cancer or raised blood pressure, are symptomless.

Suchman's (1965) description of the stages of illness experience is displayed below. The lay referral system allows the individual to relinquish certain obligations but official sanction for this can come only from a doctor.

Another perspective regards sickness as a maladaption of organisms to their environment (Dubos, 1965). Mankind has evolved from the stage of hunter/gatherer to agriculturalist and finally to industrial man. Each stage has provided different dietary patterns and immunity patterns. Usually accommodation takes place fairly quickly.

What defines a symptom

It should be apparent by now that health is not easily defined. Secondly, together with sickness, when it is defined it is with reference to social norms. Twaddle (1977, pp. 108/9) presents an analysis of symptoms, isolating the factors which define them:
1. Assumptions of causality. Here the main question is what 'caused' the disease or illness. Was it voluntary, the result of natural causes or was it 'sin'? Was it self-inflicted or accidental?

SUCHMAN'S STAGES OF ILLNESS EXPERIENCE

	I Symptom ex- perience	II Assumption of the sick role	III Medical care contact	IV Dependent-pa- tient Role	V Recovery and rehabilitation
Decision	Something is wrong	Relinquish nor- mal roles	Seek profes- sional advice	Accept profes- sional treatment	Relinquish sick role
Behaviours	Application of folk medicine, self-medica- tion	Request profes- sional validation for sick role from members of lay referral system—con- tinue lay remedies	Seek authorita- tive legitimation for sick role— negotiate treat- ment procedures	Undergo treat- ment proce- dures for illness—follow regimen	Resume normal roles
Outcomes	Denial (flight into health) Delay Acceptance	Denial Acceptance	Denial Shopping Confirmation	Rejection Secondary gain Acceptance	Refusal (chronic sick role) Malingerer Acceptance

SOURCE: Rodney M. Coe, *Sociology of Medicine* (New York: McGraw-Hill, Inc., 1970), p. 108. Reprinted with permission of McGraw-Hill, Inc.

2. Assumptions of treatability. Some diseases are untreatable and become classified as handicap or part of the aging process.
3. Assumptions of prognosis. This includes the length of time the disease is expected to last, the degree of impairment, and the probability of death resulting.

   If a disease is self-induced and socially disapproved (e.g. venereal disease) the more likely the individual is to be stigmatised, (Goffman, 1963).

Factors related to the presumed severity of the symptoms are as follows:

1. Physical manifestations. The more visible the symptoms the more likely they are to be regarded as severe;
2. Impression management. The more the individual conveys signs of pain etc. the more serious his condition will be regarded;
3. Familiarity of the condition. The more familiar the condition the less severe it will be regarded.

How health professionals view illness and the patient Many theories used in contemporary medical settings are based on the biological models of disease. Undoubtedly, the scientific nature of the models and the framework used by doctors, nurses and so on, owes much of its success to being closely linked with the scientific areas of biology and chemistry. The use of scientific diagnosis provides a prediction of how the patient will fare from having a particular kind of illness, an aetiology of the illness in question, and lastly may suggest a course of treatment for the illness. David Mechanic states 'correct and reliable diagnosis is the basis of the sound practice of scientific medicine'. Sometimes a diagnosis can be made and a course of treatment effectively carried out, such as in the case of pernicious anaemia. At other times, however, even though a diagnosis is made, no substantial prediction can be made of the disease's course, the aetiology is doubtful and the treatment ineffective. Mechanic (1968) cites Boeck's sarcoidosis as an example, and adds, 'although it is helpful to make the diagnosis, it does not lead to a clear course of action' (p. 93). Similar problems are presented by the diagnosis of raised arterial blood pressure. In itself a correlation between hypertension and mortality is statistical rather than individual, and high blood pressure is a measurement more than anything else (Jones, 1985). The first stage of hypertension shows no organic change in the cardiovascular system and generally no treatment is prescribed. Indeed, because 10 % of the population display raised blood pressure at this stage such treatment would be very expensive. The second and third stages reveal left ventricular hypertrophy and ischaemic heart disease, but those making the diagnosis are usually aware of such traps as the false positives of the electrocardiogram and some of the negative side effects of the treatment with hypertensive drugs. In addition, there are difficulties involved in the measurement of hypertension by the two most commonly used methods, the intra-arterial method and the cuff and sphygmomanometer. The individual's own blood pressure may vary according to such factors as his emotional state, room temperature, previous physical activity and so on. Several factors emerge in this area which have a bearing on the biological model such as the difficulty of diagnosis (after about fifty years of age, for example, it is normal to have abnormal blood pressure), the quantitative relation between raised arterial pressure and mortality, divided medical opinion as to whether to have treatment intervention at stage one, and so on.

The diagnosis made by the doctor is based on his previous medical knowledge, both clinical and arrived at by scientific research, but also his observation of the patient and the latter's account of his symptoms. Therefore, interpretation and selection enter into the area of diagnosis and disease. Individuals differ enormously according to age, socio-economic status, climate, sex, culture and so on, which in turn affect the patient's and the health professional's interpretation and selection of criteria.

The reliability of diagnosis

Many psychiatrists, for example, differ in regard as to what constitutes sickness. R.D. Laing is one psychiatrist whose views often ran counter to orthodox psychiatry. The interview and the consultation are situations very open to errors of interpretation. Some surveys have suggested that agreement between psychiatrists on the diagnosis can be as high as 55 % and as low as 28 %. Other surveys have suggested that agreement between psychiatrists can sometimes be as varied as 0,05 per hundred to 51 per hundred as, for example, in the case of military psychiatry (Mechanic, 1968 Blum, 1962). In two British

THREE-BED HOSPITAL
Fifteen-Century manuscript from Florence. Biblioteca Medica, Luarenziana, Florence, Italy

studies of psychiatric diagnosis differing levels of agreement were reached for various diagnoses as follows: schizophrenia (68 %), manic depressive psychosis (69 %), mental deficiency (70 %), etc. In contrast poor levels of agreement were found for such diagnoses as paranoid psychosis (29 %) (Norris, 1959). The second study (Kreitman, 1961) found high agreement in cases of affective psychosis, organic conditions and psychosis of old age, but low agreement on schizophrenia, neurotic depression and anxiety states. Less than 50 % agreement was found in some diagnoses but in the case of depression it reached 85 %. In terms of psychiatric diagnosis it appears that psychiatrists have greater levels of agreement than mere chance would expect (Brown, 1966).

Scheff (1966) talks of a basic 'decision rule' which states 'if in doubt, presume illness'. This is particularly so in the diagnosis of physical illness. The opposite appears to be the case with psychiatric diagnosis. Two examples cited by Scheff was a study of the advisability of tonsillectomy for school children among 1 000 pupils. Of these 611 had their tonsils removed. The remainder were examined again and a further 174 were sent for tonsillectomy. The final 205 children were examined and a further 99 were judged in need of a tonsillectomy! In the second example, in a study of 14 867 films screening for tuberculosis signs, there were 1 216 positive readings which materialised as being negative and a mere 24 negative readings which turned out to be positive. The over diagnosed conception of the patient is clear. Many patients are forced into a sick role which is unnecessary. Yet another example occurs in X-ray readings in which as many as 25 % of films displaying abnormalities can be missed. One study of emphysema displayed very different clinical assessments.

Uncertainty in diagnosis can be of two kinds (Davis, 1960): Clinical uncertainty exists between diagnosis and prognosis; the latter where, although the doctor knows the diagnosis and the prognosis, he refrains from telling either the patient or the family.

ILLNESS AS DEVIANCE AND DEVIANCE AS ILLNESS

In every society there are some individuals and groups whose behaviour is regarded by others as deviant, odd, peculiar or in some way a problem. Such behaviour can vary to the extent that in one society it may be regarded as odd but in another as perfectly normal. The kind of behaviour regarded as odd can also vary both within and between societies. Furthermore, one kind of behaviour may be unacceptable to one group in society and yet fully welcomed by another group or even encouraged. The period of early socialisation is important for the later behaviour, and when people suffer some trauma in early childhood this often has a considerable effect on later behaviour, resulting in an abnormal or deviant pattern. But although what happens in the biography of each individual is obviously important, great variation already exists in society; a great range of behaviour can be regarded as 'normal'. There is also a variation among the different social classes and groups in society. In addition, the frequency of deviance in society may vary. For example, crime and suicide rates can vary from one period of the year to the next and from one year to another. What some university students may do on Rag Day may well be regarded as a prank, but the same actions carried out by working-class youths may be seen as delinquent. Thus, the concepts of *meaning* and *interpretation* enter into the sorts of actions which we may or may not regard as abnormal. Certain types of abnormal behaviour are largely confined to one stratum of the population. For example, robbery with violence is a working-class crime; embezzlement is more often a middle- or upper middle-class phenomenon.

Illness as deviance
Medicine as a discipline is applying the medical model to areas not traditionally belonging to it. Mental disorder, for example, was at one time thought to be due to demon possession. The fact that medicine has extended its influence to that area is an example of *medicalization*. Areas that were regarded at one time as legal, religious, biological or moral are now the province of medicine. These include child abuse, alcoholism, drug addictions, kleptomania, sexual abnormalities and attempted suicide. Recently smoking and obesity have come to be regarded as medical problems. Another recent example is the area of transsexualism or gender confusion. Hyperkinesis, or over-activity in children, is now regarded as a disease, partly because ritalin, a stimulator has been found to have the effect of pacifying them. It appears that some forms of deviance come to be medicalised when some drug or other is found which can cure it. One advantage of the medicalization of deviance is that these individuals are now regarded as *sick* rather than *bad.* (Conrad P, Schneider JW., 1980).

Medicine is what sociologists define as an agent of social control, that is, it defines the norms and forces conformity on deviants. Homosexuality offers a clear example of a deviation which has undergone a chequered career. From the New Testament onwards homosexuality was regarded as a moral sin until, in the nineteenth century, it was an imprisonable offence (but only homosexual males as Queen Victoria did not regard it seemly among women!) More recently in history it was regarded as a sickness but professional psychiatric associations, under pressure from homosexual liberation movements, have designated it as an alternative life style. No doubt perspectives will change again.

The other side of the coin is to regard illness as deviance from a biological norm of health and general feelings of well being. Diagnosis by the doctor reveals abnormalities from the norm of health. In medical sociology illness is viewed as a deviant social state 'brought about by disruption of normal behaviour through disease'. (Cockerham, 1978, p. 88) By defining illness as deviance we impute a social judgement.

Illness, from the functionalist perspective, is dysfunctional because the stability of the social system is under threat.

The analysis of deviant behaviour Deviant behaviour is any behaviour that fails to meet some specified standard which is socially or culturally expected by a society, social group or system. Obviously in everyday behaviour we witness a large number deviations, for example when people are too early or too late in turning up for an appointment. In one sense the idea of deviance is a departure from an ideal statistical norm or standard and as such is atypical. But a purely statistical approach to the problem does not help us very much. Another approach to a definition is to refer to deviant behaviour as the kind of behaviour which violates institutionalised expectations (expectations shared and recognised as legitimate within a social system, a departure from culturally expected rules of conduct).

We tend to assess nonconformity by the degree of the deviation from some specific standard, and its direction. For example, people who are two minutes late for an appointment are regarded differently from those who are one hour late, and those arriving early are regarded differently from those who arrive late. The standards from which behaviour deviates allows only a certain amount of deviation and to become too deviant can involve the introduction of sanctions by the group or society. The situation in which an action occurs plays a part in determining whether it is called deviant. For example, people may become intoxicated at parties and on Christmas and New Year but not at other times, people may kill others in wartime but not in peacetime, and so on. The limits which are tolerated by groups and societies are constantly changing, and behaviour regarded as deviant a generation ago may not be so regarded today.

Some deviations are **approved** by society and some **disapproved**. We therefore tend to look at society as shown below:

DISAPPROVED DEVIATIONS	APPROVED DEVIATIONS
the poor	the wealthy
the sick	the healthy
the intellectually stupid	the intellectually able
the ugly	the beautiful
the aggressive	the meek

Jones, 1975

One of the problems in analysing deviance is how to define the specified or accepted standards from which people deviate. In the case of criminality which involves the infringement of a law, the problem is still with us, but to a lesser extent. In the case of **crime** we have a legislative set of laws and an intricate machinery for dealing with infringement. When deviance is also **illegal**, as were suicide and homosexuality some time ago, the problem is less acute (although there are still problems). In terms of more ordinary kinds of deviation, however, because the norms or rules are not codified or written down,

FROM: *SUNDAY TIMES*, 19 JUNE 1988

CAPTIVE OF THE FINGER CHOPPER

I was drunk when he cut them off, says woman in ordeal

A woman who allowed a one-armed pawn-broker, with a fetish about severed limbs, to amputate three of her fingers while she was drunk, spoke this week of her horror, humiliation and pain.

Mrs Hannah Damons, of Robertson in the Boland, also claimed in an interview with the Sunday Times that the pawnbroker, Mr Phillip Morkel-Brink, kept her captive in his flat.

Her three-month nightmare ended recently when police 'rescued' her from Mr Morkel-Brink and later charged him with assault with intent to do grievous bodily harm and for illegally possessing two firearms.

Mr Morkel-Brink, who employed three one-legged women and dreamt of one day holding a party of one-legged, one-armed and fingerless people, failed to appear in court this week after having been granted R300 bail at an earlier hearing.

His attorney told a Cape Town magistrate that the accused had fled South Africa to seek sanctuary in Greece. A warrant of arrest was issued, and the hearing was adjourned to the end of the month.

Lonely

Mrs Damons, 33, who was to have testified at the trial, said she prayed every night for the matter to end.

'He must be sentenced and sent to jail. I never gave him permission to cut off my fingers,' she said.

Mrs Damons recalled how her 'affair' began with Mr Morkel-Brink on a November night, and ended with him saying that he loved her three months later.

He had invited her to his flat as he was 'lonely and needed company'. 'Once in his flat we started to drink and he asked me if I wanted to have one of my fingers amputated,' Mrs Damons said.

'He showed me his hand, from which a finger had been amputated, and said it was a 'wonderful feeling' to have fingers amputated. 'I refused at first but, because I was a bit drunk, I told him to wait until the morning for my final decision.

'However, I couldn't get out of the flat because it was locked and there was a bull terrier guarding the door. 'Though I was drunk, I realised I was in trouble,' she said, 'and after some more drink he persisted.

'In desperation I told him: 'If you want my finger, take it.' 'I didn't think he would do it, but he gave me an injection and I felt nothing. He gave me three headache powders and I lost consciousness.'

The next day, Mrs Damons said, she went to a doctor for treatment. Mr Morkel-Brink had offered to look after her and to buy her anything she wanted even after she left him and returned home. She said that he made a 'nuisance' of himself by phoning her continually and showering her with small gifts.

Help

She said she had given up her job as a domestic servant and decided to go home to Robertson, and she asked him to help her move her luggage.

'There was nobody else to help me. He took my daughter and some of our luggage back to Robertson and then offered me a job in his shop. He said he would show me how to work with the books and I thought that would give me an opportunity to improve myself.

'However, one night while I was staying with him, he told me to take a pair of bolt-cutters to the room. He suddenly turned to me and told me to put two fingers between the blades. I was scared, and wanted to get out, but couldn't.'

it becomes more difficult to discover just what standards are held by any group. One suggestion that sociologists make is that we should try to deduce what the commonly accepted standards of society are, and Emile Durkheim suggested that the deviant was a 'moral frontiersman' who acted as the agent through whom society was reinstated on the right track.

Learning to be deviant The problem of how we come to learn to become deviant, to learn deviant actions and beliefs, involves a number of approaches, some of which see deviance as **achieved** by the individual and others as **ascribed**. That is, either one becomes deviant through one's actions, or one is regarded by others as or belonging to a deviant context. We can list the major theories as follows:

1. Conditioning

A child can be punished for doing something wrong by the withdrawal of affection or approval, and because children (and all humans) are constantly seeking to achieve pleasure and reduce pain most children learn by this method of conditioning **not** to do the wrong thing. This kind of theory is popular with behavioural experimental psychologists such as Trasler and Eysenck.

2. Imitation

Individuals simply copy the behaviour of approved models and reproduce such behaviour in similar conditions. Such a theory involves not simply a straight copying but a consideration of the decisions involved in whether they should or should not copy.

3. Definition of the situation

The learner, according to this theory, is encouraged to make sense of the situation with which he is confronted. He interprets previous rewards in order to apply such conditions to a present or future situation.

4. Differential association

Sutherland tried to discover the epidemiological characteristics of deviance by relating behaviour to the degree of disorganization or organization in the environment. He summed up his theory in the phrase 'crime causes crime', by which he meant that individuals reared in a criminal environment were **more likely** to become deviant than those who were not. He did not suggest a direct causal link, because individuals act both to **define a situation** and to place a **meaning** on events. Situations which evoke associations of the criminal environment would be likely to elicit criminal behaviour.

5. The learner's contribution

Individuals do not simply absorb the external world without discrimination. They possess their own values and beliefs, meanings and interpretations, and the result is a continuous interchange between reality and subjective experience. This has two consequences: firstly, an individual does not become deviant overnight but undergoes a series of assimilations and accommodations, with the result that two individuals subjected to the same reality may react differently. Secondly, although a pattern or norm of behaviour exists in society, individuals perceive it differently.

Sociology has been anxious to explain how deviance arises in society rather than in the individual. Therefore, the four major theories of deviance are outlined below. Together they try to explain why deviance arises in society, why it takes specific courses, and why some actions are regarded as deviant while others are not.

Cultural transmission theory According to this theory deviance is learned in the same way as conformity by the process of social interaction. Sutherland's differential association theory mentioned above is one of the contributions to this perspective. Individuals are socialised into deviant behaviour simply by associating with deviants. As we do not exclusively associate with deviants their influence will be determined by:

1. The **intensity** of the association.
2. The **ratio** of contact with deviants versus contact with conformists. By this is meant that individuals are more likely to be influenced by family and friends, when young, and by deviants only if they mix with deviants most of the time.

This theory certainly explains *recidivism*, or continual relapsing into deviant patterns, because the released prisoner, for example, simply rejoins the criminal networks. It is helpful in explaining the pull that certain **subcultures** have on individuals and also the way in which a delinquent gang may be the norm for a teenager but deviant from the point of view of the larger society.

One of the weaknesses of the theory is that many individuals are exposed constantly to deviant subcultures, for example, but never become deviants themselves. Furthermore, people become deviant without being exposed to a subculture. A modification to the theory has suggested that some deviance can be learned by imitation or incidental contact. However, even if we accept this modification, cultural transmission theory does not explain how deviant acts are defined as deviance initially or how they arose in the first instance.

Structural strain theory This theory explains deviance as social strains which arise in society and incline people to be deviant. Such theory takes the view that Durkheim's notion of *anomie* describes a state of society in which norms are weak, conflicting or entirely absent. Robert Merton has taken this further. According to this theory (sometimes called *social disorganization theory*) society is seen as a system consisting of an ordered relationship of parts. From time to time this ordered system fails, generally in three main ways:

1. **Normlessness**: a lack of specific rules on which action can be based.

2. **Culture conflict**: the existence of at least two opposing sets of rules on how to act.
3. **Breakdown**: rules exist but conformity to them does not produce the expected rewards.

The basis of social disorganization is **social change**, which results in some parts of the ordered system becoming out of joint with other parts. Such social change may be caused by technological or cultural changes which produce a change in the relationships between individuals.

If a society is socially disorganised, this produces stress, with the result that persons in the society experience personal disorganization and adopt behaviour patters such as alcoholism or mental illness. In South Africa stress due to uncertainty about the political future and other factors makes this country one of the highest in the world in stress-related diseases and crimes. South Africa's divorce rate is the third highest in the world, its heart disease rate is the highest, as is urban black alcoholism. (South Africa is third in the world for alcoholism across all races.) *Sunday Times*, June 14, 1987).

Merton constructed a typology which was concerned with **cultural goals** and **institutionalised means**. An individual or group can reject either one of these, resulting in a fourfold classification.

Anomie usually occurs when there is an imbalance between the availability of socially approved means for achieving certain socially approved goals. Merton's typology envisages five possible courses of action depending on whether the individual rejects or accepts the means. Conformity occurs when people accept both the means and the goals; innovation occurs when individuals accept the approved goals but do not possess the means for obtaining them, e.g. wanting to pass an exam but having fallen behind so much one resorts to cheating; ritualism occurs when people still cling to the means even though the goals have long been displaced, e.g. petty insistence on rules as is required of civil servants; retreatism is rejection of both the means **and** the goals, for example the hobo or Skid Row alcoholic are retreatists. Rebellion occurs when both the accepted goals and means are rejected, and others are adopted.

There is much in this theory to recommend it because it accommo-

MERTON'S TYPOLOGY OF DEVIANCE

Modes of Adapting	Accepts Culturally Approved Goals	Accepts Culturally Approved Means
Conformist	yes	yes
Innovator	yes	no
Ritualist	no	yes
Retreatist	no	no
Rebel	no (creates new goals)	no (creates new means)

Merton, 1968, p. 194

dates deviance within the social structure. Albert Cohen's study of the gang gives a lot of support to this theory. However, such a theory does not explain why the rich, for example, having both means and also acceptance of the goals, embezzle money. In addition, it is not always so easy to distinguish clearly between means and goals nor is it obvious that such means and goals are held in common by any group or society. Because he adopts a functionalist perspective Merton assumes a consensus of values in society. In actuality there are differing perspectives and conflicting values in abundance.

Labelling theory This theory explains deviance by describing it as a process by which some individuals and groups successfully define other individuals and groups as deviant. Labelling or *typing* can be summed up in the saying 'Give a dog a bad name and hang him'. A person or act becomes deviant only when categorised or labelled as such by others. Deviance is, in this view, relative and socially constructed.

The distinction is made between **primary deviance** and **secondary deviance**. The former refers to commonplace, everyday deviance such as fiddling travel expenses, which all of us do from time to time. By the latter we refer to persistent nonconformity or deviance. If the primary deviance is discovered it becomes amplified, the individual is degraded and labelled (as 'queer', 'liar' 'prostitute' etc.). The secondary deviant is forced into the company of those who share a similar deviant perspective.

This theory has a lot to recommend it and offers sufficient explanation for marijuana use and alcohol abuse. It can be used, for example to explain varying social attitudes towards drug use. In most societies the use of tobacco and alcohol is approved (despite the enormous physical and social damage they cause) while the use of marijuana is not.

Despite its usefulness there are many shortcomings to this theory. Many deviants have never been aware of being labelled and yet perpetually deviate. It is also possible for some individuals to label themselves. After the initial or primary deviation the embarrassment of being apprehended may 'cure' the deviance once and for all.

Control theory Deviance, according to this theory, is a failure of society to control the individuals within it adequately. Those individuals who are bonded to their society or community in some way will show greater control and conformity than those who are more isolated or detached. Individuals who have an **attachment** to society, a greater **commitment** to society because of what they have invested, an **involvement** or participation, and a **belief** in the moral values, will display more reluctance to deviate.

This theory offers a solution as to why certain kinds of individuals might become deviant (e.g. hoboes). Juvenile delinquency, too, occurs at a time when the young are loosening their bonds with their families. The theory does not explain why those with apparently strong bonds are often deviant. It may well be the case that some people have weak bonds because of their particular kind of deviancy and not vice versa

Social pathology It may be relevant here to make a few comments on the **social pathology** model of society. According to this view, now a very out of date perspective indeed, society is seen as a system analogous to an organism. Moreover, it is an organism in a healthy state. Deviant situations or individuals are seen as the 'disease' within society and a danger (usually moral) to its wellbeing. The key to this perspective of society lies in the process of socialisation through which the moral norms are transmitted. In the early years of the theory deviants were regarded as deliberately rejecting the teachings of society, but subsequently they came to be regarded as having learned the wrong values. Early theorists saw deviance as inherited by in-breeding and confined to lower strata in the population, but later this view was modified to mean that social pathology was rarely to be found without a bad environment.

The new deviancy theorists, such as Young and Cohen, have not been happy with the idea of deviance as a pathology. 'It is simply not possible to regard all the various activities popularly considered as deviant (for example, homosexuality, communism, heavy drinking, marijuana smoking, sexual promiscuity, abortion, prostitution, petty theft) as diseases in the body of society, for if we were to extract all these deviants there would be precious little left of the organism which the absolutists postulate! Rather they suggest, what is a deviant form of behaviour is a matter of opinion, and opinions vary. The use of the word 'pathology' and organic metaphors, are subtle means by which one group (who consider themselves normal) combat the values of those they consider different from themselves.' (Young, 1987, p. 418)

Deviance in the We shall deal elsewhere with two types of behaviour that some socio-
medical setting logists would designate as deviant, namely illness and death.

Those engaged in medical and paramedical occupations are inevitably thrown into contact with illness in one form or another. Illness is itself an extremely good example of a type of deviance, and the medical categorization of a sick person fulfills in an admirable fashion the classic sociological exploration of deviant behaviour. Other forms of deviation are distributed throughout the population, not necessarily randomly but certainly to the extent that such deviant behaviour contains other elements of physical impairment that require medical treatment and diagnosis. For example, alcoholism eventually produces a variety of diseases including cirrhosis of the liver and peripheral neuritis. Again, an addict may appear several times in the same casualty department feigning symptoms which he knows will result in his obtaining the drug he requires.

Situations such as the ones we have mentioned require a knowledge of both the deviation concerned and also some knowledge of how to deal with the deviants themselves, who in most cases are not alien beings, but unfortunate individuals who have surfaced from a pool of latent deviants in the general population. 'Often those engaged in the treatment and care of such individuals can exhibit quite damaging prejudice which interferes with the quality of the relationship required.' By recognising the subtleties of the process by which a person becomes a deviant, much can be done to benefit both staff and patient.

There still remain a number of other categories of deviant behaviour which are of concern, namely role and status conflict in old age, alcoholism, drug addition, delinquency and crime, mental disorder, suicide and sexual deviance. There may well be other types of deviance arising out of extreme prejudice, marital and family conflict, and so on.

In the remaining part of this chapter we will discuss some of these categories in detail.

SEXUAL BEHAVIOUR

Human beings **learn** their sexual behaviour through the socialization process. The sex drive is very similar to the hunger drive in its flexibility, i.e. there is a wide variation in what human beings can eat just as there is a wide variation in sexual attachment. In order to obtain some idea of the complexity of human sexual behaviour we can consider the findings of two fairly recent studies (Ford and Beach, 1951, and Gregersen, 1982) who did a cross-cultural comparison based on several anthropological, ethnographic studies. From their findings it appears that there are three *cultural universals* which are found in all the 294 human societies which they studied. These are *the incest taboo* (prohibition against sexual contact between parent and child or brother and sister and often other close relatives which can also be **homosexual**), *heterosexuality* (sexual orientation towards the opposite sex), although there is a continuum of homosexual practices in most societies, i.e. sexual orientation or attraction towards one's own sex, and even **bisexuality**, sexual orientation towards both sexes), and *marriage* (a legalised mating arrangement between two or more individuals). The variety of sexual behaviour includes the extreme differences societies display in the degree of **restrictiveness** and **permissiveness** which we find. Traditional values about sex have historically been influenced by religion and the Church, mostly to the extent of prohibitions regarding frequency, position, and manner of sexual intercourse. (Forster and Ranum, 1975). It is frequently mentioned that a **double standard** exists in sexual behaviour in advanced industrial western societies; the extra-marital and premarital experiences of males are viewed with tolerance, while such behaviour is regarded as immoral amongst women.

The measurement of human sexual behaviour

It is difficult to measure human sexual behaviour. People are often unwilling either to volunteer for experimental studies or to answer truthfully in response to various surveys. The most successful survey was that of Alfred Kinsey who submitted a questionnaire to 18 000 people, and claimed to have produced a 'scientific' survey of the sexual life of Americans. Although this study is probably the most comprehensive, it is not entirely valid. There have been queries about its statistical accuracy, the sampling procedure, and the fact that it is a biological and not a sociological study. Some of his findings are difficult to believe, for example that 50 % of males and 4 % of females living in rural areas had experienced **bestiality** (sexual intercourse with animals) and that 28 % of women and 37 % of men had experienced sexual desire towards the opposite sex a proportion of whom to the point of orgasm. Another criticism of Kinsey is that his sample contained an over-representative number of Jews and college-educated.

Nevertheless, it is worth citing some of the findings here in order to give some indication of the extent of social behaviour.

1. **Masturbatory behaviour** was practiced by 93 % of males and 62 % of females, and is more common among better educated urban dwellers and less common among devoutly religious believers. Males worry and experience guilt feelings while females do not appear to do so.

2. **Extra-marital** sexual relationships were allegedly experienced by 50 % of males and 26 % of females by the age of 40. Males felt more strongly about such relationships if experienced by their wives, and 51 % thought such behaviour was grounds for divorce while only 27 % of females thought so. Such behaviour did not seem to vary much with social class differences, although devout females appeared more inhibited than those who were not devout.

3. **Homosexual behaviour** to varying degrees was experienced by 50 % of males and 28 % of females by the time they reached 45, and was found to increase with the level of education for both sexes, and especially among single females.

4. **Bestiality** was experienced by 8 % of males and 4 % of females by the age of 21, primarily those living in rural areas. In some populations this rose to as high as 50 %, although this dropped to almost zero in the males after 21 but only by 50 % in the females (mostly unmarried).

In modern industrialised societies **unmarried teenage pregnancies** are on the increase, and until recently **sexually transmitted diseases** were also increasing. With the advent of **AIDS** virus the trend is to less promiscuity. In countries which allow a certain level of 'soft' **pornographic** materials to be in general circulation the debate still continues as to whether this inhibits or promotes bizarre sexual behaviour, especially that associated with sexual violence.

The sociological perspective Sociologists regard sexual behaviour as a part of social action because it not only influences, and in turn is influenced by, other factors, but it also supplies a motive for action. Often it interferes with other social behaviour, and in the case of deviants can be interpreted as often **disruptive** to normal societal processes. Researchers such as Kinsey and Masters and Johnson (1980) are working mainly in the physicalist tradition and place a heavy emphasis on styles of sexual behaviour and the ecology of the sex act. Sociologists differ from this view because they tend to concentrate on institutionalised forms of sexual behaviour. For example, the importance of procreative behaviour lies in its demographic consequences and the institutional arrangements a society establishes for the birth and rearing of children.

Some sociologists have talked of the *eroticised role*, by which they mean that we possess social roles such as lover, wife, prostitute and so on, which have a heavily sexual element embedded in them together with economic or affective exchange. Sexual behaviour, because it is under the control of the cortex, is regarded as implying a degree of normative and decisional control. Urination and defecation are associated with the sexual motivation of infants during the process of socialisation. The work of many researchers has provided strong evidence that although sexual behaviour may be biogenic in origin the particular aspects adopted by persons in order to achieve sexual gratification is socially learned. Because social disapproval induces anxiety, most of us refrain from pursuing a deviant career. Because of the eroticised role we interpret sexual behaviour as being meaningful to the actor and capable of being understood by the observer in placing it in the context of other aspects of the personality of the individual.

Individuals are recruited to the eroticised role (i.e. they become wives, husbands, lovers, and so on) on the basis of social norms, personality and societal mechanisms of control . ariances, disturbances of the personality and various breakdowns in the mechanisms of the process of socialization and societal response result in a breakdown of sexual relationships, or sexual malfunctioning.

Norms of recruitment to the eroticised role

Recruitment into the eroticised role is constrained because of the proscription and prescription of social norms. For example, white does not usually marry black, royalty does not marry commoner, and Roman Catholics do not marry Protestants. Special rules may be in force prohibiting some of these marital ties, as was the case until recently in South Africa. Individuals may, as is almost universally the case, be excluded from incestuous relationships, or forming endogamous or exogamous ties. Numbers of any individuals in society are excluded from recruitment to the eroticised heterosexual role, for example, the inmates of prisons or asylums, or those in certain religious orders. Certain occupational conditions may also make it difficult to become recruited into the eroticised role, such as a migrant labourer or sailor.

Another important aspect of recruitment is the means of sexual communication used, for example language, dress, ritual courtship and makeup. Deviant sub-groups, for example homosexuals, develop private signalling systems to cue a potential partner.

Society controls the types of sexual behaviour as well as the recruitment by such mechanisms as attitudes which reflect disapproval, by gossip, and by scandal. Social control may also be institutionally arranged, as for example in the Nazi youth camps in Germany, various community prohibitions among religious orders, and by chaperonage.

Sometimes there is control over the form of the sexual act, such as the prohibition against oral/genital contact built into the legislature in some American states. Some of the population such as dwarfs, the crippled, the blind and deviants, present a special problem because their identity is 'spoiled' but their sexuality unimpaired. Erving Goffman's *Stigma* (1963) gives a good account of how such problems are managed by cripples, prostitutes, homosexuals, ex-mental patients, alcoholics, unmarried mothers, and so on.

Deviant occupations Some sexual deviations tend to be linked in the mind of the general public with certain kinds of occupations. Actors, for example, are thought of as being proportionately over-representative among homosexuals than perhaps boxers or bank managers. One study of homosexuality suggested that it was linked to the stratification system in a society. Because of the seasonal variation of the entertainment industry such work offers a low level of average earnings, insecurity, and low male economic status. Unless actors are very successful they are generally accorded a low level of prestige by the general public (Plummer, 1981). Societal norms regard many of the theatrical accoutrements as more appropriate for women (e.g. makeup), and although the same economic conditions apply, such recruitment characteristics as 'good breasts', 'beauty', and so on, are carried over into the non-theatrical world and ensure female entertainers greater access to higher levels of the stratification system. Consequently, the male entertainer is a less desirable marriage choice and furthermore has to compete with males of a higher socio-economic status. This considerably inhibits the male entertainer's access to the females with whom he works. Obviously some males are attracted to the entertainment world **because** it offers opportunity in a homosexual career.

An American study of striptease artistes showed, as one might expect, that their physiques were more generous than the average women, that they were Caucasian and generally urban, and that almost all were first-born children. They also had a high rate of homosexual behaviour compared with the general population because their occupational choice made it difficult to formulate normal relationships with the male sex. A further study of burlesque comedians gives additional substantiation to this idea.

Statistics of sexual offences in South Africa and the world It is important to realise that recorded criminality is only a sample of the total criminality. Sociologists rely heavily for their data on what are known as **official statistics**, i.e. statistics collected mainly by government agencies. However, caution must be exercised when dealing with such statistics. Durkheim's *Suicide*, first published in 1987, used official statistics on suicide, treated as **social facts**, as the main data for the study. Such an approach has been severely criticised in the last few years for a number of reasons:

1. There is a 'dark figure' of undiscovered crimes ranging from blackmail to rape, which are **not** reported for a number of reasons, and one estimate is that only 10 % of offences are actually reported.
2. Increase in crime can mean an increase in the **detection** of crime.
3. Statistics can be manipulated to distort the situation.
4. Further research has shown how statistics are partly **created** by prejudice, e.g. discrimination on the grounds of colour, social class or sex.

As regards statistics for suicide, for example, Douglas (1967) and Atkinson (1971) have both criticised Durkheim's reliance on official data. The former accuses Durkheim of not questioning the **subjective meanings** held by the officials and social actors, i.e. that the statistics themselves fail to understand the rules and meanings which both these categories give to behaviour within a concrete situation. Atkinson studied the meanings that coroners attribute to suicide. Coroners use indices to decide what constitutes suicide. These indices include suicide notes (to determine that it was not murder), although only 30 % leave such notes; modes of death (e.g. a car crash may or may not be a suicide); location and circumstances of death (a genuinely suicidal individual would commit the act in a place where he/she would be unlikely to be discovered); and life history and mental condition. The low rate of recorded suicide in Roman Catholic countries was found to be directly attributable to suicide being regarded in such countries as a mortal sin against God and therefore coroners were reluctant to label a death as such out of deference to the surviving relatives.

However, taking into consideration the above, it is still the case that statistical information in relation to deviance gives us at least a broad indication of trends in sexual behaviour. There is clearly no uniform picture. The pattern in Europe and America seems to be that one third of heterosexual offenders are under 21, compared with one tenth of homosexuals. Of those convicted of heterosexual offences, 7 % were over 60. Quite a number of homosexual and heterosexual offenders are married with three or more children (17,7 % and 34,2 % respectively). Most cases of indecent exposure occur among males with one child or during the wife's first pregnancy (nearly 45 %). One in five of homosexual offenders were engaged in some form of personal service, domestic work or entertainment (16 % were domestic workers, hairdressers, cooks, waiters and barmen, and 5 % were actors, musicians and artists).

Homosexuality   Homosexual behavior is the establishment of sexual relationships with members of one's own sex. As Kinsey suggested, possibly a significant number of both males and females have some experience of reaching orgasm with a member of the same sex at some stage in their lives. However, it is useful to distinguish adolescent experimentation from the act of socially identifying with homosexuals, for it is only a small proportion of the former who become homosexuals. Deviation of this type is classified by some, as we mentioned earlier, as *primary* (sporadic, situational and unorganised) or *secondary* (deviant behaviour organised as part of a deviant identity). Primary homosexual behaviour can develop into secondary behaviour according to a variety of contingencies such as frequency (how often), visibility (it is 'spotted') and according to the reaction, tolerance or exclusion from normal channels. Lemert (1967) sees primary deviance as having only marginal implications for the psychic structure of the individual, whereas secondary deviation is deviant behaviour.

The homosexual, once labelled, tends increasingly to have all his/her actions interpreted through the homosexual framework. Gay or homosexual men tend to be more visible than their female counterparts. This is probably because male homosexuals are much more promiscuous (as are heterosexual men), fewer females engage in homosexual or lesbian behaviour, and so on (Plummer, 1981). McIntosh (1968) discusses gay men's visibility in terms of their having what she calls a 'more well developed role' than lesbians. However, research demonstrates quite clearly that while the average white male heterosexual has five to nine sexual partners over the course of his life, his homosexual counterpart has 1 000, most of them strangers. (Bell and Weinberg, 1978).

The search for the aetiology of homosexuality has led to a number of interpretations:

1. **Early experiences**. Although a proportion of homosexuals had some form of homosexual experience while young this cannot be the whole answer because many homosexuals had no such experience (in fact they may have had heterosexual experiences). Also some form of primary homosexual experience is undergone by many who develop into heterosexuals.

2. **Family environment**. The class psychoanalystic interpretation is to view homosexuality as a 'sickness' or pathology resulting from a weak or absent father and a strong and dominating mother.

3. **Social learning**. The individual learns that some experiences, i.e. homosexual, are more sensually rewarding than heterosexual ones. In terms of general rewards and punishment, however, society tends to punish homosexual behaviour. Also a number of homosexuals do not find their life style rewarding and in fact want to abandon it completely.

4. **Self labelling**. If, after an initial homosexual encounter, the individual labels him/herself as normal but simply going through a phase, this is a confirmation of a heterosexual orientation. If, on the other hand, the self label is 'I'm enjoying this. Perhaps I'm gay' then people become 'trapped within their own self definition of their sexual orientation.' (Robertson, 1987). Evidence from prison studies shows that heterosexual males can engage in homosexual activity **while maintaining a heterosexual identity**. Similarly,

studies of male prostitutes highlights the same notion: 'No matter how many queers a guy goes with, if he goes for money, that don't make him queer. You're still straight.' (Gagnon and Simon, 1967)

Homosexual individuals tend also, contrary to popular opinion, to manage their lives fairly well. The labelling perspective appears to contain two paradoxical elements: on the one hand, deviants are not disturbed, sick or pathological but on the other hand, because of tensions in the social fabric, they encounter negative sanctions throughout their deviant careers which in fact lead to these conditions. In the early stages of a deviant career homosexuals experience problems of secrecy, doubt, guilt, access, identity, and so forth, which create the 'potential for pathology, despair and tragedy'. In the later stages access to a supportive subculture appears to be the answer, and individuals embracing such a subculture will not display signs of pathology and disturbance. (Plummer, 1981). Because of the stigma, and until recently the fear of prosecution, attached to being a homosexual, it was little wonder that such individuals tended to frequent disreputable places such as public lavatories, parks, empty lorries, etc. and found what little comfort they could in transitory and promiscuous relationships. The coming out period of a homosexual, the self-recognition of a homosexual identity, is generally a period of excessive sexual activity. It is at this time that many appear to go through a crisis of femininity. The period of aging is another crisis in the life cycle of homosexuals because they realise they have become unattractive to younger homosexuals.

Is there a genetic basis for homosexuality? The genetic basis for homosexuality is uncertain, although many still regard it as an inherited constitutional abnormality. Kinsey's investigations showed that homosexuality and heterosexuality were not mutually exclusive categories but overlapped.

Contrary to popular opinion there is no necessary connection between one's sexual activities and the social roles one plays. 'Male/male sex is more able to ignore the so-called 'natural' connection between sexual position (inserter, insertee, for example) and gender role . . . In male/female sex there is more likely to be an automatic link between sexual position and gender role. And since there is a power differential between heterosexual women and men, the 'use' of the woman by the man is more likely to occur than in male/male sex where, if 'use' does occur, it is more likely to be mutual.' (Plummer, 1981). Similarly, lesbian sexual roles of 'butch' or 'femme' are very infrequent. 'There are few lesbians for whom a masculine identification is terribly important . . . few lesbians become committed to this totally masculine role as a near permanent life style'. (Gagnon and Simon, 1967)

The construction of the homosexual identity can be approached in two ways. The first approach is found among geneticists, clinicians and behaviourists who all agree that such identity is firmly established before puberty. Some, such as Money (1977) argue that such identity is established by the age of three. This is the *sexual orientation model.* The other approach, the *identity construct model,* stemming from the symbolic interactionists, argues that our identities are flexible and negotiable in adult life. Dank (1974) in his study of 377 self-identified homosexuals found that they varied greatly at the age at which they constructed a homosexual identity:

HOMOSEXUAL IDENTITY ESTABLISHED (MALES)				
Age	15	20	25	25+	
%	12.2	35.3	30.7	21.8	
No.	45	130	113	80	Total = 377

Source: Dank, 1974

Some studies distinguish between homosexual *activities* and homosexual *identities,* such as are often stated by respondents:' . . . the Dilly Boy is anxious not to be labelled a homosexual for, in his view, homosexuals are effeminate and contemptible. The Dilly Boy aims to keep his cool, letting the customer do what he wants, while he himself proves his masculinity by avoiding emotional involvement.' (Evans, 1979). Weinberg (1978) looked at activities, identities and self suspicions in a sample of 30 male prostitutes. He found four patterns as follows:

1. E to S to L
   Engaged in activity to suspected himself to be homosexual to labelled self as a homosexual
2. E to L
   Engaged in activity to labelled a homosexual
3. S to E to L
   Suspicious of being homosexual to engaged in activity to labelled as a homosexual
4. S to L to E
   Suspicious, labelled, engaged

Of the thirty men 'only four definitely thought of both their behaviour and themselves as homosexual at the time they were first engaging in sex with other males.' (Weinberg, 1978, p. 151)

There is certainly no reason to suppose that homosexuality is determined by a specific gene. Male homosexuals were found in one study to have more elderly mothers, and to arrive later in their families than their brothers and sisters, and even to have a higher brother-sister ratio than was expected. Female homosexuals are also found to have an excess of sisters compared to the general population, and to have older mothers. Lang put forward the idea that homosexuals were 'intergrades' which appeared to be males but had a female chromosomal pattern, which would account for the excess of brothers and elderly mothers. However, Pritchard, after examining the Y chromosomes of a number of male homosexuals, found no evidence of any abnormality, male homosexuals having a male chromosomal pattern and female homosexuals a female chromosomal pattern.

The challenge of gay militants to the American Psychiatric Association diagnosis

Since the first *Diagnostic and Statistical Manual of Mental Disorders* was published in 1952, which in turn was based on the *International Classification of Disease*, published by WHO, homosexuality was identified as a medical pathology, and homosexuals are defined as ' . . . individuals whose sexual interests are directed primarily toward objects other than people of the opposite sex . . . ' In 1970 a survey of public attitudes towards homosexuality revealed that 62 % of Americans agreed, and called it a 'sickness that can be cured'. Increasingly, both male and female homosexuals began to disagree with the medically attributed label of 'sick'. Homosexuals 'felt it bore little resemblance to their lives, except as they were disturbed by harassment and discriminatory treatment, and more to the point, as it actually contributed to their problems in attempting to live 'normal' lives in the society . . . this medical diagnosis of pathology was perceived as a barrier to those rights. If they were 'sick', their legal and moral currency was thereby called into question. '(Schneider and Conrad, 1980, p. 29). Over the next two decades groups of homosexuals worked to challenge the psychiatric label. In 1969 in New York's Greenwich Village, police and homosexuals confronted each other. The two homosexual groups were the Gay Liberation Front (GLF) and Gay Activists Alliance (GAA)). By increasing disruption of psychiatric and medical association meetings, pressure was brought to bear, which, together with an emerging support from an influential minority of psychiatrists, resulted in an eventual decision by the Psychiatric Association to remove the designation 'sickness' and to regard homosexuality as a 'lifestyle'.

Transsexualism

'The typical transvestite is a man who'll dress in suspenders and stockings, become excited by this and masturbate or make love with his wife. Unfortunately, most wives are turned off by this, so it becomes a clandestine thing.' *Scope*, October 9, 1987, p. 80.

Gender identity, in psychiatric and psychoanalytic terms of reference, becomes established within the first five years of life. It is an integral part of adult identity that individuals clarify and strengthen gender identity.

The biology of sex gender

The biological determinants of sex gender lie in the presence of an X or Y chromosome in the fertilising agent and the joining of this with the X chromosome in the ovum. Evidence points to a predisposition at birth to a male or female gender orientation but such a predispositional pattern can be modified by subsequent socialisation procedures. Subsequent changes in gender assignment after the age of two and a half 'are very likely to create serious problems for the child' not least because by that age 'the identity of the child as a boy or girl is already well ingrained in the child's awareness and behaviour' (Lidz, 1968). The child thus develops a sex identity initially through a process of modelling where he uses his parents as identification figures. The establishment of sex/role standards by assimilation from the culture in which he is raised involves a series of role-playing activities as part of the total process of sex role identification. Eventually the individual regards or perceives himself as feminine or masculine, which is the stage of *sex role identity*.

The *transsexual* is a term referring to an individual's identity as male or female not corresponding to their anatomical sex. Transsexuals feel distinctly ill at ease living in the sex role which corresponds to their anatomy. The difference between homosexuality and transsexualism is simply that 'The criterion of homosexuality . . . is sexual behaviour involving individuals of the same sex, while the criterion of 'inversion' is a personality in which the person's thinking, feeling and acting are typical of the opposite sex.' (Brown, 1958). *Transvestism* refers to the action of cross dressing, while *hermaphrodites* appear to possess both male and female sex organs. Some would argue that transvestites and transsexuals are types of homosexuals. Gender identity forms a continuum of sex and gender role orientation formulated by Benjamin (1966). The term *gender dysphoria syndrome* (Fiske, 1973) describes the presentation of the symptoms and biographies of those desiring sex reassignment. The physical and psychosocial aspects of sex reassignment 'usually include hormone treatment with

---

FROM: *SCOPE*, 1 JULY 1988

THINGS THEY ARE A-CHANGIN'!

For five days a week, Ray and Vera of Wimbledon are exactly what they appear to be—a perfectly normal, retired, middle-class couple. But on weekends this relationship undergoes a dramatic change.

For husband Ray becomes Vera's attractive and sophisticated best girlfriend—Rona!

Ray is among the estimated 200 000 full or part-time transvestites in Britain today, who, in the increasing climate of sexual glasnost, are coming out into the open and declaring their predilection for taking on the clothing and lifestyle of the opposite sex.

Like the great majority of transvestites, Ray remains a perfectly normal and adequate husband to Vera during the week, but he prefers to play his sexual role as Rona to the hilt during the weekends. She only found out about Ray's 'other self' comparatively recently, but finds that she is able to accept it fairly easily.

'There's just one tiny problem,' she says with a laugh. 'As Rona, Ray's a great deal prettier than I am—and that's really not terribly fair!'

masculising or feminising hormones, changes in clothing and hair
style, voice practice with a tape recorder and speech therapist, electrolysis for beard removal in male to female transsexuals, and, finally,
surgery' (Oles, 1977). The stages in transformation outlined by Oles
reveal the order of identity change. 'When a person begins taking
hormones he or she is beginning to make the sex change a reality and
sometimes finds that the reality does not match the dream . . . There
is the realisation that the sex change will not be a total transformation
of either personality or physique'. When finally a decision is made to
'declare' one's adopted identity then 'The decision to cross dress in
public is an important step in the sex change process . . . By appearing
in the clothing of the desired sex role the transsexual is publicly
expressing his or her identity and experiencing other people's reactions
to it.' (Oles, 1977, p. 69)

Conversion surgery

Surgery becomes the final and irrevocable step in sex reassignment
although such 'conversion surgery' is only a 'confirmation and com-
pletion of what has already proved to be successful' (Money and
Gaskin, 1971). The presentation of the self for surgery invariably
requires the fulfillment of three criteria: (a) the desire to dress in the
manner of the opposite sex; (b) seeking to be regarded and socially
accepted as a member of the opposite sex; and (c) a persistent desire
to undergo a conversion operation. The prevalence of transsexualism
in the population is difficult to gauge. Before gender reassignment was
surgically performed a group of Singapore transsexuals had to demonstrate that they had never had any heterosexual inclinations, that
they had been living the life of a woman for the last three years, and
that they were psychologically female in every respect (Tsoi, 1977). Of
the fifty-six cases in the Singapore sample 58 % underwent 'the sexual
reassignment operation, which consisted of at least penectomy, female
external genitalia and construction of an artificial vagina following
castration. Some cases were followed by operations to enlarge their
breasts'. Certainly for the Singapore transsexuals their condition 'did
not appear to be related (a) to the lack of father figure or undue
attachment to the mother, as reported by Stoller (1968) or, (b) to cross
dressing and rearing'. Socarides (1960) appears to argue in an opposite
fashion that 'there is no evidence that gender identity confusion, a
gender identity contrary to the anatomical structure, is inborn'. In fact,
and perhaps not surprisingly, those who advocate the inborn nature
of transsexuality also tend to be supporters of surgical conversion,
whereas those who assign its aetiology to sociological variables tend to
be advocates of psychotherapeutic treatment. The aetiology, it is
argued, is not treated by surgical and endocrinal methods. 'Are those
patients free of their former conflicts, no longer homosexual, transves-
titic, or schizophrenic, or do they now pursue these drives without
conflict, having only altered their external anatomy?' (p. 131).

Transsexual biographies

The biographies of transsexuals such as Agnes (Garfinkel, 1967), Jane Fry (Bogden, 1974), Roberta Cowell, (Cowell, 1954), Jan Morris (Morris, 1974), and Christine Jorgensen (Jorgensen, 1967) are possibly more illuminating than the clinical data of a number of psychiatric studies. Agnes, for example, was absolutely convinced that she was a woman born with a man's body. 'Much of the instrumental realism that she directed to the management of her chosen sexual status was concerned with so managing her circumstances as to avoid what she regarded as a mistaken and degraded identity' (Garfinkel, p. 130). An elaborate system of 'passing' (as a woman) was developed after 'Agnes's commitment to an external signification in the form of feminine attire at the age of seventeen. Jane Fry voices similar sentiments when she says, 'I am a female with a birth defect. I am a woman but I have the organs of the other sex. I want to be a whole person again' (Bogden, 1974, p. 21). Jane asks, 'What is a person? Is a person what he is on the inside? Or what he is on the outside? . . . The only thing I want to change is my body, so that it matches what I am' (p. 19). Roberta Cowell writes that 'for the first thirty years of my life I was Robert Cowell, an aggressive male who had piloted a Spitfire during the war, designed and driven racing cars, married and become the father of two children. Since May 19th, 1951, I have become Roberta Cowell, female. I have become a woman physically, psychologically, glandularly and legally' (Cowell, 1954).

Gender identity is an integral part of adult identity, of the sense of oneself as male or female. Gender role 'includes everything you feel and think, everything you do and say, that indicates, to yourself as well as to others, that you are male or female. Gender identity and gender role are not two different things; they are different aspects of the same thing . . . ' (Money and Ehrhardt, 1972, p. 9). The newborn are wired but not programmed for gender identity and the gender identity option is open at birth even for normal infants although after the age of three or four 'When the gender identity gate closed behind you it locked tight' (p. 119).

The actual process or mechanisms of becoming a transsexual are described in detail elsewhere (Jones, 1984, pp. 202, 215). These mechanisms include objectification (the goal of becoming a complete sexual person), commitment (to conversion surgery), the creation of myths (the opposite gender is ascribed attributes and qualities which in reality do not exist), and the mechanism of ritual (the ritualistic elements of the adopted sex). In the case of the last, some have commented that the male to female transsexuals sound 'not like a woman, but like a man's idea of a woman . . . like a woman in a TV commercial' (West, 1974, in Money and Tucker, p. 206).

ALCOHOLISM

We have mentioned elsewhere the high rate of alcoholism in South Africa. There are 52 000 estimated white alcoholics, a rate of 32 white male adults per 1 000. Urban blacks are the highest in the world, 98 per thousand, compared with France 94, Italy 59, Canada 23, USA 22 and the UK 19. South Africans, between 1961 and 1981 increased their spending on food by five times whereas for alcohol the increase was 27 times greater.

To a large extent alcoholism is a cultural product being very much the most suitable means that individuals have to help them overcome various social or psychological difficulties. Tension is found to some degree in all societies, although distributed among individuals in unequal degrees, and because alcohol is a means of relieving tension then theoretically the probability of becoming alcoholic is distributed according to the degree of tension. However, it is not quite as simple as this. A **social learning perspective** makes the following assumptions:

1. **Drinking alcohol is mainly functional**. It is aimed at attaining pleasant effects or avoiding unpleasant ones. Pleasant effects could include feeling 'high', a 'warm glow', 'feeling relaxed', etc. Unpleasant effects include frustration, stress and anxiety.
2. **Drinking is learned**, from parents, books and films.
3. **Learning to drink heavily will be influenced by compensatory adaptive processes**, psychological or physical dependence.
4. **A learned habit can become a learned compulsion**. Alcohol-related problems such as health, finance, self esteem, personal relationships, provide strong reasons to continue drinking **and** strong reasons to abstain.
5. **Cognitive control will tend to be impaired**. A condition of 'learned helplessness' sets in, in which motivation is sapped, emotionality heightened and pessimism prevails. This results in an impairment in cognitive control, i.e. thinking, planning, goal setting and making commitments; the ability to regulate drinking is thus also impaired.
6. **The nature of the relapse process will change as drinking progresses**. This will tend to be in three phases: (a) psychosocial cues such as arguments, anxiety, social pressure and frustration, (b) the person's reactions to taking just a few drinks become more extreme as they experience the desire for more, and learned helplessness; (c) the expectation of withdrawal symptoms and drinking which is motivated by the desire to escape from or avoid them. (Hodgson and Stockwell, in Heather, Robertson and Davies, 1985, pp. 17–34).

In traditional societies alcohol aids social cohesion. It also aids certain forms of religious actions and rituals. When drunkenness does occur it usually takes the form of a shared revelry. The authors of *Drunken Comportment* attempt to demonstrate that the form our behaviour takes after exposure to alcohol is culturally determined. Horton studied 118 primitive cultures in Africa, Asia and North and South America and related the frequency of drunkenness to two indices of social anxiety: insecurity about food supplies and stresses of acculturation from contact with Western civilization (which weakened social patterns and kinship ties). The more these factors operated the more Horton discovered there was a high rate of drunkenness. Hallowell shows from the literature of the seventeenth and eighteenth centuries that the Northwestern Woodland Indians of North America were suffused by anxiety because the witchcraft of sorcery systems which they had were, in fact, a highly institutionalised means of aggression. When alcohol was introduced by the white man this simply made the situation much worse.

Definition of terms A few people are teetotallers. Some are social drinkers. Some are excessive or heavy drinkers. A number are alcoholics. The World Heath Organization (WHO) defines alcoholics as:

... those excessive drinkers whose dependence on alcohol has attained such a degree that they show a noticeable disturbance or an interference with their bodily and mental health, their interpersonal relationships, and their smooth social and economic functioning, or who show prodromal signs of such developments.

Ignoring the causes but concentrating on the effects this definition led to the inclusion of alcoholism as a mental illness in the *International Classification of Diseases*. (Thorley, 1981)

The medicalization of alcoholism was encouraged by the view, until recently widely held among experts, that alcoholism was a *disease*. Shaw (1979) attacked the notion of an alcohol dependence syndrome on two counts:

1. Only the psychobiological changes could be confirmed scientifically;
2. 'Its use in research and treatment would be at best superfluous but more probably misleading and confusing.'

Alcoholics Anonymous, in the *Big Book*, also support this notion:

Alcoholics ... have one symptom in common ... they cannot stop drinking without developing the phenomenon of craving. This phenomenon ... may be the manifestation of an *allergy* ... it has never been, by any treatment with which we are familiar, permanently eradicated. The only relief we have to suggest is entire abstinence ...

Not only does the religious atmosphere of the A.A. organization deter many (Jones, 1970a, 1970b, 1984) but the 'disease' concept is apparently without foundation:

The notion of physical allergy offered an advantage over competing medical conceptions of such deviant drinking as a type of mental illness or psychiatric condition. Although AA ideology agrees that a compulsion to drink drives the alcoholic, it rejects the idea that such conduct is merely a symptom of under-

The Citizen, 19 April 1990

Alcoholism gene has been discovered: claim

CHICAGO. — Researchers say they have pinpointed for the first time a gene that may make people prone to alcoholism, adding weight to the argument that alcoholism is a disease and not a moral weakness.

Government scientists called the finding 'provocative and promising', even if it requires more study, but a leading investigator in the field declared it was impossible to say an 'alcohol gene' had been identified. The researchers reported in yesterday's *Journal of the American Medical Association* that they found a particular gene on a chromosome previously linked with alcoholism to be far more common in alcoholics than in non-alcoholics.

If verified, the finding would represent the first specific identification of a genetic root for alcoholism.

Alcoholism, which afflicts an estimated 18 million Americans, tends to run in families, and previous studies of families and of adopted twins have suggested that environment and genetic factors contribute to the disorder.

Scientists exploring possible genetic factors have previously implicated three chromosomes as possibly having a role, but no one before has isolated any gene on those chromosomes as likely culprits, the researchers said. — Sapa-AP.

A FRAMEWORK FOR PREVENTION OF DRINKING-RELATED PROBLEMS

Problem⇒ ⇓Aim of Prevention	Type 1: Alcohol-related	Type 2: Context-related	Type 3: Interaction-related
Stop	Prohibition Abstention Non-harmful Minimal integrated consumption	Utopia Perfect people's lives Relabel	Impossible without either 1 or 2 being stopped
Hinder	Safer alcohols Safer drinking practices Antidotes Antabuse More damaging alcohols Rationing Restrict availability Safe limits Food	Conceptualise alcohol use and meaning Tackle cultural drug reliance Coping, living skills, training Find new scapegoat Special drinking contexts	Special drinking contexts Ease transitions Safer cars, roads for pedestrians, drivers Combination of previous Location of and transport to and from drinking settings Insulation of drinking contexts Combat alcohol/aggression myth Increase natural constraints
Curtail progress	Unemployment Conflicting attitudes Poverty Affluence	Living standards Harmonious living Integrate drinking	Combination of previous

(McKenzie, 1985)

lying psychiatric disturbance. The concept 'mental illness' has never enjoyed quite the stature of 'real' i.e. physiological diseases in the world of medicine. (Schneider and Conrad, 1980, pp. 30–33)

The concept of dependence is 'essentially a less dogmatic version of the disease concept of alcoholism.' (Shaw, 1985). Shaw goes on to quote Davies (1974, p. 132):

To call the alcohol dependence syndrome a disease does not do justice to the complexities of the problem, and, by ordering medical thought along the lines of symptoms and signs, it (would be) largely to blame for the late recognition of the condition. It militates against the shift of emphasis to the non disease state of (harmless) dependence, where preventative measures of a social kind may be most effective in the long run . . . the alcohol dependence syndrome tends to focus on the metabolic processes rather than on the social and psychological conditions which favour high consumption of alcohol . . . it (also) needlessly confuses the non medical, professional people, who are concerned with helping alcoholics.

Detrimental effects of alcoholism There are an estimated 1 million South Africans suffering from some degree of alcoholism, all of them economically active. It is further estimated that days off from work due to alcohol cost the country some R500 million per annum. It is possible to categorise the consequences of alcohol consumption as follows:

1. **Alcohol-related consequences**. These are a *direct* result of imbibing alcohol, for example, alcohol-induced liver cirrhosis, intoxication and alcoholic poisoning;
2. **Context-related consequences**. The context can be defined on a cultural, social, interpersonal or individual level, thus any drinking by a member of an abstinent family may be viewed as a drinking problem;
3. **Interaction related consequences**. Examples are drinking and driving, or Monday morning absenteeism.

Some occupations are considered 'high risk' because they exhibit high rates of alcoholism and high mortality rate from illnesses associated with alcoholism. Bar workers have some five times the normal rate, and sailors and commercial travellers also have a high rate.

The physical effects include malnutrition, loss of appetite accompanied by morning nausea which results in an inflamed stomach (gastritis), and a diseased liver (cirrhosis). However, between the alcoholic and the non-alcoholic there appear to be no differences in anatomy, physiology or pathology, nor any abnormalities of metabolism or of tissue chemistry. There is no evidence of an allergic factor in alcoholics. Similarly there is no evidence to support endocrine factors. There is slight evidence for loss of brain substance, and nutritional factors (N1 factors) have been evidenced, as also has metabolic disturbance. The reason why the children of alcoholics are more prone (one survey estimated 11 %) is not biological or genetic but due to example.

There remain social and cultural theories of causation. These fall into three categories: incitement, opportunity and example. Opportunity consists in increased leisure and money, and in the way a particular society is structured and organised. Included here are the occupational opportunities and the distribution of bars. Wine-producing countries such as France, Germany and South Africa are high on the table of alcohol consumers and also high on the list for alcohol related diseases. The characteristics common to high rates of alcoholism include social pressure to drink, inconsistent or nonexistent social sanctions against excessive drinking, convivial or utilitarian goals, drinking outside a family or religious setting, and ambivalence towards drinking moderately. The most effective cause appears to be the power of example.

The alcoholic's family Do alcoholics select certain types of wives and are those women particularly attracted to alcoholics? The wife of an alcoholic is much more frequently than chance the daughter of an alcoholic. Alcoholics frequently marry women older than themselves, and it is much less common for a wife to leave an alcoholic husband than vice versa. The children of alcoholics stand a very good chance of being abusers themselves.

Treatment Among the resources consulted for treatment are the GP, the hospital doctor, the psychiatrist, Antabuse, psychotherapy, group therapy, aversion therapy, and so on. Davies (1985) has typologised therapists' and clients' views on the success of treatment as follows:

	General hospital (n = 25)	Therapist (n = 25)	Client (n = 25)
Advice, direction, explanation, help with drinking	12	14	26
Questions and talking	8	6	14
Psychiatry group therapy	0	4	4
Medications	0	3	3
Physical examination	1	1	2
Other (controlled drinking, occupy time, be locked up)	2	3	5
Don't know	6	5	11

PATIENTS' VIEWS OF THEIR INITIAL CONSULTATION

	Favourable	Unfavourable	Neutral	N/A
General psychiatric hospital patients	11	4	8	2
Specialist ATU patients	21	0	0	4
All patients	32	4	8	6

Criteria of *Favourable*
classification
Found it helpful
Pleased
Was told something
Not disappointed
To my liking
What I wanted/expected
Good
Factual
Learned something
Received an opinion
Surprised (favourably)
It allowed relief

Unfavourable

Disappointed
Haven't learned anything
I gave more than I received
Not very helpful
A bloody waste of time

Neutral

Alright/OK
Straightforward
Uncomplicated
What anyone would have asked me
Just a question and answer session

THERAPISTS' VIEWS ABOUT TREATMENT FOR ALCOHOL PROBLEMS

	General psychiatric hospital therapists (n = 11)	Special ATU therapists (n = 4)	All therapists (n = 15)
Counselling (advice-giving, explanation, guidelines)	8	4	12
Detoxification (management of withdrawal)	6	2	8
Working with spouse and families	3	2	5
Pursuing abstinence	3	0	3
Treatment of primary problems (psychosis, depression)	3	0	3
Behavioural methods	1	2	3

(McKenzie, 1985 *in* Heather, Robertson and Davies, p. 203)

SUICIDE

Psychiatrists are more likely to commit suicide than most of their patients. They have an annual suicide rate of 70 in 1 000 000 compared with 11 in 100 000 in the general public. Other surveys have shown that doctors in other fields are also likely to kill themselves more frequently than other professional men. Up to the age of 39 one in four deaths among doctors was suicide compared with one in ten in the under 30s for the general public. 1 in every 50 doctors takes his own life. In England and Wales 5 000 people kill themselves each year and 40 000 attempt to do so. Suicide rates vary between nations, with West Berlin one of the highest and Italy and Southern Ireland among the lowest (although in Catholic countries authorities may be loath to return a suicide verdict because of the stigma involved). Suicide also varies according to the time of the year, the social class of the individual concerned, and in the methods used. All this suggests what has long been recognised, that is a social tendency to suicide.

Many studies have found suicide to be positively correlated with the following factors: male sex; increasing age; widowhood; single and divorced state; childlessness; high density of population; residence in big towns; a high standard of living; economic crisis; alcohol consumption; history of a broken home in childhood; mental disorder; physical illness. Among factors adversely correlated to suicide rates are female sex; youth; low density of population (but not too low); rural occupation; religious devoutness; the married state; a large number of children; membership of the lower-socio-economic classes; war. The most common factor appeared to be social isolation.

The incidence of suicide showed distinct seasonal variations. Contrary to what might be expected the peak season for suicide are not autumn and winter but the spring and early summer. One suggestion for this has been that it may be the time when a rhythmical biological change is manifested, but a sounder suggestion is that it is also the most 'popular' time for depressive illness, which would partly account for the seasonal increase in the incidence of suicide. It may also be because it would be a time of the most marked contrast between the internal state of an individual who was feeling depressed and the external state of nature at its sunniest and best.

Freud postulated a 'death instinct' which existed alongside the sexual drive and which manifested itself as a tendency to disintegration and destruction. Another factor which has been suggested is that of imitation, which might be true in suicide epidemics and suicides that run in families but not applicable to the majority of suicides.

Psychological signs Some, although by no means all, would say that a person must be mentally ill in order to undertake suicide. If we consider the four broad categories of mental impairment—the neuroses, psychoses, mental retardation and the abnormal personality—some substantiation might be made for associating suicide with mental illness, as one-third of people who kill themselves are estimated to be suffering from a neurosis, psychosis or personality disorder. Suicide is rare among those suffering from *organic dementia* and mental defectives. Psychologists and psychiatrists would generally look for the following criteria indicating suicide, according to many: (1) depression with guilt feelings, self-deprecation and self-accusations associated with tension and agitation; (2) severe hypochondriases, i.e. tendency to continuous complaining, usually about physical symptoms; (3) sleeplessness, with great concern about it; (4) previous suicidal attempt; (5) fear of losing control; (6) suicidal preoccupation and talk; (7) suicides in the family; (8) life in social isolation; (9) serious physical illness; (10) alcohol or drug addition (there is a high incidence of drug taking among doctors, which might partly account for their high suicide rate); (11) the end of a depressive illness; (12) dreams of catastrophes; (13) unemployment and financial difficulties.

Suicide notes and coroners' reactions to suicide A number of studies of the notes left behind by suicides reveals them to be far less dramatic, and much more matter of fact, than simulated notes. Such notes are among the criteria used to arrive at the real suicide rate in society which lies beneath the official statistics. However, recently serious doubt has been thrown on this real suicide rate as it has become apparent that different societies and different groups in society view the behaviour designated 'suicide' differently. It is really a blanket term used to cover different kinds of behaviour which has different meanings attributed to it. A further suggestion is that coroners act as 'front-line' individuals who help to establish a shared definition of suicidal situations by interpreting the meaning of the evidence. A similar role is served by the mass media who popularise or focus attention on a particular kind of suicide (for example, among students) which then becomes fairly established in the mind of the general public.

Durkheim's contribution

One of the earliest sociologists to point out the social tendency of suicide was Emile Durkheim. He postulated three types of act.

1. *Egoistic* suicide, arising from the individual's lack of integration with his group. He had in mind here the lack of social controls as illustrated by the single being more prone than marrieds, Protestants (with the stress on individualism) being more prone to suicide than Catholics, and so on.

2. *Anomic* suicide represents the failure of the individual to adjust to social change and the weakening of social constraints. The limits society imposes on the individual's desire make them more reasonable and realizable. High employment in wartime is an insufficient cause of the drop in the suicide rate, and rather (a) there is more opportunity for disguised suicide, (b) there is an increase in 'causes' and 'partisanship'.

3. *Altruistic* suicide is when the group's authority over the individual may be so compelling that he loses consciousness of his own personality and its claim upon life. Examples are the aged Eskimo going into the snow to die, the captain going down with his ship,

SUICIDAL YOUNGSTERS

KOBUS HERBST'S death has again highlighted the problem of teenage suicides. Since the beginning of the year, more than a dozen teenagers around the country have killed themselves, at least three after being accused of theft.

This week senior specialist at Tara, Dr David Norris—he deals mainly with problems in adolescents—spoke of the possible reasons for teenage suicides.

'One has to look at the whole family setup, at the stresses within the family unit. Today, there is great difficulty in maintaining family ties,' said Dr Norris.

He added that suicide gets worse, not in war time where the stresses are obvious, but when stress becomes undefined, where there are hidden conflicts and perhaps unemployment.

'Teenagers feel the brunt of that burden. Suicide attemps in adolescents are common. Some are due to true depression, but most come from a feeling of not coping, a feeling of alienation, having no one to turn to.

'Also, the availability of successful methods has increased—more guns, gas, drugs are available,' he said.

Dr Norris said the peak period for para-suicide (where the victim is making a plea for help) is between the ages of 15 and 25.

'These deaths seem to go in cycles, rather like copy-cat deaths. 'Teenagers must be made aware that there are crisis centres they can turn to—hospital emergency services, Life Line, or crisis clinics.'

As a pointer to parents, Dr Norris said they had to recognise the needs of teenagers under stress. 'Modern society is so competitive, we expect the best of everybody. A child doing well at school might not be thought to be a problem if he gets good marks. But pushing for good marks could put great pressure on the child.'

CHILLING LIST OF TEENAGE SHOOTINGS AND HANGINGS

Here is a list of some of the suspected schoolchild suicides reported this year:

- FEBRUARY 28: At Atlantis School of Industry near Cape Town, teenager Martin Booysen, 15, is found hanged by his pyjama top in a punishment cell. Reports say he was depressed after being forced to remain in his cell as punishment while his schoolmates took part in the school's sportsday.

- MARCH 2: Roodepoort Standard 9 pupil Pieter Swanepoel, 15, dies after being shot in the head at his parents home.

- MARCH 10: A 17-year-old Nelspruit youth is found shot shortly after being detained by a Heidelberg traffic inspector for alleged car theft.

- MARCH 11: Johannesburg schoolboy Anthony Wright, 18, found dead from a gunshot wound in his head in a car outside a Kibler Park block of flats.

- MARCH 17: Wesdene bus disaster hero, Daniel du Toit, 17, found shot at his parents' Triomf home. Friends say there was no apparent reason for his suicide.

- APRIL 11: Matric pupil Barend Jacobus Basson, 17, found shot in his bedroom after returning from a rugby tour of the Eastern Cape. He is believed to have been scolded earlier by a teacher for ordering a beer.

- APRIL 21: Rustenburg primary schoolboy, Johan van Vuuren, 11, is found shot dead with his father's firearm. Police say Johan and other pupils were accused of stealing stationery from the school and that Johan shot himself while the school's deputy head searched his home for stolen items.

- APRIL 23: Virginia schoolboy, 14-year-old Pieter Steyn, found hanged with a rugby bootlace in his bedroom cupboard. Police say Pieter had been extremely depressed.

FROM: *SUNDAY TIMES*, 15 MAY 1988

and the Indian widow's suttee—all exemplifying a suicide which is socially and culturally imposed.

Other contributions

Cavan formulated a combination of factors that caused suicide: (1) a personal crisis that either disturbs the individual's customary ways of realizing his needs or introduces a conflict between them, for example when one's spouse dies or there are rows; (2) a personality factor when a rigidity in some people makes for difficulty in adjustment; (3) the factors arising from social disorganization.

Psychoanalytic explanations

Four determinants of personality may be distinguished: (1) *constitutional*—the inherited and biological aspects of personality; (2) *situational*—chance and accidental events and experience such as being an orphan or only child; (3) *role*—the cultural determinants of how statuses are to be put into action or performed on the basis of age, social class, occupation, and so on; (4) *group membership*—of school, class, nation and so on. The psychoanalytic approach talks in terms of a wish to kill some unidentifiable characteristics within the self or a wish to be killed or atone. Sometimes this is expressed as a wish to die and seek reunion with a loved one or God. There is some evidence that some suicides wish to identify with a parent or parent surrogate who died at a crucial time in the child's development.

Ecological studies

Sainsbury's study of suicide in London boroughs found the following factors associated with the act: *social status*—poverty, unemployment, overcrowding, and middle-classness were none of them important by themselves but there was a tendency for the poor to commit suicide less frequently than the middle class; *social isolation*—people living alone, living in boarding houses, and lodging-house keepers were found to be of significant numbers; *social mobility*—people entering and leaving, those of foreign birth, that is, all transients, were significant; *social disorganization*—divorce, illegitimacy and delinquency were factors, and there was a correlation of suicide with the rate of admission to mental hospitals, increasing age and rapid changes in an individual's economic position.

DRUG ADDICTION

There appears to have been a successive tradition of drug use throughout history. The Sumerians, the Chinese and the Incas all used drugs extensively. Cannabis is used in many religious rites, as is also peyote. The Peyote religion is found in over 50 North American Indian tribes.

Terminology The word *drug* denotes a chemical substance used medicinally. A secondary meaning associates it with addiction. In 1950 the World Health Organization described *addiction* as a state of periodic or chronic intoxication which was detrimental to the individual and subsequently to society, and which was produced by the repeated consumption of a drug which was either natural or synthetic. *Habituation* differs from addiction because it creates a desire (but not a compulsion) to continue taking the drug for the sense of improved well-being. In 1964 the World Health Organization recommended that *drug dependence* be substituted for these two terms.

Drugs themselves fall into two categories: *hard* or dangerous restricted drugs such as heroin and cocaine and *soft* drugs such as barbiturates (phenobarbitone), amphetamines (pep-pills, benzedrine), cannabis, and LSD 25 (d-lysergic acid diethylamide).

The growth in the rate of addiction is one of the significant factors in addiction with the average age of new addicts becoming less. There are more male addicts than female addicts, and there is some indication that new addicts in Britain are male rather than female. In America addiction is mainly a problem associated with minority groups, whereas in Great Britain this is not the case.

Narcotic addiction is more of a problem in some countries than others. In Hong Kong the rate is 120 times the rate in Great Britain, and in Iran it is 264 times the rate. In America the problem is 12 times that in Britain. It has been estimated that the number of new addicts doubles every one and a half years. Naturally the increase of this nature is purely statistical and the process of levelling out inhibits any such phenomenal growth. Addiction growth seems to have been stimulated among 'non-therapeutic' addicts (obtaining the drug from another addict) as compared with 'therapeutic' addicts (who obtain their drugs from medical treatment), the latter being a comparatively static group. The former seem to have begun as a small group in the late 1940s or early 1950s who were aided by Canadian and American addicts, and the over-prescribing of some GPs in Great Britain. ·

SMOKING DAGGA
Cape Town, 1982,
P Alberts

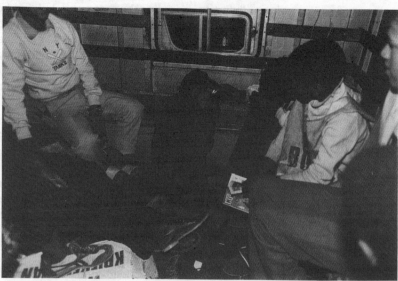

The sociology of It seems that one has to work hard to become an addict. Not all who
the addict come into contact with addicts become so themselves. Some are not
really affected in any significant way, others simply do not attempt it
even though given ample opportunity, and so on. An experiment in
which two successive doses of morphine were given to 150 healthy
young men resulted in only 3 being willing for the injection to be
repeated. One researcher has stated that the danger of addiction
'resides in the person and not the drug'. Even addicts realise that the
positive aspects of heroin last only for some 18 months, after which
time the doses are to prevent withdrawal symptoms.

Different societies at any one time entertain a variety of beliefs and
attitudes towards certain drugs. Certain individuals whose use of
drugs differs to some extent from the norm are labelled by others as
deviant. This encourages such individuals to identify with others like
them in order to form a drug sub-culture. Such sub-cultures tend to
fall into two distinct kinds comprising those from the educationally
and culturally under-privileged and those from the educated middle-
class 'rebels'.

Drug addicts are generally young people who live in large urban
areas and who occupy a minority status in society. The high rates in
America are generally to be found among ghetto Negroes and Puerto
Ricans, but the addicts themselves do not differ in education and
intelligence from others who share their position but are non-addicts.
Because of the economic demands of being an addict, most of them
tend to be unemployed and living on the fringe of society.

Generally, addicts seem to come from homes where the mother is
dominant and the father weak and ineffectual. Addicts also appear to
entertain more than their fair share of negative attitudes, of 'opting out'
of the male ideal, to experience difficulty in establishing social relationships, being easily depressed and frustrated and so on. Three factors
seem important in any individual becoming an addict; (1) a psychological, predisposing inadequate personality, (2) a crisis such as a
death or other traumatic event, (3) the timely offer of the drugs.

MENTAL ILLNESS

There is evidence that mental illness occurs in all cultures. We must
be careful to distinguish *social concepts* relating to mental illness, such
as madness, lunacy, from *medical classifications* such as psychoses
and schizophrenia. The three main causal classifications are as follows:

1. Mental disorders resulting from organic lesions (for example syphilis of the central nervous system).
2. Mental disorders resulting from psychological experiences.
3. Mental disorders resulting from social experiences.

The main areas of traditional demarcation are:

Psychoses entailing a gross derangement of mental processes and
inability to evaluate external reality correctly;

Neuroses entailing some impairment of functioning, often of a segmentary nature but involving no distinct break with reality;

The psychosomatic disorders entailing organic malfunctioning. Examples of psychoses include schizophrenia, of neuroses, various anxiety reactions, and of psychosomoses, asthma, rashes and hypertension.

Aetiology The old explanation in terms of mental illness arising from the strain of modern living is no longer tenable. Research of incidence over a century found no evidence of a rise in rates over this period below the age of 50. The hypothesis that people living in a *gemeinschaftlichten* community are less prone is not tenable either. Eaton and Weil's study of the Hutterite settlements in Montana and the Dakotas showed the same rate of mental disorders as for New York State. Mental illness seems to be societally distributed, and the mental disorders known to western psychiatry occur just as much among primitive peoples throughout the world. Wherever schizophrenia, for example, has been reported, the society in question has been in the process of *acculturation*, a sociological concept involving further concepts of culture conflict, marginality and shock.

The following social characteristics have been found in a number of studies to be associated consistently with a relatively high incidence of diagnosed schizophrenia: aged between 20 and 35; low socio-economic status; living in anomic urban area; being a migrant; unmarried; being introverted. There is inconclusive evidence of the relation of mobility to functional psychoses. The aetiology of schizophrenia is now regarded as arising from various combinations of hereditary vulnerability and stress from the environment, the former arising from a combination of genes rather than from a single one. Other theoretical formulations include the *double-bind* theory, in which the individual is regarded as being involved in an intense emotional relationship in which two contradictory orders or messages are sent, for example, from the mother to the child. This seems to have support in a situation in which a mother cannot tolerate an affectionate relationship with her child but cannot accept the feelings that she has. Absence of a strong father figure who might help the child discriminate messages is also conducive to this. Wynne developed a similar theory. He observed the extent to which the families of schizophrenics attempt to maintain an illusion of complementarity that does not in fact, exist, denying differences and directing joint efforts towards achieving what Wynne calls *pseudo-mutuality*.

Social class, occupation and education Social class is an important indicator of the kind of experiences to which an individual has been subjected during his life and his expected reactions to these experiences. One theory, concerned with schizophrenic patients, suggests that their generally low socio-economic status can be accounted for by their drift down to that level. Another theory suggests that low status of many schizophrenics is the result of their being born into a socially disadvantaged situation. One survey found that in the USA 91 % of schizophrenics were in the same social class as their family of origin compared with 36 % of the general population; which suggests a remarkable absence of general mobility. Morrison found that the occupations of schizophrenics were distributed normally as one might expect for the general population. It is more than likely that the origins of the patient determine the care he receives from his relatives. The fewer the letters and visits a patient gets the more likely he is to stay in hospital. The patient's treatment has been shown to be related to his social class. In America, at least, the middle and upper classes are more likely to get psychoanalytic treatment and the poor, physical treatment. A patient's socio-economic status may influence the physician in his diagnosis either by the *parataxis* of the socially disadvantaged (inability of expression) or reluctance on the part of the physician to diagnose schizophrenia in those who approximate closest to his own socio-economic status.

Family environment and mental illness

In cases where the nuclear family is not properly formed, as we indicated in our discussion of the work of Bowlby and the Harlows, there is a slightly higher tendency to produce schizophrenics. Various adverse features occur in schizophrenic-producing families, basically what Lidz and others have called schism and skew. Usually the mother forms a close though anxiety-ridden relationship with the child while the father is excluded; the reverse occurs occasionally when the patient is a daughter. Disturbances in family life in early years can and do produce varying degrees of disability and often characteristics of a psychotic type.

Mental retardation, long thought to be organic in origin, is in some cases brought about by faulty family mechanisms. The feeble-minded, the educationally sub-normal and the defective can come from high intelligence, high socio-economic homes, but also, of course, from low intelligence, low socio-economic homes. At one time these facts were explained by reference to the theory of multifactorial inheritance, i.e. that the child inherits gene combinations which are unfavourable. Another explanation will refer to environment. Relatively severe mental defects can be caused by what Bourne has called 'grossly perverted rearing'. The mother may be of low intelligence (and therefore incapacitated) but it is difficult to pin down the causal or associative factors involved. Children from poor homes also suffer more in childhood from bronchitis, pneumonia, infective diarrhoea, and vomiting. They also have more home accidents than children from good homes. The mothers of defectives from good homes tend to have experienced disturbances in their relationships with their own parents during adolescence and to have entered into marriage and motherhood with generally unfavourable attitudes. A great deal of research indicates that the essence of mental illness might lie in the area of disturbance in interpersonal relationships.

Social behaviour of mental patients

The behaviour of mentally disturbed individuals is a result of their illness and also a means of recognizing and diagnosing their particular disturbance.

Schizophrenics stand at odd distances from others when engaged in interaction; their posture and gesture are utilised to express the bizarre; they lack gaze contact; their speech fails to synchronise and there are long pauses; they are introverted in a very special way and do not engage in social behaviour; they give no reward in interaction and resent criticism; they lack social skills.

Depressives are miserable, sombrely dressed but neat and clean; their posture is drooping with lowered head; they speak little and their voice is low and slow; they can engage in social behaviour; they show little interest in the opposite sex; they are socially unrewarding and lack confidence; 10–15 % try to kill themselves.

Manics are cheerful and wear loud clothes; they have a dramatic gaze; they speak a lot; they are dominant, extroverted, and possess poor social skills; they misperceive situations and cannot see anyone else's view; they can be rewarding or non-rewarding.

Paranoics are introverted; they dress to suit the mood they are in; they don't trust or revel anything; they are socially unrewarding, and are arrogant and touchy; they have poor social skills and misperceive situations.

Anxiety neurotics have a tense and awkward posture; their movements are jerky; they indulge in face-touching, speak fast with breathy voices; their faces are tense; they show lack of poise and don't enjoy social occasions; they worry what other people think; their social skills are strange and destructive; their perception is over-sensitive and they are afraid of rejection.

Hysterics take great care of their clothes and general appearance; they emphasise bodily complaints; they blink excessively; they are extrovert but socially unrewarding; they are flirtatious.

Therapy Some studies have suggested that individuals recover under psychotherapy and also when under no treatment. 70 % of neurotics are self-cured after two years and 90 % after four years. Reasons for this vary from the suggestion that they adopt a new style of life, or have amateur help from friends. Sometimes there is improvement for no apparent reason, for example when a great number of mentally ill people recovered at the death of George V! Three methods of treatment are generally used: *psychoanalysis*, which involves interpretation; *non-directive therapy*, in which no direct help is given; *existential therapy*, in which the patient is directed to his own goals.

In the 1950s there seemed to be no faster rate of recovery for those treated compared with those on the waiting list, but since 1960 those treated have a greater rate of recovery than those not treated. One suggestion is that psychiatrists and psychoanalysts have improved, and that recovery does depend on the *manner* of psychoanalysis rather than any particular school. Young and intelligent psychoanalysts produce a greater degree of confidence and a higher rate of recovery. *Behaviour therapy* has had some success (88 %) with enuresis by the use of avoidance therapy. *Aversion therapy*, mainly with drugs, has had some success with bizarre forms of sexual deviation. *Desensitization* has been very successful (some 81 %) and uses a light hypnotic state to discover what factors are found upsetting (for example, a fear of death) and gradually subjecting the patient to increased 'doses' of the fear stimulus (starting with photographs of cemeteries and finally ending with the glimpse of dead bodies). *Assertion therapy* is the acting out of dominant situations. *Social skills therapy* consist of neurotics being put in a situation where they are required to talk, and involves the use of role-playing, feedback, social-skills training which are utilised to deal with different age and personality categories. Individuals are taught to emit appropriate signals and simple social situations are explained to them.

Mental illness as a social role Lemert's conception of primary and secondary deviance is important because it may determine whether mental illness is a transitory phenomenon or whether it becomes part of the identity of the individual concerned. In other words, subsequent social experience may in fact *worsen* one individual whose handicap is identical with that of another. One example is when some children with polio are more socially disabled than another group even though their actual physical handicap is less.

Thomas Scheff has argued that mental disorders are residual deviant behaviour and emerge from very different sources. He also argued that the amount of illness recognised and treated is a tip of a much larger iceberg the existence of which is denied, not recognised, or is so transitory as to change quite rapidly with the change of circumstances. The behaviour which comes to notice, however, is the result of particular social forces which induce the individual to grasp on to the notion of playing the role of the mentally ill, often because such individuals have retained a stereotyped image of the behaviour associated with such illness. Various rewards may accrue to individuals who adopt such roles which, once undertaken, may in the long run prevent a return to the 'normal' role. It is very often the case that when a mental patient denies that he is sick, this is taken as a further indication of the illness he is thought to be suffering from. To try to revert to the original and normal role is difficult because of the stigma and suspicion attached to the role of the mentally ill. Finally, Scheff thinks that the transition from the primary to the secondary type of deviation can occur during crisis, when the individual is most open to suggestion.

Thomas Szasz believes that the term 'mentally ill' is used in modern society to designate areas that have no foundation in biological malfunction, and that such designation is based upon ethical or psychosocial criteria. Despite Szasz's criticisms the disease concept of mental illness may still be useful.

Erving Goffman described the mental hospital as a *total institution* comparable with a prison. The criteria which qualify for admission vary enormously and include the seeing of visions and the hearing of voices. However, there are still important contingencies which determine admittance within certain limits, such as the socio-economic class of the patient and the extent to which his offence is 'seen' by others. But Goffman sees the whole situation as a dramatic occurrence in which the patient is gradually relieved of his freedom, and the 'self is systematically, if often unintentionally, mortified'.

CRIME AND DELINQUENCY

A.K. Cohen's theory of delinquent behaviour sees it occurring as a result of thwarted status problems faced by working-class youths. Children learn to become delinquent by becoming members of groups in which delinquent conduct is already well established. Within each age group cultures exist which are shared by only a few, and these are termed *sub-cultures*. There are sub-cultures within these again, belonging to neighbourhood cliques and so on. What Cohen is saying is that in many ways becoming a delinquent is like becoming a Boy Scout. The characteristics of delinquent sub-cultures lie in its non-utilitarianism, maliciousness and negativism. Taking its norms from the larger culture it actually turns these upside-down, and the conduct of a member becomes right precisely because it is wrong in the eyes of the larger culture. Such a sub-culture is also versatile in the sense that stealing often goes hand in hand with vandalism, trespass and truancy. It is also a form of short-run hedonism, in which pleasure is immediate and transient. It exhibits group autonomy because social pressures comes from within the group.

The middle-class values which are presented by society to working-class youths are for the most part unobtainable. There is no thought in the working-class culture of postponing gratification for future rewards, nor are they encouraged to be rational, responsible, ambitious or have a respect for private property. Denied status in the world outside, such youths create their own status systems in which values are prized which are not accommodated in the larger culture.

Cloward and Ohlin distinguish three types of delinquent gang: (1) *criminal* gangs are chiefly engaged in theft and money-making activities; (2) *conflict* gangs look upon violence as a major source of status; (3) *retreatist* gangs stress drugs as a means of escaping from the immediate. Basically the origin of these three types stems from the gulf which exists between goals and opportunities.

Factors in delinquency Barbara Wootton selected twenty-one major investigations and found twelve different factors connected with delinquency: (1) the size of delinquent's family; (2) the presence of other criminals in the family; (3) club-membership; (4) church attendance; (5) employment record; (6) social status; (7) poverty; (8) the mother's employment outside the home; (9) school truancy; (10) a broken home; (11) health; (12) educational attainment. None of these, says Wootton, are *causes* in the accepted sense, but there is a correlation in the sense that some of these factors accompany the fact of being a delinquent.

Some have argued for the existence of *formal* and *subterranean* values in society. The former are deferred gratification, planning, routine, predictability, non-aggression, for example, and the latter are short-run hedonism, spontaneity, new experience, excitement, aggressive masculine role, peer-centredness and so on. Although we all hold subterranean values to some extent and usually express them in our leisure pursuits, certain groups such as working-class youths tend to accentuate these values at the expense of the formal ones.

David Matza and Gresham Sykes have tried to account for a theory of delinquency by suggesting that working-class youths do not set out to violate the formal values of society but try to be accepted by the system by adopting a set of strategies or justifications which he thinks will be accepted by the wider society. These *techniques of neutralization* are five in number: (1) responsibility is denied, for example, 'I'm sick'; (2) denial of victim, 'we weren't hurting anybody'; (3) denial of injury, 'people like that can afford it'; (4) condemnation of the condemners, for example, 'everybody does it'; (5) appeal to higher loyalties, 'I didn't do that because of myself'.

Individuals become delinquent (or deviant) as a result of exercising certain choices in the context of *affiliation* (contagion or conversion) and *signification* (being signified or identified as a thief as opposed to becoming one). Matza goes on to give a picture of the delinquent as not essentially very different from normal youths in society. 'The delinquent is casually, intermittently, and transiently immersed in a pattern of illegal action.'

Wardrop suggested five categories of delinquency as follows.

1. *Organic*–largely the result of brain damage due to an early history of birth trauma, early injury, illness involving encephalitis. There is a persistent tendency to hyperkinetic behaviour with poor muscular co-ordination. In adolescence the behaviour form is outbursts of temper, overtly delinquent behaviour which is often motiveless, together with a lack of ability to form stable relationships. Subjects also possess a poor *self-image* due to poor abstract reasoning ability.

2. *Grossly deprived delinquent*–illegitimacy and rejection produces an affectionless character and hostility resulting in poor impulse control. Such children, with a history of statutory child care and

fostering, have a low tolerance of frustration and require immediate impulse gratification.

3. *Emotionally disturbed delinquent*–this group is sick, as opposed to the first two, which are disturbed: (*a*) neurotic reaction–a history of rejection and a delay in psychosocial development which takes the form of stealing in boys and promiscuity in girls (both are attempts to identify with a sex role); (*b*) psychotic reaction–taking the form of 'odd' behaviour or persecution.

4. *Family problem delinquents*–delinquency in this case is reactive to interpersonal tension in family relationships.

5. *Situational delinquency*–typical problem delinquents produced by culturally and economically deprived backgrounds without any psychiatric or emotional problems.

The genetic basis of crime and delinquency Following on Lombroso's work on the 'atavistic' criminal in terms of skull shape and size were the attempts of Kretschmer and later Sheldon to distinguish body types, namely *ectomorph, mesomorph* and *endomorph* to which a particular kind of temperament was attached. The endomorph preferred comfort, the mesomorph was aggressive and active, and the ectomorph introverted. Subsequent research found that there were twice as many mesomorphs among delinquents than could occur by chance. One answer is that delinquent gangs and behaviour is more suitable to those with a mesomorphic physique and such children are more likely to be admitted to gangs than more 'weedy' children.

A recent suggestion that genetics may be a clue to violence is the result of research showing a link with genetic abnormalities in the sex chromosomes. Patients in a special security hospital in Scotland included a group sharing a genetic abnormality–their bodies contain two Y male sex chromosomes instead of one. They also shared gross personality disturbance and had a history of early conflict with the law. Although physically healthy (but unusually tall) the majority were mentally subnormal, from normal home backgrounds, but given to violent temper and unresponsive to treatment. A study of Rampton prisoners revealed an extra X chromosome (female) resulting in cunuchoid proportions, a tendency to breast development and infertility. In the general population XXY is 1 in 1 000 or 1 in 1 500 but at Rampton it was 1 in 200 and in some places 1 in 100. Klinefelter's syndrome, XXY, is found 1.3 times in every 1 000 male babies. Although such theories as these may explain a small proportion of pathological offenders they still leave much unexplained. XYY males, because of their height and build, may be singled out in societal processes and be victims, partly at least, of societal reaction, labelling or typing processes.

STIGMA

By *stigmas* Goffman (1963) does not mean simply a physical blemish such as scars, deformities and so on. Prostitutes, homosexuals and dustmen have stigmas to a larger or lesser degree. But a person can have a scar, for example, which can be interpreted as something positive (he gained it in the war). Generally, 'by definition, of course, we believe the person with a stigma is not quite human. On this assumption we exercise varieties of discrimination, through which we effectively, if often unthinkingly, reduce his life chances'. He goes on to suggest that on the basis of the original imperfection we impute a wide range of further imperfections.

Such stigmas are gross physical defects, defects in character, and stigmas associated with membership of some particular group which is looked down upon by society. These stigmas are ascribed at birth or acquired in the course of a life, and although people receive their stigmas at different periods they nevertheless share basic common problems and adopt common strategies which help them to manage their spoiled identity. Having a stigma such as a colostomy does not necessarily in itself produce a peculiar way of life, but this may result from the way the person is viewed by others.

People with a stigma such as prostitution may (1) refrain from mixing with 'normals', (2) refrain from telling 'normals' the true facts, (3) meet the situation directly. In other words, a prostitute can mix with others of the same occupation or with sympathetic 'normals', an illiterate can pretend to be actually literate, a limbless man can ostentatiously light a cigarette with his artificial hands with is 'sufficient to warn the audience that there is no need to go beyond the normal set of social understandings'. In a similar vein, which we shall discuss in more detail later, the sick person is often stigmatised, especially in the hospital setting, and 'talked down' to by the staff.

Courtesy stigma Some people, simply because they share a web of affiliation with a stigmatised person, are themselves spoiled in their identity. They are 'normal' and yet very 'different' in many ways. Often such individuals manifest their differences by conversation, slips of the tongue, and so on. In any society there are people who are friends or relatives of stigmatised individuals and groups such as homosexuals, criminals, and deformed children. Different types of adaptation are possible for those with courtesy stigmas. They can affiliate wholeheartedly with the stigmatised; they can eventually cease to be regarded as 'normal' by society; they can try to convey that they are unsoiled or unconnected. One study of the mothers of mentally retarded children showed how their adaptations were in fact examined through their relationships with family, friends and other parents of retardates. These mothers helped to maintain membership of the 'normal' community by altering the meanings of these relationships and limiting participation in the organised world of mental retardation. Further, by recognizing the priorities of conventional family life they helped to provide additional ways of conveying an image or normality.

THE SICK ROLE

Generally, diagnosis takes place within the context of the *medical/disease hospital model* which is one which:

generally implies the perception of the consumer of a human service as a *sick patient* who after *diagnosis*, is given *treatment* for his *disease* in a *clinic* or *hospital* by *doctors* who carry primary administrative human management responsibility, assisted by a hierarchy of *paramedical* personnel, and *therapists*, all this hopefully leading to a cure.
(Shore, in Jaco, 1979, p. 346)

The sickness career or sociological forms of illness Parson's (1951, 1958, 1964) classic representation of the sick role shifted the focus away from a *medical* perspective to the *sociological* qualities. In this analysis 'sickness' becomes a *dependent variable*. We must view Parson's analysis in the broader terms of his concern with two major problems: the modernization of societies and the manner in which deviant behaviour is controlled. In relation to the former, Parsons saw the professional role emerging at the same time as the businessmen rose to a dominant position. The two groups were distinguished from one another both in their orientations and in the kinds of relationships they had with the public. The person defined as 'sick' was presented with a variety of expectations, and Parsons viewed these people as the prototype of the professional client. Such a client is vulnerable to exploitation and requires some form of institutionalised protection. In relation to the control of deviant behaviour Parsons argued that sickness requires to be separated from other forms of deviant behaviour such as crime. The primary focus was in differentiating the sick from the criminal. Accordingly, in reading each of the following expectations posited as characteristically held for the behaviour of sick people, the meaning will be clearer if the phrase 'relative to the criminal, the sick person is expected to' is used as a preface.' (Twaddle, 1977, p. 117)

Parsons analysis of the sick role can be reduced to four basic conditions:

1. **The sick person is exempt from the normal social roles.** Naturally this depends on the degree and severity of the illness. Exemption tends to be the prerogative of the doctor as the authority on what constitutes sickness. Because sickness requires legitimation this prevents society from malingering.

2. **The sick person is not responsible for his or her condition and cannot 'pull himself together'.** Sick people need specialised intervention and need to be taken care of.

3. **The sick person must try to get well and regard the sick state as undesirable.** Stages 1 and 2 are conditional on the third. Exemption is temporary.

4. **The sick person has an obligation to seek technically competent help.** They must go to physicians and cooperate to the full.

Thus, to claim the sick role gives us an excuse not to perform certain responsibilities, puts upon others the obligation to look after us, makes us reluctant to be ill and anxious to get well, and makes us seek the help of a doctor or other qualified person. Sick role variations are bound to occur in instances where individuals are not given or expected to have exemption from normal roles, the degree to which they are expected to 'get well', the extent to which they cooperate with the treatment agent, and finally the degree to which they are held responsible for their condition.

Criticisms of the sick role

There are a number of criticisms which have been levelled against Parsons' formulation:

1. Freidson argues that Parsons' conceptualization of the sick role is heavily tailored to modern Western industrial society, and that the extent of the exemption is a *consequence* of the seriousness imputed to the condition. In a trial classification of deviance the following might emerge:

		Imputation of responsibility	
		Individual held responsible	Not held responsible
Imputation of seriousness	**Minor deviation**	Parking offence	A cold
	Serious deviation	Murder	Heart attack

(Jones and Jones, 1975)

The degree of the seriousness of the deviation reflects middle-class views. However, Freidson makes the point that often the medical profession holds individuals responsible for medically labelled illness as in the case of venereal disease, abortion and attempted suicide. Furthermore, the above classification merely distinguishes between 'crime' and 'illness'. A more sophisticated table is presented by Freidson. The Parsonian definition of the sick role occurs in cell 5, Goffman's stigmatised roles are in cell 4, and chronic sick or dying roles are found in cell 6.

Imputed seriousness	Illegitimate (stigmatised)	Conditionallyl egitimate	Unconditionally legitimate
	Cell 1	Cell 2	Cell 3
Minor deviation	'Stammer' Partial suspension of some ordinary obligations; few or no new privileges; adoption of a few new obligations.	'A cold' Temporary suspension of few ordinary obligations; temporary enhancement of ordinary privileges. Obligation to get well.	'Pockmarks' No special change in obligations or privileges.
	Cell 4	Cell 5	Cell 6
Serious deviation	'Epilepsy' Suspension of some ordinary obligations; adoption of new ones; few or no new privileges.	'Pneumonia' Temporary release from ordinary obligations; addition to ordinary privileges. Obligation to cooperate and seek help in treatment.	'Cancer' Permanent suspension of many ordinary obligations; marked addition to privileges.

(Adapted from Freidson, 1970, p. 239)

2. The sick role applies to a limited range of illnesses. It appears to be limited to chronic illnesses.
3. The way in which the sick role is formulated makes it biased towards consultations with doctors. In practice, however, much of the behaviour of sick people is self-help or consulting with non-professionals.
4. There is a lack of uniformity among persons and groups. Such behavioural differences can relate to pain (which varies among ethno-cultural groups) and to personal and religious definitions of 'being sick'.

Culturally induced illness In society there are many factors which help towards a culturally induced illness. Waitzkin, (1983, pp. 62–85) mentions such examples of social structures of medical oppression, i.e. social class and economic cycles, stress, work and profit, and racism and sexism. *Society* and *culture* are closely linked concepts in sociological theory. *Culture* refers to all the shared products of society, both **material** (artefacts, books, space rockets) and **non-material** (language, ideas, beliefs, etc.). *Society* refers to the totality of social relationships between people. Obviously we cannot have a society without culture nor can we have culture without a society.

A clear example of a culturally induced illness is the disease *kuru*, which until recently was found in abundance among the Fore of Highland New Guinea. This disease produced extreme difficulties of muscular coordination and resulted, always, in death. Subsequent research showed it to be a slow virus infection affecting women and children of either sex but seldom adult males. The answer lay in the cultural practice of cannibalism. The Fore women and children prepared human flesh for consumption. The virus was not destroyed when cooked because water boils at a low temperature in the New Guinea highlands. the transmission was probably through cuts in the skin rather than through ingestion. (Gajdusek, 1957, 1973)

Examples which show how the customs of a people affect their physical health are legion. It is scarcely surprising that tetanus neonatorum is common among those African peoples who apply a herbalist's mixture containing powdered dung to the cut cord of each newborn baby, or where tetanus spores shed by domestic animals lie thick about the huts with their caked dung floors. Nor is it surprising that men of the Karamajong tribe of East Africa, whose diet includes a daily pint of blood drawn from the jugular veins of their cattle, should be better nourished, with higher red cell counts, than men of neighbouring tribes who do not have this custom.
(Susser, Watson and Hopper, 1985, p. 137)

The role of cultural differences in illness behaviour has been well documented. People learn different responses to pain, for example, and there are both social class variations and cultural variations in response to symptoms. Mechanic (1968, p. 119) writes:

. . . it seems fair to conclude that cultural and social conditioning plays an important though not an exclusive role in patterns of illness behaviour, and that ethnic membership, family composition, peer pressures and age/sex role learning to some extent influence attitudes toward risks and the significance of common threats, and also the receptivity to medical services.

Thus the intensity of pain does not follow necessarily from the nature and extent of an injury but rather has to pass through every individual's cultural 'filter' which transcends the biological basis of the injury. Lewis (1981) describes the cultural influences on behaviour in a New Guinea village.

The conflict view of medicine stresses inequalities in health due to the unequal distribution of resources and the differential access to health care. Waitzkin (1983) has documented culturally and socially induced illness in modern American capitalist society relying on the theoretical foundations established by Friederich Engels, Rudolph Virchow and Salvador Allende. Engels documented mostly occupational diseases in nineteenth century England, while Virchow emphasised most strongly the social contradictions of the class structure in nineteenth century Germany. Allende, a Chilean writing in the first half of the twentieth century, discussed specific diseases within the social and cultural environment:

The individual in society is not an abstract entity; one is born, develops, lives, works, reproduces, falls ill, and dies in strict subjection to the surrounding environment whose different modalities create diverse modes of reaction, in the face of the etiologic agents of disease. This material environment is determined by wages, nutrition, housing, clothing, culture, and additional concrete and historical factors . . .
(Allende, 1939, p. 75)

In South Africa cultural and social conditions discriminate widely. De Beer (1985, p. 66) asks:

1. Why are there so many cases of TB, cholera and malnutrition in the homelands and almost none among the white population of South Africa?
2. Why do children all over South Africa get measles, and yet almost exclusively it is the working class who die as a result of the illness?
3. Why do so many people get ill and die from preventative and curable diseases?

Susser, Watson and Hopper (1985) present an analysis of health under the ideology of apartheid, and seek to disentangle socio-economic factors from the distinctly separated racial categories. 'Blacks and Whites live in different worlds. Whites die of developed world diseases; Blacks die of Third World diseases.' The former die from ischaemic heart disease, lung cancer and suicide, while the latter die from gastroenteritis, TB, nutritional disorders and homicide. One set of disorders points to the 'culture and behaviour of a wealthy society, while the other points to the structure of a caste society (infectious and parasitical diseases). A third set of disorders is related to the distribution of medical care. The health patterns of South African can be seen as a faithful reflection of its economic, social and political structure . . . ' (Susser, Watson and Hopper, 1985, p. 582)

Religious influences on disease result in profound differences for various categories. Thus Protestants, Catholics and Jews have different rates for a number of physical and mental disorders. Mormons and Seventh Day Adventists have a low incidence of cancer, and few Mormons are alcoholics. (Jones, 1984, p. 83). Zborowski (1969) examined a group of hospital patients who had a common diagnosis and one would expect equivalent levels of objective pain. He found that Jews, 'Old American', Irish and Italian patients exhibited different responses to pain.

In relation to South Africa, in the Durban area a number of studies (Kuper, Watts and Davies, 1958) showed that even with two distinct cultural groups existing side by side, considerable differences in still-birth and infant mortality rates were displayed. In low- and high-economic housing projects African mothers had a number of advantages over Indian mothers such as having a more formal education, being younger, bearing fewer children, and making more use of antenatal and midwifery services. African babies also tended to be heavier than Indian babies.

Cancer

We have mentioned elsewhere the prevalence of carcinoma of the esophagus amongst certain cultural groups such as the Xhosa of the Transkei. Another form of cancer, cervical cancer, is also distributed in the population according to social and cultural factors being associated with frequency of sexual intercourse, both marital and extra-marital. Thus it is extremely low in nuns, Jewesses and high among prostitutes and venereal disease clinic patients:

CERVICAL CANCER RISKS REPORTED IN VARIOUS STUDIES

Low Risk	High Risk
Moslem	Women prisoners
Jewish	Prostitutes
Amish	Venereal disease clinic client
Seventh-Day Adventist	American negro
Italian American Immigrants	Puerto Ricans
Irish American Immigrants	Mexican immigrants
Churchgoers (Protst. & Cathlc.)	Non-churchgoers
High social class	Low social class
Rich	Poor
Rural	Urban

Source: Martin (1967), from Susser, Watson and Hopper (1985, p. 153)

Yet another form of cancer associated with social and cultural influences lies in the area of carcinoma of the bronchus. Smokers have a 70 % greater overall chance of death than non-smokers, and smoking is associated with cancer of other organs of the body such as the pancreas, kidneys and bladder. Smoking caused one death in eight among men 45 to 54 in Britain in 1975 and smokers in America run a 20 times greater risk than do non-smokers.

Feeding practices Feeding practices differ between and within societies. Breast-feeding varies according to social class and among various cultures. These practices also change with time and with different social conditions.

Finally, doctor-patient interaction is also conditioned by social and cultural influences. Various studies have shown that doctors are happiest with middle-class patients and unhappy with working-class patients, i.e. patients from the same cultural background as themselves and those from a dissimilar background). There are many reasons for this, one of the most important being communication (Tuckett, 1976, p. 190). The findings of these various studies can equally be applied to nurse-patient interaction, with socio-economic background being very important. In South Africa racial factors also influence the power and status of health professionals in their helping relationship with patients.

SUMMARY

1. 'Sickness', 'illness' and 'disease' mean different things, 'sickness' being a sociological concept.
2. Illness experiences and behaviour are viewed differently by doctor and layperson.
3. The reliability of diagnosis varies considerably between physical and mental symptoms.
4. The medicalization of deviance is an example of medicine, as an agent of social control, defining the norms and enforcing conformity on deviants.
5. The process of learning to be deviant is due to conditioning, imitation, definition of the situation, differential association or the learner's interpretation. The main theories are: cultural transmission theory, structural strain theory, and labelling theory. Deviance as a pathology is itself a mechanism of social control.
6. Sexual behaviour is learned. However, the process of sexual deviation has led to a number of theories, although there appear to be no grounds for a genetic basis. Gay militants have concluded a successful campaign to have the term 'homosexual' removed from the 'sick' category.
7. Transsexuals who are committed to changing their sex undergo conversion surgery although controversy exists as to whether this is legitimate.
8. The process of becoming an alcoholic is made reasonably clear by the social learning theory, and the disease concept of alcoholism is seemingly losing credibility.
9. Suicide is not an individual action but one associated with a number of social factors.
10. Drug addiction and mental illness can also be fitted into deviancy theories such as Lemert's. Some, such as Scheff and Szasz, are critical of the application of the concept at all.
11. Parsons' sick role was important in shifting illness into a social context, although subsequent criticisms make us treat it with some caution.
12. Many examples abound of culturally induced illness, a classic case being that of the disease *kure* among the Fore of Highland New Guinea.
13. Other cultural factors inducing illness are socio-economic.
14. Such social and cultural factors can also influence doctor-patient or nurse-patient communication.

IMPORTANT TERMS

disease	social pathology
sickness	incest taboo
illness	homosexuality
cognitive dissonance	heterosexuality

negative valences
signs
symptoms
deviance
subculture
recidivism
anomie
social disorganization theory
normlessness
culture conflict
breakdown
cultural goals
institutionalised means
labelling theory
primary deviance
secondary deviance
control theory
psychosis
neurosis
psychosomatic neurosis
mesomorph
medical/disease model
culture

bisexuality
marriage
bestiality
eroticised role
stigma
official statistics
sexual orientation model
identity construct model
transsexuality
transvestite
hermaphrodite
gender dysphoria syndrome
conversion surgery
alcoholic
egoistic suicide
anomic suicide
altruistic suicide
subterranean values
formal values
endomorph
ectomorph
society

SELF-ASSESSMENT QUESTIONS

1. 'The social distribution of 'good health' closely reflects the social distribution of wealth and income.' Discuss
2. We all have notions of 'femininity' and 'masculinity'. How far do these notions affect the treatment and expectations of the sexes?
3. Durkheim's interest was not in individual suicides but in suicide as a social act. How far was he successful?
4. How far is illness socially constructed?
5. Outline the main theories in relation to deviance.
6. Critically discuss the disease syndrome model of alcoholism.

CHAPTER
THREE

PATIENTS AND PROFESSIONALS

- medical institutions
- the professions
- the interactions of patients and professionals
- becoming a patient

MEDICAL INSTITUTIONS

In all societies health care facilities appear interrelated in the sense that they are socially organised responses to disease 'that constitute a special cultural system: the *health care system*.' (Kleinman, 1980 p. 24)

Kleinman goes on to say that:

'In the same sense in which we speak of religion or language or kinship as cultural systems, we can view medicine as a cultural system, a system of symbolic meanings anchored in particular arrangements of social institutions and patterns of interpersonal interactions.'
(Kleinman, ibid.)

He sees medicine as having a 'symbolic reality' and regards the medical system as one which 'structures the experience of illness and, in part, creates the form the disease takes.' (Kleinman, 1973, p. 206). Similarly, Douglas (1973) states:

The social body constrains the way the physical body is perceived. The physical experience of the body, always modified by the social categories through which it is known, sustains a particular view of society . . . the care that is given to it . . . must correlate very closely with the categories in which society is seen.
(Douglas, 1973 p. 93)

Kleinman, whom we follow closely in this section, is arguing that the health care system *integrates* all other aspects of society concerned with health, including socially legitimated statuses, institutions, interaction settings, power relationships, roles, beliefs about the causes of illness, and norms governing the choice and evaluation of treatment. Patients and healers, together with illness and healing, cannot be understood outside the cultural meanings and social relationships which constitute a system of health care.

However, this health care system is a conceptual model rather than reality and we derive this model from a number of procedures:

1. We *observe* the manner in which people *act* in it and *use* its components.
2. It includes people's tacit beliefs and overt behaviour.
3. Their beliefs and behaviours are governed by cultural rules.

It is similar to other cultural systems in the sense that we can understand it in terms of its instrumental and symbolic activities and that such beliefs and behaviour are influenced by a number of factors. These include:

(a) social institutions (clinics, hospitals, doctors' and nurses' associations, health bureauracies).
(b) social roles (sick role, healing role);
(c) interpersonal relationships (social networks, patient-doctor, patient-family);
(d) interaction settings (home, clinic, ward, surgery);
(e) economic and political constraints; and
(f) available treatment interventions and type of health problem.

Health care in context The relationship between culture and medicine has been studied on a number of levels, including linguistic and symbolic analysis. Nevertheless there are three main constraints operating against an attempt at a holistic view of health care systems:

1. The domination of the biomedical model has had the effect of excluding social science answers to social problems. The total environmental context provided by enthnographic studies has not been accepted as an appropriate scientifically based approach for medical research, and health care has been viewed as restricted to the modern medical profession and biomedical science.
2. Health professionals working in developing countries have taken the idealised model of professional care in technologically advanced societies and applied it to the Third World. It is clearly inappropriate for a number of reasons, including the tendency to exclude indigenous healers. Most illness episodes in developing countries are treated in a family context. Furthermore, the appropriateness of the health care system model to developing countries would include a sociopolitical, economic and cultural element.
3. There is a tendency to treat healing as an acultural phenomenon devoid of context rather than as a core function within specific social and cultural context

Kleinman goes on to suggest that health care systems ought to be studied in the context of their cultural settings, particularly as they are socially and culturally constructed. We must also remember that social 'realities' differ according to a variety of socio-economic factors. Health care systems and the clinical reality created by these systems can be studied at different levels, both micro and macro:

... the health care system is created by a collective view and shared pattern of usage operating on a local level, but seen and used somewhat differently by different social groups, families and individuals. Social factors such as class, education, religious affiliation, ethnicity, occupation and social network all influence the perception and use of health resources in the same locality, and thereby influence the construction of distinctive clinical realities within the same health care system.
(Kleinman, op. cit., p. 39)

We must not forget, Kleinman adds, that various factors shape the *content* of health care systems, such as cultural, historical, socioeconomic, and political influences. He cites the examples of alcohol and drug abuse which have now been taken over by health care systems whereas previously they were managed by legal and ethical systems. Similarly, he cites Foucault's study of the redefinition of mental illness, albeit over a much longer historical period. We have dealt with this elsewhere under the theme of the *medicalisation of life*, i.e. Illich's main argument.

Kleinman's argument is that there are several different kinds of reality, as follows:

1. *Social reality* (the social and cultural world, social reality, per se)

2. *Psychological reality* (the inner-world of the individual)
3. *Biological reality* (the infra-structure of organisms, including man)
4. *Physical reality* (the material structures and spaces which constitute our reality)
5. *Symbolic reality* (which bridges the social and cultural world with the psychological and biological reality)

(Kleinman, op. cit., p. 41)

It is widely recognised nowadays that health systems are shaped by a number of factors including their cultural settings. Kleinman separates such influences into *internal* and *external* factors. Examples of the latter include political, economic, historical, social structural and environmental determinants. Each of these can further be broken down. Thus for example environmental determinants include: geography, climate, demography, environmental problems, such as famine, flood, population growth, pollution, and agricultural and industrial development.

Most studies that fall under the heading of the 'political economy of health' are concerned with indicating the political and economic factors which intervene in the health process. These are discussed more fully in Chapter Ten. Work has also gone on in the area of illness and life-stress and the correlation of admission to mental hospitals and periods of economic depression. Certainly, although it is recognised that health care systems are influenced by external factors, there is presently an insufficient understanding of the mechanisms at play.

The internal structure of health care systems Kleinman's model of the *internal* structure of health care systems falls into three sections. The *popular* sector is the least understood by researchers and yet is the major of the three sectors by far:

It can be thought of as a matrix containing several levels: individuals, family, social network, and community beliefs and activities. It is the lay, non-professional, non-specialist, popular culture area in which illness is first defined and health care activities initiated. In the United States and Taiwan, roughly 70 to 90 percent of all illness episodes are managed within the popular sector.
(Kleinman, op. cit., p. 50)

By far the most popular therapeutic measure is self-treatment within the family setting. A number of steps occur once disease is encountered:

perceiving and experiencing symptoms
labelling and evaluating the disease
sanctioning a particular kind of sick role (acute, chronic, impaired, medical, psychiatric, etc.)
deciding what to do and engaging in specific health care seeking behaviour
evaluating the effects of self-treatment and therapy obtained from other sections of the health care system
(Kleinman, op. cit., pp. 51–52)

If the context of the popular sector appears to be insufficient then the individual must resort to either professional or folk practitioners. However:

The clinical realities of the different sectors and their components differ considerably. Popular, professional and folk cultures and their subcultural components shape the illness and therapeutic experiences in distinct ways. But the power to create illness and treatment as social phenomena, to legitimate a certain construction of reality as the *only* clinical reality, is not equally distributed. The professional sector is paramount because social power is in large part a function of institutionalisation, and the professional sector is heavily institutionalised whereas the popular sector is diffused.
(Kleinman, op. cit., p. 52)

The professional sector consists of the organised healing professions comprising mostly western medical organisations but sometimes various indigenous medical systems are also included. For example, in Transkei, herbalists are recognised by the legislature and exist as an alternative choice to western scientific medicine. A number of studies have been carried out on native healing groups and such systems as chiropractic and homeopathic healers. (Jones, 1985). A tendency has been to ignore the existence of alternative healing systems and to regard societies as utilising only the services of orthodox medicine. This results in a tendency to ignore the effects of alternative healing professions.

The folk sector consists of non-bureaucratic, non-professional specialists whose practice is usually divided into the *sacred*, or religious (e.g. Shaminism and ritual curing) and the *secular* (e.g. herbalists, manipulative surgeons). (Elling, 1981).

In terms of tangible health systems we must obviously consider the social organisation of the modern hospital, which we have done in Chapter Seven. Other aspects are also referred to elsewhere. We have chosen to adopt a theoretical perspective in this section because it facilitates an overall view of medical institutions, including practitioners, organisations, and physical settings, in a cross-cultural manner. Hence we realise that *our* system is not the only one or the correct one and that others with perhaps an equally sufficient claim also exist. We also come to realise, perhaps, that a number of systems exist side-by-side, often in total ignorance of each other. This is particularly true in many developing countries where western and traditional forms of therapy vie for customers.

THE PROFESSIONS

It is commonplace in today's world to refer to a wide variety of occupations as *professions*, for example lawyers, doctors, nurses, estate agents, bank employees, teachers and so forth. One definition in a classic work written in 1925 suggested, 'A profession may perhaps be defined as an occupation based upon specialised intellectual study and training, the purpose of which is to supply skilled service or advice to others for a definite fee or salary.' (Carr-Saunders, Vollmer and Mills, 1966). However, this is too wide a definition and merely lumps together a variety of occupations. Clearly the notion of *profession* elicits some kind of service idea in which 'devotion to the client's interests more than personal or commercial profit should guide decisions when the two are in conflict'. (Wilensky, 1964). There seems to exist some kind of ideal type of profession and thus some occupations have attributes which single them out as professions. Greenwood (1957) lists five characteristics of a profession. Firstly, professionals acquire a *systematic body of theory*. Secondly, the professional 'knows' what is best for the client or patient (as opposed to the customer who knows what he wants) and thus exercises *authority*. The authority is reinforced by means of professional control over entry into the profession by the restriction of *admission.* Control of admission is accompanied by a *code of ethics* which, if violated, could mean expulsion from the profession. Finally, each profession has its own values, norms and symbols; its *culture.* Millerson (1964) shows, from a review of a number of sociologists that the three traits most commonly identified are:

'adheres to a professional code of conduct';

'organised'; and

'skill based on theoretical knowledge'.

Power relations and professionalism   In modern societies the professions have grown in numbers and are consequently a characteristic feature of the growth of the service sector. It is common nowadays to classify professionals into two categories, thus:

- *Higher professionals*: doctors, dentists, lawyers, scientists, university teachers, engineers.
- *Lower professionals*: teachers, social workers, nurses.

Differences between the two groups are reflected in the stronger market position of higher professionals, and a tendency to work autonomously rather than for government, although private practice is becoming rarer. Traditionally, professionals have been viewed as giving a qualitatively superior service to the community than non-professionals. The functionalist (or 'trait' or 'attribute') approach gives a rosy picture of professionals as providing a superior service based on specialised expertise and exhibiting a primary commitment to community rather than self-interest. The two approaches are, in effect, slightly different as the 'trait' approach simply lists the characteristics of a profession. It is one which fails to analyse professions as being intricately involved with power relations in society and with monetary interests. In medieval times professionals were attached to rich patrons. However, with the coming of the industrial revolution they achieved new status and power, which meant that they could regulate the supply and cost of professional services by controlling entry:

The difference between professions and other occupations is that they have succeeded in convincing the public of their special skills and importance and of their need for corresponding privileges, whereas others have not. (O'Donnell, 1981).

A Marxist or power-conflict view of professionals considers them in relation to power and control in three areas of interaction: central and local government; the client; other colleagues.

With respect to government, the twentieth century has created an influx of professionals as government employees, for example, doctors, social workers, nurses and teachers. With the introduction of the National Health Service in Britain most professional medical workers became employees of the government. Inevitably the professional associations are torn between exercising negotiations over pay and conditions through trade unions or through associations.

Power and control in interaction with clients: As most professionals are employed by large organisations they have become increasingly subject to control by the overall authority of management. This can be seen in a number of bureaucratic situations, for example doctors versus administrators in hospitals, university academics versus university administrators, and so on. Increasingly, the authority of professionals has become eroded, for example the professional accountant finds that his work is now codified, standardised and routinised. Sociologists such as Herbert Gintis have suggested that bureaucracies, just as much as industries, produce fragmented (specialised) and alienated labour. Increasingly, according to the power-conflict analysis, the professions are being forced to maintain their traditional notions of power and status whereas in effect perhaps they are now simply well-paid workers.

A second aspect of client interaction is the *relationship of professionals to their individual clients*. Many see professionals as engaged in the process of 'mystifying' or manipulating the client. This is particularly clear in the doctor–patient relationship when drugs are often prescribed as a *cure* rather than as a treatment. Very often patients are not only not told what is wrong with them but they are also not aware of what the prescribed drugs are called and what they are for. In most cases, when blood pressure is taken, the patient is merely told 'its a bit high today' rather than the diastolic and systolic readings. The third area concerns the *professional control of professionals*. Entry is still controlled and censure, in theory, still exercised. In effect, of course, censure is rarely exercised and only for the most severe of offences. Frequently, when a number of professionals are together, such as in a hospital team, the senior consultant or surgeon is at the top of the hierarchy. As O'Donnell says:

Recent analysis suggests that for the public to hold professionals in awe serves only to perpetuate the myth that their work is incomprehensible to most and deserves unquestioning respect. This sense of mystery serves as an ideological cloak beneath which professionals can pursue their own interests which need not coincide with those of others. Increasingly, clients are bringing professionals to account on the same practical basis as other occupations, that is, in terms of the quality of their work. Nevertheless, professionals do remain relatively wealthy and privileged partly because there is an objective basis to their claims to be especially competent in difficult skills.

(O'Donnel, op. cit., p. 384)

The professions and nursing   The work a person does tells us a great deal about other aspects of that person's life. It helps us to place him or her quite firmly in a whole pattern which we have learned to associate with that work, including the *stereotypes* that we have. Equally importantly, the kind of work that a person does to a large extent determines activities in the non-work sphere. For example, we would be very surprised if a barrister lived in a council house or frequented dog races.

We spend most of our lives working. Sometimes we find it intensely satisfying but most people, unless they fall into this lucky category, 'each day sell little pieces of themselves in order to try to buy them back each night and weekend with the coin of fun'. C. Wright Mills was referring to the monotony of work that so many in the population face as a daily occurrence. We have moved away from the *gemeinschaft* economic existence of pre-industrial times to the large impersonal technical work situations of the twentieth century. The whole pattern of work has changed. Now people no longer work in isolated folk communities but congregate in large masses in factories and offices.

Because it is difficult to arrive at a definition of *work* as a term, partly because some people are lucky enough to enjoy what they are doing but also because a large number of people such as housewives work without being paid, then sociologists prefer to use the term *occupation*. This latter term refers to that which a man does to determine his *market situation*, i.e. which enables him to receive services and goods for money or some other form of exchange. Some work, of course, falls outside the market situation. By this we mean the kind of work that people might perform in their leisure time, such as decorating their house. Another way of classifying work is to designate it as either *expressive* (enjoyable or intrinsically satisfying) or *instrumental* (merely a means to an end).

The social system has the task of filling the multiplicity of job-roles available in a given society. Depending on the society in which we live, this can be achieved either through coercion or socialization. In many societies there are few options available to large sections of the population, because individuals are coerced, either by force or by a severe limitation placed on the options to enter certain occupational categories. In a more open society, however, individuals are brought up in particular socio-economic strata of the population, which nevertheless theoretically offers them an unlimited choice of occupations. In a society such as this other factors enter into the freedom of choice, such as education. In other words, children of working-class parents usually choose the occupations of their parents, their friends or relatives, and very rarely either wish to break away from this or indeed have the necessary qualifications to do so.

Realism of aspirations Sociologists of occupations have argued that working-class children, whether consciously or unconsciously, limit themselves to their class horizons, regarding it as natural that they move into the same occupational level as their parents. They do not choose from the whole range of occupations because their *milieu* has dictated to a considerable extent the possible occupations in terms of which they think. Other research has shown that children from non-selective schools rank very low in the scale of ambitiousness, and working-class children set the horizon of their expectations at the level of their classmates, neighbours and friends. The working population tends to fall into three categories. Firstly, those with high aspirations who obtain the jobs of their choice. Secondly, those who have no great expectations of work. Thirdly, those who use work as a means of achieving status and remuneration.

Occupations and the economy Occupation, because it has implications for the non-work sphere, is the most important indicator of the position an individual occupies in a market situation. It also gives a strong indication of a person's status and also his income. In modern industrial society some sociologists such as Marx have argued that highly impersonal modes of production have led to man being alienated. Even non-Marxist sociologists of work have argued that men employed in industrial occupations are alienated, that is, alienation is used as a shorthand description of the impact of modern industrial life on the manual worker. Generally speaking, the word alienation can be broken down into the following categories:

1. In a factory technology the workers are dominated and their alienation expressed in their relative *powerlessness* before the machine system.
2. Robbed of a sense of purpose due to the fragmentation of the work task, the worker develops *meaninglessness*.
3. Having no claim to the property institutions of capitalism there arises the employee's sense of *isolation* from the system of organized production and its goals.
4. Modern technology and capitalist economic institutions have negated the human perspective in the work situation, resulting in *self-estrangement*. However, most social scientists today would argue that alienation is not a consequence of capitalism *per se* but of employment in the large-scale organizations and impersonal bureaucracies that pervade all industrial societies.

Within modern industry a vast process of structural differentiation has taken place, resulting in variations in the form and intensity of alienation. The best example of alienation is probably among car assembly workers, as many as 61 % in some surveys claiming that their work is monotonous all or most of the time. Alienation refers particularly to the quality of personal experience which results from ways in which the social world is organized, and in particular the socio-technical settings of employment. When men feel that they are manipulated as objects, are without either control or power, and are without the *gemeinschaft* type of community that could compensate in some way for this feeling, they develop symptoms of fragmentation which we call alienation.

Some sociologists have pointed out that alienation follows a U-curve. During the old cottage and craft industries, when the *gemeinschaft* community was at its greatest, alienation was at its lowest. The industrial revolution, with the mass exodus from the agrarian division of labour to the cities, saw the end of the cottage industries and an increase in alienation. In the twentieth century with a large section of the labour force in assembly-line industries the feeling of alienation is at its highest, but already, in fully automated industries such as chemicals, there is evidence of a counter trend as the labour force is thrown back upon its own resources. The work of Goldthorpe on Vauxhall car workers bore out much of the research on alienation, but the particular factory studied had a long record of good relationships at the time of the study, and possibly the sample used (229 affluent workers) was too small to draw any valid conclusions. In the words of the French writer Albert Camus 'Without work all life goes rotten. But when work is soulless life stifles and dies.'

Work satisfaction
Work satisfaction varies greatly by occupation, and as one might expect, the greatest satisfaction is displayed by professional and business occupations. The same pattern is displayed for those asked whether they would enter the same occupation again (mathematicians 91 % to unskilled car-workers 16 %) and those asked whether they would continue working after the age of 65 (professionals 68 % to unskilled 16 %). Although similar results are born out by a number of studies the samples in most of them tend to be quite small.

There are many factors which account for occupational differences in satisfaction. Firstly, occupational prestige which is invariably carried over into the non-work area. Secondly, control over time, physical movement and place of work, or control over the technical and social environment (coalminers and steel workers appear to derive some satisfaction from this), or control as the freedom from direct supervision (which appears to give satisfaction to miners, lorry drivers and railwaymen). Thirdly, integrated work groups where the evidence suggests that the greater the extent to which workers are members of integrated work groups on the job, the higher the level of job satisfaction and the less the degree of work alienation. Fourthly, occupational communities such as those described in *Coal is Our Life* and *The Fishermen* have a high level of off-work association which is rarely found among urban factory workers, and in which the occupation itself is used as a reference group utilizing its standards of behaviour, its system of status and rank, as a guide to conduct carried over into the non-work area. This stands in marked contrast to the alienated assembly worker, who is characterized by a separation of his work-sphere from his non-work-sphere.

Occupational values   Different occupations carry with them differences in the prestige allocated to them in society, so that we normally rank unskilled and manual work as prestigiously low and non-manual work as high. There is considerable agreement from the surveys completed in this area that members of the general population tend to rate occupations roughly on the same point of a prestige scale so that professionals are ranked higher than middle-management who in turn come higher than skilled manual workers. Income by itself is not a sufficient criterion upon which to base a judgement. A poorly paid nonconformist minister of religion will be credited with more prestige than a second-hand car dealer, for example. Such notions as 'service' and 'usefulness' to society are also important in evaluating occupational rankings.

Bureaucratic organizations   Many people spend a large part of their working life in what are termed bureaucratic organizations in both the public and the private sector. Bureaucracy emerged in China, but it now characterizes much of present-day western industrial society. Because such organizations vary, sociologists find it useful to employ an ideal type of bureaucratic system based on the work of the German sociologist Max Weber, and which includes (a) carefully defined *offices* or positions, (b) a *hierarchical* order with clearly distinguished lines of responsibility and opportunity, (c) selection of personnel by methods based on *technical* or *professional* qualifications, (d) *rules* and *regulations* for social action, (e) security of *tenure* and the possibility of *career* and (f) a minimum of emotional involvement. All procedures are carried out by a *rational* procedure. Obviously an ideal type does not really exist and instances only approximate to it. We can all think of instances in which the system breaks down, when for example a firm sends out several reminders which cost more than the small amount owing. We can also envisage employees without technical competence, confusion and conflict among roles, and arbitrary and ridiculous rules.

Generally, bureaucratic systems are criticized for dampening personal growth, developing conformity and the 'organization man', and because they are hierarchical. There are dysfunctional and unintended consequences of bureaucracies, which are often inefficient and fail to achieve their intended goals. (See Chapter Seven for further analysis.)

Professions   Professions stand out from occupations and the surveys of occupations carried out on them as distinctly different. A profession is a very different type of occupation from all others, particularly in the distinction that a professional has the right to control his own work, that is he possesses a deliberate autonomy to such right and is granted such rights as to be able to deliberately ignore outside intervention. There remains a distinction between 'scholarly' professions and 'practising' professions and between professions and paraprofessions, which it is hoped will become apparent.

Some professions, for example dentistry and pharmacy, are autonomous in their own right, without being as prestigious as medicine. Others are very much dependent on the paradigm profession of medicine and are called *paramedical*. Nursing is a good example of a paramedical profession because although it becomes legitimate for nurses to receive orders and be evaluated by members of the medical profession the opposite is not the case. Nursing therefore becomes classified as a paramedical profession because, in the words of Freidson, they specifically and generically occupy positions round a profession. The search for full professionalism by paraprofessionalists is usually instituted by the latter setting up roughly the same standards as the profession that they are trying to emulate, principally training and licensing.

Characteristics of a profession
A profession is usually characterized as possessing the following characteristics, derived from William J. Goode: (1) the profession determines its own training and educational standards; (2) the practice of the profession is generally recognized by some form of licensing; (3) the boards which grant the licence are manned by members of the profession; (4) legislation is decreed by the profession; (5) standards and their control are laid down by the profession. Training in particular is prolonged, specialist and relatively abstract. The nursing profession on these criteria fails to possess the autonomy and control over training, and neither is it felt to create the knowledge, despite claims to the contrary. Even the possession of a criterion of 'service organization' is not felt sufficient to warrant the label of profession, because it is basically an institutional attribute rather than an individual one. It is only when society acquiesces in granting an autonomy from supervision by lay personnel that the category of profession can be awarded.

The divisions of medical labour
Medicine historically sought the exclusive right to practise its arts. Many other kinds of healing art became dissociated with such a claim and with the state of monopoly which accompanied it. It has now become established that it is illegal for anyone to practise medicine who is not qualified to do so.

Many tasks of medical healing, which were once thought the sole prerogative of physicians, are now practised by non-medical personnel, but it is the *control* of the situation and of the division of labour which is distinctive. One of the categories of occupation falling under this control is designated as paramedical, by which is meant the healing activities controlled obtrusively or unobtrusively by physicians. Freidson distinguishes such control by the amount or degree of technical knowledge 'released' by physicians, the extent of the assistance of paramedical workers, the subordination of paramedical workers is less than that given to physicians.

Consequently, Freidson argues that paramedical workers are to be distinguished from established professions by their lack of responsibility, autonomy, prestige and authority. Some occupations, such as herbalism, society designates as 'quack' or 'freaky'. It must be remembered that the designation 'paramedical' is a sociological one and not in any way implied as denigrating these occupations. Historically, through the university and the guild, the medical profession has consolidated its predominance in the areas of diagnosis and prescription.

Even the paramedical division of labour is hierarchically stratified with nurses ranking far higher than medical technicians and attendants. Other factors to be taken into consideration are that many paramedical occupants are *women*, and that prerequisite qualifications such as 'A' levels for university entrance are usually required for the former, that is the medical profession.

The training of personnel appears to be closely associated with the prestige of the occupation, and training geared to a university or in some way connected with one invariably occupies a higher position in the division of labour. Recruitment to medicine and nursing training is not a particular problem in either America or Europe, as the difficulty seems to lie in getting women to *stay* in the job and to reconcile the labour pattern with the competing demands of marriage and family life.

Friedson argues that professional autonomy is more easily developed by occupations that can successfully operate *outside* the confines of organizations. Traditionally the nurse has cared for the sick on the orders of, and in the absence of, a physician. Historically, the separation of secular nurses from the religious orders did not give the former any special claims based on the profession of skills and technical training until the middle of the nineteenth century. Because of the development of the modern nursing system under Florence Nightingale, the roots were firmly established in the subordinate position of the nurses of the Crimea under the military physicians. Even after her initial success at Scutari, the basis of the ideology of nurses was based on their social class and morals.

Nightingale . . . refused to allow any of her nurses to undertake to give any service at all on their own initiative. Her nurses' services were to be granted only when specifically requested by the doctors. No nurse could give food to any patient without the doctors' written order. No nurse could soothe or clean a patient without the doctors' order. Nuns were forbidden to engage in religious visiting. Nightingale thus required that what the nurse did for the patient was a funciton of what the doctor felt was required for the care of the patient. . . . *Nursing was thus defined as a subordinate part of the technical division of labour surrounding medicine.*
(Freidson, 1970, p. 61)

The dilemmas of nursing   While anxious to establish itself as a new and independent division of labour, nursing has had to face the dilemma that its work is not controlled by the occupation itself but stands in direct relation to the orders of the attendant physician. Increasingly, however, it has become recognized that the occupation of nursing possesses many tasks and a body of special knowledge that makes the nurse a surrogate doctor. The traditional model of the bedside attendant has given way to one of supervision, and a concomitant growth of occupations such as *practical nurse or nursing assistants* or others with fewer qualifications and training in an essentially subordinate position to fully registered nurses.

Now in a state of change, the occupation of nursing sees a route of social and occupational mobility up the hierarchy through an essentially administrative function. In many respects nursing is moving towards its own autonomy and self regulation, although its real dilemma still resides in its members being subordinate to the authority of the physician.

Teaching as an occupation The foregoing analysis of the occupation of nurses beings out the sociological implications of professionalization. Such implications are not confined to nursing but shared by other occupations such as

'FIFTY YEARS'
'Then' and 'Now': images of nurses in 1838 and in 1888.

teaching, from which many researchers would wish to withhold the title of 'profession'.

Clearly nursing fulfils far more acceptable criteria than teaching with its professional register, control over entry, a firm body of special and esoteric knowledge and so on. The one unsatisfied criterion appears to be that of autonomy and the particular relationship of nursing to the physician, although there is some indication that nursing authorities and associations are taking steps to remedy this.

The nursing profession We turn now to looking at the occupation of nursing by trying to apply some of the perspectives we have discussed above. It is an impossible task to look at the occupation *in vacuo* because we must constantly relate it to the broad structure of the occupations within the social structure and market situation of a country.

Characteristics of recruits Recruits to nursing tend to be predominantly female. Nowadays about 10 % of recruits are males who work mainly in mental and mental subnormality hospitals rather than general hospitals. Student nurses are generally drawn from the Registrar General's Classes I, II and II, are unmarried and in the 18–20 years of age range. One in four nurses in training in Britain come from abroad; English and Welsh nurses form the largest section and Irish and Scottish nurses comprising a minority. Recruits stem from a wide range of educational levels, with the majority possessing no formal school-leaving certificate but above average in educational attainment and a wide range of IQ according to Jillian Macquire in a fairly recent survey.

The majority of recruits appear to have chosen nursing as a first choice, and in a positive manner, at an early age, and generally to have had some work experience or voluntary experience relevant to their career choice. On the whole those who opt for nursing appear to know more about different kinds of training and career opportunities in nursing than potential recruits. As in many other occupations the choice of career is relevant to encouragement from relatives and information being passed on to them by friends and relations. With most recruits to nursing the over-riding reason for choosing nursing is because it is seen as helping people in a practical way.

Characteristics of intakes Intakes into non-teaching hospitals tend to be based on the immediate geographical locality supplemented by recruits from overseas. Such rely heavily on cadet courses, whereas teaching hospitals have a higher level of education in their recruits while those at the lowest level are in non-teaching hospitals.

Nature of attrition

Attrition or 'wastage' or 'withdrawal' is mostly due to voluntary withdrawal from training rather than nursing, and there are differences between types of nursing schools. Such withdrawal is higher in the first year than in the two subsequent years, and particularly high in the Introductory Courses. Male recruits have higher attrition rates, according to Jillian Macquire's survey, but it makes no difference to either male or female recruits what age they were at entry or how near they live to their home. Grammar-school recruits have less attrition than other recruits but those from abroad have the highest rates. Lowest rates of attrition are from children's nurses and general nurses. As we might expect, those with positive attitudes are more likely to complete their training than those possessing negative attitudes.

The attitudes of the general public to nursing

Nearly 26 % of the general public in the U.K. regard nursing as a suitable first choice but rate secretarial and teaching work as higher. This same general public, however, had three out of five members who knew what SRN stood for, and only two out of five who knew what SEN stood for. Nursing was generally agreed upon as being harder than teaching or being a bank clerk, and a much more worthwhile job than these other occupations. Adults in the general population entertained a general image of nursing which included the idea that nurses worked harder than others. The majority thought nurses were underpaid but nevertheless would encourage their daughters to nurse. One third of all women develop an intention to nurse at some time, and this can be as many as 77 % in those of school age. One in six develop a strong interest in nursing, and this reaches its peak between the ages of 13 and 16. Jillian Macquire's survey also showed that there was no interest in nursing which could be related to social class. The main deterrent was felt to be the hours worked and the pay, although the better educated tended to be more critical of the general conditions. The main positive factor was that nursing was worthwhile.

The selection of recruits

As we might expect those who apply for nursing are a highly self-selected group. The degree and kind of selection varies from hospital to hospital, and the ratio of those accepted to those rejected out of those who apply is greater in the U.K. for RHB (Regional Hospital Boards) hospitals than it is for teaching hospitals. Obviously, prestige of training establishment is an important in the choice of where a recruit chooses to do training as it is in choice of university, that is Oxbridge over Redbrick, large Civic over small Civic, and so on. Many hospitals set academic standards above the preliminary minimum set by the General Nursing Council, and some hospitals use batteries of tests in selection of students.

The career pattern of the qualified nurse

All but a small minority of those qualified work as staff nurses, half working less than one year in a staff nurse grade. Within two and a half years one third of females are married and two thirds of these are not working. This can be compared with the Plowden Report's comment on young women teachers: 'We can expect that of every hundred women who enter the training colleges, only 47 will be in the schools after three years' service and after six years only 30.' With the changing institutions of society, and the changing role of women, the wastage pattern of women in trained occupations appears somewhat alarmingly high, but if we take the training of nurses in a wider context we can argue that it is not only a training for an *occupation* but also an education for life and motherhood. Two and a half years after qualifying 44 % are working in hospitals as compared with 81 % of males working. The average staff nurse is single, works full-time, is among the youngest and most recently qualified, and is more mobile than other trained staff. The majority of married staff nurses work part-time, and nearly half of the total number of staff nurses are working in their own training school. Only a small percentage become ward sisters.

Enrolled nurses are usually under twenty-five, but more than a quarter are over-thirty-one. Most married nurses of all kinds have a break in service, either with childbearing or marriage. The longer the break the less likely they are to return. Family commitments, the age of children, and the lack of career prospects for part-time nurses are the main factors determining the pattern of employment.

The nurse in the hospital environment

In traditional training programmes there is a constant conflict between the educational requirements or needs of students and the staffing requirements of the ward. As we might expect, and sharing a pattern with teacher training, for example, there is substantial confusion about the desired end product of the training process and about the definition of the 'good nurse'. We would expect the attitudes of nurses to be linked to the training that they have received, but evidence for this view was only established by Jillian Macquire between the attitudes of mental nurses and the therapeutic organization of the institution for which they are working. Discipline in hospitals tends to be externally imposed and authoritarian, which produces conflict and makes adaptation difficult for entrants schooled in a society which is becoming increasingly permissive in relation to authority.

The turnover of qualified staff depends, it appears, not on the characteristics of individuals but on some institutional effects peculiar to a specific hospital, probably the communication system of the hospital. Absence rates were 80 % due to sickness for all grades, but were greater for the student nurse than for the trained ones. These sicknesses tended to be for respiratory and non-specific gastro-enteritis, which emerged as the major 'causes', and the absence for non-residential nurses was surprisingly greater than for residents.

Structure and ideology We have outlined some of the characteristics of recruits and the qualified nurse. The general features of the occupation present a picture of nurses as composed almost wholly of women employed not only in hospital wards but also in administrative capacities. They are mostly employed in salaried positions in subordination to physicians. The occupation in general has a relatively open recruitment (almost any woman can enter *some form of* nursing) and a spatial transferability of skills (they can move about the country if they so wish). The majority of nurses, both in Britain and America, work in hospitals, public health sectors or private homes. The occupation is embedded within a hierarchy of authority which stretches upwards to the physicians and the nursing hierarchy and downwards to student and ancillary nurses. Nurses are found in a number of diffuse occupations such as teaching, administration and bedside nursing. They also specialize within the hierarchical lines of the hospital or agencies and within the clinical specialization of medicine itself. It appears, then, to be predominantly a woman's occupation, with a relatively open recruitment and a high degree of geographical mobility.

The nursing reform movement, which paved the way for the near-professionalization of nurses, led eventually to sweeping changes in both the role of the nurse and her task within the hospital organization. Nurses no longer, in theory, were regarded as a pool of potentially cheap labour to be drawn upon at the discretion of physicians, and neither were they any longer anything approaching a nineteenth century description, which said they were 'Ward-maids . . . in much the same position as housemaids, and require little teaching beyond that of poultice-making.'

Pervasive imagery of bedside nursing

The image of the nurse as one whose task is that of providing bedside comfort for the sick and dying is one which still persists despite the increasing pattern, especially in America, of nurses as administrators. The persistence of this imagery has something to do with the sacred character of the occupation stemming both from its religious and secular origins, which Florence Nightingale did little to dispel. The religious significance and influence of the concept of 'vocation', for example, finds its most obvious example in the nursing world. Olesen and Whittaker's account of this world brings out a parallel between the nurse's Hospital Training School and a convent. Both are comparatively total institutions, in Goffman's sense of the term, in which the novices are depersonalized and resocialized. Values and personality attributes are deliberately manipulated to designated ends. 'Inevitably, in this secluded company, notions so much a part of both occupations arise: sisterhood, committed purpose, dedication of one's life to a 'calling', and a sanctity of one's trust.' The image of the administering angel, the Lady with the Lamp, coupled with the *affective* nature of women (so the cultural stereo-type would have it) as sensitive creatures, has in modern times led to the formulation of various socio-psychological approaches such as 'total patient', 'the communicative approach', 'psychological needs', 'the psychodynamic' and that of 'interpersonal relations'.

This has in turn led to certain ambiguities in the nursing administrator. Indirect patient care is believed to be as important as direct patient care, with the consequence that the nurse as supervisor is playing as vital a part in the overall nursing structure as her colleague who acts in a direct relationship. Nevertheless, the hospitals and public health authorities have made administration the route into professional viability and visibility, and also institutional power. Most women enter the profession seeing themselves as bedside nurses and yet the dilemma or ambiguity lies in the fact that promotion and salary beyond a particular level depend on an upward mobility through the administrative route.

Organizational context of nursing care

Hospitals and the employees of hospitals in theory cannot practise medicine. Only the physician is licensed to do this, with the consequence that this represents an extreme concentration of a given function around a position which, to some extent at least, is part of a complex institutional division of labour.

Because the 'private duty' model of nursing care gave way to the institutionalized (or incorporated into an institution such as a hospital) model, we had the result that there was an increase in categories of nursing staff. 'Functional' nursing as perceived from the perspective of the nurse herself meant that her duties were assigned according to the level of competence of the nurse and the needs and requirements of the situation. The 'system' itself acted as a deterrent to professional nursing because the organization of the hospital was bureaucratic and hierarchically structured.

This has led some, such as Isabel Menzies, writing in 1961, to postulate that certain psychological defences are erected by nurses in relation to patient care. She argues that because of the emotional intensity of the nursing act, certain psychological barriers are unconsciously built up, making it difficult for nurses to engage in significant relationships with patients. Her study of some London hospitals concludes that even the social organization of the nursing service has been evolved, largely without conscious awareness, for the express purpose of avoiding any activation of those emotions arising from patient contact. Thus, the organization aims at preventing nurses from having long or intense contact with patients. The often distasteful and frightening tasks that confront a nurse in the hospital setting arouse strong feelings of both a positive and a negative kind. The organization of the modern hospital, in order to shield the nurse, creates socially structured defences. Each nurse is asked to perform only a few of the nursing tasks, thus giving her a comparatively restricted contact. Simultaneously the patients are depersonalized, for example by being called the 'liver case' or by their bed number. It is almost an 'ethic' that patients are to be treated and viewed as alike. The uniform, furthermore, is a symbol of expected behavioural conformity, and of the attempt to establish an operational identity among all nurses in the same category in the hospital. thus nurses are interchangeable in staff assignments. In this way, Isabel Menzies argues, there is built into the institutional setting of the hospital and the role of the nurse, a 'safety valve' which ensures that no nurse has a contact nor involvement such as to allow her to develop any intensity of emotional commitment to the patient.

From the patient's point of view 'functional' nursing has the effect of increasing his anxiety. On admittance to a hospital he is anxious both about his condition, his new 'communal' situation, and his family whom he has left. From his very admittance he finds himself in an impersonal atmosphere and very often whatever personal treatment he might receive merely seems to accentuate his anxiety. Sometimes he is left for a long time on his own before anyone attends to him. He finds an added anxiety from the multiplicity of staff because he has not had time to recognize the different categories. He suffers, above all, a loss of independence and self-identity which results in a craving for individual identity and attention. Most of the problems of these different perspectives arise from the nurse and the patient viewing the situation within the hospital from two different viewpoints.

The nurse in the modern organizational context has a role which clearly recognizes a set of tasks which may be exactly or almost exactly specified and which involve a specialized and easily defined expertise. Nevertheless, there is a distinct boundary around the nurse's role beyond which she cannot go simply because to do so would involve a knowledge of the skills of the medical technician, the physician, the laboratory technician, and so on. But these are part of her role-set, the web of other roles with which her own interacts within the institutional setting. The old view of the nurse's role as being purely instrumental no longer applies. Her role is also expressive, that is, concerned not simply with a person's sick nature but with the *total* patient over a period of time. The role is affective in the sense that Isabel Menzies is talking about. The nurse cannot help but *feel* for the patient she is caring for but is guarded by the institutionalization of the role from the dangers of extreme affectivity.

The nurse is constantly subjected to some of the conflicting values in industrial society, some of which we have discussed in a previous chapter, such as religious, political and cultural values. Like all other role-incumbents the nurse must resolve, within the framework of role within the modern hospital, the dilemmas of general social interaction designated by the sociologist Talcott Parsons: affectivity versus affective neutrality (the emotional tone or level of a relationship); specificity versus diffuseness (should the nurse act as simply an aid to healing or should she see the role as a wider one incorporating a counselling or 'friendship' type of approach); universalism versus particularism (should she regard one patient just like another or can she 'particularize'); quality versus performance (does the nurse relate to the patient on the basis of the latter's sex or age or colour or on the basis of the latter's progress in health); self-orientation versus collectivity orientation (does the nurse put her own needs first or the requirements of the profession). Obviously we cannot go into these pattern variables, as they are called, in too great a depth here, but the pattern which emerges is that of the nurse's role as one involving a choice between these variables both from her own individual point of view and also from the institutionalization of the role by the hospital organization in which she finds herself. (For further elaboration see Chapter Seven.)

Conclusion Our discussion has examined the sociological concept of occupation in modern industrial society with particular reference to some of the implications of the concept to others such as status. The profession was regarded as a special category of occupation having special criteria which marked it off from other occupations. Nursing was analysed in order to bring out some of the nuances of the concept of profession, and perhaps the only drawback to nursing being accepted as a fully fledged profession was its lack of autonomy. Teaching appeared to fail several criteria for qualification as a profession. It may appear rather strange that both nursing and teaching, both generally regarded by the layman as professions, failed a sociological 'test' but we must remember that we were engaged in a kind of sociological exercise which was using the word in a strict sense. It is obvious that those criteria used were themselves open to debate, and perhaps there is a happy medium between using 'profession' as loosely as the general public does to refer to virtually any occupation, and as strictly as the sociologist does, which severely limits its use. Nevertheless, an analysis of the concept and its application did throw some interesting light on the role of the nurse in the modern hospital setting and the relationship of her occupation to that of the physician and other medical and paramedical personnel. The sociology of occupations clearly recognizes that many new 'professions' are emerging in keeping with the growth in the complexity of modern industrial and technological society which are termed *qualifying associations*. Nursing is clearly in a very strong position to consolidate its strengths and to achieve either professional autonomy in the near future or at least some form of alternative to the present position. Nursing in the above analysis shares a category similar to that of pharmacist and slightly below that of optician, but only if we use the criterion of being able to prescribe. There are many other criteria we could opt for, such as service orientation, which nursing undeniably shares with physicians. We have tended to adopt the criterion of occupational autonomy in this chapter, following Freidson and others, which was as much intended as an exercise in the sociology of occupations as it was a stand for one particular criterion.

THE INTERACTIONS OF PATIENTS AND PROFESSIONALS

Health practitioners usually encounter their patients when the latter are in a vulnerable position, i.e. being ill. During what Krause (1978, op. cit.) calls the 'politics of diagnosis', it is the former who do the defining (how ill?, what of?) but certain characteristics of the patient will determine the quality of the relationship, for example, his or her race, sex, cultural background, financial status, and age. Formerly, because medical practitioners had virtually no contribution to make to the preservation of human life, their major role was that of comforter, hence the Greek *klinikos*, from which we derive *clinician*. The essential humanity of the role of the physician gave way in the twentieth century to that of the medical scientist and universal expert. We have discussed elsewhere the concern by some, such as Zola and Illich for example, of the increasing medicalisation of life. The growth of what some call *medical imperialism* includes numerous instances of medical intrusion into hitherto distinct areas, such as the American prison or elementary school (tranquilisers given to unruly prisoners and schoolchildren). Krause (1978, op. cit., p. 91) cites a study of two groups of surgeons, one salaried and the other given money for each operation. As we might expect, the latter group performed twice as many operations as the former.

The doctor–patient relationship is central to the practice of medicine. The traditional view regards the patient as inferior, to be taken care of by the doctor, whereas the modern view regards the patient as equal. Krause discusses a number of areas which affect the doctor–patient relationship, such as racial prejudice (blacks discriminated against in terms of doctor–patient ratios, access to hospitals, quality of service), sexism (abortion, exploitation of female psychiatric patients by therapists) ageism (most illnesses of the elderly are chronic, non-curable and consequently regarded as uninteresting or unrewarding), and cultural chauvinism (despising the patient because he/she comes from what is regarded as inferior culture).

Very often there exists between patient and doctor what is known as a *competence gap*, because the patient usually lacks the medical knowledge of a doctor. This puts the doctor in a position of power over the patient, and the possibility of exploitation arises. The functionalists introduce the notion of 'trust' (e.g. Parsons) but others see in the stratified distribution of technical knowledge the potential for professional dominance. (Freidson, 1970). Alienation also arises in the doctor–patient relationship because becoming a patient involves surrendering one's role as an independent adult as well as one's body.

Waitzkin (1974) further discusses the stratification within the doctor–patient relationship in respect of information control. The relationship is fraught with uncertainty, and although doctors may experience uncertainty in relation to the outcome of illness, and in medical research and training, it is nevertheless infinitely greater for the patient because of the competence gap. Medical uncertainty is experienced in three areas. Firstly, the effect of service on any individual; secondly, lack of consumer expertise on the sources and quality of treatment; and, thirdly, a lack of information for consumers regarding drugs, treatment and diagnosis. Studies in America have shown that even when doctors are certain about the course a disease will take they still tend to prolong uncertainty. For example in the communication of prognosis to families of children with poliomyletis, stating the expected date of discharge to T.B. patients, and withholding the facts from dying patients. One explanation for the maintenance of uncertainty lies in the reluctance of people to communicate bad news that was being withheld.

Waitzkin explains it in relation to the source of the physician's power: 'Physicians' ability to preserve their own power over patients in doctor–patient relationships depends largely on the ability to control patient's uncertainty.' The more knowledge the patient has about his condition the less power the physician can exercise.

Another source of control is that of the social class differences that invariably exist between patient and doctor. Cartwright explains the diffidence of working class patients as resulting from the following:

1. their perception that doctors do not expect them to answer questions;
2. a sociolinguistic deficit, particularly in the use of technical medical language;
3. the awe with which the working class regard doctors; and
4. the social distance between patients and doctors, stemming from the latter's high social status.

Cartwright discovered no real difference in the strength of the desire for information between the working and the professional patients, except the former's reluctance to ask questions.

Micro-politics of the doctor-patient relationship Waitzkin's study of the micro-politics of the doctor–patient relationship (1983, op. cit.) highlights the fact that it is not merely a problem in itself but part of a wider social and historical context.

. . . research portrays doctor–patient interaction as a frequently dismal process, filled with misunderstandings, insensitivity, and frustration. Patients often leave the medical encounter with their perceived needs for information unmet. Even when highly motivated, doctors tend to underestimate patients' desire for information and to overestimate their own communicative skills. Communication barriers seem greatest when professionals and clients of different class background, sex or race try to interact.
(Waitzkin, 1983, p. 143)

He argues that because doctor–patient encounters are embedded in a social context, 'messages of ideology and social control in medical encounters are rife':

Such communications carry certain distortions; although they tend to be nontechnical these messages convey the symbolic trappings of scientific medicine and the impression of the professional's superior technical knowledge. This communicative pattern supports the professional's dominance within the encounter, to reinforce current social arrangements in work, the family, leisure, pleasure, sexuality, and other facets of social life. A primary, though implicit, goal is the husband's client's continued participation in economic production. For women, this goal extends to the maintenance of the husband's economic role through housework and other familial responsibilities. Doctors make decisions about the certification of medical disability and eligibility for welfare payments. They also manage anger, anxiety, unhappiness,

loneliness, depression, and related emotions: in the process, the social origins of many of these emotions escape notice.
(Waitzkin, op. cit., p. 180)

The social organisation of a visit to the doctor When one visits a doctor the patient's interaction with him is only one of many interactions that make up the social organisation of the experience. (Amir, 1980). For example, there are special settings (waiting room, examining room, doctor's office), complying with procedures (making an appointment), and dealing with a number of people (nurse, receptionist, bookkeeper)

The generalised visit to the doctor entails the component parts of negotiating access through claiming procedures: establishing physical presence within the premises; waiting; being served; and exiting.
(Amir, op. cit., p. 258)

Amir highlights the spatial, temporal and interactional components of the process.

The medical model in doctor–patient interaction Danzinger's study (1980) of the pregnant patient's career, views it within a series of interactional events. She notes that many of the concerns of the patient fall outside the range of medical deliberation. Furthermore, 'the form and content of the pregnant patients' career is inextricably linked with the presentation of the power and authority of medical expertise.' The patient is treated as 'physically and emotionally traumatised.' Most of what was learned in prenatal classes is never subsequently touched upon, and the pregnant patient is forced into a stringent time schedule. Three types of patient-processing mechanisms are introduced to structure the patient's career. Firstly, 'documentation as a case according to diagnostic classifications provide a chronology of conditions into which the facts of particular cases must be fitted.' Secondly, practitioners stereotype patients, either by moral categories or social distance distinctions. Thirdly, the practitioner displays moral imperatives, and what doctors suggest is usually adopted unquestioningly:

. . . in terms of their usual work routines, doctors carry on similarly to social workers, dieticians, nurses, educators, plumbers, car mechanics, scientific researchers, medical and laboratory technicians, or lawyers. What is unique to a medical practitioner is the sacred right to violate or assault another human being's body, or to order someone else to execute the assault.
(Op. cit. p. 302)

The doctor–patient relationship The initial encounter between doctor and patient is one of negotiation, the former having several built-in advantages such as status, technical knowledge and the tools of the trade (white coat, stethoscope, large desk, etc.). The encounter involves negotiation or bargaining, with power playing an important part in this. Usually, the patient has very little with which he can bargain, except the refusal to co-operate.

However, the role of the doctor is not without a number of built-in conflicts.

1. The doctor must appropriate his interests equally among his patients giving none more time at the risk of the neglect of the others.

2. Medicine, including doctor's time, is composed of scarce resources. Sudnow, for example, noticed that more attempt was made to save the life of a 20 year old than a 40 or 70 year old when admitted to the casualty departments of two American hospitals:

   'Among other categories of persons whose deaths will be more quickly adjudged, and whose 'dying' more readily noticed and used as a rationale for apathetic care, are the suicide victim, the dope addict, the known prostitute, the assailant in a crime of violence, the vagrant, the known wife-beater, and, generally, those persons whose moral characters are considered reproachable.'
   (Sudnow, 1967)

3. Another area of conflict lies in the doctor needing to balance 'the interests of any one patient at any point in time with the same patient's interest in the future.' (Tuckett, 1976.) This usually takes the form of an evasion of the truth if a poor prognosis is discovered.

4. Sometimes a patient's welfare has to be balanced against that of his family or household, as for example when someone may have to be compulsorily committed as a mental patient.

5. On occasion the doctor is faced with situations over which he has no control, such as the patient presenting himself with an incurable disease, or a patient complaining about some social concern such as an unhappy marriage or inadequate housing.

6. Doctors have their own career aspirations which may not accord with the post they hold. Thus in Britain and America most hospital work is carried out by junior or immigrant doctors because the career orientated enter more glamourous fields.

7. Sometimes doctors may feel conflict between an obligation to help a patient and being an employee of the state, such as the issue of when a sickness certificate should be withheld or extended.

8. The role of doctor makes perhaps more demands than other occupations. Conflict may arise between the occupational role and that of tennis player, husband, father, etc.

The context of medical practice The meeting of doctor and patient within the context of medical practice shows clearly that the former is often assessed by the latter in lay terms. Mechanic's (Mechanic, 1968) work on the issue of physician choice and qualities of a good doctor, shows that high on the list of priorities (as seen by the city of Madison's mothers) were *competence, personal interest,* and *general behaviour* towards the patient. The choice of doctor was usually on the recommendation of friends or neighbours, recommendation of another doctor, and accessibility of the doctor's office. Highest among the reasons for dissatisfaction was that the doctor *failed to do what seemed indicated.* Among other reasons given was a *lack of interest* which was displayed, and a *wrong diagnosis*. Mechanic's work seemed to indicate that a number of physicians do not adequately meet their patients' expectations, and fail to explain, to their patients' satisfaction, procedures and assumptions in the treatment process.

We have mentioned above that patients often present problems to doctors which are far beyond the competence of the doctor concerned. This appears to be very much the consequence of society moving from a *gemeinschaft* construction to a *gesellschaft* arrangement with the consequence that whereas previously social problems were handled within the family and kinship settings the bureacratisation of social institutions means that such problems must now be dealt with by others. The family doctor appears to have borne the brunt of this shift.

The problem of conflict and conflict resolution in doctor–patient interactions has been looked at by Bloor and Horobin (1975). They question the belief that the doctor–patient relationship is fundamentally reciprocal, but rather that it contains elements which are likely to generate conflict. The source of the conflict 'lies in two basic assumptions held by doctors as to how their patients should behave. They believe patients should use their own judgement as to when it is appropriate to seek medical advice; however patients are later expected to defer to the doctor's judgement when undergoing medical treatment. Because doctors appear to hold these conflicting expectations this produces in the patient a *double-bind* situation (a contradiction in expectations)'. (Bloor and Horobin, 1975, p. 280)

The main complaint that doctors have against their patients is that their time is often taken up by trivial conditions. In one study 26 % of doctors regarded 50 % of their patients as bothering them with unnecessary problems. It is obvious that doctors expect a higher awareness of medical conditions among the general public and that they should be well-informed about when to enter into health-seeking behaviour. There is some suggestion that doctors do not like to be questioned or challenged about their diagnosis and treatment and will, when threatened, hide behind a professional facade. Such challenges are more likely to come from the educated classes.

Freidson (1962) takes the view 'that the separate worlds of experience and reference of the layman and the professional worker are always in potential conflict with each other.' The physician is at pains to impose a professional diagnostic and palliative framework upon the patient. The patient, from the perspective of his own lay position, tries to *control* what the doctor is doing to him. Conflict, which may arise in this situation, is also more likely to do so when the patient defines his condition as critical rather than ordinary or minor, Freidson sees three ways in which the conflict might earlier be dealt with. Firstly, the doctor may agree more and more with the demands of the patient (but then if he does so extensively he ceases to be the doctor!). Secondly, the patient may take a crash course in health education in order to meet the doctor's viewpoint (however, the more the education the more the patient may seek to control the doctor's work!). Finally, the doctor may strive to achieve 'such relatively high social standing as to gain an extra-professional source of leverage for controlling the patient, but the patient tends to answer by only superficial co-operation and covert evasiveness.'

Becoming a patient
We generally speak in loose terms about a society being 'sickly' or 'healthy'. However, it is extremely difficult to arrive at a true or accurate picture of the health of a population. The question itself is full of difficulties. For example, are people ill when they display physical symptoms of illness but do not themselves feel ill or vice versa, when they do in fact feel ill but have no diagnostic symptoms? Are trivial complaints those designated as such by the doctor, or by the patient? Some complaints can be 'trivial' and yet cause considerable discomfort or pain, and yet other complaints can actually be serious but the discomfort and pain well controlled. Post-mortems have often revealed advanced diseases which during the life of the individual caused little or no discomfort.

The problem of measurement of the extent of disease in society is problematic. For example, if we take a simple count of sickness certificates this may not give anywhere near an accurate picture because not all people who are sick, stay off work or seek a sick note. Problems of measurement also call into question whether we are guaging the extent of illness or disease.

Several studies have, in fact, tried to estimate the extent of illness and disease. One survey found that out of a total of illness recorded only 25 % had consulted a doctor. Other surveys range from 'under one third' to 'less than half'. Wadsworth (1971) showed that in a community of a thousand, between 750 and 900 would, in any two weeks, experience at least one painful and distressing symptom. Less than 200 of these would visit a doctor during the same period, and of them 28 would attend as out-patients in a hospital, and only 5 as in-patients. In another survey a random sample, thoroughly screened and examined, revealed that 52 % who had been receiving no treatment at all, required further investigation and possibly treatment. Several questions are raised by such studies, such as why certain individuals seek help while others do not. It is certainly not the case that only the more seriously afflicted seek care, as the last study mentioned bears out.

One factor which determines whether individuals or families engage in health-seeking behaviour is to do with the *tolerance level*. Such levels are experienced differently by different groups and cultures and also by certain individuals. We are required to feel perceived needs before action is taken. Many individuals bear symptoms regarded by most doctors as pathological and yet do not seek medical help of any kind. Various studies of pain thresholds reveal 'that quite discrepant amounts of morphine were required to reveal pain in people with apparently similar injuries.' (Tuckett, op. cit. p. 165)

Another factor which we touched upon earlier is that individuals may seek help from other than western medicine, for example witch-doctors and herbalists. And yet others may deliberately stay away from doctors from a fear of what they might be told.

Mechanic views illness behaviour as culturally and social learned responses. Thus the higher the social class of the individual the more likely he/she is to seek help. Certain ethnic groups have an exagerated response to pain. The socio-economic background of individuals to a considerable extent determines responses to illness and pain. Common symptoms tend to be ignored more than atypical ones. One study of pain referred to above revealed that similar wounds requiring surgery elicited different responses to pain on the part of soldiers and civilians. Different 'stress' groups reveal different inclinations to utilise medical facilities, thus high-stress individuals utilise medical facilities far more than low-stress individuals. Mechanic (op. cit., pp. 130–131) lists ten factors affecting the response to illness:

Factors affecting the response to illness

1. Visibility, recognizability, or perceptual salience of deviant signs and symptoms.
2. The extent to which the symptoms are perceived as serious (that is, the person's estimate of the present and future probabilities of danger).
3. The extent to which symptoms disrupt family, work, and other social activities.
4. The frequency of the appearance of the deviant signs and symptoms, their persistence, or their frequency of recurrence.
5. The tolerance threshold of those who are exposed to and evaluate the deviant signs and symptoms.
6. Available information, knowledge and cultural assumptions and understandings of the evaluator.
7. Basic needs which lead to autistic psychological processes (i.e. perceptual processes that distort reality).
8. Needs competing with illness responses.
9. Competing possible interpretations that can be assigned to the symptoms once they are recognised.
10. Availability of treatment resources, physical proximity, and psychological and monetary costs of taking action (included are not only physical distance and costs of time, money, and effort, but also such costs as stigma, social distance, feelings of humiliation and the like.)

People naturally do make visits to their doctor, and on average, in the U.K. for example, men make on average three visits and women four per annum. (Dunnell and Cartwright, 1972). Tudor Hart (1971) argues that a large number of visits to the doctor are merely seeking legitim-ation for the illness by obtaining a doctor's certificate. These are predominantly working class patients and thus the 'purpose' of the visit is more economic than medical. He notes that during the working years middle-class patients paid 53 % fewer visits than working-class people, although at 75+ this had changed to 62 % *higher!* This suggests that many visits, especially by the working-class, are indeed trivial but that such visits are to do with the larger economic structure of society where many individuals are concerned about their finances. Perhaps also important is the strong suggestion that only *some* symptoms are presented to the doctor at any one visit.

If in addition to being ill the patient requires hospitalisation this adds an entirely new dimension. (Tagliacozzo and Mauksch, 1980). In the modern hospital patients remain relatively strangers to each other. This gives greater power to the hospital functionaries and this 'power which is vested in them can inhibit the patient to seek clarification and guidance. The roles of doctors and nurses assume that of *significant others.*' Such significance is derived from different sources:

The physician represents authority and prestige. His orders legitimise the patient's demands on others and justify otherwise deviant aspects of illness behaviour. The physician is not only the 'court of appeal' for exemption from normal role responsibilities, he also functions as the major legitimizing agent for the patient's demands during hospitalisation . . . Although the physician's authority ranks supreme in the eyes of most patients, they are also aware that he is only intermittently present and thus not in a position to evaluate the behaviour of both patients and nurses and to sanction this behaviour during the everyday procedures of hospital care.

The significance of the nurse stems not only from her authority in interpreting, applying and enforcing the orders of the physician but, in addition, from the fact that she can judge and react to the patient's behaviour more continuously than the physician. From the patient's point of view, he also depends upon the nurse as an intermediary in the provision of many other institutional services. (Tagliacozzo and Mauksch, op. cit., pp. 186–187)

Constantly, patients desire to please the nursing staff but at the same time play off the nurse against the physician. Patients felt that both nurses and physicians required *co-operation* from them. Most patients, however, thought that nurses expected of them 'not to be demanding', to be 'respectful' and to be 'considerate'. It was a constant worry, to patients that they might be attracting services from the nursing staff that were seriously needed by those who were sicker. Both nurses and doctors were seen as 'constantly on the go'. Interestingly, cardiovascular patients expressed criticism of nurses and physicians much less frequently than other patients. Interestingly, also, women were more critical of nursing care than men, 'and more frequently expressed fear of negative sanctions from nurses. Women, more than me, emphasised personalised relationships when they discussed the needs of patients.' Many male patients identify the nurse with the images of 'sister' or 'mother' or 'homemaker'. These conjectures may also help to explain the well-known preference nurses have for male patients.'

Finally, a study by Lorber (1970) found that, from a sample of 103 surgical patients admitted to hospital, most were found to have entered with the feeling that they should be 'obedient, cooperative, objective about their illness, and expect attention only if they are very ill.' The patients with 'deviant' attitudes tended to be better educated and younger and argued more with the physicians and nurses, and tended also to complain about minor discomforts as a way of obtaining attention. 'Good' patients were considered to be those who were cooperative, uncomplaining and stoical, although staff expected to be informed if they were needed medically. 'Problem' patients were those who were uncooperative and overemotional and complaining, although they were categorised as such only by the staff who had to bear the brunt of their time-consuming requests. These were generally patients who did not respond to sedation or tranquilisers (the chief methods of dealing with pain or discomfort) and who, instead, required lengthy verbal reassurances and explanations:

In sum, doctors and nurses expect to carry out their work by well-established routines, with a minimum of interruption from patients. Those patients who make no trouble at all, who do not interrupt the smoothness of medical routines, are likely to be considered *good* patients by the medical staff . . . good patients usually had routine surgery and were out of the hospital within a week, or had major surgery and accepted whatever was done to them cheerfully and cooperatively. Doctors and nurses tend to consider *average* patients those whose complaints are medically warrented, who respond to established routines for handling such complaints, and who therefore take up the expected amount of time for their type of illness.

Problem patients are two of a kind. Those who are seriously ill, and who complain a great deal, are very emotional, anxious and need a lot of reassurance, encouragement, and attention from the staff are problematic, but 'forgivable' because their situation is not of their own making . . . Patients who are *not* seriously ill in the eyes of the staff, but who nevertheless act as if they are by complaining, crying and refusing to cooperate with medical routines, are the mostly profoundly condemned by the staff. Such problem patients, in this study, were tranquilised, sometimes discharged early, and, in one case, referred to a psychiatrist . . .

Thus, the consequences of deliberate deviance in the general hospital can be medical neglect or a stigmatising label, while conformity to good-patient norms is usually a return home with only a surgical scar.
(Op. cit., pp. 214–215.)

SUMMARY

1. Medicine is a cultural system with symbolic meanings.
2. Health care systems integrate other aspects of society.
3. We are hampered from arriving at an holistic view of health care systems by (1) the dominance of the biomedical model; (2) a predominance of the 'professional care' model; and (3) the treatment of healing as an acultural phenomenon.
4. The internal health care system comprises the *popular* (informal), the *folk*, and the *professional.*
5. Professions are analysed from a functionalist and a power-conflict perspective.
6. A profession is a special category of occupation with specifically framed sociological criteria which exclude some occupations normally regarded as 'professional'.
7. Physician–patient interaction invariably displays characteristics of power and control in which the doctor exercises dominance by virtue of utilising such ploys as witholding information, exploiting the deference of working class patients, etc.
8. Physicians generally complain that they are presented with essentially trivial complaints, although what appears so to the doctor is not necessarily perceived as such by the patient. The opposite can also be the case.
9. Many social factors affect the response to illness including the tolerance threshold and the interpretation of symptoms.
10. In hospital settings the nursing and medical staff often have different expectations vis-a-viz the patient than the patient has of them, including the general belief than some patients are 'problems'.

IMPORTANT TERMS

symbolic reality
biomedical model
secular
medical imperialism

ethnography
sacred
profession
double-bind

SELF-ASSESSMENT QUESTIONS

1. Outline the effects that the dominance of the biomedical model has had in supplying answers to social/health problems.
2. What are the defining characteristics of a profession? From your experience of the health professions how far would you agree with the power-conflict model?
3. Give a critical account of Waitkin's analysis of the doctor–patient relationship.
4. Describe the sociological process of becoming a patient.

5. What factors affect the response to illness?
6. What does Kleinman mean by saying that the health care system *integrates* 'all other aspects of society'?

CHAPTER FOUR

PEOPLE AND WORK

- social differentiation
- occupation and disease
- lifestyles
- work and community

SOCIAL DIFFERENCES

There have already been indications that people differ from one another in a number of important ways, some of which may include differences in income but also such things as power and prestige. Every society allocates these and other things according to their own distinctive criteria, and during the course of history both the criteria and the system of social stratification might change. By social stratification, we will mean the way in which people are *ranked* on a scale of inferiority/superiority, which results in differences between them of privileges, rewards, obligations and restrictions. The term itself is taken from geology, where it refers to successive layers of rock, but when we talk of people as being socially stratified the problem becomes much more difficult because people think, feel and sometimes act about the way they are stratified and about their social position. Moreover, each stratum interacts with every other, producing a conflict of interests.

The patients that are seen by nurses and doctors obviously differ in a number of ways. They are fathers, mothers, brothers, sisters, male, female, tall, short, old, young, good-looking, ugly, and so on. Most of these differences are determined in a way that it would be almost impossible to alter, but social stratification is not concerned with these kinds of criteria (although they may enter into it) but more with the problem of *scarcity*, and more particular the scarcity of positions in society which individuals desire.

Stratification in subhuman and simple societies It is well known that animals try to exert social dominance over each other. Among birds this is commonly referred to as the pecking order. When a new bird is introduced into a cage or pen full of other birds he has to fight at least one of the birds in order to establish which one will become dominant. Once such dominance has been established the defeated bird, on subsequent meeting, retreats from the victor. Research suggests that social dominance is established by a number of such factors as strength, size, degree of fear, familiarity with the territory, and the general state of health. As far as chickens are concerned, to be at the top of a pecking order establishes a number of privileges such as the first choice of a partner or the best food. Observations of rodents, dogs and primates revealed very different patterns of social domination according to such measurements as intensity, duration, and so on. In insect societies there exists a very rigid structure of stratification.

Many simple societies operate a system of stratification based on age sets. The Australian aborigines have such a system, and it is one in which the social status (the relative degree of honour or prestige which individuals accord to other individuals who occupy a social position) of any one aborigine is the same as that of another of his own age. Contrary to what we might think such a society is *open* because no individual is able to remain in the same position all his life, all have a chance of working through each position, all do the same type of work associated with each position, and so on. This stands in marked contrast to a *closed* stratification system such as caste (a stratification system where individuals are accorded a permanent rank at birth and in which contact between categories is severely restricted).

Major systems of social stratification

Generally, sociologists have isolated three major systems of social stratification: caste, estate, and class systems. In one sense there are what are known as ideal types (constructs or models of the real world) because they do not exist in a pure form in any society and are used rather as ways of comparing any actual system of social stratification both with other systems and with the pure form itself.

Caste

The caste system is composed of a number of horizontal strata each responsible for a number of functions within a society. Every caste or sub-caste has specific functions it can perform and others that it cannot. Thus a member of a high caste cannot become 'contaminated' by performing a function or an occupation reserved for one from a lower caste. The ranking order of such a society is usually the result of some struggle of powerful groups in the society at some time in history, or the result of military conquest by an outside power.

The best known example of such a system is the Hindu caste system in India, which is usually divided into four main categories (although there are an estimated 10 000 caste groups) of *Brahmins* or priests, *Kshatriya* or warriors, *Vaisya* or merchants, and *Sudra* or workers and peasants. In addition to these four main groups there exist the *Untouchables* or *outcastes* who have been expelled from their caste (either themselves or through some action of the ancestors which violated the rigorous caste rules). It is estimated that 6 % of the Hindu population of India are Brahmins, and 20 % untouchables. These four traditional *Varnas* (the term originally meant *colour*) are held by some to be very similar to the next major system we shall discuss, the estate. There is evidence that passage between castes was always possible either by intermarriage or some other means and that they were not as closed as is popularly thought. Today caste lines are being considerably weakened in the big cities and by government legislation.

Theoretically caste is ascribed and fixed for life and marriage is endogamous. Social interaction between members of different castes is rigidly fixed by a series of rules meant to consolidate the purity of the Brahmin and the impurity of the Untouchable. Some of these rules prohibit the entry of the lowest class into the city walls between 3 p.m. and 6 p.m. for fear that their shadows, lengthened by the afternoon sun, would contaminate a member of a superior caste. Untouchables were not permitted within 124 feet of a Brahmin, and for them to even glance at a cooking pot necessitated the destruction of the contents. This was particular attention paid to a set of complicated rules governing eating behaviour of Untouchables (Harijans) and Brahmins.

FROM: *SUNDAY TIMES*, 1 MAY 1988

INSTANT WHITES!
6 Indians change their race

AT LEAST six Indians successfully applied to the Government to become white, a report tabled in Parliament shows.

This and other statistics are contained in the report of the Department of Home Affairs for the 18-month period from July 1, 1986 to December 31 last year.

The report also reveals that during the period under review, 438 'Cape coloureds' became white.

But whether their coloured brothers and sisters or relatives of colour would even be able to visit them is another question.

During the same period, 464 Africans became 'Cape coloured,' presumably allowing them to live in comparatively better developed coloured suburbs.

Twelve coloureds became Chinese.

Whereas only one 'white' decided to turn 'Chinese', at least 17 Chinese decided to become fully-fledged 'whites' — instead of being only 'honorary whites'.There are also four whites who became Malay — probably for reasons other than just preferring bobotie to biltong.

Some of the other race switches were: Indian to Cape coloured, 87; Cape coloured to Indian, 85; Indian to Malay, 42; Malay to Indian, 50.

Cape coloured to black, 17; Black to 'Other Asian' (no particulars what that means) three; black to Indian 10; Black to Griqua, 22; Cape coloured to Malay, 30; Malay to Cape coloured 27; Black to Malay; two; Griqua to black, two; coloured to Griqua, four.

The total race changes were 1 356 compared to 1 054 the previous year.

Generally, the caste system appears to be closely tied to occupation with the Harijans occupying the very low-status jobs such as road-sweepers and basketmakers and the Brahmins or priest at the top followed by warriors, herdmen, fishermen and so on. Many Harijans have made fortunes, and by the process of *Sanskritization* or the spread of Hindu influence on tribal ritualized beliefs, whole groups have bettered their caste position. Caste is, however, not just an occupational group but an example of a closed status group because individuals who perform the occupations are designated inferior/superior by others. Social mobility (the extent to which an individual or group moves up or down the social stratification system) is usually achieved by a group or collectivity rather than by individuals.

There are two ways that are frequently used to explain the caste system. Firstly, the historical explanation for the existence and persistence of caste refers to the original Aryan invaders who brought their system of ranks into a highly tribalized society through the introduction of food taboos, subsequently consolidating their social distance by these food taboos. A religious and magical system later consolidated their maintenance of social distance from the conquered people. The second explanation lies in the relationship between *Jati* (the social reality of caste life for Hindus) and *Varna*, the former being the actual division of the local community, endogamous, and often having the same occupation, and being able to 'fit' into the Varna system. The system of division is supported by the *Karma* (which teaches that membership of a particular caste is deserved) and *Dharma* (the rules or code of duty). Some have seen the caste system as being fundamentally indebted to the rules and regulations governing pollution while others have tries to distinguish between Hindu religion and Hindu law, seeing the latter as the main factor behind the caste system.

What does seem to be the case is that the dominant castes sustain their superior position, both social and economic, by also controlling the religious system of the country. In a country where the majority of the population is still desperately poor and illiterate this has been comparatively easy for a period of some three hundred years. Recent social change following the departure of the British had led to some erosion of the caste system, although some sociologists would argue that there is evidence that caste-consciousness and organization have *increased* in modern India, and point to the proliferation of caste shops, banks, papers, and so on, in support of this.

Slavery

Very brief mention must be made of slavery which, although not a major system of social stratification, is nevertheless treated by some sociologists, notably Bottomore, as being able to contribute to the approach as a whole. Slavery is a system whereby an individual and his labour are regarded as capital. These systems can vary from one of extremity in which the slave has no rights to one in which he is protected to some extent by laws. The basis of slavery is economic, and the individuals concerned are subjected to a system of social inequality in which he is compelled to work as the property of an aristocratic group.

Modern examples of caste slavery. In modern times the caste system has been introduced into countries other than India, such as South Africa and the Southern States of America. Similarly with the Jews under Nazi Germany. In all these examples a certain group of people are categorized as inferior in relation to superior groups on the basis of some criterion.

Slavery was introduced on a large scale into the plantations of the Southern States of America and some of the British colonies. This is usually known as *commercial* slavery and associated with plantation agriculture in areas of the world with a labour shortage. The nineteenth century saw the introduction of *domestic* slavery into industrial nations, basically a large group of people providing domestic or household services in addition to personal service for a small privileged section of the population. The rise of Nazi Germany saw the introduction of largescale slavery in Europe, although it has always persisted in Moslem countries to some extent.

Estate

Another closed system is the estate system, similar to the caste system but less rigid. It was at its most prominent during feudal times in

Europe and, like the caste system, consisted of ranking various positions according to a classification based on functionalism. It was a less rigid system because the different estates, orders or categories were held to be of equal or near equal importance. The estate system comprised a horizontal group or orders, namely politics, military, religious, economic and peasant. Each horizontal division also contained a hierarchical stratification; for example, in the peasant order the yeomen were at the highest position and the serfs at the lowest.

There was legitimate interaction between the orders such as when the religious order, due to celibacy, sought recruits from the peasant order. Girls, also could transfer from one estate to another through marriage. The serf, at the bottom of the vertical order of an estate, had no right of appeal to the king over his chattels, and so on. Some social historians would argue that there were only two estates in classical feudalism, the nobility and the clergy, while others would recognize that the burghers formed a group before they finally took over the entire system.

Like the caste system the estate system was supported by religious ideology and a legal system, and the church was an essential force in maintaining the feudal society of the middle ages.

Class

Class systems are usually found in advanced, market-oriented societies and are generally described as groups possessing the same economic position in society. A section of the general population sees itself, and is seen by others, as differing from other sections of the population in value orientations, prestige, possessions, occupation, education and life style. Compared with caste and estate systems this kind of system is relatively open and allows individuals to transfer from one section to another.

The importance of social class Class is one of the terms used by sociologists which has a different meaning to the non-sociologist or man in the street. It is important to the sociologist because it helps to bring out a number of theoretical issues. It is also important because it concerns all of us and affects many other social processes such as behaviour, political habits, religion, ability and educational opportunity, manner of dress, accent, and so on. It is not, however, simply an intellectual concept, but embraces our eating habits, our thinking, our way of copulating, our choice of marriage partners—in fact all our behaviour as humans. Very often people from one social class find it very difficult to communicate or understand a person from a different social class. Upper class people may be regarded as 'cissies' by working-class men who in turn might be regarded as uncouth and barbaric by the upper or middle classes. Middle-class psychiatrists, for example, have less success in the treatment of working-class patients than in that of middle-class ones, and middle-class teachers are not the most successful in coping adequately with working-class children.

In terms of health, individuals who belong to the middle class are likely to live longer, be generally healthier, suffer from fewer crippling diseases, and have a secure pension in their old age. In more general terms social class is now known to be associated with mortality rates, the educational level reached by individuals, one's likelihood of becoming physically or mentally ill, juvenile delinquency, one's occupational level, and crime and divorce rates. Social class factors are also seen to be important in the degree to which any one individual seeks to *achieve* something, and levels of achievement are seen to vary with social class.

Different strata of the population seek to 'get on' more than others (although even in the same class there are differences in the stress on achievement).

Social class also enters into religious affiliation and behaviour, and into the values and attitudes held by people in society in relation to politics, education, thrift, and so on. It also enters into the degree and type of social participation so that leisure patterns vary enormously in relation to the different social classes, as do reading habits and viewing habits.

Theories of social class Karl Marx (1818–83), a German sociologist and social theorist who laid the foundations of the Communist movement, was very concerned with social class, and because he was also interested in economics he came to the conclusion that members of a society who have in common the same relationship to the means of production belong to the same class. He argued that to produce something affected social relationships and that an individual's class position depended on his position in the economic system. Marx saw capitalist society as ultimately composed of two opposing groups possessing different interests:

1. the bourgeoisie or owners—who owned and controlled the industrial and commercial means of production; and
2. the proletariat or non-owners—who owned nothing but their labour, which they sold to the bourgeoisie for wages.

Marx was not describing an actual society here but offering an analytical tool for examining what he termed capitalist societies. Endemic to such societies is the notion of *conflict*. The two main classes are constantly at war because the interests of capital and the interests of wage labour are diametrically opposed.

Max Weber (1864–1920), a German sociologist and politician, built upon Marx's work and distinguished between three dimensions of social class:

1. Class—the amount and source of individual income in so far as these affect the chances of obtaining other valued things, mainly property and services.
2. Status—the unequal distribution in society of social honour, and particular styles of life and the consumption of commodities. Status is obviously tied to class, particularly occupations. Thus a second-hand car salesman may have a higher income than a nurse or

school-teacher and therefore in Weber's sense a higher class, but his status is lower.

3. Power or parties—the ability to influence the actions of others. This includes trade unions, political parties, professional associations, and so on.

Any individual can be rated along each of these three dimensions, but generally speaking a high position in one of the dimensions usually brings with it a high position in the other dimensions, for example, a consultant surgeon may have high status and high class. However, incongruities can occur, such as the example of the member of the aristocracy who has lost his material wealth and possessions (low class), his ability to enforce decisions in society (low power), but is still regarded as having a 'good standing' in society (high prestige or status).

Talcott Parsons, the American sociologist, saw social stratification as being potentially conflicting, but in reality it integrates society and makes it cohesive. What we have is not two great conflicting classes but a series of gradations in which social honour is given to members of society by other members of society. This view, of integration and cohesion, is known as the *functionalist* theory of society, which sees society as relatively stable, and its individual members as being in consensus or agreement about certain values which they hold in common. The stress is on the inter-relationships in society.

Some others of the functionalist school have suggested that social stratification is important for the maintenance of society, especially in the way in which occupations vary in their degree of importance, and that such importance is attached, generally, to those occupations which occupy a *scarce* position in society and where recruits to such positions need to undergo a prolonged course of training. Differential rewards are important in order to induce people to undergo such a training.

The number and determinants of social class rank Until now we have been discussing theoretical models of social class. A great amount of work is undertaken, however, on distinguishing the social classes in society from one another and deciding the limits of each category of social class.

Determinants

In terms of specific examples of the kinds of behaviour, accomplishments, possessions, and so on, that we normally use to decide a person's social class, we look at his education, income, occupation, type of housing and so on. A second, and more theoretical way of looking at the problem, is to try to gauge the relative power which an individual is accorded by others in society.

Number

The *continuum* theory states that social classes are not sharply distinguished from one another, but overlap. While a number of sociologists might agree with this they feel that in terms of analysis it is not much help. The *three-class* theory sees society as composed of an upper, middle and lower class. Others who felt that such a theory was too simple and did not distinguish strata sufficiently suggested a *six-class* theory in which the upper class becomes divided into upper-upper and lower-upper, the middle into upper-middle and lower-middle, and the lower into upper-lower and lower-lower.

More recent studies of social stratification and *social mobility* between different strata have been carried out largely in terms of occupational-prestige scales. In Great Britain scales of occupational status are usually based on some modification of the Registrar General's Classification.

I–II	Professional and managerial
III	White collar
III (Man)	Skilled manual
IV	Semi-skilled
V	Unskilled

Although occupation as a measure of an individual's class position is a fairly accurate measure in itself, we must still be wary of equating occupation exactly with class status. Also certain confusion can easily arise, for example in placing a musician in class III—whether he is a member of the Royal Liverpool Philharmonic Orchestra or a member of an insignificant pop group.

Moser and Hall attempted to rectify some of the confusion in the Registrar General's scale below, with percentages of the working population in each class shown on the left.

3,0 %	I	Professional and high administrative
4,5 %	II	Managerial and executive
10,0 %	III	Inspectional, Supervisory, and other non-manual (high grade)
13,0 %	IV	Inspectional, Supervisory, and other non-manual (low grade)
41,0 %	V	Skilled Manual, and routine grades of non-manual
16,5 %	IV	Semi-skilled manual
12,0 %	VII	Unskilled manual

The percentages are based on the Hall and Jones study in 1950, but it gives some idea of the relative *spread* of individuals into the different categories. Another way of doing this is to compare the occupational categories with the percentage of the male population and in terms of social class, as in the next table.

Occupational categories	% of male population	Social class
I	3,0	Upper middle class
II	4,5	Middle middle class
III and IV	23,0	Lower middle class
V	41,0	Skilled working class
VI and VII	28,5	Semi-skilled and un-skilled working class

This gives 30,5 % of the population (male) as being middle class and 69,5 % as being working class.

Other measurements

Other ways of measuring class position in the relatively open societies with which we are most familiar are the *life-style* approach, the *subjective* approach, and the *reputational* approach. The life-style approach uses the criteria of who a person mixes with, what he owns and what he wears and eats, and so on. This approach assumes that people tend to mix 'like-to-like' and also that their social behaviour or the way they live tends to distinguish them. The reputational approach usually entails people with a knowledge of a society acting as judges and placing individuals into social-class categories. The subjective approach is merely to ask an individual what category he would classify as his own. There are, in fact, various faults in each of these approaches and researchers tend to use a *multiple-index approach* (two or more of the above approaches) when working on data.

Subjective aspects of stratification As opposed to the *objective* aspects of class—how individuals relate to the means of production and how this affects their lives—sociologists also show interest in the *subjective* aspects—how people see their society as being socially stratified, whether they agree with this, and so on. One well-known example of this subjective element is derived from Marx and involves the notion of *class consciousness* (the realization that a number of individuals share the same interests but that these interests are in opposition to other groups in society).

Individuals who share this class consciousness have an image or picture of the way society is run, ordered and held together. For example, some might see virtually everything in society as being dominated by evil and wicked capitalists who manipulate and control the destinies of everyone and everything. Elizabeth Bott, writing about the family and social networks some years ago, gave a vivid picture of complementary and independent family activities with 'close-knit' and 'loose-knit' networks. Although she was arguing about the degree of segregation in the relationship of roles between spouses and how this varies directly in relation to the degree of connectedness of the social network of the family, she also, in addition, gave a graphic picture of the way in which the people she was studying 'saw' society. Various studies of communities in rural Wales, England, and working-class communities in Britain as a whole often give quite clear descriptions of the way the people 'see', through their ideologies and so on, the way *they* or their group view the construction of society. David Lockwood described three types of workers, each with their different images of society. The proletarian worker adopts the power model of society, the deferential worker adopts the status hierarchy as his perception of social inequality, and the privatized worker adopts the pecuniary model of society. These images are determined by the work situation and the way it is organized, how the work is related to the community in which the worker lives, and the way in which status is allocated.

Class and values

To belong to one social class rather than another can imply a number of different life-styles, different types of social relationship, and different values and norms. For example, the degree to which one uses the educational system and succeeds in it depends to a very large measure on social-class influences. Florence Kluckholn suggested a model of the different ways in which different social strata answered different fundamental questions about the environment. These fundamental answers, which are accepted and unchallenged by the strata, she termed *life orientations*. For example, the lower classes tend to live in the immediate period of time and think not of the future but of the present and its problems. The middle classes think constantly of the future, and hence *defer* their gratification, while the working-class requires *immediate* gratification. The middle class, also, sees nature as capable of manipulation, while the lower class sees itself as being manipulated by nature. We therefore can expect the working class to be relatively fatalistic and to use such expressions as 'it had to be' and to invoke the concept of 'luck' a little more often. Sociologists have subsequently applied these *models* to the achievement of children from different classes in terms of a 'getting on' ideology (middle class) and a 'getting by' ideology (working class).

Orientations or problems	Range of variations		or possible solutions
1. Relationship between man and nature	Subjugation to nature	Harmony with nature	Mastery over nature
2. Time	Emphasis on the past	Emphasis on present time	Emphasis on future time,
3. Activity	Emphasis on being	Emphasis on being in	or becoming
4. Significant relationships	Individualistic	Collectivity	
5. Human nature	Evil	A mixture of good and evil	Good
	Lower class	**Lower-middle class**	**Middle class**

Some sociologists have argued that class cultural differences may involve differences in language and intellectual approaches to problems. Basil Bernstein, following a long tradition among anthropolog-ists, has argued that working- and middle-class people use linguistic codes that are different both in their grammar and in their words. Working-class people use what he terms a *restricted code* for example, a limited and restricted use of adjectives and adverbs, frequent use of personal pronouns rather than impersonal ones ('we', 'you', rather than 'one', 'it'), small use of conjunctions, poor grammatical sentences, and so on. Middle-class people use an *extended code*. He points out that middle-class people sometimes also use a restricted code (at church services, cocktail parties, etc.) but they can alternate and switch to an extended code. He is not suggesting that the working class have not got a richly expressive syntax, but in a society in which middle-class extended codes are dominant (especially in the educational system) then they are obviously at a distinct disadvantage. Experimental work has tended to support his general theory. Work with English mothers of small children has shown that different social classes use their speech for different ends and in varying degrees of effectiveness (even when the intelligence of the participants was held constant). What these studies mean is that middle-class children have an ability to control verbalized behaviour which can help in producing a high achievement and success in planning for long-term goals. Some ex-perimental work by Bernstein himself gives further support for his theory because he found that middle-class mothers verbalize with their children far more and that such extensive 'talking to' children help in a number of ways.

Gesture

One implication of Bernstein's theory of the two codes may be that the working-class restricted code is more effective as speech (rather than written form) and that the working-class support their speech through the use of elaborate gesture. Working-class people may be expected to have different speech structures and accents than middle-class people but they also have different facial and gestural movements. One example is the manner in which a working-class man holds a cigarette in a cupped hand, usually behind his back, while a middle-class man probably holds it well in front of him between his index and middle finger. An elaborate analysis of facial expression, hand movements, body posture, head position, the distance a speaker positions himself from the person he is speaking to, and so on, has been carried out by Michael Argyle and others.

Social stability

We would expect the working class to be anxious to overthrow the upper strata of society if what the sociologists described was true, that is that the latter dominated and in terms of wealth and income controlled the destinies of the former. On the whole, however, they tend to support the present order of society and its institutions such as the monarchy and turn out in thousands to support royal weddings and funerals. Several theories have been suggested to account for why the deprived of a society don't become more radical. One answer is known as the *relative-deprivation* theory and suggests that men compare their condition not with society as a whole, or the very wealthy, but with their nearest reference group. For example, an old car may not occasion envy, jealousy or rage when seen alongside a number of other old 'bangers', but surround it with limousines and it is more likely that frustration and enmity will arise. This still leaves us wondering why it is that these groups make such a limited comparison, and some sociologists have even suggested that they couldn't face the true realization of their situation. When Marx suggested that religion was the opiate of the people he was suggesting that it dulled the senses so that they were unable to see their real situation. He was, in fact, suggesting another argument as to why the deprived are not more radical. The values and expectations created by religion prepare, it is argued, the main body of society for the very values and social expectations requisite for an industrial economic system. This particular argument is discussed at greater length in the chapter on Beliefs Values and Norms.

Education and class

Working-class children are generally educationally under-privileged as a direct result of the economic under-privilege of their parents. They are under-privileged in the schools that they attend, many of which are Victorian in construction and without adequate facilities such as toilets. Teachers, being merely human, have less desire to work in these areas (unless very dedicated) than in the more splendid surroundings of the suburban school. Urban schools in the inner areas, especially of large cities, were recently designated as Educational Priority Areas, and given extra finance for staff and facilities. In relative terms, however, this was very inadequate and of very little use unless the living standards from which the children came was also changed. In Britain children are not given the same educational treatment, for some are assessed and selected for special *kinds* of education in specialized schools, and the school system is itself stratified into different types of schools with different ability classes. Many of the middle classes opt out of the state education system (just as they opt out of the NHS) and send their children to private and public schools. Because schools are staffed mainly by middle-class teachers (if they were not middle class to start with, they are by virtue of their education and occupation) they often impute *meanings* to the children they teach. One study showed that head and class teachers of secondary modern schools saw their C stream pupils as dirty, smelling and stupid, aggressive and lacking in ambition; in other words they might have interpreted the pupils' behaviour differently, or given a different meaning to it, had it been exhibited by middle-class children.

Correlates of   Many of those who occupy high social-class positions in society feel
stratification   that they deserve much of what they receive as extra recompense
because of the responsibility that they have to bear. But the disparities
in social class are reflected in the income they receive and also in
patterns of health. For one thing, certain occupations carry with them
a high risk of mortality and also a high risk of crippling diseases. Infant
mortality rates are higher the lower the social class involved. Mental
or psychiatric disorders show a social-class distribution.

The pattern of sexual intercourse varies not only from culture to
culture but from social class to social class within any given culture.
For example, the working class are more likely to experiment less in
sexual positions, have sexual intercourse with the lights out, and with
some of their clothes still on. Michael Schofield found that the lower
classes learned the facts of life later than the middle classes (respectively 12,7 for boys and 12,5 for girls as compared with 12,3 and 11,9).
One reason suggested for class differences is implied by the fact that
middle-class girls reach puberty earlier which, coupled with the extended way of talking mentioned by Bernstein, may mean that the facts

BABIES	MOTHERS AND SOCIAL CLASS				
	Profes-sional managerial (I–II)	White collar (III)	Skilled manual (III Man)	Semi-skilled (IV)	Unskilled (V)
	%	%	%	%	%
Mother's age 21 or less at first birth	24	25	40	46	53
Breastfeeding at 1 month	60	50	50	51	34
Breastfeeding at 3 months	39	34	24	22	12
Breastfeeding at 6 months	20	12	11	11	7
No bottle after 6 months	10	9	4	1	1
No bottle after 12 months	50	47	29	21	15
Dummy at some time	39	53	71	75	74
Dummy still at 12 months	26	38	55	57	46
Bottle or dummy to go to sleep	23	36	47	52	51
Bottle or dummy if wakes	24	36	40	47	42
Bedtime: 6.30 p.m. minus	47	31	29	24	31
Bedtime: 8.0 p.m. plus	7	12	20	23	26
Sleeps in room alone	54	42	20	18	3
Diet inadequate	5	10	13	13	32
Potty training not started (12 months)	12	16	17	13	32
Potty trainingg of those started	never successful	36	38	46	42
Genital play checked	25	50	57	69	93
No smacking	56	38	32	42	35
General smacking	39	53	60	54	58
Frequent tantrums	9	8	14	15	23
Father's participation high	57	61	51	55	36
Father's participation little or none	19	6	16	18	36
Baby-sitting once or less p.a.	25	36	42	42	59

Source: J & E Newsom, Patterns of Infant Care in an Urban Community. London, Penguin, 1965, p. 229

of life were explained to them earlier. Probably middle-class parents are more aware of the need for sex education. Similar patterns can be seen with delinquency and crime, which we examine in more detail elsewhere. Several studies have been done on the way in which social class affects child rearing. Some of the ways in which it does can be seen by examining the above table.

Social mobility   The degree to which a society exhibits movement between social classes or strata is termed *social mobility*. Two types are generally noted. When movement is up or down from one stratum to another this is termed *vertical mobility*, and when it is from one social position to another without in fact changing the social stratum it is known as *horizontal mobility*.

The causes of mobility

There is a high social mobility when certain conditions prevail in society, for example in periods of rapid social change such as we have during revolutions or war or conquest of some kind. Large immigrations can change the pattern of social mobility, as for example with the influx of European peasantry into America or the Asians into Africa. A political revolution can change the mobility pattern in quite a drastic manner, as occurred in the revolution in Russia in 1917. Sociologists tend to classify the factors as follows:

1. Opportunity structure—in relatively open societies there is opportunity to move which is lacking in closed societies such as the caste system. Very advanced societies have educational, business and entertainment mobility.
2. Demographic factors—new immigrants, coloured or white, generally tend to push the older inhabitants automatically up the social ladder. Similarly, internal migration from the countryside to the towns or from one part of a country to another is often done for the purpose of improving one's position.
3. Automation—tends to displace blue-collar workers and attract white-collar opportunities.
4. Levels of aspiration—Achievement varies from one stratum to another, and although it might well be present in all social classes it tends to be higher in the middle classes.

The achievement of social mobility

Vertical or horizontal mobility can be achieved in a number of ways. For example a person can gain much from attendance at a school with a good reputation, from staying on at school beyond the statutory period, by going on to higher education, and so on. Degree of mobility is directly related to education, which in turn is closely tied to occupation. One of the ways in which one can achieve a higher social status is by being recruited to a higher-status occupation. Yet another way is by economic success, which can open many avenues to social mobility if not in itself (at least in Britain) a very important factor. To control power, for example political power, can also bring social mobility, but power in a general sense is usually tied to the above avenues of social mobility such as education and economic success. Finally, new ways have appeared through show business and pop music, and through athletic and sporting prowess.

Social-mobility studies tend to be concerned with differences in social mobility between different countries, increase or decrease in social mobility, and the theory known as *embourgoisement* (the convergence of the working class towards the middle class), and finally the suggestion that there are a number of 'top people' who are firmly entrenched as the ruling elite in both the political, religious, social, military and economic spheres.

Are we all middle class now

As societies become more industrial there is a tendency towards equilibration, in which the members of one stratum become more like others in some respects. This is usually taken to mean that the working class is crossing the threshold of the middle class either by acquiring material possessions, acquiring new norms, values and standards of the middle class, and that the members of the working class are being accepted as social equals. Much of the research brought to bear on this argument is far from satisfactory. It is further complicated by the fact that many who are working class tend to consciously identify themselves with the middle classes by their voting behaviour. The answer seems to lie along the lines that while there has been a general trend in both America and Britain towards a general equalizing of wages, there is no evidence that middle-class life styles have been aspired to in any significant form, for example in entertaining, visiting, social participation and so on. Evidence from work dissatisfaction, work conditions, and other areas suggest that a gulf still exists. The child-rearing philosophies, from work both in England and Detroit, suggests further large gulfs between the social classes. In some ways—for example, by ownership of a television set—the working class are catching up with the middle classes. But this is not to take into account the actual viewing habits. Other indices such as the ownership of a car, telephone, and so on are also seen by some as indicative of a narrowing of the gulf. But it appears that as the gulf starts to close the middle classes jump one step ahead (for example by having two cars, two telephones, a colour television, holidays at home in England and not in Spain where the working class go to in increasing numbers). Further division is maintained by the middle classes being able to purchase social advantage in the form of private education and private medical treatment.

Occupational ranking studies

Cross-cultural studies tend to display a certain similarity of ranking between different occupations. However, there may be many reasons why we should cast some doubt on any claim for such studies *really* proving anything because often the occupational titles vary and inter-

OCCUPATIONAL RANKING IN 4 COUNTRIES

Indonesia	Rank	USA	Rank	Great Britain	Rank	USSR	Rank
Physician	1	Physician	1	Medical officer	1	Doctor	1
Univ. professor	2	College professor	2				
Engineer (chemical civil, architect)	3	Chemist/architect/civil engineer	6			Engineer	2
Lawyer	4	Lawyer	6	Country solicitor	3		
Member: People's Representative Council	5	United States Congressman	3				
Head of government department	6	Head of department in government	4				
Military officer	7	Army Captain	10			Officer	armed forces
Director of private corporation	8	Director of large corporation	6	Company director	2	Factory manager	3
Airline pilot	9	Airline pilot	8				
High school teacher	10	Instructor in public school, 11		Elementary-school teacher	6	Teacher	5
Newspaper reporter	11	Reporter, daily paper	14	News reporter	7		
Artist, pianist, author	12	Artist	9				
Farm owner operator	13	Farm owner operator	12	Farmer	5	Chairman of collective farm	6
Non-commissioned officer	15	Corporal in army	18				
Electrician, machinist	16	Electrician, machinist	13	Fitter (electrical)	10		
Owner-operator lunch stand	17	Owner-operator of lunch stand	17	Newsagent tobacconist	8		
Policeman	18	Policeman	16	Policeman	9		
Truck, bus driver	19	Taxi driver	19	Carter	11		
Labourer (servant, messenger, janitor)	20						

Source: Murray Thomas R. Reinspecting a Structural Position on Occupational Prestige. *American Journal of Sociology* March 1962, 67, p. 564

viewing procedures may be incomplete or dubious. Certainly it appears that professions come at the top with semi-skilled and unskilled occupations ranking low.

Status We tend to get our initial status from our family of origin. This ascribed status can, in time, become achieved status as we leave the family of origin and carve our own way through the world. A nurse from working-class parents, for example, may well mix in very different circles from her own colleagues whose parents are middle class. In other words, the social status of an occupation may be different from that of the person who occupies it. Some occupational groups rise suddenly in the status hierarchy, for example technologists. The behaviour of individuals often reflects their status. Thorstein Veblen coined the term *conspicuous consumption* to describe the competitive way in which wealth was used to portray one's social status. In advanced societies such as America and Britain, economically unproductive occupations or behaviour, such as fox-hunting, often carry with them high social prestige, while the opposite is the case for economically productive work. It seemed to Veblen, writing at the very end of the last century, that the very highest prestige was given to those who did not need to work in order to live. Very 'flashy' diamonds and cigars are examples of conspicuous consumption or pecuniary emulation. It seemed to him, moreover, that women were attributed high social status if they possessed a useless beauty, and dogs gained a high value if bred into an ugliness out of all proportion to their actual utility. In many ways society, with its insistence on accrediting high status to often utterly useless people and objects, was in effect emulating or resembling some tribal societies, notably the Kwakiutl tribe's custom of *potlatch* (involving either the destruction or giving away of such items as blankets, which brought with it an enormous status) and the Melanesian yam display and *kula*. In these complicated processes status was maintained by ostentatious displays of wealth. Similarly, the colonial British felt obliged to give cocktail parties which were successively better and more elaborate than the previous one. Not to do so was to lose face. Again, to fail to return in like kind a birthday or Christmas gift is regarded as a loss of honour and a slight in western countries.

In England the kind of vocabulary used (as well as the accent, of course) is regarded as an indicator of whether a person is middle or lower class. Some examples are given below.

U	Non-U
pudding	sweet
sick	ill
wireless	radio
master	teacher
luncheon	dinner

Conclusions Every person employed as a nurse or doctor both comes from a family occupying a position in the social strata and is also in an occupation which is itself socially ranked. Furthermore, the patients who come into contact with medical and para-medical staff come from a wide variety of social background. In many cases, the health services get a gross distortion because the 'elite' have tended to purchase their treatment elsewhere. Many of the patients may appear coarse and vulgar to a nurse or doctor from the middle classes, and often some difficulty may be experienced in even understanding the speech of some patients. Very often, too, communication relating to illness may be severely hampered due to lack of understanding and the attributing of different meanings by the participants involved. Some of the implications of social differences are encountered here.

OCCUPATION AND DISEASE

Epidemiologists, and social scientists in general, noticed a correlation between the types of work people do and the risk of being afflicted with certain kinds of disease. As early as the 1840s Friedrich Engels, who worked so closely with Karl Marx, noticed a connection between social origins and illness. He held that the British capitalist system forced most of the population to live and work in conditions which induced disease. He followed closely the work of early social reformers such as Chadwick (1965) who documented the connections among poverty, disease, mortality and environmental pollution in 1841. Chadwick was particularly concerned about sanitary conditions in industrial Britain. Another pioneer who was concerned with socio-economic factors was Abraham Hume.

Engels (1973) was initially concerned with the effects of environment toxins and the lack of dispersal systems for human animal wastes resulting in severe air and water pollution. Engels also regarded infectious diseases such as tuberculosis and typhus as the result of lack of basic sanitation, poor ventilation and overcrowding. Similarly, when discussing nutritional diseases such as rickets and scrofula Engels drew connections with social conditions. Occupational or industrial accidents also drew his attention, such as amputation of various limbs by contact with unguarded machines; further complications resulted in tetanus. Chronic musculoskeletal disorders were also the product of repetitive work as were also varicose veins, leg ulcers and flat feet:

All these affections are easily explained by the nature of factory work . . . The operatives . . . must stand the whole time. And one who sits down, say upon a window-ledge or a basket, is fined, and this perpetual upright position, this constant mechanical pressure of the upper portions of the body upon spinal column, hips and legs, inevitably produces the results mentioned.

This standing is not required by the work itself.
(Engels, in Waitzkin, 1983, p. 69)

Engels dealt in detail with pottery workers' poisoning which resulted from absorbing toxic chemicals from lead and other heavy metals. The results included 'severe abdominal pain, constipation, and neurologic complications like epilepsy and partial or complete paralysis. These signs of lead intoxication occurred not only in workers themselves, according to Engels, but also in children who lived near pottery factories.' (Op. cit., p. 70.)

The textile workers' contraction of pulmonary disease (what is known today as byssinosis) manifested the following symptoms:

. . . The most common effects of this breathing of dust are bloodspitting, hard, noisy breathing, pains in the chest, coughs, sleeplessness—in short, all the symptoms of asthma . . .
(Op. cit., p. 70.)

Similar manifestations are apparent in 'grinders' asthma, a disease of the respiratory system caused by inhalation of dust particles in the manufacture of knives and forks. Again, Engels was the first to point out that 'black lung', or coal miners' pneumoconiosis, was preventable if working conditions were improved.

It is now quite clearly recognised that there are a large number of diseases which are occupationally induced, such as welders' beryllium poisoning, 'black lung', asbestosis, industrially caused cancers, metal and solvent poisoning, and many more:

And, well, my father worked in a chemical plant right next door to the one I work for: about twenty years. He's dead now. I had an uncle: he also worked in a chemical plant, the same plant right next door to me. He dies of cancer, this cancer in the throat. He had a tube in his throat, and it was a result of working in this chemical plant; and he didn't have it before he went there. But a certain chemical that he inhaled got in his throat, and his throat was a mess and he died . . . We're a small bunch but we've got a problem. These chemicals are going to kill us all.
(Quoted in Krause, 1978, p. 308)

Over twenty years ago, in 1968, the U.S. Public Health Service, estimating from a study of California, a national rate of 336 000 cases of job-caused illness per year, 'which didn't include in the estimate diseases not found in California, such as coal miner's black lung or pneumoconiosis.' (Op. cit., p. 308.) In 1972 the American Institute for Occupational Health and Safety estimated that 100 000 Americans die each year as a result of industrial employment and another 390 000 are incapacitated. Krause goes on to document, both in Britain and America, the long struggle mine workers have had to get pneumoconiosis recognised as a disease with respective compensation.

The extent of mercury poisoning, lead poisoning, gases such as sulphur dioxide and pesticides are widespread. Blacks have a higher industrial illness and death rate than whites. (Op. cit., p. 310–311.) However, both in Britain and America, unionised labour is traditionally more concerned with wage increases than with such issues as occupational safety from accidents and disease, and increased educational opportunities.

The hazards of work Although the distribution of acute sickness does not vary so drastically between occupational groups, chronic sickness certainly does:

SICKNESS BY AGE AND SEX IN OCCUPATIONAL CLASSES: GREAT BRITAIN, 1974–1976							
	Acute sickness: days of restricted activity (person/year)			Chronic sickness: long-standing limiting illness (rates per 1000)			
	Age-group			Age-group			
	0–14	15–44	45–64	0–14$^\alpha$		15–44	15–64
	M	F	M	M	M	F	M	M
Profes-sional	12	8	9	13	92	76	60	168
Em-ployers	14	8	11	13	106	73	75	161
Other non-ma-nual	13	11	11	21	95	78	84	261
Skilled	12	11	15	23	102	81	88	248
Semi-skilled	12	11	14	21	108	70	91	275
Unskilled	10	11	19	29	123	107	109	880

$^\alpha$Limiting and nonlimiting, long-standing illness, disability, and infirmity.
Source: Morris JN (1979). Social inequalities undiminished. *Lancet*, 1, 87–90.

The problems inherent in studying occupational disease are many and can be listed as follows:

1. Inadequate detection and under-reporting of workplace accidents;
2. Lack of provision for independent monitoring of industrial and occupational disease;
3. The reluctance of industry about acknowledging the toxicity of the large numbers of chemicals constantly being added to its products;
4. The difficulty in obtaining good statistics about exposed workers from industrial sources;
5. The difficulty in establishing cause and effect;
6. Fragmentation (in some countries) of agencies responsible;
7. Greater eagerness to look at industrial accidents rather than diseases;
8. A 'conspiracy of silence', directed by employers, towards workers and unions;
9. Government reluctance to upset industry;
10. In some countries difficulty in gaining access to work site.

(Compiled from Susser, Watson, and Hopper, 1985, p. 243, and Krause, op. cit., p. 315.)

In addition many workers under-report their illness or injury for fear of losing their jobs. Just over ten years ago one tenth of the American labour force reported an industrial illness or injury, and 8 in every 100 000 workers died. One estimate puts the number of workers in America presently out of work due to work-related diseases or accidents as 2 million. The groups most at risk are: industrial workers, agricultural workers, non-union workers and workers in small firms (under 25 employees). Migrant workers in America, because of the poor working conditions combined with inadequate living conditions, experience an infant mortality rate 60 % above the national average and a life expectancy of only 49. (Susser, et al. op. cit., p. 243.)

Psychosocial factors, such as stress, boredom, fatigue, alienation and dissatisfaction, increase the risk of injury. The elaborate social rituals introduced in an attempt to circumvent such routinisation, boredom or alienation, is nicely summed up by Alan Sillitoe's description of working-class life in Britain in the 1950s:

At a piecework rate of four-and-six a hundred you could make your money if you knocked-up fourteen hundred a day—possible without grabbing too much—and if you went all out for a thousand in the morning you could dawdle through the afternoon and lark about with the women and talk to your mates now and again. Such leisure often brought him (Arthur, the hero) near to trouble, for some weeks ago he stunned a mouse—that the overfed factory cats had missed—and laid it beneath a woman's drill, and Robboe the gaffer ran out of his office when he heard her screaming blue murder, thinking that some bloody silly woman had gone and got her hair caught in a belt (big notices said that women must wear hair-nets, but who could tell with women?) and Robboe was glad when it turned out that it was nothing more than a dead mouse she was kicking up such a fuss about. But he paced up and down the gangways asking who was responsible for the stunned mouse, and when he came to Arthur, who denied having anything to do with it, he said: 'I'll bet you did it, you young bogger! 'Me, Mr Robboe?' Arthur said, the picture of innocence, standing up tall with offended pride. 'I've got so much work to do I can't move from my lathe' (Sillitoe, 1958, p. 67)

Work hazards need not be confined to the workplace but spread to family and community:

Families of asbestos workers have developed mesothelioma, most likely the result of contamination by asbestos fibres adhering to work clothes brought home. Communities surrounding concentrated industries may experience high rates of specific cancers: bladder and liver cancers around petro-chemical industries, respiratory cancers around foundries. Children living near copper smelters show raised body levels of arsenic; those living near lead smelters show raised levels of lead, with effects on the neural system that are certainly not healthy.
(Susser, et al. op. cit., p. 243)

Morris (1975) cites a number of other occupations at risk, especially that of the sandblaster (because of silicosis they have a 75 % greater death rate than the national average), but also those of steeplejack, window-cleaner, bullfighter, fisherman, and anyone working with asbestos. The table reproduced below gives figures from two physically active occupations. It shows clearly occupation as a factor in health and ill-health, physical, mental and social.

SICKNESS ABSENCE OF MEN IN TWO PHYSICALLY ACTIVE OCCUPATIONS: BRITAIN 1961–1962 Rates for all men=100		
Agricultural workers	Diagnosis	Coal miners (face workers)
67	all causes	188
40	acute upper respiratory infections	234
60	influenza	234
47	bronchitis	205
55	chronic sinusitis	300
33	coronary heart disease	61
45	psychosis, psychoneurosis	196
60	arthritis and rheumatism	338

Source: Morris, op. cit., p. 152

A study carried out by Morris among different occupational groups in London showed clear differences in occupational health. Thus the incidence of ischaemic heart disease was much higher among London busdrivers (a largely sedentary occupation) than bus conductors, both for all forms and for sudden death. Similarly, a casual diastolic B.P. over 100 mm.Hg was considerably higher among drivers over fifty years of age than conductors. In nearly all instances heavy manual workers are less likely to die of ischaemic or coronary disease. A Czechoslovakian study of 1 469 railwaymen aged between 40 and 49 displayed the following:

Percentage with casual systolic blood pressure greater than 180 mmHg
drivers 13 %
stokers 6.3 %
shunters 2,5 %
Source: Morris, op. cit., p. 168

Fatalities are difficult to estimate, as we mentioned above. The *1972 Report of the Committee on Safety and Health at Work* (the Robens Report) stated:

Every year something like 1 000 people are killed at their work in this country (U.K.). Every year half a million suffer injuries in varying degrees of severity. Twenty-three million working days are lost annually on account of industrial injury and disease.

Kinnersly (1973) put the figure at 2 000 dying from injuries received at the workplace, 1 000 dying from industrial diseases, 1 000 000 off work for at least three days through injury or disease, and 10 000 000 injured to the point of requiring first aid. Note that these are yearly figures and not accumulative. The number of former employees receiving an industrial disablement pension in 1975 was 203 000, with 31 000 widows receiving an industrial death benefit. Mining fatalities are particularly easy to identify:

Mining deaths and injuries, 1975–1976
killed: 59
seriously injured: 538
injured and off work: 52 946

As we mentioned earlier, there are a variety of industrial diseases which can be categorised, many of which appear only a number of years after initial contact. Apart from byssinosis, a respiratory disease, industrial chemicals such as beta-naphthylamine and vinyl chloride monomer can be assimilated. The former chemical was common in the rubber and cable industries until 1950 but we now know that it can lead to bladder cancer some fifty years later. 'Vinyl chloride monomer is the major ingredient of PVC and it has now been discovered that exposure to this chemical can eventually cause a very rare form of liver cancer known as angiosarcoma.' (Doyal and Pennell, 1979). Doyal goes on to indicate that the high incidence of asbestosis and mesothelioma in the 1970s, following the 1969 asbestos control regulations, resulted in an *increase* in this type of cancer of at least 68 % between 1970 and 1976. This is because there is an incubation period of between five and 35 years.

The importance of work to disease/mortality patterns is demonstrated by an American report entitled *Work in America*:

In an impressive 15-year study of aging, the strongest predictor of longevity was work satisfaction. The second best predictor was overall 'happiness' . . . Other factors are undoubtedly important—diet, exercise, medical care, and genetic inheritance. But research findings suggest that these factors may account for only 25 % of the risk factors in heart disease, the major cause of death. That is, if cholesterol, blood pressure, smoking, glucose level, serum, uric acid, and so forth, were perfectly controlled, only about one-fourth of coronary heart disease could be controlled. Although research on this problem has not led to conclusive answers, it appears that work role, work conditions, and other social factors may contribute heavily to this 'unexplained' 75 % of risk factors.

(Special Task Force to the Secretary of Health, Education and Welfare, 1973, p. 77)

STANDARDIZED MORTALITY RATIOS FOR DIFFERENT OCCUPATIONS IN THE UK, 1961 (MEN AGED 15–64)						
Occupation	All causes	All TB	Lung Cancer	Coronary Heart Disease	Bronchitis	Accidents other than motor vehicle and in the home
A. MANUAL						
fisherman	144	171	188	115	148	480
coal-face workers	180	294	140	144	293	522
engineering fitters	99	76	111	107	87	86
textile process workers	133	111	116	129	161	127
bus and train conductors	105	162	103	110	138	31
dock labourers	136	180	169	105	220	368
engineering labourers	139	169	151	115	217	112
kitchen hands	130	410	88	102	165	185
all semi-skilled manual workers	103	108	104	96	116	128
all unskilled manual workers	143	185	148	112	194	193
B. NON-MANUAL						
mining managers	66	18	56	91	33	28
personnel managers	67	40	44	89	64	150
chemists, physical and biological scientists	88	21	56	111	33	65
government ministers	75	29	69	97	28	9
university teachers	56	50	12	65	-	43
judges, barristers	solicitors	76	33	40	93	24
medical practitioners	89	64	48	118	23	55
all intermediate non-manual occupations	81	54	72	95	50	56
all professional and administrative	76	40	53	98	28	43

Source: Registrar General, 1969: 91, 132–199

OCCUPATIONAL AND ENVIRONMENTAL DISEASE
Sir George Baker's 'consummate proof' that the Devonshire colic was due to lead poisoning

Clinical Observation	Epidemiology	Laboratory Study
(1) Baker (1767) recognised that the 'endemial colic of Devonshire', commonly ascribed to the acidity of the local cyder that was drunk in large and increasing quantities, often terminated in palsy; especially of the arms, and epilepsy; a recognisable syndrome and 'precisely the same disease which is the specific effect of all saturnine preparations' . . . Yet another epidemic from the contamination of feed and drink by lead	(2) He observed that the colic was rare in other cyder-producing countries, and commonest in parts of Devonshire where most cyder actually was made. Suspecting adulteration with lead to be responsible, he found that lead indeed was used in the construction of the presses in Devonshire. The apples were in direct contact with the metal, which was slowly dissolving during grinding or later stages. In other countries lead was rarely so used	(3) 'Sine experimentia vanna omnis theoria.' Be that as it may, Baker showed by chemical test that the local cyder did in fact contain lead. On his initiative, its presences in Devonshire cyder, and absence in others, was independently confirmed in London. (Baker recognised that he himself was 'under the influence of a preconceived opinion')

'In this instance, cognitio causae morbum tollet' (Baker). 'Under the influence of his discovery a grievous endemic affliction rapidly became extinct' (Simon), despite local opposition because of the threat to their livelihood.

CAUSES OF CANCERS
Chemical carcinogenesis—Occupational epithelioma of scrotum

Clinical Medicine	Laboratory Experiment	Epidemiology, Occupational Health, Public Health
In 1775, Pott, a leading surgeon of his day, found far too many scrotal cancers in chimney sweepers among his patients and described 'a most noisome, painful and fatal disease . . . peculiar to a certain set of people' from puberty on. The chimney sweeps themselves recognised the condition as 'soot wart'. Pott pleaded eloquently against this exploitation of the 'climbing boys' who had often been forced to do this job from 5 or 8 years of age. Pott emphasised the long incubation period of the growth. Later, it was observed that the disease may develop many years after exposure to the hazard had ceased.		Beginning in 1788, Parliament passed a series of laws to prevent children being employed as chimney sweeps: this was the first modern official intervention on behalf of children. Enforcement was slowly effective, though Dickens was still writing about the scandal 50 years later.

Clinical Medicine	Laboratory Experiment	Epidemiology, Occupational Health, Public Health
		In 1892, Butlin demonstrated that while still prevalent here, sweeps in other countries do not suffer from scrotal cancer: because they wear protective clothing and because, he claimed, the nocuous material is removed every day by thorough washing.
	1915–18 Yamagiwa and Itchikawa produced squamous-cell carcinoma of the skin in the rabbit by repeated paintings with tar. 1924–33 Kennaway and co-workers identified the 3:4-benzpyrene as the carcinogen in tar. This, it is evident, is the responsible agent in the soot. Skin cancer was again reproduced in animals with the benzpyrene. A group of carcinogenic polycyclic aromatic hydrocarbons has been defined.	In 1946, Henry analysed available mortality data on scrotal cancer and followed up the death certificates, taking detailed occupational histories—'shoe-leather' epidemiology. He confirmed that in 1911–39 there was still a gross persisting excess of the disease (nearly 200–fold) in men who had been chimney sweeps. Comparable data are not available for more recent years. Obviously, however, the occupational tumour is now quite rare: methods of domestic heating have improved, soot is removed mechanically, no one climbs chimneys for a living. In general, people are cleaner, and they would tend to wear adequate clothing in such a situation. Moreover, precursor tar warts, should they occur, are likely to be recognised early and cured.

CHEMICAL CARCINOGENESIS
Cancer of bladder in dyestuffs workers—and rubber workers and cable workers and . . .

Clinical Observation	Laboratory Experiment	Epidemiology: Occupational Health

(1)
In 1895 Rehn described bladder cancer among a small group of workers engaged in the manufacture of magenta from aniline. He considered inhalation of that to be the most likely agent— whence 'aniline tumours'.

(2)
In 1937 Hueper et. al reproduced the tumour in dogs by feeding them β-naphthylamine, an aromatic amine

(3)
Ad hoc cohort studies, delayed because of the Second World War and beginning in 1948, by Case and colleagues, soon revealed a gross excess incidence of bladder cancer in dyestuffs workers making and handling β-naphthylamine, α-naphthylamine, and benzidine; though not aniline.

Manufacture of dyestuffs in Britain had been increased when German supplies stopped in World War I. National occupational mortality statistics failed to reveal the problem because the population-at-risk is small and, therefore, included with larger groups.

These tumours characteristically occurred at younger ages ('anticipation') than non-occupational bladder cancer. Their 'incubation period' was found to be variable, but mostly between 15 and 20 years.

Clinical non-observation has been a serious problem, the occupational origin of bladder cancers being missed. Industrial medical officers, coroners, the staffs of government departments of Employment and Social Security are involved as well as all parts of the NHS.

Individual risk of workers developing the disease in conditions prevalent during the 1920's to 1940's was found to be exceedingly high, between 1 in 10 and 1 in 5 (and even up to 1 in 1, one hundred per cent, in a small group of men distilling β-napththylamine). i.e., it is many times the national average. There is no evidence of any immunity to the industrial disease.

The death of a *cable worker* from bladder cancer, the inquest and consequent publicity (1965), the discovery of other such cases, aroused public anxiety and led to new investigations.

Serendipity.—During these studies, Case *et al..* discovered a high mortality from the cancer in *rubber workers* who had been chosen as 'controls'

Analysis of death certificates over a period of 15 years established that *cable workers* also have an excess of the disease (rubber is used for insulation).

Clinical Observation	Laboratory Experiment	Epidemiology: Occupational Health
		Control of the Hazard.—Manufacture in Britain of β-naphthylamine, the most lethal substance was stopped by 1952. Primary neoplasm of the bladder due to industrial exposure was prescribed as an industrial disease.

Exfoliative cytological *screening of individuals-at-risk*, for precursor papillomata, and for cancer, was begun by industry in 1950 and is now widely used. The method may not be sufficiently sensitive.
  Surveillance of workers and ex-workers in affected industries continues to be essential. Cases are still occurring in rubber and cable workers; it is not clear if these are residual from known carcinogens that have been controlled, or if other chemicals, or foreign importations (e.g. of rubber for retreading) are responsible. Adequate control of the dangerous chemicals is inadequate in many countries |
| Perhaps as many as 1 case of bladder cancer in 5 is due to occupation. A high index of suspicion is necessary in *genitourinary practice*, and it is important to take adequate occupational histories: 'Of what trade is he?' (Ramazzini) | *A carcinogenic group of aromatic amines* has been defined but is not necessarily exhaustive. Meanwhile, it does not seem likely that a satisfactory method of screening suspected chemicals for their potential carcinogenic activity on bladder and kidney will be found. | *Epidemiological methods* have still to be used to identify high-risk groups |

HORMONE DEPENDENCE IN BREAST CANCER

Clinical Observation	Laboratory Experiment	Population Studies
1713: Ramazzini noticed that breast cancer was especially common in nuns.	A. *Hormones and Normal Mammary Function.* Around the turn of the century, the old theory of 'neural' control of breast growth and lactation was supplanted by 'hormonal' theory. It is now known that many endocrine factors are involved, including oestrogens, progesterone, etc.	1842: Stern showed that cancer of breast was relatively commoner among single women; and particularly so among nuns.

Clinical Observation	Laboratory Experiment	Population Studies
1739: Heister wrote that breast cancer was commoner in nuns, single women, and married women who had borne no children.		1915: Hoffman showed that mortality from breast cancer was close to 10 times higher in England and Wales than in Japan. There was immediate interest in possible hormonal factors.
1895: Beatson produced regression of recurrent breast cancer by removal of ovaries.	B. *Hormones and Breast Cancer* 1913 Lathrop and Loeb showed that pregnancy protects against experimental breast cancer in mice. Subsequently, the action of oestrogens in influencing the growth of breast cancer in animals was demonstrated.	1915: The Registrar General published figures showing that mortality is higher in single women than married; and higher in childless than in fertile married women.
Huggins introduced adrenalectomy in treatment (1945)		
Olivercrona introduced hypophysectomy (1952)		Age-trends show a striking levelling at the menopause
	Multiple Causes The synergistic action of *genetic* and *hormonal* factors together with a *virus-like-agent* (Bittner) is most effective in producing a high yield of mammary cancer in mice.	It was for a long time further postulated that *prolonged lactation* protects against breast cancer and so partly explains the connections of the disease with marital status, fertility and geography. But a study in USA (1960) found no difference in lactation history between breast cancer patients and controls
		A comparative study, using standardised methods, is in progress in several countries. This has shown that it is age at first pregnancy that matters. Lactation does not protect, early age of bearing first child does. MacMahon and colleagues have postulated altered ratio of oestrogen fractions as possible underlying hormonal lesion; and they are making international comparative studies of this—geographical biochemistry—which are confirmatory

Clinical Observation	Laboratory Experiment	Population Studies
		A prospective survey in women of Guernsey aged 35–54 by Bulbrook and colleagues found that low excretion of androgen metabolities is associated with high subsequent incidence of breast cancer. This suggestion of a possible precursor abnormality should be tested in a larger population

A NEW CAUSATION DISCOVERED
Production of congenital malformations by rubella

Clinical Observation	Laboratory Study	Epidemiology; Community Diagnosis; Community Health
Gregg, ophthalmologist, then others in Australia, taking clinical case-histories, connected an unusual frequency in infants of congenital malformations—cataract, heart disease—with rubella early in mother's pregnancy (the rubella syndrome, RS). This was in 1940–1 when rubella had been unusually common after a long period of low incidence. Clinicians recognised the significance of the observation, which opened up a new era of research into possible environmental causes of malformation.	*Embryology.*—By animal experiment, and special observation on man, *ethology*, it has been demonstrated that during a critical period of early embryonic life, when organ differentiation and growth are taking place, they are specially vulnerable to damage. The specific malformations associated with rubella commonly are multiple and they are found when maternal infection has occurred during the first trimester, and particularly the 4th to 8th week, of pregnancy; i.e. the period of organogenesis in the human embryo.	*Testing of the hypothesis.*—Looking back, and making use of routine official census statistics, a high rate of congenital deaf-mutism was identified in the cohort of births exposed to the epidemics of rubella that occurred in Australia during 1898–9 and other years, as well as in 1938–41

Serologic Epidemiology.—Surveys have shown that in urban Western populations 15–20 per cent of women of child-bearing age are susceptible to rubella. |

Clinical Observation	Laboratory Study	Epidemiology; Community Diagnosis; Community Health
Other anomalies, such as deafness and psychomotor retardation gradually were added to the rubella syndrome; as well as congenital diseases—thrombo-cytopenic purpura, meningitis, etc.	*Teratology.*—Congenital malformations have been produced in animals by many different agents, singly or in combination, but always be degree of malnutrition or other damage insufficient to kill the embryo. It can be postulated that it is the mildness of the infection, in the case of rubella, which is responsible for the frequent malformation rather than death of the embryo.	*Individual Risks.*—Prospective clinical survey by British Medical Officers of Health before virologic and serologic tests became available found these risks *of malformation to infant:* 567 *Pregnant Women with Rubella* All these mothers: Risk to infant = 1 in 14 Maternal rubella in first 12 weeks: Risk to infant = 1 in 6 Maternal rubella at 13–40 weeks: Risk to infant = 1 in 34 5 611 mothers who did not have rubella: Risk to infant = 1 in 36 There was also an excess of abortion, stillbirth, infant death, and low birth weight, in the rubella cases.
	Virology.—Rubella virus infects the placenta via the blood stream; then invades the foetus where it was isolated 20 years after Gregg. A chronic infection persists throughout foetal life, is present at birth, and may continue up to 3 years of age. Virologic investigations since 1962 have confirmed the observation that RS in the infant can occur even though the *maternal infection is inapparent. Laboratory diagnosis of infected women and infants* is now quite practicable	A later *audiometric survey* of children exposed in utero who appeared normal at birth detected considerable subclinical hearing loss in addition to the clinical deafness
		Estimate of proportion of malformation that is due to rubella is difficult to make, but it probably is quite small
		Search for evidence of special incidence of congenital anomalies in relation to *other viral infections* in pregnancy has so far yielded little, excepting with cytomegalovirus

Antenatal diagnosis permits termination of affected pregnancies
A vaccine has been developed and immunisation is now being widely used

CAUSES OF GOITRE IN TASMANIA (CLEMENTS)
Its prevention and ecology

Clinical Medicine	Epidemiology and Public Health	Nutrition; Molecular Biology
Observation in 1949 of high frequency of goitre in Tasmania	A special survey in 1949 during routine school medical inspection confirmed the clinical impressions of high prevalence of goitre among children in Tasmania. Mass distribution of KI tablets was organised, but re-survey five years later showed a further rise of prevalence in the children, i.e. the customary response to iodine was not obtained. Moreover, boys were affected as much as girls, unlike the picture in iodine-defiency goitre.	
	In the period between the two surveys there was considerable increase in milk consumption by children. To meet the demand for milk, production of a forage crop choumollier—a kale—was greatly increased	Twenty-five years before, Chesney had demonstrated the goitrogenic action of an agent in brassica seeds (e.g. kale). However, local attempts to isolate substances from cow's milk with strong enough goitrogenic activity were unsuccessful.
	Selective distribution of the goitre suggested that personal susceptibility was also involved.	
The number of cases of thyrotoxicosis in the island's two clinics quickly more than doubled. Most of the patients were over 40 years of age and had nodular goitres rendering them susceptible to toxic change from rapid increase of iodine intake.	In due course, incidence of goitre fell but not in some regions where inefficient distribution of the tablets was blamed. So in 1966, potassium iodate was added to bread; and the incidence throughout Tasmania has fallen to that of non-goitrous regions.	
The standard Glasgow system of clinical assessment was used, and special studies made to validate current vs. previous diagnosis of thyrotoxicosis.	Particular efforts were made to ascertain all cases by collaboration between the special clinics and local doctors. During recent years the incidence has fallen, suggesting a cohort effect.	Modern methods of diagnosis using I131 up-take studies, T3 resin uptake, etc.

Source: Morris, J.N., 1975, *Uses of Epidemiology*, Edinburgh: Churchill-Livingstone, pp. 251–261

Lifestyles We have discussed elsewhere that the introduction of vaccinations and antibiotics over the last century has had no particular impact on the overall death rates in western societies. (McKeown, 1979). As we discussed earlier the decline in mortality was due to improved standards of nutrition and hygiene, i.e. largely public health measures. The overall extent of disease is not declining.

As we discussed elsewhere, the ecological theory of disease has largely replaced the germ theory. That is, death from infectious diseases is at its lowest in advanced industrial and post-industrial nations. Most people now die from diseases of old age such as heart disease, cancer and strokes. As is shown elsewhere in this chapter, many diseases are work-related or environmentally-related. Diseases at the latter part of the twentieth century appear in some way to be related to diet, nutritional balance, weight, occupation, genetic background, lack of exercise, and other factors. There are also stress-related diseases such as gastric ulcers, high blood pressure and asthma, and socially based psychological or psychiatric illness. Many illnesses are due to cigarette smoking, the over-consumption of alcohol, or drug-taking. The tables below are taken from a famous study of cancer and smoking which was conducted on British doctors by Sir Richard Doll.

Individual risks and chances in relation to smoking habits
Experience of British Doctors 1951–8: Men

(1) Risks of Dying from All Causes Within the Next Ten Years

Decade	Non-smokers	Ex-smokers	Cigarette smokers	Other	All doctors
45–54	1 in 27	1 in 19	1 in 13	1 in 19	1 in 16
55–64	1 in 8	1 in 7	1 in 5	1 in 12	1 in 7
65–74	1 in 3	1 in 3	1 in 2	1 in 3	1 in 3

Later data, up to 1965,, shows that at age 35,, the risk of the cigarette smoker dying within a decade ranged from 1 in 47 in light smokers (1–14 per day) to 1 in 22 in heavy (25 or more per day); etc. The figures for non-smokers, referred to in the text, were now 1 in 75 instead of 1 in 90, etc.

(2) Chances in 100 (%) at Age 35 of Surviving to Age 65

  Non-smokers: 85
  Ex-smokers: 81
  Cigarette smokers: 73
  Other smokers: 86
  All doctors: 79

The later figure for non-smokers was 82 %.

Doll R, Hill AB. (1962 & 1971). In *Smoking and Health* and *Smoking and Health Now*, London: and personal communications.

(Source: Morris, 1971)

It is clear that individuals very often create their own illnesses through eating the wrong food, refusing to wear seat belts, infringing speed limits, and smoking and drinking to excess. In this section we will look at some of these problems.

Illich (op. cit., p. 89) maintains:

. . . in rich countries the life expectancy of those between fifteen and forty-five has tended to stabilise because accidents and the new diseases of civilisation kill as many as formerly succumbed to pneumonia and other infections.

He goes on to claim that a change in life-style, particularly among the aged, for example to be removed from their accustomed surroundings to an institution, results in an earlier death. If we include breast-feeding as a life-style then the switch from the breast to the bottle produced tragic consequences:

As the bottle became a status symbol, new illnesses appeared among children who had been denied the breast, and since mothers lack traditional know-how to deal with babies who do not behave like sucklings, babies became new consumers of medical attention and of its risks.
(Op. cit. p. 95.)

Obviously, life-styles are closely linked to our occupation, and as a result of the combination of the two we arrive at a life-chance. If we contrast the two extreme occupations from the earlier table showing the standardised mortality ratios for different occupations in the U.K. for 1961, we arrive at the following.

	All	T.B.	lung cancer	CHD	bronchitis	accidents
Coal-face worker	180	294	140	144	293	522
Medical doctors	89	64	48	118	23	55

The **SMR**, or *standard mortality ratio*, is calculated above or below 100 (the average) so that in terms of accidents, for example, coal-face workers are 422 per cent more likely to die from an accident than average whereas a doctor is 45 per cent *less* likely to die from one. When and how we will all die is very much the result of the category of social class we are and our occupational group. The two are closely linked in the sense that occupational group is the main factor for placing an individual in a social class and that those from a middle-class background are more likely to go to good schools, enter a university and subsequently qualify as a professional. Infant mortality is closely linked to occupation and although the overall rate has declined in western nations the differential rates between classes has remained fairly constant. Occupation also influences our utilisation of health services so that preventative services such as radiography, pap smears, immunisation and prevention, are not taken advantage of by the lower occupational groups as they are by the middle and upper groups:

Cartwright's scholarly review of the evidence in fact leaves little room for doubt that the middle class are the main beneficiaries of health services. To select a few of the findings she reviews: they are more likely to benefit from ante-natal examinations, more likely to attend a family-planning clinic, and more likely to discuss birth control with their G.P.. Middle-class individuals are more likely to have had post-natal examinations. Middle-class old people are twice as likely to have had help from a chiropodist and a visit from their doctor. Middle-class individuals are more likely to have their own teeth; they are usually found in the better endowed geriatric and psychiatric hospitals. Furthermore, doctors in 'well to do' areas write more expensive prescriptions and spend longer (on average 6,1 minutes compared with 4,4 minutes) with middle-class patients.
(Tuckett, op. cit., p. 114.)

A review of the literature reveals that the professional and intermediate classes are considerably superior to those at the other end of the social-occupational scale in a number of ways. They generally live in larger houses in more pleasant areas, their work usually takes place in nicer surroundings and they enjoy social relationships with others outside the home. (Manual workers never mix, socially, either within or outside the home.) In summary, it might be said that the majority of authors in this field argue:

... that, despite changes in affluence and industrial work, it still makes sense to draw a quite sharp distinction between the life-experience and norms common among manual and non-manual workers respectively.
(Tuckett, o cit., p. 142)

Goldthorpe and his colleagues (1969) following Florence Kluckholn whom we mention earlier, have developed a typology of 'typical' class orientations, as in the following table.

TYPICAL CLASS ATTITUDES

Working-class (manual) perspective	Middle-class (non-manual) perspective
(i) The basic conception of social order is a dichotomous one: society is divided into 'us' and 'them'. 'They' are people in positions in which they can exercise power and authority over 'us'. The division between 'us' and 'them' is seen as a virtually unbridgeable one: people are born on one side of the line or the other and very largely remain there. Life is seen as something to be 'put up with'.	(i) The basic conception of the social order is a hierarchical one: society is divided into a series of levels or strata differentiated in terms of the life-styles and associated prestige of their members. The structure is, however, seen as a relatively 'open' one: given ability and the appropriate moral qualities—determination, perseverance, etc.—individuals can, and do, more up the hierarchy. What a man achieves in the end depends primarily on what he 'makes of himself'. Moreover, it is felt that the individual has an obligation to assume responsibility for his own life and welfare and to *try* to 'get on in the world' as far as he can.

TYPICAL CLASS ATTITUDES

Working-class (manual) perspective	*Middle-class (non-manual) perspective*
(ii) Complementary to the idea of 'putting up' with life is that of 'making the best of it'; that is, of living in and for the present. As Hoggart (1957) observes, 'working class life puts a premium on the taking of pleasures now, discourages planning for some future good'. This emphasis on the present and the lack of concern for 'planning ahead' are, moreover, encouraged by the view that there is in fact little to be done about the future, that it is not to any major extent under the individual's control. A certain amount of fatalism and acceptance, as well as an orientation to the present thus hold together as a mutually reinforcing set of attitudes.	(ii) The emphasis placed on 'getting on' implies, on the part of the individual or family, a marked orientation towards the future. Major importance is attached to looking and planning ahead and, where necessary, to making present sacrifices in order to ensure greater advantages or benefits at a later stage. Such deferring of gratification, say, in the furtherance of a career or business undertaking—is approved of as a matter of morality as well as expediency.
(iii) In so far as it is felt that purposive action can be effective, the emphasis is placed on action of a *collective* kind aimed at the protection of collective interests—trade unionism being, of course, the most developed form. A prime value is that set on mutual aid and group solidarity in the face of the vicissitudes of life and the domination which 'they' seek to impose. This value in turn confirms the shared, communal nature of social life and constitutes a further restraint on attempts by individuals to make themselves 'a cut above the rest'. Such attempts, in the form, say of conspicuous consumption or occupational advance, are likely to be interpreted by the community as threats to its solidarity, as expressions of group or class disloyalty. Even in the case of children, parental concern that they should 'do well' is confined to achievement within the context of working-class values and life-styles—as, for example in becoming established in a 'trade' or a 'steady' job. Aspirations do not extend to levels of education nor types of job that would result in children being taken away from their family and community in either geographical or a social sense.	(iii) The middle-class social ethic is thus an essentially *individualistic* one: the prime value is that set on individual achievement. Achievement is taken as the crucial indicator of the individual's moral worth. However, achievement is also regarded as a family concern: parents feel an obligation to try to give their children a 'better start in life' than they themselves enjoyed, and then anticipate that their offspring will in turn attain to a still higher level in the social scale. In other words, the expectation is that advancement will be continuous—between generations as well as in the course of individual lifetimes. Indeed, through parental aspirations for children, it is possible for desires and hopes for the future to become virtually limitless.

(Adapted from Goldthorpe *et al..*, 1969: p. 118–121)

An area of difference according to social class is that of leisure. The working-class couple is more likely to spend a substantial part of leisure time indoors whereas the middle class spend more time eating out and going to the theatre. Gardening is reported as more popular with the middle class, and entertaining friends as opposed to neighbours.

The different life-styles of individuals within different social classes:

... can influence an individual's susceptibility to disease. For example, the fact that manual workers and their wives are less likely to plan their families by spacing births ... and the fact that the early years of their marital relationships are unlikely to be of the kind where partners feel they can confide in each other about *any* kind of problem means that they are more vulnerable to depression

following a life-crisis. Similarly, the fact that the perspectives of working-class people do not emphasise *individual* action to secure future ends, offers one reason for working-class parents being less likely to visit welfare clinics with their children . . . or to take preventive action in relation to pre-natal . . . or dental care . . .
(Tuckett, op. cit., p. 151.)

Work, community and disease

Generally, we can arrive at three basic definitions of community:

1. A locality or a specified geographical area

as a basis of social organisation. We might think of Prince Albert, in the Karoo.

2. A local social system

or set of relationships that concentrate upon a given locality. What is highlighted is the concentration of social relationships.

3. A type of relationship

Producing a strong sense of shared identity.

However, Hillery (1955, p. 119) after reviewing 94 definitions of *community*, reached the conclusion that 'beyond the concept that people are involved in community, there is no complete agreement as to the nature of community.' Nevertheless, we will take the concept in the three ways outlined above.

The two sociologists most concerned with the notion of community were Ferdinand Tönnies and Emile Durkheim who were both concerned with the transition from traditional to modern society. In 1887 Tönnies described in his book *Gemeinschaft and Gesellschaft* the distinguishing characteristics of the *Gemeinschaft*, a community in which most people know each other, and the *Gesellschaft*, in which people are in 'association', more like strangers to each other.

GEMEINSCHAFT	GESELLSCHAFT
1. Intimate face-to-face contact	1. Impersonal contacts
2. Strong social solidarity	2. Individual, not group loyalties
3. Very traditional	3. Slackening of traditional ties and val

Durkheim had a similar scheme in 1893 in his book *The Division of Labour*, where he distinguishes between *organic solidarity* (a kind of social cohesion based on the *differences* between members) and *mechanical solidarity* (a kind of social cohesion based on the *similarity* of members).

Talcott Parsons developed Durkheim's mechanical and organic solidarity in terms of *pattern variables*, as follows:

PATTERN 'A' VARIABLES	PATTERN 'B' VARIABLES
TRADITIONAL SOCIETY	MODERN SOCIETY
Ascription	Achievement
(status at birth, e.g. king)	(earned status, e.g. film star)
Role Diffuseness	Role Specificity
(*Gemeinschaftlich*)	(*Gesellschaftlich*)
Particularism	Universalism (equally treated,
(treated in a personal way)	e.g. by competition)
Affectivity (emotions importantly	Affective neutrality (emotions
displayed)	concealed)
Collective orientation	Self-orientation (personal
(shared family and community	success)
interests)	

Most societies, it is important to note, display a mix of types *A* and *B*, but generally the former is predominant in a tribal society whereas the latter is typically industrial.

This section is concerned specifically with community-based illnesses, that is, disease arising out of the community environment or a community which is work dominated, such as a coal mining town or a fishing community. The concentration of the motor car in urban areas in most countries has resulted in an enormous concentration of petrol fumes. Inhabitants of urban areas therefore have this problem, over which they have little control, to contend with in addition to many other health problems. Thus death rates for lung cancer are higher in urban (more polluted) areas than rural (less polluted) areas, and studies have revealed that immigrants from England who enter South Africa, New Zealand and America have a higher rate of lung cancer than the indigenous population with comparable smoking habits. This could well be because of the polluted air of most British cities. Recent studies in Britain showed abnormally high lead levels in children living near inner-city motorways. Benzo-a-pyrene is a carcinogenic agent produced by car fumes and is found in high levels in major cities. Petrol fumes attack other parts of the body apart from the lungs. Esposito (1970) states that the consequences of living in a large city are equivalent to smoking a packet of cigarettes a day. Yet another problem is that the increase in lung cancer, due to sulphur dioxide pollution which occurred on Staten Island, is estimated to be 33 % higher.

As Doyal and Pennel state:

The hazards of production extend well beyond the workplace, transforming the material environment and contributing to what are often termed 'pollution problems'.
(Doyal and Pennell, 1979, p. 75)

Most probably a pollution-free world is an impossible ideal. Doyal and Pennell go on to discuss three types of industrial pollution and their effects on health. Firstly, many workers bring home with them a variety of toxic substances. For example, one study in England found that the fathers of children working in a large rechargable battery factory were bringing home with them traces of lead. Consequently, the level of lead in these children's blood was much higher than other children living in urban areas. The workers were bringing home lead on their clothes, shoes and hair. An American study of the families of asbestos workers showed the following alarming results:

Last year Selikoff's group started to look at the families of Peterson Asbestos workers, who received slight exposure to fibres brought back by the wage earners in their hair and clothing. To date, the team has X-rayed 210 people and the results are disturbing indeed. Almost 40 per cent of the subjects were found to possess abnormalities in their lungs, of the type common to asbestos workers. Even more alarming is the fact that some of the abnormalities have shown up in the lungs of subjects whose asbestos industry kin spent no more than a few days at the Paterson plant.

The problem is not restricted to lung abnormalities. Recent months have seen three cases of mesothelioma among the asbestos workers' families who were indirectly exposed to the mineral fibres, and Selikoff fears an increase in such cases in years to come.

(*New Scientist*, 1974, October 3)

Other effects, not immediately apparent, produce congenital birth defects. A Canadian study showed that workers in hydrocarbon-related occupations, including painters, machinists, miners and motor mechanics, produced an abnormal number of children suffering from malignant disease.

Doyal and Pennell go on to examine the polluting of communities through factory waste. Pollution of this sort is not confined to large-scale disasters such as the wastage of dioxin which occurred at Seveso, in Milan in 1976, the mercury poisoning of Minamata Bay in the 1950s or the widespread chromium pollution in Tokyo. In the mid-1970s, for example, a little Yorkshire village called Hebden Bridge experienced an 'epidemic' of asbestosis which spread through the whole community, and not just workers and their immediate families. Communities are known to have been affected by copper, lead and zinc smelting. Community arsenical poisoning in communities with these industries, throughout America, shows a mean increase in lung cancer mortality of 17 per cent for males and 15 per cent for females. (Op. cit., p. 78.)

The third type of pollution considered is the diffuse atmospheric pollution found in urban areas. This is found to be an accumulation of 'irritant gases such as sulphur dioxide, combined with atmospheric suspensions of tars and resins and with matter such as cotton or asbestos fibres'. (Ibid.) It is well documented now that this type of pollution causes optic and bronchial irritation and increased susceptibility to infection in the young and the old. It also produces chronic bronchitis and emphysema. We mentioned above the high lead concentration of children living near inner motorways in Britain. A report of one study showed that atmospheric lead pollution can become attached to sticky foods, sweets, and hands, and that it was quite possible for a child to consume ten times its tolerable daily lead intake in as many sweets. (Ibid.)

A number of other epidemiological factors enter into differences in the distribution and concentration of disease. Communities differ as to quality of life and these differences are used by Government to exercise positive discrimination. Thus *area mortality* exists on a regional basis, so that people simply live longer in some areas of a country than they do in others. In other instances we talk of population density, and that air pollution in 'dirty' areas results in a higher mortality for respiratory diseases. As we mentioned above, certain occupations are prone to a much higher national average death rate, such as disabling back injuries among farm workers, plastic workers' liver cancer, brain disease from mercury poisoning, asbestos workers' lung disease and cancer and many more. Even the last category can be broken down as follows:

Chronic lung disease due to exposure to different types of dust
aluminosis (bauxite lung) from aluminium in smelting, explosives, paints and firework manufacture;
baritosis from barium sulphate in mining;
beryllium disease from beryllium in aircraft manufacturing, metallurgy, and rocket fuels;
byssinosis (brown lung) from cotton, flax, and hemp dust in textile manufacturing;
coal miners' pneumoconiosis (black lung) from coal dust in mining, coal trimming, and the graphite industry;
kaolinosis from hydrated aluminium silicates in china making;
platinum industries asthma from platinum salta in electronics and chemical siderosis from iron oxides in welding and iron ore mining;
silicosis from silica in mining, pottery, sandblasting, foundries, quarries, and masonry;
stannosis from tin oxide in smelting; and
talcosis from hydrated magnesium silicates in the rubber industry.

Waitzkin *in* Eisenberg and Kleinman (1980, p. 357)

Stress disorders

These disorders also vary from region to region and from job to job, as also do *hypertensive disorders* which also differ in rural and urban settings.

Ischaemic heart disease

This is associated with sedentary work whereas men in physically active jobs have less ischaemic heart disease during middle age. A clinical sample of men living in hard and soft water ares showed that the mean blood pressure by age was higher in the soft water areas for both casual diastolic and supine diastolic. There is also some connection recorded between high blood pressure and fishing communities with a high rate of salt intake.

Cardiovascular disease

This is to some extent the result of local culture-patterns, as well as lack of exercise, obesity, cigarette smoking and metabolic and carbohydrate levels.

Alcoholic rates

These vary from community to community and from country to country. Communities which tolerate alcohol consumption and are themselves producers of alcohol have high rates, as also the areas within these countries. For example, France and West Germany have the highest rates of alcohol consumption (and cirrhosis of the liver). In Zambia, although the majority of the population does not consume alcohol, such consumption as exists is concentrated around the Copper Belt.

Cigarette smoking

Smoking is directly related to lung cancer and other illnesses but is very much tied to social class, and consequently to occupational groups. Thus the semi-skilled and unskilled smoke considerably more than their professional and white-collar counterparts. They also display considerably less interest in any form of vigorous exercise in their leisure time.

Pollution and urban development

It is generally much more unhealthy to live in towns than in rural areas, particularly in Britain, Europe and America. This is due to such factors as pollution and overcrowding and perhaps also to the poverty-large family syndrome seen in inner-urban areas. The rediscovery of byssinosis among the cotton communities showed that it was related to other respiratory diseases, also. Deaths from lung-cancer in metropolis, town and country over a three year period in England and Wales show it to be highest in London County, next highest in the conurbations and urban areas and lowest of all in 'truly rural' Wales. Although London men have four times the rate of cancer of their counterparts in rural Britain, cancer of the stomach is extremely high in North and West Wales. Cancer of the oesophagus is the highest in the world among the Xhosa of Transkei. Male cancer of the stomach and lung are much higher among social class IV and V than 1 and 11, but the reverse is true of cancer of the prostrate and testis. Female cancer is higher among social class 1 and 11 for lung and breast, lower for cervical cancer and slightly higher for uterine cancer. For females, cancer of the breast, uterine cancer and ovarian cancer is more prevalent amongst those who are married but infertile, and those who are single.

Surprisingly, wide ranges of incidences of cancer are to be found among the top ten developed nations. Also, diseases are found to 'cluster' among certain populations and groups, e.g. cancer of the stomach in Japan, liver in the Bantu, and pancreas among American blacks. With immigrant Japanese entering America the high rate of stomach cancer and the low rate of cancer of the colon and breast which is the common pattern in Japan, settles down to the typical American pattern.

The concept of community

The concept of community is important because in epidemiological research mapping is used to trace and locate the spread and incidence of various diseases. It is important, secondly, because it shows us the availability and utilisation of health services.

(Community) place is important because it refers to the physical environment in which we live, both natural and man-made. It has been suggested that 'well' people may have an 'immunity' by which they can 'tolerate quite a range of differences in 'arrangements of physical phenomena' without adverse results. (Anderson and Andersen in Freeman, 1972, p. 408)

These authors go on to say that:

. . . there is a logical explanation for the fact that community mental health service is most fully developed up to now in medium-sized country boroughs. These communities have populations sufficiently large to support a complete range of facilities, except for the most specialised, and these facilities can be located within fairly easy reach of the whole community. Rural areas have neither of these advantages, and the cities face concentrations of intractable social problems and large immigrant groups.
(Op. cit., p. 409–410.)

Communities reveal differences in social class which in turn reflect differences in occupation. Thus Koos (1954) found significant differences in the symptoms reported by different social classes in his small, fictitiously named, rural community.

Thirdly, a community can be viewed as a social system, with health as one of the major agents of interaction. If we view health as a major community system we assume that it has identifiable characteristics such as:

1. A structure, or related set of agencies, organisations or establishments;
2. Manifest and latent functions;
3. Health functionaries;
4. An ideology or rationale;
5. Equipment and other material resources for carrying out the activities expected; and
6. Links with other systems, such as the economic system. (Op. cit., pp. 411–417.)

SUMMARY

1. The three major systems of social stratification are caste, estate and class, the last being the important concept in western societies.
2. The deteminants of social class generally include education, income, and occupation.
3. The social class to which an individual belongs permeates nearly all aspects of life, including language, gesture, the distribution of psychiatric and physical disorders and life chances in general.
4. Social mobility is possible, either vertically or horizontally, although this is determined by the opportunity structure and demographic factors, on the whole.
5. The early work of Chadwick and Engels, and later Waitzkin and others, linked occupation and disease. This showed that certain occupations were directly correlated to disease and mortality even within the same social class, i.e. bus drivers and bus conductors.
6. While infectious diseases account for few deaths in western nations, people's behaviour or lifestyle, e.g. smoking or drinking to excess, considerably influences our morbidity and mortality. The general division is thought to be between manual and non-manual occupations.
7. Community-based illnesses (communities which exhibit illnesses specific to that community) can also include abnormally high lead levels in urban dwellers, etc. Area mortality exists on a regional basis not only for physical but also stress-related diseases.

IMPORTANT TERMS

commercial and domestic slavery   conflict
social class rank   class consciousness
life-orientations   extended and restricted codes
relative deprivation   horizontal and vertical mobility
status   life-style
community   pattern variable

SELF ASSESSMENT QUESTIONS

1. Outline the major systems of social stratification and indicate the importance of social class to the study of health and illness.
2. What are the connections between poverty, disease and mortality?
3. In what ways is sickness related to occupational class?
4. Why might life-styles be important in relation to disease and mortality?
5. Discuss the concept of community and community-based illnesses.
6. In what ways might the transition from *Gemeinschaft* to *Gesellschaft* societies affect illness and the treatment of disease?

CHAPTER FIVE THE FAMILY

- sociology of the family
- family breakdown
- socialization and gender
- formation
- the family and illness

ALEXANDRA TOWNSHIP BABY CLINIC

THE SOCIOLOGY OF THE FAMILY

The family is a complex, ancient and basic social institution which is universally found wherever there are human groups. Today, in many advanced countries such as South Africa, Britain and the U.S.A., the family structure is under considerable pressure. The number of live births to unmarried mothers and the spiralling rate of divorce are some of the factors that exert pressure. There are many different forms of family organisations, and some examples of these different structures can be found among the Hopi, the wandering Bushman of the Kalahari and in European societies. We also find a rudimentary form of such a structure among other animals such as free-living chimpanzees and apes. Social groupings involving mating and a relationship between a mother and infant have been variously described in birds, rabbits, dogs, cats and rodents. The social organisation of the family is based upon fundamental biological functions, but man's rich cultural nature results in a greater variation within his species.

Some characteristics are common to *all* family forms. Firstly, the family is constituted of a group of people who are related to one another in some way. Secondly, its members live together in close proximity for relatively long periods of time. Thirdly, the family is an economic unit which consumes goods and services and often produces goods and services. Fourthly, children resulting from the union of the adults are cared for and are their responsibility.

The family The family is a social structure, or sub-system, which commences when marriage has taken place or kinship ties have been established, and of which society approves. Generally, members of a family live together and interact socially according to norms, roles and status positions prescribed by the greater society. More clearly, we can think of it as a particular grouping of persons united by socially sanctioned kinship, marriage or adoption ties, who tend to live together and interact together according to well-defined social rules.

It differs from other sub-systems in society in a number of different ways. Firstly, it is generally the group which the individual encounters from the outset. This is called the *family of orientation* (the one into which we are born) as opposed to the *family of procreation* (the one which we later create ourselves). The individual encounters this group over a period of time. (S)he is in the family for primary socialisation and usually has the family as a base for the period of secondary socilisation, although with the latter the emphasis is on other groups with whom the individual mixes or is influenced by. Because of this extended and intensive period during which the individual is living with the family we can expect the time to be one in which vitally important influences are brought to bear on the formation of the individual's behaviour and personality, and one which leaves a lasting pattern of loyalty and deep affection on all of us.

Every society clearly distinguishes between children born within wedlock (legitimate) and those born out of wedlock (illegitimate). Legitimacy is encouraged because it makes the economic and social roles and responsibilities easier to allocate. Society *knows* who is responsible for looking after the young. Births which are illegitimate tend to result in some confusion as to who is the father and often the affective role is allocated to welfare agencies or the mother's eldest brother. Secondly, of all the groups of which we are or become members, the family is the smallest or one of the smallest. This is certainly true of the *conjugal* family, which is the name given to the typical family structure found in industrial society. Thirdly, some of the other systems in society would find it difficult to function without the family. In modern industrial society functions of the family are gradually being eroded and taken over by specialist agencies. Lastly, the emotional intensity of family relationships and the control of members makes it particularly suitable to act as a vehicle for the exercise of constraint.

Functions of the family Although there are many variations in types of marriage and the forms that families take, nevertheless the *functions* of the family are considered as essential for the fulfilment of certain social requirements. A functionalist view of the family would include the following six functions:

1. The family provides the setting for the socialisation of the young by conveying values, modes of behaviour and social traditions on the one hand, and attitudes and cognitive content on the other.

2. The family provides for the regulation of sexual and parental behaviour or requirements.

3. The family provides a basis upon which private property in the broadest sense can be passed on with the minimum of conflict.

4. The family provides a group of people who are expected to give affection and love.

5. The family provides care and training for the otherwise helpless young.

6. The family is the means by which society passes on its titles or statuses which are ascribed to the young.

Although nearly all these functions could be performed by other agencies only the family can perform them all so effectively.

A conflict view of the family   Not all sociologists would agree with the functionalist views of the family. Conflict theorists such as Marxists maintain that the family contains the primary instance of one group's domination over another, in this case male over female. Marital relationships are viewed as reflections and reinforcements of gender inequalities. It is true that until recently women were socially and legally subservient to men. However, there is a move towards greater equality among spouses in post-industrial societies. However, it is not only gender conflict which is attracting the attention of conflict theorists. More and more evidence is emerging of deep-rooted family violence between husband and wife, parent and child, and child against child. In America, for instance, it is estimated that seven million spouses each year go through a violent episode in which pain or injury is inflicted on the partner. A good percentage of all murders is committed by a relative. Child abuse, whether physical or sexual, has reached alarming dimensions both in South Africa and in Britain and the U.S.A. Sexual abuse constitutes a quarter of those who are also physically abused. Often, there are forms of sexual abuse which leave no physical signs. Often physical abuse arises from family stress due to financial problems. It may well be, of course, that such a dramatic increase is a reflection of a more aware society rather than any *actual* increase.

Conflict theorists criticise functionalism on a number of grounds:

1. It confuses function with cause or with explanation. Although this is to some extent true, sociologists have attempted to get round it by using words such as 'competences'. Functional analysis is seen by most as only one of many possible modes of analysis. No item is irreplaceable.

2. Functionalism is conservative. This is not true because Marxist analysis often incorporates a functionalist perspective as well as a conflict one.

3. Functionalism ignores social conflict, cannot analyse human action or meaning, and cannot analyse power.

4. Functionalism reifies certain institutions. This is true but so does certain Marxist analysis.

Marriage Marriage is distinguished from mating, and is to be regarded as social rather than biological. It implies, primarily, a relatively *stable* relationship between one or more men and one or more women. The form of family which we think predominates, the *monogamous* family (one wife to one husband), is in fact not found in 80 % of societies throughout the world, and in these societies *polygamy* (the existence of more than one legal spouse at the same time) is common. In 80 % of societies where polygamy is the structure, the most common type is *polygyny* (one man is legally contracted to more than one woman) although we can still find examples of *polyandrous* marriage (more than one husband to one woman) in certain parts of India, for example the Toda. This last example of a marriage form is very rare and occurs among the Toda because their practice of female infanticide produces a surplus of males in the society. Economic circumstances can shape sexual if not marriage arrangements, as we can see with the Xhosa. Over 20 % of the male population are absent at any one time thus resulting in a surplus of women.

As we have already mentioned, an important element in defining marriage is the *principle of legitimacy* by which a relationship between a mother, father and child is socially approved or legitimated. Sexual relationships between various members of society are given legitimate approval by some form of *incest taboo*, which prohibits sexual intercourse between designated members. The family has given rise to the social institution of marriage and not the other way round. Marriage is a contractual agreement based upon certain regulations and rules which govern the rights, duties and privileges of a wife to a husband and vice versa, and of both to their offspring, their relatives (*extended family*), and society at large. It would be incorrect to think of marriage as regulating sexual intercourse. It is more helpful to think of it as a means for making the reproduction of offspring legitimate. It becomes obvious, also, that to become pregnant (or even give birth) before marriage is in some societies a signal of fertility and has full social approval. The variations in the structure of marriage we have mentioned means that sexual behaviour is not uniform but can vary enormously. Many societies have a system of 'privileged relationships' which can allow a man to have sexual relationships with the wife of his brother (some 34 societies), with his wife's sister (some 28 societies) and with his mother's brother's wife (six societies). In the Old Testament the Hebrews had a form of marriage (*levirite*) which provided that a childless widow should be retained in the husband's clan by marrying his brother or kinsman. These 'extra-marital relationships', although socially prescribed, may surprise some more used to the western form of marriage, yet in many ways they can be seen as providing a means of giving security to the woman, and also binding together various tribes and clans. Even in western society many see it as less shocking for a husband to have an affair than a wife, and in Japan sexual relationships are socially approved between a man and a woman other than his wife, although not the other way round.

Kinship Kinship is the social network of individuals related together in some way, usually by marriage, adoption or ancestry. The *extended* family of traditional societies has kinship as the basis of social organisation. Here the kinship group is large and individuals are closely involved with its members. In modern societies the isolated *nuclear* family predominates and the entire family network rarely, if ever, comes together. Primary, secondary and tertiary relatives can run into several hundred and consequently societies have various mechanisms for dealing with such large numbers, for example counting *only* the mother's or the father's side as kin.

Romantic love Romantic love between man and woman is a comparatively new phenomenon and does not appear to be known in Europe before the rise of the *trouveres* and the troubadours. Many societies have no notion of romantic love, and in such societies marriages can be 'arranged' by reason of family background or wealth. People without such a concept find it very alien. The Samoans, when told the story of *Romeo and Juliet*, were reduced to laughter. Far from taking romantic love for granted we must realise that it is a purely cultural manifestation. It does, however, fulfill a number of functions in the maintenance of the institution of the nuclear family. These functions are seen as three in number:

1. A transfer of loyalties away from their family of orientation to a new family of procreation.
2. The notion of romantic love provides emotional support in the new life a couple has to face together.
3. Romantic love provides an incentive to marriage in a modern world where there is a choice to marry or not.

Forms of marriage and types of family One of the questions that immediately spring to mind is why there are so many variations in the forms of marriage and types of family, and indeed why there should be any variation at all. The answers cannot be framed in terms of individuals but in the way in which cultural conditions pre-empt the entry of the individual into society and determine to a large extent the social patterning of his life. Monogamous marriage is generally universal and found in societies which also practice a more dominant form. Usually in such circumstances the practitioners of monogamy are far too poor to afford more than one partner. Very often forms of marriage denote the social status of an individual so that polygynous practices reflect wealth, status and power manifested in a large number of wives belonging to a high status person or chief. On the other hand polyandrous practices are nearly always a sign of poor social conditions because of which a number of men pool their labour in order to establish a household.

Differences also occur in the way in which marriage partners are selected. *Endogamy* requires a person to marry within a specified group of which he is a member. Such groups are usually based on race, religion or social class. Until recently, in South Africa, legislation controlled inter-marriage between different races. *Exogamy* refers to the prohibition of marrying within certain groups of which an individual is a member. The incest taboos which we have mentioned, deliberately exclude certain groups from being eligible, namely close blood relatives. The manner in which mates are selected varies enormously from society to society. In many areas of the world it is still the accepted practice to choose a spouse for one's own children of marriageable age. Thus the elders, in this case the parents, choose the marriage partners of their children because of the cultural belief that love, if these societies entertain such a notion, is something which is expected to develop from rather than precede the marriage.

The children of marriages require a social placing in order to facilitate such matters as inheritance and status succession. One way of doing this is to relate offspring to already existing positions, namely the father's, mother's, or both. These lines of decent can be counted solely through the male line (*patrilineal*), the female line (*matrilineal*), or through either (*bilateral*). Quite broad patterns are to be seen in the places where those married take up residence. In a system favouring a *patrilocal residence* the newly married take up residence near or with the parents of the groom or husband, whereas in one favouring *matrilocal residence* they live near the wife's family. *Local residence* means that residence is socially sanctioned with either the bride or groom's family, usually on a permanent basis. A small number of societies have a pattern known as *avunculocal residence* where the newly weds live with the family of an uncle. The practice which we are most familiar with in South Africa, the States and Europe is known as *neolocal residence*, in which a household is established separate from both parental families.

Some social anthropologists have attempted to relate residential practices with other, and especially economic, activities. For example, matrilocal residence is claimed by some to be predominantly found among agricultural societies where women both tend and own the land. Very often, of course, two or more of these patterns exist side by side.

A further distinction occurs between the *extended* and *nuclear* family. The former includes a married pair and their offspring, and is a socially recognised kinship unit that in addition includes one or more others related who are defined as kin. The nuclear family is a kinship unit limited to a married pair and their children.

If we take a cross-cultural perspective we find that many of our cherished values are drastically challenged. In most societies the notion of romantic love does not exist and individuals have their spouses chosen for them. In the West we have legalised one wife to one husband at a time. Of all societies in the world only a small percentage insist on this. Similarly most societies regard it as amusing that individuals should not have extra-marital or pre-marital sexual experience. Also in many societies age differences of the partners are grossly in excess of the twenty or twenty-five years that the West allows.

The traditional family form has undergone substantial transformation in the present century primarily because the nuclear family is more adapted to the changing social and economic conditions. This is mainly because of the following reasons.

1. Loss of functions

There is a loss of functions which were formerly the province of the family. Many affective and educative functions of the family are now taken over by schools and welfare institutions.

2. Geographic mobility

Fluctuations in the economic market has meant increased mobility in the labour force. Both in Western societies and traditional societies the labour force is attracted to where work opportunities exist. This is not possible if obligations are maintained to a patrilocal residence.

3. Social mobility

Unlike previous centuries modern society is mobile, with increasing emphasis on improvement of status. Individuals within a family may well draw away in terms of life-style and social enhancement.

4. Advantages of small families

Increasingly, the small family with a very limited number of dependent children makes the nuclear family less of an economic liability.

There are several dysfunctions connected with the nuclear family, however. These include a high emotional expectation which is not always fulfilled; over-dependence on one breadwinner; in times of emotional upset a nuclear family is thrown in upon itself; and the old have no real meaningful role.

	Female population in millions	% of women in labour force	% of women who are lite-rate	% in elementary and second-ary school	% in University	Female life expectancy	Estimated births per woman	Females as % of national legislature
AUSTRALIA	7,6	33	99	74	25	78	1,9	10
BRAZIL	68,2	23	76	64	18	67	3,7	1
CHINA	519,0	37	55	38	1	72	2,3	21
DENMARK	2,6	38	99	81	29	78	1,6	27
GHANA	7,0	41	43	44	*	55	6,5	*
HUNGARY	5,6	43	98	77	13	75	2,0	31
ITALY	29,4	29	95	72	23	77	1,7	7
MOROCCO	11,9	16	22	36	4	62	5,7	0
U.S.	120,1	39	99	84	61	78	2,1	5
U.S.S.R.	147,1	49	98	69	22	75	2,4	33

*Not available
Source: Selected countries from Women . . . A World Survey by Ruth Leger Sivard

Courtship and marriage patterns in the marriage market

With increasing freedom in the West to court with and engage in sexual experimentation, it is a little surprising to discover that individuals tend to marry partners who share similar social characteristics. Sociologists call this process *homogamy*. It is called a 'marriage market' by some because both sexes normally try to 'sell' their wares, whether it be physical attractiveness, humour, intelligence, career prospects or one's family status.

1. Age

We tend to marry spouses of a similar age. Usually the male is older than the female and the average age difference is 2.1 years.

2. Religion

We generally marry those of the same religious faith although inter-denominational marriages between Protestants is quite common. In certain social situations such as Northern Ireland, it is taboo for a Protestant to marry a Roman Catholic.

3. Social class

We tend to marry within the same social class because generally we mix and live socially with similar classes and share the same general outlook on life, including class-specific tastes and interests.

4. Education

We generally marry those with the same educational background or the same level of intelligence.

5. Race

We tend to marry within our own racial and ethnic background. Although in most countries there is no longer legislation against interracial marriages it is still very much socially disapproved of.

6. Propinquity

We marry people from the same neighbourhood or workplace, usually, rather than from more distant areas.

Family breakdown

It we take four main functions of the family held to be of central importance, the sexual, the economic, the 'reproductive' and the educational, we can examine them in relation to a popular thesis that in modern urban and industrial society such functions have been eroded.

The sexual function

Evidence to substantiate extra-marital or pre-marital intercourse and its frequency abounds. We must, however, realise that we must exercise caution in relation to the material which by its very nature is open to misinterpretation and error. If we accept the evidence of Kinsey (which is open to criticism) there is some suggestion that pre-marital and extra-marital behaviour has increased, but of course we are lacking any real base figure from which to draw any conclusions as to

FROM: *SUNDAY TRIBUNE*, 27 SEPTEMBER 1987

DEADLY DADDIES

The Volk's fatal flaw . . . family men who kill their loved ones 'for kindness'

File of family murders

IN the past six months, there have been at least seven family murders:

- A Malvern man killed his pregnant wife and himself.

- A Secunda police sergeant's young widow gassed herself and her three children.

- A Bryanston man killed his wife and two teenaged sons with a crossbow and shot himself with a pistol.

- A Tarlton man killed his wife, wounded his daughter and son-in-law, and then shot himself.

- A Randfontein woman has pleaded guilty to provisional charges of shooting her husband and gassing three of her five children.

- An air force officer shot himself and his son.

- A man killed his Rustenburg lover and her two children and, some time later, himself.

A DEVOTED, gentle family man and head of the home—who believes in life after death and is feeling hopeless and helpless—could turn into the killer of his own family.

This is the view of pastoral theologian Jan van Arkel, who has done a study of an increasingly and seemingly peculiarly South African phenomenon: family killings.

Mr van Arkel, a senior lecturer at the University of South Africa, believes that the South African community is heading for more such killings.

His research has shown that the group who potentially could commit this type of crime—murder of family members before the murderer commits suicide—seems to be urban Afrikaans men.

This is partly because of the nature of Afrikaner families, which are often close-knit and patriarchal while English families tend to be 'more democratic and companionable,' he says.

He argues against the theory of other concerned experts that family killings are an extension of the pattern where violence is found in homes.

'People who kill members of their family before killing themselves can be extending their love to those they kill.

'They are the sort of people who normally would never harm anyone in their family.

'The warning signs are when these people send out a message of hopelessness and helplessness in crisis situations. They might tell someone that they see no future for themselves,' Mr van Arkel said.

In Protestant homes where the teaching of churches often portray life on earth as less rewarding than in Heaven, the desperate potential killer may make the decision that death is a better option than life, he argues.

'Even if they are not religious they may regard death as a better option.

'Their reasoning, when it comes to their families, is that the option they choose for themselves is also the best option for other family members and killing them in preparation to their own suicide is an act of mercy,' he said.

'Then they usually go through with it.

'At the time there is an extreme upsurge in violence. They might pump three to six bullets, almost emptying the firearm, into a loved one, not because they do not want that loved one to feel pain or harm—death must be instantaneous,' he said.

'Once they have killed their spouse and the eldest child, they reason that leaving younger children as orphans would be wrong, so they are also killed.'

After each such case, surviving relatives, the police and experts give jealousy, financial ruin, potential criminal charges or other factors as the reasons for the killings.

Mr van Arkel believes that these are only the final triggers that leads to the deaths.

He has tried to find out why these killings are prevalent in South Africa and why, because of the dearth of literature overseas on the subject, it seems to be more of a problem locally than elsewhere.

'In our society there is justification for violence—if it is for a good cause. Justified violence is the message we get from the Government and from the liberation movements.

'Killing is justified if it will help create a better option.

'Ours is also an individualistic society where we are expected to deal with our own pain and not ask for help.

'Whites also feel very uncertain about the future of the country and what is in store for their children.'

MOM TELLS OF HER SHOOTING ORDEAL

JOSEPHINE KINNEAR cannot forget the terrible evening 14 months ago when—in a moment of confusion and utter despair—she put a gun to the chest of her three-year-old daughter and pulled the trigger.

Seconds later she shot herself while her husband's lover taunted her on the telephone.

But fate intervened and both survived.

This week Mrs Kinnear (34) told The Sunday Tribune of those terrible seconds as her daughter, Clariss, lay covered in blood at her feet and she felt death was the only answer to her problems.

'I shot my baby daughter as an act of love. I could not leave her alone with all the problems and the hell on earth.'

After shooting Clariss, Mrs Kinnear turned the firearm on herself. The bullet penetrated her breast and missed her heart by a fraction.

Last November the attractive blonde was given a suspended three-year sentence for attempted murder.

'People asked me how I could have done such a thing, but at that moment when I pulled the trigger I didn't think of anything,' Mrs Kinnear recalled.

'I cannot describe the pain and suffering I went through after the shooting.

'Everytime I see little Clariss playing or look at myself in a mirror I remember that dreadful day.

'But looking back at the shooting I can only thank God that we are still alive.

'I realise it was totally selfish to do such a thing.

'But I feel good that God gave Clariss and I a second chance to live. For this I cannot thank Him enough'.

Mrs Kinnear said she paid dearly for what she did.

'But all I think of now is the happiness of my kids . . . and that life goes on'.

how great the trend has been. Sexual permissiveness is the result of the separation of the *procreational* function of sex and the *recreational* function. The fact that contraceptives are freely available means that the recreational aspect can be practised without fear of pregnancy even outside of marriage. The notion of exclusive and mutually gratifying sexual relationships solely with one's partner is being drastically eroded.

The economic function

The industrial revolution has meant that the centre of production has moved from the home or 'cottage industries' to the factory system, necessitating a process in which only selected members of the family are employed. This process of industrialisation away from the home is for consumption within the home, and the family as an economic unit has changed to one which consumes rather than produces. The family appears to be the chief unit of consumption in society, spending most of the wage on such needs or requirements as food, clothing, housing, and so on. The family is also of importance in the passing on of inherited wealth or property and a vehicle for legal arrangements to facilitate the inheritance of capital.

The socialisation function

In many ways this function is the most apparent. In the last century the educational system has grown at an enormous rate with specialised institutions providing pre-school, school and post-school facilities. Thus many of the processes that were previously carried on inside the home are now catered for far away from the family. Nevertheless, much of the work in the sociology of education is concerned with the way in which the home and family situation complement the educational system rather than existing independently of one another. It might be better to use the word 'interact' rather than 'complement' because many families, principally those of semi-skilled and unskilled manual workers are at variance with the educational system and its values and consequently tend to perform more badly, or get less out of, the school and other institutions.

The productive system

We mean by this not the biological reproductive function of the family but the way in which the family 'passes on' its social statuses and positions. In spite of preventative contraceptive methods illigitimacy is greater than ever. In many cases the fetus, instead of being aborted is retained by the mother after birth and forms an incomplete nuclear family. In a great number of instances the child is adopted by a nuclear family other than its own procreative one. A large number of children become institutionalised or fostered. All these instances of the impairment of the family's reproductive function demonstrate the way in which legitimate social statuses and positions, in other words social descent, is not carried out in the normal manner.

The decline of the nuclear family One of the problems sociologists and social historians concern themselves with is whether the emergence of the nuclear family facilitated the development of industrialisation or whether it emerged as a consequence of the industrialisation process. The first view sees the emergence of a mobile, untied and 'rational' labour force as a pre-condition for industrialisation. Such a force would be best provided for by the nuclear family, with its stress on allocation by achievement rather than ascription. The second view sees the industrial process as rendering superfluous the extended family, by a process of social evolution. In other words, because the industrial process required ease of mobility and lack of encumbrance, the extended family became less of a necessity. It is difficult to reach any real agreement. Some studies, for example, have shown that the family of the seventeenth and eighteenth centuries was not so very different from that of today, with an average size of between four and five.

The nuclear family contains elements of both *consanguine* (related by blood to all members of the family of origin) and *conjugal* (the parents in the nuclear family must *not* be related by blood) relationships. Some sociologists have said that it is the conjugal element that was conductive to industrialisation. Such a system allows greater flexibility and mobility in terms of the labour market. Because it is neolocal (each couple sets up its own household) the conjugal family has weak kinship networks, which permit greater flexibility and mobility. However, these neolocal, independent households themselves produce problems such as the ambiguity of the older people in society, the denigration of 'wisdom' as opposed to specialised technical knowledge, and the inability to deal with disruptions such as the children left over from divorce or separation. The effect of women forming a large part of the labour force of any industrialised country—and of that labour force a large number are married—produces problems for women in carrying the burden of both a household and work. Industrial societies are striving, also, to produce some sort of balance between population and fertility, and nations undergoing industrialisation are attempting to reduce the birth rate.

Evidence from several empirical studies shows that so-called nuclear families see their kin quite frequently (67 % once a week and 20 % more than once a week). Other studies have stressed the importance of family 'friends' and suggested that 'isolated families are largely a figment of the imagination.' The main thrust appears to be that the extended family is still thriving but in a social rather than an occupational form. Bell showed the middle-class extended family in Britain to be a functioning social entity. Some studies have shown this contact to as high as three quarters of children (married) who have contacted their parents within the period of one week. American data suggests that the higher the social class the greater the contact. The Firth studies in London and the Young and Wilmott research in Bethnall Green and in Woodford have shown that in these areas nuclear families in the usual sense simply do not exist, and the existence of the extended family must be assumed for the purposes of analysis.

Divorce: an institutionalized arrangement for the erosion of family groupings South Africa rates third in divorce in the world but the U.S.A. and Russia are higher. Over 50 % of all recent American marriages will end in divorce, the average length being seven years. The introduction of legal aid for divorce helped to accelerate the incidence. A 'no fault' divorce is a recent introduction in most countries and allows divorce on the grounds of incompatibility. Childless marriages which feature in divorce constitute under 30 %, the remainder leave behind children who inevitably suffer. Divorced individuals suffer from extreme loneliness, feelings of inadequacy and isolation. The mortality rate for the divorced is considerably higher than for the married. Although the mothers are usually awarded the custody of the children, fathers may also obtain custody, or joint custody may be arranged in certain circumstances.

Those who get divorced are usually those who marry very young, those who marry after only a brief acquaintance, urban residents, and where the wife is in good employment. Divorce does not represent a vote against marriage as most of the divorced remarry within a short period of time. Divorce itself exists in society as a socially sanctioned arrangement when the marriage contract can be terminated and the family dissolved.

Causes of marital breakdown Those who marry very young inevitably change their personalities and 'grow out' of their partners. Often the person one has married is unable to cope with new demands, or is perceived as being unable to do so. Similarly with marriages that dissolve after the children have left the home where individuals are thrown back upon each other after a busy period of child-rearing and find it difficult to re-orientate their lives to each other. Apart from the homogamous process mentioned above we could mention one's parental image or one's personality needs. Sometimes this choice is reversed; that is, people will become attracted to those with an opposite or dissimilar personality, and who are opposite or dissimilar to one's parental image.

An undisputed contribution to marital breakdown is made by sexual difficulties, whether it be non-consummation, failure of coitus or sexual deviation. Under this heading we can include sexual permissiveness. Very often doctors and health workers in general are ill-equipped to deal with marital breakdown.

In general we can list some main social factors, as follows:

1. A greater tolerance of the divorce action resulting in less stigmatisation;
2. The existence of alternatives for either partner; for example, a divorced woman can either support herself or claim maintenance in a way she certainly could not have done fifty years ago.
3. There are correspondingly fewer social pressures to stay married.

More specifically we can list the following points as contributing to divorce:

1. A more tolerant religious climate due to secularisation;
2. A more tolerant legal climate;
3. A high density of urban living with the accompanying anonymity of social behavour;
4. The growth of industrialisation has meant the minimisation of the family as a productive unit, and a stress on its consumption;
5. Greater geographical mobility has decreased neighbourhood constraints;
6. High expectations of romantic love engendered by advertising and television may not be met in reality;
7. The growing economic independence of women;
8. The over-dependence on mutual support within the nuclear family cannot always be sustained.

Adjustment to divorce

Divorce, like death, erodes the family unit. Goode (1964) has listed six ways in which the life situation is affected by either death or divorce:

1. Sexual satisfaction ceases;
2. Loss of security, love, friendship;
3. The children lose an adult role model;
4. The domestic work-role for the remaining spouse is increased, especially when there are young children involved;
5. Economic problems increase, especially if the husband has departed;
6. Household tasks and responsibilities are redistributed.

Current issues in the family

Black families are invariably one-parent families headed by a female. Half of black births are to teenage mothers who are unmarried. The cycle of poverty and deprivation has serious social implications of crime, violence and delinquency.

In America the question of abortion is seriously disputed, usually on moral or religious grounds. It is estimated that over 4 000 abortions are carried out each day. The two camps of pro-choice and pro-life are distinguished from each other by a number of socio-economic characteristics.

There are millions of children of divorced parents. Marital disorganisation can be directly related to delinquency, inadequate socialisation, sexual deviance, lack of success in later marriage and poor school performance. The social consequences are enormous.

Changing and future family patterns

In this century marked differences can be discerned in the pattern of the family in all modern, industrialised, and post-industrial countries:

1. Women have improved their status considerably both in the politico-legal field and economically. More and more are now released

into the labour force, benefit from higher and further education, and so have attained a degree of independence previously unknown.

2. There is a more egalitarian sharing of household tasks where the woman is herself employed in the labour market, although this tends to vary according to the socio-economic class of the spouses.

3. The nuclear unit is gradually being replaced by single-parent families. In 1986, in South Africa alone, there were 23 134 divorces, over 60 % of which occurred in the Transvaal. In America over 20 % of all births are illegitimate and over 26 % of families are one-parent. In Britain in the last thirty-five years there has been a growing number of *households* (from 15 million to 20 million) which is not due simply to the increase in population. One of the reasons is that many women who have either survived their husbands, are divorced or are rearing children out of marriage, are finding themselves playing the role of household (or family) head.

4. More and more couples are *cohabiting*. In America over 2 million unmarried people of the opposite sex share a household. This figure tripled between 1970 and 1983.

5. Children are increasingly viewed as not merely an economic asset but as humans in their own rights, and this results in greater permissiveness in child-rearing techniques.

6. Serial monogamy, where people marry more than once, is on the increase as divorce becomes easier to obtain.

7. There is increasing concern by people entering marriage to 'make it work'. This is done by a variety of methods including preparatory classes and a greater interest in sexual variation and techniques that will improve intercourse.

8. Greater geographical mobility has fasciliated increased flexibility in choice. We no longer have to marry people from our own village.

9. Many couples now make a conscious decision to remain childless.

10. Experimental patterns have been introduced such as communes, open marriage, and even homosexual couples marrying and adopting.

Socialisation and gender formation The important groundwork of what makes us feel, think and act is firmly laid down in the early years. The distinguishing characteristic of humans is that their behaviour, apart from that which is instinctual, is learned during the lifetime of the individual. It is this learning which sociologists term *socialization*, the study of which brings together sociology, social psychology and social anthropology. Individuals become socialized by interaction with others in the society; that is, the sum total of what makes us human is learned from social interaction with others, with certain limits which might be set by heredity. Childhood, or initial or primary socialization, refers to the learning process which takes place in the earlier years of a person's development, usually the first ten years. Adult or secondary socialization refers to learning through interaction which occurs after childhood.

An important part of this process is the physical handling which an individual experiences from the mother or mother-surrogate. This is generally termed maternal love or affection. As we shall see later, children reared in institutions tend to be maladaptive both in childhood and in later life.

The distinguishing characteristic of learned behaviour itself is the acquisition of language, which begins with the child's crying. Once the child realises that this alters the behaviour of others towards him, because they now give attention, the baby receives a further impetus.

Part of the process of socialization is by imitation. We learn to imitate the behaviour of our parents, siblings and peer group. Any impairment in this learning process generally results in some impairment in development and consequently in the individual.

Role learning

Role learning is an attempt to determine how we can later play certain adult roles. The little girl learns to be like her mother, or to play the mother role, just as the little boy learns to be like his father by playing father roles. These roles consequently become part of our total behavioural repertoire.

The process by which a distinct *self* emerges is one which is unique to humans. Cooley (1864–1929) saw the self as emerging in early childhood and then being constantly reevaluated during the course of our lives. He introduced the term *looking-glass self* which refers to a social mirror in which we can view how others react to us. By watching the way in which others react or respond to us we can tell whether we are ugly, popular, beautiful, etc. There are three steps to the development of the self:

1. We imagine how we appear to others. Generally there are significant others such as our family or close friends. Do we appear intelligent, loving and respectable?
2. We interpret the actions of others. Do they see us as we are trying to present ourselves or not?
3. We develop a self-concept by using our interpretation of others' judgements to develop impressions or feelings about ourselves.

These ideas were taken further by GH Mead (1863–1931) who developed the concept of *social interaction* which is the interaction between people through various symbols such as language, signs and gestures. The mind itself, Mead argued, is a social product. He introduced the idea of *role-taking* (taking the role of other people in order to understand better either our own or others' viewpoints), *particular other* (we internalize in childhood the expectations of our parents), and *generalized other* (attitudes, expectations and viewpoints of society as a whole). By an examination of children's activities Mead distinguished three stages of role-taking:

FROM: SUNDAY TRIBUNE, 24 AUGUST 1986

THE BISEXUAL WAY

So what's wrong with sharing one's body with a friend after a tough game of rugby?

WOMEN'S lib move over—a new revolution in sexual behaviour is on our doorstep: bisexuality.

The new generation of young people is not about to be forced by the fears and fancies of the Moral Majority into believing that sex for procreation is the only type of sex there is, nor into accepting the 'straight' stereotype as the only valid means of sexual expression.

The claim that we are 'born' heterosexual is as blatantly false as the rest of our insecure straight society's pet prejudices: in truth it is culture, not nature, which forces the straightjacket of sexual roles and stereotypes upon us.

I can think of few sights as pitiful as an adult man calling upon religious claptrap and unscientific mumbo jumbo to justify his stultifying rigidity of sexual orientation and hysterical fear of gay people—it certainly failed to engender any respect for my parents into me.

After all, what could be more relaxing and natural than to share one's body with a friend after a tough game of rugby or demanding session in the gym? Why, indeed, should any red-blooded male be denied the pleasures of such full friendships, yes, even of masculine love, with his fellow men, merely for the sake of your insecurity?

Like the great civilisations of Europe before us, we refuse to sacrifice our minds and freedom for the chains of straight society's small-minded definitions or categories: nor will we clamber into the closet with you on those balmy days when you are prepared to waive your moral objections in the name of discreet pleasure.

Keep your approval: we do not need it. There is more fulfilment to be gained from a year of freedom and sheer good fun than from a lifetime of subservience to any of society's holy cows. We are young, free, and the future is ours.

Why not join us in our celebration of life, instead of condemning us idly from the sidelines?

LOVER BOY
Port Elizabeth

Imitation

This occurs up to the age of three and consists of the child imitating someone near in a spontaneous but only occasional gesture or word.

Play

Later the child learns to dress up as 'mummy' or play at being 'teacher' thus developing the ability to view the world from another perspective.

Games

Yet later children learn organised games which consist of rules, anticipating other players, etc.

Formation and changing of attitudes

Attitudes are learned from experience, both direct and indirect. They are states of readiness or predispositions to action, which means that to say that someone has an attitude means that there is a probability of a defined behaviour in a defined situation. To say that an individual is patriotic does not mean that this attitude is being constantly displayed but that given certain conditions such as the national flag being displayed, it will be. Attitudes are favourable or unfavourable behaviour tendencies to objects, persons, situations or ideas. They are *personal* if possessed only by oneself; they are *social* if they are shared by a number of individuals or large groups of people.

Attitudes form an important part of both our everyday lives and our socilization process. The nurse has attitudes towards patients, the shopkeeper to the customers, and the teacher to the pupils. We also have attitudes towards capital punishment, the ANC, pre-marital sex and birth control, these concepts acting as stimuli that produce a variety of feelings that cause us to think and act in particular ways.

It is generally agreed that attitudes are formed and developed as follows:

1. In the first five years of life in the parent–child relationship and in the child-rearing programme;
2. In later life by influence by association between individuals, groups and institutions;
3. Throughout life, by individual and unique experiences.

Social anthropology has brought us a wealth of instances of varying attitudes. The late Margaret Mead, in an early study, studied the mountain dwelling Arapesh, the river dwelling Mundugumor, and the lake dwelling Tchambuli, all of whom show an amazing diversity of attitude formation. The New Guinea Tchambuli, for example, have reversed the normally accepted male role in society. The women in this tribe are dominant, aggressive and industrious, while the men are effeminate, graceful and artistic. The women also dominate in both economic and sexual matters, and in the latter take the initiative. We will see below when we look at *gender*, that this is different from biological sex. Mead demonstrated quite clearly that we have built-in expectations of males being aggressive and females submissive.

The socilization process, through which individuals acquire personality and learn the way of life of their society, is acquired through social interaction. *Language* is an important element of the socialization process to which we will return. In addition the individual has to learn how to *think* and how to *feel.* The intellectual function of thought has been analysed as developing in four stages, as follows:

1. The sensorimotor stage

Until about the age of two the intelligence of children is expressed solely through physical and sensory contact. Initially unable to differentiate themselves from the world they still cannot think about the world without possessing language.

2. The preoperational stage

The child is unable to perform many simple mental functions because he or she lacks concepts such as speed, weight, causality, number, etc. This lasts until the age of about seven.

3. The concrete operational state

From seven until twelve the child cannot reason abstractly or hypothetically but can handle concrete operations.

4. The formal operational stage

During and after adolescence we achieve abstract, formal, thought.

Although all individuals are capable of proceeding through these stages not all do so because they may be largely absent from their own cultures. Also, although the process is similar the actual content of what we learn is dependent on the social world around us.

We learn to feel in much the same way, mastering through progressive stages, primarily related to age, feelings such as empathy, hate, love and envy. We must consequently learn to interpret our emotions and, very importantly, under what social conditions to express them. Obviously, different cultures 'allow' different emotions to be expressed at certain times and by specified individuals.

Agents of socialization

These include a number of categories such as individuals, organisations and groups, which are particularly important in the socialization process.

1. The family

To the child the family offers an all-encompassing environment through which it learns its emotions, language, norms and values. It often is an instrument for passing down *personality traits.* Thus children of divorced parents are more likely themselves to become divorced, children who are abused are more likely to have one or both parents who were abused, and children of alcoholics or heavy drinkers are themselves more likely to become so. Also, being born into a family means being born into a particular point in the social structure, acquiring an ascribed status of religion, class, race, etc. To a large extent this pre-determines the kind of social interaction the individual will experience. The social class of origin thus 'programmes' a whole set of values and norms.

2. The school

The educational process is formally manifested in the school where a whole barrage of both explicit and implicit values are conveyed. Indoctrination can be overt or covert, the latter in the form of the *hidden curriculum* (children learn a whole set of practices and values which prepare them for whichever society they are being 'schooled' for).

3. The peer group

This is a group of the same age and characteristics as the individual. Increasingly, and especially after adolescence, this becomes a dominant influence in terms of attitudes and values.

4. The mass media

This has an increasingly powerful socializing influence on the young but whether the effects are positive or negative, is not clear.

The nature/nurture ratio

A totally barren debate among social scientists has been the relative influence of *nature* (heredity) and *nurture* (learning). Quite obviously, we realise now that both influences are vital to the socialization process. However, to say that one is 60 % and the other 40 % or vice versa is not only futile but impossible to guage.

Socially deprived environments: human impairment

Feral children

Feral children have been reported from time to time. These are children reportedly discovered running wild and having being reared by animals, usually wolves. When found these children were reported to have the posture and characteristics of animals. None of them survived after captivity. Unfortunately the evidence for such children is open to dispute, for instance they were never examined by skilled investigators. Also, their history *before* their discovery is not documented and therefore we cannot rule out some form of handicap such as autism.

Children reared in isolation

Children reared in isolation offer clearer evidence as to the *learnt* nature of human development. Animals when reared in isolation are still recognisably cats, dogs and budgerigars. This is because they rely not so much on *language* but on innate mechanisms which transmit the developmental messages. There are a number of examples of children reared in extreme isolation. A girl called Anna was discovered in 1937 who had been deprived of normal contact and care for almost all of her first six years of life. She died in 1942, aged approximately ten and a half, of haemorrhagic jaundice. When found she could not walk, talk, or exhibit any intelligent human behaviour. Two years after being discovered she had grasped the rudiments of social living, and could walk, although she was unable to talk. A comparable case was that of Isabelle, discovered shortly after Anna, and approximately six-and-a-half years old. She was unable to speak and to all intents and purposes her actions were those of a six-month old infant. By the age of fourteen she was almost normal.

Both these and similar children, being deprived of social interaction, lacked normal physical, psychological and social development. The interactive process can be divided into **non-verbal** (*visual*) **communication** and **verbal communication**. In the former we include bodily contact, physical propinquity (nearness), bodily orientation, posture, physical appearance, facial expression, head and hand position and movement, and direction of gaze. In the latter we include all spoken commands and praises, etc. An individual reared in such socially deprived circumstances is denied a situation in which any of these can be learned.

The Harlow experiments

These experiments were carried out in Wisconsin, U.S.A., with socially deprived rhesus monkeys. Previous experiments had been performed on sheep, goats and puppies. The Harlow experiments achieved social isolation by not allowing individual monkeys any means of approach to monkey playmates. Monkeys reared in this way developed unusual and psychotic behaviour such as (*a*) passive sitting and vacant staring; (*b*) repetitive stereotyped movements; (*c*) hands clasped on head and constant rocking backwards and forwards, a pattern also displayed by orphanage children.

From 6 to 12 months more severe social effects appear, and when placed with normal monkeys the deprived lack any noticeable demonstration of friendship. None of the deprived monkeys (male) developed adequate heterosexual behaviour, although for females the prognosis was 50 %. Impregnated females rejected their offspring.

Next raised were monkeys without mothers but with access to other infant monkeys. No sexual abnormality resulted because lack of normal mothering was compensated for by infant play and affection. The Harlows went on to compare monkeys raised by dummy or *surrogate* mothers and those raised by real mothers. Although the former were slow in developing patterns, as time progressed there were no noticeable differences. Next, infants with their own mothers were prevented from contacting other infants. The mothers became over-solicitous, although they provided compensation for infant deprivation.

Finally, the effects of total deprivation were studied with the results shown in the table below. Although these experiments are important, we must temper our conclusions by reminding ourselves that these are monkey communities, and that there may be no direct analogy with human society.

DURATION	RESULT
After three months	Total shock and self-imposed starvation
After six months	Delay and repression of capacity for social interaction
After twelve months	Cessation of all play: incapable of survival

Institutionalised and motherless children

These were studied in England by John Bowlby. His work showed that certain experiences in the socialization process produced characters that were affectionless and delinquent. These experiences were (a) lack of opportunity for forming an attachment to a mother figure during the first three years; (b) deprivation lasting from three to more than six months during the first three or four years; (c) changes from one mother figure to another during the same period. The adverse effects of the deprivation could last either during the period of separation, during the period immediately after restoration to maternal care, or permanently.

Bowlby stressed the necessity of having a psychic organiser, the mother figure, during certain critical periods of a child's formation. These critical periods include that when the child is in the process of establishing a relationship with a clearly defined person, usually achieved by six months of age, and up to his third birthday, during which stage the child needs the almost constant presence of the mother figure. The final critical period is when the child is becoming capable of maintaining a relationship with the mother in her absence. The work of the Harlows appears to substantiate any move away from too rigid a connection between mother and child. In monkey infants, at least, lack of a mother relationship can be adequately compensated for by allowing for periods of play with other monkeys of the same age.

The social formation of ability

A study of socially deprived environments is not limited simply to large-scale psychological effects. Studies of canal boat and mill children have shown that a poor social and cultural environment produce a correspondingly poor I.Q. (intelligence quotient). Studies of orphanages have shown that when children are removed from an inferior background to an enriched nursery-school environment a considerable increase in I.Q. results, although little improvement is evident after the age of seven.

Bernstein's socio-linguistic theory

This is an important step in the sociological study of language origins and development (socio-linguistics). Bernstein suggests that there are two types of language spoken in any country, that of the working and that of the middle class. The latter is articulate, rich and flexible, and provides a vehicle for logical argument by its vocabulary and form. The former is limited in vocabulary, adjectives, conjunctions, adverbs, and

FROM: SUNDAY TIMES, 23 OCTOBER 1988

LIFE AFTER THE MAN OF THE HOUSE BECOMES A WOMAN

Bill wants to become Billie—and the Campbell family is learning to cope with his sex-change

Instead of recoiling in horror, Christine Campbell is sticking by her husband as he undergoes a sex change. In fact, she says they will remain best of friends for the rest of their lives. LIZ HODGKINSON reports

TO outward appearances, the Campbells seem like any other ordinary, happy family. There is Bill, a management consultant, who goes off to work every morning in a neat, dark business suit; his American wife Christine, 35; and their three young children Susie, Kenny, and William. They live near Manchester in a pleasant semi-detached house which has bikes in the hall, toys on the floor, and all the usual clutter of family life.

But they are not quite ordinary. At least, Bill Campbell isn't. For slowly and deliberately, in front of his family, he is changing into a woman.

Over the next few weeks Bill will give up his job and throw away his male clothes. Instead of being called Bill, he will be known as Billie. He has had his last man's haircut and is letting his locks grow.

He has started hormone treatment at Manchester's Gender-Identity Clinic to soften his male outline, strip his body of masculine hair, and give him female-type breasts.

He still looks and talks like a man, but over the next few months his whole appearance will undergo a dramatic change. Electrolysis treatment will remove facial hair, and his voice, thanks to speech therapy, will become more like a woman's. Eventually his male organs will be surgically removed.

Bill is biologically and anatomically a normal male, and his interests have always been those usually considered masculine. As a younger man he was a lightweight boxer. He is keen on maths, physics, mech-anical things, inventions, motoring and photography. He is not effeminate, and has never been gay.

An estimated 1 000 Britons in every generation suffer serious confusion over their sexual identity, and Bill is not the first man to undergo the sex-change treatment.

His case is unusual in that he has his wife's support and sympathy. Usually, married transsexuals divorce before the irrevocable transformation, but Bill and Christine intend to stay together.

The usual reaction of spouses is to recoil in horror when they learn that the man they married wants to become a woman. But Bill and Christine reckon they are now closer than ever. They are setting up a business, a petrol and service station. It will be run by two directors called Ms Campbell, who are legally husband and wife.

The two older children have already been put in the picture. Eight-year-old Susie said: 'Mummy and Daddy wanted me to realise that my Daddy still loves me, but that he's got to change and I might lose a few friends. But I won't be losing Lindsay (her best friend), will I, Mummy?' Kenny, seven, declined to comment.

Bill, 38, was born in Manchester, where his parents kept a pub, attended Manchester Grammar School, and went to Oxford Polytechnic. After that he worked in the American solar energy industry and met Christine while running a sales force in Phoenix, Arizona.

Christine said: 'I had just told my mother that I would never ever marry, and six weeks after meeting Bill we got married. Six weeks after that, I became pregnant.'

The Campbells moved to Los Angeles where they set up a solar energy company, eventually employing more than 200 people. When the oil price dropped, they moved to Fiji, and then spent six months in Hawaii. They decided to move to England with their two children four years ago.

Three years after moving to their present home, William, now one, was born. 'Although we are very close, and have always been best friends, we hadn't made love as man and woman for years,' Bill said. 'Then one crazy night we did, and William was the result.'

There won't be any more children, though. The huge doses of female hormone that Bill is taking mean that he can no longer perform as a man.

On the sunny Saturday afternoon when I met Bill and Christine at their home, Bill was wearing a yellow shirt and jeans. He looked completely masculine, apart from two aspects: he was wearing white wedge-heeled women's sandals, and women's breasts were visible through the loose shirt.

This was a 'Bill' rather than a 'Billie' day, although Bill says that as the months go by, it is becoming increasingly difficult for him to wear a man's shirt and tie.

'Now that we've finally come to accept the inevitable, we are happier together than ever,' Christine said. 'Life has been agonisingly stressful for Bill over the past few years because of the strain of trying to live two lives. He feels natural as a woman, but has had to go out into the outside world as a man, and trying to keep the other side secret.'

She still had not got completely used to Bill being a woman. 'I didn't marry a woman, and it will be a major adjustment. The best thing is, that when it's all above board, Bill will be much happier.

'My next challenge will be to start calling him 'Billie'. And then for the rest of my life, I shall have to refer to my husband as 'she'. That's not going to be too easy.

Christine said that, in their marriage, physical sex had never been important. 'We feel that we are meant to be best friends, and professional partners, and this will continue for the rest of our lives.'

Liz Hodginson is the author of Bodyshock: The Truth About Changing Sex, published by Columbus Books, £5.95.

CHRISTINE'S STORY

'WE married in 1979, and as far as I knew Bill was just the same as any other man. Then one night he got into bed wearing one of my nightgowns, which I thought was extremely odd. It puzzled me a lot but at the time I knew nothing about transsexualism, and had hardly even heard of the word.

'After that, I tried to ignore Bill's occasional dressing up in my clothes. I suppose I imagined it would go away in time. But then he told me that all his life, ever since he could remember, he had wanted to be female.

'I was horribly shocked, but I tried to come to terms with it and as time went on, I came to realise it was something deep-seated, rather than an occasional aberration. Bill started to see a counsellor when we were in California, and I went too, as I wanted to share what he was going through, and try to understand it.

'It took me ages to accept that Bill was a transsexual, and I had to get things clear in my own brain. I thought: if I'm not married to a man, what am I? If we stayed together would we be considered lesbian, or what? There have been many times when I've thought: Why me?

'But then I realised I had fallen in love with a person, with Bill's character and personality, rather than his body, and that won't change. The essential part of him won't alter. So now, particularly over the past year, I've accepted that we soon will be two women living together. We won't divorce, we won't separate, but will see this through together.

'One of the reasons we are setting up our own business, rather than being employed, is because then it doesn't matter who you are so long as you are providing a good service. We decided we had to do this, as Bill can no longer go to work pretending to be a man.

'The children will have a father who no longer looks like a father, and this will be difficult for them. We've also got to cope with what other people might think and say. Some of our friend's know, others don't, and we have agonised over the best way of telling everybody. But really, there is no easy way, no best way.

'But I know that Bill, there is no choice. He cannot continue to live as a man.'

BILL'S STORY

LIKE most transsexuals, Bill Campbell knew from the age of about four that something was badly wrong, and that he should have been a girl. 'As with most people like myself, the feeling has come and gone in waves.'

'When I met Chrissie and we started a family, I hoped it would all go away, that I could put it behind me. But every now and again, the beast would rear its head and now I know I have got to go through with the complete transformation. life is simply unliveable in any other way.

'My mother has called me selfish and asked if I can see what I'm doing to the children. She said I would have to move away. But for me, to leave my family would be the same as committing suicide.

'I know that many transsexuals have had to leave their families, and often never see their children again. But just the thought of never seeing my children brings tears to my eyes. For a while, before they knew, life was truly terrible. As soon as I got home from work I would want to change out of my male clothes and put on my female ones. But as I couldn't do it in front of the children, I had to wait until they went to bed.

'One day, though, we decided to let them see me dressed up as Billie, and they laughed and laughed. Then afterwards, they would say: when are you going to dress up as Billie again? I have two different wardrobes, and am looking forward to having a ceremonial bonfire of all my male clothes.

'Chrissie and I have worked out a schedule of things to be achieved, and are going about the changeover in as businesslike a way as possible. We are trying to plan and prepare for it not to be a major upheaval.'

often consists of stereotyped phraseology, one phrase having to perform many functions.

Bernstein distinguished between two types of code, the *elaborated* and *restricted*. In the former, the speaker selects from a relatively wide range of alternatives; in the latter the range of alternatives is severely limited. In both codes the distinguishing characteristic is one of *predictability*, the restricted code possessing a high level of predictability and the elaborated code a low one. The middle class are advantaged because they are socialized into both codes, while the working class is confined to only the restricted code. Ability tests and the academic school curriculum are heavily biased towards the elaborated code.

Children from the relatively deprived environment of the lower working class are also severely handicapped in terms of attitudes and aspirations, these being constantly lower than those of middle-class children with the same I.Q.. Studies of school leavers, for example, have shown that working class children invariably aim at occupations well below their actual level of ability. Children do not choose from the whole range of occupations. Their perceived ability, together with the social and educational milieu in which they grew up, have fixed the area of choice within which they operate.

Although we have concentrated on primary socilization we must not forget the secondary process which continues until death. Many writers have pointed out that the notion of adolescence is a creation of industrial societies. Other less fortunate cultures subject the individual to marriage and employment at an early age. Thus the onset of secondary socilization varies, although in industrial societies it can be said to commence in the mid twenties.

Socialization is viewed as a *morphostatic* process. That is, social structure (the network of social positions to which are assigned tasks and responsibilities) carried on in time, even though the occupants of social positions change. Society changes the raw biological individual into a socialized being because individuals learn roles in an interactive situation. By taking the roles of others we adopt the perspectives of others in relation to ourselves. These others vary in significance and the others become merged or generalised over time. Some, such as Dennis Wrong, have argued that we are *over-socialized*, by which he means that we must not forget our biological nature. Very often the transmission of culture can do violence to our socialized bodily drives. This results in the repressed and frustrated individual whose actions are subsequently designated as deviant. Impairment often produces deviance.

Gender socialization

This is yet another aspect of the process we have discussed above. The sexes differ biologically in *genes* (males have an X and a Y chromosome, females have two X chromosomes), *hormones*, and *anatomy*. Psychologically there are also differences in evidence from infancy. John

FROM: *SUNDAY TRIBUNE*, 24 AUGUST 1986

AT LAST, I WILL BE A REAL MAN!

The pain, trauma and the tears of a girl's long battle to shed her female form and live as a man

NINETEEN years ago Catherine 'Junior' Schwerin was born at the Groote Schuur Hospital in Cape Town, in December this year she will be born there again—this time as a man.

Her life, since the tender age of nine, when she realised she was not what people would term a normal little girl, has been nightmarish.

Junior has lost everything in her unending battle to try to make those around her realise that all she wants is to be a complete male.

This need has driven her to two unsuccessful suicide bids, into the dark world of gay clubs where she felt at home with people who understood her, through harrowing days of loneliness and months of shock treatment at Tara Mental Hospital in the Transvaal and finally jail.

Her parents have disowned her and former friends now shun her. Often when people see her in the streets dressed as a man, they shout abuse at her and on a number of occasions she has been assaulted.

And her latest attempt to show her family and the world she can be a man landed her with a criminal record.

Junior was convicted for theft and fraud in the Durban Regional court this week after stealing a cheque book from a family member and writing a R19 226 cheque to buy a car.

She was sentenced to 18 months' imprisonment, suspended for three years.

Junior told the court she was going through a slow process of a sex change and that she is half man and half woman.

'I know it was a crazy thing to do but when I bought that car I did so as Clifford Junior Schwerin. No questions were asked. My appearance is that of a man and this caper was proof that I could be part of this world as a man.

'It has caused me much pain. Three days after I bought the car I was arrested and put into jail.'

Here Junior was humiliated, a humiliation that has caused her to lose her confidence in coping with the transitional stages of her sex change.

'The prison officials did not know what to do with me. They were in a quandary as to whether to put me in the men's section or the women's. Eventually I was put into solitary confinement, where I felt like a monkey behind bars, every warder in the place came to have a peek at me. Obviously word had spread that they had a transsexual in their midst.'

Junior said she experienced her first lesbian relationship during her first year at high school. 'It was a relationship where I was the dominant partner. Although I was female, I felt like a male and to the best of my ability I tried to behave as one, most of the time it came naturally.

'It was a boarding school so we could get away with being together but eventually we were discovered and separated. By that time I had realised fully what I was and all I could do was spend hours in the library reading as much as possible on sex changes.'

A year later Junior was sent to a school in Johannesburg where, at 15, she became involved with lesbians and homosexuals.

She frequented gay clubs where she met a lesbian of 19. 'I loved her so much that I wanted to give up my schooling and move into her flat. This was when my mother found out and she put an immediate stop to the relationship.

'My father reared me as a son. I was not allowed to wear dresses and I played rugby and cricket. I looked like a boy and often people would ask my sister if I was her brother. It must have been my father's greatest dream to have a son.'

She had a mental breakdown during the first term of her matric year and was taken to Tara Mental Hospital after an overdose. At the hospital she befriended a doctor who understood her secret desire. After months of treatment, the doctors treating her concluded that the only way she could lead a normal life was to have a sex change.

As she was underage one of her parents signatures was necessary before the operation could go ahead. Her mother refused and Junior had a nervous breakdown.

'I wrote my final matric exams at Tara and a day before I was discharged I got my results—a pass with four distinctions, one of the very few things in my life I am proud of.

Junior flew to Cape Town and, after months of gruelling skin grafts, blood tests and mental assessments at Groote Schuur Hospital, she was told she was a true transsexual.

'I now had the go-ahead to have the operations. I had enough money—all I needed was that one signature.

'I decided to tell my father and ask him to sign for me but when I approached him all hell broke loose. He was extremely angry. He said he would disown me and that I should change my name as I had brought shame upon my family.'

Junior said her father threatened to have her declared insane but before this could happen her doctors stepped in and overruled her parents.

In February this year she began hormonal treatment which has changed her physical appearance.

'I have become more masculine, I now have to buy shoes two sizes bigger, my voice is changing and I occassionaly have to shave. It is a weird feeling but at least I know my life is taking a definite course.'

In December Junior will undergo a series of operations. She said her uterus will be removed and at a later stage the ovaries will be used to form the testicles. She believes a mastectomy is not necessary as her breasts have diminished due to her hormonal treatment.

The third part of the sex change will be done over three weeks and involves a number of small operations. 'Skin from the inner side of my left leg and flesh from my right hip will be removed to form the male organ. This will then be grafted onto a hole under my arm and after two weeks, if all goes well, it will be placed.'

According to a Durban doctor who has performed numerous sex change operations, the skin and flesh forms a flabby tube in which, at a later stage, plastic tubes are inserted causing the tube to be constantly rigid.

After the operations Junior's dream is to get married. 'I want to get married soon after leaving hospital and one of my main ambitions is to sport a large moustache as I walk down the aisle.'

Money concludes that humans are psychosexually neuter at birth and that gender is independent of biological characteristics. Gender identity is an integral part of adult identity, of the sense of oneself as male or female. Gender role includes 'everything you feel and think, everything you do and say, that indicates—to yourself as well as to others—that you are male or female. Gender identity and gender role are not two different things; they are different aspects of the same thing . . .' (Money and Ehrhardt, 1972) The newborn are wired but not programmed for gender identity and the gender identity option is open at birth even for normal infants, although nothing much can be done after the age of three or four. (Jones, 1984). Gender socialization is learned in the family setting and reinforced throughout one's lifespan by the mass media and other agencies of reinforcement. We are conditioned to accept a gender role that coincides with our biological equipment, we imitate those around us, regarding them as sex models, and we undergo a process of *self-definition* whereby we assign ourselves to one of the sexes and around this choice fashion our social roles and personalities.

In rare instances gender identity does not correspond to an individual's anatomical sex. Such individuals are termed *transsexuals* and often describe themselves as being trapped in the wrong body. Some psychiatrists and sociologists espouse the view that this is an 'inborn' association while others assign its aetiology to sociological variables which have been in some way impaired. (Jones, 1984). Following extensive examination, a decision is sometimes made to reassign the sex, a process usually ending in surgery.

The family and illness The family of procreation not only provides the initial or primary socialization base but biologically endows each of us with a unique combination of genes. Such genes may carry *fragilitas ossium* or *diabetes* in the population generally. Specific genetic disabilities among blacks in South Africa include Transkei Foot, characterised by lateral deviation of the fifth toe and found in the Mpondomise Xhosa community, and Wadoma Foot, a form of ectrodactyly ('ostrich feet') found in an isolated group in the Zambesi Valley. Other genetic diseases common to blacks in other parts of Africa, although rare in Southern Africa, include sickle cell anaemia and glucose 6 phosphate dehydrogenase deficiency. In contrast the whites have a relatively high prevalence of Huntington's Chorea and fibro-cystic disease. Even more common is diabetes, which can also be inherited, although there is a strong environmental factor also present such as lifestyle and family diet.

The family influence on disease can also reach back into the fetal and even pre-fetal stage. Such factors as herpes, malnutrition, and cytomegalovirus all affect the condition of the fetus. More recently Aids has been found to be passed on to the fetus. On perhaps a more common level it is generally well known that smoking slows fetal growth and reduces fetal size. Alcohol consumption and particularly excessive alcohol consumption can lead to fetal malformation.

What some medical sociologists such as Waitzkin (1985) have dubbed 'the second disease', by which they mean diseases which are the result of poverty but which are preventable, is also linked directly to the family. A family's *socio-economic environment*, level of income, education, housing, diet, etc. provide social reservoirs for carrying diseases such as rheumatic fever, T.B. and polio.

As we have mentioned above, the family is the primary agent of socialisation. It is here that attitudes and behavioural responses are generated and assimilated. Neuroses and psychoses are generally believed to be rooted in the family and early or primary socialisation. Schizophrenia, for example, is nowadays largely viewed as a combined set of factors such as lower social class position, genetic susceptibility to stressful life conditions and poor coping patterns. There is some support for the *drift hypothesis* which states that individuals with a predisposition to schizophrenia may 'drift' into lower socio-economic classes than the background of their family or origin would warrent. There is probably a combination of genetic and environmental factors associated with this illness.

There is a family connection with a number of psychiatric and chronic degenerative diseases. Under the former we can include schizophrenia, alcoholism, psychopathy such as child abuse, manic-depressive psychosis and various forms of mental retardation and a host of other psychiatric disorders. The latter includes gout, heart disease, hypertensive disorders, diabetes and ulcerations.

One of the major problems associated with the family and illness is the separation of heredity and environment. In one sense the environmental factor is both what we have at present and also the past history of how this came to be. In this sense it is *very* difficult to separate the two. However, social scientists have endeavoured to do this by a number of methodologies. If we can attempt to summarise these very briefly the steps are as follows:

1. Establish a familial aggregation or ocurrence. This is done by observing the excessive frequency of a trait as compared with the population at large.
2. At the same time, search for indicators of genetic effects or genetic effects linked to family recurrence:
3. Search for indicators of genetic effects in the *absence* of family recurrence;
4. Search for indicators of environmental effects in the presence of family recurrence;
5. Search for indicators of environmental effects in the absence of family recurrence.

Finally, illnesses differ in their effects according to their severity and also according to which member of the family is ill. In some societies the illness of the man, as the sole breadwinner, can have disastrous consequences. Illness becomes 'disabling' when the illness, whether psychological or physical, leads to an *impaired role* in which the individual is unable to carry out his or her role obligations. For example, an arm injury in a schoolteacher will presumably have less devastating effects than on a professional tennis player.

When disabilities become permanent, such as in the case of blindness, then family members have to adjust their expectations. The extent of the disability may affect the individual's family role more so than the occupational role and vice versa. In long term chronic diseases family involvement in the form of care tends to be long and frequent. In addition to additional financial burdens such situations tend to disrupt family roles (in the case of the mother, for example) and in the case of the elderly sick in the presence of the nuclear family. Furthermore, hospitalisation of different members may present different strains on the nuclear family. Entirely different strains and coping mechanisms may have to be brought to bear in the case of mental illness within the family.

SUMMARY

1. The family varies considerably in structure and organisation.
2. The family is a relatively small unit comprising members living in close proximity over time, and forming an economic unit which provides for all members.
3. The family is a universal phenomenon because it provides for a number of functions such as socialization, social placement, sexual regulation, and the replacement of members.
4. The family of orientation (the one into which we are born) is the basis of primary socialization whereas the family of procreation (one which we make ourselves) becomes the basis for the process of secondary socialization.
5. Legitimate (born into wedlock) is preferred to illegitimate birth (born out of wedlock) because it makes the economic and social roles and responsibilities easier to allocate.
6. Conflict theories of the family view it as primarily dysfunctional and the root of many problems whereas Function theorists view it as necessary and beneficial.
7. There are many forms of marriage and types of family which are usually regarded as the result of economic conditions.
8. The traditional, extended family, has declined in industrial societies because it has lost its educative and affective function, it is not geographically mobile, it is less socially mobile, and it is more of an economic liability, than the nuclear family which has emerged.
9. Courtship and marriage patterns in the marriage market are not arbitrary but socially defined.
10. Family breakdown encompasses the erosion of various functions such as sexual, economic, and reproductive.
11. Divorce is at its highest rate ever, partly because of greater tolerance for dissolution and better opportunities.
12. The pattern of the family is changing rapidly and future patterns may include reconstituted families, childless couples, single parent families and those who choose to remain single.
13. Primary and secondary socialisation determine our personalities and make us what we are. This is done by role learning and social interaction.
14. Attitudes vary from culture to culture and are acquired in the primary stage and also throughout life by encountering unique experiences.
15. Human impairments occur in primary socialization and by inadequate acquisition of language and abilities.
16. Gender is considered to be independent of biological characteristics.
17. The family can genetically transmit disease and also provide the environmental basis for disease. However, it is difficult in many instances to differentiate the two factors.

18. The social implications of disease for the family setting varies greatly. It also affects differently the roles and obligations for each member.

IMPORTANT TERMS

family	family of orientation
family of procreation	legitimate birth
illegitimate birth	kinship
marriage	monogamy
polygamy	polygyny
polyandry	endogamy
exogamy	neolocal residence
patrilocal residence	matrilocal residence
principle of legitimacy	incest taboo
extended family	nucleur family
bilateral	avunculocal residence
homogamy	consanguine
conjugal	primary socialization
secondary socialization	looking glass self
social interaction	role taking
particular other	generalised other
gender	hidden curriculum
'nature' and 'nurture'	peer group
elaborated and restricted codes	morphostatic
drift hypothesis	non-verbal and verbal communication

SELF-ASSESSMENT QUESTIONS

1. Give a brief summary of *two* sociological perspectives on the family.
2. Why is divorce on the increase in industrial and post-industrial societies?
3. Discuss the view that the family as a social institution is declining.
4. To what extent is it true to say that the nucleur family is best suited to modern industrial societies?
5. Discuss the importance of the socialization process in the creation of individuals.
6. How important do you consider the role of the family in health? Carefully examine all aspects.

CHAPTER SIX IDEOLOGY AND MEDICINE

- the nature of ideology
- medical ideology
- marginal medicine
- medical sects

Charles II touching sufferers from scrofula (The King's Evil).
Source: BBC Hulton Picture Library

THE NATURE OF IDEOLOGY

Ideology is generally defined as a distinctive pattern of beliefs and concepts which purport to explain complex social phenomena with a view to directing and simplifying socio-political choices facing individuals and groups. The term became used by Marx and Engels to imply 'false' consciousness, so that Marx writes that ideology is consciousness of reality in which 'men and their circumstances appear upside down as in a *camera obscura*'. Karl Mannheim (1936, pp. 238–239) states that 'the study of ideologies has made it its task to unmask the more or less conscious deceptions and disguises of human interest groups . . . ' Ideologies can be 1. *particular*, i.e. taking place on a psychological level and structurally resembling lies; 2. *total*, i.e. mental structures in their totality, a man's whole mood of conceiving things as determined by his social and historical setting. Ideologies aim at total explanation in a manner similar to viewing the entire world through spectacles of a particular tint.

The 'end of ideology' debate has tried to argue that the belief patterns that supported extremist and political movements are now out of favour with intellectuals. '. . . We have witnessed an exhaustion of the nineteenth century ideologies, particularly Marxism, as intellectual systems that could claim *truth* for their views of the world.' (Bell, 1960, p. 16). Ginsberg (1962 p. 12) usefully distinguishes between *open* and *closed* ideologies. He means by 'closed' ideologies 'self-contained systems demanding all-or-none commitment, of the kind demanded by, for example, Bolshevist communism.' On the other hand 'open' ideologies, such as liberalism, non-Marxist socialism, and conservatism, are open in that they are 'often criticised from within and that they also learn from each other. If, as a result, they recognise their onesidedness, and discover areas of agreement this may indicate not exhaustion, but healthy advance.' However, there is much more to the concept of ideology than what we have said so far. The symbolic interactionists, for example, held that the importance of significance of objects and events for any individual is determined by the meanings he/she attaches to them. Thus, in a sense, we possess a *repertoire*, or stock, of meanings, e.g. language, although some of these stocks or repertoires lie outside language. It is important just to note that some philosophers such as Ludwig Wittgenstein, have argued that the limits of language are the limits of our world, that is, we cannot conceive of anything outside, and without using, language.

This, therefore, presents us with another perspective on the concept of ideology, that is as a system of meanings with which individuals become involved, or as a particular stock of meanings on which we all draw to interpret our experience of the world. The place we hold in society structures our interaction, as a consequence of which we develop some views rather than others. Often the social organisations we find ourselves a part of, such as the educational system, or the economy of a country, limit the choice of those who participate in them.

And yet, somehow, the millions of people who comprise any one society, with all their definitions and interpretations of social situations, still do not themselves constitute a society. Berger and Luckman (1967, pp. 47–48) explain how all these typifications come together to form the *social structure*.

The social reality of everyday life is thus apprehended in a continuum of typifications, which are progressively anonymous as they are removed from the 'here and now' of the face-to-face situation. At one pole of the continuum are those others with whom I frequently and intensively interact in face-to-face situations—my 'inner circle', as it were. At the other pole are highly anonymous abstractions, which by their very nature can never be available in face-to-face interaction. Social structure is the sum total of these typifications and of the recurrent patterns of interaction established by means of them. As such, social structure is an essential element of the reality of everyday life.

What we might term 'world views' differ across society according to the social positions which individuals occupy. As we see elsewhere, our occupation and income place us into certain social categories which in turn has the effect of producing in us different ways of looking at various facets of society, such as the educational system, religion, etc. In effect, an individual's subjective interpretation and definition are also accompanied by large-scale societal interpretations and definitions. These are on-going, and inherited by us, when we become affiliated or members of social structures such as social class, and the educational system. Consequently, when we come across a system of ideas working in a social structure and helping to keep it going, we call it an ideology, belonging to that structure. Education is an important social structure because it very much colours our view of the world. It is one of the foremost agencies for the promulgation and perpetuation of ideas.

If we take occupation as pinpointing our position in the social class system we will see that very different views on education are entertained according to whether one is an unskilled factory worker or an orthopaedic surgeon. It is often argued, for example, that lower working class children tend to *externalise* authority, and to see it as physically retributive. On the other hand, middle-class children *internalise* authority into a personal sense of right and wrong, and to see it as psychologically retributive. Our social position within the system of social stratification influences our thinking and our degree of motivation, in other words our *construction of reality*, and consequently determines our level of achievement in education.

What we have said so far may be summarised as follows:
1. Ideology is *not* to be defined as a set of opinions, even if these opinions are shared by a number of individuals.
2. An ideology represents the interests of a social group.
3. Fascism is an example of an ideology.

The marxist theory of ideology In Marxism, ideology helps to protect the vested interests of certain groups in society, or helps to justify various systems of inequality. For example, *slavery* was assumed the natural 'lot' of the vast majority of the population throughout the ancient world, and even the great philosophers of ancient Greece, Plato and Aristotle, assumed it to be a natural condition which would exist for ever. Consequently, this is an example of an ideology, i.e. supporting the existing social order and the interests of certain groups.

An important theorist in the Marxist tradition is Antonio Gramsci (1971). He saw the capitalist class as using two kinds of socio-political control. First of all there is direct domination or physicial coercion such as that held by the state, i.e. police, army, courts, prisons, and other institutions. However, such repressive and totalitarian regimes cannot last for ever. Second, an important mechanism of social control is what Gramsci terms *ideological hegemony*. By hegemony he means bourgeois or middle-class domination in its widest sense, not only in intellectual life and the political field, but also in what we usually term 'commonsense'. In a complicated statement Gramsci tries to show that the middle-class have managed to incorporate their view of the world into the commonsense view of the world held by the working class.

This usually involves the notion that there is such a thing as a natural order to the world—the implications of this being that if the subordinate class believes something to be natural then it cannot be changed. Within capitalism the idea that the upper and middle classes have 'breeding' serves as a commonsense explanation that they are born to lead.

Gramsci does not see ideologies in terms of their truth or falsehood, but according to their power to bind together the members of social classes and to put into practice particular views of how society should be organised. He also recognises the importance of an ideological apparatus which helps to secure the consent of the dominated class. In capitalist society this involves institutions such as the family and the education system which help to spread and maintain the dominance of ruling class ideology.
(Boronski, 1987, p. 17)

Such hegemonic institutions as schools, churches, mass media, and family, are instrumental in promulgating particular values, beliefs, attitudes, and morality that are to be found in abundance in societies. 'This ideologic system supports the established order and the class interests that dominate it. The same ideologic forces achieve acquiescence and mute resistance from groups who are oppressed.' (Waitzkin, op. cit., p. 139)

The concept of *ideological legitimation* is directly related to the Marxist theory of class struggle. If the Marxist theory is correct, and the working class are constantly exploited in every conceivable society (apart, one assumes, from socialist countries) why do they put up with it. Quite clearly in some military dictatorships such as we find in Central and South America (and some would argue South Africa) they simply have no option. These countries are not democracies in the sense that the majority of the population are not allowed to vote.

The answer to why the working class acquiesce, lies in the importance of ideas, values and beliefs, according to the Marxists. The ideologies into which the working class are so successfully socialised are on the whole totally unobtrusive. They are, for the most part, unaware of them. If the ideological support for a society is removed that particular social structure would collapse.

In the Marxist view, a class society's superstructure is indispensable to its survival. It represents the society's cultural characteristics and the institutions that promote these characteristics. Its *infrastructure*—its class-based mode of production—only survives so long as the reality of its class character remains unrecognised, or is considered legitimate, by those whom it subordinates.
Scource: Jones, 1985, p. 48

Capitalism survives because of the existence of institutions which divert 'the attention of the exploited away from the reality of their condition.' Popular literature and music, television and radio, the cinema, and thriller novels, are all singled out for diverting the attention of the working class away from the stark reality of their existence. Newspapers and other news media are simply, to Marxists, distorting the actual and trivialising reality.

Consumer behaviour, and consequently capitalism, depends upon the reproduction of demand. This is for the most part brought about by means of advertising, where, from an early age, children are socialised into consumerism.

Ideology in the family and at school The family plays an important role in socialising individuals into a subordinate role. It is within the family that we first learn obedience and authority. When we submit to the wishes of parents we are rehearsing for the later role of submitting to the wishes of our employers. the whole process is reinforced by the educational system. Among those who have written about the relationship between the family and education and the work process we must mention some. Zaretsky (1976) attempts an analysis of the family which stands in stark contrast to that offered by Talcott Parsons. Although both see the family in modern society as one of the few arenas for personal expression, and as developing in relation to the needs of the wider society, Zaretsky's Marxist approach relates changes in the family to changes in the process of production. Inevitably, for Marxists, the gender distinctions in the family are reflective or gender relations in the economy. Zaretsky doubts the quality of the family and its relationships under capitalism.

Willis (1977) views unquestioning conformity as favouring the middle and upper classes at the expense of the working class. He writes about working class male sub-culture in Britain, and finds strong parallels between the workplace and the school because they are concerned with similar values. He finds the following characteristic of working class life-style:

a cult of masculinity (pronounced sexism);
gaining, quickly, control over work and school;
rough and witty humour; and
being practical, as superior to being theoretical.

Braverman (1974) argues that (he is referring to the American system) the majority of people are over-educated for the work that they do. In just twenty years the median years of schooling rose by two years. He argues that the educational system has a primary function in preparing people for the work force. He regards most work as being capable of being carried out with no skills at all, and consequently he rejects occupational training as a function of education. The three R's are helpful at work but they are also very necessary for urban existence. The fact that the illiterates in British and American society manage to do their work perhaps supports his thesis. The functions performed by schools is as follows:

1. They socialise and 'child mind' while the parents are at work.
2. Increased educational expansion removes millions from the work force and consequently reduces unemployment figures.
3. Schools provide jobs for middle class teachers and administrators.
4. The weakest in the job market can now stay on at school.
    Finally, ideological legitimation justifies inequality.

It is in *the classroom* that we first encounter both the inevitability and the justice of inequality. Here we learn that people do not just possess *different* abilities. they possess *better* or *worse* abilities. 'Clever' children succeed and are rewarded with good grades and exam results . . . Experiences in school can only encourage people to believe that inequality of reward is just.

In a fundamental way, then, education, with its intrinsic emphasis on competition and selection . . . teaches members of a capitalist society the justice of inequality.
(Jones, 1985, p. 51)

Both the educational system and the mass media have been cast in the mold of ideological legitimators. Jones captures the essence of what Marx meant when he said: 'The ideas of the ruling class are, in every age, the ruling ideas.' The working class subscribe to the dominant ideologies, constantly perpetrated by institutions such as the mass media and education, and emerging as stereotypes. Thus the middle and upper classes are 'good' and the working class is 'bad'. The upper-class stereotype is associated with a particular:

- *demeanor*—a lofty disdain for all ordinary mortals and a complete ignorance of the word 'self-doubt'.
- *mode of dress*— . . . this often involves, among males, what Ralf Dahrendorf has called a kind of 'cultivated dishevellment'. Typically it includes very old baggy cords or cavalry twill trousers; noisy shoes; tweed jackets-old-with patches on the elbows; check shirts (Viyella) and cravats . . .
- *manners*—described by Nancy Mitford as 'U' as opposed to 'non-U'.

- *language*—usually known as the 'OK yah' mode of speech. In his novel *The Rachel Papers*, Martin Amis captures this nicely. 'The doors opened. A tall ginger-haired boy in green tweed moved gracefully down the steps. He looked at me as if I were a gang of skinheads . . . Behind him at a trot came two lantern-jawed girls, calling

  "Jamie . . . *Jamie.*" Jamie swivelled elegantly.

  "Angelica, I'm not going to the Imbenkment. Gregory shall have to take you."

  "But Gregory's in Scotland" one said

  "I can't help thet." The ginger boy disappeared into an old-fashioned sports car.

  The students were pouring out steadily now.

  Each and every one of them was shouting.

  "Caspar, yah, Ormonde Gate, not possible, super, Freddie, five o' clock, *rather*, tea? Bubble, later, race you there, beast, at Oswald's? Double-parked Alfa Romeos, Morgans and M.G.s jostled and revved . . .

  (Jones, P., op. cit., p. 52–53)

Althusser: structuralism

Althusser is what is known as a structuralist Marxist. He has written extensively about the relationship between the economic base and the superstructure. He is not as determinist as Marx and sees elements of the superstructure as being independent of economic forces. For Althusser every process of production is an interaction between the economy, ideology and politics. The ideological and political aspects are part and parcel of the superstructure. In order to develop this notion he utilises two concepts. Firstly, *repressive state apparatuses* (RSAs) are the police, army, law courts, and other institutions that keep control of society by repression or violence. Secondly, *ideological state apparatuses* (ISAs) are all the institutions that put forward dominant ideologies in the population. ISAs include the family, the educational system, cultural systems, the legal system, and the mass media. Neither RSAs nor ISAs appear in a pure form, and often the ISAs are used to legitimate the actions of RSAs.

Habermas: critical theory

The third writer working within the Marxist framework is **Jurgen Habermas**, who introduced his *critical theory* which shares an origin with Althusser's structuralism (i.e. classical Marxism) although it differs in maintaining that individuals have the capacity to reflect critically about society and can take purposive political action. Althusser and other Marxists tend to see individuals as incapable of critical action and more as puppets moulded by external forces, in particular economic forces. Habermas argues that there are three kinds of knowledge: (1) *empirical-analytic* (positivist); (2) *historical-her-*

meneutic (interpretist); and (3) *self-reflection* (philosophical knowledge of a critical kind).

Thus, in addition to scientific sociology and interpretive sociology, Habermas adds self-reflection, which he breaks down into

(a) individual self-consciousness whereby we examine critically our own social life. Unlike (1) and (2) above, this involves going beyond the given.

(b) Hebermas suggests that there is an objective or ideal standard by which we guage approximations to 'cruelty', etc.

Habermas singles out science as being the prime example of ideology because of its claim to be the epitome of objectivity:

. . . scientific ideology has defined an increasing range of problems as amenable to technical solutions. For this reason, science tends to depoliticise these issues by removing them from critical scrutiny. According to Habermas, science legitimates current patterns of domination, including the class relations of production.
(Waitzkin, op. cit., p. 140)

Science has become a fetish. Scientific ideology creates legitimation via cultural symbols in the educational system and the mass media. Unfortunately, Habermas's work suffers from lack of example of scientific ideology. However, if we look at social control and ideological manipulation we see that these become very closely related in medicine. The medicalisation of a number of areas of life is such an example. In particular, the doctor–patient area of interaction shows clearly social control over human emotions and the asymmetrical nature of the relationship itself:

From a position of relative dominance, doctors can make ideologic statements that convey the symbolic trappings of science. These messages reinforce the hegemonic ideology that emanates from other institutions—the family, educational system, mass media, and so forth—and that pervade a society. The same messages tend to direct clients' behaviour into safe, acceptable, and nondisruptive channels; this is the essence of social control in medicine.
(Waitzkin, op. cit., p. 142)

Medical ideology Generally speaking, it has been noted that ideology is more strongly represented among the middle-class groups in society and rarely among the poorer elements. The former are rarely likely to be in fear of losing their jobs:

. . . the poor are often politically conservative, especially if they have gained the first foothold on the ladder of respectability and security as members of a union of health workers . . .

'Position effect' is a summary concept describing this phenomenon: the elite can afford to be radical because they do not risk much and can always opt out if the going gets too tough; those in the middle occupational ranks—nurses, technicians, and others—are often sources of internal controversy within unions or outside of them, acting some times in unity with the unskilled and at

other times apart from them . . .
(Krause, 1978, p. 78)

In a country such as America with a limited amount of public medicine
the hospital strike of 1970 in San Francisco revealed that the interns
(trainee junior hospital doctors) were striking for two demands, initially
their own higher pay, and secondly for greater community control of
the hospitals. They were told that if they called off their second demand,
i.e. greater community involvement, they would be granted an increase
in pay. They were pressured to concede the second demand by medical
schools connected to the striking hospitals, which threatened to refuse
certification of their internship period as being valid.

In the middle ranks of the occupational hierarchy, the nurses' and technicians'
associations were beginning to act as labor unions . . . The . . . American
Nursing Association . . . is structured to use its state branches as collective
bargaining units in the classic union sense, and has even lobbied in many
states to pass legislation giving nurses the right to formally unionize, strike, and
bargain with hospitals.
(Op. cit., p. 79)

Krause's contention is that the very manner in which the health system
and its constituent parts are organised is the result of a particular
ideology:

Patterns of service, such as the precise way a community's doctors' offices,
hospitals, and patients are arranged with respect to one another, are ultimately
the consequence of an operating political philosophy, which is then translated
into the way power and control is exerted in the system.
(Op. cit., p. 124)

Change can be brought to bear on the patterns of service in one of three
ways:
1. By changing the ideology of the wider society, e.g. from a laissez-
   faire capitalist to a welfare state or socialist ideology;
2. Changing the structure or the formal relationships, in the sense of
   'who does what to whom';
3. Changing the existing programme: 'the priorities in terms of who is
   seen first, or most respectfully treated'. It is clear that:

philosophy justifies programs and the priorities within them; change at any of
the three levels, to be successful, necessarily involves change at the other two.
(Op. cit., p. 125)

Any health system entertains a number of goals which are prioritised.
But who, exactly, does the prioritising? Is it the patients, the community or the medical staff? Or is it in fact the pharmaceutical giants?
The underlying philosophies justify prioritisation and do, in reality,
become *ideologies*. Different ideologies will result in a rearrangement
of health services and priorities. Krause points out that ideologies are
emotional as well as intellectual. People cling to them tenaciously and
are hurt when they are questioned. Engels, in a letter to Mehring (14
July, 1893) defined ideology as an intellectual process which is:

accomplished by the so-called thinker consciously ... indeed, but with a false consciousness. The real motives impelling him remain unknown to him, otherwise it would not be an ideological process at all. Hence he imagines false or apparent motives.
((Marx-Engels, 1933, p. 388)

This is akin to Freud's concept of self-deception or *rationalisation*. Krause divides ideologies into four groups, the entrepreneurial, the technocratic, the radical populist, and the pragmatist.

The entrepreneurial ideology

The entrepreneurial ideology is pluralist and stems from the old capitalist laissez-faire system of free competition. It has as its philosophical background Social Darwinism, or the survival of the fittest and in its extreme form would justify not providing sanitation or food for starving workers as 'the strongest would make the best workers, and death would weed out the poorer producers and the weak.' As free competition is the order of the day this takes place between 'large and small settings, between the employee class and the poor, and between the powerful and the weak in their struggle for health care.' Different providers also compete with each other.

The technocratic ideology

This ideology emerged as in part a reaction to entrepreneurial ideology:

Here the central idea is the desirability of expert control of the system through rational planning from a central position of power, in a situation where the expert planner actually has direct (or close indirect) power over the social situation for which he is planning.
((Krause, op. cit., p. 128)

Technocratic ideologies are generally represented in Communist or socialist countries. An important element is the blueprint (special plan) which is followed to the letter. Often, however, such plans or blueprints are merely justifications for a particular interest group's attempt to gain political support from those who believe that the planners and the planned are truly neutral. An example would be an attempt to centralise all power and control over the health care system firmly within the university or medical school.

Radical populism

Although not quite the 'revolt of the client' the emphasis is 'on the power of the health-care consumer over the health-care system.' Although different groups will operate differently in the interests of citizen control, 'all share the belief that the technical experts in health care do not necessarily work in their interest.' (Krause, 1978, p. 130) Ultimately, however, health-care systems can simply withhold their services, an action that will hurt the poor more than the middle class, who often have a wide range of alternative systems to which to turn.

Pragmatic ideology

Pragmatic ideology is concerned with getting the job done. The pragmatist may embrace each of the other three ideologies should the occasion be appropriate.

An excellent analysis of a medical sector and the various competing ideologies involved in the creation of a National Health Service is to be found in Navarro (1978). Navrro gives a good example of an ideology (or rationalisation as we mention above) justifying an increase in the cost of health care. The then secretary of the Department of Health and Social Services, Sir Keith Joseph, stated that 'increased dental charges . . . would give a financial incentive to patients to look after their teeth . . . They would therefore have a beneficial effect on dental health. As Tudor Hart has noticed, that rationale could very well lead to governments raising the tax on coffins to reduce mortality.' (Navarro, 1978, p. 139) Medicine has successfully sold the ideology of its apparent success, as outlined by Waitzkin, below. However, in practice the 'concentration of economic power and its consequent process of industrialisation creates dislocation and diswelfare . . . the main function of medicine in present-day capitalism is not to solve or cure, but to take care of and administer the diswelfare that is created by the social relations of production.' (Op. cit., p. 92). Navarro maintains that there are **two functions of medicine**:

On the one hand it ameliorates and makes palatable the diswelfare created in the sphere of production and consumption. Therefore, it has been incorporated into the realm of demands made by the working population to reduce the damage that is imposed on our population. On the other hand, medicine also has a legitimation function, i.e. to make people believe that what is politically and collectively caused can be individually and therapeutically cured. These two functions explain, to a large degree, the growth of medicine and its ineffectiveness.
(Op. cit., p. 92)

There are various ideological mechanisms at work which *exclude* conflicting ideologies that are at variance with the system:

This is clearly shown in the lack of attention to and the lack of research in areas that conflict with the requirements and needs of the capitalist system . . . much priority is given to the assumedly individual causation of disease . . . most research on heart disease—one of the main killers in society—has focused on diet, exercise and genetic inheritance . . . millions of pounds . . . have been spent. However, in a fifteen-year study of ageing . . . it was found that the most important predictor of longevity was work satisfaction.
(Op. cit., p. 118–119)

A dominant ideology in many spheres of life is that the individual is responsible. Thus he/she is responsible for being out of work, for seeking his/her own health care, and many others.

The emergence of community care ideologies

These as well as 'human relations' and 'mental hygiene' ideologies are ideological movements concerned with the care of the mentally ill, 'and proponents are sometimes carried away in their enthusiasm. For the most part, however, community care technologies are still undeveloped, and in returning impaired patients to the community, we do not eliminate illness or the social problems that illness may cause.' (Mechanic, 1968, p. 390). Ideological groups include Alcoholics Anonymous, Recovery, Inc. and Neurotics Nomine, as well as Make Today Count, and groups for homosexuals, transsexuals and nearly every -*ism* that one can think of. (Jones, 1984).

Ideologies are the 'spectacles' through which one views the world. The Marxist perspective sees virtually everything as being economically determined, the 'born again' Christian will also view the world from a very distinctive perspective, as will the racist and the homosexual subcultures. As we have seen ideologies are important for maintaining the social relations of production and various patterns of domination. Waitzkin (1983, pp. 56–58) identifies a number of areas of medical ideology:

1. Disturbances of biological homeostasis are equivalent to breakdowns of machines

This assumes a mechanistic view of the human body at the cost of causes of disease that originate in the environment, work processes and social stress; 'it also reinforces a general ideology that attaches positive evaluation to industrial technology under specialised control. This ideologic component helps justify costly and complex medical approaches that depend on advanced technology, as opposed to mundane but potentially more effective practices.' (Op. cit., p. 56)

2. Disease is a problem of the individual human being

Waitzkin says the reductionist approach focuses on disruptions in individual biology instead of emphasising the illness-generating conditions of society. A similar criticism is laid against the equally reductionist perspective of seeing disease as caused by the lifestyle of individuals (see Chapter 4). Being a Marxist, Waitzkin sees disease and illness as the products of class structure and the relations of production.

3. Science permits the rational control of human beings

By correcting the defects of individuals, medicine makes individuals more controllable. Medicine is seen as helping people to stay in the work force, thus working hand-in-hand with capitalist economic interests!

4. Many spheres of life are appropriate for medical management

We have referred to this earlier as 'the overmedicalisation of life', which is another way of describing medicine's increasing social control. We have described elsewhere the tendency towards medical imperialism when increasingly areas such as child-abuse, hyperactivity, aggression, alcoholism, and so on, are placed under medical control.

5. Medical science is both esoteric and excellent

Modern medicine is seen as an extraordinary example of scientific knowledge and research practices. Its functionaries hold elite positions in an occupational category known as professionals. Even if they are highly educated, non-medical or lay-persons are wholly dependent of doctors for the interpretation of medical data. 'The health system therefore reproduces patterns of domination by expert decision makers in the workplace, government, and many other areas of social life.' (Op. cit., p. 58)

Marginal medicine Marginal medicine is often talked about under different labels such as fringe medicine or quasi-and limited practitioners. A recent addition to such labels is that of *alternative medicine*. However, little serious sociological analysis has been carried out on what we shall call marginal medicine in contrast to the abundance of material produced on the new religious movements (NRMs). One such reason for this neglect is that orthodox western medicine claims a total monopoly of 'truth' over marginal medicine in a way that orthodox churches cannot claim a monopoly over the numerous sects that exist in the matter of salvation.

We cannot hope to cover all of marginal medicine and will concentrate on a few main alternatives to western orthodox medicine. In the next section, however, we offer a broad socio-historical account of the rise of orthodox medicine, and show that it has as many serious challengers as there were religious sects in the emergence of Christian orthodoxy. Wallis's study (1985) of the Human Potential or Growth Movement, shows it to have arisen from a number of sources, including humanistic psychology (with its origins in psychoanalytic therapy). It overlaps with

meditation; dance; forms of martial art and movement, such as T'ai Chi; other oriental practices devoted to spiritual and physical growth, such as Yoga; massage, etc.
(Op. cit., p 27)

The Human Potential Movement has much in common with other groups of activities, as follows:

Physical: Bates eye method, Alexander technique, vegetarianism and other dietary practices, natural birth.
Meditative practices: TM, Yoga, martial arts
Occultism: Astrology, Eckankar, Benjamin Creme, Theosophy, Gurdjieff's Work.
Social Change: Ecologism, Feminism, Gay Lib, 'Participatory Politics'.
'Traditional' therapy and counselling: Psychoanalysis, Jungian Analysis, marriage guidance and other counselling.
(Op. cit., p. 27)

**The human
potential
movement** This movement consists of a collection of different groups without a common structure or organization of membership. Participants may join more than one similar group at the same time or sample what each has to offer. There is considerable commercial enterprise visible in the Growth Movement. These groups may operate in an almost commercial way, each one offering a product, which is marketed as unique and effective, the solution to one's problems. An interesting aspect mentioned by Wallis is the Movement's steps towards *professionalisation.* Thus there is a Master's programme in Humanistic Psychology run by a branch of the American Antioch University in London, and there are formally organised courses of training, lasting two to three years, and culminating in a diploma. There is also, apparently, concern to establish standards of practice, supervision and ethical conduct. The Foster Report of 1971 recommended the establishment of a British Psychotherapy Council, although this has not, to date, been implemented. Attempts at accreditation and certification have met with little success, indeed many view such attempts as running counter to the exploratory spirit of humanistic psychology.

**The trend towards
spirituality** This has been explained by the Stark-Bainbridge theory of religion and development in the Human Potential Movement. This theory is a complicated one but it is saying essentially that there are *rewards* and *compensators*. The former is defined as 'anything humans will incur costs to obtain' (Stark-Bainbridge, 1980, pp. 114–128). If the desired reward is absent 'explanations will be accepted which posit attainment of the reward in the distant future or in some other nonverifiable context.' (Op. cit., p. 121). *Compensators* are 'postulations of rewards according to explanations that are not readily susceptible to unambiguous evaluation'. (Ibid.) Thus:

. . . The failure of rewards to be forthcoming from some group or movement of a naturalistic kind on which one's hopes were pinned, may lead one to be willing to accept religious compensators instead, and thus provide a strong incentive for the leaders of such groups and movements to respond to failure by shifting what they have to offer in a supernaturalistic direction. (Wallis, 1978, pp. 36–37)

Whatever the reasons, and Wallis is in disagreement with the Stark-Bainbridge argument, the Human Potential Movement incorporates much of the disease of modern society, such as individual anxieties and self-doubt; inability to develop or maintain satisfactory interpersonal relationships; and a general sense of underachievement.

Alternative healing Easthope's study (1985) of marginal healers examines alternative healing practices in Britain, Canada, the Philippines and Australia. Healers are characterised by having no choice in the matter. They were called to the vocation. 'Healing is seen as a gift which the healer finds himself compelled to accept. Sometimes early resistance to the gift is punished by some affliction, such as paralysis, but eventually the recipient is forced to accept the gift of healing. Often the gift is intimated through the hearing of voices or by means of visions. Easthope never witnessed the direct payment of money to a healer, even though patients sometimes raised the issue. '. . . the claim that they did not choose to become a healer and that they get no monetary reward from the fact of being a healer is part of the impression of personal disinterest that is projected . . . many healers say that healing is physically, emotionally and mentally exhausting . . . they are, like doctors, always on call.' (Easthope, 1985, p. 55) Personal disinterest is further established by the scene setting, usually featuring the healer's disciples rather than himself, a further attempt to project a lack of self-interest. In the healer–patient interaction,

Healers listen to their patients in a manner that is distinctly different than that of doctors. The doctor initiates a consultation by an open question, 'How are you?', but he does not expect a full answer, only a starting point from which he can put further questions to solve a diagnostic puzzle . . . Healers, although they often use the same question, do expect a full answer and usually spend most of a consultation listening rather than questioning. They allow and encourage the patient to talk about themselves at length, offering only supportive cues to the patient to encourage them to talk further . . . In addition healers, unlike doctors, are often careful to accept the patient's description of their symptoms verbatim rather than translating, as a doctor does, such symptoms into their own terminology.
(Op. cit., pp. 55–56)

Healers maintain that orthodox medicine does not practice a holistic approach 'but only with the symptoms and disease for which the individual constitutes a site'. It is an important part of the healer's image that he is seen to possess knowledge and authority, either the language and symbols of science or religion. Some use both. One of the most famous healers, Harry Edwards, wore a white coat and conducted 'his healing in a room that resembled a chapel containing an altar and cross (religious symbols). This duality was further expressed in the fact that his spirit guides (religion) were Lord Lister and Louis Pasteur (science).' (Op. cit., p. 60)

In a discussion of the *placebo effect* (from the Latin, 'I will please') Easthope argues, from a range of evidence, 'that it was not the sugar pill but the doctor–patient relationship which caused the placebo effect.' He goes on to maintain that healers are not quacks because the placebo really works. It is also used in orthodox medicine. Kleinman and Sung (1976 and 1980) are among the many who have emphasised the importance of symbolic reality in the healing process.

Christian science healing practitioners This religious sect, founded by Mrs Mary Baker Eddy, holds that man (and presumably woman) is spiritual and cannot be sick. When we conceive of ourselves as sick, and subject to decay and death, this is illusory, 'although it is an illusion so powerful that it causes man to see, feel, suffer just the conditions which it specifies.' What is healed is in fact a false belief which we entertain, or which others entertain about us. (Wilson, 1961). Rather than being curative the system is, 'rather preventative of ill-health, accident and misfortune, since it claims to lead into a state of consciousness where there things do not exist.' (Op. cit., p. 63)

The notion of *malicious animal magnetism* is actually evil thought, operated by people consciously or unconsciously thinking badly about someone. Healing or physical improvement is brought about by the denial that the physical exists.

Christian Science uses practitioners whose treatment 'is a process of argument, affirmation and denial.' Christian Science is the ultimate panacea.

The practitioner begins by allaying the fear of the patient—'if you succeed in wholly removing the fear, your patient is healed.' The arguments which a practitioner may use vary from case to case and from practitioner to practitioner but generally they are a reaffirmation of God's allness and goodness, mental insistence that harmony is the fact . . . The practitioner will argue, and may explain to the patient, that since man reflects God, Spirit, he cannot be sick, that causation is in Mind, is according to spiritual law, and that Mind controls body. Sickness is a dream from which the patient must be awakened. Such treatment may be given in the presence of the sick person, or *in absentia*. (Op. cit., p. 70)

The practitioner does not name the sickness as this would give it reality. Practitioners are not confined to those who have received class instruction, and are mostly female.

Chiropractors Basically, chiropractic theory holds that all diseases are caused by dislocated bones in the spinal column. By a process of manipulating these bones pressure is released from the nerve. Chiropractors have been attacked as 'quacks' by the medical profession in all countries.

Chiropractic has developed outside the medical field. Nevertheless, in many American states, for example, they must pass the same basic science examinations as physicians, they are able to sign employee sick leave, some states recognise them for medical aid, and they qualify for Workman's Compensation claims in forty-eight states. Wardwell (1952, 1972) indicated several factors which contributed to the marginality of the role of the chiropractic.

1. Chiropractors realistically unite to fight for self-protection, legal recognition, and public acceptance;
2. Treatment failure is a reflection on the individual practitioner or that the case didn't get to him soon enough;
3. If the occupation is so different from that of the physician then the chiropractic need not feel inferior. Also he should not be expected to study the same subjects;
4. Chiropractors share an 'ideology of an oppressed minority'.

Chiropractors are not professionals:

Although in a narrow sense there is a codified body of knowledge, most of it has not been scientifically demonstrated to be accurate. Open to more serious question, however, is the service orientation of many chiropractors . . . In view of the fact that chiropractic is often seen as a means of upward social mobility,

as a way of improving one's status, it seems unlikely that the service motive could be very strong ... (the) recognised national association ... does not exercise the same professional control over its members as does the American Medical Association ... collegial relationships which are crucial to the organisation of medicine and osteopathy are absent among chiropractors; rather, they are in competition with each other. Finally, chiropractors can obtain licences in most states, but in only a few is the licensing decision in the hands of other chiropractors.
(Coe, 1970, pp. 221–222)

Osteopathy Although Osteopathy started life as a pseudoscientific cult with a philosophy of manipulation of dislocated small bones in the spinal column, in America they are on a par with physicians:

Gradually, the new concepts were introduced into the schools of osteopathy; new forms of treatment, such as hydrotherapy, electrotherapy, and even drugs, were added to manipulation. There was ... a change from 'osteopathic manipulation to osteopathic medicine:' Course work in medical subjects and in surgery was added to the curriculum along with extended training in internships and residencies. Along with the improved and increased academic and laboratory training, osteopathic students are exposed to a new ideology which holds that they are 'as good as anybody' (meaning doctors of medicine) and that 'osteopathy is not a deviance from, but a 'speciality of' medicine.'
(Op. cit., p. 218)

Osteopathy, then, is apparently well on the way to professional status although the vast majority oppose a merger with the medical profession. Finally, 'there are indications that in some localities osteopaths are coming to occupy the role of the disappearing general practitioner.'
(Wardwell, 1972, p. 261)

In America there is no marked difference between osteopathy and medicine. Entrance requirements and the curriculum are identical, except for osteopaths there are sections on osteopathic theory, diagnosis and treatment. However, certain cultist healing elements were still to be found among osteopaths, rendering it difficult to completely bring the two professions together. (AMA Committee for the Study of Relations Between Osteopathy and Medicine, 1953).

Wardwell (1952 and 1972) attempted a successful analysis. *Limited practitioners* are those whose health services are generally confined to particular aspects of the human body. *Marginal practitioners* are those who, although focussing on the whole range of the body's functions, employ unorthodox techniques and therapies. *Quasi practitioners* are those who use pseudoscientific or religious techniques or therapies. Chiropractors are limited practitioners, together with osteopaths.

PHARMACY

This is a special case because of its commercial and professional role, subordination to the physician, etc.

LIMITED PRACTITIONERS
dentists
podiatrists (chiropodists)
optometrists
clinical psychologists

MARGINAL PRACTITIONERS
osteopaths
chiropractors

QUASI-PRACTITIONERS
faith healers
primitive and magical healers
quacks
Christian Science practitioners

The development
of medical sects
It is now fairly well established that there appear to exist strong parallels between the emergence and development of sects of a religious nature and those that are distinctly secular. Thus Budd's analysis of the Humanist societies, Jones's description of ex-mental patient groups, the SPGB and Alcoholics Anonymous, O'Toole's account of Maoists and De Leonists, as well as other work, give some idea of the extent to which overtly secular movements and groups approximate in organisation and structure to avowedly religious or transcendental groups. (Jones, 1985) Thus these two separate classifications, religious and secular, have in common particular elements that associate them together in an analytical series of parallels, as distinct from other groups within society as a whole. (Jones, 1985)

But obviously societies can be looked at apart from such stark polar differentiations as secular and transcendental. For example, medicine as a corpus of 'knowledge' and as a 'practice' can be seen in a historical context to parallel the development and fragmentation of the church. Like the church, it too has had its schisms and sects defined by and relating to the main corpus of what is regarded, by being defined and perceived as such, as legitimate knowledge. Thus Inglis writes:

Medicine, like religion, became plagued with sects, each regarding itself as the possessor of the one true interpretation, and each requiring from its practitioners obedience to the one true faith.
(Inglis, 1965, p. 32)

There is certainly no lack of precedent for attempting to locate the 'dynamics of sectarianism' in nonreligious phenomena, and Berger indicates that it can be found 'at work in places far removed from religion proper—in politics, art, literature, and even within the sacred precincts of science itself.' Again, Wilson regards manipulationist sects as 'much more congenial to the prevailing secular culture,' and he characterises such sects as 'being much more instrumental in their concerns' which is not a community as such but the 'gathering of an association of like-minded and like-instructed people, who use a common method in coping with the world. The manipulationists have found a method by which to achieve salvation, but salvation is largely seen as the ability to realise the good things of the world, and particularly long life, health, happiness, and a sense of superiority or even triumph.' Medical sects, it will become clear, more closely approximate to this category than to the other six described by Wilson. Nevertheless, medical sects not only conform to the relatively established definition of voluntariness, exclusivity, merit, self-identification, legitimation, and so on, but also reflect a system of sub-classification within the maniuplationist category itself. (Wilson, 1970)

The origin of medical sects

The complexity of the early beginnings of the history of medicine is well documented.

Briefly, the Dogmatists adhered to the physiological basis of disease, and were closely allied to the Empirics, who were experiential and noncausative. Both sects were Hippocratic, descriptive, and rational. The Methodists regarded health as the balance between tension and relaxation (later manifested in the eighteenth-century Brunonian theory of sthenic and asthenic, and the Broussais theory of 'inflamation' in the nineteenth). The Pneumatists held to the doctrine of mental causation with pneuma or breath as the vehicle of the 'mind'. Although initially followers of Erasistratus, they were early forerunners of Mesmer, Stahl's seventeenth-century Animism, Van Helmont, and possibly psychoanalysis. The Eclectics adopted any or every theory to meet their current requirements. The distinctive characteristic of these sects is their adherence to the principle or article of faith that there existed a single therapy for all ailments. It is not to be assumed that these early sects are merely of historical interest, for as we shall see, many nineteenth-century sects such as homeopathy, chiropractic, and osteopathy were direct doctrinal descendants.

Galenism: the development of orthodox doctrine

Galen (c. 130 A.D.) was an anatomist who embraced the Pythagorean structure, and he is regarded by many as setting the seal for the development of medicine in succeeding centuries. His concept of 'life force' can with little effort be equated with 'God' and consequently can be regarded as the New Orthodoxy. In effect his writings became blue-prints for survival, underwent a period of relative decline, and experienced a restoration of his system which was exemplified by the Salerno School that emerged in the eleventh-century. Nevertheless, sorcery, magic, astrology and the supernatural in general were inexorably intertwined throughout this period without any attempt at a rational medical diagnosis and treatment. The theory or doctrine of humors and the works of Galen (and to a lesser extent Avicenna, c. 890 A.D.) dominated the prescribed system of training required of aspiring medical men who, after training, subscribed to the doctrine of contraries which, suitably embellished with ritual, is exemplified by the practice of 'bleeding'.

From time to time the orthodox doctrine invariably encountered its challengers. Roger Bacon, for example, questioned the dominant traditions of the day which included Scholasticism, Galenism and Aristotelianism. The Renaissance heralded the heterodoxy of Von Hohenheim (later known as Paracelsus), Vesalius, Pare, and Fracastoro, as well as Eustachio and Fallopius. Von Hohenheim (described by Osler as the 'Luther of Medicine') prefaced his lectures by burning the works of Galen and Avicenna, thereby signifying a break from the current orthodoxy that had dominated medical practice for so long. His followers, who became known as the Paracelsists and kept his work alive in England and Germany, were often members of the Rosicrucians. (Jones 1985) Vesalius, in the fields of anatomy and surgery, both broke with his original adherence to Galen and Aristotle and favoured a more experimental approach. Surgery found a most humane Luther in Pare, who utilised astute observation combined with practical experience, and Fracastoro anticipated nineteenth-century bacteriological discoveries. With these four the whole structure of medieval medical orthodoxy lay in ruins.

One of Galen's major achievements was the unification of the early sects into a dominant orthodoxy which gave a legitimation and framework to practicing adherents and a theoretical yardstick by which deviance could be measured and adjudicated and punishment meted. That the number of increasing challenges to this orthodoxy occurred during this period was compatible with those that threatened the authority of the church itself, and in many instances was met with the same ruthless resistance. Men began to return to the ancient theorists but not with any fundamentalist stance; this time they were questioning and rejecting. Naturally, like any dominant and deeply embedded corpus, affections and sometimes financial investments, perceived by the challengers as misplaced, were strongly resisted. Thus, it is important to realise that the overthrow of medieval medical orthodoxy was neither a singular nor swift occurrence but a tandem event. That is, although erosion began to occur on a large scale, the process was a gradual one that took place over a number of centuries. Belief in humors, alchemy, astrology, and pneumatism still persisted alongside the new knowledge of many of these 'revolutionaries'.

The rebuilding process

The erosion of Galean orthodoxy necessitated a reconstruction on a grand scale. Harvey's description, in 1628, of the circulation of the blood had to wait ten years before it was felt that the medical world would not reject it out of hand. Similarly, Thomas Sydenham's adherence to Hippocrates and the subsequent rejection of the doctrine of contraries and polypharmacy meant that his contributions were largely ignored during his lifetime, and some were bitterly attacked. But with the decline of Galenism, Catholicism, and sorcery, medical communities were more than ready to look for new messiahs.

The early sects, the Dogmatists, the Empirics, and the Methodists, having flourished intermittently and in a sublimated fashion, broke out anew under the guise of the iatrochemical, iatrophysical, and vitalistic schools.

The new systematists of the seventeenth century

Three main secretarian groups appeared in the seventeenth century and continued to dominate fractionalised medicine, often with heated consequences. Iatrophysicists or iatromechanists preached the application of mechanics to human physiology, for example, regarding the heart as a pump. They were influenced by advances in mechanics, the work of Galileo, and Descartian philosophy. Their origins can probably be traced to Sanctorius's invention of a number of instruments such as the first clinical thermometer and the pulse clock, but the founder is generally regarded as Borelli (1608–1679 A.D.) with his explanation of muscular substance as 'succus nervens'. Another exponent was Baglivi, who espoused the simile of the various organs of the body as resembling various mechanistic devices. This led him eventually to a more patient-centred theory in the manner of Hippocrates. Boerhaave, a self-styled eclectic, did much to bring about iatrophysics as a substantive sect in Europe. Diderot and the French 'Encyclopédie' were also iatromechanists.

The iatrochemists, as the name implies, were concerned to apply chemistry to medicine and introduced 'acids' and 'salts' into medical description. The work of Bryle and others was used as a contrasting model to mechanics. The four humors of the body were replaced by saliva, pancreatic juice, and bile, and health was explained entirely in terms of chemical changes. Helmont, the founder, lived from 1577–1644 and held to a Paracelsian theory of 'life force' or 'Blas' which generated bodily malfunctioning. He believed that the doctrine of contraries was a dangerous delusion. His writings were influenced by alchemy and mysticism, and he died while awaiting trial by the Inquisition. Sylvius (1614–1672) regarded the acids and alkalis as capable of providing treatment. The English Wallis compared the physician with the brewer, always looking for irregularities in the fermentations of the body. However, most iatrochemists were vitalists.

Vitalism was the name given to a belief held by a group of men who propounded a view similar to that of Stahl, who claimed discovery of a substance named phlogiston and who adhered to the Aristotelian tradition as organistic, believing in a 'sensitive soul' similar to the Greek 'psyche', governed by neither mechanistic nor chemical laws. Some have described the vitalists as a rival faction of the iatrochemists. Stahl's writings were mystical and obscurantist, and the whole group was criticised by Cullen as not 'doing' anything. A colleague of Stahl's at the University of Halle, Hoffman, supported the life force theory which he called 'tonus' (tonic), and developed what was virtually a sub-sect. Other variations included Haller's 'irritability' principle. Perhaps the most important sub-sect stemmed from the writings of John

Brown, who stated that ill health, a maladjustment of stimuli, has two categories: asthenic, requiring a stimulus for the life force and stehenic, requiring sedation. His followers, known as the Brunonians, administered massive doses of drugs, and sectarian antagonism was at times so great that it required police intervention. Brunonian theory was disseminated in America under the leadership of Benjamin Rush. We should not mistake these three schools as mere fancy nor their sub-sects as aspects of frivolous fashion. All these schools laid claim to a monopoly of truth and persist to the present day in one form or another.

Institutional orthodoxy and the dilemma of new discoveries

The story of Jenner's fight to get inoculation accepted is typical of the resistance of both the medical establishment and 'conventional wisdom'. But it was not always these factors that limited the revelation of a discovery. For example, the obstetrical forceps was probably invented by Peter Chamberlain (the Elder, 1560–1631) but was kept a secret by succeeding members of the family until the death of Hugh Chamberlain in 1728. This example is an indication of the limitation of a discovery owing to private greed.

In many examples in the history of medicine it is clear that lack of medical advancement is due to simply ignorance. Thus, the slow realisation by naval medicine that scurvy was preventable by vitamin intake. Although Lind is credited with this realisation in 1753, it is documented a century earlier. The implementation of Lind's proposals was put into effect forty years later by the British Navy, but American sailors had to suffer for a further century because of their lack of enthusiasm for 'limeys'.

The history of the discovery of anaesthetic is a relatively clear example of orthodox opposition. It had been known for a thousand years that opium, hemp, and alcohol were pain killers. Since they were disliked by some of the medical fraternity in their 'primitive' form, most operations, including amputation and brain surgery, were performed without benefit of even these. The puzzle lies in the fact that a number of individuals such as Davy, Faraday, and others, although attempting to publicise the use of nitrous oxide and its beneficial application to surgery, met with little success. In America Morton's achievement with 'letheon' in 1846 at the Massachusetts General Hospital was kept secret, together with the active agent diethyl ether. Some controversy surrounded the particular incident, and it is unclear whether Morton, a dentist, wished to patent the anaesthetic for gain or 'sat' on it in order to make more money eventually. Similar reactions of ridicule and contempt greeted Elliotson's attempt to introduce mesmerism and Esdaile's surgical work with mesmerism and hypnotism. Americans such as Clarke, Lang, and Wells all attempted experimental surgery and molar extractions, although the first operation under general anaesthetic in England was carried out by Liston in 1846. Chloroform, following the pioneer work of Soubeiran, Guthrie, Leibig, and Simpson, rapidly replaced ether, despite theological and fanatical opposition. Thus, Simpson of Edinburgh 'was obliged to defend chloroform against its antagonists who opposed it . . . alleging that it would 'rob God of the deepest cries' of women in labour.' Despite the controversy, Snow became the first British anaesthetist.

Ironically, it was Simpson who opposed the Listerian system of antisepsis which was to revolutionise the practice of surgery. Others, such as Ernst von Bergmann of Berlin and Lawson Tait of Birmingham, were among the violent antagonists of Listerian antisepsis. The opposition to Semmelweiss resulted in his being dismissed from his post, and in its strength is not unlike the ridicule and scepticism encountered by Pasteur with his micro-organisms and also the subsequent battle between the 'germ' and 'terrain' schools.

It is worth recording that penicillin, discovered by Fleming in 1929, was not fully realised as a potential antibiotic until 1944, owing to the efforts of Florey, Chain, and their assistants from Oxford. They persuaded the American government to utilise it with the armed forces rather than civilian personnel, owing to its scarcity. Even this decision was not without its problem, for it involved a dilemma 'between using it for sulfa-fast gonorrhoea or for infected war wounds . . . (the) Chief Surgical Consultant . . . opted for use in those wounded in battle. The Theatre Surgeon made the decision to use available penicillin for those 'wounded' in brothels . . .'

Finally, it is worth illustrating the length and degree of orthodox opposition to two seemingly innocuous types of medical techniques and instruments. Percussion was discovered by Auenbrugger (who used it initially to check the level of his father's wine barrels). It was not overtly opposed, for this time opposition took the form of simply ignoring it, and it was not revived for over twenty years, by Corvisart in 1808. Loennec, Corvisart's pupil, developed ascultation (listening to body sounds) from which he developed the stethoscope. It took some years to break down prejudice and opposition to its use, although retrospectively it is regarded as one of the great inventions of medical science, replacing uroscopy as the physician's symbol.

Cultic quackery

Medical professionalism was formed more out of greed and malice than any genuine desire to establish rigorous standards. Hence, 'its most obvious characteristics were envy, malice and uncharitableness.' Besides the long and historic enmity between physicians and surgeons, there was also enmity between those who practiced with a university qualification and those who did not, usually clerics and apothecaries. Professional monopoly was established in England by Linacre, who founded the Royal College of Physicians of London. This guild of physicians 'immediately instituted restrictive practices, limiting the number of doctors and so enabling them to charge inflated fees.' No doubt it was the literate and ambitious who singled themselves out from the numerous claimants as having the sole prerogative to treat human suffering, claiming as their right and passport to prosperity the title of 'doctor'. 'The medieval university thus, for the first time in history, created definite and distinct administrative criteria for establishing a single occupational identity within the vague collection of healers who were in practice at the time.' The rivalry between surgeons and physicians ended with each establishing professional autonomy, but the former were still threatened by the 'short robe' barbers who were often preferred by the general public, as, of course, were also the 'quacks'. Struggles also persisted between apothecaries and physicians.

Quacks were not always rascals, and many practiced surgery on areas of the body considered too risky by the orthodox. The most famous quacks included Cornelius à Tilbourn, or Tilburg, who became a physician to William III. Another was Abraham Souberg, who specialised in cataract operations. Perhaps the most famous was William Read, whose ability as an oculist earned him a knighthood from Queen Anne and an appointment as oculist-in-ordinary to George I. Another oculist was Bannister, who wrote a distinguished work on the diseases of the eye. Yet another was John Taylor, who became oculist to George II. Joshua Ward was a highly successful quack, using his 'drop' (antinomy) and 'pill' (arsenic); and John Hill was made a knight of the Swedish Order of Vasa for his work on vegetarianism. In America Elisha Perkins used 'metallic tractors' in Connecticut, with great profit. Perhaps the most flamboyant was Crazy Sally Mopp of Epsom, who for a time was eminently successful. Quacks proliferated, and in Prussia, for example, the number of professional quacks rose from 269 in 1876 to 4 104 in 1902, (Inglis, 1965) that is, one quack for every five qualified doctors. The proportion was probably higher, for these figures refer only to those who reported under the prevailing regulations.

Several groups emerged in what might be termed the manipulationist area of the treatment of human ailments, notably chiropractic and osteopathy—which we shall return to later. No doubt the 'bone setters' constituted less of a threat to orthodox medicine than some of the other groups.

Christian Science has been more than adequately dealt with elsewhere, but perhaps we can mention its connection with the magnetisers, the most famous of whom was Perkins, an ex-doctor. Phineas Quimby of Maine became a mesmerist, and it was a patient of his, later known as Mary Baker Eddy, who founded Christian Science, a vitalist development of mesmerism. Spiritualist healers, too, attracted a substantial following.

Another curious quack was Hercules Sanche, credited with patenting the Oxydonor or Electropoise in 1892, and as late as 1952 he was still operating in Florida a business known as Hydrotonics, Inc. Another notorious quack was Albert Abrahams, who developed Electronic Reactions and, together with his 3 500 disciples, made thousands of dollars a week from 'patients' whose complete profile and diagnosis he purported to be able to give from a drop of blood, including disease, sex, age, race, and religion.

Quackery of the kind described above approximates to the concept of 'cult' and should not be coupled with 'sects' such as homeopathy, osteopathy, and chiropractic, to which we will turn below. Both categories are located in relation to the dominant orthodoxy and are defined, 'by the definers', as non-conformist and excluded from a monopoly of practice. If we follow Wallis and argue for a pluralistic legitimation for the cult by its subscribers, the above deviances from medical orthodoxy are seen as 'one of a variety of paths to the truth or salvation'. Cults are 'temporary associations of seekers and are seen as orientated towards the problems of individuals: loosely structured; tolerant; and non-exclusive.' The fragility and transience of cults imply difficulty in establishing authority, and they are service-orientated with a loosely structured boundary and faint commitment. Quackery fits into the concept of cults not only in these respects but because it also lays claim to some secret formula or gadgetry, an immediacy of cure, and a special gnosis gleaned from the cultic milieu.

Phrenology and mesmerism

Both phrenology and mesmerism were a mixture of quackery combined with genuine scientific research. Following early work on cerebral localisation, notably by Willis in 1664 and Robert Boyle in 1691, Franz Joseph Gall (1758–1828), a student of Van Swieten, lectured in Vienna on localised mental faculties that affected the surface areas of the skull and brain. With his pupil Spurzheim, Gall founded the cult of phrenology, whose primary claim was that a person's personality or character could be gleaned from various 'bumps' or prominences on the head that could be charted or graphed. originally an attempt at a serious study, it subsequently became exploited by unscrupulous quacks. Phrenology had a large popular following, and some thirty 'faculties' were purported to be 'discovered', for example, a large amount of acquisitiveness in a person produced a rise on the surface of the skull. Until fairly recently 'phrenological heads' or busts, and charts, could be purchased. Despite the cultic element, phrenology pinpointed the localised nature of cerebral function and spurred others such as Rolando and Flourens. At the time, phrenology caused a great deal of debate, and a paper read at the Royal Medical Society of Edinburgh in 1823 by Combe resulted in further popularisation. Later attempts to revive phrenology in a diluted form included the view that the heads of criminals conform to a particular shape.

Mystic and romantic fantasies in Germany gave rise to animal magnetism or mesmerism, which originated in the eighteenth century. Its principal advocate was the Schwabian Franz Mesmer, who revitalised the connection between medicine and mysticism after being influenced by Father Gassner. (Mesmer's doctoral thesis described the mystical influence the planets exerted on the pathology and physiology of the body.)

Magnetic medicine has a close relation to sympathetic medicine. It originated, probably, with William Maxwell, an English doctor, about 1650. He postulated a soul that reacted outside the human body on the radiations of the latter's forces—which he also claimed were found in blood and secretions. Mesmer held that bodies contained a magnetic fluid, and this belief resulted in his 'magnetic therapy' stemming from the laying on of hands.

Magnetisers multiplied, composed of some who wished to give magnetism a scientific basis by linking it with natural philosophy. The remainder were charlatans and quacks. Solar brains and postulated spiritual fecundations were hotly debated. The period appeared to encourage the miraculous cure by 'touching'. England, for example, witnessed many cures for rheumatism performed by the Irishman Valentine Greatrakes, and France could boast of Franfois de Prazis, a Jansenist, who received postmortem visits to his tomb from numerous followers. All this was in the tradition of the 'royal touch'.

Mesmer achieved great success by using somnambulism and clairvoyance to prevent pain, and his reputation was so great that he attracted both the patronage of the King of France and the following of many famous individuals such as Lafayette, Hegel, and Schelling. Opposed by the Academy of Medicine and the whole of medical orthodoxy, mesmerism caused great controversy, but gradually Mesmer's disciples gave way completely to fantasy and created a cosmological theory of a magnetic universe, the recurring tragedy of reduction to a unitary system. Caught in an outdated theory which was rationalist and speculative, he was also 'ahead' of his time with his theories of scientific hypnotism. He can be credited with being a forerunner of psychiatry and psychotherapy, and true hypnosis is regarded as being the discovery of one of his disciples, Puysegur, although the final transition of mesmerism into scientific hypnotism is credited to Bertrand in 1820. His present-day followers (now known as 'magnetopaths') maintain a distinction between suggestion and spiritual transference on the one hand and successful healing by animal magnetism on the other.

An example of a mixed thaumaturgical and manipulationist sect of recent origin is that of the Antoinists on the Continent. Occultist, mystical, and obscure, it arose from the conviction of Antoine Louis that he possessed magnetic fluids which had the propensity to overcome all illness and even death. Combining healing and dietetics, the sect has an estimated '50 000 followers in France and perhaps twice the number elsewhere—particularly in Belgium, Italy and Brazil,' including three temples in Paris.

Osteopaths, naturopaths, chiropractors, and homeopaths: sectarian challenges or quasi-and limited practitioners

Hahnemann's revelations, in 1796, that 'similia similibus currentur'—'let likes be treated by likes'—was beyond doubt, had been suggested to him by scientific research long before. It arose from a genuine desire to save orthodoxy from the charge of iatrogenesis which was later to be laid against it. Instead of heeding what might well have been a warning, however, the medical fraternity literally hounded Hahnemann from district to district, regarding him as a threat to allopathic tenets. Chemists, seeing their livelihood threatened, were even more vociferous.

The introduction of homeopathy to England came through Quinn, a student of Hahnemann, and led to the foundation of the homeopathic hospitals, though not without vehement opposition. The cholera epidemics of the 1840s led to a substantially more successful treatment by homeopathic than by orthodox means to the extent that the statistics were suppressed by the president of the Royal College of Physicians.

The Hahnemanns divided into the 'pure' homeopaths, that is, literalists who accepted Hahnemann's texts as 'God-given', and 'eclectics' who accepted the allopathic remedies or prescribed large doses. Thus, in 1871, of 75 homeopaths in Chicago, six out of ten were 'pure' and the remainder 'eclectic'.

The origins of osteopathy began with the manipulative techniques (which in turn were grounded in the ancient craft of bone-setting) that were practiced by the Misses Mapps and the Herbert Barkers. But medical orthodoxy closed ranks and consolidated its opposition, culminating in the striking off of Axham, Barker's anaesthetist. But when Barker died in 1950, manipulative surgery was still unaccepted in Britain. In America the fundamentalist arterial doctrine of Andrew Still resulted in the founding of an osteopathic school. In both countries osteopathy took over manipulative techniques that medical orthodoxy either could not or would not practice.

Palmer's chiropractic doctrines are not essentially distinguishable from osteopathy. 'Some Osteopaths continue to assert Still's Rule of the Artery, while some Chiropractors insist upon Palmer's Rule of the Nerve, but in fact nerves and blood supplies are so interlinked that the distinction is less important than both groups have tried to make it appear . . .' (Inglis, 1965)

Nature cures, originally centred around the Greek temples of health and later around the supposedly medicinal spas of European watering places, have as a core belief the redemptive qualities found in the natural and organic elements such as the sun or herbal foods. Although naturopathy is not embraced by the medical profession in Britain, it is claimed that in Germany, for example, as many as one in five doctors are naturopaths. Various branches such as herbalism and the prescription of honey as a panacea for all ailments, have reinforced the scientific view that, with a further variation of nudity, naturopathy is the epitome of quackery.

Wardwell as described above, has developed a classification of the above groups as follows. 'Ancillary practitioners' are those function under the autonomy of orthodox medical practitioners, and include nurses and physiotherapists. 'Limited medical practitioners' are those whose practice is not supervised by medical practitioners but is limited to treatment of certain parts of the body, and include dentists and chiropodists. 'Quasi-practitioners' are those who claim validation of their treatment and success by reference to some nonempirical attribute such as God or the mysterium tremendum, and include Christian Science practitioners and faith healers. 'Marginal practitioners' function independently 'of medical supervision . . . (and) . . . do not limit themselves to ailments affecting only a particular part of the body. Propounding a conception of health and illness at variance with that of orthodox medicine, they challenge its central tenets, are designated 'sectarian' by it, and are consequently marginal to it. The most prominent examples have been osteopaths, naturopaths, and chiropractors.' (Wardwell, 1952, 1972)

The cultic claims of marginal practitioners tend to cluster around a hostility to allopathy, and a rejection of bacterial and germ theories of disease, in favour of a monocausal theory. Historically, at least in America, osteopathy and chiropractic are being absorbed into medical orthodoxy and given practice under state license. Thus, osteopathy in its training syllabus follows the path of orthodox medical training, with the addition of osteopathic training. Chiropractic, on the other hand, although recognised by insurance companies and Medicare and state licensed, is still rather marginal, and in America has tended to absorb the remaining naturopaths. Homeopathy, in both Britain and America, is perhaps the least marginal of all these groups.

SUMMARY

1. Ideologies claim to explain complex social phenomena and can be regarded as 'closed' or 'open'.
2. Ideologies can also be regarded as a system of meanings entertained by individuals. Although not simply a set of opinions, an ideology represents the interests of a social group.
3. Gramsci viewed capitalists as using physical coercion, for example the police and the army, as a kind of socio-political control. However, he also viewed what he called *ideological hegemony* as perhaps a more pervading and long-lasting means of social control.
4. Various ideological mechanisms thrust us into various hierarchical positions in society and justify inequality.
5. Krause's argument is that health systems are organised as a result of a particular ideology.
6. Krause divides ideologies into four groups, the *entrepreneurial, technocratic, radical populist* and *pragmatist.*
7. Marginal medical movements are those not accommodated within the dominant ideology.
8. the medical profession exemplifies the dominance of the biomedical model to the exclusion of most others.

IMPORTANT TERMS

ideology	hegemony
repressive state apparatuses (RSAs)	infrastructure
entrepreneurial	radical populist
false consciousness	ideological legitimation
stereotypes	ideologic state apparatuses (ISA)
technocratic	pragmatist

SELF-ASSESSMENT QUESTIONS

1. Explain what is meant by the *end of ideology* debate.
2. How valid and how useful is it to regard ideology as a system of meanings?
3. What is the Marxist view of ideology? To what extent do you agree with it?
4. Examine South Africa's health system from Krause's perspective that it is the result of a particular ideology.
5. Waitzkin identifies a number of areas of medical ideology. Expand on all five areas using examples with which you are familiar.
6. Give an account of the development of modern medicine outlining the sectarian nature of marginal medical movements.

CHAPTER
SEVEN

THE ORGANISATION AND EVALUATION OF HEALTH CARE

- the structure of the hospital
- the primary health care team
- health services in Southern Africa
- a critique of health services

Nuns at work on a ward at the Hôtel Dieu, Paris, c. 1650
National Library of Medicine, Bethesda, Maryland

THE SOCIAL STRUCTURE OF THE HOSPITAL

We generally think of the study of organization as something connected with efficient management in industry. Sometimes we are led to think of schools, the army, social clubs, political parties, and so on, as exhibiting a form of social relationships and control which we feel resembles the large corporation or organization. At other times some of us might be led to the view that there are certain characteristics which seem similar to all these which are also to be found in the growth of the modern hospital. Indeed, in a modern hospital we find many of the features which sociologists claim to belong to organizations as such, including bureaucracy, professionals, the existence of rules and control by seemingly impersonal forces.

The concept of Max Weber regarded modern industrial society as being characterized
bureaucracy by bureaucracy and it was he who developed a systematic theory of bureaucracy in organization. Weber conceived of a bureaucracy as having the following characteristics:
1. Tasks are specialized;
2. Authority is hierarchical;
3. There is a system of rules;
4. Employees are technically qualified and career-oriented;
5. The system is impersonal;
6. The system is efficient.

A bureaucratic organization becomes, then, more than a 'rule by officials or office'. In the way that Weber develops the idea it becomes a *model* or *ideal type* to which actual existing organizations might approximate. Weber appears to use 'bureaucracy' in three distinct ways: (*a*) as a type of organization in which there are fixed and official areas of jurisdiction, a graded system of authority, a system of central files, a set of special skills called office management, full-time personnel, a set of rules for defining procedure; (*b*) as the ideal type of rationality in organization which possesses clearly conceived goals, and which is also impersonal (office and incumbent are separated) and routinized (activities and relationships are simplified and regularized).

Some sociologists would claim that there is a certain ambiguity in Weber's use of the term 'bureaucracy' to imply a kind of rational organization. If he meant by it an organization that maximized administrative efficiency, then the above list *is* ambiguous. For example, some studies have shown quite clearly that efficiency is often best served by informal personal relations among staff and by unofficial practices. However, Weber is *not* in fact, equating rationality with efficiency. What he is most concerned with is the idea of authority, by which he means *charismatic authority* (based on some sacred or outstanding quality of the individual), *traditional authority* (based on a respect for custom), or *rational legal authority* (based on regulations and a code of legal rules).

Growth of the
modern hospital

The modern hospital is regarded by sociologists as an example of a modern institution exhibiting many of the characteristics of a complex organization. It is not surprising, therefore, that one of the organizational features it exhibits is a form of Weber's bureaucracy. The hospital that we recognize as such today can trace its origins back nearly two thousand years. Medicine was formerly regarded as an ancillary branch of religion, and in its beginnings its activities were defined in terms of a narrow and restricted religious dogmatism. Such a state continued until after the Middle Ages. The very word *hospitalis* (from the Latin noun *hospites* meaning guests) gives a clue to the function of the early hospitals, which were more akin to monasteries providing food and shelter for their guests. These buildings were in the charge of a hospitaller or chaplain who was aided by women, generally from a religious order. Such seemingly remote beginnings have had some considerable influence on the development of the modern hospital and its 'ethic'. For example, the foundation of Christian charity has emerged in modern times as 'working for others', as 'service' and 'welfare', and so on (although this is not to suggest that such considerations are restricted to Christians). Another idea which has survived is that hospitals and their personnel do not discriminate but are 'open' to all.

During the Renaissance period hospitals declined with the fall of the monastic orders and the conditions that consequently prevailed led to the passing of the English Poor Law in 1601. It was not until the development of the scientific outlook that hospitals became measurably better than under the monastic orders—some two hundred years later. One interesting feature of the period is that through their professional association physicians have gained control over the standards practised in the hospital setting.

The modern hospital became established as a remarkable improvement on the institutions of previous years, partly because of medicine becoming established on a scientific basis (for example, the evolvement of bacteriology and physiology) but also with the development of anaesthesia and antisepsis. A third and important development was the establishment of a trained and highly competent nursing staff originating with Florence Nightingale. As a result of the enhanced social status of the medical personnel, more and more of the affluent sectors of society were willing to entrust their prognosis and treatment to the hospitals. Furthermore, hospitals began to be seen as institutions for teaching and research. Today, the location of hospitals is mostly determined by existing buildings, mostly in inner urban areas, and which comprise the most famous of our teaching hospitals. New hospitals, however, must locate themselves in relation to the centres of population, the recruitment of appropriate staff and so on. In order to manage a vast and complex organization such as the modern hospital, staff and techniques are required which maximize efficiency. Consequently, a sociological concern has arisen towards the processes of decision-making which are carried out in hospitals and the way in which social roles are allocated, how they interact with each other and how they change over time.

The increase in the technological efficiency of the modern hospital has also meant an increase in the specialization of the roles within it. For example, at the end of the eighteenth century there were nine basic roles to be found in British hospitals. Gradually, with the increase in human skills and technological 'know-how', many additional categories were attached to hospitals, such as radiologists and cardiologists. Similarly, original categories became subdivided and multiplied. Coe gives the example of the nurse. 'At first, nurses did not only patient care and administrative duties but housekeeping tasks as well. Gradually, they were relieved of these lesser chores by personnel who filled a series of positions of orderlies, attendants, maids, and others. Today, skilled nursing consists mostly of coordinating the activities of many skilled and semiskilled personnel and supervising the execution of physicians' orders for technical care of their patients.'

The growth of the hospital industry and medical manpower

Between 1946 and 1963 the number of hospitals in America increased by 16,5 %. Such hospitals of the 7 138 in existence at the latter date as are designated voluntary, non-profit short-term institutions had, in the seventeen years' interval, increased the number of hospital personnel per patient by 56,4 % whereas the number of personnel employed had increased by 154,4 %. This meant that the number of personnel to every patient in 1963 was 244, as compared with 156 in 1946. The total expense had increased by 574,5 % to R22 000 million. Similarly, the trends in Great Britain between 1949 and 1964 show a pattern which follows that of the American hospital industry. By 1969 there were approximately 701 280 whole-time employees in the hospital services in Britain which included the following:

*   hospital medical staff, 25 657
*   hospital nursing staff, 300 598 (including 80 000 in training)
*   hospital midwifery staff, 19 438
*   hospital ancillary staff, 257 351
*   approximately a further 50 000 were clerical and administrative staff. These figures give an indication of how complex an organization the modern hospital has become.

The social structure of the modern hospital We began by sketching the characteristics of Weber's bureaucratic model, and in the next section we will examine the extent to which it is accurate to claim that hospitals are bureaucracies. Before we do so it will be useful to outline some of the practices which are carried out in this complex medical setting, paying particular attention to the authority system of the modern hospital which many sociologists have highlighted.

The division of labour within a hospital generally comprises seven sections as follows: (1) physicians; (2) paramedical, divided as (*a*) nursing ward and therapeutic personnel who serve the patient directly;

A MEDIEVAL HOSPITAL
Park-Davis Division of Warner-Lambert Co., Morris Plains, New Jersey

(b) laboratory and technical staff; (3) service workers such as those employed in the laundry and kitchens; (4) clerks; (5) administrators; (6) governing body; (7) patients. These categories, listed by Freidson, interact with one another in a highly complex manner within the organization of the hospital. Such an organization has been described as a prototype of a multi-purpose organization: 'it is a hotel and a school, a laboratory and a stage for treatment'. Because it is an organization a hospital processes goals or aims which might include the care of the patient. However, such goals may be various and include some which are important and some which are minor, such as saving on laundry costs. Whatever the goals there is a need to create and sustain an organization which can realize them. Apart from the formal goals which might be held by the majority of personnel there exist a number of sub-goals and informal goals which might be entertained by only a minority or specialized category of hospital staff.

Within the bureaucratic framework there exists a *dual* line of authority as mentioned by Coe, which consists of the administrative section and the medical section. Unlike other bureaucratic institutions it is the medical staff who have the control of the authority system (in the former the management would direct the line workers). 'Thus the medical staff usually directs the 'line' in its activities while the management's authority is often restricted to matters concerning providing the means by which the doctor's orders may be successfully carried out.' Traditionally, the patients are the physician's. This has the result that the nurse is receiving orders from the physician while at the same time being herself an employee of the hospital, and the added peculiarity that the position of the former is that of a 'visitor' or 'guest' stemming from the days when the hospital was completely separate. 'Often the demands of patient care, especially when they are of an emergency nature, cannot be accomplished within the framework of administrative rules; thus the nurse is caught in a conflict between the expectations of the physician that his orders be carried out and the expectations of the administrator that administrative procedures will be complied with.' Two other features of the hospital mentioned by Coe include the extreme division of labour with many specialities and the authoritarian nature of the hospital, which apparently can only survive in a setting in which orders are given and not questioned and where expertise is the keynote for action. Freidson goes so far as to suggest that physicians often intrude into ambiguous areas of hospital life on the grounds that these constitute an emergency 'so as to gain the aid or resources he believes he needs'. Again, such is the charismatic authority of the physician that his line of authority (defined by those to whom he gives orders) often extends to other personnel in the hospital to whom he is not a bureaucratic superior.

The modern hospital is no exception to other organizations which contain conflicting perspectives held by the personnel within it. For example, the patient has a highly personal and emotional involvement in his own illness which he is generally prevented from seeing correctly due to his lack of technical expertise in such areas as diagnosis. The medical staff, on the other hand, cannot *afford* to see the patient as an individual to the extent that they become emotionally involved with him. Hospital ancillaries are another example of a group of non-professionals who cannot be expected to have very much of a share in a professional ideology. Freidson sees the nurse as the 'intense focus of conflicting perspectives' because she provides the professional perspective on the ward and the locus of both administrative and medical authority. In the process of bargaining with the physicians she has the advantage of knowing her patients intimately, and in bargaining with the latter she can make full use of her access to the physician. 'Thus, while she may serve as a troubled focus of conflicting perspectives, she also may very well hold the balance of power in determining the outcome of bargaining among patient and staff.' Finally, the physician can well act as a hierarchical authority within an ostensibly democratic setting. As Freidson puts it, 'There is no court of appeal from superior training, knowledge, and judgement; technical decisions are not made by vote.'

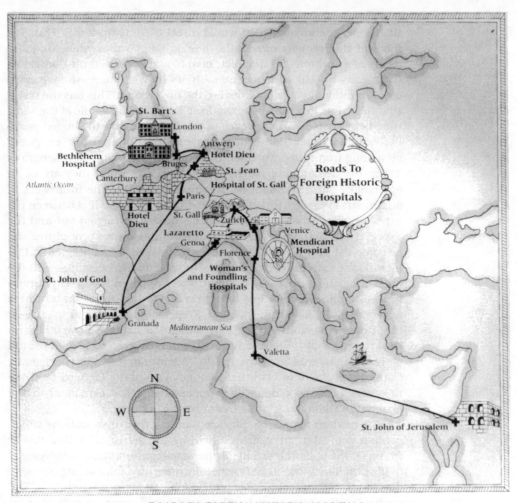

ROADS TO FOREIGN HISTORIC HOSPITALS

Patterns of ward care and models of patient care

Some hospitals contain more than one pattern of ward care, but generally such patterns can be broken down into three categories, as described by Freidson:

domestic service pattern (feeding, clothing, amusing—found in badly staffed institutions, mental and nursing and geriatric institutions)

medical-intervention pattern (medically dominated, generally excluding socio-psychological treatments)

therapeutic interaction (therapeutic milieu, rehabilitation).

Coe presents these models in table form and under different names. They are still, however, basically the same three which Freidson describes, and arise from the goals entertained by the organizations, certain ideological assumptions about disease, and a set of role expectations. Obviously there is not a complete overlap in the two sets of terminology but the similarities are sufficient to equate the two.

DIMENSION (Domestic Service Pattern)	CUSTODIAL	CLASSICAL (Medical interven- tion pattern)	REHABILITATION (Therapeutic intervention)
1. Stated goals	Comfort	Cure	Restoration
2. Assumptions about the disease process (a) Therapy (b) Sick role	Sporadic Permanent	Central Temporary	Supplementary Intermittent
3. Patient motivation	Obedience to in- stitutional rules	Obedience to 'doc- tor's orders'	Achieve mastery
4. Resulting institutional model	Total institution	Acute general hos- pital	Rehabilitation centre
Source: Adapted from Coe (1970), p. 283.			

Hospitals as bureaucracies

Weber's model of a bureaucracy was based more on the way work was organized (the administration) than the actual performance of tasks. Moreover, his model was heavily influenced by the Prussian government of his day and the almost complete absence of client-serving organizations in his time. Nevertheless, his model has influenced sociological studies of hospitals on the basis of its main features which we outlined at the beginning of this chapter, namely a hierarchy of authority which is official rather than personal, a series of impersonal relationships, a career which is clearly guaranteed, and an equally clear area of authority. Several reasons spring to mind as to why Weber's model is illuminating but not *exactly* appropriate. For example, the physician in the hospital often gives orders to those to whom he is not a bureaucratic superior. This has the affect of breaking the 'line of authority' which Weber conceives of as unilinear and necessary for efficient and organized performance in the day-to-day running of the hospital. Rosengren and Lefton (1969) suggest other reasons. Weber, for example, talks about authority residing in the 'hierarchy of offices *and* in demonstrated expertise', although in practice the more complex the organization the more likely it is that expertise is held by individuals who come from *outside* the administrative line. This is what has been termed the dual-authority system of the hospital. Again, hospitals may approximate more to the bureaucratic model depending on the type of hospital. Thus many hospitals are *total institutions* in Goffman's term in which control of the patient is improved by bureaucratic organization, for example mental hospitals. It is true to some extent, also, that wards within hospitals differ from each other to the extent that they approximate to the bureaucratic model. One study suggested that medical wards in hospitals 'conformed more closely to the bureaucratic model with a clearly demon-

THE WARD, NEW ORLEANS, 1859
The Bettmann Archive, New York

strated hierarchy of authority from the residents to the interns.
Autonomy in decision making at the nursing level was minimal.
Specific 'orders' and 'commands' stemmed from routinised and standardised channels. On the surgical side, however, the authority system
was considerably more flattened.' Consequently, the nurses were able
to, and indeed expected to, exercise more authority, autonomy and
inventiveness than medical nurses. One of the reasons given for the
differences between the two types of wards is that surgical wards have
patients whose illnesses are more specifically defined, and where
diagnosis is not so ambiguous. Other studies of surgical wards have
suggested that it is they that are more highly bureaucratized.

Bureaucracies and the psychiatric milieu

Some studies have suggested that bureaucratic features are dysfunctional to the goals of psychiatric hospitals because they create stresses and tensions and are not fitting to the flexibility required by the treatment. Further, the traditional lines of hospital bureaucracies based on a hierarchy of authority aggravate psychiatric patients.

Authority and influence structure

Several factors can affect the power structure as it exists within the hospital organization. Mechanic cites such factors as expertise, effort and interest, attractiveness (personality), location and position, coalitions and rules. The larger and more complex the organization the more inevitable it becomes that responsibility is delegated with the consequence that lower-ranking personnel often assume power in areas that the planners and the experts have opted out of due to other priorities. The lower-ranking personnel 'must see to it that the daily and more mundane activities progress. In taking this responsibility they assume considerable power which may appear trivial in the light of long-term organisational policy.'

Decision making and organizational structure in the British health Service

Kogan and Balle have listed some fourteen organizational activities which might be carried out in a hospital as follows: (1) board and housing; (2) general nursing services; (3) medical diagnosis; (4) in some hospitals the provision of treatment prescribed by a GP; (5) paramedical services; (6) training facilities; (7) development; (8) research facilities; (9) in psychiatric hospitals the provision of facilities for compulsory detention; (10) pre-registration facilities or training for doctors; (11) post-registration training facilities for doctors; (12) pre-registration training for nurses; (13) medical laboratory facilities; (14) public health education. They reiterate a point made before that out of the 20–30 professions that constitute a hospital the doctor occupies a dominant place because he is the only one able to prescribe within a legal framework. The group officers include the HMC, the Group Secretary and the Chief Nursing Officer. The last two work in a collateral relationship because in theory neither can instruct the other. Kogan and Balle present each hospital as possessing two (at least) executive hierachies, that of the hospital secretary and the senior nursing officer, both built upon superior-subordinate relationships.

The registrars and housemen are accountable to consultants, but consultants themselves are 'not accountable to any role within the hospital or within the group. They are employed and deployed by the RHBs'. Relationships between medical and paramedical staff (chiropodists, medical laboratory technicians, occupational therapists, physiotherapists, radiographers and remedial gymnasts) can take a variety of forms as follows: (1) paramedical workers subordinate to an administrator; (2) paramedical workers subordinate to a consultant;

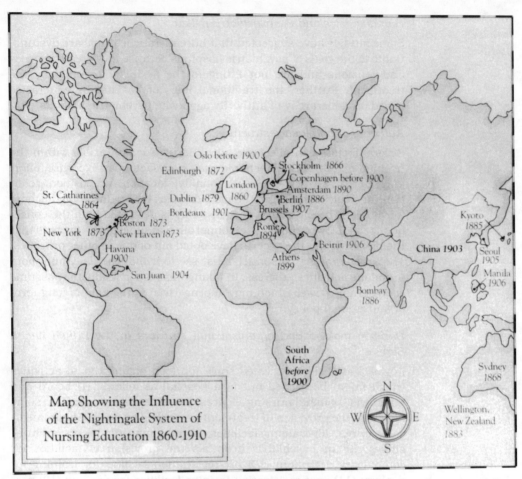

Map Showing the Influence of the
Nightingale System of Nursing Education 1860–1910

(3) paramedical workers subordinate to heads of department who are
also paramedical but not clearly subordinate to anyone; (4) when the
paramedical department does not have a medical head a lot of the work
is prescribed by a doctor although he leaves a great deal of discretion
to the paramedical worker; (5) when the paramedical department does
not have a medical head the doctor and the paramedical worker may
work collaterally. the dual-authority system of the medical and administrative personnel means that there are a limited number of criss-
cross points which consist of a common manager 'with authority to
determine issues between subordinates', for example the first criss-
cross point in a dispute between ward sister and a catering manager
would be the hospital management committee.

Hospitalization   When an individual becomes ill he or she will undergo a number of
changes both in the bodily state and in a psychologial sense. For

example, there may be actual pain or bodily discomfort due to the physical nature of the illness and, in addition, a perceived change in how others regard the patient, which results in loss of status, feelings of inferiority, uselessness, and so on. Admittance to hospital entails entry to an institution that is very different from the world outside. Not only are routines, attitudes, dress and so on abnormal, but a previously active individual is now reduced to a state in which physical movements are extremely limited. In addition, the admitted individual carries with him anxiety about the family he has left behind, certain tasks which have to be completed by others, and, in the case of admission to a mental hospital, some stigma. As Coe points out, however, certain cases of admission may actually reduce the strain on the remaining family who had found it almost impossible to cope.

Most institutions of this nature have the characteristic of totality in the sense that 'all aspects of life are conducted in the same place and under the same single authority'. Goffman's analysis of such a total institution is more applicable to mental hospitals, which allow the inmates to be treated in 'batches'. General hospitals are not quite the same. For example, patients are not as 'long-stay' as in mental hospitals and the 'batch' approach is carried out only in a few activities such as 'feeding, administering medication, bathing, assessing vital signs (blood pressure, temperature, pulse), arising and retiring . . .' Both medical establishments are socially stratified with the administration and medical branches separated. As Coe says, 'The main points of convergence are the significant distinction between those who give care and those who receive it and the kinds of occupational groups found in the organization and the ways in which these groups are stratified.'

When an individual enters a hospital he brings with him what Goffman has termed a 'presenting culture' of the whole way of life that he had before his entry. In order for the hospital to function effectively, however, and to obtain its goals, it is necessary for the patients to be assimilated into the organizational processes of the hospital. These are described by Coe as stripping, control of resources, and the restriction of mobility. The stripping procedure results in 'every distinctly personalising symbol, material or otherwise . . . (being) . . . taken away, thus reducing the patient to the status of just one of many'. The second organizational process, the control or resources, 'is concentrated in the hands of the staff. This enables them to manipulate the physical environment (including patients, regardless of the desires or expectations of the patients) for the purpose of regulating the patient behaviour . . .' Such control is not only over physical items but extends to severe limitations being placed upon knowledge. '. . . more often it is the patient who is deprived of information about events in the hospital and particularly information concerning himself.' Lastly, the patient is severely restricted as to where he can or cannot go within a hospital. More often than not a patient is confined to a small physical space such as his bed or his ward.

SICK WOMAN IN WARD OVERRUN BY RATS IN BELLEVUE HOSPITAL
Engraving from Harper's Weekly, 1860. Museum of the City of New York, New York

There are four ways of adjustment to the process of hospitalization which are mentioned by Coe. The first way is by physical or psychological withdrawal. Secondly, the patient can contravene the hospital and staff's rules by overt aggression. Thirdly, the patient may integrate himself into group and institutional activities. Lastly, patients may acquiesce by complying with the institutional way of life. The degree and combination of these modes of adjustment vary according to age, sex, race, degree of illness, and so on.

Patient care and the influence of organizational factors

The type of organization in which a patient is 'housed' can have a varying affect on the care he receives. One simple example is that a mental patient in a large custodial and bureaucratic nineteenth-century institution receives a totally different course of treatment (if any) than someone perhaps in a small 'open' psychiatric hospital. Several studies have shown considerable variation between mental hospitals in the treatment of patients, for example in the degree of physical freedom allowed to ward inmates, the amount of locker space, personal effects. Another factor influencing patient care is the attitude of relatives. When there is no one at home to care for him a patient may be retained in hospital even when his symptoms have disappeared. It has also been found that frequency of visitors was correlated with a shorter stay in hospital, a patient with fewer visits being more likely to stay in hospital for a longer period. New trends in community care have meant that it is now easier to relocate patients in the community.

One study, by Emerson (1970), deals with how definitions of reality are sustained in gynaecological examinations by the elaborate medical ritual and organization. 'The medical definition grants the staff the right to carry out their task. If not for the medical definition the staff's routine activities could be defined as unconscionable assaults on the dignity of individuals.' Such examinations are carried out in 'medical space' (hospital or doctor's office). 'The staff wear medical uniforms, don medical gloves, use medical instruments. The exclusion of lay persons, particularly visitors of the patient who may be accustomed to the patient's nudity at home, helps to preclude confusion between the contact of medicine and the contact of intimacy . . . The patient's body is draped so as to expose only the part which is to receive the technical attention of the doctor. The presence of a nurse acting as 'chaperon' cancels any residual suggestiveness of male and female alone in a room.' Any threat to the medical detachment is counteracted by appropriate responses by the gynaecologist and his team nurse.

A further substantiation is provided by Frankfort (1972) in her decription of what she terms the 'gynecological ritual'.

The receptionist, the magazines, the waiting room, and then the examination itself—being told to undress, lying on your back with your feet in the stirrups, looking at a blank ceiling while waiting in an orderly air-conditioned room (the doctor isn't the one without clothes, after all) for him to enter—and no one thinking that meeting a doctor for the first time in this position is slightly odd. (p. xii)

Hospitals and patients and environments

Hospitals sometimes pursue goals which are in conflict with one another, such as trying to provide a service while at the same time attempting to maintain the system. While the organization attempts to depersonalize the patient, the latter combats such moves by various strategies available to him. Sometimes the patient has to acquiesce to the demands of the institution even though they are presented as an aid to the maintenance of the social system rather than to any improvement in his health.

Relationships between staff and between staff and patient differ according to the medical setting in which they occur. Rosengren and Lefton suggest that 'special' cases such as a metabolic unit, a tuber-culosis unit, a children's hospital, a rehabilitation unit, and a terminal ward or hospital all present changes in relationships because the patients or clients are specially selected for care or treatment.

Finally, hospitals exist within communities and are to be regarded as to some extent the product of various ecological, demographic and economic characteristics of the area which they serve. The *community morphology* approach tends to view them as micro-structures of the community they serve.

The architecture of the hospital

Prior (1988, p. 86) argues that the spatial divisions which are expressed in buildings 'can best be understood in relation to the discursive practices which are enclosed in their interiors.' The architectural form of a hospital building is 'inextricably bound up with the forms of medical theorising and medical practice which were operant at the hour of their construction.' Consequently:

All subsequent modifications to hospital design can be seen as a product of alterations in medical discourse. As a corollary of this . . . architectural features have no existence outside and beyond the forms of thought and practice which produced them and that it is therefore erroneous to speak of the 'logic of space', or of spatial properties which are independent of observers and actors.
(Ibid., p. 110)

Prior traces the development of the children's ward which only appeared in 1852. The Pavilion Design was an expression of the miasmic theory of disease with its emphasis on free air ventilation. With the advent of the germ theory of disease at the end of the nineteenth century the emphasis was on the operating theatre, the laboratory and the isolation cubicle. Other concerns are with the diffusion of light, the distribution of space per bed, as well as ward ventilation.

The early asylums demanded a very special architecture. It was an era of physical constriction. The architecture of madness had a certain constancy:

Enclosure of the inmates from the external environment and the internal partitioning of space. And, more importantly, in each of the asylums the emphasis is upon certain cells.
(Ibid., p. 102)

The regulation of the body, together with control and segregation, were the result of disciplinary spacing.

However, as madness transposed into illness throughout the nineteenth century the architecture of the asylum came to approximate more and more to that of the general hospital.
(Ibid., p. 106)

Theories of nursing

The South African Council of Nurses has described nursing science as follows:

Nursing science is a human clinical health science that constitutes the body of knowledge for the practice of persons, registered or enrolled under the Nursing Act as Nurses or Midwives. Within the parameters of nursing philosophy and ethics it is concerned with the development of knowledge for the nursing diagnosis, treatment and personalised health care of persons exposed to, suffering, or recovering from physical or mental ill-health. It encompasses the knowledge of preventive, promotive, curative and rehabilitative health care for individuals, families, groups and communities and covers man's life span from before birth.

The first theory of nursing was formulated by the English founder of nursing, Florence Nightingale, who emphasised what subsequently became known as the *nursing paradigm*, that is *person, nursing, health* and *environment*.

The Nightingale System soon spread throughout the British Empire, including South Africa, and emphasised the Matron of the hospital as having total responsibility for patients, personnel and training, domestic staff and laundry, linen and kitchens. The Matron was responsible only to the Hospital Board. Nurses lived in nurse's homes and were divided into probationer nurses and educated probationers. Nightingale believed that nursing schools should be attached to medical schools and teaching hospitals, probationer nurses had to be impeccable in their behaviour, and the matron (now Nursing Service Manager) was responsible for the entirety of the operation, including teaching and domestic supervision.

The American System was essentially an adaptation of the Nightingale System and is to be found principally in North America. It, also, adheres to the concept of training schools being attached to hospitals, with the responsibility being focussed on the superintendent of nurses. However, a dietician has responsibility for the catering department and its personnel, with a domestic matron controlling housekeeping.

The Motherhouse System has developed from the old female religious orders with substantial 'on the job' training. Retired nurses are accommodated in nurse's homes attached to the organisation.

The Continental System appropriated aspects of both the American and Nightingale system and exists parallel with the Motherhouse System. Head Nurses of each block report directly to a doctor and also to the hospital's director, who may be medical or lay. this system is to be found in Latin America and the European Continent. (Mellish, 1988, pp. 162–164)

The major contributor to nursing theory and practice in South Africa is Charlotte Searle, who emphasises the following:

1. Care for the sick by 'folk art' (not for gain);
2. Home-nursing and first aid as a voluntary social duty;
3. Formal training.

These qualities form the essential element in the concept of nursing.

The nurse practitioner has to develop her own ability and sensitivity as a nurse. This sensitivity is based on the personal philosophy of the nurse, how she sees her role as a nurse and the needs of those for whom she has to provide care. The cultivation of values and sensitivity in the nurse–patient (person) relationship is basic to the development of empathy, sympathy and personal and professional integrity. Every action, every verbal or non-verbal act of communi-cation, influences the way in which the patient sees himself, the nurse and his interaction with her. It influences him in the choices he makes for his health care. The figure below demonstrates this interactive concept.

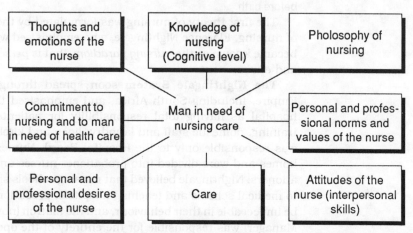

Diagram to show the interactive processes in nursing, showing the importance of 'the self' in nursing care and how this interacts with the patient and how the patient inter-acts with all dimensions of nursing
(Searle, 1987, p. 64)

Two further nursing theorists require mention. Imogene King's Inter-action-Transaction Systems Model views ill-health as the inability to function in various prescribed social roles. These she describes as:

1. Personal systems (perception, self, growth, and development, body image, space and time);
2. Interpersonal systems (human interaction, communication, trans-actions, role and stress);
3. Social systems (organisations, authority, power, status, decision-making).
(King, 1981)

Madeleine Leininger's theory of *transcultural nursing* embodies the concept of care as a universal human need necessary for human beings to survive. She constructed a caring classification system containing a series of verbal cultural caring symbols as follows:

A Psychological caring symbols:
1. affective;
2. cognitive;
B Practical caring symbols:
1. social organisation;
2. technical;
C Interactional caring symbols:
1. physical;

2. social;

D Philosophical caring symbols:

1. spiritual;
2. ethical;
3. cultural.

(Leininger, 1984)

Types of
organisations
We have mentioned elsewhere sociological distinctions concerning various types of organisations. One useful way of distinguishing between organisations was devised by Parsons (1960) as follows:

1. Integrative organisations. These function to maintain social control. These generally are organisations concerned with the law such as South Africa's judicial system.
2. Goal attainment organisations. These are generally aimed at the attainment of political goals such as government undertakes when it bestows power on certain individuals and groups.
3. Adaptive organisations. These are generally organisations concerned with the generation of economic activities, such as a small general dealer or the Ford Factory at Port Elizabeth.
4. Pattern maintenance organisations. These are organisations concerned with cultural inheritance. For example, the family is responsible for passing on the process of socialisation, and schools for passing on the pattern of education.

Parson's neat classification is very typical of the functionalist approach which relies heavily on goals and needs and sees society as ordered and regulated. Such an approach is conservative and sees society as harmonious and integrated. Consequently Parsons views the sick person as deviant and the admission to hospital as signalling the cessation of the normal role.

The hospital as an organisation

The hospital exhibits the core characteristics of authority, communication, formality, rigidity and division of labour:

1. Authority.

In addition to Weber's three types of authority mentioned earlier it is clearly useful to distinguish between *staff and line authority* (Du Toit, unpublished M.A. thesis). Thus an example of line authority among medical personnel would be as follows:

medical superintendent
deputy medical superintendent/s
chief surgeon/physician/gynaecologist/urologist/paediatrician, etc
registrars
senior housemen
housemen

CARTOON OF A MAN-MID-WIFE OR A NEWLY DISCOVERED ANIMAL,
DEPICTING A MIDWIFE BISECTED INTO MALE AND FEMALE HALVES.
From S.W. Fores, *Man-midwifery Dissected*, London, 1793.
Wellcome Institute for the History of Medicine, London, England.

Authority of this type is clearly hierarchical with a distinctive and descending order:

The staff authority originated from a need for specialised knowledge and skills usually unknown to the people in the line organisation. The staff organisation thus includes, in the context of the hospital, specialists like medical practitioners, nurses, paramedical personnel (professional personnel) and others.

However, in the hospital the line and staff organisation are in a unique relationship to each other; the line organisation includes persons in administrative positions, but these persons have specialised knowledge and skills, for example, the medical superintendent of the hospital. The medical superintendent is an administrator as well as a professionally qualified medical doctor, and wields authority over administrative as well as professional personnel. Despite the differences in authority between the staff and line organisations, one cannot exist without the other. The administrative (line) organisation personnel is responsible for the procurement of resources necessary for the functions of the professional personnel. These resources include personnel and stock . . .

Apart from staff and line authority, two other lines of authority can be identified in the hospital . . . On the one hand, there is the 'collegial' organisation of the medical and nursing staff and the ethical and professional prescriptions issued by the professional bodies of these professions. On the other hand there are the administrative rules and regulations of the hospital often referred to as 'red tape'.
(Ibid.)

2. Communication.

Du Toit and Van Staden (1989) describe communication within a hospital setting as being *vertical* and *horizontal*. The former is both upwards and downwards within the line of authority while the latter is between persons of the same hierarchical level.

3. Formality and rigidity.

In the hospital environment, where strict adherence to rules is essential, there are bound to be a number of situations in which *over-adherence* causes depersonalisation to staff and students.

4. Division of labour.

It goes without saying that each member of staff has a precisely allocated role in which prescribed tasks are performed.

The primary health care team Primary health care is essentially health care at ground level or, to put it another way, the initial or first level of health provision. Primary health care (or PHC) has been defined by the World Health Organisation and the United Nation's Children's Fund (WHO/UNICEF Report to Alma-Ata Conference, September 1978) as follows:

Primary Health Care is essential health care made universally accessible to individuals and families in the community by means acceptable to them, through their full participation and at a cost that the country and the community can afford. It forms an integral part, both of the country's health system of which it is the nucleus and of the overall social and economic development of the community.

It is essential that PHC includes the following areas of provision:
1. A safe environment, including water and sanitation;
2. Adequate nutrition;
3. Basic preventative health care such as immunisation, antenatal and postnatal care, obstetric care, family planning, health education;
4. Care for the aged, handicapped and chronic sick;
5. Screening of persons, treatment and referral;
6. Provision of services for *all.*

The general nurse is the mainstay of PHC although there is no longer provision for a singly qualified general nurse. There are currently some 11 000 still remaining on the SANC register. (Mellish, 1988). The midwife, in recent times, became established firmly in England with the foundation of the Midwives Institute in 1881. In South Africa, due to the pioneering efforts of Mary Hirst Watkins, registration of midwives first occurred in the Transvaal in 1896 and Natal in 1899. By 1986 there were 51 774 registered midwives in South Africa as follows:

Whites, 22 338
Coloureds, 5 087
Indians, 1 169
Blacks, 23 180

Another category of nursing is that of psychiatric nursing which came into its own in 1975 when the Mental Health Act, 1973, was promulgated.

Community nursing

Community nursing embraces a number of categories in its historical development, such as the school nurse, tuberculosis nursing and industrial nursing. Mellish (1988) sees three main contributions to the emergence of community nursing in the South African context. Firstly, the work of the *Vrouevereniging* in all four provinces led to the establishment of district nursing and midwifery services, particularly in rural areas. Secondly, the establishment of the Cape Hospital Board in 1912 aimed to improve the health of the community by providing health education, primary health care in homes or at clinics and domiciliary midwifery service. Thirdly, voluntary organisations emerged and developed.

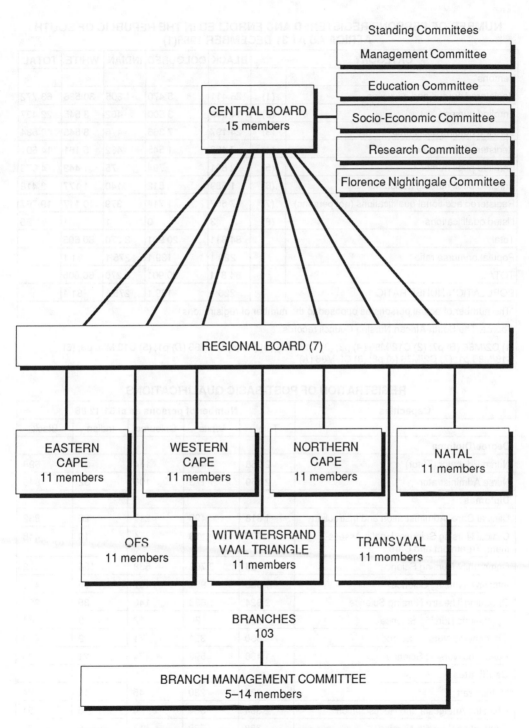

**STRUCTURE OF THE SOUTH AFRICAN NURSING ASSOCIATION
(AN ELECTED POLICY-MAKING BODY)**
Searle, 1987, p. 98

NUMBER OF PERSONS REGISTERED AND ENROLLED IN THE REPUBLIC OF SOUTH AFRICA AS AT 31 DECEMBER 1985(1)

CATEGORY		BLACK	COLOURED	INDIAN	WHITE	TOTAL
Persons*						
Registered nurses and midwives	(1)	26 411	5 470	1 305	30 586	63 772
Enrolled nurses	(2)	14 930	3 500	462	3 545	22 437
Enrolled nursing assistants	(3)	24 197	7 366	476	8 545	40 584
Registered student nurses	(4)	7 463	1 545	432	5 161	14 601
Enrolled pupil nurses	(5)	2 661	794	75	1 443	4 973
Enrolled pupil nursing assistants	(6)	1 589	512	140	1 177	3 418
Registered additional qualifications (not persons)	(7)	7 557	1 714	379	10 117	19 767
Listed qualifications	(8)	3	0	1	31	35
Total		84 811	20 901	3 270	60 605	
Population/nurse ratio		220.1	139.1	275.1	81.1	
TOTAL		84 811	20 901	3 270	60 605	
POPULATION/NURSE RATIO		220:1	139:1	275:1	81:1	

*The number of actual persons as opposed to the number of registrations.

Source: The South African Nursing Council records

(1) C2/M86 (*B*) p7; (2) C12/M86 (*A*) p2; (3) C17/M86 (*A*) p1; (4) C3/M86 (*D*) p1; (5) C13/M86 p3; (6) C18/M86 p1; (7) C2/M86 (*J*) p8; (8) C2/M86 (*K*)

REGISTRATION OF POST-BASIC QUALIFICATIONS

Capacities	Number of persons as at 31/12/86				
	Total	White	Coloured	Indian	Black
Degree/Diploma					
Nurse Educator (Tutor)	2 068	1 489	144	37	698
Nurse Administrator	2 159	1 173	106	32	848
Diplomas					
Clinical Care, Administration and Instruction	1 618	493	217	26	882
Clinical Nursing Science, Health Assessment, Treatment and Care	475	13	4	10	448
Community Nursing Science	5 328	2 762	538	156	1 872
Intensive Nursing Science	1 665	992	167	35	471
Operating Theatre Nursing Science	2 824	1 636	146	35	907
Ophthalmic Nursing Science	318	36	12	9	261
Orthopaedic Nursing Science	830	321	71	9	429
Paediatric Nursing Science	1 488	598	174	21	695
Certificates					
Mothercraft	430	280	45	11	94
Obstetric Analgesia and Recuscitation	394	334	4	5	51
Occupational Health Nursing	388	328	17	6	37
(Mellish, 1988, P. 83.					

The Role of the The following factors will have an increasing influence upon this role:
South African The work of international health agencies such as the World Health Organi-
nurse sation is opening up new fields of health care.

The philosophy of humanitarianism prevalent in the Western World, and which demands that health care must be available to all by the year 2000, is extending the role of the nurse. This will go far beyond that envisaged at present. The responsibility that nurses in remote areas will have to bear will be greatly increased. At the same time, knowledge of these factors is creating a deep awareness among nurses of the importance of their role, their responsibility for establishing sound human relations in communities and meaningful patient–nurse interpersonal relationships. It is also engendering a new awareness of the vital necessity of continuing education that relates to their particular field of work, as well as to professional growth and development in general.

In certain societies the feminist movement could have disastrous effects for the nurse practitioner, whilst in others it could lead to the gradual emancipation of women. Wisdom in dealing with the inequalities in male and female status must characterise the attitudes of the nurse practitioner in Africa. Similarly so, great wisdom is necessary, particularly in traditional societies, to develop a philosophy of sharing the burden of family relationships and responsibilities between husband and wife. Burn-out, both in professional and private life, is bound to increase if, in this era of increasing pressure in the work situation and in family life, the family partners do not acknowledge that the burden of being wife, mother and professional practitioner is an excessively arduous one and that the successful professional practitioner needs a stable, co-operative family life. In some areas the feminist movement will lead to greater assertiveness and even aggressiveness on the part of nurses.

The increase in the world's population, which is expected to reach 8 000 million by the year 2020, will drastically increase the demand for health services. This is already escalating so rapidly that the demand for all categories of nursing personnel is increasing dramatically. The result will be that the registered nurse practitioner will inevitably face serious competition in the employment field, for the numbers in the sub-professional categories of nurses exceed those in the professional categories and their services are less costly. The increased use of these categories will place a greater supervisory burden on the registered practitioner, whilst the risk to the public will inevitably increase.

The ideal 'health for all by the year 2000' requires that the nurse practitioner adjusts her philosophy of care so that she can provide a comprehensive service in the preventive, promotive, curative and rehabilitative fields. The practitioner must view man as a person with a life-span of health with possible episodes of sickness.

The human rights theory that every human being has a right to health is having a profound effect on the work of the nurse/midwife, who has to educate the individual, the family and the community at large to protect and promote their own health through safer life-styles, responsible collaboration with health professionals and, through the cultivation of a sense of personal responsibility for their own health, the health of their families and their communities. The nurse practitioner is playing a key role in this field and is in the vanguard to educate the public about family planning, nutrition and promotive and preventive health measures and to provide services for the early detection and treatment of ill-health as an essential measure to prevent regression of the health status of the individual.

The increased facilities for communication in the health field, for example computer-based assistance in providing health care information and continuing education even in remote areas, will also affect the nurse practitioner. The use of television, radio and the plethora of professional journals, books and research reports available will provide such a volume of information to every practitioner that she will not be able to cope with it, as well as with her work, unless she learns how to select information that applies to her particular sphere of practice and to her profession in general. This is a skill every practitioner must acquire.

The nurse practitioner's image is crucial in the demanding health situation. Every practitioner must be a well educated person who commands the respect of and can hold her own with other health professionals, as well as with her patients and the community. Every nurse practitioner has a leadership role to play in her community.

The realisation of the public and other health professionals that nurses/midwives hold a great deal of social power will gradually affect their roles. In many developing countries, including part of South Africa nurses/midwives are the main group of educated women. These practitioners have learnt how to command difficult situations, have managed large numbers of patients and personnel, have coped with disasters, have confidence in their own ability to handle the health affairs of mankind, know the needs and aspirations of women and know the communities they serve. They have the basic knowledge and abilities to meet the escalating demands of the health care situation. All nurse/midwife practitioners must brace themselves and face the task ahead of them.

The ability to develop co-operation on a collegial basis with the medical and other health professions is of paramount importance. The multi-disciplinary health team is a feature of modern health care. To be successful, the team must work on an equal partnership basis. If the nurse/midwife practitioner in the team is timid, unsure of herself and adopts a *handmaiden* approach, she will be a handmaiden not only to the doctor, but to all the other health professionals in the team. If she is incompetent and lacks the requisite knowledge about patient care that other members of the team have, she will be overlooked by them.

The role of the nurse/midwife practitioner as a *social developer* in her area is also of major importance. Health care forms an integral part of social development in any area. The nurse practitioner has a major role to play in identifying health needs, advising on the distribution and adequacy of coverage of the available health facilities, the efficacy of the intervention, the observable benefits derived from the utilisation of resources, the acceptability of the service to the community, the extent and potential of community involvement, the questions that need answers, the availability of local resources and the relationship of the work of *all* sectors in the social system to resolve major problems.

The available health resources and the effectiveness of health planning will inevitably have a major impact on the role of the nurse practitioner. She has a duty to concern herself with the concepts, trends and costs of health care, the reasons for escalations in costs, the quality of health care, the nature of public expectations, the changing epidemiological picture, the organisation and structure of the health care delivery system, the economic developments or retardation arising from the health status of an area and the measurement of the effects of the health care work with which she is involved. The nurse practitioner is concerned with all aspects of the quality of human life and health, for this is essential to socio-economic development. Every nurse practitioner makes a contribution to the development of health services and must be knowledgeable about the provision of health care and the needs of the relevant community.

The cultural and religious beliefs of the people the nurse serves will require her to provide services within such parameters, but will also require her to involve herself increasingly in decisions concerning the artificial termination of pregnancy, the problem of the newborn with gross congenital defects, the use of human foetuses in research, sterilisation of humans, castration, artificial insemination, human experimentation, trials of therapeutic substances on human beings, euthanasia, tissue and organ transplants, the moment of death, psycho-surgery, environmental protection, compulsory immunisation for health protection, family planning, compulsory self-protective measures, detention for treatment in medical institutions, and the threatened loss of professional secrecy through the use of computers in the health care situation.

The utilisation of the nurse/midwife practitioner as an agent of change within the profession, the health services and the community will be a major factor in health service development and social change. Epstein maintains that nurses have a significant role to play in the process of social change. They combine a high level of health knowledge with a keen awareness of the psycho-social problems associated with health care. The nurse practitioner generally has a high level of personal skill in relating to patients and their families (Epstein 1974:79). Nurse practitioners have a duty to involve themselves In community planning, development and public policy formulation through service on commissions, councils, committees and in parliament. The nurse practitioner has a major role to play in health and social education, particularly of women and children, and through research and professional publications.

The contributions of 'space-medicine' to health care might well result in a vast array of new techniques and new principles in health care, necessitating up-dating and continuing education on an extensive scale. This will result in a reorganisation of the traditional approaches to post-basic nursing education at all levels. The traditional time factor of a one-year course in a speciality will inevitably be replaced as modern educational technology to expedite the learning process becomes available. Smaller units of learning to meet the rapid change in specialised health care knowledge will be the general method of approach to formal post-basic and continuing education in the practitioner's employment situation.

There is already a notable increase in patient expectations arising from the prepaid health care movement, rising levels of education and political awareness and improved health education. In addition to dealing with patient problems of increased complexity, the nurse practitioner will have to equip herself to function in such a demanding situation. Patients are demanding greater availability of health services, a higher quality of care, more personal involvement in care and a greater depth of understanding from nurse practitioners. The changing patterns of ill-health are resulting in increased chronic illnesses, new sicknesses and multiple problems regarding care, all of which demand more expert nursing observations, better counselling and more complex treatment.

The fact that patients are becoming more involved in decisions about their health care necessitates that nurse practitioners adopt a co-operative instead of a maternalistic role.

The relationship between the roles of doctors and nurses is changing. The population explosion demands more health services, but such key personnel as doctors and pharmacists cannot be produced as rapidly as the population growth demands. The nurse practitioner has perforce to take on duties that are normally the purview of a doctor and/or a pharmacist. This broadens the nurse's scope of practice, but at the same time increases her legal liability. The nurse's education must equip her to meet this growing need.

The increase in the multiplicity and the multi-dimensionality of health problems requires a major change in the attitudes of health personnel, particularly of nurses, to ensure multi-faceted, personalised 'patient care' instead of so-called 'health care'.

The increase in the multiplicity of interprofessional relationships arising in the health team situation is resulting in the overlapping of functions between the various disciplines represented on the health team. This frequently leads to discord among the members of the team. Status conflicts arise as the levels of education of the various professional groups improve and approximate that of the doctor more closely. Much of modern health care does not consist of 'doctoring', but falls within the purview of other health professions. The doctor finds it hard to accept that he need not always be on 'top', but must always be on 'tap'.

The changing patterns of health care such as the increase in ambulatory care; the privatisation of health services; the use of hospitals as 'intensive care settings'; the extension of home care services; the development of health centres, day and night hospitals, mobile services and private practice; new patterns of staffing; increased utilisation of nurses; and increased flexibility in the use of nursing personnel and the provision of health care will all have a major impact on the role and functions of the nurse practitioner and *ipso facto* on her education and levels of responsibility.

(Searle, 1987, pp. 319–323)

Health services Mellish (1988) has adequately sketched the implications of the Health
in Southern Act for nurses and the establishment of a National Health Policy
Africa Council. Searle and Brink (1982) state:

> The aim of this Council is to ensure that the various authorities which provide
> health services in the Republic shall carry out all such activities as they are
> authorised to do so under the Health Act and any other applicable law, 'to
> promote the health of the inhabitants of the Republic so that every person shall
> be enabled to attain and maintain a state of complete physical, mental and
> social wellbeing, and which shall exercise such other powers and perform such
> other duties as may be conferred or imposed upon it by this Act.

Mellish sees the constitution of this Council as providing for a
Minister of Health and including members of the Executive Committee
for each province, who are charged with Hospital Services. This creates
a mechanism by which health problems peculiar to a province can be
presented directly to the Government of the day. Mellish goes on to
explain:

> (The Health Matters Advisory Committee) is of vital importance. It is composed
> of representatives of the Department of Health and Welfare, including the
> Director-General, the Director of Hospital Services of each provincial adminis-
> tration, Medical Officers of Health of local authorities rendering services in
> urban as well as rural areas, and the Surgeon-General of the South African
> Defence Force. The Committee considers health matters and makes recom-
> mendations to the National Health Advisory Council.
> (Mellish, 1988, p. 178)

There are twenty-five different categories of nurses registered with the
South African Nursing Council in 1988 only the following being
numerically significant:

General nurse	11 067
General nurse (males)	1 212
General and psychaitric nurse and midwife	6 517
General nurse and midwife	45 998
Midwife and enrolled nurse	1 547
TOTAL NUMBER OF NURSES ON 31/12/88	69 347
TOTAL NUMBER OF NURSES ON 31/12/87	67 088

(Figures supplied by SANC, 1990)

The real implications for nurses arise out of the Sub-committee on
Nursing which consists of representatives of the Department of Health
and Welfare, the South African Military Nursing Service, the Department of Prisons, the four provincial Departments of Hospital Services,
local authorities and the South African Nursing Association. With the
exception of the Chairperson all members of the Sub-committee are
nurses and are concerned with the totality of nursing and nursing
services. Consequently the establishment of such a committee means
that nurses have a major role to play at the policy-making level of
Government.

Mellish goes on to elaborate the distinct advantages of the professional composition of such a committee:

They consider matters related to nursing in depth and make recommendations to the Health Matters Advisory Committee. This Committee, in turn, makes recommendations to the National Health Policy Council.

It may seem that the new dispensation is rather far removed from the average professional nurse in practice, but the members of the Subcommittee on Nursing have the fullest right to consult any member of the profession, at any level, for advice or information on specific aspects of the rendering of nursing services. This power or right is spelt out in the provisions of the functions of the Health Matters Advisory Committee, which states: 'the committee may at its discretion, in regard to any matter falling within the scope of its functions, consult any person, body or authority and may take evidence from or hear representations by such person, body or authority' (section 3 (2) of the Health Act). The same provisions apply to the members of the subcommittees. Thus the members of the Subcommittee on Nursing can also institute inquiry into specific problem areas. This type of inquiry or investigation could involve many nurses, even though only by completing a simple questionnaire. It is also possible for nurses to bring specific problem areas to the attention of the members of the Subcommittee, who then have a truly broad base of relevant information upon which to debate and base their recommendations regarding policy.

(Mellish, 1988, pp. 178–179)

The Health Act specifically recommended certain functions for various Departments of Health and Welfare:

The various departments of health and welfare

The functions of the Departments of Health and Welfare include:

- the coordination of health services rendered by the Departments, with due regard to health services rendered by provincial administrations and local authorities
- the establishment of a national health laboratory service
- promotion of a safe and healthy environment
- the promotion of family planning
- the provision of services for the procurement of evaluation of evidence of a medical nature with a view to legal proceedings
- any other functions as may be assigned to it by the Minister.

The practical implications for nurses, especially those employed by the Departments, are thus related to assisting in the coordination of services and the promotion of family planning, as well as undertaking or participating in relevant research programmes.

The provincial administrations

The functions of the provincial administrations include:

- the provision of hospital facilities and services

- the provision of an ambulance service within its province and, where necessary, the coordination of services with adjacent provincial services

- the provision of facilities for the treatment of patients suffering from acute mental illness

- the provision of out-patient facilities in hospitals or other places where patients are treated for a period of less than 24 hours

- the provision of maternity homes and services
  the provision of personal health services, either on its own or in cooperation with local authorities

- the coordination of services with a view to the establishment of a comprehensive health service in the province, taking into account the services rendered by others providing health services

- any other functions assigned to it by the Minister.
(Mellish, 1988, p. 180)

The positive benefits to nursing in the sense of greater involvement are apparent:

Here the practical implications for nursing practice are perhaps more obvious, as the nurse is heavily involved in rendering nursing care and supplying nursing services at a visible level.

The Act indicates that the function of the provincial administrations shall be to provide certain facilities or services, but does not actually state that they themselves render such services. This means that the facilities of other existing organisations may continue to be used, being duly compensated monetarily therefore by the provincial administration budget.

From a nursing point of view this means that much closer cooperation between services is possible and that the services should no longer consider their functions in separate 'compartments'. It should also make it possible to assess the services being rendered by the various authorities and thus to eliminate unnecessary duplication.

Another factor to be considered is that the provincial authorities can become involved in more primary health care centres where patients are not accommodated overnight and in incorporating immunisation services and family planning clinics into their existing hospital out-patient or detached clinics. This is already being done, but with more careful consultation and planning among the various authorities much more coordination could be achieved, which would benefit patients and clients and ensure the prudent allocation of scarce resources, both human and material.
(Op. cit., p. 180)

The functions of the local authorities

- These include the maintenance of its district in a clean and hygienic condition at all times

- the prevention of the occurrence of any nuisance within its district
  when a nuisance has occurred, abating it or causing it to be abated, or remedying it or causing it to be remedied

- preventing the pollution of water intended for the use of the inhabitants of its district

- the prevention of communicable diseases, the promotion of the health of persons, and the rehabilitation in the community of persons cured of any medical conditions and participation in the coordination of such services.

A nuisance is defined and other provisions are laid down, including aspects such as the appointment of medical officers of health, nurses, health inspectors and other health personnel.

Provisions are also made for the making of regulations which add flesh to the skeleton provided by the Act with which to carry out the intentions of the Act without it being necessary to resort to amendments of the Act each time—a quite impractical state of affairs.

Again it can be seen that there is provision for the coordination of health services, which has very obvious implications for nursing practice.

In November 1980 the Minister of Health announced that a National Health Services Facilities Plan had been drawn up. This plan was formulated by the Subcommittee for Health Service Buildings and submitted to the Health Matters Advisory Committee. This Committee, in turn, placed the matter before the National Health Policy Council, which approved the plan. Thus it is clear that the coordinative system instituted by the Health Act does play a role in the formulation of policy which should not be underestimated.

The underlying principle of the National Health Services Facilities Plan is the need for a policy which provides not only for *facilities*, but for the *actual delivery* of health services and *the provision of funds* for the development of a comprehensive service.

- Other principles incorporated in the plan are the following:
  Centralisation of policy formation and planning of health services, facilities and strategy

- Decentralisation of services and facilities in which the promotive, preventive, rehabilitative and curative components all take their rightful place

- Shifting of emphasis from a curatively oriented service to a service in which attention is also given to basic needs, the promotion of health and other facets of health care

- Community involvement

- Coordination of services and collective utilisation of facilities by different authorities

- Recognition of the task of the private practitioner and the integration of his services with those of the public sector.
  (Mellish, 1988, p. 181)

A more detailed summary can be found in Searle and Brink (1982) and Strauss (1981).

THE NATIONAL
HEALTH PLAN
AND ASSOCIATED
VARIABLES

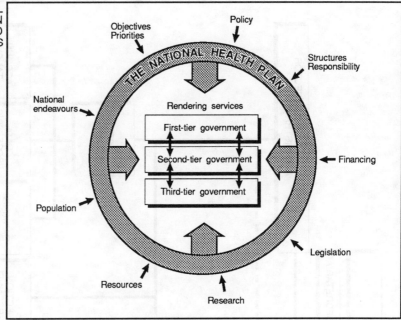

The national health plan

The National Health Plan was devised in 1986 with the implicit aim of creating a comprehensive health service for South Africa. It formulated the major objectives regarding health as:

- a centralised policy for achieving national health goals and priorities;
- centralised responsibility for the provision of health services;
- decentralised implementation based on the National Plan for Health Service Facilities.

It states that the process of rendering comprehensive health services involves:

- the identification of national health objectives and priorities;
- acceptance of a national policy to achieve the health objectives in a coordinated manner;
- the implementation of the national health policy means of the *National Health Plan*;
- continuous monitoring of the rendering of health services and modification of national health objectives and priorities as called for.

The National Health Plan and associated variables
Administrative structure of the South African Nursing Association
(Searle, 1987, p. 102)

The most critical components which have a bearing on the Plan are:

- the national health policy, health objectives and priorities;

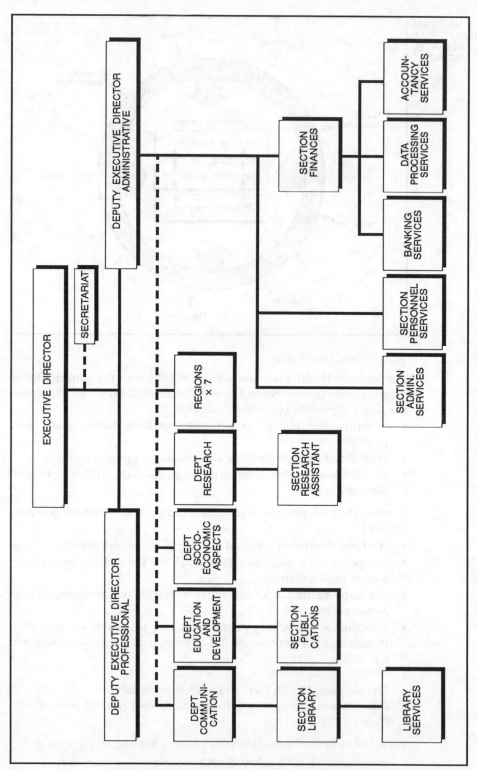

ADMINISTRATIVE STRUCTURE OF THE SOUTH AFRICAN NURSING ASSOCIATION
Searle, 1987, p. 102

- the responsibility of the authorities assigned to the rendering of health services;
- health financing based on the national health policy, objectives and priorities.

Responsibility for rendering health services

Levels I-III

These are to be managed by the Administrations:

- House of Assembly
- House of Representatives
- House of Delegates
- the Department of National Health and Population Development, but for delegated execution by the Provincial Administrations.

Level I — Provision of basic subsistence needs

- Safe drinking water and wider environmental health
- Sewerage and waste disposal
- Food supplementation
- Infrastructure and basic housing

Level II — Health education

- Minimum educational level
- Training and education
- Guidance

Level III — Primary health care

- Self-care
- Community nursing services
- Community health centres

[diagram]

Administrative structure of the South African Nursing Association (Searle, 1987, p. 102)

Levels IV-VI

These are to be managed in the following way:

Delegated services are to be executed by Provincial Administrations, which also act as agents for other authorities, within the framework of the total health plan.

Hospitalisation

- Level IV — Community hospital
- Level V — Regional hospital
- Level VI — Academic hospital

Under this plan it is envisaged that in future a comprehensive health service will be rendered cost-effectively to all the peoples of South Africa. Preventive, promotive, curative, maintenance and rehabilitative health will be *one service*.

The formulation of The National Health Policy

(Mellish, 1988, pp. 181–184)

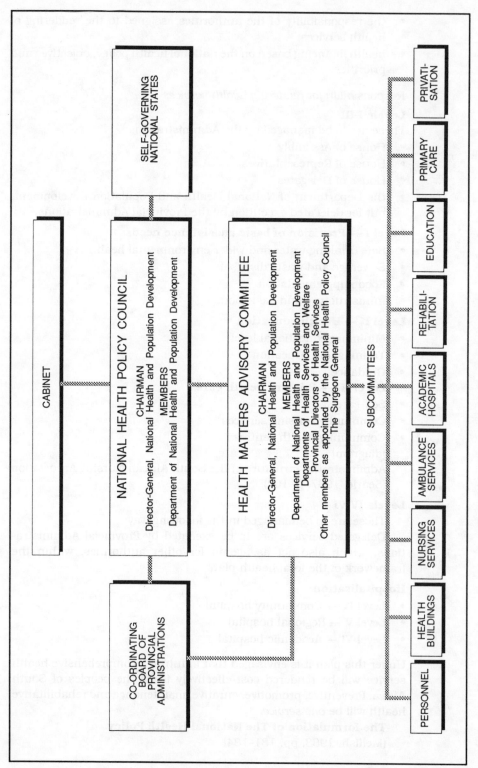

THE FORMULATION OF THE NATIONAL HEALTH POLICY
Searle, 1987, p. 103

A critique of health services

Overview   One of the overall criticisms of health services in South Africa is directed not against the health services themselves but against various socio-economic deprivations in Southern African society. A clear example is that of the unresolved problem of tuberculosis. It was not until the 1950s that the first effective drug became available in South Africa. Undoubtedly TB is more prevalent amongst the poorer population groups. In 10-year-olds it is found to be greater in the coloured and black groups (10–20 %) and lower in the Asian and white groups (–5 %). Among the rural populations in Transkei, Ciskei and Bophuthatswana it is considerably higher, ranging from between 50 and 100 children per 1 000, twenty years ago to about 30 per 1 000 currently. (Jones). The sheer task of reducing the number of TB-infected people is a practical impossibility. The importance of health education in teaching people to recognise the early symptoms of the disease and to present themselves for early treatment cannot be overemphasised. Non-presenters remain a problem and among the methods used to trace TB carriers, the contact follow-up method appears the most effective. Non-compliance to stipulated treatment remains problematic and up to 30 % of patients undergoing treatment absconded. Various procedures such as the appointment of TB counsellors is efficacious and also cost-effective. (It costs eleven times the salary of a counsellor to actually hospitalise a patient.) Large-scale preventative TB treatment is not cost-effective. Independently of socio-economic factors such as malnutrition, Blacks are 20 times more susceptible to TB than are other groups in South Africa. Studies are under way on immune recognition genes and disease susceptibility genes. Approximately 50 % of the Third World is infected with tubercule bacilli but the most important task remaining is to identify those most at risk.

South Africa displays both a Third World disease pattern resembling that of Nineteenth Century Europe and a First World pattern such as strokes, diabetes, heart disease and cancer. Rural Blacks display a typically Third World pattern which manifests itself as gastro-enteritis and tuberculosis while urbanised populations display the more Westernised profile. Nutritional diseases in the very young (kwashiorkor, marasmus, and protein-energy malnutrition) are attributable to calorically inadequate bottle feeds. This can be remedied by improving the educational standard and the health education input.

In the field of epidemiology, pioneer work in South Africa was carried out by Professor Wyndham and Dr Irwig which showed the very high death rate among African children as opposed to white children. Improvements in basic living conditions and primary health care are necessary to improve the mortality rates. General awareness particularly through the mass media has made people assume some control over adverse factors such as hypertension, hypercholesterolaemia, and cigarette smoking, all of which can lead to IHD (ischaemic heart disease).

Clearly, it is impossible to separate a nation's health from a nation's economic prosperity. What many others such as Navarro have convincingly argued (see Chapter Twelve) De Beer puts succinctly in the Southern African context.

The economic organisation of medicine reflects and contributes to the basic political and economic divisions in our society.
(De Beer, 1984, p. 68)

Are health policies adapted to the practice of medical care?

Kervasdoué (1981) was innovative in introducing the notions of equality and control. He argues that equality of access is not a new concept but dates back to the turn of the century when insurance programmes were introduced to compensate for inequalities of income. Limitations of access have become increasingly eroded, and furthermore equality has come to mean geographic equality whereby there is equal availability of medical care. Increasingly equality in this latter sense has come to mean the ratio of patients per doctor or hospital beds per thousand inhabitants. Various cash incentives are built in to help doctors to locate their practices in areas where medical care is scarce.

Control is more recent a notion and was applied initially to costs. In order to control costs attempts were made to limit the numbers of medical personnel, equipment and drugs. There is considerable difficulty in trying to measure medical results. Resources also vary greatly from country to country.

When we examine Africa specifically, we can see graphic examples of socio-economic developments affecting health status, as follows:

1. General development

The growing interdependence of industrialised and developing countries has meant that economic set-backs in the former have a direct affect on the latter. By 1984 roughly one quarter of the African population was dependent on imported grain. In some African countries production in agriculture is much less than it was twenty years ago. Such a crisis is a reflection of high unemployment among the labouring forces in Africa, too fast a population growth, continued soil erosion, and insufficient support given to agricultural production. Political instability has characterised many African states together with an ever increasing number of refugees (currently estimated at some five million in Africa alone).

2. Demographic trends

Population size and growth rates are extremely important factors in determining the health of a nation. Africa, for example, has double the crude birth rate of the average of all countries and also double the fertility rate. The population sex ratio in Southern Africa, for example, is influenced primarily by labour migration and mortality rates. Children in Africa account for nearly half the total population. In Africa the urban populations have increased by 75 % in the last decade. All these factors contribute to dramatic changes in life-styles, particularly changes in the functions and structure of the family and in patterns of family breakdown and formation.

3. Economic and social trends

Recent years have shown increasing economic disparity as a result of economic instability. Many African countries are bankrupt or owe such large debts to the World Bank or International Monetary Fund that they cannot hope to repay them. As a consequence their currencies have been devalued. Absolute poverty is estimated by the World Bank to trap some one thousand million people thus increasing the risk of disease and disablement. Although some promising decline was shown in the level of illiteracy the overall level was increased as the sheer numbers also increased. Most of the illiterates are women. Developing countries continued to supply less food and some, previously exporters, became net importers although often unable to purchase food because of their balance of payments. As a consequence many of Africa's population receive less than 90 % of their daily nutritional requirements, and diseases of malnutrition are rife.

Hunger thus exists in the modern world in spite of ample food supplies at the global level. The complexity of the problem is illustrated by the evidence of imbalances in supply, bottlenecks in delivery, and political and administrative constraints and failures that complicate the struggle against hunger and starvation at the regional and national level. Relief work is often hampered by political conflict and the lack of infrastructure . . .
(WHO, 1987, p. 23)

Women are still grossly unequal and young children die at an alarming rate. In Latin America alone 40 million children live without families. Many children are exploited as child labourers.

Issues affecting the role of the health professionals
1. The probable inability of the health care system and the available nurse practitioners to provide for the health needs of the community, bearing in mind the population explosion which is accelerating rapidly.
2. The cut-back by the state on financial support for the health care delivery system in order to meet the exigencies of the stagnation of the economy in South Africa and in other Western countries, with a resultant decrease in the number of available posts for all grades of nursing personnel and a reduction in the available services.
3. The need to design new modalities of health care to meet public needs and escalating costs with full awareness that preventive health care and care of the sick will always be a basic responsibility of the state. Modalities of health care will affect the scope of practice of the nurse/midwife practitioner.

4. The fundamental public morality, which requires the general availability of high standards of health care, but which as a result of economic services may be diluted to such an extent that the practitioners are unable to practise with 'due care'.

5. The inadequacies of health care system that could enhance inter-professional and inter-collegial co-operation which could lead to improved consumer and personnel satisfaction.

6. The maldistribution of the available health manpower, which results in the absence of personnel in some areas and unemployment in others.

7. The shortage of medical, dental, pharmaceutical and supplementary health service personnel and the fact that the nurse practitioner has to fill the vacuum.

8. The trend towards reversal of the socilisation of health care to a system of greater privatisation resulting in changing patterns of employment for nurse/midwife practitioners, as well as changes in their role and functions and socio-economic circumstances.

9. The increased unionisation of workers that will result in increased health benefits and an increase in the number of persons participating in medical aid schemes and thus demanding private health services.

10. The need for individuals, families and groups to develop their own basic self-help health care system for promoting health, preventing disease and dealing with minor illness. The nurse/midwife practitioner will have to undertake the main burden of health education to promote this.

11. The need for society to effect a greater balance between life-styles and environmental ecology. This, too, requires an increased health education contribution from the nurse/midwife practitioner.

12. The transition from a predominantly disease oriented health care system to a health-wellness oriented system with due regard to the pool of ill-health that exists will necessitate changes in the attitudes of nurse/midwife practitioners, who will have to see their role and functions as embracing preventive, promotive, curative and rehabilitative dimensions at all levels of care.

13. Health care for all by the year 2000 is not possible unless all health practitioners try to influence the political will and the people to work towards this ideal. The nurse/midwife practitioner has a major role to play in this process of persuasion.

14. The nurse/midwife practitioner can assist in giving the media a positive approach to the problems of the health care system and of her own potential contribution to social change.

15. The resistance to change in the health care sector will require a positive approach from all nurse/midwife practitioners in order to reduce this resistance, otherwise delays in improving the system will inevitably result in a magnification of the problems.

16. The nurse/midwife practitioner will have to play a major role in obtaining consumer co-operation and satisfaction with the health care system.
17. The nurse/midwife practitioner will have to equip herself with the knowledge to help attain optimal health care objectives at minimal cost and to contribute to health care research and the development of a modern health care information system. This could revolutionise the work of nurse/midwife practitioners.
18. The nurse/midwife practitioner will have to develop the ability to make a contribution to the health care policy of the nation at local, regional and national levels.
19. The nurse/midwife practitioner will have to equip herself to provide the greater share in the humanisation of the health care system.
20. The development of standards and quality control systems that acknowledge both the needs and constraints of human and material resources fall primarily within the role and functions of the nurse/midwife practitioner.
21. Nurse/midwife practitioners can make a major contribution towards the understanding of cultural differences and interracial relationships. They have to serve all sides with neutrality and with concern, compassion, integrity, knowledge and skill.
22. the constitutional changes in this country will lead to an increased level of decentralisation of health care; a marked increase in the regulations which will govern scarce resources and the quality of health care; and the development of new social and political options in respect of health care. The nurse/midwife practitioner will be in the forefront of the personnel who will have to make the new constitutional approaches work in so far as health is concerned. (Searle, 1987, p. 311–313)

Other areas of concern facing the health practitioner are as follows:
1. The trend away from the socilisation of the health care system towards greater privatisation of health care and such issues as the fact that the health of the nation is at the mercy of the profit element in health care, the expensive state health care facilities will not be properly utilised and thousands of nurses and other personnel who will move from secure posts with excellent pensions and educational conditions of service to posts which do not have such favourable prospects in the long-term and that have more job insecurity because the private sector is not bound by the personnel protection mechanisms of the public service will become economically and socially insecure.
2. The probable inability of the health care system to provide for the health needs of the community, bearing in mind the tremendous population explosion which has already commenced and which will accelerate markedly towards the year 2000.
3. The constitutional change in this country, which will lead to increased decentralisation of health care and a marked increase in

the regulations which govern the scarce resources and the quality of health care. This must inevitably lead to the development of a number of social and political options with regard to health care. Society's values and needs will determine the development of social and political priorities in health care.

4. The fundamental public morality that requires the general availability of high standards of health care. This may result in an attempt to provide this universally available service at a minimal level of care, for the financial situation will force this type of development which the nurse practitioner will have to implement.

5. The need to develop a balance between human life-styles and environmental ecology which, if neglected, will have disastrous consequences for man's health.

6. The implications of the slow transition from a predominantly disease-oriented health care system to a health-wellness-oriented system, with due regard to the problems of the pool of ill-health that exists.

7. The designing of various systems of health care bearing in mind that the care of the sick will always be a basic responsibility and an essential aspect of the health care system.

8. The increase in the unionisation of workers, with a resultant increase in the percentage of citizens of all races who are members of medical aid schemes.

9. The maldistribution of and the shortage in certain categories of health manpower.

10. The knowledge explosion in the health sciences and the lack of resources to utilise such knowledge to the full.

11. the need for individuals, families and groups to develop their own basic self-help health care system for promoting health, preventing disease, dealing with minor illness, participating in the rehabilitation process and developing health promoting life-styles.

(Searle, 1987, p. 311–313)

SUMMARY

1. Weber's *ideal type* of bureaucracy has important bearings on the kind of organisation that constitutes a hospital with its distinctive division of labour and lines of authority.
2. Modern hospitals are complex organisations with their authority and influence structure. Such a perspective has important bearings on the way in which decisions are made within the hospital, the way health services are organised and on the process of admission, patient care and discharge.
3. The hospital as an organisation exhibits the core characteristics of authority (staff and line), communication (vertical and horizontal), over-addictive rule following, and a clearly defined division of labour.
4. Primary Health Care, or front-line health care, embraces areas not immediately connected with health, such as the supply of fresh water and sanitation, nutrition health education and screening.
5. The various schools of nursing still dominate the approach and organisation of health care.
6. New developments in statutory health bodies have meant that nurses are more directly represented on a national level.
7. Provision of health services in South Africa must be considered in terms of the profound socio-economic differences which exist in this society. Such differences are based on racially dictated segregation and role allocation.
8. South Africa contains both First and Third World disease patterns.
9. The pattern of developing countries shows the major areas of *underdevelopment* which contribute to basic health deficiencies such as malnutrition and tuberculosis.
10. Apart from global implications in development, South Africa faces similar problems and must devise effective strategies for coping.

IMPORTANT TERMS

Bureaucracy
traditional authority
dual line of authority
community morphology
primary health care
motherhouse system

ideal type
rational legal authority
total institutions
vertical and horizontal communication
nursing paradigm
interaction-transaction systems model

SELF-ASSESSMENT QUESTIONS

1. What is meant by 'bureaucracy'? How effectively can Weber's model be applied to the modern hospital?
2. What new demands will be brought to bear on the nursing profession in South Africa as a result of social and economic changes in society in the year 2000?

3. Why are socio-economic factors important in any approach to health?

4. Outline the strengths and weaknesses of the theories of nursing mentioned in this chapter.

5. 'The nurse practitioner has to develop her own ability and sensitivity as a nurse. This sensitivity is based on the personal philosophy of the nurse, how she sees her role as a nurse and the needs of those for whom she has to provide care . . . Every action, every verbal or non-verbal act of communication, influences the way in which the patient sees himself, the nurse and his interaction with her. It influences him in the choices he makes for his health care.' (Searle, 1987, p. 67–68) Is this a true estimate of the importance of the nursing profession?

6. How could the health services in South Africa become more egalitarian?

CHAPTER
EIGHT

DEATH AND DYING

- medical diagnosis
- the social organisation of death
- a time to die
- individualised death

VICTORIAN VAGINAL EXAMINATION
Royal Society of Medicine, London

MEDICAL DIAGNOSIS

Medical diagnosis occurs on a continuum of health and death. Long (1984) articulates this with the following diagram.

Adapted from:
Lillenfeld & Lillenfeld,
1980, p. 60

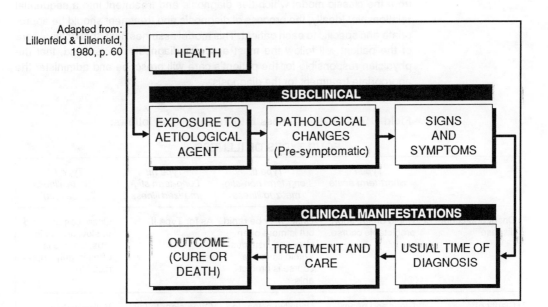

HEALTH

SUBCLINICAL

| EXPOSURE TO AETIOLOGICAL AGENT | → | PATHOLOGICAL CHANGES (Pre-symptomatic) | → | SIGNS AND SYMPTOMS |

CLINICAL MANIFESTATIONS

| OUTCOME (CURE OR DEATH) | ← | TREATMENT AND CARE | ← | USUAL TIME OF DIAGNOSIS |

Diagnosis is essential in recording illness, whether it is lay-diagnosis or self-diagnosis. In other words, the person must present him/herself in a way which communicates his/her perception of being ill. The notion of the lay person's definitions of health and illness thus enter into the picture. It is important to stress here the difference which exists between disease and illness, the former being a *medical* diagnosis based on signs and symptoms while the latter is a person's subjective interpretation of certain feelings of pain and discomfort they perceive themselves to possess. Thus, diagnosis can relate to *illness* and to *disease*, although, as we shall see below, both mean very different things. Dingwall (1976) states that

there are no illnesses or diseases in nature. Illness is the outcome of human classificatory activity. It is moreover a deeply moral one, since health is identified as desirable and illness as undesirable ... 'illness' and 'disease' are evaluative terms applied by man to natural circumstances that precipitate death.
(Dingwall, 1976, p. 82)

Feeling ill may or may not be disease. The concept of disease is very much part of the medical model. Illness behaviour takes place within a social context, and to say that someone is 'ill' is stated within such a social context. The medical pathological notion of 'disease' is distinct from the notion of 'illness', by which we mean individual experiences and perceptions. The formal and classical model of disease and its diagnosis is summarised by Duff and Hollingshed (1968):

From the perspective of theoretical medicine, the best patient care is derived from the classic model which ties diagnosis and treatment into a sequential relationship. Ideally, the process of diagnosis and treatment should be appropriate and specific to each patient. This model assumes, first, that optimal care of the patient will follow the most accurate diagnosis . . . second, that the physician responsible for the patient's care will prescribe and administer the appropriate treatment for the diagnosis.

Field (1976) divides illness into four types as follows:

FOUR TYPES OF ILLNESS

	Type I: Short-term acute	Type II: Long-term non-stigmatized illness	Type III: Long-term stigmatized illness	Type IV: Mental illness (see text)
Onset and course of disease	Rapid onset, short, predictable course.	Onset may be rapid but is more often slow and insidious. Within limits the course is predictable.	As for Type II.	Onset can be rapid or slow and insidious. Course is often largely unpredictable.
Clarity of symptoms	Clear and unambiguous to both lay public and physician.	Usually unclear to lay public and to physician until a number of sophisticated diagnostic tests have been made.	Often clear to lay public, although they may be unable to interpret them. Clear to physician once diagnostic aids used.	Varies widely. Usually ambiguous both for public and physician.
Medical diagnosis	Highly certain and reliable as the underlying biological processes are well understood.	Usually certain and reliable. The unfolding of the biological course of the disease fairly well established.	As for Type II	Uncertain and unreliable as the processes are not well understood.
Medical treatment	Effective and curative. Illness is reversible.	Effective to moderately effective but not curative. The disease process may be halted or controlled, but not reversed.	As for Type II.	No unequivocally effective treatment. Although it is sometimes reversable it often is not.

	Type I: Short-term acute	Type II: Long-term non-stig- matized illness	Type III: Long-term stig- matized illness	Type IV: Mental illness (see text)
Physician's role	(a) To identify the disease. (b) To legitimate temporary release from social obligations. (c) To certify the short term impact of the disease.	(a) As type I (b) To legitimate indefinite release from social obligations. (c) To aid in the definition of the long term impact of the disease.	(a) As type I. (b) To legitimate permanent release from social obligations. (c) As type II, especially with regard to the rehabilitative process.	(a) To certify the individual as different. (b) To legitimate others' definition of the individual as being incapable of fulfilling social obligations. (c) to construct a social identity and ways of acting acceptable to others.
Impact on self-conception	Minimal as the label is temporary even though it may be all-pervasive at the time.	Variable, depending on the degree to which the illness is internalized. However, there is always some effect since the label persists.	Considerable and unavoidable. The illness often becomes the central organizing aspect of identity for both the individual and others.	Variable, ranging from slight to severe. The extent to which the label 'mentally ill' becomes central for the individual and others varies widely.
Social consequences	In short run the individual is released from a wide range of social obligations while retraining most of his rights. Minimal long-run consequences.	Short-run consequences are as for type I. Long-run consequences are variable and to some extent under the individual's control.	Severe. Due to the visibility of the physical consequences, The individual cannot exert much control over placement into a 'spoiled' or stigmatized category. Illness inevitably becomes disability.	Vary widely. At best may be short run and minimal, at worst an all pervasive and permanent discrediting of the individual as a competent and normal actor.

Field goes on to comment on the diagnostic process as an important aspect of the physician's work. Once an individual has tentatively identified themselves as ill they may well seek out a professional diagnosis as opposed to their lay-diagnosis. The professional diagnosis will, once made, condition the way the individual will view their illness. The medical profession is under constant pressure to present a diagnosis: 'If in doubt, presume illness.' He quotes Scheff's study of physicians' judgements on whether tonsillectomies were to be performed on a thousand children.

The thousand children were screened by one group of physicians and about 60 per cent of them had their tonsils removed. The remaining children were then examined by a second group of physicians and nearly half of them were recommended for the operation. Finally, this last 'healthy' group were examined by yet another group of physicians and again nearly half of them were recommended to be operated on.

(Field, 1976, pp. 357–8)

AFTER DEATH
Theodore Gericault, 1818. The Art Institute of Chicago, Illinois.
A. A. Munger Collection

Scheff's second example involved a study (1966) of 14 867 films screening for TB symptoms. 'There were 1 216 positive readings which turned out to be negative and only 24 negative readings which turned out to be clinically active.' Scheff's argument is that the reluctance of a physician to make a diagnosis often forces the individual into a sick role. Once the diagnosis is made it can fundamentally alter an individual's life style, as in the case of diagnosing hypertension, despite the fact that 'there is no conclusive evidence that high blood pressure inevitably leads to clinical malfunctioning.' (Scheff, 1966, in Field, 1976 p. 358).

The final aspect of diagnosis covered by Field is that it is essentially a mechanism for resolving the uncertainties of both doctor and patient as to the nature of the illness, and how it ought to be treated. He quotes Davis's distinction (1960) between two types of uncertainty: *clinical* and *functional.* The former is the genuine uncertainty as to the diagnosis and prognosis. The latter term refers to a situation where the physician knows the diagnosis and prognosis, but keeps the patient and family in a situation of uncertainty.' The latter type of uncertainty might be because the physician is reluctant to be the bearer of bad news.

The classical model of diagnosis is clearly deficient in a number of ways, not least because it does not take cognizance of the personal and social influences that relate to disease.

Navaho Wyman's study (1966) of diagnostic techniques among the Navaho
diagnosticians Indians is directed to that aspect of diagnosis which relates to causes of disease with no obvious symptoms, and falls into three types: motion-in-the-hand star-gazing and listening. Although it is possible to be practiced in all three diagnostic forms it is more usual to concentrate on one. The function of the diagnostician is to search for the causative agents and also to recommend treatment. Usually the treatment specifies a chant to sing over the patient but sometimes it is the recommendation of specific therapeutic treatment. Most illnesses are believed to be caused by one of two influences; the obvious, such as the accident that causes broken bones, and an unknown influence which attacks the patient in his weakened moments and perhaps as the result of some taboo which has been transgressed.

Freidson (1960) talks of the professional and lay systems of evaluation and referral. An individual experiences some form of symptom for which he prescribes for himself some home remedy. When other people, such as members of the household, are drawn into the situation by having their attention focussed on it then diagnosis becomes *shared.* There is a system of referrals through a hierarchy of authority. Thus in actuality diagnosis is initially lay diagnosis. There is often a long system of lay diagnosis, perhaps from the nuclear family 'through successively more select, distant and authoritative lay-men until the 'professional' is reached.'

The drug doctor Balint (1957) introduces an examination of what he terms the 'drug doctor'. He was particularly anxious to stress the harm done to the patient by treating physical symptoms only, without recognising the social and emotional context in which they arise. This relationship, and the manner of *examination* of the patient by the doctor is also important.

Our experience has invariably been that, *if the doctor asks questions in the manner of medical history-taking he will always get answers—but hardly anything more.* Before he can arrive at what we called 'deeper' diagnosis, he has to learn to listen.
(Balint, 1957, p. 121)

Often, individuals may try to overcome problems in living by resorting to becoming ill.

If the doctor has the opportunity of seeing them in the first phases of their becoming ill, i.e. before they settle down to a definite 'organised' illness, he may observe that these patients, so to speak, *offer or propose various illnesses*, and that they have to go on offering new illnesses until between doctor and patient an agreement can be reached . . . The variety of illnesses available to any one individual is limited by his constitution, upbringing, social position, his conscious or unconscious fears and fantasies about illnesses, etc.
(Balint, 1957, p. 122)

The point made by Balint and his colleagues is that the doctor him/herself is a kind of 'drug':

. . . by far the most frequently used drug in general practice was the doctor himself, i.e. that it was not only the bottle of medicine or the box of pills which mattered, but the way the doctor gave them to his patient — in fact, the whole atmosphere in which the drug was given and taken.

Naming the illness The patient is primarily concerned with obtaining both reassurance and a label which can be attached to his pain and fear. The patient wants to know 'What does the book say?'

I wish to emphasise here that nearly always this is the chief and most immediate problem; *the request for a name for the illness, for a diagnosis*. It is only in the second instance that the patient asks for a therapy.
(Balint, 1957, p. 123)

The problem of simple communication and shared understanding of what medical terms mean is therefore quite important. A study by Pratt et al. (1961) showed that patients were poorly informed about their own condition and the ten most common diseases. Patients gave little evidence of conscious demand for further information about their condition. Physicians assumed, and wanted patients to possess, more knowledge about symptoms, aetiology and treatment of diseases, than was actually the case. A further study by Boyle (1970) found significant differences between patients' and doctors' interpretations of all terms except 'a good appetite'. An important factor, as one might expect, is the educational level of the respondent as the correlation between educational attainment and vocabulary performance is high.

Withers (1946) showed the popularity of small-town diagnosis by an analysis of the home diagnosis of children in a small midwestern community. Usually the wife performs the diagnosis:

The five primary diagnostic points are these: (1) Testing the sick person's brow with the back of the hand for fever. If the brow feels much hotter than the hand, the 'patient' is 'feverish'. (2) Examining the tongue to see if it is coated. (3) Asking 'when did your bowels move last?' (4) Asking, 'Does your head ache?' and (5) asking, 'do you hurt anywhere else?'
(Withers, 1946, p. 238)

The diagnostic A further emphasis on the importance of interpersonal skills during
interview diagnosis has been made by Twaddle (1980). The single most important
source of information which can lead to a diagnosis is the *interview* or
history taken from the patient. Although estimates vary it is thought
that 90 % of diagnostic skills come from the initial interview.

Laboratory tests and observation serve only to confirm the diagnosis or to help
select among a few alternative possibilities. It would be expected that considerable attention would be given in the medical curriculum to skills of interviewing. Yet this is not the case. Instead, medical schools emphasise the laboratory
skills, and attention to interviewing is limited . . .
(Twaddle, 1980, pp. 121–2)

He goes as far as to suggest that the interview itself need not necessarily
be carried out by a physician, and indeed in many instances such
initial history taking was grossly defective:

Physicians failed to hear what the patient was telling them; by their conduct
they blocked certain kinds of information from being provided. The result was
that the interviews did not generate the data needed for accurate diagnosis.
(Ibid.)

The notion of *disease* is, according to Twaddle, a Western one because:

The conceptualising of disease requires a rational model in which means and
ends are separated and related, a cultural feature that developed in Europe
during the eighteenth century in conjunction with the idea of progress and
philosophical positivism.

. . . When people think of disease, they presume it is not a figment of someone's
imagination. It is real and can be observed, classified, explained and acted on.
(Twaddle and Hessler, 1977, pp. 50–51)

The concept of medical practice as a labelling process emerges quite
clearly when we talk about disease. *Making a diagnosis* is at the heart
of scientific medicine. (Op. cit., pp. 51–2; Mechanic, 1968, p. 91). The
diagnostic procedure requires the fitting of various signs and symptoms into prescribed categories:

The process of Patient complaints
diagnosis Patient behaviour   Doctor identifies
Physical examination   symptoms and names
Laboratory findings   the disease = **diagnosis**
(Adapted from Twaddle and Hessler, op. cit., p. 52)

Diagnostic This was introduced early this century in the form of chest X-rays and
technology by the 1930s the technique was considered highly sophisticated. If we
remember that until the end of the Second World War, tuberculosis
was the greatest killer among the 15–35 age group, then this particular
diagnostic technology was used very frequently with profound social
consequences arising from the readings. For example, teachers were
not allowed to teach or doctors to doctor if their X-ray showed an

abnormal density. The first attempt at validation was made by Yeru-shalmy et al. (1951) who found that

> in making this x-ray interpretation, in one out of three cases the physician would not only disagree with a second or third 'reader' but in 20 per cent of the cases would not even agree with himself. That is to say, when confronted on two different occasions with the same pair of x-ray films, he would give diametrically opposing answers. Yet is was on this supposedly 'decisive' technology that decisions radically affecting the lives of people were made.
> (McDermott, 1977, p. 143)

Another example, during the same period, was the introduction of a serologic diagnostic test for syphilis which was introduced by Wasser-mann. However, the test was too sensitive and half of those displaying positive reactions were not syphilitic at all! Such a discovery was made much later, to the profound embarrassment of many of those falsely diagnosed. It was also discovered later that the antisyphilitic treatment used was an important source of hepatitis. Thus forty years later

> the particular bit of unvalidated technology . . . led to this . . . unfortunate mistake (but which) represented the practical application of basic principles of the new science of immunology.
> (Op. cit., p. 144)

Diagnosis today Many theories used in contemporary medical settings are based on the biological models of disease. There are other, and sometimes similar, models used by such practitioners as faith healers and herbalists. Undoubtedly, the scientific nature of the models and the framework used by doctors, nurses and others owes much of its success to being closely linked with the scientific areas of biology and chemistry. The use of scientific diagnosis provides a prediction of how the patient will fare from having a particular kind of illness, an aetiology of the illness in question, and lastly may suggest a course of treatment for the illness. Sometimes a diagnosis can be made and a course of treatment effectively carried out, such as in the case of pernicious anaemia. At other times, however, even though a diagnosis is made, no substantial prediction can be made of the disease's course, the aetiology is doubtful and the treatment ineffective. Mechanic cites Boeck's sarcoidosis as an example, and adds, 'although it is helpful to make the diagnosis, it does not lead to a clear course of action'. Similar problems are presented by the diagnosis of raised arterial blood pressure. In itself a correlation between hypertension and mortality is statistical rather than individual, and high blood pressure is not itself a cause of death or of a person being admitted to hospital. The first stage of hypertension shows no organic change in the cardio-vascular system and generally no treatment is prescribed. Indeed, because 10 % of the population display raised blood pressure at this state such treatment would be very expensive. The second and third stages reveal left ventricular hypertrophy and ischaemic heart disease, but those making the diag-nosis are usually aware of such traps as the false positives of the electrocardiogram and some of the negative side effects of treatment with hypertensive drugs. In addition, there are difficulties involved in the measurement of hypertension by the two most commonly used methods, the intra-arterial method and the cuff and sphygmoma-nometer. The individual's own blood pressure may vary according to such factors as his emotional state, room temperature, previous physical activity and so on. Several factors emerge in this area which have a bearing on the biological model such as the difficulty of diagnosis (after about fifty years of age, for example, it is 'normal' to have 'abnormal' blood pressure), the quantitative relation between raised arterial pressure and mortality, doubts about effective treatment at stage one, and so on.

The diagnosis made by the physician is based on his previous medical knowledge, both clinical and arrived at by scientific research, but also his observation of the patient and the latter's account of his symptoms. Therefore, interpretation and selection enters into the area of diagnosis and disease. Individuals differ enormously according to age, socio-economic class, climate, culture and so on, which in turn affect the patient's and the health professional's interpretation and selection of the criteria.

Mental illness   In a number of areas there is substantial controversy as to the reliability of diagnosis, for example in the case of mental illness (Szasz, 1964). The biological basis for a diagnostic model is particularly unreliable when referring to *problems of living*. Szasz has put forward the theory that what we term mental illness is observed and diagnosed from patterns of behaviour and thinking which deviate from the normal rather than by a systematic study of organic brain lesions. *Mental illness* is a term usually used to classify problems associated with problems of living rather than problems related to a biological break-down of some sort. Often diagnosis which masquerades as medical or psychiatric diagnosis is actually social diagnosis.

The reliability of   Apart from problems associated with raised arterial blood pressure
diagnosis   there are many other instances of difficulty associated with diagnosing illness. Many psychiatrists, for example, differ as to what constitutes 'sickness'. R. D. Laing is one psychiatrist whose views often ran counter to orthodox psychiatry. The interview and the consultation are situ-ations very open to errors of interpretation. Some surveys have sug-gested that agreement between psychiatrists on the diagnosis can be as high as 55 % and as low as 28 %. Other surveys have suggested that agreement between psychiatrists can sometimes be as varied as 0.05 per hundred to 51 per hundred, as, for example in the case of military psychiatry. The diagnosis of different mental conditions varies very much. Schizophrenia, psychosis and mental deficiency have a high agreement, but paranoid psychosis and cerebrovascular psy-chosis have a low agreement level.

Medical diagnosis is, as we might expect, higher among specialists than in general practice in the degree of accuracy. Mechanic cites the example of between 20 to 25 % error in even a well-trained person's reading of X-rays. Many other areas of research have shown varying differences in both the kind and the accuracy of medical diagnosis.

Illness as social deviance

Illness is viewed by many sociologists as social deviance because it is not only deviant statistically but also from some standard or norm. Although it is true that disease can be 'there', what really matters is how we think or conceive it. Freidson puts it this way: 'Diagnosis and treatment are not biological acts common to mice, monkeys, and men, but social acts peculiar to men. Illness as such may be biological disease, but the idea of illness is not, and neither is the way human beings respond to it. Thus, biological deviance or disease is defined socially and is surrounded by social acts that condition it.' (Freidson, 1970, p. 209) Illness as deviance contains both a biological and a social aspect. The sociologist's task is not to accept illness as something which indisputably exists but to try to explain the social processes whereby certain symptoms and signs arise in the first place, how we call such signs and symptoms 'sickness', and how the person designated as 'ill' adopts the role of the sick person, cripple, dying, incurable and so on. The situational theory of deviance, which we discuss in the chapter on deviance, throws light on the concept of illness as social deviance by regarding deviance as imputed (rather than 'out there'), not necessarily motivated by the individual, and responses to it are organized or managed socially. Like beauty, deviance to a considerable extent is in the eyes of the definer.

Freidson argues that Parsons' conceptualization of the sick role is heavily tailored to modern Western industrial society, and that the extent of the exemption is a *consequence* of the seriousness imputed to the condition. In a trial classification of deviance, the following might emerge (adapted from Freidson, 1970, p. 231).

IMPUTATION OF SERIOUSNESS	IMPUTATION OF RESPONSIBILITY	
	Individual held responsible	Individual not held responsible
Minor deviation	Parking offence	A cold
Serious deviation	Murder	Heart attack

The degree of seriousness of the deviation reflects middle-class views. However, he makes the point that often the medical profession holds individuals responsible for medically labelled illness as in the case of venereal disease, abortion and attempted suicide. Furthermore, the above classification merely distinguishes between 'crime' and 'illness'. A more sophisticated table is consequently presented by Freidson (1970). In the following table, adapted from p. 239, the Parsonian definition of the sick role occurs in cell 5, Goffman's stigmatized roles are in cell 4, and chronic sick or dying roles are found to cell 6.

Imputed seriousness	Illegitimate (stigmatized)	Conditionally legitimate	Unconditionally legitimate
	Cell 1	Cell 2	Cell 3
Minor deviation	'Stammer' Partial suspension of some ordinary obligations; few or no new privileges; adoption of a few new obligations.	'A cold' Temporary suspension of few ordinary obligations; temporary enhancement of ordinary privileges. Obligation to get well.	'Pockmarks' No special change in obligations or privileges.
	Cell 4	Cell 5	Cell 6
Serious deviation	'Epilepsy' Suspension of some ordinary obligations; adoption of new ones; few or no new privileges.	'Pneumonia' Temporary release from ordinary obligations; addition to ordinary privileges. Obligation to cooperate and seek help in treatment.	'Cancer' Permanent suspension of many ordinary obligations; marked addition to privileges.

The lay conception of illness and disease

To a very large extent it is true to say that illness behaviour is a culturally and socially learned response. Thus middle-class people are quicker and more eager to seek medical advice than working-class people, and in certain cultures the witch or folk-doctor is relied upon in preference to the medical practitioner. Illness differs in response and recognition according to ethnic differences, and response to pain also varies according to ethnic culture. The higher the socio-economic class the greater the possibility of reporting illness behaviour. Such classes, Mechanic reports, 'were move likely to buy health insurance, to get a periodic medical check-up, to receive polio immunisation, to eat a balanced diet, and they more frequently had eye examinations and dental care'.

Not only are the signals of distress (what we will call pain) felt or interpreted differently by different cultural and ethnic and social groups but they are also interpreted differently. Other symptoms, such as tiredness or irritability, are also interpreted differently and have different *meanings* attributed to them. Some cultures regard certain symptoms as of little consequence and do not follow these up by reporting them to the medical authorities. In a sub-culture of violence any individual act of violence is unlikely to be regarded as symptomatic of mental disturbance.

The lower the social class of the group concerned the more likely they are to be ignorant of the functioning of the human body. 'They are prone to think of and describe their experience with illness in the now-antiquated notions still exploited by patient-medicine advertisements—notions of qualities of the blood, of the necessity to 'purge the system', of the importance of the state of the liver and kidneys to health, and the like.' Freidson suggests that such a person is more likely to seek the help of folk or patent remedies. The group to which one belongs determines to a large degree the extent to which any one lay-person refers to (a) his fellows, (b) a medical practitioner.

Mechanic has found it useful to distinguish between *self-defined* and *other-defined* illness, the major distinction being that in the latter case 'the person tends to resist the definition that others are attempting to impose upon him'. He uses this distinction in listing ten factors affecting the response to illness, as follows:

1. Visibility, recognizability, or perceptual salience of symptoms.
2. The perceived seriousness of symptoms.
3. The extent to which symptoms disrupt family, work, and other social activities.
4. The frequency of the appearance of symptoms, their persistence, or frequency of recurrence.
5. The tolerance threshold of those who are exposed to and evaluate the deviant signs and symptoms.
6. Available information, knowledge, and cultural assumptions and understandings of the evaluator.
7. Perceptual needs which lead to autistic psychological processes.
8. Needs competing with illness response.
9. Competing possible interpretations which could be assigned to the symptoms once they are recognized.
10. Availability of treatment resources, physical proximity, and psychological and monetary costs of taking action.

Mechanic cites the example of a man who has occasionally become inebriated. This may become more frequent and persistent, and his behaviour or situation will probably become more evident to his family and colleagues. His behaviour will become more disruptive and people will become less tolerant. Information will be sought, and the perceived seriousness will, most probably, overcome the perceived stigma. The final exemption from obligations is death. It is also when illness, seen as an active struggle by individuals to control their life situations and environments, ceases.

DYING AND DEATH IN THE MEDICAL SETTING

Julius Roth's study, *Timetables*, is concerned with the way in which the inmates of a tuberculosis hospital structured the passage of time. When individuals are uncertain about what might lie ahead of them they tend to draw upon the experiences of others who have either been through the same experiences or are at that time experiencing the same. The formation of group norms focused upon reference points becomes an essential part of the *career* of the inmate. Roth means by the *career* of the institutionalized TB patient, 'a series of related stages or phrases of a given sphere of activity that a group of people goes through in a progressive fashion (that is, one step follows another) in a given direction or on the way to a more or less definite and recognisable end-point or goal'. The group norms that are formed serve to measure the progress of the individual and are, in fact, *benchmarks* or events of significance that occur in the average career. In a hospital setting two groups of people, those in authority and the patients, each construct *career timetables*. By this Roth means that 'when many people go through the same series of events, we speak of this as a career and of the sequence and timing of events as their career timetable'. The authority group and the patients both establish a timetable for the same series of events, but because they 'see' the same events differently (professional versus lay, hospital versus patient) and differ in their goals the timetable norms developed differ from each other to some extent. Hence there arises, according to Roth, a constant bargaining relationship between 'the expert, the professional, the authority, the controller on the one hand, and the client, the subordinate, the controllee on the other hand'. Roth's study can be usefully applied to a number of medical settings other than a tuberculosis hospital. Elizabeth Gustafson applies the concept of career to a study of the dying nursing-home patient (1972). In such an institution the majority of patients are terminal cases who although perhaps not willing to admit the fact at least know that they are in that setting until they die. 'For the aged patient, the passage of days itself beings him noticeably closer to the end of the road. Admission to the nursing home immediately launches him into a new, regressive career ending in death.' Timetable scales in a nursing home career are illustrated by Gustafson:

PHYSICAL DETERIORATION SCALES			MENTAL DETERIORATION SCALES
Social activity	Mobility	Functional control	Mental control
1. Passes to 'outside'	1. Walks	1. Continent	1. Occasional forgetfulness
2. Responsibility for own affairs; social contacts			
3. Hobby or job	3. Hobbies		
4. Physical recreation			4. Occasional incoherence
5. Spectator recreation	5. Wheelchair	5. Incontinent	5. Considerable disorientation
6. Minimal activity	6. Bed		
7. Lassitude	7. Extreme weakness		7. Total *non compos mentis*
8. Coma	8. Transfer to general hospital		
Source: Adapted from Gustafson, 1972, p. 229.			

Bargaining as a process of interaction with authority is not so firmly articulated as described by Roth because, as in terminal wards, many may have become too ill to maintain a bargaining position. Anyway, the nursing staff have little control over the terminal outcome. The process involves in many cases bargaining for more time 'directly with his disease, or death, or God'. Despite the forced cheerfulness of the medical staff the patient 'finding the staff unresponsive to the real meaning of his bargaining, becomes frantic and eventually lapses into despair . . .' The distinction between a *social phase* of death and a *terminal phase*, preceding the final termination occasioned by psychological or biological death, enhances the value of the social phase during which the patient is reacting against the desire of relatives, staff, visitors and peers to force him into a premature social death. 'This kind of bargaining will and should continue in the best of institutions. But it will become effective and wholesome when the staff members and visitors respond by doing all they can to facilitate the preservation of the patient's maximum status according to the timetable scales. The staff member with this positive goal will find it easier to acknowledge (sometimes directly to the patient) that death is the inevitable end of the career. The patient who feels he has been valued and respected during this phase will find it easier to approach the end of his life willingly.' When the terminal phase is reached medical staff can help the patient move into a positive position *beyond* the process of bargaining in a full acceptance of death. 'It should become the common goal of staff and patients that each dying career should end in this positive way.'

A different setting for dying is offered by Glaser and Strauss' study (1965) of a terminal cancer ward. In such a setting the articulated bargaining process suggested by Roth may not apply. In contrast there may arise a certain amount of *confusion* about the form that staff–patient interaction should take. For example, the patient may feel that he will survive but the nurse knows that he will die. A form of mutual pretence exists when both know that the outcome will be terminal but both act as though it will not be so.

A time to die David Sudnow's study examines the way in which dying is socially organized in the hospital setting. From the observation of 250 deaths he concluded not only 'The categories of hospital life, e.g. 'life', 'illness', 'patient', 'dying', 'death', or whatever, are to be seen as *constituted by the practices of hospital personnel* as they engage in their daily routinised interactions within an organisational milieu', (Sudnow, 1967, p. 43) but we also see that the very way of handling the dying patient may itself be a reflection of the needs of the staff to attempt to cope with their routine work. Occasionally this may result in the committing of improprieties such as the closing of a terminal patient's eyelids before death (it is more difficult after), and leaving a patient near to death in a room not adapted to terminal cases such as a laboratory or supply room. Sometimes, on a busy ward, 'portions of the wrapping are done before death, leaving only a few moments of final touch-up work with the dead body . . . they will occasionally go into the room of such a patient (one they believe will die shortly), change the bedsheets, insert dentures, and, in several cases I know of, diaper a patient who is still 'alive'. Such predeath treatment is likely to occur only during the night shift when aids are assured that relatives will not visit and discover their work'.

Glaser and Strauss' later study, *Time for Dying*, written in 1968, is concerned with dying as a temporal process which takes place 'over time'. A secondary consideration of the study is that the process of dying in hospitals is influenced by the training and codes of the medical staff. Lastly, an individual's death is a *social* event to the extent that it influences others and is noticed and recorded.

Dying trajectories Glaser and Strauss talk of the course of dying as a *trajectory* (the path made by a body moving under a given force—a term used in physics) which has duration (it takes place over time) and shape (it can be plotted or graphed). The hospital, doctors and nurses must deal with a series of critical phases during the process of dying: '(1) The patient is defined as dying. (2) Staff and family then make preparations for his death, as he may do himself if he knows he is dying. (3) At some point, there seems to be 'nothing more to do' to prevent death. (4) The final descent may take weeks, or days, or merely hours, ending in (5) the 'last hours', (6) the death watch, and (7) the death itself. After death, death itself must be legally pronounced and then publicly announced.' Often the relationships between doctors and nurses is such that the latter are not taken into full medical confidence and have to pick up 'cues' about the patient's condition. Such cues are gleaned from the physical state of the patient himself and from temporal references made by nurses or doctors.

The dying trajectory is a status passage. Originally the term was used by Van Gennep to describe the passing of a person from youth to adulthood, or from spinsterhood to marriage, and so on, which is characterized by clear and precise rules. Such passages from one status to another are scheduled, regulated and prescribed, although some are not. Furthermore, to move from one status position to another may or may not be desirable, inevitable, reversible, repeatable, individual, shared, clear, voluntary, controlled or legitimate. Dying as a trajectory 'is almost always *unscheduled*: second, the sequence of steps is *not institutionally prescribed*; and third, the actions of the various participants are only *partly regulated*'. Generally, we regard death as undesirable.

Improving the care of the dying

More people than ever before are dying in institutionalized settings such as hospitals or nursing homes. Often the care given to terminal cases is described in the popular press as 'inhuman', 'insensitive' and so on. Nevertheless, the care and devotion lavished by nurses and doctors on terminal cases is of a high order. The Glaser and Strauss works are part of a six-year study specifically concerned with the dying patient. The second contribution in the series is by Jeanne Quint, *The Nurse and the Dying Patient* (1967). Certain general recommendations arise from the research.

1. 'Training for giving terminal care should be greatly amplified and deepened in schools of medicine and nursing.' Sociological and psychological approaches to death and dying with regard to the dying patient and his family should be introduced with particular reference to the 'web of social relationships that grows up around a patient who lingers while dying'

2. 'Explicit planning and review should be given to the psychological social and organizational aspects of terminal care.' Particular patterns of dying as demonstrated by the different types of trajectories require varying organizational efforts.

3. 'There should be explicit planning for phases of the dying trajectory that occur before and after residence at the hospital.' Often the patient is dying and yet well enough to be only an out-patient visitor to the hospital. Similarly, post-mortem grief is no longer supposed to be the concern of the hospital. New mechanisms offering some form of trained therapeutic service could be introduced to care for the relatives of the dead, and perhaps even for those who die at home.

4. 'Finally, medical and nursing personnel should encourage public discussion of issues that transcend professional responsibilities for terminal care.' Such issues as the withholding of addictive drugs until near the death and the apparent senseless prolonging of life are, according to the researchers, public issues which are neither the province nor within the capabilities of the medical and nursing professionals.

Conclusions   Diagnosis of illness is based firmly on the biological model. The process of bargaining can enter into diagnosis just as much as into the setting described by Roth. For example, Balint's study shows how the diagnosis made by a general practitioner results from a kind of negotiation made between the patient and the doctor which entails the patient making 'offers' of various symptoms and illnesses which the doctor can reject, accept or modify until there is a kind of common agreement satisfactory to both. Part of the process involves some sort of reconciliation between the lay and professional perspectives of illness, but the interpretation and selection of data are also important. The acceptance of a diagnosis of illness excuses us the performance of certain roles. Generally speaking, individuals are not normally held responsible for illnesses and are exempted from obligations.

The concept of career timetables as developed by Roth, although applied initially to a TB unit, was extended by Gustafson to death and dying. The varying trajectories of dying as studied by Glaser and

Strauss resulted in some concrete recommendations for improving the care of the dying.

THE SOCIAL ORGANISATION OF DEATH

Social networks, human survival and mortality

Social network is a term employed by Walker et al., (1977, p. 410) to refer to 'that set of contacts with relatives, friends, neighbours, etc. through which individuals maintain a social identity and receive emotional support, material aid, services and information, and develop new social contacts.' Generally, social networks are utilised by individuals engaged in a *help-seeking career*, who have a real or perceived problem and are on the way to treatment, recovery, rehabilitation or even death (McKinlay, 1980). Mitchell (1969, pp. 1–50) discusses two main classifications as follows:

- *anchorage* (the particular individual being observed within a network)
- *density* (extent of individual contacts without a focal individual)
- *reachability* (the extent to which individuals can use relationships with others)
- *range* (distribution of experience, age, ethnicity, attitudes and information within a social network)
- *morphological* (relationship of links with one another)
- *content* (inferable meanings of individuals to each other within a network)
- *directedness* (extent to which contact is undirectional or reciprocal)
- *durability* (amount of time, emotional intensity, intimacy and reciprocal services in the tie)
- *frequency* (amount of contact within the network)
- *interactional* (nature of the links themselves)

The concept of *career* has been used to trace the stages from person to patient to person.

It is clear that the notion of social network is an epidemiological variable. The lack of a social support system, or loss of such a system, makes people much more susceptible to tuberculosis, female depression and anxiety, coronary heart disease, strokes, schizophrenia, accidents, suicide, rheumatoid arthritis, high blood pressure and pneumonia. (McKinlay, op. cit, pp. 80–81). The experiencing of certain symptoms prompts most people to help-seeking behaviour, particularly when such symptoms deprive them of some valued social activity. The individual consequently resorts to discussing the symptoms with someone else (75 %) in what Freidson has termed the 'lay referral system'. Network ties which are strong are invariably found in working class (lower socio-economic) neighbourhoods, whereas weak network ties are found in more middle-class, affluent neighbourhoods. Such lay referral systems facilitate help-seeking careers until, by a process of accepting or rejecting the lay diagnostic labels, a point is reached

Diagrammatic repre-
sentation of a typical
sequence of stages in
help-seeking.
(McKinlay, op. cit.,
p. 79)

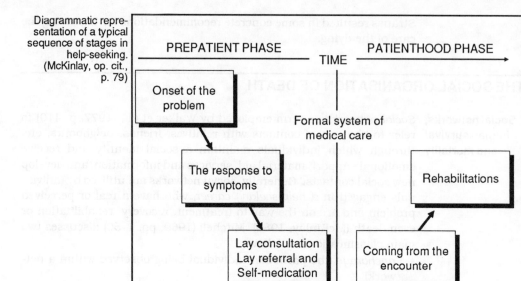

where appropriate professional organisations and persons are identified.

Once the professional target has been reached, the network system
still influences the *formal encounter* in three ways. Firstly, by 'pulling
strings' or identifying 'people in the know'; secondly, by influencing the
expectations that are carried into the encounter; thirdly, the presence,
as opposed to a request to 'wait outside', the network system person,
probably influences the content of the exchange between the professional and the client. Often, by excluding friends and relatives from
the primary encounter the professional is insensitive to the apprehen-
sion of the client. Even after diagnosis, and during treatment or
rehabilitation, social network support has been shown to be beneficial.

Social networks, Apart from the work of McKinlay and others a recent review of support
death and systems by Pilisuk and Parks (1986) places them in the broader context
bereavement of interpersonal analysis. Contrary to popular opinion, support systems in terms of the extended family and similar ties did not wither
away with the Industrial Revolution but remain abundant if slightly
dissimilar in form (e.g. emotional stroking groups).

In the final step in the help-seeking careers, death and bereavement
have also been found to be related to social networks. Firstly, the
characteristics of the network size, strength of ties, frequency and

content have been shown, independently of related socio-economic variables, to influence the risk of death. For example, the death rate of surviving spouses within the first year of being widowed, is ten times higher than among married people who are comparable in sex and age. (Parkes et al., 1969). Another study showed that within fifteen months of widowhood older persons suffering from diabetes and heart disease did so much more severely than those of similar age who were not widowed, and high rates of illness and death were found far more in the separated, the divorced and the single, rather than the married. (Brody, 1979).

Secondly, social networks determine the manner in which the crisis of death and bereavement is responded to. Anthropological data show quite clearly that death and bereavement rituals in non-Western societies have aspects which are far more conducive to coping with death.

The German poet Rainer Maria Rilke wrote that 'In hospitals, where people die so agreeably and with so much gratitude towards doctors and nurses, one dies a death prepared by the institution: they like it that way. If, however, one dies at home, one chooses as a matter of course that polite death of the better circles with which, so to say, the funeral first class and the whole sequel of its touching customs begin.'

A time to die There are as many perspectives on death and dying as there are people who die. However, it is useful to narrow these perspectives down into seven major ones, falling into two categories, *sociological* and *philosophical/psychoanalytical*. (Charmaz, 1980. This section is heavily indebted to her work.)

All of us entertain death conceptions which are generally held to be either *developmentally* or *socially* caused. For example, studies of children's conceptions of death seem to suggest that they are related to mental development, although recent studies of terminally ill children seem to suggest that these children are able to correctly identify and interpret signs given by others which indicate that they are soon to die. Researchers 'argue that children's views of death reflect the information available to them and the situation in which it is acquired.' (Op. cit., p. 97.) They conclude that dying children's perceptions of the events are simply reflections of the thoughts and feelings of the adults surrounding them. Studies of the other researched group, the aged, reveal that they accept the dying process and consequently exhibit less fear: death is within them rather than without. Death talk reveals to us many of the meanings attributed to death. Similarly, gesture is significant. The majority of individuals both fear and deny death, the former includes loss of experience, one's body or self, or ceasing to *be*, while the latter is the result of either an individual adaptation to one's mortality or a response which is culturally situated.

Charmaz argues that the experience of dying, like most experiences, is closely tied to the social setting in which it occurs. As we shall explore in the next section most deaths take place in a medical institution such as a nursing home or hospital. The fact that emotional support for the dying is best given in the 'bosom of the family' means that institutionalised and technological dying misses out in this respect. Institutionalised death very often means that terminal patients are treated as socially dead before they are actually so. Numerous research studies, e.g. Sudnow (1967) reveal that in institutional settings the routinization of work tasks for the staff takes precedence over patients' personal concerns, and consequently it is staff work priorities which shape the patients' dying process. Dying people are estimated for their social value so that consequently age and social class affect the quality and quantity of care given. Thus the young with a high social status receive more care. (Op. cit., p. 168)

In all societies and in varied settings there are individuals who specialise in death work. The management of death becomes routinized in a number of ways. One way is to separate the dead and dying from the living 'so that death remains hidden and its effects are minimised,' the assumption being that death is disruptive:

Consequently, workers devise strategies that make it routine, including (1) the separation of the physical setting of death work from other parts of the organisation or community, (2) separation of workers who commonly handle the dying and dead from other workers, and (3) the removal of those who are dying or dead from ordinary settings. Two other means of minimising the effects of death on the world of work are (1) the development of *self-protection* strategies to control interaction and (2) claims of *professional status*. (Op. cit., p. 205)

Such claims to professional status for funeral directors is denied because they do not conform to the sociological model of professional work, namely extensive expertise and abstract theoretical knowledge (see Chapter 3). Charmaz discusses at length two other modes of death and dying: 1. the routinization of extraordinary death—(a) murder, (b) capital punishment, and (c) war; and 2. suicide.

Finally, the expression of grief is culturally structured, with different nations expressing their sorrow in very diverse ways. 'What grief is, how it is felt, and what is to be done about it are culturally defined.' To westerners who have absorbed the Protestant Ethic grief is private and individual, a personal problem that has to be worked out alone. To Africans, Latins, and others, the culture allows it to be shared and externalised.

In any man who dies there dies with him
His first snow and kiss and fight.
It goes with him.

There are left books and bridges
And painted canvas and machinery

Whose fate is to survive.
But what has gone is also not nothing:

By the rule of the game something has gone.
Not people die but worlds die in them.
(Yevtushenko)

MAJOR PERSPECTIVES ON DEATH

Sociological Perspectives	Focus or Emphasis	Theorists	Consequences
1. Symbolic Interactionism	Actor's *meanings*	Blumer, Strauss, Denzin	Death and dying realistically handled (active)
2. Structural functionalism	Institutional	Parsons, Lidz	Individual negated by institutions (passive)
3. Dramaturgy	Actor's *actions*	Burke, Goffman	Death and Dying realistically handled (active)
4. Marxism	Institutional *and* actors	Sudnow, Giddens, Zeitlin	Social and political action (active)

Philosophical and psychoanalytic approaches	Focus or Emphasis	Theorists	Consequences
5. Existentialism	Individual *acceptance*	Harris, Sartre, Heidegger	Social and individual action (active)
6. Phenomenology	Subjective *confrontation*	Brogden, Taylor, Psathas	Death and dying realistically handled (active)
7. Psychoanalysis	Individual *actors*	Freud, Gifford, Pincus	Denial of death and reality (passive)

(Adapted from Charmaz, 1980, pp 61–63)

INDIVIDUALISED DEATH

Although death comes to us all it manifests itself in different disguises and appears along different pathways. Such differentiation is historical and sociological for the simple reason that:

The social body constrains the way the physical body is perceived. The physical experience of the body, always modified by the social categories through which it is known, sustains a particular view of society . . . The care that is given to it . . . must correlate closely with the categories in which society is seen.
(Douglas, 1973, p. 93)

Kleinman (1973, pp. 206–213) takes this idea further when he describes medicine as having a 'symbolic reality' whose 'systems function along the lines of the cultural dialectic, relating and treating both individual and social realities . . . A given medical system . . . structures the experience of illness, in part, creates the form disease takes'. We will argue that death, also, is a social construction, which in turn affects our style of dying and the values and meanings which accrue to it. Death challenges the 'taken-for-granted realities and accoutrements of everyday life' (Berger and Luckmann, 1967, p. 119). The cultural recipes for correctly dying are provided by the legitimations of death which in turn sustain the social order. The medical act of healing obviates the threat that death brings to the social order.

Furthermore, as a concomitant of this, most recent studies in death and dying have tended to emphasise that dying as a total experience is at variance with the hospital emphasis on the disease process and the diseased organ, where the termination of life is viewed as failure on the part of the personnel involved. The Death System (the totality of words, actions and attitudes concerning death, typified in the *Ars Moriendi* and the Tibetan *Book of the Dead*) is socially constructed and perpetuated, varying from age to age and generally a reflection of the current social structure and institutions.

The social history of death The rise of widespread interest in thanatological (death and dying) concerns was a characteristic of the seventies, and not limited to those who practice cryogenics. Historically, 'infectious, acute diseases were an important source of death in the premodern world' (Lofland, 1978, p. 21), the key factor being the absence of 'early diagnosis' and the 'likelihood that diseases or potentially fatal conditions would be 'identified' rather late in the dying-to-death trajectory'. The modern shift in the social pattern of dying meant that:

not only was the family as a socially-supporting institution altered by the impact of industrialisation and urbanisation, mortality and morbidity rates shifted such that death in childhood sharply declined whereas dying by lingering, chronic illness showed a remarkable rise.
(Benoliel, 1978, p. 6)

Illich (1977, pp. 179–214), following Aries, distinguished six stages of *natural death*: (a) the fifteenth-century 'dance of the dead'; (b) the 'Dance of Death'; (c) 'Bourgois Death'; (d) clinical death; (e) medical intervention; (f) intensive care death. Illich utilises the concept of *industrialisation* to explain the perceived evils of modern society, particularly medical practice and the depersonalisation of dying. But whereas Illich is essentially an advocate of changed *lifestyles*, others, such as Navarro, would argue that this is basically a conservative approach and that the real solution lies in political change. Hence:

the greatest potential for improving the health, of our citizens is not primarily through changes in the behaviour of individuals, but primarily through changes in the patterns of control, structures and behaviour of our economic and political system.
(Navarro, 1975, p. 361)

Society's attitudes to death consist of normative responses to death and the dying, and are calculated to function as constraining mechanisms. Historically, Aries (1974) has typified the attitude of the twelfth century as 'tamed death' when the dying embraced their fate as an inevitable aspect of life. The Middle Ages regarded death as familiar and public and its catechism and ritual were firmly rooted or located in the family setting. In the twentieth century's attitude death is hygienic and unobtrusively private. On average, for example, an American experiences a family bereavement once every twenty years (Dumont and Foss, 1972). The avoidance of death, where death is forbidden, manifested itself in 'the displacement of the site of death. One no longer died at home in the bosom of one's family, but in hospital, alone' (Aries, 1974, p. 87). Thus 'Death is no longer an occasion of a ritual ceremony . . . Death is a technical phenomenon obtained by a cessation of care . . . determined in a more or less avowed way by a decision of the doctor and the hospital team' (Aries, 1974, p. 88).

That a bureaucratic method of dealing with death is currently practised should not, as Blauner (1966) indicates, really surprise anyone. It is, after all, the western world's 'characteristic form of social structure' rather than a manacious plot, as Illich might express it, on behalf of the Medical Establishment. Nevertheless, depersonalised, institutionalised death is concomitantly a shift in focus, away from individual decision-making in life and death:

Dying in the nursing home meant removal from a life-stimulating environment and loss of personal control over intimate decisions to a company of strangers. The technologising of death increased the dehumanising outcomes for dying patients . . .
(Benoliel, 1978, p. 11)

Lofland quite rightly points out that a combination of factors such as (a) a reaction against impersonalism, (b) the rise in chronic illnesses, and (c) an early identification of the soon-to-be-dead, manifests itself among a number of individuals and groups in an attempt to exert an existential *choice* as to the form and meaning that death will take:

It is only very recently that any significant portion of human beings find themselves 'dying' for a long enough period of time for the issue of how best to go about it meaningfully to be raised. That a new role possibility—that a new 'core category' around which identity may be formed—has emerged and that this new role possibility is unencumbered by much historic structuring, engenders action problems for those who take it on.
(Lofland, 1978, p. 35)

The process of becoming dying

Berger and Luckmann stated that:

Life expectancy varies with social location . . . there is considerable discrepancy between the life expectancies of lower-class and upper-class individuals. Furthermore, both the incidence and the character of pathology vary with social location. Lower-class individuals are ill more frequently than upper-class individuals, in addition they have different illnesses. In other words, society determines how long and in what manner the individual organism shall live.
(Berger and Luckmann, 1967, p. 181)

Death is socially constructed and appears at least to be constrained by a Durkheimian cohesiveness or social integration (Seligman, 1974). Thus Phillips and Feldman (1973) found that deaths were less frequent before significant ceremonial occasions. And Alderson (1975, p. 151), utilising mortality data for England and Wales for 1972, found that persons over seventy-five displayed a consistent trend in deaths 'with an excess in birth month and the following three months'. This suggested the hypothesis that in the elderly 'a birthday may in some subtle way influence the general morale of an individual'. Finally, Engel (1971, p. 771) mentions that sudden death follows a precipitating life situation.

Studies of healthy populations have suggested 91 %–92 % have bodily disorders requiring treatment (Pearse and Crocker: 1944; Hinkle: 1960; Schenthel: 1960). The presentation of perceived symptoms to a doctor takes place in a complex system of social life which gives 'meaning' to the potentially sickly facets of existence. Thus Zola states that 'Instead of it being a relatively infrequent or abnormal phenomenon, the empirical reality may be that illness, defined as the presence of clinically serious symptoms, is the statistical *norm*' (Freidson, 1972, p. 392), which is also suggested by Mechanic's view (1968, p. 149) that 'being ill is not an unusual state of being, and much illness is ignored and tolerated'. Twentieth century man has at his disposal a highly technical medical machine able to diagnose his symptoms which, combined with a cultural acceptance of entry to the stage of the 'chronic sick' and treatment capable of prolonging life, produces a 'monstrous regiment' of the soon-to-be-dead.

Validation of the status dying While Scheff (1963) maintains that there is considerable evidence that physicians facilitate illness after ostensibly minor symptoms are diagnosed, it is probably not the case that this is so of dying itself. Apple (1960), Mechanic (1962), Gordon (1966), Kosa and Robertson (1969), Zborowski (1969), Robinson (1971) and Twaddle (1977) have written extensively on the sick role, some of them suggesting that it be abandoned entirely as a valid concept. The grounds for rejection of Parson's analysis are generally that: (1) the sick role lacks uniformity when applied to a variety of social groups and individuals; (2) the sick role is more appropriate to acute illness; (3) Parson's view of patient-physician interaction is traditional and one-to-one; (4) Parson's model has a middle-class orientation; and (5) it does not take into account non-western societies.

A radical extension of the sick role views it as providing:

a convenient mechanism of social control by which institutions can allow deviant behaviour within carefully controlled limits. Because the sick role reduces potential opposition directed against the institutional structure itself, it fosters institutional stability.
(Waitzkin and Waterman, 1974, p. 65)

Nevertheless, Parson's sick role formulation offers useful insights into the sickness career. If we start at the 'being well' state there are points which are culturally defined as 'not being well'. Generally these points consist of 1. not feeling well; 2. inability to perform some task; 3. other more important symptoms (Baumann, 1961). Thus it appears that individuals first realise that they are sick when their symptoms interfere with their daily lives, in particular their day-to-day activities, when their tolerance threshold breaks down, and when their symptoms cannot be located in the realm of the familiar. Friedson's (1961) 'lay referral system' is but the first step before the symptoms are professionally legitimated. One of the alternative routes to 'getting well' is dying, a status validated by the following conditions:

1. recognition and validation by physicians;
2. impairment of normal activities;
3. chronic rather than acute symptoms;
4. uncertain or poor prognosis.

The contemporary pariah Aries's analysis of the changing attitudes towards death begins with the sparing of the sick person the truth of his own death and ends with the initiative of death being placed in the hands of the doctor and the hospital team, away from the family. Consequently, those who control death attempt to elicit 'an acceptable style of living while dying' (Aries, 1974, Gorer, 1965). Blauner (1966) mentions that 'many writers have commented on the tendency of relatives to avoid the subject of death with the terminally ill' and that one way of combating this meaninglessness is by adopting Glaser and Strauss's (1965) 'open awareness context' where both physicians and patient express an acknowledged awareness of the terminal situation. Contemporary man 'hides his death as he hides his sex, as he hides his excrements' (Morin, 1951, p. 331). Even in terms of physical place, 'the hospital morgue is best located on the ground floor and placed in an area inaccessible to the general public. It is important that the unit have a suitable exit leading onto a private loading platform which is concealed from hospital patients and the public' (Owen, 1962, p. 304).

The negotiation of the terminal situation Blauner (1966) writes about the dying, especially those from a higher social status, as being 'in a better position to negotiate certain aspects of the terminal situation.' Again, he mentions that:

> The dying patient in the hospital is subject to the kinds of alienation experienced by persons in other situations in bureaucratic organisations. Because doctors avoid the terminally ill, and nurses and relatives are rarely able to talk about death, he suffers psychic isolation. He experiences a sense of meaninglessness because he is typically kept unaware of the course of his disease and his impending fate . . . He is powerless in that the medical staff and the hospital organisation tend to program his death in keeping with their organisational and professional needs; control over one's death seems to be even more difficult to achieve than control over one's life in our society.
> (Blauner, 1966, p. 89)

Pacing and styling the dying role Three characteristics of the dying role mark it out as *singular*. Firstly, it is a transitional status passage; secondly, it is generally irreversible; and lastly, it is a non-graduating condition in the sense that no one returns to bear tidings as to the quality of the experience. There are also clearly defined rules of *entry* such that one has to be *admitted* by the gatekeepers of death and the 'actors have to accept the admission as accurate' (Lofland, 1978, p. 45). Why the label 'dying' should be ascribed to some and not others in our society is *socially* determined and prescribed, and the label 'dying' is imputed or applied depending on the dying person's location in a variety of social structures and the labeller's involvement in a mesh of organisational, interactional and professional situations (Sudnow, 1967, pp. 68–72). Some, such as Kübler-Ross, have postulated *phases* of the dying role or 'stages of death': denial, anger and rage, bargaining, depression and acceptance, although these only describe the possible course of reaction of the soon-to-be-dead to their impending fate. Noyes's (1974) model of the death experience postulated three stages, namely (*a*) resistance; (*b*) review; and (*c*) transcendence.

Lofland, in her study, further elaborates on the process of *styling* to include 'cultural scripts', provide some specification for how one is to act when one is in the category' (Lofland, 1978, p. 48). Other aspects include *space* (what proportion of the individual's identity is to be labelled 'dying'), *population* (whether the dying role is to be played in a privatised or communal setting), *knowledge* (who shares the knowledge of the individual's admission to the dying role) and *stance* (the verve with which one enacts the role). Further, the degree of panache with which we can control or manage the dying role is determined by four external conditions, namely, '(1) the disease process, (2) the social organisation and culture of medical practice, (3) available resources, and (4) surrounding others' (Lofland, 1978, p. 58).

The biomedical model
The growth of the biomedical model manifests itself in a number of ways:

objectification of the doctor–patient relationship through formalization of the patient history and physical examination; use of technical procedures to assist in diagnosis; utilization of machines in treatment; clinical experimentation; and the appearance of multiple fields of specialized medical practice ... According to (Engel's) argument, the biomedical model of disease has acquired the status of dogma such that all members of society are influenced to a greater or lesser extent by a belief system that defines disease in terms of biomedical and physical deviations from established norms and a reductionist approach to the problem of defining illness.
(Benoliel, 1978, p. 5; Engel, 1960, 1971)

Perhaps Illich puts it more graphically:

... the man best protected against setting the stage for his own dying is the sick person in the critical condition ... The medicalization of society has brought the epoch of natural death to an end. Western man has lost the right to preside at his act of dying ... Mechanical death has conquered and destroyed all other deaths.
(Illich, 1977, p. 210)

Arluke (1978, p. 109) states that 'death can challenge the efficacy of the individual practitioner as well as the profession as a whole'. The medical personnel buttress themselves against the intrusion of a death event by 'concentrating the work of review on the post-mortem course of patients' and its significance is 'diminished by directing instructional interest on the events that lead up to death' (Arluke, 1978, p. 114). Physicians not only determine the circumstances of death but the exact moment at which it occurs. The routinisation of death in the hospital setting is a process of disengagement from a perspective of the dying as a social object. Staff enter into a series of avoidance procedures which have been documented by Sudnow (1967). There is some evidence that the medical model enables the student physican to become socialised to death:

. . . the clinician learns to view dying patients not as people with feelings, but as medical entities, specimens, or objects of scientific interest. By adopting a scientific frame of mind, utilized so effectively in their previous work with dead bodies, clinicians can effectively avoid the uncomfortable inner feelings which occur when they are exposed to dying patients.
(Coombs and Powers, 1975, p. 258)

The Mask of Professionalism, with its special language, attire, cynicism, material objects (e.g., stethoscopes), ritualised and impersonal action, and hospital routine, are addenda to the socialised perspectives on death (Bowers et al., 1976). Death has become shrouded, softened, in a bureaucratic system because the 'death specialists' have taken over various handling procedures (Blauner, 1966). However, an inevitable dichotomy exists between the rational-bureaucratic model and the affective implications of grief and mourning. Furthermore, hospital personnel can become 'acclimatized' to death and dying, usually when 'Death Saturation' occurs and the staff become overloaded with too many deaths (Pattison, 1977).

Thus Benoliel speaks of a 'counterculture against impersonal death', probably beginning with Feifel's (1959) work, culminating with Kübler-Ross (1969). *Death and Dying* courses not only appear in the high school curriculum but also in newspapers, notably in California. Lofland speaks of the same counterculture as the 'Happy Death Movement':

Listed among the agencies pledged to combating the shift in control, from the individual to a medicalised, technologised, impersonal mode of medical engineering, are such groups and organisations as the Euthanasia Education Council, the Foundation of Thanatology, Ars Moriendi, the Forum for Death Education and Counselling, Shanti, Threshold, Inc. Bereavement Outreach, the Widow-to-Widow Program, Hospice of Marin, California, Hospice, Inc., of New Haven, Connecticut, and Compassionate Friends. The informal death talk therapy in such movements follows the well-heeled pattern established by Alcoholics Anonymous and Recovery, Inc (Jones, 1970, 1975) 'My name is Kevin and I am an alcoholic. I have been drinking for as long as I can remember', or 'My name is Pat and I am an ex-mental patient. Last week I couldn't leave the house without palpitations'. One description is as follows:

Each meeting opens with an affirmation of personal tragedies in the style of Alcoholics Anonymous: 'My name is Ernie Freireich and I am a bereaved parent. I lost my son Mark in an automobile accident.' Each lasts as long as members want to air feelings and think they can provide mutual support.

'Only in such settings,' explained Freireich, whose 16-year-old son was killed two years ago, 'do you feel able to talk freely with another person who's been down the same street you've been down, without having judgement passed on you.' Knowing that their listeners understand the participants feel free to express the depths of their pain and bitterness.

(Seligman and Agrest, 1977, p. 89)

Self-help groups Groups concerned with self-help have mushroomed dramatically in the last few years, particularly in North America, developing, generally, from 'grass-roots origins, their faith in group dynamics as a source of individual change and their reliance on the sharing of common experiences rather than professional expertise . . .' (Lusky and Ingman, 1979). Some have classified the self-help group occurrence as a 'collective response to an irrational and fragmented society' (Katz and Bender, 1976, p. 37). Such groups possess the following attributes: (1) they involve other persons on a small-group, face-to-face basis; (2) they arise usually spontaneously; (3) they are sometimes ad hoc or short-lived; (4) they vary in functions and characteristics; (5) they involve personal participation; (6) they emphasise the *meaning* of participation; (7) they supply a reference group; (8) they require some form of action; (9) they usually begin from a condition of powerlessness.

Developmentally self-help groups emerge from social movements, emphasising *change* as their main orientation. The characteristics of self-help groups appear to approximate to two of Blumer's (1951) categories of social movements, namely that they are *specific* and *expressive* rather than general. Katz and Bender (1976), using a primary focus framework, construct a typology of self-help groups, namely: (1) groups whose primary focus is on self-fulfilment or personal growth; (2) groups whose focus is on social advocacy; (3) groups focusing primarily on the creation of alternative patterns for living; (4) 'outcast haven' or 'rock bottom' groups. Cressey (1955) adds a further dimension, namely *rehabilitation*, while Sagarin (1967) supplies 'conforming' and 'reforming', 'inner-focused' and 'out-focused'.

Happy Death Movements as self-help groups arose principally as a reaction against the bureaucratisation of death:

In the main, movement proponents and sympathisers have not found these arrangements satisfactory. They have argued . . . that hospitals' emphasis on 'cure' makes them poor settings for prolonged dying: that the needs of the dying are submerged to the routine of instrumental care . . .

(Lofland, 1978, p. 84)

THE CLASSIFICATION OF SELF-HELP GROUPS

Primary Focus	Inner Directed	Outer Directed	Conforming	Reforming
Self-orientated	Recovery, Inc.	—	Yes	Yes
Socially orientated	—	Welfare Rights Organisations	—	Yes
Alternative-orientated	Gay Liberation	Women's Liberation	—	Yes
Omega or 'Rock Bottom-orientated'	X-Kaley	—	Yes	Yes

There seems little doubt that the reaction against the routinisation and bureaucratisation of death has manifested itself in a quest for autonomy, in a desire for the power of negotiation to determine one's death. Crane (1975) sees such a reaction as forming a loose social movement which as two primary goals, (a) improvement of the quality of interaction between, and with, the dying; (b) seeking a legislative right to refuse treatment.

Rational - bureaucratic aspects of terminal care Kübler-Ross's emphasis has been on death as the final stage of growth, a legacy of an essentially developmental model (Charmaz, 1976), in the belief that 'When you are dying, if you are fortunate enough to have some prior warning . . . you get your final chance to grow, to become more truly who you really are, to become more fully human'. The inexorable drift away from the humanisation of death towards a rational-bureaucratic management where the dying are technologically processed is noticed by a large number of writers. Thus Reiser (1977, p. 229) states:

Machines . . . direct the attention of both doctor and patient to the measurable aspects of illness but away from the 'human' factors that are at least equally important . . . the problems of illness snatched from beliefs, illusions, values and other facets of cultural and mental life . . . are as forceful and significant as the biological problem of illness approached through technology and scientific learning.

Technology's 'prolonged assault on death' can be evidenced from four examples: (a) we will compare the numbers of those dying in hospitals over the last ten years and if it is the case that a greater percentage are now dying in a hospital situation, and hospitals are highly technologised institutions, then the dying act is itself becoming more technologised; (b) we will cite evidence from a contemporary sociological account of hospital dying; (c) we will cite evidence from a dying 'timetable' and a dying 'event'; and (d) we will record a personal description of one woman's death by her son.

A dying timetable

A dying 'timetable' could be described as follows:

8:20 p.m.   Admitted to the hospital.

11:15 p.m.   Emergency operation for cerebral damage following a
               road accident which caused a posterior fossa frac-
               ture resulting in swelling in the occiput and com-
               pression.

2:10 a.m.   Operation complete; intravenous feeding.

6:30 a.m.   Machine-controlled life by being placed on respirator.

7:15 a.m.   Prognosis for recovery nil.

6:00 p.m.   Neurological administration of electroencephalogram
               reveals no cortical activity or evidence of viability.

10:00 p.m.   Operating room. Normal body temperature, pulse,
               blood pressure and respiration.

11:00 p.m.   Removal of respirator.

11:15 p.m.   Patient pronounced dead. Removal of heart and kid-
               neys for recipients.

This is clearly a case of dying without knowing that one is dying, as
the patient, after the initial operation, has no perceived awareness.
Nevertheless, the prominence of technology is obvious, and the dying
process can be compared with the account below:

> The woman lay half-naked on the bed, hooked up on tubes, a tracheostomy,
> and a respirator, staring desperately around the room. The psychiatrist's first
> impulse was to cover her with a bed-sheet, but a nurse appeared and said,
> 'Don't bother—she will push it off again in a minute.' The psychiatrist ap-
> proached the patient, who took her hand and pointed to the ceiling. The
> psychiatrist looked up and asked if the light was bothering her . . . when the
> psychiatrist asked for the light to be switched off, however, the nurse reminded
> her of the rules and regulations of the intensive treatment unit, which required
> that the light stay on. Then the psychiatrist asked for a chair for the mother to
> sit with her daughter. She was told that they could not give her a chair anymore
> because during the previous visit the mother had stayed more than five
> minutes. The woman died eight hours after the physicians had informed the
> parents of her imminent death—she died with the room light in her eyes, the
> tubes in her mouth and veins, and the parents sitting outside in the waiting
> room.
> (Vaatch, 1977, pp. 319–320)

Sudnow's distinction between 'clinical death' (the appearance of
'death signs'), 'biological death' (the cessation of cellular activity) and
'social death' (the patient is treated as a corpse) is of interest here (1967,
p. 74):

> A nurse on duty with a woman she explained way 'dying' was observed to spend
> some two or three minutes trying to close the woman's eyelids . . . When
> questioned about what she had been doing, she reported that a patient's
> eyelids are always closed after death, so that the body will resemble a sleeping

person. After death, however, she reported, it was more difficult to accomplish a complete lid closure . . . she always tried . . . to close them before death; while the eyes are still elastic they are more easily manipulated. This allowed ward personnel to more quickly wrap the body . . .

Most of Sudnow's observations were of sedated, comatose, deaths. Indeed, of 200 deaths observed, no 'deaths were of the Hollywood version, wherein the person's last sentence is interrupted by his final breath' (Op. cit., p. 89.) He cites a passage in support of his observations, to the effect that 'the classical deathbed scene, with its loving partings and solemn last words, is practically a thing of the past; in its stead is a sedated, comatose, betubed object, manipulated and subconscious, if not subhuman' (Fletcher, 1960, p. 141).

While hospitalised deaths in America have been variously given as 73,1 % (Lerner, 1970) and 50 % (Morrison, 1973), in Britain the percentage of deaths that occurred in hospitals in 1967 and 1977 was as follows:

HOSPITAL DEATHS AS A PERCENTAGE OF TOTAL DEATHS IN GREAT BRITAIN IN 1967 AND 1977

		Total Deaths	Hospital Deaths	%
1967	M	307 732	165 706	53,84
	F	294 307	163 014	55,38
1977	M	321 053	186 760	58,17
	F	317 169	194 250	61,24
Source: Office of Population Censuses and Surveys, 1979.				

This shows an increase of 4,32 % for men in ten years, and 5,85 % for women. The total of deaths by all causes according to type of institution for England and Wales for 1967 and 1972 shows the same pattern of increase:

TOTAL DEATHS BY ALL CAUSES, AND SEX, ACCORDING TO TYPE OF INSTITUTION IN ENGLAND AND WALES, 1967 AND 1972

	Total Deaths		Psychiatric Hospitals (i)		Other Hospitals (ii) etc		Home (iii)	
	M	F	M	F	M	F	M	F
1967	277 178	265 338	6 728	9 980	149 085	149 623	121 365	105 735
1972	300 389	291 500	6 150	9 294	173 016	179 974	121 223	102 232

Source: Registrar General's Statistical Review of England and Wales, 1967 and 1972, Part 1, Appendix H.4.
Notes: (i) including N.H.S. and non-N.H.S.; (ii) including other institutions, both N.H.S. and non-N.H.S.; (iii) at the deceased person's own home, other private houses and other places.

In terms of percentages relating to two categories, viz. institutional and non-institutional deaths, we have:

**INSTITUTIONAL AND NON-INSTITUTIONAL DEATHS IN ENGLAND
AND WALES EXPRESSED IN PERCENTAGES 1967 AND 1972**

	Institutional Death		Non-Institutional Death	
	M	F	M	F
1967	56,21	60,15	43,78	39,84
1972	59,60	64,92	40,35	35,07

Thus in 1972 the percentage of deaths in England and Wales that occurred in institutions was 59,60 % for men, an increase of 3,39 % from 1967, and 64,92 % for women, an increase of 4,77 %. Undoubtedly, therefore, the increasing tendency is towards a highly technologised death in an institutional, rather than a domestic, setting.

Finally, a personal account of one woman's death by her son further emphasises the impersonal aspect:

7 p.m. Mother took ill soon after a light tea. The doctor visited her at 11 a.m. and, after examining her, suggested that she be kept on the oxygen. As soon as he had gone she lost her speech. I presumed that she had had a stroke. I telephoned the ambulance which arrived in a short time. The men said that my mother would be admitted to the new Royal Country Hospital but, half way there, they were informed by radio that there were no beds available and that they were to proceed to Shire Hospital. The doctor at Shire said, 'Your mother has had a stroke but isn't ill enough to be detained in hospital. What's more we have no spare beds and so we'll send her home as soon as an ambulance is available.' I waited until 9 p.m. She was kept in a cubicle for six hours without my seeing her again that night. I went home to await her return and shortly afterwards the hospital rang to say that my mother had had another slight stroke and that they were admitting her to a ward. It later transpired that she had pneumonia. She died two days later . . . I must add that the doctor was frightfully arrogant. I had been nursing my mother for the last two years, day and night. I slept on the couch so that I could minister to her bodily functions and clean her, and to give her oxygen frequently throughout the night. I know my mother had to die sometime, but not to be treated in such a despicable manner before doing so, after all my devoted attention.
(From: The diary of a Mr A.A. Philips.)

Making today
count

The increased rational-bureaucratic management of death invariably results in episodes of dehumanisation such as those described above. The counterculture against such technological intrusion is well represented by a group called Making Today Count (MTC), Inc., which has 136 Chapters across the United States. The founder Orville Eugene Kelly, gives an account of his own cancer and the subsequent beginning of the movement in *Make Today Count*, published in 1975. Kelly's own reaction to the diagnosis of malignant lymphoma closely parallels Kübler-Ross's concept of stages of death. He writes: 'I wanted to know why I was being shortchanged'. Following his newspaper account of his illness the initial MTC meeting of eighteen cancer patients and their families was held at the Elks Club in Burlington, Ohio. Kelly's primary aim was that:

Cancer has to be faced. Death has to be talked about openly . . . Only that way can we give ourselves a chance to take pleasure in our daily lives, and give our lives some sense of meaning and accomplishment.

Organisation

Membership of MTC increased rapidly. The format of the meetings is similar to that of A.A. and other self-help groups—namely a sharing of experiences, the appearance of guest speakers, and the ability of the member to make a decision that they *want to be helped*. Information is shared by the production of a monthly newsletter.

Beliefs and practices

Kelly (1975, p. 127) claims that:

The entire thrust of MTC, both as a philosophy and as a movement, is to improve the quality of life for people whose terminal illness is a real and personal matter—and those are, of course, the terminally ill and their families.

He is convinced that most people fear death because they don't talk about it freely:

Probably because I live so close to the knowledge of my own death, I have become particularly sensitive to the ways people try to deny death, and . . . that it leads ultimately to a denial of life itself (op. cit., p. 129).

The emergence of this new core category, the chronically dying, is a relatively new phenomenon, as Lofland points out above, and, as a reaction against the technologising of death and its concomitant dehumanisation, the soon-to-be-dead are encouraged, in groups such as these, to make a conscious choice as to the form that their remaining days will take. By such conscious measures the dying obviate what Blauner describes as the psychic alienation so commonly experienced: in sum they establish control over their dying.

The major problems accompanying cancer are largely emotional. However, the success of MTC, as reflected in its phenomenol growth, is indicative of many things:

the need of the terminally ill to share their problems and to learn from one another; the growing willingness of our society to deal with the problems of illness and death; our growing unwillingness to tolerate cover-ups, whether political or medical. It also reflects, I think, another development: a growing independence among patients and their families . . . We are no longer content to be treated like children . . . the best treatment for us as human beings . . . is compassionate honesty (op. cit., p. 146).

Death can be more tolerable if it can be publicly discussed and society can be made to change its attitudes. MTC thus is comprised of individuals the major part of whose identity is labelled 'dying' who are playing their roles in a communal setting in a flamboyant announcement of their dying status.

The basic tenets of the group are crystallised in its goals and philosophy. MTC is not a religious organisation nor is it involved with any religious sect or denomination. This does not mean that the organisation prohibits the sharing of a variety of spiritual or religious experiences. Kelly himself is a religious person but MTC does not have a mandatory belief to which members have to subscribe. The organisation is emphatic that it does not become involved in any recommendations regarding certain kinds of treatment, and neither does it provide ancillary services such as nursing and homemaking.

The dynamics of anticipatory death MTC is not the only self-help group for the terminally ill. For example, Reach for Recovery is composed of women who have had mastectomies and who are committed to helping others. The Parents' Sharing Group, while not composed of the soon-to-be-dead, 'is a group process designed to help parents of children suffering from leukemia cope with some of the human threats that accompany diagnosis, treatment and hospitalisation of the disease' (Kerney, 1974, p. 316). The usual type of group is composed 'of three to eight mothers, and is fluid in nature, with new persons coming in and others dropping out'. (Op. cit., p. 319.)

The dynamics of all such groups, however, are concerned not only with anticipated death but also with anticipatory grief. Such grief, as documented by Aldrich (1974), has something to teach us concerning the quality of experience felt by the soon-to-be-dead. For one thing, in comparison with conventional grief, anticipatory grief accelerates rather than decelerates. There is a certain amount of unresolved *ambivalence* attached to it, also, which serves merely to increase the prevalence of *denial.*

Certain characteristics are common to all aspects of the dying role:

Over an extended time, therefore, the family members may (1) experience depression, (2) feel a heightened concern for the ill member, (3) rehearse his death, and (4) attempt to adjust to the various consequences of it. By the time the death occurs the family will, to the extent that they have anticipated the death dissipated their grief, display little or no emotion.
(Fulton and Fulton, 1974)

The formulation of the personal and social meaning of an anticipated death involves not only questions of the type asked by Kelly but also coming to terms with the significance of certain values in the life that one has hitherto led. It includes, also, a certain adjustment to the personal time-space dimension because 'anticipatory grief involves a profound sense of loss of the future' (Ramshorn, 1974, p. 248). Neither does anticipatory grief, in the usually short period it is with us, allow the soon-to-be-dead and his family to revamp their emotional orientations. 'Anticipatory grief is a period of intense involvement, which requires suspension of normal roles within the family, work and community systems.' (Op. cit., p. 249.)

Finally, professional treatment of the sick relates acutely not only to the patient's physiological status but also to his social situation (Crane, 1975, pp. 68–84). The terminally ill fluctuate between seeking treatment actively or not, and the attitude of the patient is an important factor in the physician's decision-making process, apart from the evidence that a number of patients have difficulty in conveying their attitudes to the medical staff. The family's attitude is regarded with some ambivalence by the physician, with the exception perhaps of the treatment of an unsalvageable patient. A number of variables influence the decision process. High status patients are differentially treated as against low status patients—but not if they are unsalvageable. Deviants such as prostitutes or addicts, contrary to Sudnow's experience, did not appear in the Crane study to be discriminated against. Finally, age seems to influence the degree of active treatment so that those showing serious illness at the middle of the life-cycle were more likely to be accorded suitable treatment than those at the end of the life-cycle.

We have argued that an increasing depersonalisation of death, arising from a highly technological approach, has resulted in a quest for autonomy manifested in some form of personal control of the dying event. This reaction, displayed in concrete terms in the growing number of dying groups such as MTC, arises out of an inevitable dichotomy between the rational-bureaucratic model and the affective implications of the dying role. At present self-help groups for the terminally ill coexist alongside the medical profession in an uneasy truce. Their very existence probably implies the latter's laxity in supplying the affective dimension to merely physical treatment. The work of Cicely Saunders in London, Brown in Minnesota, Twycross in Oxford, Gusterson in Sussex, Hadlock in Orlando, Florida, Lamers at Marin in California, Mount in Montreal, are just some of those active in the field of terminal care *within* the medical profession. Currently there are about forty hospices in England with others emerging in North America and Europe. Movements such as MTC have an important lay contribution to make because they see their programmes from the perspective of the dying patient. They are singular movements emphasising a positive approach for the soon-to-be-dead, creating a situation where the latter can negotiate their own identity.

SUMMARY

1. Disease is a medical diagnosis based on signs and symptoms while illness may or may not be a disease but a subjective feeling. Diagnosis based on the classical model often fails to take account of personal and social influences.

2. Lay and professional systems of evaluation and referral exist in a social context. Usually the initial diagnosis is self-diagnosis leading to family or friends' denial or confirmation and ultimately ending in professional denial or confirmation.

3. Lay and professional definitions of medical terms differ very much from each other.

4. Dying in a hospital setting takes the form of a *trajectory* which takes place over time and can be described in a number of critical phases.

5. People within a social network can generally rely on a social support system and the intensity of such a system influences the mortality and morbidity rate. The experience of dying, however, is closely tied to the social setting in which it occurs.

6. The social history of death has shown a shift from a family centred experience to a bureaucratic one in which the initiative of death is placed in the hands of physicians and the hospital team.

7. The growth of self-help groups specifically dealing with the dying appear to have arisen as a reaction against the bureaucratisation of death.

8. Groups such as Make Today Count mobilise a number of coping mechanisms to deal with anticipatory grief.

IMPORTANT TERMS

disease	illness
diagnosis	drug doctor
dying trajectory	career
timetables	social network
symbolic reality	biomedical model
self-help group	reational-bureaucratic
clinical death	biological death
social death	dying role
anticipatory death	

SELF-ASSESSMENT QUESTIONS

1. What are the important distinctions between illness and disease?

2. Is Twaddle correct in asserting that the notion of disease is essentially a Western one?

3. Compare and contrast *diagnosis* and *labelling*. To what extent can they both be damaging if incorrectly applied?

4. Relate the concept of social network to morbidity and mortality trends.

5. Why do sociologists tend to claim that the process of dying has become considerably more bureaucratised?
6. Discuss self-help groups in general and the way they can facilitate the death process.

CHAPTER NINE

THE SOCIAL EPIDEMIOLOGY OF DISEASE

- demography
- human ecology
- urbanisation and disease
- epidemiological techniques for the measurement of disease

DEMOGRAPHY

The current world population is currently approximately five billion. If the present rate of increase persists this will reach six billion by the year 2000. Five hundred million of this total population is malnourished and some 10 million per annum die of starvation, many of these young children. Ninety per cent of all births will, by the end of this century, be in underdeveloped or developing countries. One of the largest growth areas is that of cities. Slightly more than a century ago only London had a population of 1 million. By the end of the present century there will be 500 cities with populations of over a million, 60 of them with populations over 5 million and nearly ten of them with populations over 20 million.

Such an area of study is known as *demography*, which deals with the distribution of population, its composition (usually sex, age and marital status) and its change. Usually demography is regarded as a subdiscipline of sociology because population dynamics occur in a social context, either being affected by social factors or themselves influencing social factors. For example, religious factors may be instrumental in affecting fertility, and public health standards can prolong the life span. One of the problems facing demographers is very often the unavailability of adequate statistics, particularly in poorer countries. However, even in advanced countries population censuses are often under or over enumerated.

Measuring changes in the population: fertility rates

A crude way in which we could begin to measure changes in population is simply to count the number of children born in any particular country. The demographer, however, in order to arrive at a more accurate picture, uses *rates* and *ratios*. To arrive at a rate he divides the total of the population into the number of births in a given year, which gives him the *crude birth rate*. To arrive at what he calls the *refined birth rate* he divides the number of children born during a given year by the number of females of childbearing age (15 to 44):

$$\text{Crude birth rate} = \frac{\text{Number of births per year}}{\text{Total population}} \times 1\ 000$$

It is useful here to introduce another term known as the *population risk*, because simply to take any thousand would be a very crude way of arriving at a true picture. Thus, in order to arrive at a birth rate we would use a 'risk' population defined as women of childbearing age and not just any thousand in the population:

$$\text{Refined birth rate} = \frac{\text{Number of births per year}}{\text{Females of child–bearing age}} \times 1\ 000$$

It is also useful to give quite different figures for each sex because of different life expectancies and also to take a thousand from either sex (rather than females) would not be of much use. Similarly, different age groups are given different figures because each age group contains different numbers of the population and has different mortality rates. An example of widely differing *birth rates* is as follows:

	CRUDE BIRTH RATE	CRUDE DEATH RATE	URBAN POPULATION
LOW INCOME ECONOMIES			
Chad	44	23	18
Ethiopia	49	23	14
Tanzania	46	14	13
Transkei	38	na	na
MIDDLE INCOME ECONOMIES			
Lesotho	43	12	5
Zimbabwe	54	13	23
South Africa	38	10	53
HIGH INCOME ECONOMIES			
U.S.A.	16	9	74
U.K.	13	12	76

Source: World Population Data Sheet, 1984.

The poorer the country the higher the crude birth rate, the higher the crude death rate and the more rural the population. From the birth rate we can determine the *fertility rate* (the average number of children women are bearing as opposed to the *fecundity rate* (the number of children it is physically possible to bear, estimated at between twenty and twenty-five).

The population change in any given society can be reduced to four variables. These are fertility (births), mortality (deaths), emigration (movement from an area) and immigration (movement to an area). Any other event which affects the size of the population does so by influencing one of these *basic demographic variables*.

In the nineteenth century, Great Britain, for example, experienced the introduction of relatively sophisticated medical services, a number of scientific improvements, improved sanitary provisions, and legislation affecting general public health. The sociological changes from a nation of high fertility and mortality to one of low fertility and low mortality began at the same time. Families began to get smaller and people began to live longer; this trend began with the upper and middle classes, with their family planning and improved hygiene and dietary standards, and eventually spread to the working classes. Fears that such trends might result in a population *decline* led to the establishment of a Royal Commission on Population in 1944. In just over

100 years the number of children for marriage cohorts fell from six to two. From 1956, however, the rate increased rapidly due to a number of interesting factors:

1. There are increasingly *less* unmarried females in the population (of women between 20 and 39 in 1911, 552 per thousand were married compared with 808 per thousand in 1961).
2. More males are marrying.
3. People are marrying earlier
4. There is a rise in the number of illigitimate births.
5. Immigration.

Measuring changes in the population: mortality rates

Up to the turn of the century infant mortality rates remained fairly constant, and certainly the rate in the nineteenth century did not give a true reflection of the rapidly increasing sophistication of medical and sanitary practice. R.K. Kelsall (1967, p. 24) and others have suggested that 'It seems that it was not until the midwifery service was statutorily recognised and progressively extended in the early part of the twentieth century, and until standards of hygiene were improved that any improvement in the infant mortality rate could be achieved.' The discovery and application of penicillin and vaccines has resulted in a reduction of 90 % in post neonatal deaths (from five weeks to the first birthday) and 60 % in neonatal deaths (first four weeks after birth) compared with the early part of this century.

Life expectation tables are used by insurance companies to give a theoretical picture of the duration of life of persons born at the same time. They are calculated by taking *age specific rates* (number of deaths per thousand of certain ages) of a population and predicting a person's expected longevity. Because such tables assume the mortality rate (the current one) to remain constant they actually underestimate the lonevity of any age category. *Life span* refers to the age limit of males and females and *life expectancy* to the average length of life reached at the time of death by individuals born during a certain time. The life span has remained fairly constant because we cannot defeat the diseases of old age.

There are considerable sex differences in mortality rates. The ratio of male to female infants in all populations is generally 106:100. The general picture, however, reveals that many of these male children die off so that there tends to be an adult ratio of male to female of 95:100. There are several reasons for this including the higher rate among males of death from accidents, heart disease, T.B. and cancer, the fact that males tend to seek medical help less frequently than females, and the stresses and strains of many male occupations. In the age group of 75 and over women outnumber men almost 2:1, partly due to death in battle but also to the general mortality rate of males from a large number of specific diseases.

Measuring changes in the population: immigration and emigration

Immigration and emigration are two additional demographic variables which influence the population trends. The *migration rate* is the difference, calculated annually, between the number of immigrants and emigrants per thousand of the total population. The late nineteenth century saw a gigantic movement of populations mostly from Europe to the colonies and North America. Two factors are prominent in such movements. Those which 'force' or 'push' people to emigrate (such as the Irish potato famine which forced the Irish to America and England) and those which 'pull' people (such as the possibility of a better life in South Africa or Australia). In the case of South Africa and the neighbouring dependent and independent territories, there is constant migration and immigration. This tends to be of a temporary nature rather than permanent, and because it is basically economical it is referred to as *migratory labour.*

In the Transkei 19 % of the total *de jure* population are migratory workers, 667 499 from the rural areas and 9 860 from the urban areas. Figures for other areas are made up as follows:

Bophuthatswana	246 000
Ciskei	60 000
Gazankulu	65 000
KaNgwane	62 000
KwaNdebele	72 000
KwaZulu	308 000
Lesotho	69 560
Botswana	18 826
Swaziland	9 262
Malawi	11 491
Mozambique	37 734

Sources: Development Bank of Southern Africa, Annual Report, 1985/6, Southall (1982).

These migrations have considerable importance in terms of such factors as housing/dwelling densities, health, education, family structure, transmitted diseases and general services.

Another aspect of migration is its occurrence within a country. Generally the trend is from the poor areas to the more prosperous ones and from rural to urban conurbations. Among the reasons why there is internal migration within a country we can list: economic or work considerations; retirement; change in marital status.

Population size and living standards Thomas Malthus, writing in about 1800, was concerned with the consequences of an unchecked population which might grow at the rate of geometrical progression (2:4:8:16; . . .) more rapidly than the supply of food. Two courses of action would reduce this rate. Firstly, war, famine and pestilence. Secondly, being a Victorian clergyman, he considered celibacy and moral restraint to be important. The pessim-

DEATH OF ST CLARE, C. 1410
National Gallery of Art, Washington, D.C.
Samuel H Kreis Collection, 1952

ism of Malthus overlooked the efficiency of modern birth control methods and the technological achievements.

Nevertheless, the gap between developed nations and underdeveloped nations is increasing at such a rate that it is impossible, according to one theory, for them ever to reach the same stage. Many factors militate against the improvement of health and general standards. The most crucial is rapid population growth. Thus the poorer countries are estimated to double their populations in approximately 30 years, the world population will double in 40 years and the more developed nations in 112 years. In terms of countries this works out as follows in terms of doubling of population:

Kenya	17 years
Mozambique	25 years
Zambia	11 years
South Africa	28 years
U.K.	693 years
U.S.A.	100 years
Sweden	3 465 years

Source: *World Population Data sheet,* 1984.

The question of *optimum population* has an upper limit set by the supply of food and resources available. Similarly, if the population were not to be replaced by new members it would soon decline. The optimum size of a population, however, will be set by the scale of cultural values held in a given society at any one time:

1. Technology
2. Values relating to levels and standards of living
3. Value placed upon having children
4. Social regulation of sex
5. Post conception regulation of child survival, e.g. abortion
6. Attitudes and practices regarding health and mortality.

This means that a highly technological society can keep a large population in food and operate a surplus, will exercise constraints to keep its population within certain living standards, and will generally place the same value on either sex of its children. In countries with a strong emphasis on the male child there is usually a high fertility rate. In some societies extramarital and other sexual relationships are strictly regulated. A high value may be placed upon the males to die in battle or to enter a religious order, i.e. Thailand, thereby regulating the population. Lastly, certain foods may be culturally prohibited although nutritious.

Rapid population growth is generally caused by an inbalance and change in the ratio of births to deaths. In rapidly developing nations such as we have in Southern Africa the death rates drop dramatically with the often sudden introduction of modern sanitation, hygiene, medicine and nutrition. The village level health campaigns and the introduction of Village Extension Workers and Family Welfare Educators in Botswana are examples of the dramatic introduction of hygiene and preventative methods used in developing countries. The intensive activity by indigenous governments, WHO and international agencies has resulted in a relatively sudden drop in deaths while the birth rate continues to be high. The poorer countries are characterised by a large population under fifteen and a small population over sixty-five. These countries, already possessing a large population, are now facing rapid population growth on an unprecedented scale:

65+ AND UNDER 15 FOR SELECTED COUNTRIES

	65+	Under 15
Chad	2,6	42,0
Ethiopia	4,0	43,0
Tanzania	4,6	46,0
Transkei*	4,6	42,1
Botswana	3,7	50,0
Lesotho	5,2	40,0
Zimbabwe	1,6	48,0
South Africa**	3,9	42,0
USA	11,8	22,0
UK	15,0	21,0
Sweden	19,0	16,0

*Transkei, 1985
** All races

In South Africa, if we break down the various racial categories, we can translate these figures as follows:

TRANSKEI: 65+ POPULATION 1891–1985

Year	Female	Male	Total
1891	10 276 (3,9 %)	8 584 (3.6 %)	18 600 (3,8 %)
1904	15 788 (2,3 %)	14 088 (2,5 %)	29 876 (2,4 %)
1936	18 692 (2,6 %)	17 150 (3,2 %)	35 842 (2,9 %)
1951	31 084 (3,9 %)	20 052 (3,5 %)	52 136 (3,7 %)
1960	32 261 (3,6 %)	21 227 (3,3 %)	53 488 (3,4 %)
1970	55 941 (4,8 %)	35 554 (4,3 %)	91 495 (4,5 %)
1985	70 412 (4,1 %)	95 375 (5,1 %)	165 787 (4,6 %)

SOUTH AFRICA: 65+ POPULATION BY RACIAL GROUP — 1985

Group	Female	Male	Total
Whites	230 302 (9,9 %)	156 044 (6,9 %)	386 346 (8,4 %)
Blacks	384 494 (4,5 %)	256 166 (3,4 %)	604 660 (3,9 %)
Coloureds	55 816 (3,8 %)	40 858 (2,9 %)	96 674 (3,4 %)
Asians	11 975 (2,8 %)	10 871 (2,6 %)	22 846 (2,7 %)

It is clear from the Transkei 65+ table that very few people live to that age. The rate has been fairly constant over the last fifteen years. However, the population of the Transkei, compared with Blacks, Coloureds and Asians in the Republic, do considerably *better*. Over twice as many Whites in South Africa live to be 65+ as any other group, and only 1,6 % fewer Whites live to be 65+ compared with all the other groups combined.

TRANSKEI: UNDER 15 POPULATION 1891–1985

Year	Female	Male	Total
1891	113 774 (44 %)	112 596 (48 %)	226 370 (46 %)
1904	205 192 (30 %)	205 192 (35 %)	408 116 (33 %)
1936	275 925 (39 %)	273 947 (52 %)	549 872 (45,5 %)
1951	281 516 (35 %)	268 323 (46 %)	549 839 (40,5 %)
1960	339 724 (38,5 %)	339 111 (53,0 %)	678 835 (45,7 %)
1970	466 532 (40 %)	466 556 (56 %)	926 917 (48 %)
1985	756 395 (40,8 %)	740 708 (43,5 %)	1 497 103 (42,1 %)

SOUTH AFRICA: UNDER 15 POPULATION BY RACIAL GROUP — 1985

Group	Female	Male	Total
Whites	595 610 (25,5 %)	613 787 (27,4 %)	1 209 397 (26,4 %)
Blacks	2 856 123 (37,3 %)	2 835 691 (37,7 %)	5 691 814 (37,5 %)
Coloureds	505 113 (34,7 %)	511 718 (37,1 %)	1 016 813 (35,8 %)
Asians	137 349 (33,0 %)	140 779 (34,6 %)	278 128 (33,8 %)

The population under 15 in the Transkei is 15,7 % greater than that of the Whites in South Africa, 4,6 % greater than Blacks, 6,9 % greater than Coloureds and 8,3 % greater than Asians. On a scale of international comparison Transkei holds its own with the Low Income Economies of Ethiopia, Tanzania and the Central African Republique and the Mid-Income Economies of Botswana, Lesotho, Zimbabwe and South Africa (all races). The population under 15 for the Transkei is almost exactly *double* of that of the U.K. and U.S.A.

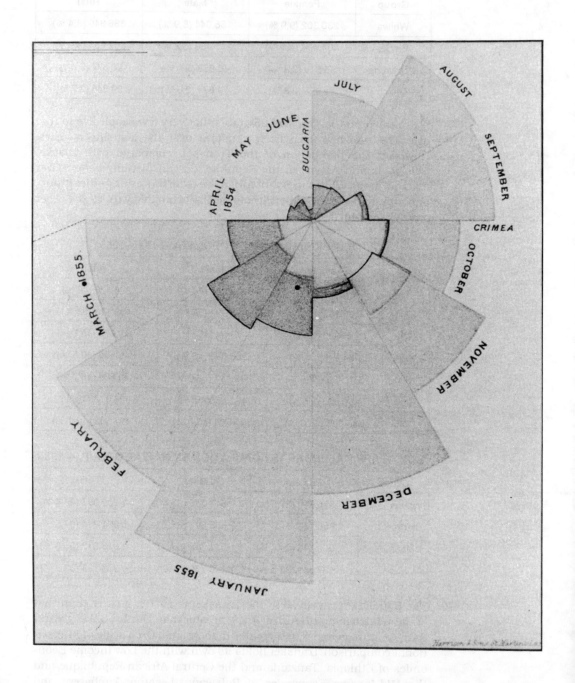

FLORENCE NIGHTINGALE'S 'COXCOMB' DIAGRAM FOR APRIL 1854 TO MARCH 1855
SHOWING THE EXTENT OF NEEDLESS DEATHS IN BRITISH MILITARY HOSPITALS.
Houghton Library, Massachusetts, U.S.A.

65+ URBAN/RURAL BY RESIDENCE—1985

	Rural	Urban
Blacks	199 500 (67,0 %)	405160 (33,0 %)
Whites	34 935 (11,0 %)	346 411 (89,0 %)
Asians	1 625 (8,0 %)	21 221 (92,0 %)
Coloureds	75 142 (22,3 %)	21 532 (77,7 %)
TRANSKEI	162 105 (97,0 %)	3 682 (2,2 %)

The birth rate remains as high as it does because developing countries are culturally bound to many traditions which place great importance on high fertility as desirable in women and fathering many children as a sign of great prestige in men. Many other factors are also important, such as the feeling that one must produce many children in order to care for one in old age. We must remember that the events taking place within one generation in developing countries took many years to develop in advanced nations.

The demographic transition   Historical demographers point out to us that in advanced technological societies such as the U.K. and America, growth rates eventually stabilised after a fall in birth rates. The question is whether, as less developed nations become industrialised, they will display the same process of a fall in birth rates. Such a process is called *demographic progression* (the tendency for birth rates to drop and population to stabilize once a society has achieved a certain level of economic and social development). As we saw in chapter five the nuclear family arose to accommodate industrialisation as too many children were regarded as an economic burden rather than beneficial. As the old values die away new values more pertinent to the process of industrialisation take their place. The problem is that there is a lag between the time it takes various traditional cultural values to become accommodated to rapidly changing economic, technical and social circumstances.

The demographic transition is characterised by three stages:

Stage one: high birth rate, high death rate

The stage is characteristic of traditional societies which the birth rate and the death rate remain relatively stable, although both are high. Child mortality is especially high.

Stage two: high birth rate, low death rate

The transition from preindustrial to industrial modes of production produces a high birth rate but a sharp drop in infant mortality and other deaths. This results in a population increase.

HEALTH INDICES FOR SELECTED COUNTRIES

	GNP %	School popula-tion per teacher	% Pop. with ac-cess to safe water	IMR 00-1	Popula-tion per hospital bed	Public exp. p.c. on health	Life expec-tancy	Pop. per physi-cian (1977)	Pop. per nurse (1977)	% Adult literates	Daily per capita intake Calories	Proteins	Fertility rate (1980)	OBR p.c. (1980)	Pub. exp. p.c. on educ.
LOW-INCOME ECONOMIES															
Chad	113	313	26	149	1 312	1	41	41 940	3 820	15	1 808	43	5,9	44	3
Ethiopia	137	271	6	147	2 672	2	40	74 910	5 320	15	1 729	58	6,7	49	2
Tanzania	264	79	39	103	482	5	52	17 550	2 390	66	2 028	48	6,5	46	5
Transkei	276	55	24	130	254**	23	41	14 735	660	33	2 950	50	2,5	38	30
Central Afr. Rep.	333	165	16	149	642	5	44	20 280	1 540	39	2 161	43	5,9	44	12
MIDDLE-INCOME ECONOMIES															
Botswana	886	55	45	83	420	20	48	8 100	n.a.	40	2 181	53			68
Lesotho	505	77	17	115	488	4	50	13 390	14 900	52	2 442	73	5,8	43	13
Zimbabwe	718	88	n.a.	74	388	14	54	6 580	1 170	74	1 911	51	8,0	54	31
S. Africa	2 387	58	n.a.	96	155	10	60	2 000	741**	65	2 826	74	5,1	18	103
HIGH-INCOME ECONOMIES															
U.S.A.	11 347	22	99	13	171	439	74	550	n.a.	99	3 652	107	n.a.	n.a.	??
UK	9 213	23	99	12	121	443	73	620	n.a.	99	3 315	91	n.a.	n.a.	??

The Transkei 1985 Sample Census gave the following total population figures: *de jure*: 3 609 962; *de facto*: 2 932 397
* De Jure Population
** Based on the 1985 Department of Health
*** White 161; Coloured 892; Black 1 172

State three: low birth rate, low death rate

In advanced technological societies, family size accommodates to the economic situation and the birth rate falls while the death rate stays low. The population rate tends towards low and balanced.

A number of demographers and development sociologists question the validity of this theory. Firstly, it does not necessarily follow that countries will follow a similar pattern either in terms of demographic stages or development. Many development theorists question whether, in fact, the underdeveloped countries will ever be able to catch up with the developed nations. There seems little chance that the 'threshold' of economic and urban development will be achieved by the poorer nations. Recessions in the world economy have severe repercussions on them. In developing countries a conglomeration of influences exist, which appear to maintain a static level of economic development and create a *cycle of poverty* and poor health. The problems are intertwined in such a complicated manner that various strata are indistinguishable from each other. Thus one cannot treat 'health' alone because it is related to other factors such as hygiene, access to safe water, education, and so on.

The poorest countries, where the population is doubling every thirty years, have the task of also doubling their income during that period, merely to *maintain* their level of existence.

Demographic characteristics of SOUTH AFRICA

1. Ethnic and racial composition of the population

The four main categories of Black, Whites, Indians and Coloureds can be further subdivided. The projected composition to the year 2000 is as follows:

RACIAL/ETHNIC COMPOSITION (%) OF THE S.A. POPULATION 1951 TO 2000

Groups	1951	1960	1970	1975	1985	2000
Whites	20,9	19,3	17,3	16,6	16,8	14,0
Asians	2,9	3,0	2,9	2,9	3,3	3,2
Coloureds	8,7	9,4	9,4	9,2	11,2	11,7
Blacks	67,6	68,3	70,4	71,3	68,7	71,2

Source: Dept. of Statistics, South African Statistics 1978. Adapted from van Rensburg and Mans, 1982.

2. Age composition of the population by race

The figures for this are given above.

3. Urban/rural ratio by race

The figures for this are given above.

4. Changes in the proportion of other race groups to whites

This varies with the numbers of whites emigrating due to political and economic conditions prevailing. Also, other race groups will tend to be underenumerated at census time.

5. Rate of urbanization

This will tend to follow the normal trend and increase.

Other demographic features to take into consideration include: the move from the cities into the suburbs; the increase in the proportion of women; the rate of industrialization; the increase in literacy and level of education; the increase of the proportion of women in the work force; and current economic status. The demographic picture for 1984 for South Africa as a whole is as follows:

Total population	31,7 million
Birth rate	35
Death rate	10
'Doubling time'	28
Population 2000	49,6 million
Infant mortality	95 (all races)
Fertility rate	5,1
Under 15/65+	42/4
Life expectancy	61
% Urbanized	53
Per capita GNP %	2,670

Source: 1984 WORLD POPULATION DATA SHEET

EXAMPLES OF EPIDEMIOLOGICAL RESEARCH CONDUCTED IN SOUTH AFRICA

FOCUS OF RESEARCH	MRC-ASSOCIATED STUDIES	NON-MRC STUDIES
Description of impact of different factors on health	Studies of causes of mortality (1979) Review of effects of smoking (1988)	Gluckman Commission (1942–44) Carnegie I: Poor white report (1932) Cancer studies (1940) Carnegie II: Studies into poverty(1983)
Identification of causes	Mseleni joint disease (1968) Oesophageal cancer	Mesothelioma & asbestosis (1950) Social dimensions of disease (1932)
Evaluation of interventions	Ischaemic heart disease (CORIS & CRISIC) (1978) Typhoid vaccination (1986) Effectiveness of primary health care nurses (1977) Chemotherapies for TB & bilharzia	Pneumococcal vaccine BCG
Dates given refer to year in which a major study commenced. In many cases subsequent studies have also been done.		

Implications of Higher infant mortality at the lower end of the social scale has been
democratic data found to be due to the higher incidence of premature births, itself
associated with such factors as early childrearing, poor antenatal care,
working too much or too hard, births close together, and a greater
postneonatal mortality due to a greater risk of infection from pneumonia, bronchitis and gastro-enteritis. Even with a general increase
in the standard of living it is likely that the same differentiation would
betray itself and that differing rates would show themselves in different
social classes. Social class variations also occur, as we see elsewhere,
in mortality rates other than those of infants. The social class gradient
in fertility rates tends to adopt a U curve, so that upper and working
class rates are higher than middle class rates.

Women today are finishing childbearing and rearing at a comparatively early age compared with last century, leaving them free to enter
into other areas of activity. They also, of course, tend to live longer than
they did half a century ago. This has considerable implications in terms
of career structure and training and for the economy in general. If we
couple this with the fact that unmarried women are disappearing,
demographically speaking, at an alarming rate then such occupations
as nursing and teaching will have to either rely on male recruitment
or adapt themselves to married women. This again will have implications in terms of training and educational provision, and it may well
be that a form of lifelong education, or recurrent education, will have
to be introduced on a large scale in advanced countries in order to cope
with these trends. The consequence of an ageing population is that
many resources from the economically viable individuals will have to
be increasingly diverted to a large section of nonproducers. Increased
numbers of ageing throws extra burdens on the health and welfare
services and the national economy.

HUMAN ECOLOGY

The study of *human ecology* deals with the manner in which community organization distributes people, services and facilities in time
and space. Adapted from a biological model it has made important
contributions to urban sociology. A *community* is a population consisting of human beings who live within a specified and limited geographical area and who have a lifestyle involving interdependence on one
another. Such a community is to be distinguished from a family or a
neighbourhood and provides systematic linkages for social and structural relationships to be created. The emphasis is upon the relationships of the community rather than the individuals who comprise it,
for communities survive both individual births and deaths and people
entering and leaving.

Community and A **neighbourhood** is a structural entity where everyone knows
neighbourhood everyone else. This is not expected in a community. Neither is the
neighbourhood a self sufficient entity providing for the whole range of

basic needs of its inhabitants. Neighbourhood interaction patterns include knowing people by face if not by name, having a 'nodding' acquaintance, a speaking relationship, visiting each other's houses, and so on.

Although there is no common agreement as to what constitutes a community it is generally held that it has a specific territorial focus. Some writers emphasise subjective criteria such as identification, whereby individuals identify with a given community. By mapping the zone to which individuals claim to belong, some sort of picture of delineation can be established. Others use the **neighbourhood cluster** method, which is an objective means by which we identify the location of each neighbourhood and the trade centres used by people in it.

Rural communities

These include settlements which are small in size and stress a *gemeinschaft* set of relationships. This kind of relationship is one in which everyone knows each other. Primitive food gathering communities are examples of this sort. A later development is the village community. This can exist as a *nucleated* village where the inhabitants cluster together. Another form is the *line village* where development is along a main track or road. The *plantation* community is one in which the workers' settlements are in relation to the employer's house. *Frontier* settlements are another form of rural settlement.

Urban communities

Urban communities are dominated not by agriculture, in the way that rural communities are, but by commerce, industry and service occupations. In urban communities there is a complex division of labour and social relationships, a high density of population, and social control is exercised by means other than kinship, such as a complex police force. The features of urban communities include a growth in impersonality, with the result that the majority of one's social contacts are superficial, transitory and segmental, and a growth in the division of labour to meet market expansion. Urban communities can be classified into manufacturing communities, retail and wholesale communities, holiday and retired people's communities and so on.

Urban communities offer a varied pattern of social interaction that is very complex. For example, *natural areas* develop by being distinguished according to some identifiable characteristics such as dockland, doctors' and hospital areas, Skid Row, China Town and so on. E.W. Burgess suggested the *concentric zone* theory, which viewed urban communities as having five zones: zone I is the central business area; zone II is the area with older houses converted into small hotels and boarding establishments and housing some of the poorer inhabitants; zone III includes better working class homes; zone IV is the middle class area; zone V is the area of fashionable suburbia. The main criticism of the concentric zone theory is the fact that urban development is not uniform. Others, such as Hoyt, argued for studying the urban community by the use of *radial sectors* stemming from the centre of cities and following major transportation routes. The nuclei analysis sees the city as exhibiting clusters of activities and population which appear in various parts of a city.

A somewhat larger but homogeneous social structure, the *region* is characterised by homogeneity related to social life, a conscious unique-ness and identification by the inhabitants, and the absence of distinct boundaries. An area becomes a region because of geographic and physiographic forces such as soil, climate and topography which often produce distinct dialects and dress. In addition certain historical developments can mold or contain people within a region such as the Karoo. Finally, cultural experiences can distinguish an area and identify the inhabitants by music or culinary specialities.

Two types of orientation have been usefully distinguished in the life style of individuals, which also dominate their personality. These are known as the *cosmopolitan* (identifies with a way of life outside local boundaries and interests and is not constrained by neighbourhood ties), and the *local* (constrained by the *Gemeinschaftlichten* of the local community with its interests). The inhabitants of the inner city areas generally fall into five classes: 1. the cosmoplites; 2. the unmarried or childless; 3. the 'ethnic villagers'; 4. the deprived; and 5. the trapped and those who are downwardly mobile. The first two categories are generally known as cosmopolitans and centralists, distinguished by a basic orientation to a large city. Locals are to be contrasted because their orientation is basically parochial and they express no interest in society at large. This kind or orientation also imposes patterns of friendship on the respective 'orienters', so that locals cultivate large numbers of friends, in whom they take a pride, while cosmopolitans are not interested in meeting as many people as possible.

Groups within cities vary, also, and it has been found useful to distinguish between *exclusive membership* groups and *inclusive spatial* groups. The former type tends to select from a total population in an area on the basis of some criterion, such as prowess or interest in sewing or choral singing, and cuts across neighbourhood lines. The latter includes all those active in a defined area.

Inner urban areas and suburbs
Because of the spatial restriction of inner city areas, people crowding into them become homogeneously segregated into distinct localities. A phenomenon known as the *ethnic villager* emerged in the inner city areas of large cities everywhere, but particularly in the great urban areas of the USA. These 'urban villagers', as they are sometimes called, lived very much as they once did in Puerto Rico or European peasant communities, exhibiting little contact with the facilities offered by inner city areas other than their place of employment. Although living in the inner city they still possess the characteristics of *gemeinschaftlichten*, that is, close kinship, lack of anonymity, weakness of secondary group contacts and of formal organisations, and are very suspicious of anything outside their immediate neighbourhood.

The suburbs of cities are more likely to be dormitory areas. They are farther away from the work and play facilities offered by cities and are more modern because they developed later. They rely quite heavily on the car as a means of transport, or other means of commuting. The density of housing is less than in the other city, and houses are single-family rather than multi-family dwellings. the population is more homogeneous, younger, has white collar (clerical and professional) occupations, higher incomes, and include a greater proportion of married people than the occupants of inner areas.

The culture of poverty and the inner city slums The last two of the five categories mentioned above, the 'deprived' and the 'trapped' have no other choice than to live in the city (unlike the first two types). The 'deprived' population are the very poor and those mentally or emotionally disturbed who live in the fringe or grey areas. The 'trapped' are those caught in a neighbourhood by industrial and commercial developments, who are unable to move out. It is to this sort of area that the *downwardly mobile* (coming down the socio economic hierarchy) gravitate. An area such as this might include the widowed and widowers of retirement age.

The distinctive behaviour exhibited by these categories differs from that of the suburban dweller to quite an extent. Such a way of life as the former may well include racketeering and gang activities which, although beyond the law, are nevertheless a part of accepted behaviour in these areas. Many sociological studies of such areas have shown that petty pilfering is an accepted way of life. The vicious circle of poverty, unemployment, low attainment, disease and ignorance, casts a blight upon these areas.

Slum areas are structured in a kind of inevitability by the economic system. Because wages are low and unemployment is high a slum area stands in marked contrast to the upwardly mobile and prosperous middle class areas. The desirable, being unobtainable, forces such individuals into what Oscar Lewis has described as the *culture of poverty*. This is an attempt to adapt, adjust and cope with the dominant values of Western society, and is thus a *sub culture*. Such township behaviour is also equally applicable to South Africa's black population. In it we see both a means of adapting and a means of reacting, by the poor deprived, to their marginal position in a society whose values are dominated by a minority of whites. It is essentially a means of coping with a statified, capital intensive society. The culture of poverty is absorbed by township children by the age of six or seven, and little else will have any real impact on them. The distinguishing characteristics of the sub culture are as follows:

1. Disengagement from the major or dominant institutions of society;
2. A chronic lack of money and employment;
3. Hostility to control agencies such as the police and welfare;
4. A sense of community;
5. Emphasis on character traits such as masculinity and localism.

ECOLOGICAL AND DEOGRAPHIC CONTRIBUTIONS TO MEDICINE

Essentially ecological studies are carried out in groups rather than individuals and involve the comparison of one set of characteristics of a population with another set of characteristics in an attempt to account for variations among the *populations* (an aggregate of objects about which certain information is desired). Such correlations are known as **ecological correlations** and are generally popular in the statistical data produced by public health departments. The census returns provide sufficient evidence on such areas as density, for example, which can be related to infant mortality, cancer and so on. However, although ecological studies can say things about populations, e.g. that a population characterised by low income and status also has high mortality, this does not in any way guarantee that persons with low income and low status will have a short life span. To impute that individuals or persons have the characteristics revealed by groups or populations is to be guilty of the *ecological fallacy*. In other words, such a fallacy imputes individual correlation on the basis of a group correlation. By far the best application of ecological and demographic data, although it has its uses in indicating areas of research on the individual, is in the area of planning of medical resources and personnel.

However, both emphasise a holistic approach to understanding disease. Disease is now viewed as a misbalance thought to be related to the total environment, both physical, social and psychological. The presence of bacillus, for example, is not a necessary factor in causing tuberculosis. The ecological approach would relate the bacillus to stress and other factors in the environment created by the industrialisation process. In other words, such an approach takes into account not simply 'germs' but environmental factors such as the food we eat, sanitary control and the regulation of births. Such an approach also seeks to highlight the principle that 'the disease condition results from a particular interaction of host, bacterial agent, and social and environmental situations.' (Tuckett, 1976).

Urbanisation Although there have been **cities** throughout history, i.e. relatively large concentrations of people who did not produce their own food, nevertheless these were relatively tiny in comparison with the cities of today. Rome, for example, was probably never more than 300 000. The process of **urbanisation** is a recent phenomenon. This is because of a number of reasons. Firstly, cities could only emerge in areas where farmers could produce a food surplus. This surplus could then be sold to the inhabitants of the towns and cities in exchange for money produced from the manufacture of non-agricultural artefacts. Secondly, adequate transportation did not emerge until the Industrial Revolution, when transport became sophisticated enough to cope with the increasing demands. Technologies for storing food, such as preservatives, the canning process and refrigeration also facilitated the process of urbanization, and these can be viewed as a third factor. Lastly, it was comparatively recently that public health measures were introduced which facilitated urban growth.

Urbanization in the developing world is increasing at an extremely rapid rate. Migration from rural areas, in certain undeveloped areas of the world, is taking place on an unprecedented scale. Epidemiological differences between urban and rural populations reflect differences in mortality, disease and health care. Some diseases are specifically rural, such as exposure to pesticides, anthrax, and so forth, while urban diseases are invariably bronchial resulting from air pollution, or mortality resulting from social disorganisation (death from violence, venereal disease and drug addiction).

In South Africa rural/urban mortality and morbidity patterns reflect vastly different causes. In rural areas distinctive diseases among blacks vary from thyroid disorders, Transkei silicosis, cancer of the oesophagus and hepatic cancer, while urban blacks display alcohol-related diseases, chronic iron poisoning, pellagra, etc. Many urban blacks are already displaying the diseases previously displayed by urban whites. (Seftel, 1977). Walker (1974) reported that dental caries, overweight, coronary heart disease and diabetes increased considerably among blacks moving from an urban to a rural setting. The variability between urban and rural disease and mortality patterns can be accounted for by a number of factors such as differential access to health care facilities and different rates of environmental exposure such as patterns of living.

EPIDEMIOLOGY

By *epidemiology* is meant **the study of the distribution and determinants of diseases and injuries in human populations**. Although originally concerned with infectious diseases, epidemiologists now concern themselves also with diseases of later life such as the vascular diseases and malignant neoplasms. Sometimes epidemics can be traced to noninfectious causes, such as the outbreak of colic among cider drinkers in Devonshire, England, which was traced to the lead piping that was used to transport the drink. The acidity of the cider released lead which in turn caused acute lead toxicity (Baker, 1767). Lind (1753) traced the incidence of scurvy among British ships to nutritional deficiency, i.e. the absence of limes, 170 years before the discovery of vitimin C. Pott (1775) isolated the high incidence of scrotal cancer among chimney sweeps and connected it to exposure to soot. However, it was not until 1854 that John Snow's classic study which connected an outbreak of cholera with a drinking pump in Broad Street, London, established the foundation of modern epidemiology.

The isolation of the germ as a causal agent led to a number of other causal agents such as:

1. Biological agents such as bacteria, insects or viruses or fungi;
2. Nutrient agents such as carbohydrates and fats;
3. Chemical agents such as dust, gases, solid particles;
4. Physical agents such as humidity, temperature and radiation.

These constitute the *disease agents*. The next important epidemiological factor is the *environment*, which includes:

1. The physical environment, such as geography, climate and weather;
2. The biologic environment which includes the presence or absence of the disease agents listed above;
3. The socio-economic environment such as occupation, education and place of residence. Finally, the *human host* is the demographic constitution such as age, sex, race and styles of life.

Epidemiology has several uses:

1. It is a study of the history of the health of populations, particularly the manner in which diseases rise and fall in a population;
2. The diagnosis of health in a community. This includes the measurement of *incidence* (the frequency with which a specific health disorder occurs in a given population during a period of time) and *prevalence* (the total number of cases of a health disorder existing at a given time). Other diagnostic indices include mortality and disability. As ways of life change so does a community's health, throwing up new groups which require attention and monitoring;
3. The functioning of health services needs to be studied with a view to their improvement;
4. To estimate from the group experience what the *individual risks* are on average for disease, accident and defect and the **chances** of avoiding them;
5. To identify *syndromes* by describing the distribution and association of clinical phenomena in the population;
6. To complete the *clinical picture* of chronic diseases and describe their natural history;
7. To search for *causes* of health and disease by comparing the experience of groups defined by their composition, inheritance, experience, behaviour and environments.

The basic variables in epidemiological research are age, sex, race and socio-economic background:

Age

This century has seen a great increase in life expectancy. Infant mortality has decreased dramatically, and people are generally living to be much older than they would have expected to do in 1900.

Sex

Females survive, on average, many years longer than males. Even in prenatal and neonatal stages male mortality rates are higher, suggesting a greater physiological weakness. Males display a 12 % greater chance of dying during the prenatal stage than females and 130 % during the neonatal states. Males also die from more accidents than females suggesting different life and occupational styles. However, women exhibit a higher morbidity, defining themselves as sick more often than males do, and showing a higher frequency, of medical consultations (excluding maternity). In terms of non-physical illness, females display more depressive, psychotic and neurotic rates than males.

Race

Across the various racial groups in South Africa there are profound differences in rates of morbidity and mortality. White South Africans live approximately 20 years longer than blacks. The infant mortality rate is considerably higher. The ratio of black physicians may be a factor in the quality of health care. Causes of death among the major racial groups in South Africa have been listed as follows:

DEATHS BY MAJOR CAUSES OF DEATH

Causes of death	Whites	%	Colour-eds	%	Asians	%	Blacks	%
Total deaths	40 194	100,0	27 069	100,0	5 476	100,0	124 688	100,0
Infectious and parasitic diseases	896	2,2	3 155	15,7	182	3,0	1 603	12,9
Neoplasms	7 425	16,5	3 278	12,1	477	8,2	9 961	8,0
Endocrine, nutritional and metabolic diseases	1 065	2,8	1 041	3,8	589	10,7	4 652	3,7
Diseases of the circulatory system	15 432	38,4	5 914	21,9	1 869	34,1	16 563	13,2
Diseases of the respitory system	4 959	12,3	3 268	12,1	521	9,5	11 909	9,6
Certain conditions originating in the perinatal period	554	1,4	2 119	7,8	252	4,6	9 763	7,8
Systems, signs and ill-defined conditions	2 644	6,5	2 281	8,4	463	8,5	23 997	19,2
Accidents, poisoning and violence	4 181	10,4	4 270	15,8	674	12,3	23 660	19,0
Other causes of death	3 038	7,6	1 733	8,4	449	6,2	8 150	6,5
(Adapted from Central Statistical Service)								

Social class

In all countries morbidity and mortality rates vary between social classes. In a way similar to being black, membership of a lower socio-economic group brings with it grave disadvantages in the frequency and type of illness and the rate of death. Even in Britain with a relatively sophisticated national health service such differences also exist. Very often such differentiation can be pinpointed as follows:

1. Environmental differences produce differences in the potential of the disease. Thus infectious diseases are much more prevalent among the lower classes where good nutrition, adequate medical care services and knowledge about disease and illness are less available.
2. There is greater exposure to disease arising out of poor environmental conditions, e.g. occupational diseases.
3. Continuous exposure to poor conditions makes the individual more susceptible to other diseases.
4. Socio-economic differences mean that the poor have inadequate access to health and welfare facilities. The lower classes can be said to be more susceptible to diseases. **The cycle of disease and poverty** means that the working class are subjected to 'economic hardship, frustrated aspirations, chronic insecurity about jobs, frequent disruption of social ties' (Susser, Watson and Hopper, 1985, p. 253).

Extremes of poverty in Europe and America have been blunted and yet widely different rates of disease persist. This is seen as a result of the quality of the social environment, in physical amenities and in differences in education. Thus lower class families are larger and more children die from violence, accidents and poisoning.

Prevention Health achievements in the West in recent years have included: the reduction of subsistence poverty; gross subnutrition in mothers and children virtually eliminated; the construction of modern housing; the Clean Air Act; reduction of maternal mortality; introduction of large scale immunisation programmes against polio, measles and rubella; Rh disease conquered; control of several occupational work related cancers; reduction of motor accidents by the introduction of the breathalyser and crash helmets, and so on. Preventative measures waiting to be applied in practice include dental caries and obesity; cigarettes, etc. (Morris, 1975). Vital to the role of preventative medicine are:

1. The quality of medical care;
2. Early diagnosis (e.g. screening for hypertension);
3. the protection of the vulnerable individual (the lowering of blood cholesterol to below 200 or so mg. per 100 ml., for example).

This section has established epidemiology within what is variously known as 'population medicine'. Such an approach contrasts with the clinical one. Mortality and morbidity rates are essential tools in the epidemiological approach. Such an approach has the ability to identify precursors which antedate the presentation of diseases which are detectable clinically, and which have the probability of developing in the future. Predispositions to disease are termed *risk factors.*

Epidemiological models Embracing both infectious and non-infectious diseases, epidemics, and also endemic and sporadic occurrences of diseases and conditions, epidemiology embraces a number of models other than the immediately obvious one of:

organism . . . man . . . disease

The older epidemiologic *triangle* (host, environment, agent) placed too much emphasis on agent. Other models were developed which stressed rather, the multiplicity of interactions between host and environment. The *web of causation* emphasises a complex interplay of chains of causation. As a consequence there is no single identifiable cause of disease. Instead, surrounding man (as host) is the environment divided into biological, social and physical. Therefore it makes little sense to ask the cause of the Irish Potato Famine when such a combination of factors were conducive to its appearance. Such factors included: scurvy and typhus, unresponsive agricultural policy, mulnutrition, overcrowding and poor sanitary conditions. Such an epidemiologic model is called the *wheel.*

We have mentioned the importance of **descriptive epidemiology** which attempts to underline the basic data on health and the major causes of disease and death. The objectives of such an approach are to provide a basis for future planning, provision and evaluation of health services and to provide comparison between countries and within countries. The importance of the *person* is demonstrated in age, sex, racial group, socio-economic status, occupation and marital status. *Place* includes climatic conditions and political and economic boundaries. The causes (or determinants) of disease are judged by five criteria: strength of the association, consistency, temporal relations, specificity, and coherence with existing knowledge.

The sources of data on community health include census information on the number of persons and their demographic, socio-economic and household characteristics. Births, deaths, morbidity and mortality are vital events.

Population dynamics and health are determined by the three major variables of birth, death and migration. Population pyramids depict percentage distribution of the population by age and sex at a point in time. Countries in transition have a high and rapid population growth.

SUMMARY

1. The demographer uses rates and ratios to measure changes in the population which he reduces to four variables; fertility, mortality, emigration and immigration.
2. Developing countries are characterised by a large population under fifteen and a small one over sixty-five years of age.
3. There is considerable debate as to whether the demographic transition will be mirrored in developing societies, partly on the grounds that they may never catch up with industrialised nations.
4. Human ecology makes important contributions to studies of social life within time and space.
5. Certain conditions had to pre-exist before the advent of large scale urbanization, such as surplus food production, transport and a food preservative technology.
6. Urban and rural morbidity and mortality patterns are vastly different.
7. The agent, the host and the environment have been largely overtaken as a model, by multi causative models. Nevertheless, the basic variables in epidemiological research are still age, sex, race and socio-economic background.
8. Preventative measures can be taken upon an epidemiological identification of health factors.

IMPORTANT TERMS

demography	refined birth rate
crude rate	fertility rate
fecundity rate	mortality
morbidity	age-specific rates
life span	life expectancy
migration rate	demographic transition
demographic progression	cycle of poverty
human ecology	community
neighbourhood	neighbourhood cluster
Gemeinschaft	nucleated village
line village	concentric zone
cosmopolitans and locals	ethnic villager
populations	ecological fallacy

SELF ASSESSMENT QUESTIONS

1. The health officer in a large city wants to start a screening and treatment programme for those with hypertension. What demographic variables should be considered in estimating the number of persons to be served by this programme?

2. What is meant by the demographic transition? Give reasons why it may or may not be applicable to all developing characteristics of South Africa and racial differences.
4. What contributions can the human ecological approach make to the study of disease?
5. What factors contributed to the growth of cities (urbanization)?
6. Discuss the main contributions made by the application of epidemiological techniques.

THE SOCIOLOGY
OF INSTITUTIONS

- religion
- education
- politics
- economics

M PEPIJN, ST ELIZABETH, GIVING HER JEWELS TO THE POOR
Panel, Koninklijk Museum Schone Kunsten, Antwerp, Belgium

RELIGION

Beliefs, values and norms: the foundations of religion All individuals possess some kind of belief and some set of values about some other people, groups, objects or ideologies. Sometimes a patient holds quite specific beliefs about the nature of disease which might be in direct conflict with those held by medical professionals. At other times, and on a broader level, any meeting between two or more individuals involves, among other things, a confrontation between the beliefs and values that each individual holds dear to himself. It may be the case, also, that certain individuals hold beliefs and values that are not only bizarre but in addition may contain a possible threat to the well-being of the community in general. Doctors, for example, may entertain a belief that the prescription of antibiotics should be delayed as long as possible. Nurses may believe that patients should or should not be 'mollycoddled'. Again, patients entering a hospital come equipped with a vast repertoire of beliefs and values that need to be accommodated to the hospital organization. In this section we shall be concerned with values as they are learned through the process of socialization and to the extent that they affect behaviour, and with articulate value systems in the form of religion.

Values The study of values has traditionally been the area of concern for philosophers; hence sociologists have studied *social values*. These are not necessarily the same as moral values. Whereas the former might be defined as an awareness that persists over time in relation to an object, the idea or person, and is also charged with emotion, the latter are not to be identified exactly (because of the criterion of *collective welfare*, which is part of the definition of social values). In a sense social values are abstractions, which are emotionally charged because they are important to the individual and relate to goals for any action that the individual might perform. Such values are not beliefs because the latter relate to the truth of falsity of certain facts in society, while the former are more like feelings about objects, ideas or persons. Some examples distinguishing between values and beliefs are given below:

Beliefs	*Values*
God exists	People should believe in God
South Africa is morally declining	Immorality is wrong

Each of us possesses a set of abstract sentiments such as 'we are all the same, basically' or 'good will out in the end' which are shared by a great number of people in society. These abstract sentiments, however, change over time and are sometimes contradictory. Another type of social value is the moral norm, which is basically a standard of behaviour which we use as a frame of reference for social action. Sometimes, as we shall see with delinquent gangs, some groups entertain norms which are in conflict with a wider society and indeed actually turn such values inside-out.

We learn values during the process of primary and secondary socialization, and sometimes we learn them so deeply that they are said to be *internalized*, meaning that we carry out a course of action associated with them in a virtually automatic manner. Obviously not all values are held in equal esteem by the individual; hence sociologists talk of *dominant* and *subordinate* values. The strength with which values are held can be measured by testing how many of the population display them in their behaviour, for how long, with what intensity and so on. A study of American society revealed a number of core values that shaped the behaviour of the mass of the population, as follows:

1. achievement and success
2. activity and work
3. moral orientation
4. humanitarian mores
5. efficiency and practicality
6. progress
7. material comfort
8. equality
9. freedom
10. external conformity
11. science and secular rationality
12. nationalism-patriotism
13. democracy
14. individual personality
15. racism and related group-superiority.

America, for example, places a great stress on physical health and great value is placed on a mastery of the environment (rather than adjustment), a concern with practical rather than mystical activities, and the idea of progress towards a goal (rather than the attainment of it). Freidson shows how the rise of a social value such as health is impossible without the rise 'of a vehicle for the value—an organized body of workers who claim jurisdiction over the value'. He is arguing that because physicians may be willing to deal with an aspect of behaviour that is problematic, that does not mean that behaviour is therefore an illness. Others could be more competent to deal with it.

Religion We turn now to the elaborate organization of beliefs and values into systems which are termed *religions*. Religion may be described broadly as a system of beliefs and practices which are usually considered as being directed towards the 'ultimate concern' of a particular society. Perhaps a better sociological definition of religion (and there are many!) is as follows:

a system of symbols institutionally organized consisting of supraempirical references that establish powerful and pervasive and longlasting moods in men by formulating conceptions of a general order of existence, and which point beyond the domain of our 'natural' reality.

A number of people would claim that religion holds the key to the ultimate 'meaning' of the central values of a society and, furthermore, is a 'power' of an ultimate nature which stands at the back of such values as some kind of sanction.

Sociology of religion The study of religion has been one of the important areas of concern of the great sociologists such as Durkheim and Weber. It is important to examine it from our point of view because it *is* so central but also because it gives one of the clearest examples of sociologists in action in an area which is both problematic and delicate.

Sir Edward Tylor attempted, in 1873, as a minimum definition of religion, to describe it as a belief in 'Spiritual Beings'. He felt that this belief could best be examined by looking at animism, which divides into two areas of dogma: (*a*) posthumous survival of souls; (*b*) the existence of other spirits up to the rank of deity. Tylor went on to develop an evolutionist theory which postulated four successive stages which arose out of the concept of the soul: animism, polydaemonism, ploytheism and monotheism.

In contrast to Tylor's now defunct theory Father Wilhelm Schmidt postulated the idea of an *Urmonotheismus*—original worship centred on the High God—all other religious forms are corruptions of this. However, what Schmidt considered monotheism was in many instances monolatry (worship of one god) and in any case monotheism is rare among primitive peoples.

A more recent theory is that of Pettazzoni, who views the monotheistic religions of Yahwism, Zoroastrianism, Christianity and Islam as having arisen from a reformist protest against polytheism.

Emile Durkheim saw religion as arising in a collective form of experience based on the supposed relation between a human group and the supernatural society and its god. The latter is the totem and is the personification of the clan. His position is sometimes termed *angelicism*. To Durkheim religious phenomena consist of beliefs and practices which are relative to sacred 'things' which are set apart from men and forbidden. All the beliefs and practices join together to form a *moral community*, which is what he called a 'church'. His real contribution in this field was to stress the identification of society with God, and his concern, unlike that of his predecessors, was with seeing the role of religion as a vast symbolic system making social life possible by safeguarding the sentiments or values of society. The role of ritual and ceremony in society was to encourage and sustain discipline, integration, euphoria, and so on.

A number of sociologists have been concerned with the *function* of religion. Although their work is of considerable interest it is, however, misleading to talk of religion as exercising a 'function' because this suggests that it is somehow necessary or inevitable. It encourages us to think of society as consisting of a number of tailor-made slots into which certain phenomena must somehow fit. Malinowski was concerned with the function of religion and magic and held that they are to be found 'whenever man comes to an unbridgeable gap, a hiatus in his knowledge or in his powers of practical control, and yet has to continue in his pursuit'. Religion is born out of 'the real tragedies of human life, out of the conflict between human plans and realities'.

A modern *functionalist*, Talcott Parsons, postulated two main types of frustration arising out of the human situation that provide a focal point for the development of religious patterns. Firstly, men are 'hit' by events that they cannot predict, control or prepare for, such as premature death or severe illness. Secondly, there is a strong emotional investment in the success of human effort but uncontrollable factors intervene, for example the weather damages the crops. These situations pose problems of meanings.

The nature of religion as a modern institution contains a number of features elaborated by Parsons; (a) beliefs; (b) symbols; (c) activities; (d) moral community; (e) rules of conduct. Thus the institution of religion helps man to overcome the 'breaking points' which confront him from time to time, namely contingency, powerlessness and scarcity.

The functionalist would argue that religion (a) provides support, consolation and reconciliation, (b) offers a secure transcendental relationship, (c) makes sacred the norms and values of society, (d) has its own independent value system, (e) provides identity functions, (f) is correlated with maturation of the individual.

However, Bryan Wilson has argued that to accept the functionalist approach is to posit some kind of unchanging psychological nature inherent in man. It completely ignores, as a theory, the changing patterns of social organization, social experience and social opportunity 'which are constantly modifying man's emotional needs and responses. If religion exists to meet certain human needs which it purports are unchanged, functionalists are faced with the fact that nevertheless religion changes. Having derived the needs from religious phenomena, it now refers to the needs in order to assert that religious practices must exist to meet them'. He goes on to say that 'if a given form of religion disappears, then some other 'religious' must be arising in its place. Thus mass-entertainment, mass-rallies, science, totalitarian political parties and ideologies, expensive consumer goods are variously accredited with fulfilling some of the functions once filled by religion'. There have been many criticisms of functionalism in religion. for one, it assumes that social systems are completely integrated and that all elements of such a system are functionable and indispensable.

Dilemmas in the institutionalization of religion

Thomas O'Dea has shown how, looking at the early church from the writings of *Acts* and *Epistles*, we can see the beginning of religious institutionalization developing into the *cult* and the emergence of *belief patterns*. At a later state we see the rationalization of belief patterns and the emergence of religious organization. By 200 AD the church had its bishops, doctrine and service of worship. However, the institutionalization of religion poses a number of dilemmas which O'Dea categorizes as follows: (a) Dilemma of Mixed Motivation—the emergence of wide range of individual motives; (b) The Symbolic Dilemma—the objectification of ritualization means a great number of people lose the 'meaning'; (c) The Dilemma of the Administrative Order—the alienation of the 'office' from the rank-and-file; (d) The Dilemma of Delimitation—concrete definition versus substitution of the letter for the spirit; (e) The Dilemma of Power—conversion versus coercion.

Religious organization

The *church* (ecclesia) and *sect* have the significant characteristics shown below according to Troeltsch and others.

Church	Sect
Membership by birth	Voluntary joining
Inclusive	Exclusive
High economic status of members	Low economics status of members
Compromising with existing society	Attitude of ethical austerity

The church is usually fully at one with the social and economic order prevailing in a given society at the time. The *denomination* can be viewed either as a sub-class of the church with a more restricted membership or as an institutionalized *sect*. Wilson sees sects as exclusive bodies who impose some test of merit on entrants. Members of such groups are kept under scrutiny and the pattern of their lives regulated in some way. Wilson offers a typology of sects:

(a) the *conversionist* sect (e.g. early Salvation Army)

(b) the *revolutionary* sect (e.g. Jehovah's Witnesses)

(c) the *introversionist* sect (e.g. various 'holiness' movements)

(d) the *manipulationist* sect (e.g. Scientologists)

(e) the *thaumaturgical* sect (e.g. Spiritualists)

(f) the *reformist* sect (e.g. Quakers)

(g) the *utopian* sect (e.g. various 'hippy' groups).

A typology such as this is based on the responses of the sect to the world. For example, the Jehovah's Witnesses are a revolutionary sect because they look forward to the passing of the present social order, whereas the Scientologists are manipulationists because they claim some special knowledge and techniques for reaching goals which are acceptable by society.

Such schemes as these by Troeltsch and Wilson are called *typologies*. They are useful for purposes of illustration and research but they do not exist 'out there'. Complex human behaviour just cannot be fitted or compartmentalized so neatly. Some sects, for example, are distinctly marginal to the categories and do in fact overlap with a number of them. Perhaps the most damning condemnation is that such schemes tend to try to reduce patters of behaviour which are very complex to apparently simple social-psychological attitudes which are then seen in terms of motivations, goals and so on.

A final addition to categorizations of this sort is what is usually called *cult*, which consist of a short-lived group which is highly individualistic. There is some disagreement among sociologists as to whether *cult* should indeed be a separate category and some, such as Wilson, have obliterated the category altogether.

Religion and social differentiation Types of religious organization are reflected in relation to the aspect of society to which they refer. For example, it was the political unity of the Church which appeared to give medieval Europe an apparent unity of *society*. Unity of *community*, on the other hand, would involve a different organization of religion. Pre-literate societies generally have religion as 'all pervading' and particularly centred around the rituals of puberty, marriage, birth and death. Pre-industrial society generally has a single religious organization which competes or joins with the state. Industrial-secular society produces a type of religious organization which is pluralistic and divided. Today, in Britain and America, very broadly speaking we can see how social differentiation leads to two very different modes of expression. On the one hand we have the intellectual and liturgical appeal of established organizations for the facilitation of 'middle-class' religious expression, and on the other hand we have the emergence of groupings stressing prayer, emotionalism and piety, principally growing in areas, and catering for segments of the population who were not accommodated by the established religious organizations.

Sociologically it is important to realize that religion (and a lot of other activities) is not a personal and individual idiosyncrasy, but socially determined. In any society which we care to look at it is public, received, inherited, learned and transmitted. The visions of the wise are themselves culturally transmitted and determined and must conform to the expectations of the listeners. One of the important factors in determining the religious experience and belief of an individual is the position he or she occupies in the social strata simply because to a large extent this position determines the way in which one looks at the world and the manner in which we accrue meaning to the life-experiences we receive.

Karl Marx was not specifically concerned with religion as such but with the social phenomenon of *alienation* which results in *false consciousness*. The discovery that man is alienated by religion gives scope for the further discovery that there are other forms of alienation such as the economic structure of capitalism. Weber was later to synthesize these ideas in his thesis that the Protestant Ethic of Calvin was the main vehicle for the emergence of capitalism in Western Europe. Marx also suggested that the bourgeois capitalism of the nineteenth century found its best form of expression in Protestantism: 'For a society based upon the productions of commodities, in which the producers in general enter into social relations with one another by treating their products as commodities and values, whereby they reduce their individual private labour to the standard of homogeneous human labour— for such a society Christianity with its cult of the abstract individual, more especially in its bourgeois developments, Protestantism, Deism, etc. is the most appropriate form of religion.'

One of the main functions of religion, in Marx's view, was as a response to frustration. Man, in his struggle against the world, pits himself initially against the 'spiritual aroma' of the world, religion. But religious suffering is at one and the same time an 'expression of real suffering and a protest against real suffering'. The economic deprivation of the working class is alleviated by adherence to religion, through Marx maintained that this adherence masked the real cause of deprivation and unhappiness, that is, the capitalist system of economics. 'Religion is the sigh of the oppressed creature, the sentiment of a heartless world, the soul of soulless conditions. It is the opium of the people.'

However, it is extremely difficult to assess whether religious activity is a response to frustration, and it is also difficult to demarcate adequately between economic and social status deprivation and other forms of deprivation, for example, impairments such as illness, ageing, and so on. Certainly, the available evidence seems to suggest that religious involvement is strongest in the middle and upper classes than in the working classes, at least in its manifest forms. In a latent way, of course, it may well be that the ideological superstructure of society makes itself felt in other, more sophisticated ways than mere attendance and observance in religious organization. This highlights an important methodological approach to the sociology of religion, that is the difference between the *objective* and *subjective* dimensions of religiosity, on the one hand between actual church attendance and on the other the attitudes and beliefs of individuals.

Weber and religion The German philosopher Nietzsche described religion as the means by which the repressed resentment of the powerless was expressed. The Christian religion in particular was the slave's revolt. Weber developed this correspondence in a more sophisticated manner and showed how the differentiation in the interpretation of salvation and suffering varied from social class to social class. Weber argued that religion provides different 'rewards' for different social strata.

1. The 'theodicy of good fortune' is expressed by those with high social and economic privileges who, rather than cultivate a theology of salvation, 'assign to religion the primary function of legitimazing their own life pattern and situation in the world'.

2. The 'theodicy of the dispossessed' or disprivileged, is concerned with release from suffering, misfortune, and so forth, and this group is particularly concerned with what it can *become* rather than with what it *is*, endeavouring to establish a principle of 'just compensation'.

Weber further elaborated the strata which he regarded as the special vehicles and interpreters of the world religions. For example, Christianity was carried by itinerant artisan journeyman, Hinduism by literati, and Buddhism by mendicant or beggar monks. This interpretation dispenses with the 'great man' theory of the origins of the world religions and instead stresses the influences of the particular strata which developed them. It is these strata which accommodated and articulated the ideology, and although the external symbols may bear resemblance to each other the interpretation is different. Weber goes on to state that even though the social situation may give rise to, and be reflected in, a religion, and economic, political and social influences shape a religious ethic, 'it receives its stamp primarily from religious sources'.

Of course, religious forms of expression do not arise in a social vacuum. Christianity's revolutionary origins were to a large extent to be expected in the context of a revolutionary age. Again, the rise of a large number of sects in the period immediately after 1800 and until the 1840s can be explained in terms of the socio-historical context of the times.

Relative deprivation Various attempts have been made to describe religious satisfaction for particular segments of the social strata in terms of a typology of relative deprivation. Glock talks about five possible types of deprivation; economic, social, organismic, ethical and psychic. *Ethical* deprivation is the lack of needed legitimizing values, and *psychic* deprivation is concerned with the search for a 'meaning' to life. *Economic* deprivation is the lack of prestige and wealth, and *social* deprivation is particularly deprivation of status. *Organismic* deprivation is deprivation of physical and mental well-being. Glock and Stark relates these 'felt' deprivations to appropriate types of religious groups, as follows.
sect (economic deprivation)
church (social deprivation)
healing movements (organismic deprivation)
reform movements (ethical deprivation)
cult (psychic deprivation)

The problem with this sort of scheme is that it is too ambitious. It tries to establish a one-one correlation between deprivation and religious groups, and one of which incorporates a multiplicity of beliefs and value systems. More important, schemes such as this ignore two important aspects of religious organization. First, religious groups have their own *dynamism* and often arise from 'internal' conflict or schisms and not from a postulated need of a number of individuals who have been deprived of some aspect of social experience. Second, one must be wary of theories which try to suggest a succession of universal needs which either are attached to people like arms or legs or which at best are unchanging.

Millenarian movements Messianic and millenarian movements flourished particularly in the Middle Ages as a response to deprivation, mostly social, although on the whole they were essentially religious and not political protests. Cohn shows how such movements as the People's Crusades, the Flagellant Movements, the Toborites of Bohemia and many more arose among the uprooted and disoriented peasantry. As Cohn says, 'Between the close of the 11th Century and the first half of the sixteenth it repeatedly happened in Europe that the desire of the poor to improve the material conditions of their lives became transfused with religious fantasies. Briefly it would seem that when the existing order or structure of a society is undermined or devalued, this process is a cumulative one; and if it has gone at all, or some major catastrophe strikes the lower and more exposed strata of the population, the way to revolutionary chiliasm is open.' (Cohn, 1961, p. 36) With the breakdown of the supporting agencies for the Feudalistic structuring of society and the emergence of a new economic and labour pattern, Cohn sees these great movements as originating through a combination of circumstances such as the following: messianic cultural elements already *in* the culture, such as the Book of Revelation (a favourite source for such groups); surplus population; no institutionalized means for expressing grievances; weakening of the authority framework in society; and the opening of new horizons and possibilities.

In more recent times the impact of European culture upon the small, simpler societies of the world has frequently inspired what are now called *nativistic* movements (variously known as millenarian, chiliasm, nativistic, messianic and revitalizing movements). Analysable in terms of culture shock, these movements have given us considerable insight into the dynamism of religion. Two examples of such movements among the modern American Indians are the Paiute Ghost Dance religion and the Peyote Cult. The former occurred at the end of the nineteenth century, in the 1870s. The buffalo had disappeared from the Great Plains, the Indians had been herded into reservations, and the Indian culture had collapsed. The originators of the movement promised a re-establishment of Indian values and life, with the proviso that recruits underwent a period of prolonged dancing. The movement led directly to the catastrophic Sioux uprisings. The rapid spread of the movement can be accounted for by the relative amounts of deprivation among the tribes. The Navaho did not succumb to the movement because, (a) they possessed a stable culture pattern; (b) ingrained in their culture was a fear of the dead and ghosts; (c) their economy was not centred on the vanishing buffalo but on sheep and goats.

The second movement provided an alternative response to deprivation because its approach was essentially peaceful. The violence of the Ghost Dance led to its being forcibly exterminated, and therefore the Peyote Cult was able to survive in areas which the Ghost Dance had been forced to evacuate. In its present form it is the largest native movement and is organized as the Native American Church, embodying a compromise between Christianity and nativism.

Worsley and others have described the emergence of Melanesian cults which have as part of their object the acquisition, for their members, of the European manufactured goods known as *cargo.* Worsley has shown a political element underlying some of these cargo cults, and in the case of the Sanusi of Cyrenaica how the movement's leaders represent a *political* response by the islanders to foreign mobilization of wealth and control. The revitalization elements are suggested by the emphasis on the magical modelling of the White Man's goods in the hope that success equal to that of the European will be forthcoming. It is difficult to discern a pattern in these diverse movements—the New Guinea Cargo Cults arose without their even having seen a white man, whereas the Ghost Dance arose in direct response to white-Indian contact. Again, the medieval movements are not nativistic, although the others are, and so on. Again, similar culture clashes among the Xhosa of South Africa and the Christians of Porto Nova have given way to a reasonable fusion process without the consequences which have arisen out of other culture clashes.

Religion as an alternative response Alternative courses of action to the 'meanings of life' are socially structured in the sense that the particular response an individual or group takes is somehow embedded in the society around him. Liston Pope in his analysis of a strike in a cotton mill in Castonia, North Carolina, in 1929, gives a graphic example of this. The religious section of the community came out unreservedly against the strike organizers and justified the practices of the management. The point he is making is that when the strikers joined the Holiness sects they might just as effortlessly have joined a political protest movement—a religious response is only one response among many. One of the reasons for an essentially *religious* response in this particular instance was the *availability* of the Holiness sects. Another was the underlying theme which a number of students of sects favour, that of *transversibility*: 'Because they have no jewelry to wear, they make refusal to wear jewelry, including wedding rings, a religious requirement. They transmute poverty into a symptom of grace.' In other words, they substitute high (religious) status for low (economic) status.

Stark has made the point that 'if reform is possible a political party rather than a religious sect will appear on the scene; if reform is a distinct *impossibility*, a religious sect rather than a political party will appear'. Stark sees sects very much as protest movements which express their economic and political discontent in religious terms. Generally, he says, sects have arisen among individuals or groups which are of low social status and he attempts to substantiate his thesis by a description of the role of textile workers in the history of European sectarianism. It is true, of course, that the working class predominate in certain sectarian movements such as Christadelphianism, Jehovah's Witnesses, and that movements such as the Elim Foursquare Gospel Church flourishes in market and seaside towns where there is often a culturally deprived population. Wilson has said that 'intense religious experience is one way of adding depth to lives otherwise shallow, insecure and difficult'. This is by no means the whole story, of course, because some sects are in fact middle class, such as the Catholic Apostolic Church and the Christian Scientists.

The protestant
ethic and the rise
of capitalism

As we have mentioned Weber suggested a link between the 'rational' capitalist enterprise and a set of fundamental beliefs because he noticed that high-status occupations, especially the leaders of big business, were overwhelmingly filled by Protestants. This led him to suggest that there was a congruence between the two 'meaning systems', that of the spirit of capitalism and that of the ascetic ethic, or what he termed an *elective affinity*. Although not the sole cause of capitalism, Weber nevertheless regarded Protestantism as one cause. His thesis has been criticized on a number of grounds. There is not sufficient evidence for postulating a *casual* link between the two meaning systems; there was nothing very peculiar about the spirit of capitalism and therefore he need not have singled it out; Calvin's ideas were not those of Puritanism, and neither was the latter a consistent body of thought. However, Weber did highlight the *transformative* aspect of Protestantism, that is, the capacity of religion or secular ideologies to legitimize, either in secular or religious ideological terms, the emergence of new social institutions and individual motivations.

Some empirical work on the Weberian thesis has been done in America. Mayer and Sharp found that both white and negro Catholics had the least economic success. Jews, followed closely by Episcopalians and Calvinists, have achieved the greatest worldly success. Lenski (1963), in his study of Detroit, found the same evidence for Catholics ranking low on the economic motivation scale. 'The Jews and white Protestants have identified themselves with the individualistic, competitive patterns of thought and action linked with the middle class . . . By contrast Catholics and negro Protestants have more often been associated with collectivistic, security oriented, working class patterns of thought and action.' (Op. cit., p. 362)

Lenski's findings have been directly challenged by Father Andrew Greeley, who found little difference in the degree of assimilation to American society of the Detroit Catholics, that Catholics increasingly approximated the American average in their values, and that once assimilated any distinctiveness disappears. In his sample, Greeley found Catholics more interested than Protestants in making money, more than likely to choose business as a career, and fully achievement oriented. We must bear in mind, however, that perhaps Greeley took his sample, a particular age-group/educational group, from those who are more likely to be achievement oriented and anxious to get on in the world.

Will Herberg (1955), in order to find out the reason why so many Americans attend church, discovered that being a Protestant, a Catholic or a Jew are three expressible ways of accepting American identity, and that being religious has become, in fact, evidence of adherence to national values. The many sects in America are, in fact, simply versions of the three main positions.

Secularization

The rise of modern pluralistic society has meant the increase of rationalization in all the spheres of life. Ironically, Christianity, particularly in its Protestant form, has accelerated the process. Some of the factors which have contributed to the decreasing embrace of religion on most areas of human life are the rise of positivism and science, the emergence of linguistic philosophy, the rise of Protestant biblical criticism, and modern behavioural psychology. Sociologists have long recognized that the process of secularization, 'a process whereby religious thinking, practice and institutions lose social significance', has not affected different strata of the population uniformly. Berger states:

> Thus it has been found that the impact of secularisation has tended to be stronger on men than on women, on people in the middle range than on the very young and very old, in the cities than in the country, on classes directly concerned with modern industrial production (particularly the working class) than on those of more traditional occupations (such as artisans or small shopkeepers), on Protestants and Jews than on Catholics, and the like. At least as far as Europe is concerned, it is possible to say with some confidence, on the basis of these data, that church-related religiosity is strongest (and thus, at any rate, social-structural secularisation least) on the margins of modern industrial society, both in terms of marginal classes (such as the remnants of the old petty bourgeoisies) and marginal individuals (such as those eliminated from the work process).'
> (Berger, 1954, p. 23)

Secular alternatives Recent work in the sociology of religion has tended to suggest that perhaps many of the characteristics to be found in religious groups can be seen in secular groups as well. Religious groups are legitimizing systems, but there are other legitimizing systems which are not overtly religious. Such groups are sometimes called para-, surrogate, or pseudo-religions and might include Marxism, Positivism or Freudianism, Alcoholics Anonymous or certain groups for former mental patients such as Recovery, Inc. or Neurotics Nomine. Often such groups have a similar organization and structure but they are ordered systems in society, also, governed by or possessing discernible rules or relationships of systems. Fringe politics, for example, often resembles fringe religion, and indeed is sometimes described in terms of sects. Black Nationalism displays both political and religious strands. Humanist societies display some of the characteristics of sects. It has been pointed out that Marxism and Christadelphianism have analogies to each other. Again, conversion to both types of belief system displays much the same patterns. (Jones, 1974)

Religion and the social construction of reality As we mentioned earlier, Durkheim saw society as though it was the *sui generis* out of which religion was made, and which both produces the fears that make men turn to religion and in turn the religion that offers some a solution. Berger is anxious to show how man is concerned with imposing 'meaning' upon 'reality'. When the legitimization for our actions is greater than the nomos (the meaning of the humanly constructed social order) this becomes the cosmos (or religion). In a

pluralistic modern technological society there may, indeed, be competing systems that can legitimize our actions and provide 'man's ultimate
shield against the terror of anomie'.

Religion and In the beginning religion provided the only explanation of disease and
medical death in society and even now, in some simple societies, a magical or
organization religious account predominates. Freidson draws attention to the remarkable similarity between Zande witchcraft and modern medical
practice, both occupations having 'gained the command of the exclusive competence to determine the proper content and effective method
of performing some task'. Further, 'the occupational group, then, must
be the prime source of the criteria that qualify a man to work in an
acceptable fashion'. Gradually we witness the general 'public belief in
the consulting occupation's competence, in the value of its professed
knowledge and skill'. (Freidson, 1972, p. 7) Similarly, Silman has
described the process whereby the priesthood (doctor) becomes separated from the believer (patient).

Glaser locates Judaism, Western and Eastern Christianity and
Islam as factors affecting the rise of the modern hospital. Buddhism
and Hinduism have mixed implications but neither appears to have
initiated a programme for mass care of the sick or for a sustained
welfare service. Religions of taboo are inimical to Western medicine and
clients prefer 'instant' cure to a prolonged period of hospitalization.
Glaser suggests that Christianity is the only major religion which has
so many functionaries employed in hospital care. He says that the
novices of religious orders 'tend to come from large, closely-knit and
religious families, from the lower middle and lower classes in towns
and rural areas, and that novices have depended heavily upon their
parish priests for advice'. There is no evidence that recruits to nursing
are any more religious than the average in the population, although
the religious nurse from, for example, the Community of the Daughters
of Charity of St Vincent de Paul, may be expected to regard nursing
itself as a means and 'her professional activity is the framework in
which she exercises her mission'. Glaser quotes a Spanish doctor
accusing nurses from a religious order (and he was not alone) of being
'usually less exact in measuring doses. They are less exact in account-
ing for time, that is, they are less careful in giving injections exactly on
time'. In their practice of nursing nuns appear to be more strict, to
avoid catheterizing patients or bathing patients, to be more hesitant
to unlock doors in psychiatric hospitals and so forth. Nuns, however,
regard 'worldly' nurses as being less dedicated, less total in their
commitment, and more likely to try to avoid very unpleasant tasks.
The work of McClelland (1961, p. 9) on *n Ach* or achievement saw it as
a function of the situation and the enduring strength of the motivation
in the individual personality. He supposed that Protestant-reared
children would be high achievers, although Catholic children would be
high on affiliation. It is 'not surprising that medicine gains many

recruits among Protestants while nursing is particularly attractive to Catholics'.

Religion is also of some importance in determining medical policy in relation to such important events as birth, death and food, so that a policy of birth control can produce severe conflicts in religious personnel whose particular beliefs prohibit such a practice, post-mortems are anathema to Arabs and often end up with a riot or occasional assassination of the dissectors, and various food taboos can arouse difficulties in preparation.

Conclusions The relationship between social status and belief systems has been graphically illustrated by Katherine and Charles George's analysis of 2 490 saints who had been canonized in the twenty centuries of the Christian era. Over 70 % came from the upper and 17 % from the middle classes. Only 5 % came from the working class. Even after death differential practices in funeral rites and decisions vary according to social class and religious affiliation, the rites of the middle class being essentially prestigious while those of the economically depressed offer facilities for the equalization of injustice incurred in this world.

Measurement of the relationship between social status and religious practice can be tackled at two levels of analysis: (a) overt religious involvement, for example church attendances; (b) covert religious involvement for example private prayer. It need not necessarily be the case that the two coincide to any extent, and thus high attendance is only *part* of the way in which people can be religiously involved. Again, attendance at religious meeting places in America is more secularized than it would seem to be here. Generally it appears that the middle and upper classes are the most active in church attendance although there is some evidence that the lower classes are more *religiously* involved, tending to have a higher incidence of personal prayer and more creedal and devotional activities. Some have made the point that a large number of the lower class have no religious commitment whatsoever, and may well have found functional alternatives to religion via political extremism.

Patients and staff who exhibit various values and attitudes at variance with the general tenor of the hospital community are doing so not because of any personal or private reason but because for one thing or another they have opted for that interpretation, and to impose that meaning system on the world around them.

SUNDAY TIMES MAGAZINE, 17 APRIL 1988

WHO WENT WHERE

Have you ever wondered where South Africa's decision-makers learnt the three Rs? Helen Lunn did some digging and discovered some interesting facts about where our politicians, civil servants, mining executives and businessmen got their education

Power and position go hand in hand, but on what educational foundations are they built? In the case of South Africa's decision makers, a few basic scholastic rules appear to have been applied in order to turn out leading politicians, successful civil servants, mining magnates and businessmen.

The equation seems to work as follows. If you're a member of the Cabinet the chances are you've attended an Afrikaans-medium Government school in a rural area, and an Afrikaans-language university. If you're a top notch civil servant you're likely to have attended an Afrikaans-medium school in an urban area, and then studied further at the University of the Free State, or at Pretoria or Stellenbosch.

If you're a mining executive you were probably schooled at a private English-language school, and at Oxford University, England. Businessmen, it seems, have varied educational backgrounds, and are drawn from either English or Afrikaans-speaking ranks.

So who went where to get where they've got? Here is an educational run-down on some members of the Cabinet and the State President's Economic Advisory Council.

THE CABINET

P W Botha—State President: Voortrekker High School, Bethlehem and University of the Orange Free State

Chris Heunis—Minister of Constitutional Development and Planning: Outeniqua High School, Cape and Stellenbosch University

Pik Botha—Minister of Foreign Affairs: Potchefstroom High School and Pretoria University

F W de Klerk—Minister of National Education: Monument High School, Krugersdorp and the University of Potchefstroom

Gerrit Viljoen—Minister of Co-operation and Development: Afrikaans Boys High School, Pretoria and Pretoria University with further degrees from Cambridge University, England and Leyden University, Holland

Magnus Malan—Minister of Defence: Afrikaans Boys High School, Pretoria and the University of Pretoria

Pietie du Plessis—Minister of Manpower: Heidelberg High School, Transvaal and Pretoria University

Cobie Coetzee—Minister of Justice: Ladybrand High School and the University of the Orange Free State

Greyling Wentzel—Minister of Agriculture: Wolmaranstad High School, Hoogenhout High School and Glen Agricultural College

Danie Steyn—Minister of Economic Affairs and Technology: Colesburg Collegiate, Steynsburg Gymnasium, Stellenbosch University and the University of Vienna

Barend du Plessis—Minister of Finance: Voortrekker High School, Boksburg and the University of Potchefstroom

Stoffel Botha—Minister of Home Affairs: Helpmekaar High School, Johannesburg and University of the Witwatersrand

Adriaan Vlok—Minister of Law and Order: Keimoes High School, Cape and University of Pretoria

THE STATE PRESIDENT'S ECONOMIC ADVISORY COUNCIL
M T de Waal—Managing Director of the Industrial Development Corporation: Paarl Boys High School, Stellenbosch University and the University of Delft
W A M Clewlow—Deputy Chairman and Chief Executive, Barlow Rand: Glenwood High School, Durban and Natal University
Dr J A Stegman—Managing Director, Sasol: Sentrale High School, Bloemfontein and Universities of Witwatersrand, Pretoria and Free State
Ahmed Sadek Vahed—Executive Chairman, A M Moola Group: Greyville Government-aided School, Durban
Ron Lubner—Chief Executive, Solaglas International: Highlands North High School, Johannesburg
Bill Venter—Executive Chairman, Altech: Helpmekaar High School, Johannesburg, Wits Technikon
R A Plumbridge—Chairman, Goldfields SA: St Andrews College, Grahamstown and Oxford University

J Ogilvie-Thompson—Deputy Chairman, Anglo American: Diocesan College, Cape town and Oxford University
Meyer Kahn—Group Managing Director, SA Breweries: Brits High School and Pretoria University
Mrs J M Green—Managing Director, Clicks: Ipswich High School, England and Grenoble University
D Masson—Managing Director, Kanhym: Goudini High School, Touws River
Dr G P C de Kock—President, SA Reserve Bank: Afrikaans Boys High School, Pretoria, Pretoria University and Harvard
Dr P R Morkel—Chief Executive, Volkskas: Paul Roos Gymnasium, Paarl, Stellenbosch University and Oxford
Colin Adcock—Managing Director, Toyota SA: Marist Brothers, Port Elizabeth and Boys High School, Pretoria, Wits University
J B Maree—Chairman, Eskom: Middelburg High School, Cape and the University of the Witwatersrand
J E D Bramwell—Non-executive Director, Murray and Roberts: St John's College, Johannesburg and the University of the Witwatersrand.

SUNDAY TRIBUNE, 2 MARCH 1986

UNISA'S ENGLISH USAGE UNDER FIRE

LECTURERS at UNISA may soon have to go 'back to school' to improve their English and avoid a communications crisis facing the university.

Although the giant university is 'bilingual' it is known that in many faculties Afrikaans speaking lecturers far outnumber English speakers.

It is not unusual for staff meetings in some departments to be conducted solely in Afrikaans—although the agenda might be in English.

One source estimates that 80 percent of the lecturers are Afrikaans-speaking while about 70 percent of the students want to receive their tuition in English.

This percentage is increasing yearly as the university's number of black students rises. Most of them prefer English.

Students have complained about the standard of English in Unisa textbooks and study material.

Some say it is clear that much of it has been translated from Afrikaans, often badly. They say that in extreme cases it is necessary to refer to the original Afrikaans text for clarity.

Now a committee has been set up to investigate the language proficiency of the lecturers, who number about 1 500.

The committee has expressed concern about the 'lack of language proficiency' of some of the new and old staff and intends to seek clarification of the university's definition of bilingualism.

Circulars dealing with the issue have been sent to heads of departments for discussion and comments. All refer to the problem of bilingualism—English and Afrikaans.

However, sources inside the university are agreed that the usage of English is the main problem.

It is now proposed to set up a language laboratory to enable the staff to improve its standard of English and Afrikaans.

The university also wants certificates issued by the Pretoria Technikon to be acceptable as proof of a lecturer's competence in the language concerned and wants its own language tests to be standardised.

An educationist said this week that 'as the black enrolment increases the demand for English will accelerate.

'The Afrikaans staff has to improve its English or the problems will increase.'

Another source said the matter was receiving attention at top level. 'There has always been some criticism of the standard of English. But now something is going to be done about it. We are working on it and I think you will see a great improvement within a year.'

CALL TO SCRAP AFRIKAANS AS COMPULSORY SCHOOL SUBJECT

AFRIKAANS must be removed from the school curriculum as a compulsory second language and the Government will have no choice but to do so, Pat Samuels, head of the 10 000-strong teachers' association of south africa said this week.

There should be only one official language—English—because Afrikaans will soon be irrelevant to a new way of life and thinking in South Africa, he said.

'The Government will have no choice in the elimination of Afrikaans because we don't expect it to hold power indefinitely.

'TASA has decided to campaign for the elimination of Afrikaans as a second com-

pulsory language because in about 10 years this language will be redundant.

'Already the large majority or unenfranchised people have clearly shown they do not prefer Afrikaans and political changes in the country will make Afrikaans unusable.'

He said in future Afrikaans would be the same status as Telegu, Hindi, French, Greek, German, etc. 'It will become a cultural language.'

TASA found it unnecessary for pupils to spend hundreds of hours in school learning a language which will have little meaning or relevance.

'The perpetuation of Afrikaans leads to tremendous amount of duplication in printed material and this is extremely costly, especially in the public service,' Mr Samuels said.

The call for the scrapping of Afrikaans is linked to a programme TASA will soon embark upon to make education 'more relevant'.

'We'll be rewriting the history of South Africa so it becomes more truthful and relevant. We don't agree with the white man's interpretation—he makes whites appear as heroes and the rest as villains.'

URGENT NEED FOR TEACHING OF AFRICAN LANGUAGES, SAYS PROF

AFRICAN languages should be taught in all schools and to the army and police to help break down racial barriers, according to Professor Noverino Canonici.

Professor Canonici, Head of the Zulu department at the University Of Natal In Durban, said: 'if we really want to communicate with the majority of people in this country, then every avenue for learning african languages should be explored, especially where the government itself is involved.'

He said if it was compulsory for army and police personnel to learn an African language 'then the Africans would no longer be the enemy. Unless we take this question of learning languages and culture seriously we are going to have problems forever.'

In Natal primary schools, only nine percent of teachers teaching Zulu were given tapes and asked to teach the subject. Ironically, those who had training in Zulu were often not assigned Zulu as a subject.

To try to remedy this, there were negotiations to get a two to three year part-time Zulu course at a local teachers' training college. This would be for teachers who were already in service.

TEACHER WITH CLASS OF 80 PUPILS, AMOUTI 1982
Photo: Omar Badsha

EDUCATION AS A SOCIAL INSTITUTION

When we compare the historical development of education from an African perspective and a Western perspective we are immediately faced with a very different set of complex problems. Two main differences stand out immediately. Firstly, many Africans still tend to be highly suspicious of their educational system because they regard it as a remnant of colonialism, or at least a form of imposition by former colonial powers. Secondly, traditional forms of educating people still persist in Africa whereas in the West they have long given way to highly evolved bureaucratic structures. A third factor to be taken into account is that much of African education is 'functional' in nature, that is, as a means for achieving something or 'getting something done' rather than as 'good in itself'. Traditional African education has predominantly been concerned with 'character-building' and socialisation procedures in a way that the British educational system, for example, has not. Yet another difference is that traditional African education is concerned with vocational training, such as the Poro and Sande in Liberia (Fafunwa and Aisiku, 1982, pp. 9–27). While the West was heavily influenced by Greek and Roman traditions a substantial part of Africa sustained an Islamic influence such as the Qur'anic school system. During the colonial period the initial educational efforts of the missionaries subsequently gave way to a more systematised and formal influence of the colonial powers, notably Great Britain, France and Germany, who had as their prime objective the preparation of the Africans for colonial domination.

Notwithstanding such differences a sociology of African education is entirely feasible.

The sociology of education The 'social improvement' notion of the sociology of education was dominant until recently. Durkheim, for example, was concerned with rectifying certain deficits created by modern industrial society by means of education. In developing countries educational programmes are very frequently linked with community development programmes and income-generating activities, and historically many social reformers in the West have believed that education could in some way compensate or rectify damage caused by social forces.

Quite clearly education *can* be conceived of as beneficial to certain social problems. How, therefore, do we separate out a clear, sociological perspective from a type of educational philanthropy? The answer, interestingly enough, was provided by another branch of sociology, the sociology of religion, in which *religious sociology*, concerned with ecumenicism, inspirational apologia and so forth, was severely distinguished from the *sociology of religion*, which was an analytical and sociological examination of religious groups, beliefs and phenomena in general. It was similarly suggested that *educational sociology* was concerned with social problem approaches while the *sociology of education* was concerned with sociological problems. The technician aspect emphasises the practitioner as opposed to the purist or theorist. In yet another branch of sociology, sociology *for* or *in* medicine is clearly differentiated from sociology *of* medicine.

The sociology of education

The sociology of education is concerned with four main areas:

1. It is concerned with the process of social interaction which takes place in education;
2. It examines the socialisation process of the child in the family, and of the acquisition of language, intelligence and ability;
3. It looks at the way other institutions interact with that of education;
4. It is concerned with the manner in which knowledge is socially organised.

There are, of course, other areas of interest which overlap with these four areas, such as the political economy of education, but these are usually part of the four main areas we have just mentioned.

Changing perspectives in the sociology of education
By 'education' we mean something considerably broader than formal schooling. We would not agree with Harris' (1979) neo-Marxist approach which regards education as:

a particular process, or group of processes that are manifested in the deliberate provision, by socially approved institutions, of sets of learning experiences that are not narrowly confined either to restricted vocational ends or to the development of particular skills. Education, then, can be taken to include the provision of learning experiences or the transmission of knowledge as it occurs in places like schools, universities, liberal arts colleges, technical colleges, colleges of advanced education and the like.

Neither can we agree that:

The key features of education, then, are that it is formal and institutionalised, that it is provided by, or sanctioned by, the state . . .
(Harris, 1979, p. 1)

Education is a wider process because it takes place in societies both *informally* and *formally*. By the first we mean that individuals absorb a great deal of knowledge about the world. They acquire over a lifetime a whole informal system of teaching and learning. Formal systems of processing individuals vary from *rites de passage* to specially constructed buildings and occupational groups whose job it is to instil a socially constructed curriculum.

Traditional sociology, as characterised by Comte, Durkheim and others, was essentially Positivist. This view was of the world as a *given*, that the human world resembles the physical world, that both worlds can be described in the same manner, and that human world concepts are reducible to physical science terms. Thus Durkheim wrote about *social facts* which exist independently of the observer. Such a view came, gradually, to be challenged. After all, it was argued, we live in an *interactive* situation and *interpret* the world around us in a meaning-

THE STAR, 26 APRIL 1990

9 OUT OF 10 PUPILS BLACK BY 2000

Of every 10 000 black children who start school in Grade 1, only about 1 300 get to matric; 270 study for matric, of whom 113 pass; 27 get matrc exemption; and one gets an exemption in maths and science. Coupled with this, about 5 million eligible black children do not even get to school. **Education Reporter JANET HEARD** reports on a recent paper presented by the national director of the Programme for Technological Careers (Protec).

There is a sense of being in the doldrums as everyone waits for political leadership to announce a strategy for education and point the way out of all the current dilemmas, Mr David Kramer, national director of the Programme for Technological Careers (Protec) said at the organisation's preliminary annual report meeting.

He said 78 percent of South africa's pupil population fell under the Department of Education and Training. By the year 2000, more than 90 percent of pupils would be black.

The qualitative problems included:

•Overcrowding and poor teacher/pupil ratios of between 1:40 to 1:55, and the declining morale of teachers.

•Another pupil disruption seemed likely with more than 60 percent of Protec branch co-ordinators forecasting a worsening of the situation this year compared with last year.

•Very few black matric pupils chose to study maths or science. Of the 196 000 DET matric candidates last year, only 18 000 were registered for maths and 24 000 for science.

•In Soweto's 63 high schools only 41 pupils took maths on the higher grade.

•Poor subject choices led to many pupils matriculating with marketable qualifications.

In 1988 about 38 000 matriculants remained unemployed.

•Only 0, 02 percent of black matrics qualifed to enter technological education at the tertiary level.

In terms of the skills crisis, about 30 percent of the workforce had no education, 36 percent had only a primary education and 3 percent had a tertiary qualification.

In August 1988 the Race Relations Survey had forecast a 200 000 shortage of skilled and semi-skilled people by the year 2000, Mr Kramer said.

"At the same time, we are facing a surplus of about 9 million unskilled or semi-skilled people. We are already in a situation where new apprenticeships have declined by 45 percent between 1982 and 1988. The supply of engineers will be half that demanded by 1991."

Mr Kramer said the country was producing only a few hundred of the 14 000 skilled black people who needed to enter the economy every year if the shortage was to be avoided.

"If South Africa is to find the skilled people it needs to create jobs and provide food and shelter for its future citizen, then it must equip the current generation of students to face the challenge."

He suggested that ways to improve the situation were: a single compulsory education department; providing black pupils with decent education; providing real skills related to the needs of the individual, the community and the country; adequate remuneration of maths and science teachers; involving commerce and industry; and developing non-formal edcational programmes.

ful way. The German sociologist, Max Weber, developed a concept called *verstehen* or 'interpretive understanding; and this can be seen as the beginning of interpretive sociology represented by Blumer, and others, who were concerned with arriving at the 'meanings' of the actors, of 'feeling one's way inside the experience of the actor.'

The field of the sociology of education also reflected changes in the overall area of sociology. Until the last decade what passed for the sociology of education found its roots deep within structural function-alism, a theory which views the world as an interlocking system of parts related to the whole and explained by reference to the whole. The sociology of education, following the influence of the Coleman Report (1966) in America and the Plowden Report in Great Britain (1967), both of which had some sociological content and analysis, began to gain popularity and became a necessary part of professional training as a teacher. However, what was taught prior to 1970 reflected the Positivist and structural functionalist perspectives rather than the interpretive perspective that was the hallmark of the 'new' sociology.

The two events which heralded the new sociology of education were the coming together of the British Open University Course Team which produced *School and Society*, and the appearance of M.F.D. Young's editorship of *Knowledge and Control* (1971). Both were to exercise a crucial influence on the subsequent framing of the subject. What had actually taken place in the sociology of education is neatly summarised by Bernstein (1972), one of the foremost exponents of the 'new' sociology of education:

From different sources, Marxist, phenomenological, symbolic interac-tionist and ethnomethodological, viewpoints began to assert them-selves . . . they share certain common features:

1. A view of man as a creator of meanings.
2. An opposition to macro-functional sociology.
3. A focus upon the assumptions underlying social order, together with the treatment of social categories as themselves problematic.
4. A distrust of forms of quantification and the use of objective categories.
5. A focus upon the *transmission* and acquisition of interpretive procedures.

There are, of course, similarities in the two approaches in that they are both concerned with the interrelationships between equality, selection and class. But the former approach concentrates on *structural* rela-tionships, usually at a macro level. The 'new' approach concentrates on a situated activity, in particular interactional contents and contexts. In particular, a large part of the sociology of education since 1970 has tended to be concerned with the social construction of educational knowledge such as curricula, pedagogy and assessment procedures. Of special interest is an examination of the ideological assumptions lying behind what passes for knowledge in society and the various forms of legitimation. (Bernstein, 1972, pp. 103–104)

African
educational
systems</div> As we have already mentioned, there is a predominance of traditional forms of education in Africa, co-existing with Western style education. In some parts of Africa tension exists between the two forms. A return to traditional education is exhorted alongside a return to traditional values. But whichever form we look at there is strong evidence that educational practices are strongly linked to stratification systems, in Africa, both pre-Colonial and post-Colonial. In some instances, for example in Botswana, the formal educational system is a mirror of the old traditional one:

> The formal education now available in public primary schools is, in its manner of approach, a perfect analogue of Tswana patterns of child training. The child learns by rote and is punished for mistakes, delinquencies, errors, or incompetence.
> (Alverson, 1978, p. 69)

The Aztec *Codex Mendoza* of the fourteenth century reveals a highly elaborate informal system of education which went on in the home where fathers taught their sons, and daughters were taught by their mothers. Even today in Mexico, in the rural areas a great amount of education is by informal methods.

Obviously, sociologists of education view the educational process as the *total learning milieu*, and not just something confined to the formal system. Thus the process of *socialisation* becomes an important area of study. This process, which makes us recognisably human, enables us to construct our own 'self'. When culture is transmitted it presents to us our world in a symbolic form:

> . . . We cut nature up, organise it into concepts, and ascribe significance as we do, largely because we are parties to an agreement to organise it in this way—an agreement that holds throughout our speech community and is codified in the patterns of our language.
> (Whorf, 1940, p. 230)

But the acquisition of culture through the socialisation process is an on-going process learned over a lifetime. It is thus useful to distinguish between childhood (primary) socialisation and adulthood (secondary) socialisation. Socialisation is morphostatic because the social structure continues on, long after individuals die.

The various roles, ideologies and tasks into which we are socialised by society may be complete or incomplete. For example, not every one does well in the educational process. We therefore construct *ideologies* to justify certain perspectives. Two such theories or ideologies are those referring to *deficit* and *difference*. For example, if someone does not do well in school, does not achieve certain goals set by society or accomplish certain tasks which are expected of them, we generally say that someone is lacking 'drive', 'personality' or intelligence. The deficit can be either *individual*, something 'missing' in the person, *institutional* or *societal*. For example, we could locate the deficit in the school or the person's country of origin. Bernstein, whom we referred to above, developed a sophisticated theory of deficit with reference to the different linguistic codes acquired by the different socialisation processes relative to the middle-class and the working-class in Great Britain. Difference theories, as distinct from deficit theories, maintain that we all have differing and unequal access to varying cultural styles. Both theories or ideologies imply an impairment in the socialisation process.

Another type of ideology was the view that talent or ability was limited in societies, and that there was a 'pool of ability' in any given society. The function of education was thought to be to 'spot' this ability and nurture it. 'Life was a hurdle race which only the most able survived, an exclusive prize to be enjoyed by a few. Hand in hand with this philosophy went a set of beliefs about intellectual capacity, and its distribution, which assumed that high ability was strictly limited in any given society.' (Swift, 1969, p. 25)

An area of increasing interest is the relationship between the educational system and the political economy of societies. One suggested function of education is to see it as an inculcator of consensus:

Thus in Third World societies, where change appears to be rapid, in effect such change is not permeated throughout that society. In such societies one could envisage the education system preparing individuals for rapid developments that it could not foresee. In slowly changing societies one could see a function of the education system as implanting a set of shared values.
(Jones, 1984, p. 34)

The consensus function of education has been attacked by a number of sociologists who maintain that most societies are pluralistic in nature, and in which competing and differing value systems exist side by side.

Another perceived function of education is as an *agent of social change*. Advanced technological societies are *achievement oriented* and mobility is *contested* rather than *sponsored*. In such societies education can quite clearly be seen as playing a major part in social change. However, the society as a whole must be educated in order for this to take place.
(Turner, 1960)

Anderson (1967) viewed the function of education as selection for the work force, whereby individuals acquire skills appropriate for particular occupations. Following from this, of course, is the perspective of education as the prerequisite for upward social mobility. In Botswana access to at least a primary education is now fairly probable:

To that extent, a larger proportion of the population have at least a chance of benefiting from the upward social and economic mobility which post-primary education brings.
(Colclough and McCarthy, 1980, p. 215)

Access to occupational slots and the amount of income entitlement is strictly related to one's educational qualifications.

Social interaction If we turn now to the description of the four main areas of the sociology **in education** of education listed above we might begin to see some way in which the subject area can be applied to both the African and the non-African area of phenomena known as 'education'. Irrespective of the broad differences between the two educational systems there are, if we apply a sociological perspective, broad similarities to be discerned. These generally fall into the category of *processes*.

In the formal educational system most social interaction occurs in classrooms, between the teacher and the pupils and between pupils and pupils. In the non-formal system social interaction occurs usually *extra-murally*, i.e. outside any formal boundary such as classrooms. Nevertheless, it does occur just as effectively but in the context of village extension teams, cultural development programmes and a host of activities which go to make up post-secondary continuing education.

Studies of social interaction in the classroom tend to regard it as social interaction taking place in a *micro social system*, a miniature of the larger society but exhibiting many of the latter's social processes. Sociologists of education first began to enter classrooms to a significant extent after the Second World War. They examined, among other processes, *teacher-centred* versus *learner-centred* environments and varying styles of leadership such as *laissez-faire, democratic* and *autocratic*. Subsequently, more interesting perspectives emerged such as an analysis of the coding of teacher-talk. The work of Waller (1932) pioneered a whole area of 'gigantic agency of social control' with elements of *conflict* arising from time to time. Other processes at work in classrooms include *differentiation*, whereby pupils are distributed (streamed) on the basis of some criterion, usually academic ability, and *polarisation*, whereby students group themselves around anti- or pro-school norms. (Lacey, 1970). It is now further recognised that teachers operate in their 'tiny worlds of reality' bounded by constraints. Procedures such as the teacher asking the questions and the pupils answering are viewed as *coping mechanisms* thus enabling the inter-actional process to continue with minimal effort and an optimum outcome. Other areas of concentration include how order is maintained (or not maintained) in the classroom and how the *cycle of teaching activity* demonstrates the use of classroom language in an effective manner:

Teacher (*soliciting*) What do we import from Denmark?
Pupil (*responding*) Modern furniture
Teacher (*reacting*) Right, and it's some of the best designed furniture anywhere in the world.
(Bellack et al., 1966, p. 166)

A second perspective of social interaction in education shifts the focus from the classroom activities of the pupil to that of the teacher. This area tends to concentrate on an analysis of teaching as a *profession* and to ask whether it fulfills the criteria of 'profession' as agreed sociologically. Further, it is useful to know the social origins and composition of those who make up the teaching profession. Some studies have concentrated on the struggle for professionalisation and the process of professional *socialisation* which takes place, whereby the trainee teacher acquires the specific knowledge and characteristics of his/her occupation. An analysis of the *role* of the teacher casts some light on how teachers are viewed by society and the particular problems that the profession experiences. Finally, sociologists of education have become interested in the process of *labelling* which takes place in schools during which various labels such as 'thick', 'stupid' or 'bright' become attached to individuals, very often on an arbitrary basis, and which influence the behavioural outcomes of both pupils and teachers.

Socialisation The first area of socialisation is that of the child in relation to the family. By socialisation we mean the process in which individuals acquire the norms, culture and values of their society of origin. Generally, we talk about the socialisation of the child within the family as *primary* socialisation. However, because it is an ongoing process we distinguish subsequent socialisation as *secondary*. *Passive* theories of socialisation have tended to view it as a process of experiential and cognitive acquisition by the child in the manner of a sponge, in which the child absorbs or 'soaks up' stimuli in a passive non-resistant manner. Opposed to these passive theories of socialisation are the *active* theories which draw a model of the child structuring and creating his/her world which would enable a 'self' or an 'I' to emerge. A number of studies have examined the socialisation process in detail (Newsom, et al., 1977; Douglas, 1964) and a significant group of longitudinal studies have emerged which study a particular cohort over time. The family of origin has also given rise to numerous studies.

The second area of socialisation has tended to concern itself with the acquisition and use of language and the way that language structures our perception of the world and establishes our intelligence and ability. The foremost exponent in the analysis of socio-linguistics is Bernstein, to whom we have already referred. He was attempting to relate the type of language used (*restricted codes* and *elaborated codes*) to differing perceptions of the world. Linked to our versatility (or lack of) in language is the concept of intelligence. What exactly we mean by 'intelligence' is not entirely clear. We do tend to imply by it the skill and speed by which we perform certain tasks. On the other hand, some have argued that intelligence simply means being able to perform adequately on certain tests, in other words, that intelligence is what is measured by intelligence tests. The main basis of contention is between those who argue that intelligence is inherited, and those who argue that it is environmentally acquired.

The institution of How do other institutions interact with that of education? Clearly, a
education in its number of factors shape the educational outcome of individuals and
social setting the goals and structure of educational institutions. We know, for example, that one' location on a scale of stratification or one's position in the social class structure has a significant correlation with one's success in the educational system. Thus children of manual and semi-skilled workers tend significantly to leave school earlier and to be

considerably less successful at gaining university places than children whose parents are professional. Some sociologists view education as a preparation for entry into the occupational structure, while others concentrate on *inter-generational* mobility (father's social status in relation to their sons) and *intra-generational* mobility (any individual's change of status during their life time). Consensus is fairly well established that education serves as a major vehicle for social mobility:

Education is still seen by an enormous proportion of the world's population as the most likely, and often only, route from rural poverty to urban affluence. Here the folklore is borne out by the facts in many countries; this generation's leaders are the most successful products of yesterday's schools; incomes of school graduates are many times those of early school leavers; and school qualifications provide access to secure jobs in the civil service and in the private sector. (Lewin, et al., 1982, p. 19)

The neglect of expenditure on education by colonial governments led to the acceleration of such expenditure immediately after independence. Access and provision tended to be grossly unequal, for example if we compare rural provision with urban provision. Furthermore, economic investment in poorer countries means that the unit costs at the university level are often twenty times greater than at the primary level. Education, particularly in developing countries, is seen as inexorably bound up with economic development, job productivity and social mobility. Marcuse's concept of *repressive tolerance* argues that certain mechanisms in society contain us but we dissipate the sources of frustration by erecting alternative routes to reach the educational goals we have established. Finally, the educational system a society possesses is invariably the result of a complex series of invisible market forces that dictate the supply and demand.

The social organisation of knowledge: the curriculum This area of the sociology of education examines the ideological basis of the curriculum. It asks such questions as why certain subjects are included but others rejected in the overall subject content of the curriculum. Some subjects carry infinitely higher status than others. How, then, does the curriculum content relate to society at large? An examination of various models of the curriculum enable us to differentiate between Bernstein's work related to the classification and framing of curriculum knowledge.

Rationalist models of curriculum tend to see the process as *received* knowledge whereas **reflexive models** tend to see the content as negotiable. A third model, **the relational model**, tends to relate curriculum content to the society as a whole. Lastly, an interesting area of study has been what is known as the *hidden curriculum*. By this is meant a body of knowledge which arises as an alternative to the formal, 'official', curriculum but is learned from being part of 'the crowd', e.g. 'good work habits'.

Conclusions Related to the four specific areas of interest in the sociology of education are specific and legitimate areas linked solely to the Third

World. Thus anyone trying to relate the four areas to Southern Africa would have to link various theories of development to education. The history of education under colonialism is also of extreme importance because of the way the latter has moulded various crucial aspects. We would have to look carefully at alternative modalities for delivering educational knowledge and also question the appropriateness of a certain amount of imposition of western curriculum on Third World countries. For countries which have only adopted western educational techniques fairly recently and housed them in institutions similar to those in the west, an application of sociological perspectives centred on the sociology of education may have a long way to go before being regarded as a distinctly African corpus of knowledge. We must content ourselves for the present at least with applying what we know already to the African situation.

THE POLITICAL SYSTEM

The political system is generally defined as an institutionalised arrangement whereby some groups or individuals acquire and consequently organise power over others. Max Weber wrote that power is 'the probability that one actor within a social relationship will be in a position to carry out his own will despite resistance, regardless of the basis on which this probability rests.' Naturally, power is not confined to politics but is apparent in a wide range of situations and relationships. Positions of power can as Weber states, 'emerge from social relations in a drawing room as well as in the market, from the rostrum of a lecture hall as well as the command post of a regiment, from an erotic or charitable relationship as well as from scholarly discussion or athletics.' (Weber, 1968, p. 238) Part of the area of politics is concerned with 'who gets what, when and how', that is, the struggle for power with the allocation of scarce resources. Involved in this struggle are a large number of *interest groups*, social groups who lobby or assert pressure on the government to either protect the interests of some groups or advance their interests. Thus the homeless, the aged, farmers, are groups in the political structure which from time to time have had very powerful lobbying on their behalf.

Although political systems exist in simpler societies they are as we might expect simpler systems than we find in more complex societies. In many remote areas, for example, there are tribes without central government, such as the Nuer, the Tallensi or the Lugbara in Africa. These societies are generally divided into small groups such as farmers, hunters or herders. Such societies have a political unity and yet they have no kings, police force, magistrates courts or chiefs. It is for this reason that some anthropologists call them *encephalic* (without a head). Generally, various lineage groups act as political units, initially as an extended family facing a common foe, but more often than not when the leaders of lineage groups (the elders) make decisions. Such decisions are obeyed because they are traditional decisions which concern the harvest or the sowing season. Another reason is that it is firmly believed by many tribes that those who disobey the elders will incur the wrath of the gods. Thus kinship and religion play an important role in the political systems of simpler societies.

The power to control other people, even against their will, is brought about by influence, coercion or authority. *Influence* is the mechanism of persuasion. Archbishop Tutu can exercise influence as can the Queen of England. A star such as Madonna exercises untold influence on young people throughout the western world. The greatest persuaders in the Twentieth Century are the newspapers and television. Earlier this century it was the influence of radio, as we are reminded by Orson Wells' famous dramatisation of H G Welles' *War of the Worlds*, after hearing which many people fled the cities and took to the mountains because they believed that Martians were attacking America! *Coercion* is exercised by some governments although most prefer to *legitimise* their force, that is, to gain the consent of the governed. There are examples of illegitimate power, such as Nguyen van Thieu's regime in South Vietnam, which collapsed in 1975 after the majority of the population had become disaffected as the war progressed, and after the withdrawal of American troops. Finally, *authority* is legitimate power agreed by all parties. Thus the system of taxation is considered a legitimate way of taking money from the population whereas looting and robbery are not.

Max Weber discussed at length three types of authority or the claiming of legitimate power. *Traditional* authority we find in such figures as the Pope, the Archbishop of Canterbury or Queen Elizabeth II. It is historical in origin and very rarely questioned. Increasingly, challenges emerge to confront this type of authority, either from within the church or in terms of the monarchy. For example, the Queen of England has very little real authority. It is mostly symbolic. *Legal-rational* authority is framed within a legal constitution and generally refers to the type of authority exercised by presidents, for example Bush and Gorbachev. Presidents can be indicted, for example President Nixon during the Watergate scandal, in a way that kings and queens never could. Also, presidents' powers cease after they vacate their offices. The third type of authority Weber termed *charismatic* authority, by which he meant those leaders who, although lacking the other two types of power, possess some kind of unique personal power. Charismatic authority arises out of the *relationship* between the individual concerned and his followers, and is not something instrinsic. Examples of charismatic authority include Jesus, Hitler, Winnie Mandela and Ghandi. After the death of charismatic leaders their charisma becomes *routinised* as traditional or rational-legal authority. An example is the charisma of Lenin which, after his death, became routinised into the rational-legal authority which characterises contemporary Soviet government and leaders.

The structure of   *The emergence of the state*
the state   The state (the highest political authority in a country) is a relatively
recent phenomenon and tied very much to industrial and post-indus-
trial societies. The state increasingly intrudes on the lives of individuals, and in some capitalist countries some 40 % of the labour force
are employed by the state (Giddens, 1982, p. 77) Another measure of
the growth of the modern state is the amount of federal expenditure a
country has. There are two main perspectives centering on the state:

The functionalist perspective views the state in terms of the function it
performs in order to preserve or maintain the social system as a whole.
These are basically four which can be described as follows:

1. *Resolution of conflict.* The state on the whole decides on the allocation of scarce resources and provides a sophisticated legal machinery to arbitrate conflicting interests;
2. *Enforcement of behaviour deemed appropriate.* The state constructs
   an elaborate legal and coercive system to ensure that agreed
   normative behaviour is maintained. These include enforcement
   agencies such as the army and police, and by a system of civil and
   criminal law.
3. *Relations with other states.* By maintaining a highly centralised
   control and authority the modern state can take part in an ongoing
   series of negotiations with other countries, such as by entering into
   trade agreements or by diplomatic censorship.
4. *Centralised planning.* The state coordinates the allocation of scarce
   resources such as health, welfare and building projects. Statistical
   records must be centralised in order for equitable decisions to be
   reached, *for the country as a whole,* on the requirements of particular areas.

The second approach is *the conflict perspective.* The principal exponent
of this view is Karl Marx who saw society comprised of various segments
which were in conflict with each other about the control of the scarce
resources of society. The two major groups are the *exploited* (the 'have
nots', the working class) and the *dominant* (the 'haves', the ruling
class). Marx saw the state as being instrumental in maintaining the
status quo and thus preserving and protecting the interests of the
ruling class. Marx viewed 'the history of all hitherto existing societies
as the history of class struggle' and identified a number of stages
through which societies had passed as follows:

1. *Primitive communism:* no classes or private property
2. *Slavery:* exploitation of one class by another
3. *Feudalism:* the exploitation of peasants by aristocratic landowners
4. *Capitalism:* the exploitation of industrial workers by the wealthy
5. *Socialism:* the overthrow of the wealthy by the exploited industrial
   workers and the establishment of the 'dictatorship of the proletariat'
6. *Communism:* the abolition of property and the establishment of true
   freedom. The state simply 'withers away'.

There have been increasing criticisms of Marx's theories, not least that the conflict function is not the only one that the state performs, and that many of the functions performed by the state overlap in capitalist and socialist/communist states. Marx's theories are neither *teleological* (having a predetermined end) nor *linear* (having an 'automatic progress' in any one given direction). Although the state preceded capitalism it has grown stronger;

Because of its role in suppressing the subordinate classes, the state's main functions are identified as repressive. Its core elements are based on organised violence (police, prisons, standind army), which is used primarily against the economically exploited classes.
(Shaw, 1985, p. 248)

If we turn to *types* of government we can see that there are three major types which can be further broken down into further forms:

Democracy

Democracy is the recognition that power lies with the electorate, the word meaning literally 'rule of the people'. Although individual participation in decision-making might have been possible in the small Greek city-states it has never been possible in modern societies. What most societies have is called *representative democracy* because the people do not rule directly but elect others to rule for them within a parliamentary system. Britain and America are the major examples of this form of democracy. Such democracies are characterised by *civil liberties* which includes the freedom to organise political statements, groups and so forth within the framework of the law. Thus newspapers and the media are subject to the law of libel and contempt.

Participatory or direct democracy in which the people take an active part in decision making was possible only in Ancient Greece and parts of Switzerland. It is also possible, perhaps, at village level or in communes such as a kibbutz. *Delegatory democracy* is that in which the elected are told by the electors what line they must follow.

Authoritarianism

Authoritarianism is a form of government in which opposition is not tolerated. It can take many forms, such as the *monarchy* (power in the hands of a hereditary claimant to the throne), a *dictatorship* (in which power is gained and preserved by an individual), or a *junta* (the military take control). Public debate is often permitted but not to the extent that the authoritarian government is challenged.

Totalitarian

Totalitarian government is that in which the leaders recognise themselves as totally supreme. Their goals are absolute. Examples of such societies are Hitler's Nazi Germany, the Khmer Rouge regime in Cambodia, and Stalin's Russia. Neither authoritarian nor totalitarian governments can be removed legally from office. Their ideologies are total, and their control of every facet of life is also comprehensive.

Yet another form of government is *oligarchy* or government by the few. An example is General Holomisa's Military council in Transkei, and yet another recent example was the Greek Colonels' military rule.

There are certain accepted conditions that must exist before a democratic government can be established. Thus it is generally agreed that modern democracies can only exist where there is an advanced economic development with the population generally sophisticated, literate and relatively affluent. Such societies tend to be highly stable because there is a large middle class with a vested interest in maintaining the status quo. It is also helpful to a democratic government if there are formal and informal constraints which limit the abuse of power. Britain, for example, does not possess a written constitution or Bill of Rights as does America and yet is a highly stable democracy. Another factor is that there exists in the society a general consensus as to what norms to follow, and an absence of major disagreements. Minority dissent, generally, is accepted and listened to, to avoid a possible overflow beyond the institutional framework. In South Africa we have a democratic system which is confined to certain groups by reason of racial classification and where even majority dissent is not heeded. Equally important in a full democracy is totally free access to information and a diffusion of power.

Interest groups   In any society with a liberal-democratic form of government *interest* or *pressure groups* exist. Their name is self-explanatory because they exist to exert pressure or influence:

Interest groups differ from political parties by their aim, which is not to take power but only to exert pressure. They differ from parties by their objects, which are usually limited in scope. They differ from parties by the nature of their membership, which is often limited to one section in society.
(Blondel, 1969, p. 26)

There are two kinds of pressure group; firstly, the *sectional* group which generally shares a common factor such as occupation, although it can also be sexual (Gay Rights) or racial (National Association for the Advancement of Coloured People). *Promotional* groups strive to further some cause such as Amnesty International or the anti-abortion lobby. Pressure groups have a further distinction into *permanent* (continuous, on-going) and *ad hoc* (formed to contest a specific issue, temporary). Interest or pressure groups have been variously criticised as being tied or aligned to the party system. Furthermore, those who are not organised can very rarely form themselves into any kind of interest group, neither can the socially disadvantaged, such as the aged and black immigrants (i.e. in the United Kingdom). Influence is brought to bear by *lobbying* (confronting decision-makers on a face-to-face basis) although sometimes this process is carried out by professional lobbyists who are paid fees on a professional basis. At the last count there were some 20 000 registered lobbyists in America.

Who governs?   C Wright Mills, in his book *The Power Elite* (1956), maintained that a small yet powerful and influential group governed America. This was not a conspiracy but a result of the fact that the leaders of government bureaucracies, corporations and the armed forces originated from the same socio-economic background; what is generally referred to as 'the old school tie'. A similar theme is pursued by Miliband (1969) and Giddens (1979). Thus Miliband states:

What the evidence conclusively suggests is that in terms of social origin, education and class situation, the men who have manned *all* command positions in the state system have largely, and in many cases, overwhelmingly, been drawn from the world of business or property, or from the professional middle classes. Here, as in every other field, men and women born into the subordinate classes, which form, of course, the vast majority of the population, have fared very poorly . . .
(Miliband, 1969, p. 47)

The leaders of the church, the professions, the military and industry are for the most part drawn from private school pupils and from the middle and upper classes.

Mill's argument was that there were three levels of power in America. At the top was the power elite which made all the important decisions, while at the second level were the heads of legislative government. At the bottom was the broad mass of the powerless who were not only unable to make any effective decisions themselves but were often unaware that these decisions were being made for them. Contrary to this Marxist view is the *pluralist model* of society which sees not a concentration of power but power exercise by many differing and competing interest groups. (Reisman, 1961, and Dahl, 1982)

ECONOMIC INSTITUTIONS

By *institution* sociologists generally mean 'the established forms or conditions of procedure characteristic of group activity.' (MacIver and Page, 1949, p. 29) The *social system* is composed of institutions. Parsons and Shils (1951) define social system as follows:

(1) It involves a process of interaction between two or more actors; the interaction process as such is a focus of the observer's attention.
(2) The situation toward which the actors are oriented includes other actors. These other actors (alters) are objects of cathexis. Alter's actions are taken cognitively into account as data. Alter's various orientations may be either *goals* to be pursued or *means* for the accomplishment of goals. Alter's orientations may thus be objects for evaluative judgement.
(3) There is (in a social system) interdependent and, in part, concerted action in which the concert is a function of collective goal orientation or common values, and of a consensus of normative and cognitive expectations.
(Parsons and Shils, p. 55)

UNSUCCESSFUL APPLICANTS FOR CONTRACTS TO THE MINES
Employment Bureau of Africa, Maseru, 1983. J. Alphers

In order to exist individuals must have certain requirements (or needs) satisfied, and thus a social institution is a group of people organised for a specific purpose. These purposes may include the rearing of children (the family), various transcendental beliefs and values (religion), the expression of secular attitudes and ideas (politics), or the organisation of knowledge (medicine or education). Thus a particular church is not an institution but 'church' is. Another way of describing an institution is as a cluster of norms, roles, values and statuses. Although at first glance the wide range of institutions seem very different from one another there are certain common characteristics shared by all of them:

1. Institutions are not subject to rapid social change except in exceptional circumstances such as the social and political revolution which occurred in 1917. Any attempt to dissolve the institutions of the family or religion in normal periods of history would be met by very fierce resistance.
2. Major institutions tend to be interdependent so that a country espousing a socialist ideology will be supported by institutions sympathetic to socialism.
3. When social institutions change, they do not usually do so in isolation. A good example is the Industrial Revolution which meant not only a shift from rural to urban places, but from the extended

family to the nuclear one and from a society dominated by religion to one espousing secular values.

4. Social problems tend to be situated within or around social institutions. For example, marital breakdown affects the institution of the family. This is often because institutions are conservative and slow to adapt to the nuances expressed by various sectors of society.

A functionalist perspective views an institution as exercising stability (representing the status quo) and, like the model of a physical organism, regarding any negative aspects as dysfunctional and in need of correction. Conflict theorists invariably tend to regard institutions as favouring one group over another.

The economic institution

The economic institution of society is that which produces and distributes goods and services. We will therefore discuss work, occupations and leisure. One school of thought is that in some simpler societies, work is not as highly valued as in Western societies. Thus the Kalahari Bushmen say, 'Why should we work when God has provided so many mongongo nuts.' (Lee, 1979, p. 62) However, such a rosy picture of these simpler societies often does not notice the constant fear of floods, drought, disease and hunger. A single-crop society, such as Ireland in the 19th century with its potatoes, was ruined when the harvest failed in 1845, resulting in famine and finally typhoid. Simple economies generally exhibit a system of mutual assistance which is essential for the group's survival. The Nuer of the Sudan, for example, eat in each others homes as often as they do in their own. Sharing is done in the knowledge that the following year it may well be your turn to require assistance.

The Turkana herders of Uganda are at liberty to use any watering place in their territory because, if the right to do so is denied, then the right to stay alive is also being denied. Small scale societies are also mostly totally independent in that they produce everything they require for their own existence. We call these societies *subsistence* economies. Once the assistance of outsiders is required there is a move to a larger, more productive economy. Wealth accumulates through a division of labour. For small-scale societies to develop they require (1) access to markets; (2) natural resources, and (3) capital equipment. The accumulation of *capital* (all those things gathered in the present to meet future needs) is found in all societies in one form or another. Land is the most important capital but hunting societies often have no capital at all with the exception of bows and arrows. Because a lot of societies have elementary technical knowledge they tend to stay impoverished. Thus in Third World countries it is estimated that one third of a woman's day is spent fetching water, gathering firewood and grinding corn.

Sectors of the economy All economies can be divided into one of three basic sectors, with the majority of those working predominating in one of the sectors. The *primary sector* places an emphasis on extracting or gathering natural resources, for example forestry, mining, fishing. The *secondary sector* is involved in turning these raw materials into manufactured goods, for example furniture, houses, tinned food. The *tertiary sector* provides services, for example teaching, nursing, shopkeepers. *Pre-industrial societies*, such as hunter-gatherer and agricultural societies, are characterised by the majority of the labour force being employed in the primary sector. In *industrial societies* the majority of the labour force is employed in the manufacture of goods, usually in factories, and are known as 'blue-collar' workers. It is important to realise that there is considerable overlap in these stages. Thus, for example, in the industrial state there are still a number of individuals who are employed in the primary sector, and even in post-industrial societies. It is the proportion or percentage which has changed.

Work It is quite difficult to define work:

'Work' can refer to any physical and mental activities which transform materials into a more useful form, provide or distribute goods or services to others, and extend human knowledge and understanding. We cannot, however, distinguish work from its various opposites—'leisure', 'idleness', 'play'—solely by reference to activities.
(Brown, in Worsley, 1987, p. 273)

It is more generally useful to use the term *employment* or *occupation* as more significant economically in terms of being paid for doing it. Unpaid work, such as domestic work, must not, however, be ignored because it is estimated that it adds some 35–40 % to the *Gross National Product*. Paid work is socially important because a number of other sociological areas tend to be dependent on it, such as the life-chances of individuals, their lifestyles and their world views. As we discuss elsewhere occupation is very much linked to morbidity and mortality rates.

Historically, in European peasant societies and Third World countries, it is impossible to separate work from other areas of social life. Among Xhosa peasant societies, for example, every member of the household, from great-grandmother to the youngest child, contributes to the household activities. Often various stages of cultivation are regulated by the magician or witchdoctor. With the coming of the industrial revolution a labour force of *employees* was created which, for the first time, was concentrated away from home. Such employees, being subject to close supervision, lost much of their previous autonomy. *Time* became increasingly important and employees were required to 'clock in' and 'clock out':

Both the availability of clocks and watches, and the emphasis on time-keeping, spending time and saving time increased greatly in the late eighteenth and early nineteenth centuries. Eventually this discipline was not only imposed from outside but *internalised* by workers themselves.
(Ibid., p. 278)

The 'formal' economy is easily recognisable but there is also an 'informal' economy which has been divided into three areas:

1. *Household economy:* production, not for money, by members of a household and predominantly for members of that household, of goods and services for which approximate substitutes might otherwise be purchased for money.
2. *Underground, hidden or black economy:* production, wholly or partly for money or barter, which should be declared to some official taxation or regulatory authority, but which is wholly or partly concealed.
3. *Communal economy:* production, not for money or barter, by an individual or groups, of a commodity that might otherwise be purchasable, and of which the producers are not the principal consumers.

(Gershuny and Pahl, in Littler, 1985, p. 248)

One of the major problems in the sociology of work is the concept of *alienation.* Many workers, especially in factories and routine office jobs, experience intense feelings of meaninglessness and personal uselessness. Karl Marx viewed this alienation from work as due to the fact that workers do not own what they produce nor the means by which they produce it. Max Weber viewed alienation as being the result of the bureaucratic *division of labour.* We mention elsewhere (Chapter 7) the characteristics of a bureaucracy as exemplified in the modern hospital or the civil service. Briefly, bureaucracies are characterised by specialisation of tasks, a hierarchical authority, efficiency, impersonality, and a system of rules or procedures. The division of labour is the specialisation by groups or individuals in their economic activities. In western societies there are nowadays approximately 20 000 different work roles compared with some 320 in the 1850s. Emile Durkheim wrote *The Division of Labour in Society* in 1893. He is particularly concerned with the social consequences of increased specialisation which he sees as having two major effects. The division of labour actually, according to Durkheim, changes the nature of the social bonds which 'cement' society together. It also encourages individualism. He describes simpler societies as being held together by *mechanical solidarity,* a form of social cohesion characterised by the individuals being similar to one another in values, kinship groups, etc. In contrast, modern societies are held together by *organic solidarity,* characterised by differences. An increased division of labour results in an emphasis on differences and individuality. The end result is *anomie,* a sense of normlessness or a lack of moral guidance to behaviour.

Alienated states	*Non-alienative states*
powerlessness	control
meaninglessness	purpose
isolation	social integration
self-estrangement	self-involvement

(Blauner, 1964, p. 63)

Socialism and   The two basic economic systems that exist in the world are *socialism*
capitalism   (public ownership of the means of distribution and production) and
capitalism (private ownership of the means of distribution and production). It is important to remember that these are ideal types (abstract
descriptions put together from a number of sources) that do not exist
in any pure form. The United States, South Africa and Canada are
examples of capitalist societies, and Russia and Albania are socialist
countries. Many countries, however, such as Great Britain and Yugos-
lavia, are a mixture of these two systems. Capitalism as an economic
system embraces the belief that the pursuit of personal profit is good
in itself, and that market competition is the basis for deciding the
production and pricing of goods. Socialism is characterised by centralised planning and the fulfillment of personal needs. Because there
are many similarities between the two systems (e.g. both are highly
urbanised with extensive bureaucracies) some writers have put forward the theory of *convergence* (that eventually the two systems will
evolve towards a common form).

The rise of corporate capitalism, legally constituted corporations
(whose powers and liabilities are distinct from their employees and
owners) and *multinational corporations* (companies with their head-
quarters in one country, which operate through subsidiaries around
the world), particularly in developing countries, has meant the emergence of a concentration of economic power and political influence.

Braverman (1974) takes a Marxist approach to labour and production processes in capitalist societies. Concentrating on labour and
labour power, Braverman sees labour as intelligent and purposive but
under capitalism the worker becomes progressively alienated from the
work process. Craft work has declined and become de-skilled labour.
Unemployment is not due to a lack of skills but to an economic system
that due to a fluctuating market has insufficient jobs. The American
Marxists, Bowles and Gintis (1976) show that the probability of
obtaining economic success is due substantially to one's socio-economic background rather than one's intelligence.

Unemployment   Finally, if we turn to unemployment within the economic system it is
clear that being in such a position exercises a considerable drain on
an individual. In modern western societies the unemployment rate
runs at between 7 and 12 %. No country has full employment because
at any one time there are individuals changing employment, entering
employment or who are off work through sickness. Apart from the
sudden change in one's economic circumstances, unemployment also
has social and psychological effects. *General rates of unemployment*
are affected by market recessions, etc. While *specific rates of unemployment* affect only certain sections of the population. For example,
the rate is higher for females than males, blacks rather than whites,
manual workers rather than office workers and migrant and seasonal
workers. One area of particular interest in the area of unemployment
is its relationship with the health of individuals. For example, in Britain

in the 1950s and 1960s, despite some technical advances in medicine, chronic illness was growing at a steady pace, together with unemployment. A small number of individuals were, in fact, experiencing the majority of days off sick. In all cross-sectional studies the health of the unemployed is more open to health problems than that of the employed. However, longitudinal studies do not show any deterioration in the health of the unemployed. Notwithstanding, a 1 % sample of unemployed, followed up for a ten year period, found that mortality was 20 % both amongst them and their wives, irrespective of their social class position and place of residence. (Bartley, 1988)

SUMMARY

1. An 'institution' is a group of people organised for a specific purpose, e.g. the rearing of children (family), various transcendental beliefs and values (religion), the expression of secular attitudes and ideas (politics), or the organisation of knowledge (education or medicine).

2. Certain characteristics are shared, such as that institutions do not change in isolation, or rapidly. They tend to be interdependent.

3. Although it is fairly easy to recognise the formal economy, an informal one also exists, which is divided into *household economy, black economy* and *communal economy*.

4. The two basic economic systems are *socialism* (public ownership of the means of distribution and production) and *capitalism* (private ownership of the means of distribution and production). Many countries are a mixture of these two ideal types.

5. Political systems exist in different forms in all societies but similar because they involve the exercise of persuasion and more importantly the exercise of *legitimate power*.

6. Legitimate authority can be of three types, according to Weber: traditional (stemming from a historical tradition); legal-rational, (such as that exercised by our State President); and charismatic (such as the authority of Jesus and Ghandi).

7. *Interest groups* are *sectional* (sharing a common factor such as occupation, e.g. being public employees) or *promotional* (advocating a cause such as Anti-Abortion).

8. Religion as a system of beliefs and practices appears to exist in all societies although in different forms.

9. The *cult, sect, denomination,* and *church,* are distinct organisations with vastly different characteristics. However, Marx saw all forms as examples of false consciousness.

10. Various categories of belief appeal to specific strata of the population possibly because of different deprivations. Thus Glock and Stark postulated a number of deprivations, i.e. economic, social, organismic, ethical and psychic.

11. Millenarian movements, from Cargo Cults, Nativistic Movements and Messianic groups, are classic responses to felt deprivation and have consequently been closely studied.

12. The emergence of capitalism at the same time as the rise of Protestantism has caused a long debate since Weber postulated the Protestant Ethic Thesis. Recent work about the values of Catholics and Protestants has not reached any firm conclusion.

13. Another on-going debate is whether the rational process is eroding religion. The secularisation process, as this is known, has its antagonists and protagonists.

14. The sociology of education is concerned with (a) the process of social interaction in education; (b) the socialisation process of the child and the acquisition of language, intelligence and ability; (c) inter-

institutional interaction; and (d) the social organisation of knowledge.

15. In both First and Third World countries the economy is seen as crucially linked to the system of education.

IMPORTANT TERMS

institution
secondary sector
industrial societies
Gross National Product (GNP)
underground or black economy
alienation
mechanical solidarity
socialism
ideal types
interest groups
legal-rational authority
teleological
participatory democracy
religion
sect
cargo (nativistic)
social fact
legitimate power

primary sector
tertiary sector
post-industrial societies
household economy
communal economy
division of labour
organic solidarity
capitalism
multinational corporations
traditional authority
charismatic authority
linear
delegatory democracy
church (ecclesia)
relative deprivation
education
verstehen

SELF-ASSESSMENT QUESTIONS

1. Describe what is meant by 'institution' and why the concept is important in sociology.
2. Explain how the economic institution pervades the other main institutions of society.
3. 'Political systems are to be found in all societies in one form or another.' Say what the characteristics of such systems are.
4. Can we say that religion has a 'function'?
5. It is usually held that modern industrialised societies are becoming more secularised. Do you agree with this statement?
6. Give an account of the four main areas which constitute the sociology of education. How has the study of the sociology of education changed since the early 1970s?

CHAPTER
ELEVEN

SMALL GROUPS, COLLECTIVE BEHAVIOUR AND SOCIAL MOVEMENTS

- small group behaviour
- collective behaviour
- social movements
- explaining social movements and their characteristics

THE BEHAVIOUR OF INDIVIDUALS IN SMALL GROUPS

Social interaction in small groups is found in a number of different species such as monkeys, apes and humans. Much of the behaviour of humans is, in fact, learned in such groups, and as individuals grow older such behaviour as they have learned in childhood groups is constrained, modified and stimulated by further contact with groups of a secondary nature.

Why study small groups? The phenomena of human interaction in societies can be viewed from a number of different perspectives. One perspective may be called 'social geography' and another 'sociology' or 'social psychology'. These are not necessarily conflicting perspectives but very often complement each other in 'rounding off' what after all is a very important study. Sometimes such perspectives break down even further into sub-categories. The study of small groups as such is commonly regarded as the special province of social psychology, and is one which overlaps with both psychology and sociology. In one sense it is useful to make such a distinction, but at a higher level such essentially artificial boundaries break down. *Social interaction* and *socialization* are areas both central to sociology and social psychology.

Sociology has traditionally been concerned with macro-scale interpretations and generalizations about large organizations of people such as societies, civilizations or nations. It has also been concerned with the movements of collectivities of people through the social structures and systems of these large organizations. However, it has been pointed out that the only historical continuity of men in society is in the small groups. Other categories such as guilds and trades have been disrupted and broken up, but small groups have survived, suggesting the latter as the basic social unit.

There has been much disagreement over what is meant by 'small group' but generally it can be taken to mean a number of persons engaged in meaningful interaction with one another in which there is some recognition of mutual expectancy.

Small groups such as the family, adolescent groups, work groups, T-groups, therapy groups, and committees are the kind studied by researchers interested in this area. Several reasons have been suggested for studying small groups. Firstly, such groups as the family provide us with our primary and basic experience in the socialization process. Secondly, some have hoped for a new sociological synthesis arising out of such study which would furnish a series of 'laws' which could eventually be applied to all human behaviour. Thirdly, small-group research is regarded by a few as perhaps providing an empirical testing-ground for sociological theory. Fourthly, a number of areas appear to converge on small groups such as counselling, clinical psychology, problem-centred groups, and so on. Fifthly, it is safe to say that many large-scale models which sociologists work with, such as the *conflict model*, can be examined in miniature. Sixthly, many pragmatic processes such as therapeutic mechanisms, so useful with groups such as Recovery, Inc. for ex-mental patients and Alcoholics Anonymous for excessive drinkers, can be scrutinized at this level. Seventh, and lastly, small-group production rates affecting output can be examined in this small and relatively concise area.

A criticism of small-group research
Before we begin to discuss the positive contributions of small-group research it might be useful to suggest some of the main weaknesses in such an approach, which often is open to attack from both sociology and psychology. Small-group research is often guilty of using obtuse and difficult language which critics regard as an attempt to cover up a weak methodology. Many small-group research situations are very artificial ones taken from the world of American boys' summer camps, girls' dormitories, bomber crews, laboratory groups and so on.

The theory of small-group research is concerned with discovering the social counterpart of the discovery of the atom in physics. Thus the small group is held by many social scientists to be the simplest unit of human phenomena—the social counterpart of the atom in physics and of the cell in biology. However, neither the call nor the atom is the simplest unit but is in fact a generic element of the biological or physical structures.

J L Moreno pioneered a method of measuring the internal structure of small groups. This method, *sociometry*, is concerned with the likings, dislikings, repulsions and attractions between members of these groups. It usually involves each member of a group specifiying, usually in private, a number of other persons in the group with whom he would like to do something (such as sit next to) and those with whom he would *not* like to participate in any activity. The limitations in the use of such methods include: (*a*) it is only *one* way of viewing interpersonal relations; (*b*) sociometry doesn't bring out the differences in 'choice'; (*c*) there is an inadequate quantitative treatment of data.

Another criticism levelled against small-group research is that the term 'small group' is itself an arbitrary classification. This is not to say that small groups cannot be studied as a religious sect, the family, and so on, but that it cannot be studied as a typical example of all the heterogeneous groups of small size. Further, a small group is not necessarily simple because of its size. On the contrary the social organization of the General Nursing Council is infinitely less complex than a hospital ward, and *gemeinschaft* communities are not necessarily more complex than Ford Motors.

The formation of social groups
It is useful to designate different kinds of groups on the basis of why they come together in the first place. For example, we talk of a leisure or interest group, a work group or a religious group and so on. B W Tuckman suggested that there are four major phases in the formation of groups and that group structure and the activities of groups develop in similar ways. He designated these as *forming, storming, norming,* and *performing*. In other words, the group locates itself around a leader, there is conflict between various sub-groups, a

development of group cohesion, and finally a resolution of interpersonal problems. Groups vary in the time they take to pass through one of these four phases and other factors such as the introduction of new members often interfere with the smooth flow. Group cohesiveness is very important in group formation because it indicates the level of attraction to a group (sometimes designated as the 'we' feeling). Individuals may be attracted to a group because of its prestige, because of other members, or because of the task that the group is performing. A group with relatively high cohesiveness displays a large amount of interpersonal interaction between members and a common agreement on the goals or task in hand.

Interaction processes in small groups Potential members of groups often share something in common, such as an alcoholic addiction problem, but having joined a particular group they also begin to develop shared ways of looking at problems, of interacting, and so on. Social groups can therefore be said to form social norms through (a) having a common (or near common) goal at which to aim; (b) the development of a specialist language to facilitate communication and goal attainment, and the establishment of quite clearly defined rules; (c) the establishment of a set of beliefs and attitudes which are held in common; and (d) the formation of a set of norms about physical appearances, clothes, etc. Thus Alcoholics Anonymous recruits share a desire to attain a sobriety and develop a special language and ritual in their groups to facilitate the achievement of this goal. They also develop the same attitudes towards their problems. The recruit to such groups must comply with such norms and later, after membership is established, the norms which initially have to be learned become familiar or internalized. Sometimes individuals in small groups do not conform to the norms. When this occurs they are either made to conform by the other members, are excluded from the group, form alternative groups of their own or become innovators in the existing group. The reasons why an individual may not conform include a number of factors such as a strong personality, a wish to challenge the leader, or the influence of another group which he regards as important. If recruits place a great deal of importance on joining a group they are more likely to conform to its norms. Also, certain personalities are more likely to conform. Argyle reports that several studies have shown that conformers are likely to be female, unintelligent, lacking in self-confidence, and authoritarian. There is some suggestion that different nationalities conform more than others and that different sub-sections vary in the degree of conformity.

Role differentiation and the structure of the small-group hierarchy Although small groups have a normative pattern, individuals in such groups often behave differently from one another because they have different tasks to perform and because their personalities differ. Very often a large group requires a firm leader, whereas a small group operates on the principle of a democratic consensus. Some groups have a system of offices, privileges and so on built in to their structure. These formal groups are distinguished from informal groups, which have an absence of such offices and titles.

There are a number of processes by which a leader emerges from a small-group situation. Leadership was initially studied in terms of the leader's attributes, but more recently it is regarded as emerging from effects induced by the demands of the situation. It is increasingly being seen as a process of interaction involving a person who influences and those who are influenced. Usually those who attempt leadership are those who successfully attempted earlier leads and who have ability to cope with the group's problems. Such individuals also display a higher self-esteem and self-accorded status. Whether or not leadership succeeds depends on the perception by other members of the similarity of this situation to ones in which the would-be leader was successful earlier. Sometimes the emerging leader is in a position to coerce other members due to his power to reward or punish them. Persuasion by a would-be leader that he can successfully lead is another factor.

The trait approach to leadership sought to identify unique characteristics in the leaders, and people were regarded as 'born' leaders. The situational approach views leadership in the life context in which it occurs. While certain minimum abilities are required of all leaders, such abilities are also distributed among non-leaders as well. Furthermore, the traits of the leader which are effective and necessary in one group or situation may be quite different from those in a different setting. Leaders tend to display a better verbal effectiveness and social perceptiveness than non-leaders. A further distinction made is between the social specialist leader whose activities are mainly constructive in contributing to group organization, maintenance and internal harmony among members, and the task specialist leader whose main concern is with the group's successful attainment of its collective aims and goals.

The two main styles of leadership normally distinguished are those of autocratic versus democratic leadership. Power and influence may be exerted in an essentially autocratic style through direct coercion and authoritative manipulation, or in a more democratic style through indirect cajoling, seduction and persuasion. Very limited and culture-bound research has tended to suggest that democratic styles of leadership are not only preferred by most people but also that they tend to facilitate the effective performance of the group.

Several factors may influence the style of leadership adopted by an individual in a group. His own personality and needs may dispose him to adopt a particular style. Characteristics of the group itself and even the pattern of communication among members may also affect the style. A person cannot display leadership functions unless others display the reciprocal role of follower. Social power is not an attribute of an individual but a relationship between an individual and others. Limited evidence suggests that good leaders are people who are (a) sensitive to specific needs and demands of their group and each of its members, (b) able and flexible enough to adapt their behaviour to suit their needs, and (c) responsible enough to initiate new actions when needed.

Status

Status is an important concept in the study of small groups for a number of reasons. Status is a position occupied by a person in the social system. This position can also be occupied by a family or a kinship group. Any position is relative to others within the social system, and determines a whole range of relationships with persons of differing status. Sociologists generally regard status as the static aspect of role and role as the dynamic aspect of status. Status entails a series of prescribed rights and duties. As we have already suggested, the bases of status differential and allocation varies considerably from society to society and from one historical period to another within the same society. Status may rest, for example, on personal achievement or on some group-recognized status-giving factor. Status may be based upon differences of birth, wealth, occupation, political power, race, IQ, and so on.

That differences exist within the system does not in itself account for status discrimination. It is the process of symbolic interpretation which gives significance. Apart from the distinction between ascribed and achieved status some have gone on to identify six main criteria: (1) birth; (2) possessions; (3) personal qualities; (4) personal achievement; (5) authority; (6) power. When there is a good 'fit' between a person's position in each of these six major rankings this indicates a high degree of *status consistency*. *Status inconsistency* is where there is a bad 'fit', for example a teacher has education but low income.

We generally talk of status as accruing to a position which any person occupying acquires or is ascribed. However, even within a given position an individual's achieved status may vary upward or downward from this base depending upon features of his performance in that position. That is, a person's role enactments or performances tend to validate his status and so may modify it. Consequently, ineptness in role enactment lead to a loss of status. An inept ward sister loses status in the eyes of the rest of the ward staff. Strictly speaking status is attributed to positions and not people. Since each person occupies multiple positions within the social system, each of which accords him a status, we can think of persons as being characterized by status.

The concept of status which we have briefly reiterated here can be related to small-group study. Every position that is recognized and continues to be recognized by the members of a group contributes in some way to the purposes of the group. Social position determines role behaviour. A position has been described by one social psychologist as a *locus of influences*. Not only this; relationships between persons in different positions influence their role relationships. In other words, positions are related along a dimension which are regarded as 'higher' or 'lower' or 'superior to' others. These are commonly referred to as status differentiations. These differentiations occur in some form in all group situations and a few of these can be classified as follows; *professional prestige* occurs between members of a group and is characterized by deference on the part of low-status members towards those of high status, and expected deference from the former on the part of the high-status members; *popularity status* occurs because people tend to associate with those who are equivalent to them in popularity status; *power and authority status* is distributed in families, organizations and so on which entail a host of concomitant behaviour patters; *knowledge status* occurs because certain groups and individuals within groups are delegated deference on the grounds of special skill or knowledge.

The basis of power in small groups is the relationship between a person and an agent (which can be another person, a role, a norm, a group or a part of a group). There are five bases of power which are important: (1) *reward power*, which is defined as power whose basis is the ability to reward; (2) *coercive power*, which is based on the individual's perception that the agent has the ability to mediate punishments for him; (3) *legitimate power* involves the individual's acceptance of a code or standard by virtue of which the agent can exert power; (4) *referent power* is based on the individual recognizing the agent as a reference group; (5) *expert power* is based on the perception that the agent has some special knowledge or expertise. Some have distinguished between power of two kinds—*behaviour control* and *fate control*. In the former, by varying his behaviour A can make it desirable for B to vary his behaviour too; in the latter, A can affect B's behaviour regardless of what B does. Thus power can be looked at in terms of the degree to which the less powerful person can affect certain outcomes on his own behalf.

A highly cohesive group possesses all or some of the following characteristics: (*a*) a high level of mutual attraction among its members; (*b*) shared attitudes and rules; (*c*) well-developed structural integration. Each of these properties confers power on the group over its members.

Communication in small groups

Communication in small groups is largely the same as that in bigger social organizations. *Horizontal communication* characterizes the majority of interaction in such groups. If we take the example of a hospital and a ward within a hospital, most communication is between individuals occupying the same status positions. For example, student nurses tend to communicate more with each other than with a staff nurse or a ward sister. Interaction takes place between student nurses on a ward in terms of cooperation and help over certain tasks. Sometimes student nurses communicate with others from other wards, and certainly individuals occupying the same status positions communicate much more with each other than with either superiors or inferiors. Communication also tends to centre around friendship and social support either in the residential quarters or coffee breaks or during leisure. *Communication downwards* in a hospital setting takes the form of information, orders or instructions. It also takes the form of communication by experts. In a bureaucratic organization such as a hospital such communication is usually filtered down through the hierarchical channels. *Upward communication* takes the form of seeking help, reporting on progress, and sometimes making suggestions.

Five different kinds of small group

The *family*, which we treat separately elsewhere, is found in some form in all species of mammals. It is in the family that the important process of socialization occurs, where positions are allocated and interaction patterns established. *Adolescent* groups are generally the first secondary associations that individuals join as completely separate entities from the family. It is in such adolescent groups that the majority of crimes, rebellion and non-conformity (to adult values, that is) occur. Some sociologists have suggested that adolescence is a creation of industrial societies and that primitive societies have no such indeterminate span between childhood and adulthood. Certain adolescents are more popular than others. For example, an American study suggests that beautiful girls and athletic boys are more popular than intelligent ones of either sex. Although generally adolescent groups have no special task they tend to be over-concerned with sex and with the establishment of an ego-identity which characterizes itself with a fastidiousness over clothes, haircuts and so on. Relationships in adolescent groups tend to be more intense than at other periods of the life-cycle.

Work-groups are essentially concerned with the performance of a task. *Problem-solving groups* usually succeed at their task better than individuals. Finally, *T-groups* and therapy groups are the setting for behaviour which, although some would regard it as atypical or abnormal, may nevertheless be a magnified example of a less obvious form of similar behaviour occurring elsewhere.

Two case studies of small-group interaction

From 1927 until 1932 the Western Electric Company carried out a series of studies under the direction of Elton Mayo into monotony, morale and fatigue. Once famous as the classic investigation, these studies are now one of the supreme examples of really bad research. The company, based at Hawthorne, Illinois, and now called the Hawthorne Experiments, were directed at the problem raised by unexpected results of the effect of lighting conditions on output. The experimenters were expecting an increase in production to coincide with an increase in illumination and vice versa. Contrary to expectations production increased not only with the improvement of lighting but also when such lighting deteriorated. To test what the 'human factors' were that apparently intruded on their experiment those involved set up another test known as the Relay Assembly Test Room. The six girls involved in this experiment, despite whatever alteration in their conditions of work, continued to improve their production. What emerged finally was that it was not a physiological relationship between the girls and their work which was important but various

BMW WORKERS ON
STRIKE,
PRETORIA 1984

Photo: Paul Weinberg

psychological factors such as the attitudes of the girls and how they regarded their work.

The Bank Wiring Room experiment was supervised by an anthropologist, Lloyd Warner, and was a study of a section of a normal workshop. Fourteen workers were studied including nine 'wiremen', three 'soldermen' and two 'inspectors'. Several findings emerged from the long and detailed observation which followed. Firstly, the men shared a set of norms which were not officially defined in any way and to some degree militated against the management. Having set their own standards of what constituted a day's work the men were very much against anyone breaking their set rate. Such norms as these were enforced by such means as group criticism and symbolic reminders that any one individual was breaking the group's norms. Secondly, the workers in the group came to regard the inspectors as superior to some extent and the soldermen as inferior. In other words, a set of social relationships and interaction was established by the group.

The impact of such a study is that it characterizes the way in which a whole series of informal relationships can develop even within a tightly regulated system. A more popular example is afforded by the BBC series *Colditz*, which demonstrates how officers held in captivity and regulated by a very strict regime can still manage to form a whole pattern of unofficial and informal activities. Another factor which emerged from the study was that the work performance to an extent depended on their social relationships. Such studies as these were the beginning of the *human relations approach*, which has tended to dominate managerial and bureaucratic studies.

The Western Electric Company study has produced the term 'the Hawthorne effect' which describes how the observer influences his object of study by merely being there. One of the reasons why the girls in the Relay Assembly Test Room showed such large increases in output was simply that they liked being observed. To put it another way they worked better when watched. A more serious criticism is summed up by Argyle: 'the results of that experiment could however be accounted for entirely in terms of uncontrolled factors, such as changed incentive arrangements, the replacement of the two slowest girls by two faster ones, and the reduced variety of work done'.

A study of the Norton Street gang by William F Whyte examined a group of Italian slum neighbourhood dwellers in Boston. The study was produced in 1943 after a number of years spent living with the group in the area. The group consisted of a number of young men (13) between 20 and 30, who were unmarried. The study showed quite graphically a small group sharing common norms and interacting together in a structural manner. There was a certain hostility to outsiders and these were safeguarded by a shared set of attitudes. The most prestigious sexual targets were Anglo-Saxon Protestant women, but women inside the neighbourhood were taboo. The group was structured into a formal hierarchy.

Evolving during the Depression, the gang was an avenue of mobility and a means of achieving social status and recognition. The group had its own corner (Norton Street) and a regular evening meeting place at a cafeteria where table positions were fixed by custom. Athletic skill and toughness were highly prized characteristics. Doc was the person of the highest status, the leader, together with his two lieutenants, Mike and Danny. These three were less restricted to gang activities than the other members. Doc was expected to lend money to others but not to borrow himself. He was expected to be fair in his dealings with others. Basically, group members derived their satisfaction from their shared activities and relationships. The study is important because it shows how a leader can effectively structure a group, and also because it highlights well-organized groups and activities even in an area which might be described as anomic or disorganized. In other words, a slum ghetto possesses a number of primary groups which offer an intimate atmosphere.

The supervisor in the small-group situation

Leadership involves some degree of supervision. It is generally felt that leaders/supervisors should be high in dominance (effectively doing the job), rewarding, skilful (in leading and supervising), and able to take the role of the other (why *did* someone act as he did). Other related characteristics that a supervisor should show are the ability to initiate structure and to show consideration for others.

Supervision in a small-group situation can take many forms, as follows:

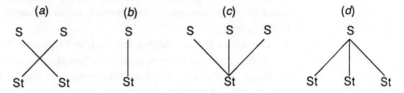

(S is supervisor and Sd is supervised) but the most common form is still (*d*). The supervisor receives little or no training in human skills or problem solving, nor in communication.

The manner or style by which a person is supervised elicits a different response in that person depending on whether the supervision is authoritarian or democratic, open or closed. It has been well demonstrated that individuals reflect supervisory styles and themselves transmit this reflection or influence. If a subordinate expects punitive or close supervision, he is not frustrated when he receives it. If he has not the normative expectation for the type of supervision he receives, then a form of conflict and resentment arises. There is very little doubt that different supervisory styles can elicit quite different results in performance. The two basic supervisory styles are the *closed* and the *open*. The former style might still be found in some of the more old-fashioned types of hospitals and medical schools. Here the supervision is formal, hierarchically differentiated and total. The latter style is found in more modern and forward-looking establishments, and here the supervisor is informal, interacts with the supervised and is relatively egalitarian.

Such work as that on supervision is directly applicable to medical settings where much of the work involves the supervision of subordinates by doctors, tutors, ward sisters and so on. Furthermore, hospitals are full of small work groups. Even hospital wards are examples of small groups where relationships and patterns of interaction can be observed and acted upon by staff. In the course of their working lives many medical staff come into contact with small groups, both therapeutic and otherwise. Despite the criticisms of small-group research mentioned above, the way in which such groups are formed and persist over time can be of immense interest to social scientists and of value to those interested in medical care.

COLLECTIVE BEHAVIOUR

Generally speaking collective behaviour refers to behaviour that is relatively ill-defined, and to emotional situations. It is behaviour characterised by moods and impulses which are unstructured, and refers to large numbers of people. It refers to a wide variety of social behaviour such as collective excitement, crowd behaviour, social unrest, fads, crazes, riots, manias, mass hysteria, rebellions, primitive religious movements, reform movements, revolutionary movements, fashions, rumours, etc. Such unstructured behaviour stands in stark contrast to bureaucratic behaviour, as in a hospital setting, for three main reasons.

1. Common moods, impulses and feelings are developed by a fairly sizeable group of people, which ties them into a collectivity;
2. Such behaviour does not conform to the norms and forms of structured behaviour;
3. Collective behaviour is fluid and emerges in an undefined situation.

One of the main theories of collective behaviour is that of Smelser (1962) which falls under the heading 'stress' or 'strain' theory, i.e. that collective behaviour is that which arises out of an attempt to alleviate conditions of stress that originate in the environment. He lists six conditions which are necessary for collective behaviour to occur.

1. *Structural strain* He has in mind such social conditions as poverty, uncertainty about the future, discrimination, and conflict. A collective movement may arise because people make a collective effort to alleviate the problem.
2. *Structural conduciveness* Society has the condition which make a particular form of collective behaviour possible in the first place. For example, the South Sea Bubble in English history or the Wall Street Crash in American history. The latter would not have been possible in an underdeveloped country that had no institution such as the stock market.
3. *Generalised belief* People must perceive their situation in a particular way, e.g. that they are discriminated against, or that people of another colour or race are a kind of economic threat.
4. *Precipitating factors* Usually some specific incident, often amplified by rumour, sparks off a riot or demonstration.
5. *Mechanisms of social control* By this is meant how the Repressive State Apparatus and Ideological State Apparatus (discussed in Chapter Six) respond by being either weak or strong. On many university campuses, for example, the authorities over-react by calling in the riot police. This over-reaction has the effect of inflaming the students even more, and in turn more drastic efforts at suppression are introduced.
6. *Mobilisation for action* The individuals involved must become organised for action. Mere physical propinquity or gathering together can facilitate action.

THE CANADIAN HUMANIST 1979; **49**: XII

SHOULD WE STEP IN?
The Problem of Deviant Cults
By Dr. Kenneth Jones

If we study the various religious beliefs subscribed to by people in our society we find we are studying at one and the same time what is considered by society to be **legitimate** belief and what is considered to be **illegitimate** belief. It is generally agreed by social scientists that such beliefs cannot simply be accepted at face value, since they may mask a whole variety of social and economic ideologies. The political, social and economic interests of people are often intertwined with their religious beliefs.

On the other hand, the officially accepted belief of a society is not something that is open to negotiation. Rather, it is a given fact, against which all unorthodox beliefs of groups and individuals are guaged. Whether or not an unorthodox belief is accepted or even tolerated, however, depends less upon the power of reason than on whether or not the governing interests in society wish it accepted or repressed. As C.R. Sharp and A. Green wrote in **Education and Social Control**: 'What seems to be crucial is whether in the last analysis one can control others and bring sanctions to bear against others, irrespective of their definitions of reality. And the ability to do this derives not from language, but from the distribution of power and authority.'

FREEDOM OF RELIGION?
Such an approach raises broad moral, legal and political issues—particularly in cases where members of minority religious groups undergo 'deprogramming'. In the U.S. such issues have already been hotly debated. In particular, the activities of 'deprogrammer' Ted Patrick have been strongly criticised. In this context familiar questions arise, e.g. how much freedom should people enjoy, how far should society go in protecting people against harmful influences, how much power should parents have over their children, and so on?

Authoritarian sects, which have rapidly increased in recent years, are seen by some as a form of psychological abduction where new members are 'brainwashed' into deviant ideologies. Deprogrammers claim their techniques, which include physical constraint and a form of secular brainwashing, are merely attempts to reinstate the recruit's reality structure. Often the deprogrammers enlist, and obtain, the support of the legislature and the police. Attempts to bring legal action in the courts against the cults have failed because they have not been shown to have infringed any known laws, although courts have successfully ruled against behaviour such as polygamy and snake handling, irrespective of the claim that freedom of religion was somehow being violated by such a ruling. Occasionally courts have ruled to interfere with actual behaviour carried out in religious groups, but nearly always this occurred where the action of the groups, in the opinion of the court, 'violated traditional standards of health, safety, or education'.

A failure to get members of religious sects classified as mentally unstable has led professional deprogrammers to apply for 'conservatorship' over sect members. In other words they claim that such persons are 'unable to manage their own affairs . . . because of debilitating factors . . .' In the U.S. a 'Legal Deprogramming Kit' is circulating and some psychologists have begun to specialize in deprogramming cases. However, members of the Unification Church examined by psychiatrists were fund to be suffering from 'coercive persuasion' rather than any psychiatric illness.

WHO ARE THE FREAKS?

'Religious freaks' espouse beliefs regarded as 'illegitimate' by the majority of society. They adopt a 'negative identity' which splits them from their families, and it is more probably the domestic schism which gives rise to their reaction rather than the attraction of the beliefs themselves. In some regards not only is the majority saying that the sects are false and they themselves true, but that the alien beliefs do not accord with the majority's view of reality. On the whole, sects hold beliefs which are circuitous, unrevisable and closed, while those of society at large are open to rational investigation, although it may be that the difference in the quality of rationality **per se** is indistinguishable, the real distinction lying in the **power** of the majority's viewpoint. As a society we continually define the reality of deviants and ignore the relative and temporal nature of the deviance itself. It may be an old truism that individuals work out their own salvation, but it is one that some are rapidly forgetting in an attempt to impose conformity.

However, although one may be intellectually sympathetic to a policy of nonintervention there do arise situations in society where intervention may well appear necessary and a course of action may mitigate against a minority definition of reality. For example, the final death toll of men, women and children in the Jonestown jungle commune reached 914 with approximately 87 survivors. The cult members took cyanide poison after the leader Jim Jones had told them: 'The time has come for us all to meet at another place.' The People's Temple had a large weapons arsenal at the commune, and Jones himself ran an international communications operation financed by generous amounts of foreign capital. Various newspaper accounts (some perhaps sensationalising their stories as a result of the Jonestown horror) alleged any number of bizarre activities on the part of Jones and his followers. In the face of such evidence, what should have been the stance of society—intervention or indifference?

SHOULD WE STEP IN?

Occurrences such as this raise very real questions about interference or noninterference. Individuals and groups perceived as constituting a danger to themselves and to other have, some would argue, a perfect right to their own view of reality and should be left alone. Others might argue that there is nothing sacrosanct about the acquisition of particular values, beliefs and attitudes. They are largely an arbitrary matter which can be equally arbitrarily altered if they appear to be in conflict with the 'legitimate' beliefs of society. Sociologists who preach that reality is a social invention should not be surprised that bizarre constructions do indeed arise. It may well be that there are occasions, such as Jonestown, when we as a society must take a caretaker approach, and re-define the reality of the more bizarre minority groups, not forgetting that history has shown repeatedly that societies themselves can often be caught up in a resemblance of W.B. Yeats' **Second Coming**: 'And what rough beast, its hour come round at last, slouches towards Bethlehem to be born.'

The bewildering number and variety of religious cults that have sprung up in Western society in the past decade has given rise to some serious questions about the limits of freedom. More and more people are coming to the conviction that some of these cults practise a form of brainwashing on their recruits and that cult members no longer have power over their own thought processes, but are manipulated by the cult leaders.

A prominent (and notorious) advocate of this view is Ted Patrick, who has taken it upon himself not only to publicise the perceived perils to which young people are subjected in certain cults, but who also makes himself available to parents—firstly, to secure the release of a son or daughter from a cult (sometimes resorting to the use of force, so that opponents of Patrick label his actions 'kidnapping'), and secondly, for the 'deprogramming' of the ex-cult member by the use of counter-brainwashing techniques (which critics likewise label brainwashing).

Since 1971 Patrick has been arrested and convicted on a number of charges, such as kidnapping and unlawful detention, and has actually served sentences in prison. But he has also won several important trials. For example, in 1974 a Seattle court ruled that the kidnapping of a cult member by Patrick acting as the parents' agent was justified insofar as he was attempting to prevent a greater harm. And in 1978 a court rules that his deprogramming techniques did not constitute an illegal act.

Not surprisingly, civil liberties groups have strongly criticised Patrick's activities—especially since some of the 'reclaimed' cult members were over 21 years of age. Civil libertarians see such acts as giving the stamp of legality to kidnapping, particularly when the police give their support and help and when judges refuse to convict even if charges are brought.

But Patrick is unrepentant: he views cults such as the Moonies, the Hare Krishna and the Church of Scientology both as dangerous to individuals and society alike, and as multi-million dollar rackets. He estimates that there have been about 3 000 religious cults in North America in the past decade with a total membership today of between ten and twenty million; and he claims to have deprogrammed nearly 1 600 people from these cults.

His basic objection to the activities of the cults is that they set out to gain control over the minds of their initiates and thereby control their lives; in fact, he goes so far as to claim that some cults exhort their brainwashed members to go to any longths (even to violence and murder) to defend the cult and to keep members firmly attached to it. The Guyana tragedy and other reports of ex-cult members being attacked or threatened give credence to such claims.

One of the simpler ways in which cult members become pliant is through the constant chanting of the same sounds—such as in the Hare Krishna. The latter reject the charge that their chanting induces lethargy and compliance and point out: 'Our members are no more brainwashed because they chant than are the nuns who say their Rosary each day or people who attend church because of the threat of fire and brimstone.'

Both the growth of pseudo-religious cults and the development of organised resistance to their activities raises some thorny questions: How can we differentiate between a legitimate religion and a dangerous cult? (For some humanists, no doubt, the answer is easy: **all** religions are dangerous!) How can we decide (and who should have the power to decide) if a person has been 'brainwashed' by a cult? How much freedom should society give to its members, and when should it step in (if at all) to prevent individual abuse? Should deprogramming be regulated—and if so, how? In these as in other related questions the march of social progress has once again outstripped our moral preparedness to deal with them.

And it is not just our humanistic tolerance that should make us wary of coming to hasty conclusions about these matters. We must also bear in mind a prime lesson of history: persecuted minorities (and not only religious ones) have often become forces for good. The Quakers, for example, nowadays among the most humanitarian forces in our society, began their history as an outlandish sect of enthusiasts guided by an obstreperous prophet whose loyalty to 'the inner light' transcended all laws and conventions.

An example of a collective movement was the People's Temple sect of Jim Jones, where more than 900 of his followers committed mass suicide by drinking Kool-Aid containing cyanide.

Rumour A *rumour* is unsubstantiated, anonymous, information. Of course, rumours can be true but they can also be false. Rumours are usually difficult to trace in terms of origin. Some rumours can be particularly forceful in stimulating crowd or mob action.

Often, especially when information is at a premium so that people do not know what is happening, for example in a large organisation such as a hospital, university or company, rumour takes the place of 'hard news' or official statements, perhaps from management. Sometimes, particularly in strained situations, there are many examples, such as the rumours that circulated in Detroit, U.S.A., during the serious riots of 1967. These included rumours that the black population was being interned in concentration camps and that some black males were being castrated. (Rosenthal, 1971, pp. 47) One of the best studies on rumour (Allport and Postman, 1958) consisted of a screen showing a slide of totally *ambiguous* scenes. For example, one shows a collection of people seated or standing on a train, with a black and a white person confronting each other in an angry manner. The subjects in the experiment are to guage what in fact they see as happening and to report it to another person who is not present. A number of individuals enter and are successively told what has occurred. After each successive telling, the *accuracy* drops phenomenally, in much the same way as does memory. The researchers listed a number of processes in operation:

1. *Levelling*—as the rumour travels down the line it becomes more concise, shorter, and easier to grasp and tell. The tendency is to use fewer words.
2. *Sharpening*—specific details tend to be singled out from the context and may become especially emphasised. An example might be that the black person is holding a knife in his hands, or that there are, in fact, five blacks confronting the white person.
3. *Assimilation*—items tend to become consistent with what is perceived as the principal theme of the story. If the knife was originally in the hands of the white person, it is quite feasible that it ends up in the hands of one of the black people in the final telling of the story.

In one study of the Deep South of America, where the condition of the negro is still inferior, it was a strong and persistent rumour that black males had larger sexual organs. Rumour often eventually becomes believed by the propogator, even through it was regarded as false in the beginning.

In telling a rumour, the kernel of the objective information that he received has become so embedded into his own dynamic mental life that the product is chiefly one of the projection. Into the rumour he projects the deficiencies of his retentive processes, as well as his own effort to engender meaning upon an ambiguous field, and the product reveals much of his own emotional needs, including his anxieties, hates and wishes.

(Allport and Postman, 1958, p. 64)

Robertson (1987) gives some excellent examples of fairly recent rumours.

1. It was widely rumoured in 1969 that Paul McCartney, one of the Beatles, had died in a motor car accident and the record company had substituted a look-alike. Human ingenuity was such that a whole series of clues 'proved' this to be the case. If Revolution No. 9' was played in reverse a ghostly voice was heard saying 'Turn me on, dead man'. If one looked closely at the *Sergeant Pepper* cover album one could see a hand over McCartney's head (a symbol of death). McCartney wears an arm-band, 'o.p.d.', which can only stand for 'officially pronounced dead', he wears a black carnation on the cover of *Magical Mystery Tour*. On the *Abbey Road* cover 'the beatles appear to be walking in the funeral procession. John Lennon was in white (the priest), Ringo Starr was in a black suit (the undertaker), McCartney was barefooted, out of step and had his eyes closed (the corpse), and George Harrison was in working clothes (the gravedigger)'. To clinch matters, a car in the background had the registration number 28IF, meaning—what else?—that McCartney would have been twenty-eight if he had been still alive.

The cause of this rumour was that because the beatles exemplified youth culture at this time, anything about them was more than likely to spread. Because they had been denied hard news fans were likely to grasp at straws as far as the group was concerned.

2. In 1982 rumours eminated from Christian Fundamentalist groups in America that Procter and Gamble, one of the largest manufacturers of household cleaning products, was actively engaged in devil worship. The logo which appeared on all their products was a satanic device when in fact it was the man in the moon surrounded by thirteen colonies (a device introduced in 1882). A television show (of which subsequently there was no trace) was rumoured to have featured an interview with the top executive of the company who stated that a percentage of the company's products was 'given to satan'. Eventually the symbol was removed from the company's products.

The reason for this rumour was that it was a 'response by some fundamentalists to a situation of ambiguity and uncertainty—the problem of identifying who their enemies are.'

(Robertson, 1987, pp. 543–544)

Often there exist a number of what Robertson calls *urban legends*, such as that Chinese restaurants serve dogs, that people have been known to eat 'Kentucky Fried Rat', that snakes can hide in imported clothing, and so on. These appear to be designed to warn against foreign products and eating fast foods. Also many stories abound in relation to lovers' parked cars, in some way highlighting adult concern with teenage morality.

Mobs are usually active and aggressive aspects of a crowd, with limited objectives. Examples are necklace murders and lynching.

Crowds are temporary collections of people and exhibit little structure. Sometimes it is difficult to distinguish between crowd and *mass*, the latter being thought of as a diffuse version of the former. The mass who heard of the murder of John Lennon or John Kennedy did so in a manner likely to suggest a loose kind of crowd.

Theories of collective behaviour There are two main theories regarding collective behaviour. *Contagion theory* can be said to have been first instigated by Le Bon in 1895, in his famous book *The Mind of the Crowd*. According to Gustave Le Bon the primary law of crowd behaviour was the mental unity of crowds. Individuals, when they come together in crowds, behave very differently than they would as individuals; they develop a 'collective' mind'. Le Bon listed other characteristics of the crows: it is always intellectually inferior to an individual, but not in terms of feelings; the crowd is very susceptible to external stimulation; the crowd doesn't think before it acts on impulse; crowds are very open to suggestion; crowds are extreme. The crowd loves, and needs, a leader. These traits possessed by the crowd are, according to Le Bon's outdated and chauvinistic theory, 'almost always observed in beings belonging to inferior forms of evolution—in women, savages, and children, for instance'.

Smelser's *value-added* theory we have already mentioned. One of its principal merits is that it encompasses a wide range of social movements and events, from the hula-hoop, Davey Crockett hats, to the appeal of certain Christian evangelists. Another important theory is Ralph Turner's *emergent norm* thesis. (Turner, 1964). He makes the point that crowds are unknown to each other before they come together. Because the crowd has no pre-existing determinants its actions can eventually take a number of different forms. Thus a crowd heckling F W De Klerk is not the same kind of crowd that would besiege Tutu. Rumours abound in crowd behaviour and triggering incidents are interpreted by the crowd amid slowly mounting tension. In other words, norms arise among crowds as a result of social interaction, and, as there are often no existing norms to tell them what rules to follow, they look to each other. This occurs in periods of uncertainty, which makes them prone to adopt whatever norm is offered. There is, says Turner, no unanimity in crowds because they are composed of very different individuals with vastly differing characteristics and motives. Crowd behaviour is open to the same explanation as other social behaviour, i.e. it is influenced by the same social norms.

Panics and mass hysteria Perhaps the most famous example occurred on October 30, 1938, when millions of Americans believed that Martians were attacking the earth. The man instrumental for this panic was the American actor Orson Welles who broadcast an adaptation of H G Wells' *War of the Worlds*. The broadcast interrupted a music concert with reports of 'atmospheric disturbances' and 'explosions of incandescent gas'. It was then announced that vast areas of America were being placed under martial law. All was delivered in a semi-realistic reporter-on-the-scene fashion.

Long before the broadcast had ended, people all over the United States were praying, crying, fleeing frantically to escape death from the Martians. Some ran to rescue loved ones. Others telephoned farewells or warnings, hurried to inform neighbours, sought information from newspapers or radio stations, summoned ambulances and police cars. At least six million heard the broadcast. At least a million were frightened or disturbed.
(Cantril et al., 1940)

A similar type of panic is amusingly dealt with in the film *The Russians Are Coming, the Russians Are Coming* (1966) which describes a Russian submarine which is grounded on the American Coast, and which subsequently turns into a panic that the Russians have invaded. Cantril analyses people's reactions which he divides into four. (1) Some took the trouble to check the internal evidence of the broadcast and decided it was science fiction; (2) some checked and discovered they were listening to a play; (3) some tried to check but carried on believing that it was actually happening; (4) some did not check at all because they were too frightened or too gullible. The importance of Cantril's study is that many of those who *believed* the programme's authenticity, had a framework into which they could fit what they were listening to. For example, they were highly religious believers who shared a fatalistic view that the world was soon to end. Others did not have the educational level against which they would check the facts. Those who panicked were those who found the broadcast convincing. We must remember, also, that America was emerging from a period of economic depression, and that Europe was on the brink of war. At that time, too, belief in Mars being possibly inhabited was widespread.

Conformity to group expectations An excellent study by Festinger (1956) describes the behaviour of a small group of religious believers which he and his colleagues had infiltrated. Mrs Marian Keech was a Lake City, U.S.A., housewife who claimed that she was constantly in touch with superior beings from the planet Clarion. She claimed that she had been warned that the world would be flooded on December 21. Festinger and his colleagues are famous for their theory of *cognitive dissonance*, a clash between belief and reality. Mrs Keech had made an announcement which in all probability would be proved incorrect. (A brilliant fictional account appears in the novel *Imaginary Friends*, by Alison Lurie). On the 20th, the day before the disaster, she was informed from Clarion that she and her followers would be picked up and transported away by a flying saucer that was parked nearby. In the waiting period the group carefully removed all metallic items from their bodies because of the known danger of travelling through outer space with metal objects.

After midnight had passed and dawn was approaching it was becoming apparent that no saucer was in fact coming. Mrs Keech received another announcement. 'And mighty is the word of God—and by His word have ye been saved—for from the mouth of death have ye been delivered.'

This message was received with enthusiasm. It was an adequate, even an elegant, explanation of the disconfirmation. The little group, sitting all night long, had spread so much light that God had saved the world from destruction. (Festinger, 1956, p. 162)

Festinger had hypothesised that if a belief was strongly held, and the believer was socially supported even when the evidence was disconforming, the belief would, nevertheless, be maintained and the believer undergo a revived period of proselytising, or converting others, in an attempt to persuade non-members that the belief was correct. Those who remained in the group did, in fact, redouble their efforts at persuading everyone in sight as to the truth of their beliefs. Those members who had not attended that day found their belief in the prophecy of Mrs Keech had either died or been seriously weakened. If we compare the account of the early Christians in the *Acts of the Apostles*, when Jesus failed to reappear, the proselytisation became, in fact, extremely fervent and intense, contrary to the expectation that the beginnings of the early Christian movement would have died away.

Extreme deprivation Collective behaviour under conditions of extreme deprivation has been described in relation to Jewish inmates in concentration camps during World War II. Amazing as it may seem, old prisoners who had survived adopted the verbal expressions of the Gestapo, together with their bodily gestures. They were responsible for actually disposing of new prisoners who appeared unfit, and appropriated for themselves portions of Gestapo uniforms. Similarly, American and British prisoners in Korea showed very different rates of 'conversion' through brainwashing. The former were converted in such large numbers that later the authorities established a commission of inquiry. The reasons for the American soldiers 'going over' to the enemy was mainly because they were more poorly educated than the British and more ignorant about the geography of their own country. Discipline and leadership were far stronger among British soldiers.

SOCIAL MOVEMENTS

Although social movements are included in the category of collective movements they are more structured, deliberate and organised. They are characterised by usually specific goals directed towards existing social institutions which are modified, maintained, replaced or destroyed. Lee has defined social movements as:

. . . collective enterprises to establish a new order of life. They have their inception in a condition of unrest, and derive their motive power on one hand from dissatisfaction with the current form of life, and on the other hand, from wishes and hopes for a new scheme or system of living . . . As a social movement develops, it takes on the character of a society. It acquires organisation and form, a body of customs and traditions, established leadership and enduring division of labour, social rules and social values—in short, a culture, a social organisation, and a new scheme of life.
(Lee, 1946, p. 199)

Blumer (1957) sees social movements as (a) general social movements, such as the labour movement, (b) specific social movements such as the Temperance Movement or the anti-slavery movement, (c) expressive social movements such as religious movements and fashion movements.

Social movements pass through a life cycle

1. In the *preliminary* stage a group of disorganised individuals are frustrated, excited and full of unrest. The typical leader is the *agitator.*
2. During the *popular* stage, the group becomes aware of itself. The *prophet* or *leader* emerges and an 'out-group' is blamed for catastrophes.
3. In the *formal* stage there is a lot of discussion and deliberation. Institutionalised arrangements are formulated. Norms, dogmas and rituals are finalised.
4. The final stage is the *institutional* stage. Organisation structures are finalised. The movement becomes the *society*, 'acquires organisation and form, a body of customs and traditions, established leadership, and enduring division of labour, social rules and social values; in short, a culture, a social organisation, and a new scheme of life'.

(Hopper, 1950, p. 278)

An example of the rise of such a group is that of the Catholic Apostolic Church which rose to prominence in the 1820s under the leadership of the charismatic Edward Irving. The Catholic Apostolic Movement arose at a time when Glasgow, in Scotland, was at the brink of civil war fanned by the revolutionary weavers and cotton-spinners. The French Revolution was a constant reminder to the British middle classes of their vulnerability.

Religion, being one of the dominant interests of society in the early nineteenth century, afforded an opportunity which was structurally conducive to the emergence of a religious value-oriented movement, but one which neverthe-less afforded a camouflaged vehicle of protest for covert political anxieties. It was an attempt at a bourgeois revolution in Britain which developed under the guise of a religious reformation specifically precipitated by the relative inflexi-bility of the governing aristocracy which was in effect blocking the social mobility of the bourgeoisie.
(Jones, 1984a, p. 107)

Wirth (1945) cites four characteristics of minority movements:

1. The *pluralistic* minority seeks to live a tolerated existence among but apart from other groups while at the same time maintaining its cultural identity by refraining from social intercourse and intermar-riage with the majority. An example is the Jew.
2. The *assimilationist* minority aspires to equal economic and social participation. An example is immigrants into America.
3. Minorities may seek *secession* either within or outside the larger society. Examples are some intellectuals and the Zionist emigration to Israel.
4. The *militant* minority. An example is a small emergent state.

Millenarian movements

Millenarian movements foretell the soon-to-be end of the present social order when the 'chosen' (usually the movement's members) will reign supreme and the wicked (their rulers) will be 'laid low'. The relationship between religion and social change is an interesting area of study. E P Thompson hypothesised that working-class millenialism was a response to the frustration 'of political aspirations, and thus repre-sented a channeling-off of revolutionary fervour in terms of a conti-nuum of activist (political) and quietist (religious) poles'. (Hill, 1973, p. 205) Lanternari is concerned with the cultural clash between de-veloping countries and advanced industrial nations. He is concerned about these 'collisions'. As one newspaper in Britain described it:

The new Messiah is usually a native who has had close associations with the best class Europeans. He has learnt their tricks and admired their gadgets and he hates their guts. The gospel he preaches . . . assures the faithful that the day of the Lord is at hand when all manner of blessings shall be their reward and the evil oppressors shall be blotted out.

The religions of the oppressed have a number of characteristics: native pagan witchcraft, sorcery, magic, followed by native spiritual healing:

The attribution of magical powers to religious healing is a feature of nearly every new messianic cult rising among people subjected to foreign rule.
(Lanternari, 1963, p. 26)

Fanon (1968) was anxious that we should always take into account the phenomena of the dance, of possession, and of supernatural visions.

Such movements as we are describing have the choice to be either militant or nonmilitant. Thus Lanternari illustrates the Maori taking militant action against the whites whereas the Australian aboriginals did not. Similarly, the Peyote Ghost Dance movement among the Plains Indians was a militant group. *Nativism* abounded as an attempt to revive certain aspects of a culture which were in danger of extinction. An example is the Peyote Cult which was less militant than its predecessor, the Ghost Dance, but which nevertheless incurred the wrath of the authorities.

In 1859 a Xhosa millenarian movement resulting in a mass cattle killing, decimated both cattle and grain, and created a massive migration to the Cape in search of a livelihood and the death of some 20 000 from starvation. The young Xhosa girl who experienced the vision, Nongqause, also dreamt that the whites would be driven back into the sea. (Davenport, 1977 and Pieres, 1987). However, Pieres suggests that the cattle killing was brought about, and determined by, the lungsickness epidemic of 1854:

The Xhosa cattle killing movements of 1856/7 cannot be explained as a superstitious 'pagan reaction' to the intrusion of colonial rule and Christian civilisation. It owes its peculiar form to the lungsickness epidemic of 1854, which carried off over 10 000 Xhosa cattle. The Xhosa theory of disease indicated that the sick cattle had been contaminated by witchcraft practices of the people, and that these tainted cattle would have to be slaughtered lest they infect the pure new cattle which were about to rise.
(Pieres, 1987, p. 60)

We have touched upon some millenarian movements in Chapter 10, particularly nativist ones. If we return briefly to the 'cargo cults', perhaps these serve to clarify such movements. The two most influential books written about this phenomena both appeared in 1957 but offer different interpretations of millenarian movements. Norman Cohn's *The Pursuit of the Millennium* deals with European social movements in the Middle Ages while Peter Worsley's *The Trumpet Shall Sound* deals with modern cargo cults.

Worsley's Marxist approach places millenarian movements reasonably firmly (but not altogether) among the lower social groups. It is a mistake to put all social movements in this category. Christian Science, the Catholic Apostolic Church and the Society of the New Church are clearly middle-class movements (Jones, 1984a) although Worsley states:

It was amongst the lowest strata, particularly amongst the uprooted and disorientated peasants who had been turned into unskilled urban workers or into beggars and unemployed, that millenarian fantasies took strongest root. (Worsley, 1957, p. 224)

Cohn argues that millenarian groups are not confined to the lower strata as there are important upper-class influences which are apparent.

Millenarian movements, Worsley claims, adopt a pacifist stance in societies which display a clear political organisation:

Where millenarism survives in countries with popular secular political organisations, it is generally escapist and quietest. It rarely looks forward to the millenium as an immediate possibility. Even the Jehovah's Witnesses movement, which still looks to an imminent millenium, is a pacifist body. (Ibid., p. 232)

'Cargo' is a pidgin English term to describe the goods brought by, and associated with, white people. 'Cargo cults' (1) believe that the world is about to end in a cataclysm; (2) believe that God or some local prophet will introduce 'heaven on earth'; (3) by ritually imitating the whites, members believe that they will acquire the mysterious spiritual powers that will enable them to obtain the white's 'cargo' or goods. As a consequence of these beliefs the members dress themselves in European clothes, acquire umbrellas or bicycles, and wait for the 'cargo' ship or airoplane to arrive. While such behaviour is regarded as insanity to whites, in that specific economic and cultural setting it makes sense. 'The sudden transition from the society of the ceremonial stone axe to the society of sailing ships and now of airoplanes has not been easy to make.' (Worsley, 1959). Natives at such a low stage of preindustrial society have little or no concept of economic and industrial production. Millenarian movements are essentially religions of the oppressed which are cultural attempts to quench feelings of injustice through magical means, this being the only recourse open to them at the time.

Explaining social movements

There are three broad theories which try to account for the emergence of social movements. These are *psychological* theories, *strain* theories and *resource mobilisation* theory.

Psychological theories

Early theorists such as Le Bon described the so-called characteristics of crowds. The very title of his book, *The Crowd: A Study of the Popular Mind*, suggests that he believed 'an agglomeration of men presents new characteristics very different from those of the individuals composing it.' Individuals as individuals cease to exist; he says, 'their conscious personality vanishes.' In its place we have *group*, or *collective mind*. The crowd becomes 'a new body possessing properties quite different from those of the bodies that have served to form it.' Unconscious impulses come to the fore once a crowd is formed. Individuals sense the power they acquire as members and become, he says, hypnotised.

Moreover, by the very fact that he forms part of an organised crowd, a man descends several rungs in the ladder of civilisation. Isolated, he may be a

Photograph by Paul Alberts

cultivated individual: in a crowd he is a barbarian—that is a creature acting by instinct. He possesses the spontaneity, the violence, the ferocity, and also the enthusiasm and heroism of primitive beings . . . an individual in a crowd is a grain of sand amid other grains of sand, which the wind stirs up at will.
(Le Bon, 1938, p. 36)

McDougall held a view of the crowd very similar to Le Bon's that it was a phenomenon displaying coarse emotions while Freud described the group ideal as the 'primal father', governing the 'ego'. Another psychological perspective is offered by Allport, who added a dimension of *facilitation* (how emotion spreads). Most theories of this type see certain individuals as more drawn to crowd behaviour, and perhaps suffering from a defective personality. Such individuals display psychological needs which are fulfilled on joining a crowd.

A recent object of sociological study is the phenomenon of the football crowd. (Dunning, Murphy, and Williams, 1988). One of the dominant myths is that football violence is a post-war phenomenon. This is not the case, however, as it originated at the same time as the game itself, at the end of the nineteenth century. The newspapers and television are amplifiers of violence in the sense that they exaggerate crowd behaviour.

Psychological theories do not explain why people with personality defects join one group rather than another, why some movements are highly successful and others not, and do not discuss the possibility of societal deficit.

Strain theories Smelser, among others, was one of the first to suggest that social movements are organised responses to certain 'strains'. Such strains can be varied. A slightly different approach is taken by those who regard people's feelings of *deprivation* as the source of social movements. Deprivation can be absolute (such as the total economic deprivation displayed by most millenarian groups) or relative (because some individuals possess less of something than others in society). Although these theories are sociological rather than psychological, they also fail to explain fully such a complex phenomenon. All societies at one time or another are subject to strain and yet this does not inevitably result in the emergence of social movements. Homosexuals have been subjected to strain since time began and yet Gay Liberation is a very recent phenomenon.

Resource- McCarthy and Zald (1973, 1977) have argued that although strains of
mobilisation theory all kinds might well exist in society, social movements will not arise unless people organise their available resources for some kind of action. Resources can include anything from money to guns. People external to the potential movement play an important part in its formulation. A clear example are professional political organisers or advisers who mobilise individual discontent into a social movement. Some outsiders are sympathetic to the movement's ideas but do not

themselves become members. Jones (1984a) examines the origins of several social movements.

There are four main types of social movements:

1. *Regressive* movements tend to be conservative. They may be groups such as the Lord's Day Observance Society which are totally opposed to any suggestion of rapid social change.
2. *Reform* movements are on the whole satisfied but would like to see some form of selective change in certain areas. Ecological groups such as *Save the Whale* are examples of this category.
3. *Revolutionary* movements display a complete dissatisfaction with the existing social order and wish to overthrow it by either peaceful or violent means. An example was the Russian Revolution in 1917.
4. *Utopian* movements seek to establish a new order. Many contemporary religious cults are examples.

SUMMARY

1. Small groups research is important because it is within small groups that many social processes occur, such as socialisation, therapy and so on.
2. Smelser's theory argues that collective behaviour will emerge only if his six conditions are met: structural conduciveness, structural strains, generalised belief, precipitating factors, mobilisation for action, and a failure of social control.
3. Crowd behaviour is important because it is a commonly observed example of collective behaviour.
4. Mobs and panics are further examples of collective behaviour, the former usually being destructive, while the latter is an example of spontaneous behaviour based on fear.
5. Rumours are informally transmitted messages from anonymous sources.
6. Social movements in pre-industrial society generally take the form of millenarian movements, while in western societies they respond to various types of strain inherent in society. Alternatively, they can be viewed as a response to psychological needs, or to individual's mobilisation of certain resources.
7. Social movements often embrace several social movement organisations within them. Social movements may be: regressive, reform, revolutionary or utopian.
8. Social movements possess their own life-cycle: a preliminary stage; popular stage, formal stage, and institutional stage.

IMPORTANT TERMS

conflict model
status consistency
mass hysteria
crowd
millenarian movements
rumour
resource-mobilisation theory
cognitive dissonance
life-cycle

status inconsistency
collective behaviour
social movement
contagion theory
cargo cult
strain theories
relative deprivation
panic

SELF-ASSESSMENT QUESTIONS

1. Compare some familiar groups: a rugby team, a street gang, a jury, a clique, some people trapped in a lift. Which generalisations hold about which groups?
2. Discuss 'communication and power in small groups'.
3. Discuss the strengths and weaknesses of Smelser's theory of collective behaviour.

4. Consider carefully Welles's *War of the Worlds* programme. Could this happen today?
5. Are millenarian movements adequately accounted for or do you think something else in the way of explanation needs adding?
6. South Africa has more religious sects that any other country. Try to account for this in the light of this chapter.

THE SOCIOLOGY OF MEDICINE: AN OVERVIEW

- models of medicine
- sickness and control
- the exploitation of health
- towards a radical sociology of medicine

MODELS OF MEDICINE

Medical practitioners, both western and traditional, espouse systems of medical beliefs and practices. We are most likely to be familiar with western practitioners, generally located in hospitals, clinics and private practice. They are trained in the western scientific discipline although the development of this is far more recent than we might suppose. Traditional systems of medical care include those used by Mexicans (the *curanderismo*), the Azande, the Dobuans, the Chinese and many South Africans, mostly black but sometimes white. Every society seems to utilize some position on the traditional/western continuum. This immediately suggests that illness and disease present a universal threat which is met by a diversity of theories and techniques for coping with them. Western societies view illness and disease as rooted in the scientifically objective world where they can be studied by scientific methods. In traditional societies the perspective is almost wholly magico-religious in which ideas about illness, disease and cure are linked to a religious, magical or superstitious framework. In Southern Africa many societies are in a stage of transition in which both systems exist side by side. In any other parts of the world, also, which are in transition, indigenous and western systems of medicine exist comfortably together. (Elling, 1981). Bomvana children wear a key on a necklace to prevent whooping cough while also having access to modern systems of immunisation (Jansen, 1973). Not only is treatment vastly different but cultural differences in symptom experience also are. Whereas in the west we would, for example, take night sweats as one of the early symptoms of TB 'it is not a sign experienced by the African as a symptom of a certain disease. To him it is a sign of hard labour (mines) or fever. On the contrary pain between the shoulders is a highly emotional sensation and is usually interpreted with the Xhosa-diagnosis of *impundulu*.' (Op. cit., p. 63). The *impundulu* or *izulu* is the lightning bird that lives in the sky and is a symbol of the powerful medicine of the female witch. The *impundulu* is thought to cause the TB patient to cough blood, which is interpreted by the diviner as evidence that the patient has been attacked by the bird. Various lumps on the body would not generally be interpreted as symptoms of cancer although constipation would be regarded with some significance.

Systems of referral also differ:

Western societies	Traditional societies
self diagnosis	first decision-taking stage
self treatment	traditional frustration period
treatment by friends or doctor	second decision-taking stage: western physician

The development of western medicine can be divided into three stages.

CLINIC SCENE FROM THE WORKS OF GALEN
Printed in Venice 1550, Achille Bertarelli Collection, Milan, Italy

The pre-germ era

The pre-germ era lasted until the 1850s and featured a number of theories which embraced the social and physical dimensions of society. The Greeks introduced a number of measures including the building of elaborate aqueducts, dietary control and the regulation of the population by the introduction of infanticide. Even before the Greeks there is evidence of practices such as cauterization and amputation dating back to 5 000 B.C. During the fifth and fourth centuries B.C. the ancient Greeks developed a more systematic approach which was less in the magico-religious tradition. The most famous Greek of this time who was writing about health was Hippocrates, who was of the opinion that 'persons who are naturally very fat are apt to die earlier than those who are slender' and 'use purgative medicines sparingly in acute diseases, and at the commencement, and not without proper circumspection'. (Glendening, 1960). His famous theory of humors postulated four: blood, phlegm, and black and yellow bile. The equilibrium of these four humors meant a healthy body. If one was too little or too much then disease would be apparent. The Hippocratic Oath is a legacy from that time and briefly includes prohibitions concerning the prescribing of fatal drugs, the performance of abortions, the practicing of surgery, sexual intercourse with patients, and divulging personal information obtained in confidence. After a brief contribution by Aristotle, the centre of medicine moved to Alexandria and subsequently to Rome. We describe in Chapter Six the development of medical sects, the major sects to emerge being the *Dogmatists* (who accepted humoral theory), the *Pneumatists* (followers of Erasistratus and his bloodletting techniques), the *Empiricists* ('if it works, use it') the *Methodists* (followers of Asclepiades who emphasised the importance of body pores) and the *Eclectics* (who stole bits from each of the other four theories although they believed that none of them as a whole contained the whole truth). The Romans also established hospitals and a programme of public health and sanitation, including private and public baths and sewers.

The most influential person at this time was Galen who through his anatomical studies of pigs and apes (human dissection was illegal) formulated a number of theories relating to the brain and the sympathetic nervous system. His book *Hygiene* contained the results.

The coming of Christianity meant a decline in the scientific approach which the Greeks has introduced. Primary concerns in the Middle and Dark Ages were spiritual well-being and the soul's salvation: health and hygiene, sanitation and scientific enquiry were disapproved of and taken as a lack of faith in God. Disease and illness, personified in the plagues and pestilences of the time was rife. In the century before the Great Plague of London in 1665 there had been four epidemics. The overcrowding in cities, a result of migration caused by poor harvests, generated the plague bacillus, *Pasteurella pestis*, carried by the rats. The people who escaped were the rich and the well nourished, while the working class and the poor became easy victims.

The Renaissance period was one in which a questioning of the Church's control over society began. It was questioned whether disease was, after all, the will of God, and the 'methodology' was criticised as being blind dogmatism. Absolute control was further challenged by several technological discoveries during the seventeenth century. In physiology, Harvey's description of the circulation of the blood was important, together with the discovery of blood cells, lymph nodes and capillaries. The invention of the microscope opened up further possibilities although at the time little connection was established between these discoveries and patient care and treatment. In the eighteenth century Jenner's smallpox vaccine was discovered and some progress was made in surgery (although this was still carried out without anaesthetic).

The germ era

The germ era began in about 1850, although by 1869 Professor Bennett of Edinburgh thought the concept of 'organic germs' was a 'daft idea'. Lister's formulation of the germ theory stated that germs were the cause of wounds' decomposing, and that germs were all around us.

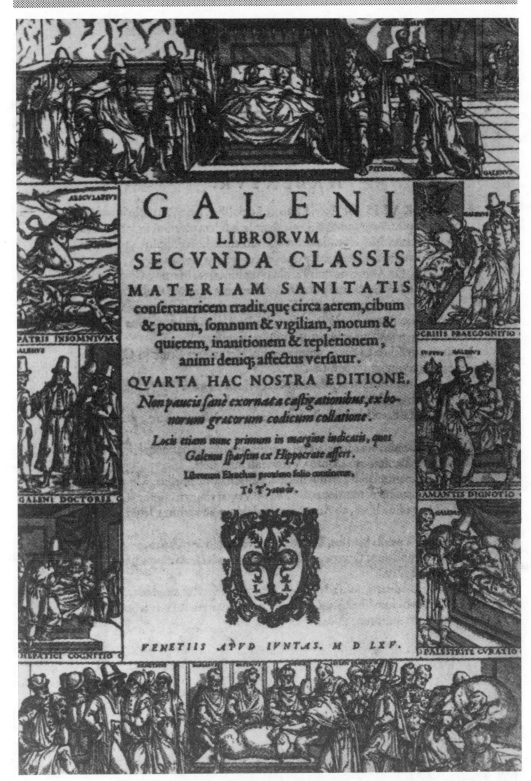

TITLE PAGE OF AN EDITION OF THE WORKS OF GALEN
Printed in Venice 1565. Achille Bertarelli Collection, Milan, Italy

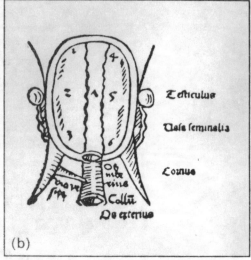

(*a*) The uterus in a ninth-century manuscript, with the 'fundus' or base, the cervix, the neck or vagina (*collam*) and the vaginal mouth (*avificiam*), all roughly labelled. (*b*) A sixteenth century illustration of the uterus copied from the *Anathomia* (1316) of Mondino dei Luzzi. (*c*) The uterus, vagina and external genitalia. (Andreas Vesalius, 1543) (*d*) The female reproductive organs according to Georg Bartisch, 1575, (left) and Scipione Mercurio, 1595, (right).
(*Royal Society of Medicine, London*)

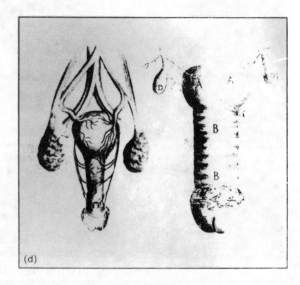

(Youngson, 1978). This was met with ridicule and controversy. By 1879 most surgeons sided with Lister, at least in a half-hearted way. In retrospect Lister's theory can be regarded as the most important single idea in the history of medicine. In effect it meant that medicine could embark on a massive immunization and treatment programme. It also meant that the shift in emphasis was away from the non-biological aspects of illness to the concept of disease. People became very optimistic that all disease could be eradicated. Finally, a new reorganization of medical training was introduced resulting in the beginnings of the modern medical school. (Twaddle and Hessler, 1977).

Another important discovery was that of anaesthetics, which, together with that of asepsis, meant that surgery could begin to make a major contribution to the conquest of health and disease. Descriptions of amputations and major surgery before the discovery of anaesthetics are shocking by today's humane standards:

When asked if he would take chloroform or not, (the patient) made no reply. Professor Syme with a pair of scissors at once cut out the cancer which was situated on the most dependent part of the scrotum. The shouts of the old man were terrific.
(Youngson, 1978, p. 26)

Masectomies were no less horrific:

The technique 'was to lift up the soft tissues by an instrument resembling a bill book, enabling the surgeon to sweep around the mass with his knife, in two clean cuts'. (Ibid.)

The first fatality under chloroform in England, after Simpson's discovery in 1848, was Heather Greener, a healthy girl of 15 who had been admitted for an in-growing toenail. The girl died because she had just eaten a large meal prior to surgery (such was the ignorance of physiology at the time), and furthermore she had literally choked to death on the water and brandy given to revive her.

The post-germ theory

The post germ theory saw the limitations of concentrating the whole of disease in an area in which the causative agent was the germ. The opposition to such a notion came from three areas, all linked more to the social sciences than to anything else. The first was the argument of Dubos, the microbiologist, who argued that health consists of the adaptation of man to his environment. When the environment changes, man is not always able to adapt immediately, (Dubos, 1959). If we believe that ill-health is cause by germs and we have the means to eradicate those germs then it follows that we can eradicate disease. Dubos, however, argued that this was not the case, firstly because some diseases arise from other causes, either genetic, environmental or nutritious. The case of TB is a well known one. Everyone who has tubercule bacilli does not contract TB. Evidence seems to show that one's *nutritional* state is the important factor; this is also the case with measles and whooping cough. Secondly, the growth of modern psy-

chiatry amply demonstrates another dimension other than the existence of germs. Finally, as discussed in Chapter Nine, it was the
emergence of social epidemiology which demonstrated the importance
of socio-economic variables. Ironically, it was the drop in acute illnesses and the concomitant rise in chronic diseases which accelerated
the growth of social epidemiology.

We will turn briefly now to the therapeutic model in the figure. We
discuss these movements at some length in Chapter Six. Suffice it to
mention that there is a wide variation in the kind of healers we
encounter among different cultures. However, all healers utilise four
elements: the symbolic, the technical, theories of disease and illness,
and the social organization of the healing role. Whether we are looking
at the Azande, the Xhosa, the Tswana or Western medicine, these
elements will appear in a particular form.

In the figure below a schematic portrayal is given of five distinct
types of healers, differentiated on the basis of symbol, technique,
theory and organisation. (Twaddle and Hessler, 1977; Jansen, 1973
and Jones, 1986).

TYPES OF HEALERS

	WESTERN HEALERS	SPIRITUAL HEALERS	CURANDERISMO	NATIVE-AMERICAN	XHOSA HEALERS
SYMBOL	stethoscope white coat Latin terms	religious trappings prayer	magical symbols wax figurines	pipe tobacco rattles	witchdoctor costumes bones
TECHNIQUES	surgery medicines	laying on of hands (gently or roughly)	foods and herbs body manipulations	use of drugs religions & spiritual action	herbal medicine *ixhwele*: sacrifice of cattle *ukuqubula*: to smear with cow-dung
THEORY	biophysical reductionist positivist	spiritual; psychological germ-mechanical; parapsychological; 'God's purpose'	imbalance of heat and cold; diseases of magic and witchcraft	human agency; supernatural agency; natural cases	cosmological balance; vital force; cause = who? not why?; witchcraft and ancestors (diagnostician)
ORGANIZA-TION	solo practitioners; fee-for-service; high technology; reliance on paramedical support	solo practitioner; one-to-one or one-to-many (mass healing); financial contribution; electronic medicine	solo practitioners to match the lifestyle of patients; payment in food if no money (i.e. formal payment); cultural congruence between healers and patients	integrative (kin involved); harmony or balance	diviner/and herbalist (healer)

HEALTH

MEDICAL MODEL (WESTERN SCIENTIFIC)		THERAPEUTIC MODEL (FOLK/TRADITIONAL)	
Focus on:		Focus on:	Acupuncture
Pre-germ	disease	patient	Homeopathy
Germ	cure	prevention	Chiropractics
Post-germ	individual	population	Osteopathy
(Biophysical reductionist model: mind/body dualism)			
DISEASE		ILLNESS	

Sickness and control   Social control in the area of medical encounters is a wide area of study covering as it does control and ideology at a macro-level to an analysis of patient–doctor interactions and negotiations as exhibiting control. We will, in this section try to describe some of these settings in which control is raised as a 'hidden' agenda item, covert rather than overt.

Roth's editing of a volume devoted to professional control of health services and the various challenges to such control merits considerable mention and discussion. (Roth, 1980). In Chapter Two we mentioned the trend towards the medicalization of deviance. This requires further explanation. The process is clearly traced in the change from 'badness' to 'sickness', a feature of increased medical control. Health itself, particularly in America, has become an instrument for the exercise of power. Clear examples of this include the legislative power of health inspectors in industry, the banning of cigarette smokers from cinemas, and the manner in which several 'deviant' behaviours, such as homosexuality, child abuse and obesity, have been medicalised. Increasingly, the medical profession seeks to create 'disease by making judgements about the world before them and applying medical categories of meaning that serve then as the bases for treatment and control.' (Schneider and Conrad in Roth, 1980, p. 4).

The fads and foibles of medical knowledge are not confined to the rise and decline of fashionable groups but more pertinently to fashionable 'diseases' and categories of 'illnesses'. Thus tonsilectomies were extremely popular until the early seventies in England and hysterectomies are only just beginning to decline in popularity. Anaemia and low blood sugar are now regarded as popular. The medicalisation of hitherto non-medical elements of our existence is an attempt to not only bring order to chaos but control, also. The problem of whether alcoholism, hypertension and neurasthenia are *diseases* is one froaght with difficulties and disagreements both from within and without the medical profession.
(Jones, 1985, p. 139)

Medical **It** is easier to understand the concept of medical control if we look
categorisation and carefully at just one example of hypertension, using the *pathological*
diagnosis model and the *statistical* model. Health and illness are relative concepts
which vary both between and within societies. However, although there
is probably little controversy as to whether carcinoma, typhoid, cholera
and poliomyelitis are diseases, it is quite debatable as to whether
alcoholism and certain kinds of mental illness are. The crux of the
problem lies in two quite different models of disease, the *pathological*
and the *statistical.* The pathological model of illness is specifically
concerned with organic malfunction 'in which disease syndromes are
defined by biological symptoms that characterise them. The pathological model concentrates on defining the nature of 'abnormal' functioning'. (Mercer, 1972, p. 79) The pathological model emphasises what is
wrong with a person, it is monocausal, and it is heavily biased towards
a biological interpretation. The statistical model 'defines abnormality
in terms of an individual's position on an assumed normal distribution
relative to others in the population being studied . . . by establishing
a statistical norm, the investigator uses the characteristics of the
particular population of people being studied to delineate the boundaries of "normal".' (Ibid.)

Hence inferences can be made from the statistical model to assume
an indication of a pathology which may be underlying without necessarily locating any pathological abnormality whatsoever. A belief that
the statistical model indicates illness implies that the statistically
larger group within society from which the indicators are drawn is in
some way 'better' or more correct than the minority group. If we define
illness in relation to the statistical model this implies that such a
definition is valid solely with reference to the group from which it was
defined (Op. cit., p. 61). Without pathological malfunctioning, deviations from a prescribed norm become an indication of illness or disease.
The implications of the dilemma of illness definition are considerable.
Firstly, what is considered an illness has consequences for the individual both in the way he or she perceives themselves and also how
they are perceived by others. (Denton, 1979, pp. 21–25) Secondly, the
broader the medical definition, the greater the power of the definers.

Kleinman suggested that:

Medical systems employ different explanatory models and idioms to make
sense of disease and give meaning to the individual and social experiences of
illness . . . A given medical system in its socio-cultural context does considerably more than name, classify and respond to illness, however. In a real sense,
it structures the experience of illness and, in part, creates the form the disease
takes.
(Kleinman, 1980, pp. 206–213).

Diagnosis and classification brings order to previously unmanageable
phenomena. Furthermore, diagnostic systems sometimes signal the
commencement of therapeutic control. Kleinman goes on to argue that
any disease, for example hypertension, is in part a cultural construct.

Disease derives much of its form, the way it is expressed, the value it is given, the meaning it possesses, and the therapy appropriate to it in large measure from the governing system of symbolic meanings'. (Op. cit., p. 209). The desire to exert medical control is based on the belief that to control hypertension it is desirable to reduce the raised blood pressure to the level approximating to that of the general population. (Posner, 1977). Unlike diabetes, however, recognisable symptoms do not manifest themselves in an ambiguous form and indeed often not in any recognisable form at all. Markedly elevated pressure is believed to lead directly to a stroke (cerebral haemorrhage, atherothrombotic brain infarction), renal insufficiency, myocardial infarction, and congestive heart failure. If such pressure can be controlled and complications retarded this is deemed the mark of success. Posner's statement about diabetes can equally apply to hypertension:

No direct correlation has been shown between the severity (of the hypertension) and the development of complications, or between the degree of control, and the development of complications. Patients with mild (hypertension) may develop severe complications. Patients who have apparently been 'well controlled' may also develop complications. It is generally admitted there is room for doubt.
(Op. cit., p. 143).

Diagnosis by itself does not necessarily lead to a correct course of action. If the physician believes that a raised arterial blood pressure level has been diagnosed there is no *necessary* prediction possible about the prognosis. A correlation between hypertension and mortality is statistical rather than individual, and high blood pressure itself is not a cause of death or of a person being admitted to hospital (apart from malignant hypertension which is totally different from essential hypertension).

The measurement of hypertension The limited specificity and sensitivity of blood pressure measurements is well documented (Waaler, 1980, pp. 53–58). Basically it is difficult to elicit 'positive response in a truly diseased individual' and there is a 'limited capability of not giving positive response in a truly non-diseased individual'. Essential hypertension is believed by the medical profession to be a *disease* rather than a risk factor despite the fact that it 'is not an either/or phenomenon' (op. cit., p. 53). The definition of hypertension 'depends upon the threshold value selected for classifying a person as hypertensive . . . In the case of hypertension the true positives can only be indirectly estimated by the excess frequency of complications following the elevated blood pressure. Thus we have the unusual and scientifically uneasy situation in which 'actual individuals with the "disease" cannot be identified, but their numbers can be estimated'. (Ibid.)

The question of whether hypertension is a disease is debatable. Pickering (1978, p. 561) has frequently emphasised that blood pressure should be regarded as a measurement exhibiting a wide range, and that an artificial and often arbitrary cut-off division between 'hypertensive' and 'normotensive' should be avoided.

The measurement of hypertension is by no means a simple operation. Factors hindering a true measurement can include the type of instrument used (the mercury manometer is preferable to the aneroid type), the size of the cuff, the heart rate, observer variation, the intrusion of previous knowledge by the person measuring, and the pressure or anxiety state of the subject. Some of these problems have been overcome by automatic pressure recordings and by intra-arterial devices.

What is arterial hypertension? What we described initially as the pathological and statistical models of hypertension can also be described as the epidemiologic and clinical models in which the latter is shown as a curve of distribution giving information about the value of group mean pressure.

One or two standard deviations above the mean can be designated as arterial hypertension based on the statistical evidence stemming from large numbers, with the added advantage that such an approach is quantitative rather than contextual.

One of the weaknesses of this approach cited by Peart is how to fit an individual into the statistics by diagnosing hypertension or whether the individual's condition is due to specific environmental circumstances. In fact, is the pressure raised only when measured and is it not, in fact, a valid measurement? Nevertheless, there is a point which physicians believe (with a great degree of variation and discrepancy) indicates that pressure is too high and will result in a shorter life-span. When to diagnose somebody as having hypertension is problematic in the extreme but it is generally recognised by the majority of physicians that a systolic measurement of above 160 and a diastolic of above 95/100 is to be regarded as hypertensive. (Julius, 1977, p. 83). A recent classification by the National High Blood Pressure Education Programme in the USA suggests that pressures below 160/95 do not require treatment.

Hypertension as a risk factor in cardiovascular disease Cardiovascular diseases account for half the annual death rate, and raised hypertensive rates are most commonly associated with such diseases. The Framingham study in the USA was undertaken in 1949 and dealt with a sample of 5 302 men and women aged between 30 and 62. Those who subsequently developed cardiovascular diseases were found to have a *mean systolic value* of 146mm Hg compared with that of 130 for those who did not. Kannel prefers to call hypertension a pathophysicologic state rather than a disease and emphasises the difficulty of finding a critical value which we can label as hypertension. Further, there is no logical point of distinction between hypertensive and normotensive. There is no doubt that hypertensives are at risk, but 46 % of premature cardiovascular disease arises in that part of the population with modest elevation. The prevalence of hypertension is estimated as 20 % of the adult USA population. In the Framingham study 40 % of male and 48 % of females displayed raised pressure. In the Framingham study 35 % of males previously categorised as hypertensive were borderline hypertensives when measured the following year. Although hypertensives develop more than their share of cardiovascular disease, nevertheless one third of all cardiovascular deaths are normotensive. Hypertension accounts for only one third of the 800 000 deaths from strokes and coronaries, although the downward trend in the USA since 1940 attributed to hypertensive mortality is now attributed to the change in the manner of death certification. Although it is undeniable that hypertension constitutes a grave risk factor in all cardiovascular disease, other factors present have to be taken into account, namely cholesterol concentration, blood glucose, cigarette smoking, ECH-LVH, in order to establish the risk profile and risk is 'proportional to the *height* of the blood pressure' (Kannel, 1977, p. 904).

It has been well documented that there is a wide range of variation in arterial pressure in any individual over a twenty-four hour period, for example during coitus and sleep, and variations occur even within periods of what are described as stable pressure. Thus an essential hypertensive could show a range of variation from 280/140 to 140/60. What, therefore, is the blood pressure of that individual? (Pickering, 1978, p. 590). Physicians believe that there is 'a fundamental difference between hypertension and normotension which is untrue. To use an artifact to interpret data is to commit the most heinous crime known to science' (op. cit., p. 650). In order to accommodate such a belief, the state of *labile* hypertension was invented to account for those who were sometimes above the arbitrary dividing line of 150/90 and sometimes below it. Unfortunately the continuous assessment of blood pressure levels reveals that nearly all normal and benign hypertensives would fall into this category. The deviation from the norm in essential hypertension is a deviation of degree rather than kind and is therefore quantitative. Pickering has this to say about the causes of hypertension:

The raised pressure in essential hypertension is due to genetic and environmental factors. The genetic factor tends to determine the arterial pressure at any age. What is inherited may be a structural or biochemical peculiarity of the vessels which may influence their response to stimuli. As life proceeds, episodes tend to occur which tend to raise or lower blood pressure. These episodes, if prolonged, tend to leave an imprint on the vessels, probably by increasing the size of the media when the pressure is high and diminishing it when it is low.

(Op. cit. p. 605)

When do diseases disappear from the medical lexicon

The clinical-pathological model is a cause–effect parameter which leads us to expect:

bacilli — sputum — TB

whereas a statistical-epidemiologic model would lead us to marshal our facts thus:

raised arterial pressure — probability of a, b, c, d,

arguing from a perceived affect to a probable cause. The first model deals with an *a priori* certainty whereas the latter model presents us with an *a posteriori* probability.

The false criteria of causality in hypertensive diagnosis and treatment

The presence of a quantitative *measurement* over a certain point is categorised as hypertension. However, even within the category of hypertension there is a necessity within the medical profession to break the category down into further sub-categories, thus:

Class	BP Level
Borderline Hypertension	occasional elevation + 160/95
Mild Hypertension	161/101–180/120
Moderate Hypertension	181/121–190/130
Severe Hypertension	191/131
Malignant Hypertension	191/131 (with Papilledema Grade IV)

Further categories such as *labile* hypertension have been created to account for those individuals exhibiting fluctuations in pressure readings above and below the arbitrary dividing line.

Hypertension *per se* is not a *cause* of anything, particularly if we regard it as a quantitative measurement and not as a disease. Large sections of the population live normal and healthy lives despite having elevated pressure and although raised arterial hypertension undoubtedly precedes a very significant number of cardiovascular mortalities, a slightly less significant number of normotensives experience cardiovascular accidents. Nevertheless, there exists an association between raised arterial pressure and a number of clinical features such as (a) an enlarged heart; (b) heart failure; (c) left ventricular failure; (d) coronary artery disease; and (e) stroke (cerebral infarction and cerebral haemorrhage). The jump to asserting a causal relationship between hypertension and associated complications is more problematic. Some might argue that 'only with experimental manipulation of the independent variables is a satisfactory causal inference possible' (Hirschi and Selvin, 1973, p. 133). Undoubtedly there exists an association between raised arterial pressure over a period of time and physical impairment although this is not a *necessary* association. However, some would argue that causality implies a chain of three links, namely, *association, causal order* and *lack of spuriousness* (Kuhn, 1962, Popper, 1959). To establish a causal relationship between hypertension and its associated complications we would have to establish one or more of the following criteria:

1. In order to be a cause of anything a factor has to be a *necessary* condition;

2. In order to be a cause of anything a factor has to be *sufficient* condition;
3. If hypertension is not a *characteristic* of cardiovascular complications it is not a cause of them;
4. *Measurable* variables are not causes.

It may well be that cardiovascular conditions appear to be epidemiologically associated with hypertension but (*a*) not all hypertensives develop such conditions; (*b*) normotensives often develop such cardiovascular conditions; (*c*) the rates of hypertension vary from place to place. To be a necessary condition for cardiovascular conditions, hypertension *must* be present although to be sufficient condition such conditions must invariably follow a consistently raised arterial pressure. We would expect hypertensives to exhibit statistically different characteristics from normotensives in the area of cardiovascular conditions—and indeed a proportion of them do; but it is equally significant that cardiovascular conditions develop in normotensives. Thus if cardiovascular conditions were a significant characteristic of hypertensives only we might be in a position to establish an important connection. But the Framingham study eighteen year follow-up of forty-year-old men showed that the probability per thousand of developing cardiovascular disease within an eight year period was a continuous one so that the higher the systolic measurement the greater the risk factor. On the other hand individuals with low blood pressure also contracted the complications (the variables of cigarette smoking, glucose tolerance and cholesterol level being held constant). Similarly Dublin (1969) et al. wrote: 'The excessive mortality among hypertensives is primarily due to the cardiovascular-renal disease.' Such tables as those of the Actuarial Society of America often include under blood pressure readings, mortality from *all* causes and not simply those from cardiovascular renal disease which alone bears relation to arterial pressure.

Many studies, too, are perhaps utilising unvarying variables where it is difficult to establish a causal factor. Again, an important intervening factor often neglected is the *meaning* of the arterial measurement to both the measurer and the measured. In recent analyses there has been a tendency to move away from measurable variables to more vague causal agents such as 'stress' and 'assimilation' which are not *non-falsifiable*. Clearly, then, the causal connection between a raised arterial pressure and causal connection between a raised arterial pressure and cardiovascular complications requires much more analysis than it is at present receiving.

Conclusion The pathological-clinical model and the statistical-epidemiologic are two entirely different ways of approaching the problem of hypertension, the former being individual, monocausal and biological while the latter is concerned with the normative distribution in a population. The statistical-epidemiologic model is group related and hence falls into the trap of deducing evidence from the group related to an individual.

Another name for this error is the Ecological Fallacy. Physicians have long entertained a number of beliefs concerning hypertension, confusing what has emerged as a continuous and quantitative *measurement* with an illness or disease. Such beliefs have drastically altered over the years but nevertheless they represent an effort to control areas of social and physical phenomena, in other words to *medicalise* all human experience. The area of hypertension is itself full of practical difficulties such as how to measure it, how to define it, how large a risk factor it is, and whether it is causally connected with cardiovascular accidents. All in all the beliefs entertained in a non-uniform fashion by physicians in relation to hypertension exhibit the same fads and foibles as they extend to other areas of the sick domain.

The history of medical control

The history of medicine in recent times has all too clearly to be seen as an over-eagerness to control non-medical aspects of human behaviour. Two further examples are those of masturbation and child abuse, the former, as we detail below, having a historical pattern, while the latter is a contemporary phenomena which illustrates the *amplification* of deviance. (Deviance is dealt with in Chapter Two). However, the contours of medical control are shaped, according to Schneider and Conrad (1980) by a number of factors which include (*a*) inter-professional debates; (*b*) inter-professional contests; (*c*) legislative politics. Thus the medical profession often *debate* about the nature of something such as mental illness, for example, as in the struggle between psychiatrists and psychoanalysts over the nature of mental disorder. The *contests* are often between social workers and physicians, for example in the case of child abuse. Legislative procedures are highlighted by the history of morphine, which was originally used as a patent medicine additive and a pain killer, and became a cause of addiction warranting legalised procedures. Similarly, heroin was first introduced as a non-addictive cure for morphine addiction! Two further stages in the medicalisation of deviance include lay challenges (for example militant homosexual groups and the rise of lay controlled ex-mental patient groups and alcohol-problem groups) and court cases in which 'the final judgements about ownership and control of 'illness' and 'disease' are made' (Jones, 1984).

As late as 1925 Professor Henry Corby, Professor of obstetrics and gynaecology at University College, Cork, Ireland, gave a warning about birth control methods:

the land will be encumbered by a weakly, degenerated race of neurasthenics and hypochondriacs, not a small percentage of whom will drift into lunatic asylums where, poor creatures, they will be in the midst of their fellow masturbators.

Dr Corby may have been rather late in expressing his views but he was not the last in a long line of those opposed to the practice. In both the eighteenth and particularly in the nineteenth century masturbation (procuring sexual excitement by manual or other stimulation of the genital organs) was viewed as a real disease. In the twentieth century, of course, many other types of behaviour are now classified as *disease*, including alcoholism and mental illness. The origin of masturbation as a disease began in Holland in 1770 when a very successful book was published with the title *Onania*. However, many centuries before that the Greek philosopher Hippocrates, the father of modern medicine, had actually associated masturbation with the occurrence of gout! In 1758 a Frenchman named Tissot published a book which stated that the loss of one ounce of seminal fluid was equal to the loss of 40 ounces of blood. It gradually became widely held by both the medical fraternity and the general public that masturbation was associated with very debilitating consequences such as physical and mental illnesses. It does not appear to have been considered that sexual intercourse had the same debilitating consequences, presumably because masturbation was against nature and consequently regarded as *unnatural*.

It was not long before the medical establishment had 'shown' beyond any doubt that such a morally reprehensive practice was also the cause of indigestion, constrictions of the urethra, epilepsy, blindness, fear of heights, deafness, ricketts and conjunctivitis. Excessive masturbation among females led to nymphomania, and this was regarded as more common among blondes than brunettes. It was further demonstrated that terrible changes in the external genitalia were to be attributed to the practice. Chronic practitioners developed enlargement of the external veins of the hands and feet, moist and variably clammy hands, stooped shoulders, a 'draggy' gait, acne, and a pale, sallow face with heavy dark circles round the eyes. It led, also, to tuberculosis and insanity. It is not surprising that towards the end of the 19th century, hospital records began to indicate that masturbation was given as a cause of death. There followed a number of attempts to classify the 'illness', and as late as 1933 it remained classified as a *functional disturbance*. The practice, in both male and female, resulted in 'constitutional shock' which seriously affected normal development. Sigmund Freud also wrote that the practice caused neurasthenia and a general malfunctioning of the nervous system.

Three main theories emerged which viewed masturbation as (1) producing disordered nerve/tone due to excess or unnatural sexual excitement. Such overexcitement led to serious physical alterations in the patient. (2) The guilt and anxiety of performing such an unnatural act produced or caused various signs and symptoms. (3) A few regarded the consequences of masturbation as merely a reaction or response of an individual in a culture which condemned the activity.

The cures very soon followed the creation of this new 'disease'. These were many and ranged from a number of restraining devices such as 'penis shields' and infibulation, or placing a ring in the prepuce so as to make the practice painful. Circumcision was advocated as were acid burns and, to make it unattractive to women, removal of the clitoris. The British surgeon Baker Brown, preferred the scissors to the knife. As far as women were concerned clitoridectomy prevented, and

THE GUARDIAN, 9 AUGUST 1988

MILLIONS DIE 'FOR LACK OF VACCINE'

MORE THAN 3.5 million children died last year because they 'didn't have 50 cents worth of vaccine in their veins,' Dr James Grant, executive director of the United Nations children's fund UNICEF, said yesterday.

He told the World Conference on Medical Education in Edinburgh that every day 50 000 people—two-thirds of them children under five—die prematurely from readily preventable causes.

Measles still kills two million a year, tetanus one million, and whooping cough 600 000, he said. Polio kills 50 000 and cripples hundreds of thousands more. Many more are killed by diphtheria and tuberculosis.

'Almost without exception, the major health threats of today can be most effectively combated by changes in human knowledge and behaviour. The toll they take among children could be at least halved by empowering people with what is already known,' Dr Grant told the conference, which aims to shift doctors' training away from high technology to using knowledge already available.

He was sceptical about the willingness of medical schools to change. In most, less than 1 per cent of medical education was devoted to topics such as community health and widescale health education.

'Is that what the corporate medical community has decided—that medical education does not include health education as a significant concern?' he asked.

The newly appointed director general of the World Health Organisation, Dr Hiroshi Nakajima, told 120 senior health experts from all over the world: 'Technological excellence must not be an end in itself for the medical profession.

'I recall too well situations in some countries where even highly qualified nurses were not allowed to give intramuscular injections. Sad to say, the only reason for this seemed to have been that there was a fee paid to the person injecting.'

At a joint press conference afterwards Dr Nakajima and Dr Grant pointed out that four million children a year are still dying from diarrhoea—much of which could have been prevented in the first place.

Holding up a packet of oral rehydration powder, Dr Grant stressed that such effective treatment cost 'a few pence.' Yet is was not 'embraced by the majority of doctors of hospitals in many countries.' It was seen as 'poor man's treatment' and in some cases also cured, such ailments as sterility, hysteria, dysmenorrhea, idiocy and insanity. A drastic cure for males was castration, which was administered liberally with ostensibly advantageous consequences. Alternatively drastic measures included needles inserted into the prostrate through the perineum and the insertion of electrodes into the bladder and rectum. More 'enlightened' cures were found in strict dietary regimes, acquiring mistresses or frequenting prostitutes. Tonics and cold baths were frequently recommended as were injections with opium.

To conclude, masturbation was regarded by the medical fraternity as a disease, which would certainly not be the case today. Yet in many ways it represented a *moral* attitude; it became for a time socially respectable to label it a disease. Another example from the same period was a disease found solely in the Southern states of America, *drapetomania*, a disease peculiar to blacks, which caused them to run away. Contemporary diseases are alcoholism, mental illness and child abuse. Many diseases come and go. Masturbation was certainly *not* a disease yet many barbaric 'cures' were inflicted on the 'sufferers'. Perhaps the painful lesson that history can teach us is that we should regard certain behaviour in society, not as illness or disease, but merely as different, unusual, or disapproved of by the Grundys of this world.

Control within the profession Extensive control is exercised by the medical profession upon itself with its division of labour within its realm of professional expertise (De Santis, in Roth, 1980). De Santis reviewed perceptions from within the profession, concentrating on four medical specialities: allergy, cardiology, dermatology, and pathology. The aim was to extend Friedson's argument (1970) that the medical profession was 'medically dominant' by suggesting that 'the profession is composed of groups of physicians whose claims to occupational expertise and demands for control are limited to specific realms. More importantly . . . these realms are not considered equal. The logical extensions of this argument would suggest that internal differentiations in power have an effect on the ultimate definition of the entire occupational realm claimed by medicine.' Weber's analysis of class was multidimensional because he breaks the concept down into *wealth* (economic status), *power* (political status) and *prestige* (social status). Several studies (Shortell, 1974) have shown that even within the medical and allied health professions there are profound differences in prestige. Medical control appears to be more a result of the politics of professional competition than the power of consensus. Specialists represent the top of the hierarchy.

At the level of micro-analysis a visit to a doctor can be viewed as a control or power situation (Amir, in Roth, op. cit.). Amir saw a simple visit as entailing several component parts 'of negotiating access through claiming procedures; waiting; being served; and exiting.' Again, the use of the medical model in doctor–patient interaction, i.e. Western medicine's monopoly of diagnosis and prescription, displays a power situation. The medical profession exercises a tightly controlled monopoly to assault the human body (Danzinger, in Roth, op. cit.). Challenges to the reign of the medical model by patient–doctor negotiation or a growth in patients' rights, would constitute a threat to medical monopoly. The existence of both lay and professional knowledge (Yedidia, in Roth, op. cit.) simply indicates, again, a situation where there exists competition and is a demonstration of the struggle for power. A history of civilisation has shown us that those who have the knowledge, exercise control (Jones, 1975, in Richardson and Houghton). Over the last hundred years 'physicians have secured a monopoly over access to and application of medical knowledge. The historical process . . . (is as follows):

1. Institutionalisation of the knowledge within the curriculum of the university.
2. Control over access to the knowledge through the regulation of medical education.
3. Limitation, curtailment, or cooptation of competing bodies of knowledge culminating in ultimate control over the right to apply medical knowledge through licensure (Yedidia, op. cit., p. 373). Illich goes as far as to say that 'as soon as medical effectiveness is assessed in ordinary language, it immediately appears that the most effective diagnosis and treatment do not go beyond the understanding that any layman can develop' (1977, p. 177).

Control in the doctor–patient relationship

Alexander (1981) shows how physicians rely on peers and colleagues mainly for critical feedback. Some without strong peer affiliation rely on patient response. Roth (1963) showed in his study of TB patients in a tuberculosis hospital how patients and staff manipulated each other. Others (Susser, Watson, and Hopper, 1985, p. 141) have shown that at the social level, medicine enters into the area of social control, e.g. in the issuing of a sickness certificate.

The situated encounters of doctors and patients display a variety of techniques in which, generally speaking, power and control is exercised by the former towards the latter. The doctor–patient bargaining process is essentially one of negotiation. In hospitals patients are managed, essentially, by the routinization of care. We discuss this aspect in more detail in Chapter Three. When patient care is put mainly into the hands of the patient, as in the case of home dialysis (Gallagher, in Jaco, 1979) a large measure of control also passes from the doctor to the patient.

THE EXPLOITATION OF HEALTH

It is becoming increasingly obvious that many diseases have their origin in society; they are socially 'caused'. This view is popular with a number of medical sociologists in Europe and America. In South Africa, also, a number of social scientists see such areas as the inequalities of health care, the extreme differentials of disease and mortality rates, and many other areas not as a law of nature or as being meant to be, but as being the direct or indirect result of social organisation which can be remedied only by a fundamental social change. A clear example is that of accidents at work. The idea of accident proneness originated about 1900. Originally this notion was statistically proved to have a scientific basis. In other words it was believed, and later scientifically demonstrated that some workers were predisposed, perhaps by some physical characteristic such as clumsiness, to be liable to have more accidents than other co-workers. Subsequent examination of the statistics has shown a number of methodological errors and a lack of knowledge of how the worker interacts with the socio-technical work environment, (Sass and Crook, 1981). Another study, (MacQueen, 1961) showed that home accidents were not random nor unexplainable but happened much more frequently to certain people on certain days of the week and at particular times of the year.

The major radical criticisms of Waitzkin and Waterman, Doyal, Krause, Waitzkin and Navarro, to mention but a few, offer a critical Marxist perspective. They argue that much medical sociology does not offer an analysis within the political economy nor does it explain differential access to health care facilities. Two major distortions require removal, namely the distortions of medicine and the distortions of capitalism (Mills, 1988). As Waitzkin argues, 'one strength of Marxist explanation is an analysis of the linkages between the health system and the broader political, economic, and social systems of society' (Waitzkin, 1981, p. 5). Such a view assumes that social reality contains structural contradictions such as social class whereby wealth and power are amassed by a few at the expense of others. Furthermore social problems occur in the context of whole societies rather than parts of societies. Problems such as infant mortality should be analysed in the context of the social structures of the entire society. Two further perspectives colour the radical approach, namely conflict and exploitation.

Health is viewed as inexorably tied to the social and economic organisation of society. The radical approach is attacking a number of basic assumptions which most of us either hold or did hold. Firstly, most people take it for granted that what determines health and illness is mostly of a biological nature. The 'cure' lies almost entirely within the framework of modern medicine. Secondly, because medicine defines itself as a natural science, the doctor/patient relationship is analogous to the relationship between the scientist and the object of study; that is, it is assumed that the doctor can *distance* him/herself in the same manner as the natural scientist distances him/herself from the subject matter. Consequently, social and economic considerations do not intrude on medicine. Lastly, it is assumed that scientific medicine is the sole mediator between disease and people (Doyal, 1979, pp. 12–13). The radicalists are at pains to refute these assumptions. Safety in the workplace, for example, implies an increased cost of production and, consequently, decreased profits. (Waitzkin, 1983).

Examples of a need for protection in the workplace include plastics workers who may contract liver cancer, and asbestos workers, who are exposed to lung disease and cancer, chronic back injuries experienced by farmworkers, and mercury poisoning and brain disease (Waitzkin, 1983).

Illich's approach (1975) is slightly different because he places what he regards as the bad effects of medicine within industrial technology and bureaucracy. He uses the term *iatrogenic* (literally 'an action that produces physicians') to denote the health damage produced by doctors and health systems generally. He means by *clinical iatrogenesis* the physical damage caused by doctors in their attempts to cure people, such as unnecessary operations and harmful drugs; *social iatrogenesis* is the belief many people entertain that medical care is the solution to all their problems; and *structural iatrogenesis* occurs when the patient's autonomy is threatened and his/her individual responsibility is expropriated. Illich is one of a number of people who is concerned with what they see as the over-medicalization of life. We have discussed elsewhere how aspects of behaviour such as excessive drinking, homosexuality and other aspects are taken over by the medical 'umbrella'. Illich's main attack is directed against such increasing political and social control by the medical profession.

The historical development of this radical approach began with Engels' *The Condition of the Working Class in England*, originally published in 1845, in which he traced tuberculosis, typhus and typhoid to malnutrition, unsafe water, overcrowding and inadequate housing. Engels' contribution was followed by Virchow's work which viewed the origins of ill health as residing in social problems. (Virchow, in Waitzkin and Waterman, 1987).

The *engineering* approach, in which separate parts of the human body can be understood very well indeed both in relationship to other organs and to themselves, has a number of serious drawbacks, not least of which is the decreasing emphasis on people and an increasing emphasis on disease. The *ecological* approach emphasises the total environment, 'the other organs of the body, the patient's feelings and experience, and the social, psychological and physical environment. Disease is seen as a misbalance, and as a breakdown in the complex and ongoing relations that exist between human beings and their environment' (Tuckett, 1976, pp. 382–385).

A pioneer exponent of the ecological view is Dubos (1965) who attributed major diseases such as tuberculosis to minute biochemical changes occuring in the human body. The emergence of the industrial age brought with it large scale stresses which altered the usual relationship of bacillus to the human organism. This view takes a similar line to that of McKeown and Powles. (In: Mills, 1988). McKeown (1971), whose work is discussed elsewhere, demonstrated that the fall in infectious diseases at the end of the nineteenth century was due more to increased standards of living, hygiene and nutrition, than to any immunisation programmes that were introduced. Powles (1973) divides history into hunter-gathering, agricultural and industrial periods. He believes, also, that the ecology is the important factor, particularly for the provision of food, sanitary control and the regulation of births. Navarro (1976) and Waitzkin (1983) tie the evils of medicine, illness and disease firmly together with the evils of capitalism.

The basic weaknesses with the above approach lie in the fact that they are too theoretical and lack any empirical support. They are criticised by Figlio (1979) as being too *utopian*. Although basically similar, the ecological exponents also differ as to whether they are liberal, humanist, Marxist or humanist-cum-radical. Within the South African context De Beer's book, *The South African Disease: Apartheid, Health and Health Services*, offers a similar view in which he places health firmly in the context of development. Tuberculosis and polio, for example, are linked firmly to the economic programmes of South Africa. These economic programmes also have an effect on homeland health services (Savage, 1980).

Waitzkin's position, as a Marxist, is that it is doubtful whether any major improvements in the health system can occur without fundamental changes in the order of society (Waitzkin, 1980). One of the major contradictions is summarized by the phrase 'diminishing returns, escalating costs', by which is meant that countries are paying *more* for less (health) service. This contradiction takes place not only in countries whose economy is characterised by monopoly capitalism (increased concentrations of large multi-national conglomerates of corporations, e.g. drug companies which control world distribution) but also in 'mixed' capitalist systems (some industries are nationalised and others are not, e.g. as in Britain) (Baran and Sweezy, 1966; and Edwards, Reich and Weisskopf, 1978). Powles (1973) has clearly shown that the decline in infant mortality and the increase in life expectancy appear to have little to do with the advancement of modern medicine, despite the dramatic increase in health expenditure. The work we have mentioned earlier in this section shows 'that with a few exceptions the technical advances of modern medicine have not led to major improvements in measures of health, illness, life expectancy, or death (Powles, 1973, p. 334). The health of large populations is, in fact, apparently more closely related to 'broad changes in society, including socio-economic development, better sanitation, other invironmental conditions, and nutrition' (Waitzkin, op. cit.). Both McKeown (1976) and Kass (1971) showed that major declines in mortality *preceded* the particular treatments of modern medicine. Thus the decline had already begun long before either identification and treatment in the case of respiratory tuberculosis, bronchitis, pneumonia and influenza, whooping cough, measles, diptheria and scarlet fever.

This decline in the rate of certain disorders, correlated roughly with improving socio-economic circumstances, is merely the most important happening in the history of the health of man, yet we have only the vaguest and most general notion of how it happened and by what mechanisms socio-economic improve-

ment and decreased rates of certain diseases run in parallel.
(Kass, 1971, p. 111)

Obviously, this is not to suggest that the decline of infectious diseases
has not accelerated. 'The point is that the most impressive improvements in these diseases have not occurred because of modern medicine' (Waitzkin, op. cit., p. 336).

Access to the medical profession is stringently controlled. Those
recruited to the occupation are, in most countries, more likely to be
male than female, to have come from professional and upper-class
backgrounds, and to have been educated at a private school. In most
countries, also, medicine enjoys the highest prestige of all the professions and is the most economically rewarding. (See Chapter 3). Especially in countries which do not operate a National Health Service the
price of medical services can rise dramatically. Because the number of
doctors is limited there is not what economists would term a healthy
competition. Referrals, consultancies, laboratory tests and X-rays, for
example, are instrumental in raising the cost of medical care although
not always essential.

Another factor in raising costs is the *medical industrial complex.* In
all capitalist countries the profits from the pharmaceutical industries
are enormous. Hospital suppliers and private hospital and nursing
homes are also extremely lucrative. In America 'two undeniable components of increasing costs, however, are the profits going to the health
professionals and private corporations' (op. cit., p. 339). Undeniably,
therefore, infectious disease declined mostly because of broad socio-
economic and hygiene conditions. As Cochrane states, this present
century has been a 'straightforward story of the ineffectiveness of
medical therapy historically' when compared to the 'layman's uncritical
belief in the ability of the medical professional at least to help if not to
cure.' (Cochrane, 1972, p. 8)

Waitzkin's second contradiction focusses on the twentieth century
shift away from *caring* to *curing* (Powles, 1973; Illich, 1976). The most
common diseases of civilzation have, on the whole, no known cure.
Thus hypertension, heart, lung and kidney diseases, for example, are
all chronic diseases for which the 'engineering' approach is inappropriate. Many of these chronic diseases, moreover, are stress related,
either occupational or economic stress. There is little evidence to show
that coronary care units are as effective so as to justify their cost, nor
that there is an effective treatment for most cancers. (Illich, 1976,
pp. 33–34). Yet the capital costs of treatment for both these diseases
far outweighs expenditure for primary health care costs in most
countries, or for that matter preventative programmes.

Waitzkin's third area of contradiction lies in the health system's
tendency to concentrate resources, resulting in maldistribution. He
distinguishes between geographical or *horizontal maldistribution.* Thus
in most capitalist countries medical facilities tend to be concentrated
in certain areas rather than others, and even within areas the tendency

is to concentrate resources and manpower within urban rather than rural areas. This is certainly the case with capital investment. Thus in South Africa, Britain and America, capital intensive investment will follow a distinctive pattern of maldistribution, with the more geographically attractive urban areas having a much greater investment than the rural areas. The simple measure of doctor–patient ratios will demonstrate this. Another form of maldistribution is called *vertical maldistribution* and is based on *income*. Numerous studies have shown that it is much more difficult for the poorer elements of any population to have access to adequate health care provision. Waitzkin isolates at least two factors in maldistribution and concentration. The first is monopoly capital investment, in the case of *health institutions*, with the trend for finance capital to be concentrated in a smaller number of medical complexes (although these are physically larger units). Secondly, the professional training of doctors and nurses takes place in organisations which emphasise technology which is advanced and specialised. Thus sophisticated diagnostic techniques demanding equally sophisticated apparatus and treatment are encouraged. These are generally found in new urban medical centres. Attempts in Cuba and Russia to rectify such maldistributions include forced assignments to underprivileged areas of the nation or a series of financial inducements to encourage health workers to practice in that area.

The final area of contradiction, according to Waitzkin, lies in the nature of capitalist health and capitalist disease. The very fact of being an industrialised nation creates a multiplicity of diseases associated with various working conditions, such as liver cancer which is often contracted by plastic workers, lung cancer and lung disease amongst asbestos workers, to name just two. Often medical treatment involves 'patching up' the patient in order for them to return to gainful employment, often to conditions which will simply make the disease recur. Certainly in times of unemployment and uncertainty it is well documented that disease increases at an alarming level.

It is generally agreed among medical sociologists, not necessarily adopting the radical political stance of Waitzkin and others, that the economy is vitally important to a nation's health and well-being. Brenner (1980) talking about the period since the mid-nineteenth century says:

. . . probably the single most consistent finding in the epidemiological and demographic literature concerns the inverse relation between socio-economic status and mortality rates. In general, the higher the income, occupational and educational levels of a population, the lower its mortality rate . . . Nor are the socio-economic differentials in mortality confined to deaths caused by infectious diseases, which have been associated with poor nutrition and sanitation and with overall poverty. In the modern era for industrialised nations, infectious diseases no longer represent a substantial risk to mortality, and mortality due to many of the principal chronic diseases constitutes the greatest source of the socio-economic differential. (Brenner, 1980, p. 372)

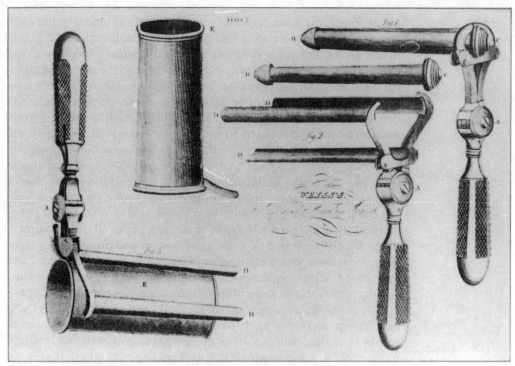

VICTORIAN INSTRUMENTS FOR VAGINAL EXAMINATION.
(Royal Society of Medicine, London)

Social class has an important bearing on health and medicine. Firstly, our occupation, our income and the type of housing in which we live is part and parcel of our socio-economic background. These in turn influence the causes and types of illnesses and our recovery rate. Secondly, life-styles of individuals vary according to which socio-economic category they fall under. The epidemiology of both chronic and acute illnesses identifies intemperate life habits as pathogenic. Such life habits include the immoderate use of alcohol and tobacco, lack of exercise and an overindulgence in food. Life styles can also include contraceptive measures (manual workers and their partners are less likely to plan their families by spacing births) and health seeking behaviour such as visits to clinics. Thirdly, in terms of communication style and the ability to relate to others from a different social class, the manual classes are at a distinct disadvantage when entering the area of negotiation within the health field, as the doctors and nurses are invariably from other social groups.

A lot of work has been carried out on the effect of unemployment and high economic instability and insecurity experienced by lower socio-economic groups (Brenner, 1973 and 1979; Eyer, 1977.) Lower socio-economic groups exhibit a far greater mortality than higher social class groups such as professional workers. This is generally thought to be a consequence of the economic instability and insecurity which produces (a) immoderate and unstable life habits, (b) disruption of basic social networks, and (c) major life stresses. (Brenner, 1980; Jenkins, 1971).

If we return briefly to the radical critique of the pharmaceutical companies this will give us perhaps some perspective as to the dangers that stem from the overmedicalisation of society. Third World countries such as Brazil, Mexico and Thailand offer an enormous variety of drugs, many of them outdated or illegal or duds (Illich, 1976, p. 72). A classic example is the drug Chloromycetin which in the 1960s was manufactured by Parke-Davis long after its toxic effects were known. Thalidomide, with its congenital effects, was only withdrawn following

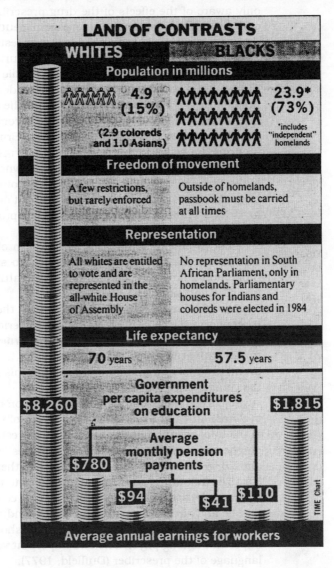

LAND OF CONTRASTS

WHITES	BLACKS
Population in millions	
4.9 (15%)	23.9* (73%)
(2.9 coloreds and 1.0 Asians)	*includes "independent" homelands
Freedom of movement	
A few restrictions, but rarely enforced	Outside of homelands, passbook must be carried at all times
Representation	
All whites are entitled to vote and are represented in the all-white House of Assembly	No representation in South African Parliament, only in homelands. Parliamentary houses for Indians and coloreds were elected in 1984
Life expectancy	
70 years	57.5 years
Government per capita expenditures on education	
$8,260	$1,815
Average monthly pension payments	
$780	$110
Average annual earnings for workers	
$94	$41

TIME Chart

a contracted legal battle. Even when drugs and 'medical devices', such as the RH Robins model of a contraceptive shield, are hazardous in First World countries, they still flourish in Third World countries where there exists no legal requirement to carry any warning as to the possible dangers inherent in the product. The consumption of pharmaceutical products has also risen astronomically in industrialised countries. (Ibid.)

Brodie (1980) attempted an economic analysis of over 2 800 branded ethicals available on the South African market. Such prescribed or recommended drugs exhibit a number of interesting characteristics such as the fact that the person paying for the drug does not order it but is *prescribed* it by a physician. The physician is usually only aware of the effects of the drug prescribed from the advertising and propaganda material of the pharmaceutical companies. Most of the costs involved in producing a new drug (estimated at approximately $55 million) are spent on the pre-manufacturing costs of research and post-manufacturing promotion costs. Brodie's analysis of the South African drug industry found it to be underdeveloped but growing rapidly. Brodie found that all but 13 % of the local industry's requirements were imported. It is therefore a 'secondary industry' in South Africa and South Africa is an 'assembler'. Brodie estimates that some 95 firms are active in S.A. with some 50 firms accounting for 97 % of the market. As one might expect, foreign ownership accounts for 50 % of the firms, with foreign market firms accounting for 86 % of ethical sales. About 24 % of sales revenue is spent on promotion (in America in 1973 $4 500 per doctor was spent on promotion). (Brodie, 1980, p. 394).

Most promotional action is in the form of 'detailmen' or medical representatives whose main function is to sell the products. Other promotional practices include mailed literature and the bestowing of free gifts and samples.

One of the main attacks levelled against the pharmeceutical industry concerns the issue of prescribing by generic (international non-proprietary) names or by brand names. The former entails a cheaper cost to the patient whereas the latter requires the chemist to supply the brand product at a premium price, often this runs from 3 to 15 times the generic price (Illich, op. cit., p. 79).

Folb's estimates put the amount spent on human pharmaceuticals in South Africa at $290 million per year (Folb, 1980). As a percentage of the total spent on health services in any country, the amount spent on pharmaceuticals in developing countries is perhaps between 17 % and 20 % whereas in developed countries the figure is approximately 5 %. The amount of government subsidies to the industry in America, for example, amounts to only about 3 % as compared with 88 % to the missile and aircraft industry and 55 % to industry in general (Op. cit., p. 433). Other South African studies have shown that brand loyalty is important among physicians and important variables are the age and language of the prescriber (Duffield, 1977).

SOUTHERN AFRICA: BASIC DATA

Country	Popula-tion 1985 ('000)	Surface area (km²)	National income per capi-ta 1984 (USA $)	Currency	Capital	Present leaders (1989)
Angola	8 000	1 247 000	$470	Kwanza	Luanda	Pres José dos Santos
Bophutha-tswana	1 300	40 000	$604	Rand	Mmabatho	Pres Lucas Mangope
Botswana	1 100	582 000	$910	Pula	Gaborone	Pres Quett Masire
Ciskei	1 000	8 000	$371	Rand	Bisho	Pres Lennox Sebe
Lesotho	1 500	30 000	$530	Loti	Maseru	King Moshweshwe II Gen Justin Lekhanya
Malawi	7 300	118 000	$210	Kwacha	Lilongwe	Life Pres Kamuzu Banda
Mozam-bique	15 000	802 000	$150	Metical	Maputo	Pres Joaquim Chissano
South Africa	27 722	1 124 000	$2 260	Rand	Pretoria Cape Town	Pres F W de Klerk
SWA/ Namibia	1 100	823 000	$1 470	Rand	Windhoek	Admin-Gen L Pienaar
Swaziland	750	17 000	$800	Lilangeni	Mbabane	King Mswati III
Transkei	1 300	42 000	$384	Rand	Umtata	Pres Tutor Ndamase Pr Min G Matanzima
Venda	450	7 000	$398	Rand	Thohoyan-dou	Pres Patrick Mphephu
Zambia	6 800	753 000	$470	Kwacha	Lusaka	Pres Kenneth Kaunda
Zimbabwe	8 400	391 000	$740	Dollar	Harare	Pres Robert Mugabe
(Copy Africa Institute)						

TOWARDS A RADICAL SOCIOLOGY OF MEDICINE

The 'manufacturers of illness', by which we mean individuals, groups and organisations which, as a by-product, also produce mortality and morbidity, are undeniably with us, as we saw in the previous section. There is sufficient documented research to show how widespread these iatrogenic affects actually are. Radical approaches in medical sociology have isolated most of these factors, either political or economic or both, as intrinsically present in the social structure of society. *Social structures* can be further broken down into (a) the family and its associated networks (b) neighbourhood and community structures, and (c) the broader political-economic spectrum. All these in some way affect the social distribution of pathology and at-risk behaviour (McKinley, 1979). The main 'enemy', particularly in America, appears to be monopoly capitalism, and the quality of health care is increasingly seen to be tied to the manner in which big business operates. Health interventions invariably are too late to do any real good, as in the case of the tobacco industry. McKinley argues that an additional factor is that the manufacturers of illness are more skilled at using social science or behavioural science techniques to 'sell' their products:

> How embarrassingly ineffective are our mass media efforts in the health field (e.g. alcoholism, obesity, drug abuse, safe driving, pollution, etc.) compared with many of the tax-exempt promotional efforts on behalf of the illness-gener-ating activities of large-scale corporations.
> (Op. cit., p. 12)

Individuals in western nations have long ago relinquished any control they might have had over the kind of food that they eat. Instead, private corporations dictate to us the kind of foods that we should eat in order to enhance their profits. Thus in America and Britain, for example, we eat about 25 % less dairy products, vegetables and fruit than a quarter of a century ago. It is estimated that approximately 40 % of U.S. adults are overweight. On the other hand we consume between 70 % and 80 % more sugary snacks and soft drinks. The food corporations, by refining flour, manage to get rid of most of the nutrition it might have contained. Pesticides used to treat food raise the concentrations found in con-sumed food. Such pesticides also find their way to the brain, liver and adipose tissue (Radomski, Deichman and Clizer; in Illich, 1976, p. 229). Furthermore, of the 2 000 additives used by the food industry in America, less than half have been tested for safety (Turner, 1970). One of the major dangers to health is refined sugar of which the average American consumes 126 pounds per year:

> The American sugar mania, which appears to have been deliberately engin-eered, is a major contributor to such 'diseases of civilisation' as diabetes, coronary heart disease, gall bladder illness, and cancer—all the insidious, degenerative conditions which most often afflict people in advanced capitalist societies, but which 'underdeveloped', non-sugar eaters never get . . .

> It seems that the American food industry is mobilising phenomenal resources to advance and bind us to its own conception of food. We are bombarded from childhood with $2 billion worth of deliberately manipulative advertisements each year, most of them urging us to consume, among other things, as much sugar as possible. To highlight the magnitude of the resources involved, one can point to the activity of one well-known beverage company, Coca-Cola, which alone spent $71 million in 1971 to advertise its artificially flavoured sugar-saturated product.
> (McKinley, 1979, p. 17)

Usually society scapegoats certain individuals and groups (more often than not ethnic minorities and the poor) as being *culpable* in some way. By not doing something they *ought* to be doing, or doing something they ought *not* to be doing they are not approximating to the 'accepted' behaviour. Clearly the notion of individual culpability is a powerful one. One often hears individuals and nations assigning blame to the individual because he/she is poor, homosexual, an alcoholic, a thief, or mentally ill, for example. Large state apparatuses are created such as welfare agencies whose function seems to be to regulate the poor (Piven and Cloward, 1971). McKinley (op. cit., pp. 18–19) goes on to stress that three factors must be taken into account. Firstly, that our societies appear to be controlled and operated in such a manner that people must inevitably fail. Often there is no choice that we are unemployed, or become sick. Secondly, even though individuals and groups lack such choice they are still *blamed* for their situation. Mrs Thatcher, the British Prime Minister, was recently reported (*Daily Despatch*, April 15, 1988, p. 12) as saying that support benefits should be provided only in 'genuine' cases and not to be taken for granted by groups such as the unemployed. 'You are not entitled to live off your neighbour if you can earn that same amount yourself. Social security is for people who genuininely cannot find a job or are sick,' said Mrs Thatcher. Thirdly, having identified the 'failures' or those responsible, society introduces welfare services which are a demonstration of how caring the system is. The irony is that it is that very system which 'had a primary role in manufacturing the problems and needs for those services in the first place.'

One of the major concerns expressed by McKinley is that having created an ideology which ascribes culpability to various groups and individuals, society creates a body of health professionals with a mandate to distinguish between good and bad behaviours, the latter open to either removal or alteration. It is quite possible to perceive health intervention as part of a wider pattern of social control or regulation.

If we desire a nonexploitive health system there are certain measures which must be advocated. We must bear in mind that nowadays it is fashionable among social and behavioural scientists in general to regard the health system as incapable of being isolated from the broader social system. Radical critics find it difficult to contemplate a humane health system within a capitalist society. (Waitzkin and Waterman, 1974, pp. 108–116). A number of **recommendations** have been presented as follows:

1. All profits (physicians, pharmaceutical companies, etc.) must be abolished. This can materialise through the nationalization of companies producing drugs and medical equipment. Private health insurance companies should be abolished and individuals made to pay for health care through a progressive taxation structure. Finally, fee-for-service practice should be eliminated.
2. The problem of local versus central bureaucracy resulting in impersonal and alienating professional service has to be surmounted.
3. Medical stratification needs to be broken down. 'The roles of orderly, physician, nurse, and aide—as well as the ancillary service roles like X-ray and laboratory technician, inhalation therapist, and so

forth—should become less differentiated' (Op. cit., p. 115). The resources and personnel available should be equalized throughout the country. In 1971 the population-to-doctor ratios varied in South Africa from 600:1 in Durban (190:1 for whites in Durban) to 40 000:1 for the remainder of the country. The net loss of doctors per year (152 in 1975) makes it difficult to have an adequate number working in primary health care (Wilson, 1980).

4. Legislative intervention. This could include removing the tax-exempt status of advertising, such as we have in America, and the restrictions on certain alcohol and tobacco advertising as we have in Britain. It is necessary to monitor carefully the activities of the *manufacturers of illness*. The American Medical Association has continually exhibited pro-tobacco sentiments 'which have been linked with the acceptance of large research subsidies from the tobacco industry—amounting, according to the industry, to some $18 million dollars.' (Nuehring and Markle, 1974, p. 515). A recent failure by the World Health Organisation to publish the results of a damaging survey on alcoholism has been traced to funding for research from the breweries.

5. The question of lobbying is fraught with difficulties because both the consumer and the manufacturer are involved in political lobbying (McKinley, 1979, pp. 24–25).

6. Public education on health matters should not just be prescriptive, such as what form of personal hygiene to follow, but analytical, in the sense of their being told the whole story. The public, and especially schoolchildren, should be constantly exposed or sensitised to the activities of the drug companies (often in areas totally unconnected to drugs) and the food and drink corporations.

CONCLUSION

Doyal (Doyal and Pennell, 1979, p. 291) states that the crisis facing advanced western countries is not a 'fiscal crisis' but a reflection of 'the obvious and growing contradiction between health and the pursuit of profit under capitalism.' A further part of the crisis are the contradictions inherent in the various types of medical practice which have emerged within capitalist societies. In Britain and America, for example, the emergence of a strong opposition to the crisis has been essentially organised as a defence 'of working class interests through protecting the right to medical care. That is to say, there has been resistance to reductions in medical services, coupled with demands for increased state expenditure on health care and a more equal social distribution of medical resources.' It is obviously very important to conserve existing services and resources but this should not inhibit us from questioning the *value* of existing services or that all medical technologies and procedures are 'good in themselves'. Neither should a desire to conserve existing resources make us ignore the social basis of health and illness. Medical technologies in use at any given time are the result of 'powerful groups in society whose various interests are furthered by the initial development and continued use of such technologies.' (Op. cit., p. 292) Illich (1976) and Doyal and Pennell have alerted us to the efficacy of high technology obstetrics and the dangers of various drugs. We must constantly reappraise current medical practice and question the export of western technologies to underdeveloped nations where it appears to be of little value in alleviating the malnutrition-related mortality from infectious diseases such as tuberculosis, cholera and typhoid. The abolition of scarcity would go some way towards an improved health system but there are many other changes which should be introduced, such as the admission policies of medical and nursing schools, the often antique content of medical education, a limit to the control exercised by doctors within the health system, and many others. 'A socialist health service would not only have to provide equal access to medical care but would also have to address itself seriously to such problems as how to demystify medical knowledge and how to break down barriers of authority and status among health workers themselves and also between workers and consumers.' (Doyal and Pennell, op. cit., p. 294). A more humane system of medical care can be introduced if we cease to adhere to the ideology of 'treating patients'. They are not passive recipients of medical expertise.

SUMMARY

1. Various models of medicine exist, and have historically existed, although the current dominant model is the western medical (scientific) model.

2. In developing countries traditional *and* western scientific models exists side by side.

3. The pre-germ, germ and post-germ stages each heralded new theories and technologies on the origin nature and treatment of disease.

4. The medical model (western scientific) is more often than not at variance with the therapeutic model (folk traditional).

5. Whatever the type of healer he/she tend to utilise symbols, techniques, theory and organisation.

6. Medical encounters can often be seen as an exercise of social control. This is particularly clear in the medicalisation of deviance such as alcoholism and homosexuality.

7. The pathological and statistical models offer differing perspectives, the former emphasising what is *wrong* with a person, while the latter emphasises deviation from a statistical *norm*.

8. Two clear examples of medical control are illustrated by the profession's response to masturbation and hypertension. A micro situation is seen in the visit to the doctor, the certification of being sick and the issuing of the sick note.

9. A number of radical medical sociologists see the origin of illness and disease as lying within the nature of society, and which can only be remedied by fundamental social changes.

10. Many diseases owe their origin to the capitalist system in which profit is maximised.

11. An analysis of the health system in the context of a capitalist society shows that there is a direct correlation between the decline of certain infectious disorders and improved socio-economic circumstances.

12. The manufacturers of illness are not simply limited to the pharmaceutical corporations but include the food, alcohol and tobacco industries.

13. The ideology of *individual culpability* deflects attention away from the social culprits such as the large corporations, inept bureaucracies and governments, etc. and lays blame on individuals and groups who are controlled by an increasing army of welfare and health workers.

14. Radical recommendations include the abolition of profits, a humanising of bureaucracies, legislative interventions, and breaking down of medical stratification.

IMPORTANT TERMS

western practitioners   traditional practitioners
pre-germ, germ and post-germ eras Dogmatists
Pneumatists   Empiricists
Methodists   Eclectics
ecological theory of disease   social control
wealth   power
prestige   situated encounters
monopoly capitalism   structural iatrogenesis
clinical iatrogenesis   social iatrogenesis
engineering approach

SELF-ASSESSMENT QUESTIONS

1. Construct a typology of healers, taking care to itemise symbol, technique, theory and organisation. What similarities and what differences are there to be found?

2. It is often said that technology and theory are inseparably intertwined. Give an account of the pre-germ, germ and post-germ eras paying particular attention to whether medical technologies can only emerge if the theory is already present.

3. Analyse two areas of medicine when viewed as an instrument of social control, e.g. the patient–doctor interaction, an aspect of deviance, etc.

4. How far would you agree that many diseases find their origin within the social structure of society?

5. What does Illich mean by *iatrogenesis*? Explore his three types and comment on the validity of what he is saying.

6. Comment on the findings of Powles, McKeown and Kass that technical advances in modern medicine have not led to major health improvements but rather that these improvements are more closely related to broad socio-economic, sanitary and nutritional changes.

BIBLIOGRAPHY

A

Abercrombie N, Hill S, Turner BS. *Dictionary of Sociology*. Harmondsworth: Penguin Books, 1984.

Adel-Smith B. *A History of the Nursing Profession*. London: Heinemann, 1969

Adel-Smith B. *The Hospitals*. London: Heinemann, 1964.

Alderson M. Relationship between month of birth and month of death in the elderly. *British Journal of Preventative and Social Medicine*. 1975; 29: 151–156.

Aldrich CK. *Some Dynamics of Anticipatory Grief*. In: Schoenberg, et al. 1974.

Alexander L. *The Double-bind between Dialysis Patients and their Health Practitioners*. In: Eisenberg L, Kleinman A. *The Relevance of Social Science for Medicine*. Dordrecht: D Reidel Publishing Company, 1981.

Allende S. *La realidad Medico Social Chilena*. Santiago: Ministry of Social Assistance, 1939.

Allport G, Postman L. *The Basic Psychology of Rumour*. In: MacCoby E, et al. *Readings in Social Psychology*. New York: Holt Rinehart & Winston, 1958.

Alverson H. *Mind in the Heart of Darkness: Value and Self-Identity among the Tswana of Southern Africa*. New Haven: Yale University Press, 1978.

AMA Committee. Osteopathy as viewed by organised medicine. *Journal of the American Medical Association* 1953; 152, 8 and 1961; 178, 2.

Amir D. *The social organisation of a visit to the doctor*. In: Roth J (Ed). *Research in the Sociology of Health Care*. Greenwich, Connecticut: Aijai Press, 1980.

Anderson CA. *The Social Context of Educational Planning*. Paris: UNESCO, 1967.

Anderson OW, Anderson RM. *Patterns of Use of Health Services*. In: Freeman HE et al. *Handbook of Medical Sociology*. Englewood Cliffs, N.J.: Prentice Hall, 1972.

Apple D. How laymen define illness. *Journal of Health and Social Behaviour* 1960; Fall: 219–225.

Argyle M. *Social Interaction*. London: Methuen, 1969.

Aries P. *The reversal of death: changes in attitudes towards death in Western society.* In: Stannard D (Ed). *Death in America.* Pennsylvania: University of Pennsylvania Press, 1978; 134–158.

Aries P. *Western Attitudes towards Death.* Baltimore: John Hopkins University Press, 1974.

Arluke A. *Social control rituals in medicine.* In: Dingwall R et al (Eds). *Health Care and Health Knowledge.* London: Croom Helm, 1978; 107–127.

Atkinson M. *Coroners and the categorisation of deaths as suicides.* In: Bell C, Neway H. *Doing Sociological Research.* London: Allen and Unwin, 1977.

Atkinson M. In: Cohen S (Ed). *Coroners' verdicts.* In: *Images of Deviance.* Harmondsworth: Penguin, 1971.

B

Balint M. *The Doctor, His Patient, and the Illness.* London: Tavistock, 1957.

Baly ME. *Professional Responsibility* (2 ed). London: Wiley, 1984.

Baran P, Sweezy P. *Monopoly Capital.* New York: Monthly Review Press, 1966.

Bartley M. Unemployment and health: selection or causation—a false antithesis? *Sociology of Health and Illness* 1988; 10, 1: 41–67.

Baumann B. Diversities in conceptions of health and physical fitness. *Journal of Health and Social Behaviour* 1961; 2 Spring: 39–46.

Beaton GR, Bourne DE. Trends in the distribution of medical manpower in South Africa. *S Afr Med J* 1980; 17 May.

Becker H. *Boys in White.* Chicago: University of Chicago Press, 1963.

Becker M (Ed). *The Health Belief Model and Personal Health Behaviour.* San Francisco: Society for Public Health Education, 1974.

Bell AP, Weinberg MS. *Homosexualities: a Study of Diversity Among Men and Women.* London: Mitchell Beazley, 1978.

Bell D. *The End of Ideology.* Glencoe, Illinois: Free Press, 1960.

Bellack AA, Kliebard HM, Hyman RT, Smith FL. *The Language of the Classroom.* New York: Teachers College Press, 1966.

Benatar SR (Ed). *Ethical and moral issues in contemporary medical practice.* Proceedings of a University of Cape Town Faculty of Medicine Symposium. Cape Town: UCT publication, 1985.

Benjamin H. *The Transsexual Phenomenon.* New York: Julian Press, 1966.

Benoliel JQ. The changing social context for life and death decisions. *Essence* 1978; 5–14.

Berger P, Luckman T. *The Social Construction of Reality.* Allen Lane/Penguin, 1967.

Berger P. *Invitation to Sociology.* Harmondsworth: Penguin, 1967.

Berger P. The sociological study of sectarianism. *Social Research* 1954; 21, 4.

Bernstein B. *Sociology and the Sociology of Education: Some Aspects*. In: *School and Society*. Bletchley: Open University Press, 1971; 95–108.

Bertrand AL. *Basic Sociology*. New York: Appleton Century Crofts, 1967.

Blalock HM. *An Introduction to Social Research*. Englewood Cliffs, New Jersey: Prentice Hall, 1970.

Blauner R. *Alienation and Freedom*. Chicago: University of Chicago Press, 1964.

Blauner R. Death and social structure. *Psychiatry* 1966; 24: 378–394.

Blondel J. *Voters, Parties and Leaders: The Social Fabric of British Politics*. Harmondsworth: Penguin, 1969.

Bloor MJ, Horobin G. *Conflict and Conflict Resolution in Doctor/Patient Interactions*. In: Cox C, Mead A. *A Sociology of Medical Practice*. London: Collier-MacMillan, 1975.

Blum R. Case identification in psychiatric epidemiology: methods and problems. *Millbank Memorial Fund Quarterly* 1962.

Blumer H. *Collective Behaviour*. In: Gittler JB. *Review of Sociology*. New York: Wiley, 1957.

Blumer H. *New Outline of the Principles of Sociology*. Lee AM (Ed). New York: Barnes and Noble, 1951.

Bogden R (Ed). *Being Different: The Autobiography of Jane Fry* (2 ed). New York: Wiley, 1974.

Boronski T. *Knowledge*. New York: Longman.

Bottomore TB. *Classes in Modern Society*. London: George Allen and Unwin, 1965.

Bowers MK, Jackson EN, Knight JA, Le Shan L. *Counselling the Dying*. New York: Jason Aronson, 1976.

Bowles S, Gintis H. *Schooling in Capitalist America*. New York: Basic Books, 1976.

Doyle CM. Difference between patients' and doctors' interpretations of some common medical terms. *British Medical Journal* 1970; 2 May.

Brady J. Marriage is good for health and longevity, studies say. *New York Times* May 7, 1979.

Braverman H. *Labour and Monopoly Capital: The Degredation of Work in the Twentieth Century*. New York: Monthly Review Press, 1974.

Brenner H. *Mental Illness and the Economy*. Cambridge: Harvard University Press, 1973.

Brenner H. Mortality and the national economy. *Lancet* 1979; September 15: 568–573.

Brenner MH. In: Eisenberg and Kleinman. *Importance of the Economy to the Nation's Health*. 1980.

Brodie J. In: Wilson and Westcott. *The Ethical Drug Manufacturing Industry in South Africa.* 1980.

Brown DG. Inversion and homosexuality. *Journal of Orthpsychiatry* 1958; 23: 424–429.

Brown GW. *Schitzophrenia and Social Care.* New York: Oxford University Press, 1966.

Brown R. *Work, Industry and Organisations.* In: Worsley P. (Ed) *The New Introducing Sociology.* Harmondsworth: Penguin, 1987.

Bucher R, Strauss A. Professions in process. *American Journal of Sociology* 1961; 66: 325–334.

Budd S. *The Humanist Societies: the Consequences of a Diffuse Belief System.* In: Wilson BR. (Ed) *Patterns of Sectarianism.* London: Heinemann, 1967.

Bulmer M. *Social Research Ethics.* London: MacMillan, 1982.

Bulmer M. *Sociological Research Methods.* London: MacMillan, 1984.

C

Cantril et al. *The Invasion From Mars.* Princetown, New Jersey: Princetown University Press, 1940.

Carr-Saunders AM. *Professions: Their Organisation and Place in Society.* In: Vollmer H, Mills DL (Eds) *Professionalisation.* Englewood Cliffs, New Jersey: Prentice Hall, 1925/1966.

Cartwright A. *Patients and their Doctors.* London: Routeledge and Kegan Paul, 1967.

Central Advisory Council for Education. *Children and their Primary Schools.* London: (Plowden Report), HMSO, 1967.

Chadwick E (1842). *Report on the Sanitary Condition of the Labouring Population of Great Britain.* Edinburgh: Edinburgh University Press, 1965.

Charmaz K. *The Social Reality of Death.* Reading, Massachusetts: Addison-Wesley Publishing Company, 1980.

Chaska NL. *The nursing profession. A time to speak.* New York: McGraw-Hill, 1983.

Chaves DE, La Rochelle DR. The universality of nursing: a comprehensive framework for practice. *International Nursing Review* 1985; 32 no. 1.

Chinoy E. *Society* (2 ed). New York: Random House, 1967.

Clendening L. (Ed). *Sourcebook of Medical History.* New York: Dover, 1960.

Cochrane AL. *Effectiveness and Efficiency: Random Reflections on Health Care.* London: Nuffield Hospital Trust, 1972.

Cockerham WC. *Medical Sociology.* Englewood Cliffs NJ: Prentice Hall, 1978.

Coe R. *Sociology of Medicine.* New York: McGraw-Hill, 1970.

Cohen S. *Folk Devils and Moral Panics: The Creation of the Mods and the Rockers.* London: Paladin, 1972.

Cohn N. *The Pursuit of the Millennium* (2 ed). London: Harper and Row, 1961.

Cohn N. *The Pursuit of the Millennium.* London: Harper and Row, 1957.

Colclough C, McCarthy S. *The Political Ecomony of Botswana.* Oxford: Oxford University Press, 1980.

Coleman JS. *Report on Equality of Educational Opportunity.* Washington DC: US Government Printing Office, 1966.

Conrad P, Schneider JW. *Deviance and Medicalization: From Badness to Sickness.* St Louis: Mosby, 1980.

Coombs RH, Powers PS. Socialization for death: the physician's role. *Urban Life* 1975; 4: 250–271.

Coser LA, Rosenberg B. *Sociological Theory: a Book of Readings.* Collier-MacMillan, 1976.

Cowell R. *Roberta Cowell's Story.* London: Heinemann, 1954.

Cox C, Mead A (Eds). *A Sociology of Medical Practice.* London: Collier-MacMillan, 1975.

Crane D. *The Sanctity of Social Life: Physician's Treatment of Critically Ill Patients.* New York: Russel Sage Foundation, 1975.

Cressey DR. Changing criminals: the application of the theory of differential association. *American Journal of Sociology* 1955; 61: 116–120.

Cuff EC, Payne G (Eds). *Perspectives in Sociology.* (2 ed). London: Allen and Unwin, 1984.

D

Dahl R. *Dilemmas of Pluralist Democracy.* New Haven: Yale University Press, 1982.

Dank B. *The Homosexual.* In: Goode E, Troiden R. *Sexual Deviance and Sexual Deviants.* New York: William Morrow, 1974.

Danzinger SK. *The Medical Model in Doctor Patient Interaction: the Case of Pregnancy Care.* In: Roth J (Ed). 1980

Davenport TRH. *South Africa: A Modern History.* Toronto and Buffalo: University of Toronto Press, 1977.

Davis F (Ed). *The Nursing Profession.* New York: John Wiley, 1966.

Davis F. Uncertainty in medical prognosis—clinical and functional. *American Journal of Sociology.* 1960; 66: 41–47.

De Beer C. *The South African Disease: Apartheid, Health and Health Services.* Johannesburg: South African Research Service, 1985.

Denton J. *Medical Sociology.* Boston: Houghton Mifflin, 1979.

Department of Health. *A new dispensation: health services in South Africa.* Pretoria: Government Printer, 1986.

Dingwall R. *Aspects of Illness.* London: Martin Robertson, 1976.

Dominian J. *Marital Breakdown.* England: Penguin Books, 1968.

Donahue MP. *Nursing, the finest art.* St Louis: CV Mosby Company, 1985.

Douglas J. *The Social Meanings of Suicide*. London: Routledge & Kegan Paul, 1967.

Douglas JWB. *The Home and the School*. London: MacGibbon and Kee, 1964.

Douglas M. *Natural Symbols*. Harmondsworth: Penguin, 1973.

Doyal L, Pennell I. *The Political Economy of Health*. London: Pluto Press, 1979.

Dublin LI, Lotka AJ, Spiegelman M. *Length of Life, A Study of the Life Table*. (2 ed). New York: Ronald Press, 1969.

Dubos R. 1965. *Man Adapting*. New Haven: Yale University Press, 1965.

Dubos R. *The Mirage of Health*. New York: Mentor, 1959.

Duff RS, Hollingshed AB. *Sickness and Society*. London: Harper and Row, 1968.

Duffield JF. *The Development of a Marketing Policy for Four Ethical Drug Types Based on the Decision Criteria for Medical Practitioners*. Cape Town: Technical Report. Graduate School of Business. University of Cape Town, 1977.

Dumont R, Foss D. *The American View of Death: Acceptance or Denial*. Cambridge, Mass: Schenkman, 1973.

Dunnell K, Cartwright A. *Medicine-Takers, Prescribers, and Hoarders*. London: Routledge and Kegan Paul, 1972.

Dunning P, Murphy P, Williams J. *The Roots of Football Hooliganism: an Historical and Sociological Study*. London: Routledge and Kegan Paul, 1988.

Du Toit DA, Van Staden SJ. *Nursing Sociology*. Pretoria: Academia, 1989.

Du Toit DA. *Die Pasient se Belewenis van die Hospital as 'n Burokrasie*. Johannesburg: Unpublished MA thesis, RAU.

E

Easthope G. *Marginal Healers*. 1985. In: Jones RK. 1985.

Edwards RC, Reich M, Weisskopf TE (Eds). *The Capitalist System*. Englewood Cliffs, New Jersey: Prentice Hall, 1978.

Eisenberg L, Kleinman A. *The Relevance of Social Science for Medicine*. Dordrecht, Holland: D Reidel Publishing Company, 1981.

Elling R (Ed). Traditional and modern medical systems. In: *Social Science and Medicine* 1981; 15a no. 2.

Emerson JP. *Behaviour in Public Places: Sustaining Definitions of Reality in Gynaecological Examinations*. In: Dreitzel HP (Ed). *Recent Sociology*. no. 2. New York: Collier Macmillan, 1970.

Engel G. A unified concept of health and disease. *Health and Disease Prevention in Biology and Medicine* 1960; 3: 450–485.

Engels F. *The Condition of the Working Class in England*. Moscow: Progress Publishers, 1973 (ed).

Epstein C. *Effective interaction in contemporary nursing*. Englewood Cliffs, New Jersey: Prentice-Hall, 1974.

Esposito JE. *The Vanishing Air: the Nader Report on Air Pollution.* New York: Grossman, 1970.

Evans H. *Harlots, Whores and Hookers.* New York: Taplinger, 1979.

Eyer J. Prosperity as a cause of death. *International Journal of Health Services* 1977; 7: 125–150.

F

Fafunwa AB, Aisiku JU (Eds). *Education in Africa.* London: George Allen and Unwin, 1982.

Fallding H. *The Sociology of Religion.* London: McGraw Hill, 1974.

Fanon F. *The Wretched of the Earth.* New York: Grove, 1968.

Farmer M. *The Family.* London: Longman, 1979.

Fatis REL (Ed). *Handbook of Modern Sociology.* Chicago: Rand, 1964.

Feifel H. *The Meaning of Death.* New York: McGraw Hill, 1959.

Festinger L et al. *When Prophecy Fails.* New York: Harper & Row, 1956.

Field D. *The Social Definition of Illness.* In: Tuckett D (Ed). *Medical Sociology.* London: Tavistock, 334-366, 1976.

Figlio K. Sinister medicine? A critique of left approaches to medicine. *Radical Science Journal* 1979; 9: 14–69.

Fiske N. *Gender Dysphoria Syndrome (the how, why and what of a Disease).* In: *Proceedings of the Second Interdisciplinary Symposium on Gender Dysphoria Syndrome.* California: Stanford University Press, 1973.

Fletcher J. The patient's right to die. *Harper's* 1960; 221, 141.

Fletcher R. *The Family and Marriage in Britain.* England: Penguin Books, 1966.

Folb PI. *The Economics of Drug Prescribing.* In: Wilson and Westcott, 1980.

Ford CS, Beach FA. *Patterns of Sexual Behaviour.* London: 1953.

Forster R, Ranum O. *Biology of Man in History.* Baltimore: Johns Hopkins University Press, 1975.

Frankenburg R. *Communities in Britain.* Harmondsworth: 1966.

Frankfort E. *Vaginal Politics.* New York: Quadrangle Books, 1972.

Freidson E (Ed). *The Hospital in Modern Society.* New York: Free Press, 1963.

Freidson E. *Dilemmas in the Doctor/Patient Relationship.* In: Rose AM (Ed). *Human Behaviour and Social Processes.* London: Routledge and Kegan Paul, 1962.

Freidson E. *Profession of Medicine.* New York: Dodd, Mead and Company, 1970.

Freidson E. *Professional Dominance.* Chicago: Aldine, 1970.

Freidson E. Client control and medical practice. *American Journal of Sociology* 1960; 65: 374–382.

Fulton R (Ed). *Death and Identity.* New York: Wiley, 1965.

Fulton R, Fulton J. *Anticipatory Grief: a Psycho-social Aspect of Terminal Care.* In: Schoenberg et al (Eds). 1974.

G

Guide to the Health Act 1977; no. 63 of 1977. Pretoria: Government Printer, 1978.

Gagnon JH, Simon W (Eds) *Sexual Deviance.* New York: Harper and Row, 1967.

Gajdusek DC. *Kuru in the New Guinea Highlands.* In: Spillane JD. *Tropical Neurology.* New York: 376–383. 1973.

Gajdusek DC. Degenerative disease in the central nervous system in New Guinea. *New England Journal of Medicine* 1957; 257: 974–978.

Gallagher EB. *Lines of Reconstruction and Extension in the Parsonian Sociology of Illness.* In: Jaco EC. *Patients, Physicians and Illness.* New York: Free Press, 1979.

Garfinkel H. *Studies in Ethnomethodology.* Englewood Cliffs, N.J.: Prentice Hall Int.

Genest J, Koiw E, Kuchel D. *Hypertension.* New York: McGraw-Hill, 1977.

Gershuny JI, Pahl RE. *Britain in the Decade of the Three Economies.* In: Littler CR (Ed). *The Experience of Work.* Aldershot: Gower, 1985.

Giddens A. *Central Problems in Social Theory: Action, Structure and Contradiction in Social Analysis.* London: McMillan, 1979.

Giddens A. *Sociology.* London: McMillan, 1982.

Ginsberg M. Facts and values. *The Advancement of Science* 1962. 1X.

Glaser BG, Strauss AL. *Awareness of Dying.* Chicago: Aldine Publishing Company, 1965.

Glaser BG, Strauss AL. *Time for Dying.* Chicago: Aldine Publishing Company, 1968.

Glaser WA. *Social Settings and Medical Organisation.* New York: Atherton Press, 1970.

Glendening L (Ed). *Source Book of Medical History.* New York: Dover, 1960.

Goffman E. *Asylums.* Harmondsworth: Penguin Books, 1961.

Goffman E. *Gender Advertisements.* London: MacMillan, 1979.

Goffman E. *Stigma.* Englewood Cliffs, New Jersey: Prentice Hall, 1963.

Goffman E. *The Presentation of the Self in Everyday Life.* Garden City, New York: Doubleday Anchor, 1959.

Goldthrope J, Lockwood D, Bechoffer F, Platt J. *The Affluent Worker in the Class Structure.* Cambridge: Cambridge University Press, 1969.

Goode WJ. *The Family.* Englewood Cliffs, New Jersey: Prentice Hall, 1964.

Goode WJ. Encroachment, charlatanism, and the emerging profession: psychology, medicine and sociology. *American Sociological Review* 1960; 25: 902–914.

Gordon G. *Role Theory and Illness.* New Haven, Conn.: College and University Press, 1966.

Gorer G. *Death, Grief and Mourning.* New York: Doubleday, 1965.

Gramsci A. *Selections from the Prison Notebooks.* New York: International, 1971.

Green RW (Ed). *Protestantism and Capitalism.* Boston: DC Health and Company, 1959.

Greenwood E. Attributes of a profession. *Social Work* 1957; 2, 3: 44–55.

Gregerson E. *Sexual Practices: The Story of Human Sexuality.* London: Mitchell Beazley, 1982.

Gustafson E. The career of the nursing home patient. *Journal of Health and Social Behaviour* 1972; 13 (3): 226–235.

Guthrie D. *A History of Medicine.* London: Thomas Nelson and Sons, 1945.

H

Harris K. *Education and Knowledge: The Structured Misrepresentation of Reality.* Boston: Routledge and Kegan Paul, 1979.

Henslin JM, Briggs MA. *Dramaturgical Desexualisation: The Sociology of the Vaginal Examination.* In: Heslin J (Ed). *Studies in the Sociology of Sex.* New York: Appleton Century Crofts, 1971.

Herberg W. *Protestant—Catholic—Jew.* Garden City, New York: Doubleday & Co., 1955.

Hill M. *A Sociology of Religion.* London: Heinemann, 1973.

Hillery GA. Definitions of community: areas of agreement. *Rural Sociology* 1955; 20: 119.

Hinkle LE, Redmont R, Plummer N, Wolff H. An examination of the relation between symptoms, disability, and serious illness in two homogeneous groups of men and women. *American Journal of Public Health* 1960; 50: 1327–1336.

Hirschi T, Selvin H. *Principles of Survey Research.* Glen: Free Press, 1973.

Hockey, Lisbeth (Ed). *Recent advances in nursing. Current Issues in nursing.* Edinburgh: Churchill Livingstone, 1981.

Holleran C. Nurses as a social force. *International Nursing Review,* 1985; 38: no. 1.

Hopper R. The revolutionary process. *Social Forces* 1950. March: 270–279.

Hughes EC et al. *Twenty Thousand Nurses Tell Their Story.* Philadelphi: JP Lippincott, 1958.

Humphreys L. *Tearoom Trade: Impersonal Sex in Public Places.* Chicago: Aldine, 1970.

I

Illich I. *Limits to Medicine.* Harmondsworth: Penguin Books, 1977.

Illich I. *Medical Nemesis: The Expropriation of Health.* London: Calder and Boyers, 1975.

Inglis B. *A History of Medicine.* London: Weidenfield and Nicholson, 1965.

J

Joint Report WHO and UNICEF to Alma-Ata Conference, September 1978.

Jaco EG (Ed). *Patients, Physicians and Illness.* New York: Free Press, 1970.

Jansen J. *The Doctor Patient Relationship in an African Tribal Society.* Assen: The Netherlands: Van Gorcum & Company BV, 1973.

Jenkins CD. Psychologic and social precursors of coronary disease. *New England Journal of Medicine* 1971; 1 and 2: 284 and 285:6.

Jones P. *Theory and Method in Sociology.* London: University Tutorial Press, 1985.

Jones RK. *A Sociology of Adult Education.* London: Gower Publishing Company Limited, 1985.

Jones RK. *Education in Development.* University of Transkei, Inaugral Lecture (unpublished), 1987.

Jones RK. *Ideological Groups.* Aldershot: Gower Publishing Company Limited, 1984.

Jones RK. *Knowledge as Power.* In: Richardson K, Houghton V. *Recurrent Education.* London: Ward Lock, 1975.

Jones RK. *Sickness and Sectarianism.* Aldershot: Gower Publishing Company Limited, 1985

Jones RK. *Some Sectarian Characteristics of Therapeutic Groups.* In: Wallis R (Ed). *Sectarianism: Analysis of Religious and Non-Religious Sects.* London: Peter Owen.

Jones RK. Alcoholics Anonymous: a new revivalism. *New Society* 1970a.

Jones RK. Sectarian characteristics of Alcoholics Anonymous. *Sociology* 1970b; 4. no. 2.

Jorgensen C. *Christine Jorgensen: a Personal Autobiography.* New York: Basic Books, Inc., 1967.

Julius S. *Borderline Hypertension: Epidemiologic and Clinical Implications.* In: Genest J et al, 1977.

K

Kannel WB. *Importance of hypertension as a major risk factor in cardiovascular disease.* In: Genest J et al, 1977.

Kass EH. Infectious diseases and social change. *Journal of Infectious Diseases* 1971; 123: 110–114.

Katz AH, Bender EI. *The Strength in Us.* New York: New Viewpoints, 1976.

Katz J (Ed). *Experimentation with Human Beings.* New York: Russell Sage Foundation, 1972.

Kelly OE. *Make Today Count.* New York: Delacorte Press (with Randall Becker), 1975.

Kelvin P. *The Basis of Social Behaviour.* London: Holt, Rinehart and Winston, 1970.

Kendall P, Reader GC. *Contributions of Sociology to Medicine.* In: Freeman HE, Levine S, Reeder LG. *Handbook of Medical Sociology.* Englewood Cliffs, New Jersey: Prentice Hall Inc., 1972.

Kerney LG. *The Ministry and a Parents Sharing Group.* In: Schoenberg B et al, 1974.

King I. *Toward a theory for nursing.* New York: John Wiley and Sons, 1981.

Kinnersly P. *The Hazards of Work: How to Fight Them.* London: Pluto Press, 1973.

Kinsey AC et al. *Sexual Behaviour in the Human Female.* Philadelphia: WB Saunders.

Kinsey AC et al. *Sexual Behaviour in the Human Male.* Philadelphia: WB Saunders, 1948.

Klein J. *The Study of Groups.* London: Routledge and Kegan Paul, 1967.

Kleinman A, Sung LH. Why do indigenous practitioners successfully heal?. *Social Science and Medicine* 1976; 138. no. 1.

Kleinman A. *Patients and Healers in the Context of Culture.* Berkeley: University of California Press, 1980.

Kleinman AM. Medicine's symbolic reality: on a central problem in the philosophy of medicine. *Inquiry* 1973; 16: 206–213.

Kogan M, Balle J. Decision making and organisational structure in the British Health Service. In: *Health.* Social Sciences Course Team, Open University. Open University Press, Bletchley, 1972.

Koos EL. *The Health of Regionville.* New York: Columbia University Press, 1954.

Kosa J, Robertson L. *The Social Aspects of Health and Disease.* In: Kosa J, Antonovsky A, Zola I (Eds). *Poverty and Health.* Cambridge, Mass.: Harvard University Press, 1969.

Krause EA. *Power and Illness: the Political Sociology of Health and Medical Care.* New York: Elsevier, 1977.

Kreitman N. The reliability of psychiatric diagnosis. *Journal of Mental Science* 1961; 107: 876–886.

Kron J. Designing a better place to die. *New York* 1976; March 1: 43–49.

Kühbler-Ross E. *On Death and Dying.* New York: MacMillan, 1969.

Kuhn T. *The Structure of Scientific Revolutions.* Chicago: University of Chicago Press, 1962.

Kuper L, Watts H, Davies R. *Durban: A Study in Racial Ecology.* London: 1958.

L

Lacey C. *Hightown Grammar*. Manchester: Manchester University Press, 1970.

Laing RD, Esterson A. *Sanity, Madness and the Family*. London: Tavistock, 1964.

Lancaster J, Lancaster W (Eds). *The nurse as change agent*. St Louis: Mosby, 1982.

Lanternari V. *The Religions of the Oppressed*. New York: Knopf, 1963.

Laslett P. *The World We Have Lost*. London: Metheun, 1965.

Lee AM. *The Outline of the Principles of Sociology*. New York: Barnes and Noble, 1946 (ed).

Lee DT. *Therapeutic Type: Recovery, Inc*. In: Katz and Bender. 1976.

Lee RB. *The Kung San: Men, Women and Work in a foraging Society*. Columbia: Columbia University Press, 1979.

Leiniger M. *Transcultural Nursing*. New York: Wiley, 1978.

Leininger M. *Care: The Essence of Nursing and Health*. New Jersey: Slack, 1984.

Lemert E. *Human Deviance, Social Problems, and Social Control*. Englewood Cliffs, New Jersey: Prentice Hall.

Lenksi G. *The Religious Factor*. New York: Garden City, 1963.

Lerner M. *When, Why and Where People Die*. In: Brim O Jr. et al (Eds). *The Dying Patient*. New York: Russel Sage Foundation, 1970.

Lewin K, Little A, Colclough C. *Adjusting to the 1980s: Taking Stock of Educational Expenditure*. In: *Financing Education Development*. Ottowa: IDRC, 13–38.

Lewis G. *Cultural Influences on Illness Behaviour*. In: Eisenber L, Kleinman A. *The relevance of Social Science to Medicine*. Holland: Reidel Publishing Company, 1981.

Lidtz T. *The Person*. New York: Basic Books, 1968.

Lippitt GL. *Visualising change: Model building and the change process*. La Jolla: Ca University Association, 1983.

Lofland J. *Doomsday Cult*. Englewood Cliffs, New Jersey: Prentice Hall, 1966.

Lofland LH. *The Craft of Dying*. Beverly Hills: Sage, 1978.

Long AF. *Research into Health and Illness*. Aldershot: Gower Publishing Company Limited.

Lorber J. *Good Patients and Problem Patients: Conformity and Deviance in a General Hospital*. In: Jaco EG (Ed). *Patients Physicians and Illness*. New York: Free Press, 1970.

Lusky RA, Ingman SR. The pros and cons and pitfalls of self-help rehabilitation programs. *Social Science and Medicine* 1979; 13: 113–121.

Lynd R, Lynd H. *Middletown in Transition*. New York: Harcourt Brace and Company, 1937.

Lynd R, Lynd H. *Middletown.* New York: Harcourt Brace and Company, 1929.

M

Machanic D. The concept of illness behaviour. *Journal of Chronic Diseases* 1962; 15: 189–194.

MacQueen I. *Home Accidents in Aberdeen.* Edinburgh: Livingstone, 1961.

Macquire J. *Threshold to Nursing.* London: Bell, 1969.

Mannheim K. *Ideology and Utopia.* London: Routledge and Kegan Paul, 1936.

Martin CE. Marital and coital factors in cervical cancer. *American Journal of Public Health* 1967; 57: 803–814.

Marx-Engels. *Selected Works Vol. 1.* Moscow: Progress Publishers, 1933.

Masters W, Johnson V. *Human Sexual Response.* Boston: Little Brown and Company, 1966.

Mauksch HO. *The Organisational Context of Dying.* In: Kühbler-Ross E (Ed). *Death: the Final Stages of Growth.* 7–24. Englewood Cliffs, New Jersey: Prentice Hall, 1975.

Mausner J, Bahn A. *Epidemiology.* Philadelphia: WB Saunders and Company, 1974.

McCarthy JD, Zald MN. *The Trend of Social Movements in America: Professionalisation and Resource Mobilisation.* Morristown, New Jersey: General Learning Press, 1973.

McClelland D. The Achieving Society. Princeton, London: Van Nostrand, 1961.

McDavid JW, Harari H. *Social Psychology.* New York: Harper and Row, 1968.

McDermott W. *Evaluating the Physician and His Technology.* In: Knowles JH. *Doing Better and Feeling Worse.* New York: WW Norton and Company, 1977.

McIver RM, Page CH. *Society.* New York: Rinehart, 1949.

McKeown T, Lowe CR. *An Introduction to Social Medicine.* Blackwell: Oxford, 1966.

McKeown T. *A Sociological Approach to the History of Medicine.* In: McLachlan and McKeown, 1971.

McKeown T. *A Sociological Approach to the History of Medicine.* In: McLachlan G, McKeown T (Eds). *Medical History and Medical Care.* Oxford: Oxford University for the Nuffield Provincial Hospital's Trust, 1971.

McKeown T. *The Modern Rise of Populations.* London: 1976.

McKeown T. *The Role of Medicine.* Princetown: New Jersey: Princetown University Press, 1979.

McKinlay J, McKinlay S. The questionable contribution of medical measures to the decline of mortality in the United States in the Twentieth Century. *Health and Society* 1977; 53: 1

McKinley JB. *A Case for Refocussing Upstream: the Political Economy of Illness.* In: Jaco, 1979.

McKinley JB. *Social Network Influences on Morbid Episodes and the Career of Help Seeking.* In: Eisenberg L, Kleinman A (Eds), 1980.

McLachlan G, McKeown T (Eds). *Medical History and Medical Care.* Oxford: Oxford University for the Nuffield Provincial Hospitals Trust, 1971.

Mechanic D. *Medical Sociology.* New York: Free Press, 1968.

Mellish JM. *An Introduction to the ethos of nursing.* Durban: Butterworth, 1988.

Mellish JM. *Ethos of Nursing.* Durban: Butterworth, 1988.

Mellish JM. Primary health care—the role of the nurse. *Curationis* 1984; March.

Menzies IEB. *The Functioning of Social Systems as a Defence Against Anxieties.* Pamphlet no. 3. London: Tavistock, 1961.

Mercer, Jane. *Who is Normal? Two Perspectives on Mild Mental Retardation.* In: Jaco EG (Ed). *Patients, Physicians and Illness: A Sourcebook in Behavioural Science and Health* (2 ed). New York: Free Press, 1972.

Miliband R. *The State in Capitalist Society.* London: Quartet Books, 1969.

Millerson G. *The Qualifying Associations: A Study of Professionalisation.* London: Routledge and Kegan Paul, 1964.

Mills CW. *The Sociological Imagination.* Oxford: OUP, 1959.

Mills J. Bridging the gap between theory and practice: a critical perspective of medical sociology within the South African context. *South African Journal of Sociology* 1988; 19 no. 1: 9–19.

Mitchell C. *Social Network in Urban Situations.* Manchester: Manchester University Press, 1969.

Money J, Ehrhardt A. *Man and Woman, Boy and Girl.* Blatimore: Johns Hopkins University Press, 1972.

Money J, Gaskin R. Sex Reassignment. *International Journal of Psychiatry* 1971; 9: 249–269.

Money J, Tucker P. *Sexual Signitures.* London: Abacus, 1977.

Morgan DH. *Social Theory and the Family.* London: Routledge and Kegan Paul, 1975.

Morin E, L Homme et al. *Mort Dans L'Histoire.* Paris: Correa, 1951.

Morison RS. *Dying.* In: *Life and Death and Medicine.* 39–45. San Francisco: WH Freeman, 1973.

Morris J. *Conundum.* New York: Harcourt Brace and Janovich, 1974.

Morris JN. *Incidence of Incapacity for Work in Different Areas and Occupations.* London: Ministry of Pensions and National Insurance, 1965.

Morris JN. *Uses of Epidemiology.* London: Longman, 1975.

Morris JN. Social inequalities undiminished. *Lancet* 1979; 1: 87–90.

N

Navarro V. *Class Struggle, the State and Medicine*. London: Martin Robertson, 1978.

Navarro V. *Medicine Under Capitalism*. London: Croom Helm, 1976.

Navarro V. The industrialization of fetishism or the fetishism of industrialization: a critique of Ivan Illich. *Social Science and Medicine* 1975; 9: 351–363.

Newsom J, Newsom E. *Perspectives on School at Seven Years Old*. (with P. Barnes). London: Allen and Unwin, 1977.

Norris V. *Mental Illness in London*. London: Chapman and Hall, 1959.

Noyes R. The experience of dying. *Psychiatry* 1972; 35: 174–184.

Nuehring E, Markle GE. Nicotine and norms: the re-emergence of a deviant behaviour. *Social Problems* 1974; 21 no. 4: 513–526.

O

O'Dea T. *The Sociology of Religion*. Englewood Cliffs, New Jersey: Prentice Hall, 1966.

O'Donnell M. *A New Introduction to Sociology*. London: Nelson, 1981.

Office of Health Economics. *The Consumer and the Health Service*. McKenzie J (Ed). (see especially pp. 11–13). 1968.

Office of Health Economics. *Without Prescription*. 1968

Oles MN. The transsexual client. *American Journal of Orthopsychiatry* 1977; 47 no. 1: 66-74.

Olesen VL, Whittaker EW. *The Silent Dialogue*. San Francisco: Josey-Bass.

Osis K, Haroldson E. *At the Hour of Death*. New York: Avon, 1979.

Owen JN. *Modern Concepts of Hospital Administration*. Philadelphia: Saunders, 1962.

P

Parkes CM, Benjamin B, Fitzgerald RG. Broken heart: a statistical study of increased mortality among widowers. *British Medical Journal* 1969; 1: 740–743.

Parsons T. *Structure and Process in Modern Societies*. New York: Free Press, 1960.

Parsons T. *The Social System*. Glencoe: Free Press, 1951.

Paterson JG, Zderad LT. *Humanistic nursing*. New York: Wiley, 1976.

Patrick J. *A Glasgow Gang Observed*. 1980.

Pattison EM. *The Experience of Dying*. Englewood Cliffs, New Jersey: Prentice Hall, Inc., 1977.

Pearse IH, Crocker LH. *The Peckham Experiment*. London: Allen and Unwin, 1944.

Phillips B. *Sociological Research Methods*. Dorsey Press, 1985.

Phillips DP, Feldman KA. A dip in deaths before ceremonial occasions: some new relationships between sociological integration and mortality. *American Sociological Review* 1973; 38: 678–696.

Pickering GW. *American Journal of Medicine* 1978; 65.

Pieres JB. Central beliefs of the Xhosa cattle killing. *Journal of African History* 1987; 28: 43–63.

Pilisuk M, Parkes SH. *The Healing Web.* Hanover, New Hampshire: University Press of New England, 1986.

Pincus L. *Death in the Family.* London: Faber and Faber, 1976.

Piven F, Cloward RA. *Regulating the Poor: the Functions of Social Welfare.* New York: Vintage, 1971.

Plummer K. *The Making of the Modern Homosexual.* London: Hutchinson, 1981.

Polsky N. *Hustlers, Beats and Others.* Chicago: Aldine, 1964.

Popper K. *The Logic of Scientific Discovery.* New York: Basic Books, 1959.

Posner T. *Magical Elements in Orthodox Medicine. Helth Care and Health Knowledge.* Dingwall R, Heath C, Reid M, Stacey M (Eds). London: Croom Helm, 1977.

Powles J. On the limitations of modern medicine. *Social Science and Man* 1973; 1: 31–48.

Pratt L, Seligmann A, Reader G. Medical vocabularly knowledge among medical patients. *Journal of Health and Human Behaviour* 1961; 2: 83–92.

Prior L. The architecture of the hospital: a study of spatial organisations and medical knowledge. *Sociology of Health and Illness* 1988; 9 no. 2: 86–113.

Q

Quint J. *The Nurse and the Dying Patient.* New York: Macmillan, 1967.

R

Radomski JL, Deichman WB, Clizer EE. Pesticide concentration in the liver, brain, and adipose tissue of terminal hospital patients. *Food and Cosmetics Toxicology* 1968; 6: 209–220.

Raison T (Ed). *The Founding Fathers of Social Science.* Harmondsworth: Penguin, 1969.

Ramshorn MT. *Selected Tasks for the Dying Patient and Family Members.* In: Schoenberg et al. 1972.

Reiser SJ. *Medicine and the Reign of Technology.* Cambridge: Cambridge University Press, 1977.

Reisman D. *The Lonely Crowd.* New Haven: Yale University Press, 1961.

Richardson K, Houghton V. *Recurrent Education.* London: Ward Lock, 1975

Robertson I. *Sociology*. New York: Worth, 1987.

Robinson D. *The Process of Becoming Ill*. London: Routledge and Kegan Paul, 1971.

Robson J. Quality, inequality and health care. Notes on medicine, capital and the state. *Medicine in Society* 1977; Special edition.

Rose AM (Ed). *Human Behaviour and Social Processes*. London: Routledge and Kegan Paul, 1971.

Rosengren WR, Lefton M. *Hospitals and Patients*. New York: Atherton Press, 1969.

Rosenstock I. Why people use health services. *Milbank Memorial Quarterly* 1966; 44: 94–127.

Rosenthal M. Where rumour raged. *Transaction* 1971. 8: 34–43.

Roth J. *The Treatment of Tuberculosis as a Bargaining Process*. In: Rose AM. 1962. 575–588.

Roth JA. *Research in the Sociology of Health Care*. Vol. 1. Greenwich, Connecticut: Aijai Press Inc., 1980

Roth JA. *Timetables*. Indianapolis: Bobbs Merrill, 1963.

Runciman WG. *Relative Deprivation and Social Justice*. London: Routledge and Kegan Paul, 1966.

S

Sacks H. *The Search for Help: No-one to Turn to*. In: Schneidman ES (Ed). *Essays in Self-Destruction*. Science House, 1967.

Sagarin E. *Odd Man In*. Chicago: Quadrangle Books, 1969.

Sagarin E. Voluntary associations among social deviants. *Criminolgia* 1967; 5: 8–22.

Sass R, Crook G. Accident proness: science or non-science?. *International Journal of Health Services* 1981; 11 no. 2: 175–190.

Saunders C (Ed). *The Management of Terminal Malignant Disease*. London: Edward Arnold, 1977.

Saunders C. *Dying they Live: St Christopher's Hospice*. In: Feifel H. *New Meanings of Death*. New York: McGraw Hill. 1977. 154-178.

Savage M. *The Political Economy of Health in South Africa*. In: Wilson and Westcott, 1980.

Scheff T. *Being Mentally Ill: a Sociological Theory*. London: Weidenfield and Nicholson, 1966.

Scheff T. Decision rules and types of error, and their consequences in medical diagnosis. *Behavioural Science* 1963; 8: 97–107. In: Freidson. 1972.

Scheff T. Users and non users of a student psychiatric clinic. *Journal of Health and Human Behaviour* 1966; 7: 114–121.

Schenthel JE. Multiphasic screening of the well patient. *Journal of the American Medical Association* 1960; 172: 1–4.

Schneider IE, Conrad P. *The Medical Control of Deviance: Contests and Consequences*. In: Roth P (Ed). *The Sociology of Health Care*; 1: 1–55. Greenwich, Connecticut: Aijai Press, 1980.

Schoenberg B et al. *Anticipatory Grief.* New York: Columbia University Press, 1974.

Schoenberg B, Carr AC, Peretz D, Kutscher AH (Eds). *Psychological Aspects of Terminal Care.* New York and London: Columbia University Press, 1972.

Searle C, Brink H. *Aspects of Community Health.* (5 ed). Cape Town: King Edward VII Trust, 1982.

Searle C, Medlen LM. *Nursing ethos and professional practice study guides NEP100 (1982) and NEP200 (1983).* Pretoria: UNISA.

Searle C. *A South African Nursing Credo.* Pretoria: SA Nursing Association, 1980.

Searle C. *History of the Development of nursing in South Africa.* Pretoria: SANA, 1965.

Searle C. The dependent, interdependent and independent functions of the nurse practitioner—A legal and ethical aspect. *Curationis* 1982; December.

Seedat A. *Crippling a Nation.* London: IDAFSA, 1984.

Seftel HC. Diseases in urban and rural black populations. *S Afr Med J* 1977; 51(5): 121–123.

Seligman J. (With: Agrest S.) *A Death in the Family* 1974; Newsweek: June 20: 89.

Seligman MEP. Submissive death: giving up on life. *Psychology Today* 1974; 7: 80–85.

Shaw M (Ed). *Marxist Sociology Revisited.* London: MacMillan, 1985.

Sheskin A. *Why Die? Extend Your Life Through Cryonics: A Study of Belief Systems and Bereavement.* New York: Irvington Publishers Inc, 1979.

Shore H. *The Psychosocial Model and Long Term Care.* In: Jaco EG. *Patients, Physicians and Illness.* Glencoe: Free Press, 1970.

Shortell S. Occupational prestige differences within the medical and allied health professions. In: *Social Science and Medicine* 1974; 8: 1–9.

Sigerist HE. *A History of Medicine.* (2 volumes). Fair Lawn, New Jersey: Oxford University Press, 1951, 1962.

Sillitoe A. *Saturday Night and Sunday Morning.* London: WH Allen, 1958.

Silman R. *Teaching the Medical Student to Become a Doctor.* In: Pateman T (Ed). *Counter Course.* Harmondsworth: Penguin Books, 1972.

Silverman D. *The Theory of Organisations.* London: Heinemann, 1970.

Smelser N. *The Theory of Collective Behaviour.* New York: Free Press, 1962.

Socarides CW. *The Overt Homosexual.* New York: Grune and Stratton, 1968.

Socarides CW. The desire for sexual transformation: a psychiatric evaluation of transsexualism. *American Journal of Psychiatry* 1969; 125: 125–131.

Social Sciences Course Team. Open University. *Health,* Decision
    Making in Britain, Part V. Bletchley: Open University Press,
    1972.

Stannard DE. *Death in America.* Pennsylvania: University of Pennsyl-
    vania Press, 1975.

Stannard DE. Death and dying in puritan New England. *American
    Historical Review* 1973; December: 1305–1330.

Stark R, Bainbridge W. Towards a theory of religion: religious com-
    mitment. *Journal for the Scientific Study of Religion* 1980; 19.2.

Stoddard S. *The Hospice Movement.* New York: Vintage Books, 1978.

Strauss R. The nature and status of medical sociology. *American So-
    ciological Review* 1957; 22.

Strauss SA. *Legal Handbook for nurses and health personnel.* Cape
    Town: King Edward VII Trust, 1981.

Suchman EA. Stages of illness and medical care. *Journal of Health
    and Human Behavior* 1965; 6: 114–128.

Sudnow D. *Passing On: the Social Organisation of Dying.* New York:
    Prentice Hall, 1967.

Suid-Afrika (Republiek). *Verslag van die Wetenskapkomitee van die
    Presidentsraad oor demografiese tendense in Suid-Afrika.* PR
    1/1983. Pretoria: Staatsdrukker, 1983.

Susser M. Apartheid and causes of death. *American Journal of Pub-
    lic Health* 1983; 73 no. 5: 581–584.

Susser MW, Watson W, Hopper K. *Sociology in Medicine.* Oxford: Ox-
    ford University Press, 1985.

Swift DF. *The Sociology of Education.* London: Routledge and Kegan
    Paul, 1969.

Szasz T. *The Myth of Mental Illness.* London: Paladin, 1972.

T

Tagliacozzo DL, Mauksch H. *The Patient's View of the Patient's Role.*
    In: Jaco EG (Ed). *Patients, Physicians and Illness.* New York:
    Free Press 185–201, 1980.

Thompson K, Jones RK. *Religion, Stratification and Deprivation.* In:
    Beliefs and Religion. Bletchley: Open University Press, 1972.

Travers A. Ritual power in interaction. *Symbolic Interaction* 1982; 5:
    2.

Tuckett D (Ed). *Medical Sociology.* London: Tavistock, 1976.

Tudor Hart J. The inverse care law. *The Lancet* 1971; 27 February:
    405–412.

Turner JS. *The Clincial Feast: a Report on the Food and Drug Admin-
    istration.* New York: Grossman, 1970.

Turner R. *Collective Behaviour.* In: Fatis REL (Ed). *Handbook of Mod-
    ern Sociology.* Chicago: Rand McNally, 1964.

Turner RH. Sponsored and contest mobility and the school system.
    American Sociological Review 1960; 25: 855–867.

Twaddle A. *Sickness and the Sickness Career: Some Implications*. In: Eisenberg L, Kleinman A (Eds). *The Relevance of Social Science for Medicine*. Dordrecht, Holland: Rydal Publishing Company, 1980.

Twaddle AC, Hessler RM. *A Sociology of Health*. Saint Louis: CV Mosby Company, 1977.

V

Van Rensburg HCJ, Mans A. *Profile of Disease and Health Care in South Africa*. Pretoria: Academica, 1982.

Virchow R. *Gesammelta Abhandlugen aus dem Gibiet der effetlichen Medizin und der Suichenlehre*. Vol 1. 1879. In: Waitzkin and Waterman, 1987.

Vollmer HM, Mills DL. *Professionalization*. Englewood Cliffs, NJ: 1966.

W

Waaler HT. Specificity and sensitivity of blood pressure measurements. *Journal of Epidemiology and Community Health* 1980; 34.

Wadsworth M, Butterfield WJH, Blaney R. *Health and Sickness: the Choice of Treatment*. London: Tavistock, 1971.

Waitzkin H, Waterman B (Eds). *The Exploitation of Illness in Capitalist Society*. Illinois: Bobbs Merrill, 1987.

Waitzkin H, Waterman B. *The Exploitation of Illness in Capitalist Society*. New York: Bobs Merrill, 1974.

Waitzkin H. *A Marxist Analysis of the Health Care Systems of Advanced Capitalist Societies*. In: Eisenberg L, Kleinman A (Eds). *The Relevance of Social Science for Medicine*, 1980.

Waitzkin H. *The Second Sickness*. New York: Free Press, 1983.

Waldron I, Eyer J. Socio-economic causes of the recent rise in death rates for 15–24 year olds. *Social Science and Medicine* 1975; 9: 383–396.

Walker ARP. Studies on sugar intake and overweight in South African black and white schoolchildren. *S Afr Med J* 1974; 48(39): 1650–1654.

Walker NK, MacBride A, Vachon MLS. Social support networks and the crisis of bereavement. *Social Science and Medicine* 1977; 11: 35–410.

Waller W. *The Sociology of Teaching*. New York: Russell and Russell (1 ed) 1932. New York: Basil Wiley, 1961.

Wallis R (Ed). *Sectarianism: Analyses of Religious and Non-Religious Sects*. London: Peter Own, 1975.

Wallis R. *Betwixt Therapy and Salvation: the Changing Form of the Human Potential Movement*. In: Jones RK. 1985.

Wallis R. Scientology: therapeutic cult to religious sect. *Sociology* 1975; 9: 1.

Walsh A. *The Prophylactic Effect of Religion on Blood Pressure Levels among a sample of Immigrants.*

Wardwell W. *Limited, Marginal and Quasi Practitioners.* In: Freeman H, Levine S, Reeder L (Eds). *Handbook of Medical Sociology.* Englewood Cliffs, New Jersey: Prentice Hall, 250–273, 1972.

Wardwell W. A marginal professional role: the chiropractor. *Social Forces* 1952; 30: 339–348.

Watson J. *Nursing. The philosophy and science of caring.* Boston: Little Brown, 1979.

Webb EJ et al. *Unobtrusive Measures: Non-reactive Research in the Social Sciences.* Chicago: Rand McNally, 1966.

Weber M. *Economy and Society.* London: Bedminster Press, 1968.

Weinberg T. On 'doing' and 'being' gay: sexual behaviour and homosexual male self identity. *Journal of Homosexuality* 1978; 4: 143–156.

Wessels J. *A progress report of primary health care in the Eastern Cape and Border, 1979–1982.* 1983.

WHO. *Evaluation of the Strategy of Health for all by the Year 2000,* 1987; 1.

Whorf B. *Science and Linguistics,* 1940; XLIV: 229-248.

Wilensky HL. The professionalization of everyone?. *American Journal of Sociology* 1964. 13 no. 1: 15–32.

Willis P. *Learning to Labour: How Working Class Kids Get Working Class Jobs.* London: Saxon House, 1977.

Wilson BR. *Religion in Secular Society.* London: CA Watts, 1966.

Wilson BR. *Religious Sects.* London: Weidenfeld and Nicolson, 1970.

Wilson BR. *Religious Sects.* London: Weidenfield and Nicholson, 1970.

Wilson BR. *Sects and Society.* London: Heinemann, 1961.

Wilson F, Westcott G. *Economics of Health in South Africa.* Cape Town: Raven Press, 1980.

Wilson T. *The Need for Health Professionals Working in South Africa.* In: Wilson and Westcott, 1980.

Winch P. *The Idea of a Social Science.* London: Routledge and Kegan Paul, 1958.

Wirth L. *The Problem of Minority Groups.* In: Linton R (Ed). *The Science of Man in the World Crisis.* New York: Columbia University Press, 1945.

Withers C. The folklore of a small town. *Transactions of the New York Academy of Sciences* 1946; series 11, 8: 234–251.

Woodruff AM. Becoming a nurse: the ethical perspective. *International journal of nursing studies,* 1985. 22 no. 4.

Worsley P (Ed). *Modern Sociology: Introductory Readings.* Harmondsworth: Penguin Books, 1970.

Worsley P (Ed). *The New Introducing Sociology.* Harmondsworth: Penguin Books, 1987.

Worsley P. *The Trumpet Shall Sound.* London: MacGibbon and Kee, 1957.

Wyman LC. *Navaho Diagnosticians.* In: Scott WR, Volkhart EH. *Medical Care.* New York: John Wiley, 1966.

Y

Yedidia M. The Lay–Professional Division of Knowledge in Health Care Delivery. In: Roth, 1980.

Yerushalmy J et al. An evaluation of the role of the serial chest roentgenograms in estimating the progress of disease in patients with pulmonary tuberculosis. *American Review of Tuburculosis,* 1951; 64.

Young J. *Deviance.* In: Worsley P. *Introducing Sociology.* Harmondsworth: Penguin, 407–450, 1987.

Young MFD (Ed). *Knowledge and Control.* London: Collier-MacMillan, 1971.

Youngson AJ. *The Scientific Revolution in Modern Medicine.* London: Croom Helm, 1978.

Z

Zald MN. Resource mobilisation and social movements: a partial theory. *American Journal of Sociology,* 1977; 82 no. 6.

Zborowski M. Cultural components in response to pain. *Journal of Social Issues,* 1969.

NAME INDEX

SUBJECT INDEX